GLOBAL ISSUES 95/96

Eleventh Edition

Editor

Robert M. Jackson
California State University, Chico

Robert M. Jackson is a professor of political science and director of the Center for International Studies at California State University, Chico. In addition to teaching, he has published articles on the international political economy, international relations simulations, and political behavior. His special research interest is the way northern California is becoming increasingly linked to the Pacific Basin. His travels include China, Japan, Hong Kong, Taiwan, Portugal, Spain, Morocco, Costa Rica, El Salvador, Honduras, Guatemala, Mexico, Germany, Belgium, the Netherlands, and Czechoslovakia.

Annual Editions
A Library of Information from the Public Press

Cover illustration by Mike Eagle

Dushkin Publishing Group/
Brown & Benchmark Publishers
Sluice Dock, Guilford, Connecticut 06437

This map has been developed to give you a graphic picture of where the countries of the world are located, the relationship they have with their region and neighbors, and their positions relative to the superpowers and power blocs. We have focused on certain areas to more clearly illustrate these crowded regions.

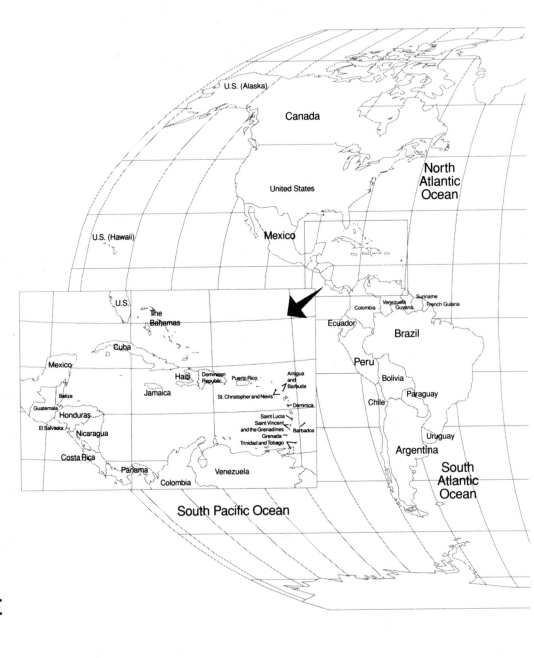

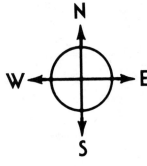

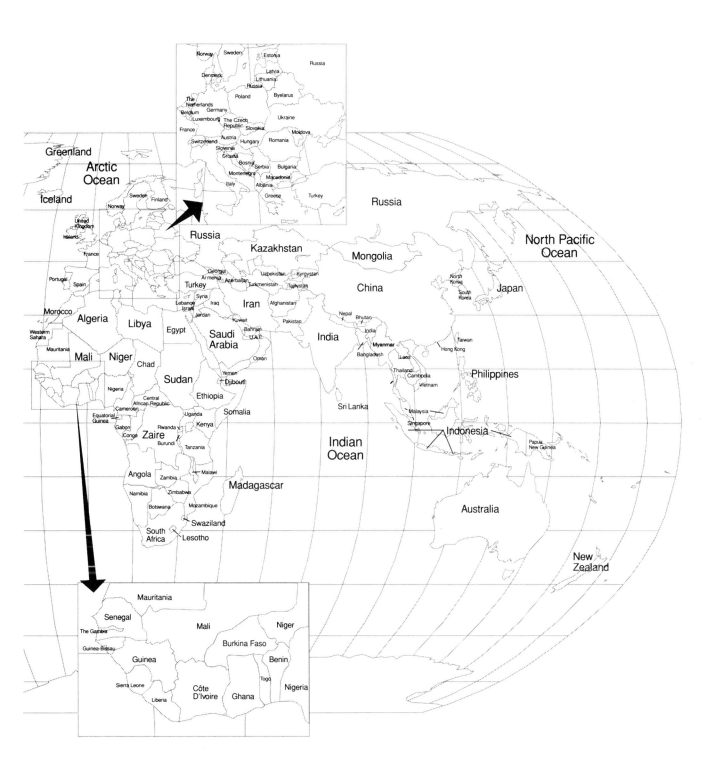

The Annual Editions Series

Annual Editions is a series of over 65 volumes designed to provide the reader with convenient, low-cost access to a wide range of current, carefully selected articles from some of the most important magazines, newspapers, and journals published today. Annual Editions are updated on an annual basis through a continuous monitoring of over 300 periodical sources. All Annual Editions have a number of features designed to make them particularly useful, including topic guides, annotated tables of contents, unit overviews, and indexes. For the teacher using Annual Editions in the classroom, an Instructor's Resource Guide with test questions is available for each volume.

VOLUMES AVAILABLE

Africa
Aging
American Foreign Policy
American Government
American History, Pre-Civil War
American History, Post-Civil War
Anthropology
Archaeology
Biology
Biopsychology
Business Ethics
Canadian Politics
Child Growth and Development
China
Comparative Politics
Computers in Education
Computers in Business
Computers in Society
Criminal Justice
Developing World
Drugs, Society, and Behavior
Dying, Death, and Bereavement
Early Childhood Education
Economics
Educating Exceptional Children
Education
Educational Psychology
Environment
Geography
Global Issues
Health
Human Development
Human Resources
Human Sexuality
India and South Asia

International Business
Japan and the Pacific Rim
Latin America
Life Management
Macroeconomics
Management
Marketing
Marriage and Family
Mass Media
Microeconomics
Middle East and the Islamic World
Money and Banking
Multicultural Education
Nutrition
Personal Growth and Behavior
Physical Anthropology
Psychology
Public Administration
Race and Ethnic Relations
Russia, the Eurasian Republics, and
  Central/Eastern Europe
Social Problems
Sociology
State and Local Government
Urban Society
Violence and Terrorism
Western Civilization,
  Pre-Reformation
Western Civilization,
  Post-Reformation
Western Europe
World History, Pre-Modern
World History, Modern
World Politics

Cataloging in Publication Data
Main entry under title: Annual Editions: Global Issues. 1995/96.
    1. Civilization, Modern—20th century—Periodicals. 2. Social prediction—Periodicals. 3. Social problems—20th century—Periodicals. I. Jackson, Robert, comp. II. Title: Global Issues.
ISBN 1–56134–357–9   909.82′05   85–658006

Eleventh Edition

Printed in the United States of America

Editors/ Advisory Board

To the Reader

In publishing ANNUAL EDITIONS we recognize the enormous role played by the magazines, newspapers, and journals of the *public press* in providing current, first-rate educational information in a broad spectrum of interest areas. Within the articles, the best scientists, practitioners, researchers, and commentators draw issues into new perspective as accepted theories and viewpoints are called into account by new events, recent discoveries change old facts, and fresh debate breaks out over important controversies.

Many of the articles resulting from this enormous editorial effort are appropriate for students, researchers, and professionals seeking accurate, current material to help bridge the gap between principles and theories and the real world. These articles, however, become more useful for study when those of lasting value are carefully *collected, organized, indexed,* and *reproduced* in a *low-cost format,* which provides easy and permanent access when the material is needed. That is the role played by *Annual Editions.* Under the direction of each volume's *Editor,* who is an expert in the subject area, and with the guidance of an *Advisory Board,* we seek each year to provide in each ANNUAL EDITION a current, well-balanced, carefully selected collection of the best of the public press for your study and enjoyment. We think you'll find this volume useful, and we hope you'll take a moment to let us know what you think.

As the twentieth century begins to draw to a close, the issues confronting humanity are increasingly complex and diverse. While the mass media may focus on the latest crisis for a few days or weeks, the broad, historical forces that are at work shaping the world of the twenty-first century are seldom given the in-depth treatment that they warrant. Research and analysis of these issues, furthermore, can be found in a wide variety of sources. As a result, the student just beginning to study global issues is often discouraged before he or she is able to sort out the information. In selecting and organizing the materials in this book, we have been mindful of the needs of the beginning student.

Each unit begins with an article providing a broad overview of the area to be explored. The remaining articles examine in more detail some of the issues presented in the introductory article. The unit then concludes with an article (or two) that not only identifies a problem but suggests positive steps that are being taken to improve the situation. The world faces many serious problems, the magnitude of which would discourage even the most stouthearted individual. Though identifying problems is easier than solving them, it is encouraging to know that many of the issues are being successfully addressed.

Perhaps the most striking feature of the study of contemporary global issues is the absence of any single, widely held theory that explains what is taking place. Therefore, we have made a conscious effort to present a wide variety of ideologies and theories. The most important consideration has been to present global issues from an international perspective, rather than from a purely American or Western point of view. By encompassing materials originally published in many different countries and written by authors of various nationalities, the anthology represents the great diversity of opinions that people hold on important global issues. Two writers examining the same phenomenon may reach very different conclusions. It is not a question of who is right and who is wrong. What is important to understand is that people from different vantage points have differing perceptions of issues.

Another major consideration when organizing these materials has been to explore the complex interrelationship of factors that produce issue areas, such as those surrounding the developing world. Too often discussions of these problems are reduced to arguments of good versus evil or communism versus capitalism. As a result, the interplay of the complex web of causes is overlooked. We have made every effort to select materials that illustrate the interaction of these forces.

Finally, we selected the materials in this book for both their intellectual insights and their readability. Timely and well-written materials should stimulate good classroom lectures and discussions. We hope that students and teachers will enjoy using this book. Readers can have input into the next edition by completing and returning the postpaid article rating form in the back of the book.

I would like to thank Ian Nielsen for his encouragement and helpful suggestions in the selection of materials for *Annual Editions: Global Issues 95/96.* It is my continuing goal to encourage the readers of this book to have a greater appreciation of the world in which they live. We hope they will be motivated to further explore the complex issues that the world faces as we approach the twenty-first century.

Robert M. Jackson
Editor

Contents

Unit 1

A Clash of Views

The three articles in this section present distinct views on the present and future state of life on Earth.

Unit 2

Population

The seven articles in this section discuss the contributing factors of culture, politics, environmental degradation, disease, and migration on the world's population growth.

The concepts in bold italics are developed in the article. For further expansion please refer to the Topic Guide, the Index, and the Glossary.

Unit 3

Natural Resources

Fourteen selections divided into four subsections—international dimensions, raw materials, food and hunger, and energy—discuss natural resources and their effects on the world community.

The concepts in bold italics are developed in the article. For further expansion please refer to the Topic Guide, the Index, and the Glossary.

Unit 4

Development

Twelve articles divided into two subsections present
various views on economic and social development in
the nonindustrial and industrial nations.

The concepts in bold italics are developed in the article. For further expansion please refer to the Topic Guide, the Index, and the Glossary.

Unit 5

Conflict

Seven articles in this section discuss the basis for world conflict and the current state of peace in the international community.

The concepts in bold italics are developed in the article. For further expansion please refer to the Topic Guide, the Index, and the Glossary.

Unit 6

Cooperation

Four selections in this section examine patterns of international cooperation and the social structures that support this cooperation.

Unit 7

Values and Visions

Six articles discuss human rights, ethics, values,
and new ideas.

Topic Guide

This topic guide suggests how the selections in this book relate to topics of traditional concern to students and professionals involved with the study of global issues. It is useful for locating articles that relate to each other for reading and research. The guide is arranged alphabetically according to topic. Articles may, of course, treat topics that do not appear in the topic guide. In turn, entries in the topic guide do not necessarily constitute a comprehensive listing of all the contents of each selection.

TOPIC AREA	TREATED IN:	TOPIC AREA	TREATED IN:
Agriculture, Food, and Hunger	16. Planet in Jeopardy 19. Landscape of Hunger 20. Can the Growing Human Population Feed Itself?	**Energy: Exploration, Production, Research, and Politics**	11. Greenhouse Effect 16. Planet in Jeopardy 22. Oil: Strategic Prize 23. Energy: The New Prize
Communications	2. Global Change 32. Triple Revolution 35. Japan's Non-Revolution 53. Global Village	**Environment, Ecology, and Conservation**	1. Preparing for the 21st Century 3. Jihad vs. McWorld 7. Optimism and Overpopulation 11. Greenhouse Effect 12. Can We Save Our Seas? 13. Sacrificed to the Superpower 14. Next Industrial Revolution 15. Green Justice 16. Planet in Jeopardy 17. Future of Water Scarcity 18. Greenwatch 19. Landscape of Hunger 47. Africa's Wildlife Poachers
Cultural Customs and Values	3. Jihad vs. McWorld 14. Next Industrial Revolution 30. Burden of Womanhood 35. Japan's Non-Revolution 40. Islam and the West 49. Long Walk to Freedom 51. Women's Role 52. Post-Communist Nightmare 53. Global Village		
Developing World	1. Preparing for the 21st Century 4. Damping the World's Population 5. Megacities 6. Rest against the West 8. Vicious Circles 9. No Refuge 15. Green Justice 23. Energy: The New Prize 26. India Gets Moving 27. NAFTA Is Not Alone 28. Chile's Economy 29. Continent That Lost Its Way 30. Burden of Womanhood 36. Global Village or Global Pillage?	**Future, The**	1. Preparing for the 21st Century 2. Global Change 4. Damping the World's Population 5. Megacities 6. Rest against the West 10. Killers All Around 11. Greenhouse Effect 12. Can We Save Our Seas? 16. Planet in Jeopardy 17. Future of Water Scarcity 18. Greenwatch 20. Can the Growing Human Population Feed Itself? 23. Energy: The New Prize 27. NAFTA Is Not Alone 28. Chile's Economy 31. Land Mines on the Road to Utopia 32. Triple Revolution 34. Future of Europe 35. Japan's Non-Revolution 36. Global Village or Global Pillage? 37. New Challenges to Global Security 39. Central Asia 40. Islam and the West 41. Rogue States, Criminals, and Terrorists 43. Dismantling the Arsenals 44. United Nations 46. Ten Keys to World Peace 50. Preparing for a Peaceful 21st Century 51. Women's Role in Post-Industrial Democracy
Development: Economic and Social	1. Preparing for the 21st Century 2. Global Change 6. Rest against the West 18. Greenwatch 26. India Gets Moving 27. NAFTA Is Not Alone 28. Chile's Economy 29. Continent That Lost Its Way 30. Burden of Womanhood 32. Triple Revolution 36. Global Village or Global Pillage?		
Economics	1. Preparing for the 21st Century 2. Global Change 3. Jihad vs. McWorld 5. Megacities 13. Sacrificed to the Superpower 14. Next Industrial Revolution 15. Green Justice 26. India Gets Moving 28. Chile's Economy 29. Continent That Lost Its Way 32. Triple Revolution 31. Land Mines on the Road to Utopia 33. We're #1 34. Future of Europe 36. Global Village or Global Pillage?	**Industrial Economics**	1. Preparing for the 21st Century 2. Global Change 13. Sacrificed to the Superpower 14. Next Industrial Revolution 15. Green Justice 22. Oil: The Strategic Prize 31. Land Mines on the Road to Utopia 32. Triple Revolution 33. We're #1 34. Future of Europe

TOPIC AREA	TREATED IN:	TOPIC AREA	TREATED IN:
International Economics, Trade, Aid, and Dependencies	2. Global Change 8. Vicious Circles 22. Oil: Strategic Prize 23. Energy: The New Prize 25. The Boom 27. NAFTA Is Not Alone 32. Triple Revolution 36. Global Village or Global Pillage?	**Political and Legal Global Issues**	3. Jihad vs. McWorld 9. No Refuge 11. Greenhouse Effect 12. Can We Save Our Seas? 27. NAFTA Is Not Alone 36. Global Village or Global Pillage? 37. New Challenges to Global Security 39. Central Asia 43. Dismantling the Arsenals 44. United Nations 45. Polio Conquered 47. Africa's Wildlife Poachers 50. Preparing for a Peaceful 21st Century
Military: Warfare and Terrorism	29. Continent That Lost Its Way 37. New Challenges to Global Security 38. Why Yugoslavia Fell Apart 39. Central Asia 40. Islam and the West 41. Rogue States, Criminals, and Terrorists 42. Contest over Asia 43. Dismantling the Arsenals 44. United Nations 46. Ten Keys to World Peace 50. Preparing for a Peaceful 21st Century	**Population and Demographics (Quality of Life Indicators)**	1. Preparing for the 21st Century 4. Damping the World's Population 5. Megacities 6. Rest against the West 7. Optimism and Overpopulation 8. Vicious Circles 9. No Refuge 10. Killers All Around 16. Planet in Jeopardy 20. Can the Growing Human Population Feed Itself? 21. Crowded Out
Natural Resources	6. Rest against the West 11. Greenhouse Effect 12. Can We Save Our Seas? 14. Next Industrial Revolution 16. Planet in Jeopardy 17. Future of Water Scarcity 18. Greenwatch 19. Landscape of Hunger 22. Oil: The Strategic Prize 24. Canada Is Ready to Exploit Huge Oil Reserves 47. Africa's Wildlife Poachers	**Science, Technology, and Research and Development**	2. Global Change 10. Killers All Around 11. Greenhouse Effect 16. Planet in Jeopardy 18. Greenwatch 24. Canada Is Ready to Exploit Huge Oil Reserves 32. Triple Revolution 43. Dismantling the Arsenals

A Clash of Views

Imagine a clear, round, inflated balloon. Now imagine that a person begins to brush yellow paint onto this miniature globe; symbolically, the color yellow represents *people*. In many ways the study of global issues is ultimately the study of people. Today, there are more people occupying Earth than ever before. In addition, the world is in the midst of a period of unprecedented population growth. Not only are there many countries where the majority of people are under age 16, but because of improved health care, there are also more older people alive than ever before. The effect of a growing global population, however, goes beyond sheer numbers, for a growing population has unprecedented impacts on natural resources and social services. Population issues, then, are an appropriate place to begin the study of global issues.

Imagine that our fictional artist dips the brush into a container of blue paint to represent the world of *nature*. The natural world plays an important role in setting the international agenda. Shortages of raw materials, drought and crop failures, and pollution of waterways are just a few examples of how natural resources can have global implications.

Adding blue paint to the balloon also reveals one of the most important concepts found in this book of readings. Although the balloon originally was covered by yellow and blue paint (people and nature as separate conceptual entities), the two combined produce an entirely different color: green. Talking about nature as a separate entity or about people as though they were somehow removed from the forces of the natural world is a serious intellectual error. The people-nature relationship is one of the keys to understanding many of today's most important global issues.

The third color added to the balloon is red. It represents the *meta* component (i.e., those qualities that make human beings more than mere animals). These include new ideas and inventions, culture and values, religion and spirituality, and art and literature. The addition of the red paint immediately changes the color green to brown, again emphasizing the relationship between all three factors.

The fourth and final color added is white. This color represents *social structures*. Factors such as whether a society is urban or rural, industrial or agrarian, planned or decentralized, and consumer-oriented or dedicated to the

needs of the state fall into this category. The relationship between this component and the others is extremely important. The impact of political decisions on the environment, for example, is one of the most unique features of the contemporary world. Historically, the forces of nature determined which species survived or perished. Today survival depends on political decisions—or indecisions. Will the whales or bald eagles survive? The answer to this question will depend on governmental activities, not evolutionary forces. Understanding this relationship between social structure and nature (known as "ecopolitics") is important to the study of global issues.

If the painter continues to ply the paintbrush over the miniature globe, a marbling effect will become evident. In some areas, the shading will vary because one element is greater than another. The miniature system appears dynamic. Nothing is static; relationships are continually changing. This leads to a number of theoretical insights: (1) there is no such thing as separate elements, only connections or relationships; (2) changes in one area (such as the weather) will result in changes in all other areas; and (3) complex relationships make it difficult to predict events accurately, so observers are often surprised by unexpected processes and outcomes.

This book is organized along the basic lines of the balloon allegory. The first unit explores a variety of perspectives on the forces that are at work shaping the world of the twenty-first century. Unit 2 focuses on population. Unit 3 examines the environment and related issues (e.g., agriculture and energy). The next three units look at different aspects of the world's social structures. They explore issues of development (for both industrial and nonindustrial societies), conflict, and cooperation. In the final unit, a number of "meta" factors are discussed. However, you should be aware that, just as it was impossible to keep the individual colors from disappearing and blending into new colors on the balloon, it is also impossible to separate these factors into discrete chapters in a book. Any discussion of agriculture, for example, must take into account the impact of a growing population on soil and water resources, as well as new scientific approaches to food production. Therefore, the organization of this book focuses attention on issue areas; it does not mean to imply that these factors are somehow separate.

With the end of the cold war and the collapse of the Soviet empire, the outlines of a new global agenda are beginning to emerge. Rather than an agenda based on the ideology and interests of the two superpowers, a new set of factors have emerged that interact in an unprecedented fashion. Rapid population growth, environmental decline, and lagging economic performance are all parts of a complex situation to which there is no historic parallel. As we approach the twenty-first century, there are signs abounding that a new era is being entered. As Abraham Lincoln said, "As our case is new, so we must think anew." Compounding this situation, however, are a whole series of old problems such as ethnic and religious rivalries.

The authors in this first section provide a variety of perspectives on the trends that they believe are the most important to understanding the historic changes at work on the international stage. This discussion is then pursued in greater detail in the following sections.

It is important for the reader to note that although the authors look at the same world, they often come to different conclusions. This raises an important issue of values and beliefs, for it can be argued that there really is no objective reality, only differing perspectives. In short, the study of global issues will challenge each thoughtful reader to examine her or his own values and beliefs.

Looking Ahead: Challenge Questions

Do the analyses of any of the authors in this section employ the assumptions implicit in the allegory of the balloon? If so, how? If not, how are the assumptions of the authors different?

All the authors point to interactions among different factors. What are some of the relationships that they cite? How do the authors differ in terms of the relationships they emphasize?

What are some of the assets that people have to solve problems that did not exist 100 years ago?

What major events during the twentieth century have had the greatest impact on shaping the world of today?

How will the world be different in the year 2030? What factors will contribute to these changes?

What do you consider to be the five most pressing global problems of today? How do your answers compare to those of your family, friends, and classmates?

Preparing for the 21st Century: Winners and Losers

Paul Kennedy

Paul Kennedy is Professor of History and Director of the International Security Program at Yale University. He is the author of The Rise and Fall of the Great Powers, *among many other books.* Preparing for the Twenty-First Century, *from which this article is drawn, is published by Random House.*

1.

Everyone with an interest in international affairs must be aware that broad, global forces for change are bearing down upon humankind in both rich and poor societies alike. New technologies are challenging traditional assumptions about the way we make, trade, and even grow things. Automated workplaces in Japan intimate the end of the "factory system" that first arose in Britain's Industrial Revolution and spread around the world. Genetically engineered crops, cultivated in biotech laboratories, threaten to replace naturally grown sugar, vanilla, coconut oil, and other staple farm produce, and perhaps undermine field-based agriculture as we know it. An electronically driven, twenty-four-hour-a-day financial trading system has created a global market in, say, yen futures over which nobody really has control. The globalization of industry and services permits multinationals to switch production from one country to another (where it is usually

cheaper), benefitting the latter and hurting the former.

In addition to facing these technology-driven forces for change, human society is grappling with the effects of fast-growing demographic imbalances throughout the world. Whereas birthrates in richer societies plunge well below the rates that would replace their populations, poorer countries are experiencing a population explosion that may double or even treble their numbers over the next few decades. As these fast-swelling populations press upon the surrounding forests, grazing lands, and water supplies, they inflict dreadful damage upon local environments and may also be contributing to that process of global warming first created by the industrialization of the North a century and a half ago. With overpopulation and resource depletion undermining the social order, and with a global telecommunications revolution bringing television programs like *Dallas* and *Brideshead Revisited* to viewers everywhere from Central America to the Balkans, a vast illegal migration is under way as millions of families from the developing world strive to enter Europe and North America.

Although very different in form, these various trends from global warming to twenty-four-hour-a-day trading are *transnational* in character, crossing borders all over our planet, affecting local communities and dis-

tant societies at the same time, and reminding us that the earth, for all its divisions, is a single unit. Every country is challenged by these global forces for change, to a greater or lesser extent, and most are beginning to sense the need to prepare themselves for the coming twenty-first century. Whether *any* society is at present "well prepared" for the future is an open question;[1] but what is clear is that the regions of the globe most affected by the twin impacts of technology and demography lie in the developing world. Whether they succeed in harnessing the new technologies in an environmentally prudent fashion, and at the same time go through a demographic transition, will probably affect the prospects of global peace in the next century more than any other factor. What, then, are their chances?

Before that question can be answered, the sharp contrasts among the developing countries in the world's different regions need to be noted here.[2] Perhaps nothing better illustrates those differences than the fact that, in the 1960s, South Korea had a per capita GNP exactly the same as Ghana's (US $230), whereas today it is ten to twelve times more prosperous.[3] Both possessed a predominantly agrarian economy and had endured a half-century or more of colonial rule. Upon independence, each faced innumerable handicaps in their effort to "catch up" with the West, and although Korea possessed a greater historical and cultural coherence, its chances may have seemed less promising, since it had few natural resources (apart from tungsten) and suffered heavily during the 1950–1953 fighting.

Decades later, however, West African states remain among the most poverty-stricken countries in the world—the per capita gross national products of Niger, Sierra Leone, and Chad today, for example, are less than $500[4]—while Korea is entering the ranks of the high-income economies. Already the world's thirteenth largest trading nation, Korea is planning to become one of the richest countries of all in the twenty-first century,[5] whereas the nations of West Africa face a future, at least in the near term, of chronic poverty, malnutrition, poor health, and underdevelopment. Finally, while Korea's rising prosperity is attended by a decrease in population growth, most African countries still face a demographic explosion that erodes any gains in national output.

This divergence is not new, for there have always been richer and poorer societies; the prosperity gap in the seventeenth century—between, say, Amsterdam and the west coast of Ireland, or between such bustling Indian ports as Surat and Calcutta[6] and the inhabitants of New Guinean hill villages—must have been marked, although it probably did not equal the gulf between rich and poor nations today. The difference is that the twentieth-century global communications revolution has made such disparities widely known. This can breed resentments by poorer peoples against prosperous societies, but it can also provide a desire to emulate (as Korea emulated Japan). The key issue here is: What does it take to turn a "have not" into a "have" nation? Does it simply require imitating economic techniques, or does it involve such intangibles as culture, social structure, and attitudes toward foreign practices?

This discrepancy in performance between East Asia and sub-Saharan Africa clearly makes the term "third world" misleading. However useful the expression might have been in the 1950s, when poor, nonaligned, and recently decolonized states were at-

SHARES OF WORLD TRADE IN MANUFACTURES[10]

percentage share

Sub-Saharan Africa: 0.4% (1965), 0.2% (1986)

East-Asia Newly Industrialized Economies (NIEs): 1.5% (1965), 8.5% (1986)

tempting to remain independent of the two superpower blocs,[7] the rise of super-rich oil-producing countries a decade later already made the term questionable. Now that prosperous East Asian societies—Korea, Taiwan, and Singapore—possess higher per capita GNPs than Russia, Eastern Europe, and even West European states like Portugal, the word seems less suitable than ever. With Taiwanese or Korean corporations establishing assembly plants in the Philippines, or creating distribution networks within the European Community, we need to recognize the differences that exist among non-Western economies. Some scholars now categorize *five* separate types of "developing" countries in assessing the varied potential of societies in Asia, Africa, and Latin America.[8]

Relative national growth in the 1980s confirms these differences. Whereas East Asian economies grew on average at an impressive annual rate of 7.4 percent, those in Africa and Latin America gained only 1.8 and 1.7 percent respectively[9]—and since their populations grew faster, the net result was that they slipped backward, absolutely and relatively. Differences of economic structure also grew in this decade, with African and other primary commodity-producing countries eager for higher raw-material prices, whereas the export-oriented manufacturing nations of East Asia sought

to keep commodity prices low. The most dramatic difference occurred in the shares of world trade in manufactures, a key indicator of economic competitiveness (see chart above). Thus, while some scholars still refer to a dual world economy[11] of rich and poor countries, what is emerging is increasing differentiation. Why is this so?

The developing countries most successfully catching up with the West are the trading states of the Pacific and East Asia. Except for Communist regimes there, the Pacific rim countries (including the western provinces of Canada and the United States, and in part Australia) have enjoyed a lengthy boom in manufacturing, trade, and investment; but the center of that boom is on the *Asian* side of the Pacific, chiefly fuelled by Japan's own spectacular growth and the stimulus given to neighboring economies and trans-Pacific trade. According to one source:

In 1962 the Western Pacific (notably East Asia) accounted for around 9 percent of world GNP, North America for 30 percent, and Western Europe for 31 percent. Twenty years later, the Western Pacific share had climbed to more than 15 percent, while North America's had fallen to 28 percent and Europe's to 27 percent. By the year 2000 it is likely that the Western Pacific will account for around one-quarter of world GNP, with the whole Pacific region increasing its share from just over 43 percent to around half of world GNP.[12]

East Asia's present boom is not, of course, uniform, and scholars distinguish between the different stages of economic and technological development in this vast region. Roughly speaking, the divisions would be as follows:

(a) Japan, now the world's largest or second largest financial center and, increasingly, the most innovative high-tech nation in the nonmilitary field;

(b) the four East Asian "tigers" or "dragons," the Newly Industrialized Economies (NIEs) of Singapore, Hong Kong, Taiwan, and South Korea, of which the latter two possess bigger populations and territories than the two port-city states, but all of which have enjoyed export-led growth in recent decades;

(c) the larger Southeast Asian states of Thailand, Malaysia, and Indonesia which, stimulated by foreign (chiefly Japanese) investment, are becoming involved in manufacturing, assembly, and export—it is doubtful whether the Philippines should be included in this group;

(d) finally, the stunted and impoverished Communist societies of Vietnam, Cambodia, and North Korea, as well as isolationist Myanmar pursuing its "Burmese Way to Socialism."

Because of this staggered level of development, economists in East Asia invoke the image of the "flying geese," with Japan the lead bird, followed by the East Asian NIEs, the larger Southeast Asian states, and so on. What Japan produced in one decade—relatively low-priced toys, kitchenware, electrical goods—will be imitated by the next wave of "geese" in the decade following, and by the third wave in the decade after that. However accurate the metaphor individually, the overall picture is clear; these birds are flying, purposefully and onward, to an attractive destination.

Of those states, it is the East Asian NIEs that have provided the clearest example of successful transformation. Although distant observers may regard them as similar, there are notable differences in size, population,[13] his-

tory, and political system. Even the economic structures are distinct; for example, Korea, which began its expansion at least a decade later than Taiwan (and democratized itself even more slowly), is heavily dependent upon a few enormous industrial conglomerates, or *chaebol*, of whom the top four alone (Samsung, Hyundai, Lucky-Goldstar, and Daewoo) have sales equal to half Korea's GNP. By contrast, Taiwan possesses many small companies, specializing in one or two kinds of products. While Taiwanese are concerned that their firms may lose out to foreign giants, Koreans worry that the *chaebol* will find it increasingly difficult to compete in large-scale industries like petrochemicals and semiconductors and shipbuilding at the same time.[14]

Despite such structural differences, these societies each contain certain basic characteristics, which, *taken together*, help to explain their decade-upon-decade growth. The first, and perhaps the most important, is the emphasis upon education. This derives from Confucian traditions of competitive examinations and respect for learning, reinforced daily by the mother of the family who complements what is taught at school.

To Western eyes, this process—like Japan's—appears to concentrate on rote learning and the acquisition of technical skills, and emphasizes consensus instead of encouraging individual talent and the habit of questioning authority. Even if some East Asian educators would nowadays admit that criticism, most believe that their own educational mores create social harmony and a well-trained work force. Moreover, the uniformity of the system does not exclude intense individual competitiveness; in Taiwan (where, incidentally, twelve members of the fourteen-member cabinet of 1989 had acquired Ph.D.s abroad), only the top one third of each year's 110,000 students taking the national university entrance examinations are selected, to emphasize the importance of college education.[15]

Perhaps nothing better illustrates this stress upon learning than the fact that Korea (43 million population) has around 1.4 million students in higher education, compared with 145,000 in Iran (54 million), 15,000 in Ethiopia (46 million), and 159,000 in Vietnam (64 million); or the further fact that

already by 1980 "as many engineering students were graduating from Korean institutions as in the United Kingdom, West Germany and Sweden combined."[16]

The second common characteristic of these countries is their high level of national savings. By employing fiscal measures, taxes, and import controls to encourage personal savings, large amounts of low-interest capital were made available for investment in manufacture and commerce. During the first few decades of growth, personal consumption was constrained and living standards controlled—by restrictions upon moving capital abroad, or importing foreign luxury goods—in order to funnel resources into industrial growth. While average prosperity rose, most of the fruits of economic success were plowed back into further expansion. Only when economic "take-off" was well under way has the system begun to alter; increased consumption, foreign purchases, capital investment in new homes, all allow internal demand to play a larger role in the country's growth. In such circumstances, one would expect to see overall savings ratios decline. Even in the late 1980s, however, the East Asian NIEs still had high national savings rates:

COMPARATIVE SAVINGS RATIOS, 1987[17]	
Taiwan	38.8%
Malaysia	37.8%
Korea	37.0%
Japan	32.3%
Indonesia	29.1%
US	12.7%

The third feature has been a strong political system within which economic growth is fostered. While entrepreneurship and private property are encouraged, the "tigers" never followed a laissez-faire model. Industries targeted for growth were given a variety of supports—export subsidies, training grants, tariff protection from foreign competitors. As noted above, the fiscal system was arranged to produce high savings ratios. Taxes assisted the business sector, as did energy policy. Trade unions operated under restrictions. Democracy was constrained by the governor of Hong Kong, *dirigiste* administrations in Singapore, and the military regimes in Taiwan and Korea. Only lately have free elections and party politics been permitted. Defenders of this system argued that it was necessary to restrain libertarian impulses while concentrating on economic growth, and that democratic reforms are a "reward" for the people's patience. The point is that domestic politics were unlike those in the West yet did not hurt commercial expansion.

The fourth feature was the commitment to exports, in contrast to the policies of India, which emphasize locally produced substitutes for imports, and the consumer-driven policies of the United States. This was traditional for a small, bustling trading state like Hong Kong, but it involved substantial restructuring in Taiwan and Korea, where managers and workers had to be trained to produce what foreign customers wanted. In all cases, the value of the currency was kept low, to increase exports and decrease imports. Moreover, the newly industrialized economies of East Asia took advantage of favorable global circumstances: labor costs were much lower than in North America and Europe, and they benefitted from an open international trading order, created and protected by the United States, while shielding their own industries from foreign competition.

Eventually, this led to large trade surpluses and threats of retaliation from European and American governments, reminding us of the NIEs' heavy dependence upon the current international economic system. The important thing, however, is that they targeted export-led growth in manufactures, whereas other developing nations continued to rely upon commodity exports and made little effort to cater to foreign consumers' tastes.[18] Given this emphasis on trade, it is not surprising to learn that Asia now contains seven of the world's twelve largest ports.

Finally, the East Asian NIEs possess a local model, namely Japan, which Yemen, Guatemala, and Burkina Faso simply do not have. For four decades East Asian peoples have observed the dramatic success of a non-Western neighbor, based upon its educational and technical skills, high savings ratios, long-term, state-guided targeting of industries and markets, and deter-mination to compete on world markets, though this admiration of Japan is nowadays mixed with a certain alarm at becoming members of a yen block dominated by Tokyo. While the Japanese domestic market is extremely important for the East Asian NIEs, and they benefit from Japanese investments, assembly plants, engineers, and expertise, they have little enthusiasm for a new Greater East Asia co-prosperity sphere.[19]

The benefits of economic success are seen not merely in East Asia's steadily rising standards of living. Its children are on average four or five inches taller than they were in the 1940s, and grow up in some of the world's healthiest countries:

A Taiwanese child born in 1988 could expect to live 74 years, only a year less than an American or a West German, and 15 years longer than a Taiwanese born in 1952; a South Korean born in 1988 could expect 70 years on earth, up from 58 in 1965. In 1988 the Taiwanese took in 50 percent more calories each day than they had done 35 years earlier. They had 200 times as many televisions, telephones and cars per household; in Korea the rise in the possession of these goods was even higher.[20]

In addition, the East Asian NIEs enjoy some of today's highest literacy rates, once again confirming that they are altogether closer to "first" world nations than poor, developing countries (see chart below).

Will this progress last into the twenty-first century? Politically, Hong Kong's future is completely uncertain, and many companies are relocating their headquarters elsewhere; Taiwan remains a diplomatic pariah-state because of Beijing's traditional claims; and South Korea still worries about the unpredictable, militarized regime in the north. The future of China—and of Siberia—is uncertain, and causes concern. The 1980s rise in Asian stock-market prices (driven by vast increases in the money supply) was excessive and speculative, and destined to tumble. Protectionist tendencies in the developed world threaten the trading states even more than external pressures to abandon price supports for local farmers. A rise in the value of the Korean and Taiwanese currencies has cut export earnings and reduced their overall rate of growth. Some Japanese competitors have moved production to neighboring low-cost countries such as Thailand or southern China. Sharp rises in oil prices increase the import bills. High wage awards (in Korea they increased by an average 14 percent in 1988, and by 17 percent in 1989) affect labor costs and competitiveness. The social peace, precarious in these recent democracies, is damaged by bouts of student and industrial unrest.[22]

On the other hand, these may simply be growing pains. Savings ratios are still extremely high. Large numbers of new engineers and technicians pour out of college each year. The workers' enhanced purchasing power has created a booming domestic market, and governments are investing more in housing, infrastructure, and public facilities. The labor force will not grow as swiftly as before because of the demographic slowdown, but it will be

COMPARATIVE LIVING STANDARDS[21]		
Life Expectancy at Birth (years), 1987	Adult Literacy Rate (%), 1985	GNP per capita, 1988 US$
Niger 45	14	300
Togo 54	41	310
India 59	43	340
SINGAPORE 73	86	9,070
SOUTH KOREA 70	95	5,000
Spain 77	95	7,740
New Zealand 75	99	10,000

better educated and spend more.[23] A surge in overseas investments is assisting the long-term balance of payments. As the populous markets of Indonesia, Thailand, and Malaysia grow at double-digit rates, there is plenty of work for the trading states. A hardening of the currency can be met by greater commitment to quality exports, high rates of industrial investment, and a move into newer, high-technology manufacture—in imitation of the 1980s re-tooling of Japanese industry when its currency hardened swiftly. Nowhere else in the world would growth rates of "only" 5 or 6 percent be considered worrying, or a harbinger of decline. Barring a war in East Asia, or a widespread global slump, the signs are that the four "tigers" are better structured than most to grow in wealth and health.

2.

For confirmation of that remark, one need only consider the present difficult condition of Latin America, which lost ground in the 1980s just as East Asia was gaining it. Here again, distinctions have to be made between various countries within the continent, with its more than 400 million people in an area almost 7 million square miles stretching from the Rio Grande to Antarctica, and with a range of political cultures and socioeconomic structures. Argentina, which around 1900 had a standard of living suggesting that it was a "developed" economy, is very different from Honduras and Guyana. Similarly, population change in Latin America occurs in three distinct forms: such nations as Bolivia, the Dominican Republic, and Haiti have high fertility rates and lower life expectancies; a middle group—Brazil, Colombia, Mexico, Venezuela, Costa Rica, and Panama—is beginning to experience declines in fertility and longer life expectancy; and the temperate-zone countries of Argentina, Chile, and Uruguay have the demographic characteristics of developed countries.[24]

Despite this diversity, there are reasons for considering Latin America's prospects as a whole: the economic challenges confronting the region are similar, as are its domestic politics—in particular, the fragility of its recently emerged democracies; and each

PER CAPITA GDP OF LATIN AMERICAN COUNTRIES[27]
(1988 US Dollars)

Country	1960	1970	1980	1988
Chile	1,845	2,236	2,448	2,518
Argentina	2,384	3,075	3,359	2,862
Uruguay	2,352	2,478	3,221	2,989
Brazil	1,013	1,372	2,481	2,449
Paraguay	779	931	1,612	1,557
Bolivia	634	818	983	724
Peru	1,233	1,554	1,716	1,503
Ecuador	771	904	1,581	1,477
Colombia	927	1,157	1,595	1,739
Venezuela	3,879	4,941	5,225	4,544
Guyana	1,008	1,111	1,215	995
Suriname	887	2,337	3,722	3,420
Mexico	1,425	2,022	2,872	2,588
Guatemala	1,100	1,420	1,866	1,502
Honduras	619	782	954	851
El Salvador	832	1,032	1,125	995
Nicaragua	1,055	1,495	1,147	819
Costa Rica	1,435	1,825	2,394	2,235
Panama	1,264	2,017	2,622	2,229
Dominican Republic	823	987	1,497	1,509
Haiti	331	292	386	319
Jamaica	1,610	2,364	1,880	1,843
Trinidad & Tobago	3,848	4,927	8,116	5,510
Barbados	2,000	3,530	3,994	4,233
Bahamas	8,448	10,737	10,631	11,317

is affected by its relationship with the developed world, especially the United States.

Several decades ago, Latin America's future appeared encouraging. Sharing in the post-1950 global boom, benefitting from demand for its coffee, timber, beef, oil, and minerals, and enjoying foreign investments in its agriculture, industry, and infrastructure, the region was moving upward. In the thirty years after 1945, its production of steel multiplied twenty times, and its output of electric energy, metals, and machinery grew more than tenfold.[25] Real gross domestic product (GDP) per person rose at an annual average of 2.8 percent during the 1960s and spurted to an annual average increase of 3.4 percent in the 1970s. Unfortunately, the growth then reversed itself, and between 1980 and 1988

Latin America's real GDP per person steadily fell by an annual average of 0.9 percent.[26] In some states, such as Peru and Argentina, real income dropped by as much as one quarter during the 1980s. With very few exceptions (Chile, Colombia, the Dominican Republic, Barbados, the Bahamas), most Latin American countries now have per capita GDPs lower than they were a decade earlier, or even two decades earlier (see chart above).

The reasons for this reversal offer a striking contrast to the East Asian NIEs. Instead of encouraging industrialists to target foreign markets and stimulate the economy through export-led growth, many Latin American governments pursued a policy of import substitution, creating their own steel, cement, paper, automobiles, and electronic-goods industries, which were given protective tariffs, government

**GROWTH OF LATIN AMERICAN INDEBTEDNESS
(SELECTED COUNTRIES)[31]**

Country	Total External Debt (billion US $)			Long-Term Public Debt As A Percentage of GNP		
	1977	1982	1987	1977	1982	1987
Argentina	8.1	32.4	53.9	10	31	62
Brazil	28.3	68.7	109.4	13	20	29
Chile	4.9	8.5	18.7	28	23	89
Guyana	0.4	0.9	1.2	100	158	353
Honduras	0.6	1.6	3.1	29	53	71
Jamaica	1.1	2.7	4.3	31	69	139
Mexico	26.6	78.0	93.7	25	32	59
Venezuela	9.8	27.0	29.0	10	16	52

subsidies, and tax-breaks to insulate them from international competition. As a result, their products became less attractive abroad.[28] Moreover, while it was relatively easy to create a basic iron and steel industry, it proved harder to establish high-tech industries like computers, aerospace, machine-tools, and pharmaceuticals—most of these states therefore still depend on imported manufactured goods, whereas exports chiefly consist of raw materials like oil, coffee, and soybeans.[29]

Secondly, economic growth was accompanied by lax financial policies and an increasing reliance upon foreign borrowings. Governments poured money not only into infrastructure and schools but also into state-owned enterprises, large bureaucracies, and oversized armed forces, paying for them by printing money and raising loans from Western (chiefly US) banks and international agencies. The result was that public spending's share of GDP soared, price inflation accelerated, and was further increased by index-linked rises in salaries and wages. Inflation became so large that it was difficult to comprehend, let alone to combat. According to the 1990 *World Resources* report, "in 1989, for example, annual inflation in Nicaragua was more than 3,400 percent; in Argentina inflation reached 3,700 percent, in Brazil almost 1,500 percent, and in Peru nearly 3,000 percent. Ecuador, with only 60 percent in-flation, did comparatively well."[30] In such circumstances the currency becomes worthless, as does the idea of seeking to raise national savings rates for long-term capital investment.

Another result is that some Latin American countries find themselves among the most indebted in the world, as the chart below shows. Total Latin American indebtedness now equals about $1,000 for every man, woman, and child. But instead of being directed into productive investment, that money has been wasted domestically or disappeared as "capital flight" to private accounts in United States and European banks. This has left most countries incapable of repaying even the interest on their loans. Defaults on loans (or suspension of interest payments) then produced a drying up of capital from indignant Western banks and a net capital *outflow* from Latin America just when it needed capital to aid economic growth.[32] Starved of foreign funds and with currencies made worthless by hyperinflation, many countries are in a far worse position than could have been imagined twenty-five years ago.[33] For a while, it was even feared that the region's financial problems might undermine parts of the international banking system. It now appears that the chief damage will be in the continent itself, where 180 million people (40 percent) are living in poverty—a rise of 50 million alone in the 1980s.

Given such profligacy, and the conservative, "anti–big government" incumbents in the White House during the 1980s, it was predictable that Latin America would come under pressure—from the World Bank, the IMF, private bankers, Washington itself—to slash public spending, control inflation, and repay debts. Such demands were easier said than done in the existing circumstances. Islands of democracy (e.g., Costa Rica) did exist, but many states were ruled by right-wing military dictatorships or social revolutionaries; internal guerrilla wars, military *coups d'état*, labor unrest were common. Even as democracy began to reassert itself in the 1980s, the new leaders found themselves in a near-impossible situation: inheritors of the high external debts contracted by the outgoing regimes, legatees in many cases of inflationary index-linked wage systems, targets of landowner resentment and/or of guerrilla attacks, frustrated by elaborate and often corrupt bureaucracies, and deficient in trained personnel. While grappling with these weaknesses, they discovered that the Western world, which applauded the return to democracy, was unsympathetic to fresh lending, increasingly inclined to protectionism, and demanding unilateral measures (e.g., in the Amazon rain forests) to stop global warming.

Two other weaknesses have also slowed any hoped-for recovery. One is the unimpressive accomplishments of the educational systems. This is not due to an absence of schools and universities, as in parts of Africa. Many Latin American countries have extensive public education, dozens of universities, and high adult literacy rates; Brazil, for example, has sixty-eight universities, Argentina forty-one.[34] The real problem is neglect and underinvestment. One citizen bemoaned the collapse in Argentina as follows:

Education, which kept illiteracy at bay for more than a century, lies in ruins. The universities are unheated and many public schools lack panes for their window frames. Last summer [1990] an elementary school teacher with ten years' experience earned less than $110 a month. An associate professor at the Universidad de Buenos Aires, teaching ten hours

13

a week, was paid $37 a month. A doctor's salary at a municipal hospital was $120 a month.... At times, teachers took turns teaching, or cut their class hours, because they and their students could not afford transportation.[35]

Presumably, if resources were available, those decaying educational and health-care structures could be resuscitated, helping national recovery; but where the capital can be raised in present circumstances is difficult to see. Moreover, in the strife-torn countries of Central America there is little education to begin with; in Guatemala, the latest census estimated that 63 percent of those ten years of age and older were illiterate, while in Honduras the illiteracy rate was 40 percent.[36] Unfortunately, it is in the educationally most deprived Latin American countries that resources are being eroded by swift population increases.

Despite these disadvantages, recent reports on Latin America have suggested that the "lost decade" of the 1980s will be followed by a period of recovery. The coming of democratic regimes, the compromises emerging from protracted debt-recycling talks, the stiff economic reforms (cutting public spending, abandoning indexation) to reduce inflation rates, the replacement of "state protectionism with import liberalization and privatization,"[37] the conversion of budget deficits into surpluses — all this has caused the Inter-American Development Bank to argue that "a decisive and genuine takeoff" is at hand, provided the new policies are sustained.[38] Growth has resumed in Argentina, Mexico, and Venezuela. Even investment bankers are reported to be returning to the continent.

Whether these changes are going to be enough remains uncertain, especially since the newly elected governments face widespread resentment at the proposed reforms. As one commentator put it, "Much of Latin America is entering the 1990s in a race between economic deterioration and political progress."[39] Whereas Spain, Portugal, and Greece moved to democracy while enjoying reasonable prosperity, Latin America (like Eastern Europe) has to make that change as its economies flounder—which

places immense responsibilities upon the political leadership.

Although it can be argued that the region's future is in its own hands, it will also be heavily influenced by the United States. In many ways, the US–Latin America leadership is similar to that between Japan and the East Asian NIEs, which are heavily dependent upon Japan as their major market and source of capital.[40] Yet there is more to this relationship than Latin America's economic dependence upon the United States, whose banking system has also suffered because of Latin American indebtedness. United States exports, which are fifty times larger to this region than to Eastern Europe, were badly hurt by Latin America's economic difficulties, and they would benefit greatly from a resumption of growth. The United States' own environment may now be threatened by the diminution of the Amazon and Central American rain forests. Its awful drug problem, driven by domestic demand, is fuelled by Latin American supplies—more than 80 percent of the cocaine and 90 percent of the marijuana entering the United States are produced or move through this region.

Finally, the population of the United States is being altered by migration from Mexico, the Caribbean, and Central America; if there should be a widespread socioeconomic collapse south of the Rio Grande, the "spillover" effects will be felt across the United States. Instead of being marginalized by the end of the cold war, Latin America may present Washington with formidable and growing challenges—social, environmental, financial, and ultimately political.[41] Thus, while the region's own politicians and citizens have to bear the major responsibility for recovery, richer nations—especially the United States—may find it in their own best interest to lend a hand.

3.

If these remarks disappoint readers in Brazil or Peru, they may care to glance, in grim consolation, at the world of Islam. It is one thing to face population pressures, shortage of resources, educational/technological deficiencies, and regional conflicts, which would challenge the wisest governments. But it is another when

regimes themselves stand in angry resentment of global forces for change instead of (as in East Asia) selectively responding to such trends. Far from preparing for the twenty-first century, much of the Arab and Muslim world appears to have difficulty in coming to terms with the nineteenth century, with its composite legacy of secularization, democracy, laissez-faire economics, industrial and commercial linkages among different nations, social change, and intellectual questioning. If one needed an example of the importance of cultural attitudes in explaining a society's response to change, contemporary Islam provides it.

Before analyzing the distinctive role of Islamic culture, one should first note the danger of generalizing about a region that contains such variety. After all, it is not even clear what *name* should be used to describe this part of the earth. To term it the "Middle East"[42] is, apart from its Atlantic-centered bias, to leave out such North African states as Libya, Tunisia, Algeria, and Morocco. To term it the "Arab World"[43] is to exclude Iran (and, of course, Israel), the Kurds, and the non-Muslim tribes of southern Sudan and Mauritania. Even the nomenclature Islam, or the Muslim world, disguises the fact that millions of Catholics, Copts, and Jews live in these lands, and that Islamic societies extend from West Africa to Indonesia.[44]

In addition, the uneven location of oil in the Middle East has created a division between super-rich and dreadfully poor societies that has no equivalent in Central America or sub-Saharan African.[45] Countries like Kuwait (2 million), the United Arab Emirates (1.3 million), and Saudi Arabia (11.5 million) enjoy some of the world's highest incomes, but exist alongside populous neighbors one third as rich (Jordan, Iran, Iraq) or even one tenth as rich (Egypt, Yemen). The gap is accentuated by different political systems: conservative, anti-democratic, traditionalist in the Gulf sheikdoms; demagogic, populist, militarized in countries such as Libya, Syria, Iraq, and Iran.

The 1990 Iraqi attack upon Kuwait, and the different responses of the Saudi elites on the one hand and the street masses in Amman or Rabat on the other, illustrated this divide between "haves" and "have-nots" in the Muslim world. The presence of millions of Egyptian, Yemeni, Jordanian, and Palestinian *Gastarbeiter* in the oil-rich states simply increased the mutual resentments, while the Saudi and Emirate habit of giving extensive aid to Iraq during its war against Iran, or to Egypt to assist its economic needs, reinforces the impression of wealthy but precarious regimes seeking to achieve security by bribing their larger, jealous neighbors.[46] Is it any wonder that the unemployed, badly housed urban masses, despairing of their own secular advancement, are attracted to religious leaders or "strongmen" appealing to Islamic pride, a sense of identity, and resistance to foreign powers and their local lackeys?

More than in any other developing region, then, the future of the Middle East and North Africa is affected by issues of war and conflict. The region probably contains more soldiers, aircraft, missiles, and other weapons than anywhere else in the world, with billions of dollars of armaments having been supplied by Western, Soviet, and Chinese producers during the past few decades. In view of the range and destructiveness of these weapons, another Arab-Israeli war would be a nightmare, yet many Muslim states still regard Israel with acute hostility. Even if the Arab-Israeli antagonism did not exist, the region is full of other rivalries, between Syria and Iraq, Libya and Egypt, Iran and Iraq, and so on. Vicious one-man dictatorships glare threateningly at arch-conservative, antidemocratic, feudal sheikdoms. Fundamentalist regimes exist from Iran to the Sudan. Terrorist groups in exile threaten to eliminate their foes. Unrest among the masses puts a question mark over the future of Egypt, Algeria, Morocco, Jordan.[47] The recent fate of Lebanon, instead of serving as a warning against sectarian fanaticism, is more often viewed as a lesson in power politics, that the strong will devour the weak.

To the Western observer brought up in Enlightenment traditions—or, for that matter, to economic rationalists preaching the virtues of the borderless world—the answer to the Muslim nations' problems would appear to be a vast program of *education*, not simply in the technical, skills-acquiring sense

but also to advance parliamentary discourse, pluralism, and a secular civic culture. Is that not the reason, after all, for the political stability and economic success of Scandinavia or Japan today?

If that argument is correct, then such an observer would find few of those features in contemporary Islam. In countries where fundamentalism is strong, there is (obviously) little prospect of education or advancement for the female half of the population.[48] Where engineers and technicians exist, their expertise has all too often been mobilized for war purposes, as in Iraq. Tragically, Egypt possesses a large and bustling university system but a totally inadequate number of jobs for graduates and skilled workers, so that millions of both are underemployed. In Yemen, to take an extreme example, the state of education is dismal. By contrast, the oil-rich states have poured huge resources into schools, technical institutes, and universities, but these alone are insufficient to create an "enterprise culture" that would produce export-led manufacturing along East Asian lines. Ironically, possession of vast oil reserves could be a disadvantage, since it reduces the incentive to rely upon the skills and quality of the people, as occurs in countries (Japan, Switzerland) with few natural resources. Such discouraging circumstances may also explain why many educated and entrepreneurial Arabs, who passionately wanted their societies to borrow from the West, have emigrated.

It is difficult to know whether the reason for the Muslim world's troubled condition is cultural or historical. Western critics pointing to the region's religious intolerance, technological backwardness, and feudal cast of mind often forget that, centuries before the Reformation, Islam led the world in mathematics, cartography, medicine, and many other aspects of science and industry; and contained libraries, universities, and observatories, when Japan and America possessed none and Europe only a few. These assets were later sacrificed to a revival of traditionalist thought and the sectarian split between Shi'ite and Sunni Muslims, but Islam's retreat into itself—its being "out of step with History," as one author termed it[49]—

was probably also a response to the rise of a successful, expansionist Europe.

Sailing along the Arab littoral, assisting in the demise of the Mughal Empire, penetrating strategic points with railways, canals, and ports, steadily moving into North Africa, the Nile Valley, the Persian Gulf, the Levant, and then Arabia itself, dividing the Middle East along unnatural boundaries as part of a post–First World War diplomatic bargain, developing American power to buttress and then replace European influences, inserting an Israeli state in the midst of Arab peoples, instigating coups against local popular leaders, and usually indicating that this part of the globe was important only for its oil—the Western nations may have contributed more to turning the Muslim world into what it is today than outside commentators are willing to recognize.[50] Clearly, the nations of Islam suffer many self-inflicted problems. But if much of their angry, confrontational attitudes toward the international order today are due to a long-held fear of being swallowed up by the West, little in the way of change can be expected until that fear is dissipated.

4.

The condition of sub-Saharan Africa—"the third world's third world," as it has been described—is even more desperate.[51] When one considers recent developments such as perestroika in the former Soviet Union, the coming integration of Europe, and the economic miracle of Japan and the East Asian NIEs, remarked a former president of Nigeria, General Olusegun Obasanjo, and "contrasting all this with what is taking place in Africa, it is difficult to believe that we inhabit the same historical time."[52] Recent reports upon the continent's plight are extraordinarily gloomy, describing Africa as "a human and environmental disaster area," as "moribund," "marginalized," and "peripheral to the rest of the world," and having so many intractable problems that some foreign development experts are abandoning it to work elsewhere. In the view of the World Bank, virtually everywhere else in the world is likely to experience a decline in poverty by the year 2000 *except* Africa, where things

1. A CLASH OF VIEWS

will only get worse.[53] "Sub-Saharan Africa," concludes one economist, "suffers from a combination of economic, social, political, institutional and environmental handicaps which have so far largely defied development efforts by the African countries and their donors."[54] How, an empathetic study asks, can Africa survive?[55]

The unanimity of views is remarkable, given the enormous variety among the forty-five states that comprise sub-Saharan Africa.[56] Nine of them have fewer than one million people each, whereas Nigeria contains about 110 million. Some lie in the desert, some in tropical rain forests. Many are rich in mineral deposits, others have only scrubland. While a number (Botswana, Cameroun, Congo, Gabon, Kenya) have seen significant increases in living standards since independence, they are the exception—suggesting that the obstacles to growth on East Asian lines are so deep-rooted and resistant to the "development strategies" of foreign experts and/or their own leaders that it may require profound changes in attitude to achieve recovery.

This was not the mood thirty years ago, when the peoples of Africa were gaining their independence. True, there was economic backwardness, but this was assumed to have been caused by decades of foreign rule, leading to dependency upon a single metropolitan market, monoculture, lack of access to capital, and so on. Now that Africans had control of their destinies, they could build industries, develop cities, airports, and infrastructure, and attract foreign investment and aid from either Western powers or the USSR and its partners. The boom in world trade during the 1950s and 1960s, and demand for commodities, strengthened this optimism. Although some regions were in need, Africa as a whole was self-sufficient in food and, in fact, a net food exporter. Externally, African states were of increasing importance at the United Nations and other world bodies.

What went wrong? The unhappy answer is "lots of things." The first, and perhaps most serious, was that over the following three decades the population mushroomed as imported medical techniques and a reduction in malaria-borne mosquitoes drastically curtailed infant mortality. Africa's population was already increasing at an average annual rate of 2.6 percent in the 1960s, jumped to 2.9 percent during the 1970s, and increased to over 3 percent by the late 1980s, implying a doubling in size every twenty-two years; this was, therefore, the highest rate for any region in the world.[57]

In certain countries, the increases were staggering. Between 1960 and 1990, Kenya's population quadrupled, from 6.3 million to 25.1 million, and Côte d'Ivoire's jumped from 3.8 million to 12.6 million. Altogether Africa's population—including the North African states—leapt from 281 to 647 million in three decades.[58] Moreover, while the majority of Africans inhabit rural settlements, the continent has been becoming urban at a dizzying speed. Vast shanty-cities have already emerged on the edges of national capitals (such as Accra in Ghana, Monrovia in Liberia, and Lilongwe in Malawi). By 2025, urban dwellers are predicted to make up 55 percent of Africa's total population.

The worst news is that the increase is unlikely to diminish in the near future. Although most African countries spend less than 1 percent of GNP on health care and consequently have the highest infant mortality rates in the world—in Mali, for example, there are 169 infant deaths for every 1,000 live births—those rates are substantially less than they were a quarter century ago and will tumble further in the future, which is why demographers forecast that Africa's population in 2025 will be nearly three times that of today.[59]

There remains one random and tragic factor which may significantly affect all these (late 1980s) population projections—the AIDS epidemic, which is especially prevalent in Africa. Each new general study has raised the global total of people who are already HIV positive. For example, in June 1991, the World Health Organization abandoned its earlier estimate that 25–30 million people throughout the world would be infected by the year 2000, and suggested instead that the total could be closer to 40 million, and even that may be a gross underestimate.[60] Without question, Africa is the continent most deeply affected by AIDS, with entire families suffering from the disease. Tests of pregnant women in certain African families reveal that 25–30 percent are now HIV positive.[61] Obviously, this epidemic would alter the earlier projections of a doubling or trebling of Africa's total population over the next few decades—and in the worst possible way: family sizes would still be much larger than in most other regions of the globe, but tens of millions of Africans would be dying of AIDS, further crushing the world's most disadvantaged continent.

The basic reason why the present demographic boom will not otherwise be halted swiftly is traditional African belief-systems concerning fecundity, children, ancestors, and the role of women. Acutely aware of the invisible but pervasive presence of their ancestors, determined to expand their lineage, regarding childlessness or small families as the work of evil spirits, most Africans seek to have as many children as possible; a woman's virtue and usefulness are measured by the number of offspring she can bear. "Desired family size," according to polls of African women, ranges from five to nine children. The social attitudes that lead women in North America, Europe, and Japan to delay childbearing—education, career ambitions, desire for independence—scarcely exist in African societies; where such emerge, they are swiftly suppressed by familial pressures.[62]

This population growth has not been accompanied by equal or larger increases in Africa's productivity, which would of course transform the picture. During the 1960s, farm output was rising by around 3 percent each year, keeping pace with the population, but since 1970 agricultural production has grown at only half that rate. Part of this decline was caused by the drought, hitting countries south of the Sahara. Furthermore, existing agricultural resources have been badly eroded by overgrazing—caused by the sharp rise in the number of cattle and goats—as well as by deforestation in order to provide fuel and shelter for the growing population. When rain falls, the water runs off the denuded fields, taking the top-soil with it.

None of this was helped by changes in agricultural production, with farmers encouraged to grow tea, coffee, cocoa, palm oil, and rubber for export rather than food for domestic consumption. After benefitting from high commodity prices in the early stages, producers suffered a number of blows. Heavy taxation on cash crops, plus mandatory governmental marketing, reduced the incentives to increase output; competition grew from Asian and Latin American producers; many African currencies were overvalued, which hurt exports; and in the mid-1970s, world commodity prices tumbled. Yet the cost of imported manufactures and foodstuffs remained high, and sub-Saharan Africa was badly hurt by the quadrupling of oil prices.[63]

These blows increased Africa's indebtedness in ways that were qualitatively new. Early, postcolonial borrowings were driven by the desire for modernization, as money was poured into cement works, steel plants, airports, harbors, national airlines, electrification schemes, and telephone networks. Much of it, encouraged from afar by international bodies like the World Bank, suffered from bureaucratic interference, a lack of skilled personnel, unrealistic planning, and inadequate basic facilities, and now lies half-finished or (where completed) suffers from lack of upkeep. But borrowing to pay for imported oil, or to feed half the nation's population, means that indebtedness rises without any possible return on the borrowed funds. In consequence, Africa's total debt expanded from $14 billion in 1973 to $125 billion in 1987, when its capacity to repay was dropping fast; by the mid-1980s, payments on loans consumed about half of Africa's export earnings, a proportion even greater than for Latin American debtor nations. Following repeated debt reschedulings, Western bankers—never enthusiastic to begin with—virtually abandoned private loans to Africa.[64]

As a result, Africa's economy is in a far worse condition now than at independence, apart from a few countries like Botswana and Mauritius. Perhaps the most startling illustration of its plight is the fact that "excluding South Africa, the nations of sub-Saharan Africa with their 450 million people have a total GDP less than that of Belgium's 11 million people"; in fact, the entire continent generates roughly 1 percent of the world GDP.[65] Africa's share of world markets has shriveled just as East Asia's share has risen fast.

Plans for modernization lie unrealized. Manufacturing still represents only 11 percent of Africa's economic activity—scarcely up from the 9 percent share in 1965; and only 12 percent of the continent's exports is composed of manufactures (compared with Korea's 90 percent). There is a marked increase in the signs of decay: crumbling infrastructure, power failures, broken-down communications, abandoned projects, and everywhere the pressure of providing for increasing populations. Already Africa needs to import 15 million tons of maize a year to achieve minimal levels of food consumption, but with population increasing faster than agricultural output, that total could multiply over the next decade—implying an even greater diversion of funds from investment and infrastructure.[66]

Two further characteristics worsen Africa's condition. The first is the prevalence of wars, *coups d'état*, and political instability. This is partly the legacy of the European "carve-up" of Africa, when colonial boundaries were drawn without regard for the differing tribes and ethnic groups,[67] or even of earlier conquests by successful tribes of neighboring lands and peoples; Ethiopia, for example, is said to contain 76 ethnic groups and 286 languages.[68] While it is generally accepted that those boundaries cannot be unscrambled, most of them are clearly artificial. In extreme cases like Somalia, the "state" has ceased to exist. And in most other African countries, governments do not attract the loyalty of citizens (except perhaps kinsmen of the group in power), and ethnic tensions have produced innumerable civil wars—from Biafra's attempt to secede from Nigeria, to the conflict between Arab north and African south in the Sudan, to Eritrean struggles to escape from Ethiopia, to the Tutsi-Hutu struggle in Burundi, to clashes and suppressions and guerrilla campaigns from Uganda to the Western Sahara, from Angola to Mozambique.[69]

These antagonisms have often been worsened by struggles over ideology and government authority. The rulers of many new African states rapidly switched either to a personal dictatorship, or single-party rule. They also embraced a Soviet or Maoist political

economy, instituting price controls, production targets, forced industrialization, the takeover of private enterprises, and other features of "scientific socialism" that—unknown to them—were destroying the Soviet economy. Agriculture was neglected, while bureaucracy flourished. The result was the disappearance of agricultural surpluses, inattention to manufacturing for the world market, and the expansion of party and government bureaucracies, exacerbating the region's problems.

The second weakness was the wholly inadequate investment in human resources and in developing a culture of entrepreneurship, scientific inquiry, and technical prowess. According to one survey, Africa has been spending less than $1 each year on research and development per head of population, whereas the United States was spending $200 per head. Consequently, Africa's scientific population has always trailed the rest of the world:

NUMBERS OF SCIENTISTS AND ENGINEERS PER MILLION OF POPULATION[70]	
Japan	3,548
US	2,685
Europe	1,632
Latin America	209
Arab States	202
Asia (minus Japan)	99
Africa	53

In many African countries—Malawi, Zambia, Lesotho—government spending on education has fallen, so that, after some decades of advance, a smaller share of children are now in school. While there is a hunger for learning, it cannot be satisfied beyond the secondary level except for a small minority. Angola, for example, had 2.4 million pupils in primary schools in 1982–1983, but only 153,000 in secondary schools and a mere 4,700 in higher education.[71] By contrast, Sweden, with a slightly smaller total population, had 570,000 in secondary education and 179,000 in higher education.[72]

Despite these relative weaknesses, some observers claim to have detected signs of a turnaround. With the exception of intransigent African socialists,[73] many leaders are now attempting to institute reforms. In return for "structural adjustments," that is, measures to encourage free enterprise, certain African societies have secured additional loans from Western nations and the World Bank. The latter organization has identified past errors (many of them urged on African governments and funded by itself), and encouraged economic reforms. Mozambique, Ghana, and Zambia have all claimed recent successes in reversing negative growth, albeit at considerable social cost.

Democratic principles are also returning to the continent: the dismantling of apartheid in South Africa, the cease-fire in Angola, the independence of Namibia, the success of Botswana's record of democracy and prosperity, the cries for reforms in Gabon, Kenya, and Zaire, the rising awareness among African intellectuals of the transformations in East Asia, may all help—so the argument goes—to change attitudes, which is the prerequisite for recovery.[74] Moreover, there are local examples of economic self-improvement, cooperative ventures to halt erosion and improve yields, and village-based schemes of improvement.[75] This is, after all, a continent of enormous agricultural and mineral resources, provided they can be sensibly exploited.

Despite such signs of promise, conditions are likely to stay poor. Population increases countered only by the growing toll of AIDS victims, the diminution of grazing lands and food supplies, the burdens of indebtedness, the decay of infrastructures and reduced spending on health care and education, the residual strength of animist religions and traditional belief-systems, the powerful hold of corrupt bureaucracies and ethnic loyalties... all those tilt against the relatively few African political leaders, educators, scientists, and economists who perceive the need for changes.

What does this mean for Africa's future? As the Somalian disaster unfolds, some observers suggest that parts of the continent may be taken over and administered from the outside, rather like the post–1919 League of Nations mandates. By contrast, other experts argue that disengagement by developed countries might have the positive effect of compelling

Africans to begin a *self-driven* recovery, as well as ending the misuse of aid monies.[76] Still others feel that Africa cannot live without the West, although its leaders and people will have to abandon existing habits, and development aid must be more intelligently applied.[77] Whichever view is correct, the coming decade will be critical for Africa. Even a partial recovery would give grounds for hope; on the other hand, a second decade of decline, together with a further surge in population, would result in catastrophe.

5.

From the above, it is clear that the developing countries' response to the broad forces for global change is going to be uneven. The signs are that the gap between success and failure will widen; one group enjoys interacting beneficial trends, while others suffer from linked weaknesses and deficiencies.[78]

This is most clearly the case with respect to demography. As noted earlier, the commitment of the East Asian trading states to education, manufacturing, and export-led growth produced a steady rise in living standards, and allowed those societies to make the demographic transition to smaller family sizes. This was in marked contrast to sub-Saharan Africa where, because of different cultural attitudes and social structures, improved health care and rising incomes led, *not* to a drop in population growth, but to the opposite. Just before independence in 1960, for example, the average Kenyan woman had 6.2 children, whereas by 1980 she had 8.2[79]—and that in a period when Africa's economic prospects were fading.

In Africa's case the "global trend" which drives all others is, clearly, the demographic explosion. It spills into every domain—overgrazing, local conflicts over water and wood supplies, extensive unplanned urbanization, strains upon the educational and social structures, reliance upon imported food supplies (at the cost of increasing indebtedness), ethnic tensions, domestic unrest, border wars. Only belatedly are some African governments working to persuade families to limit their size as people become aware that access to family planning, plus improved educational opportunities for women, produce sig-

nificant declines in birth rates. Against such promising indications stand the many cultural, gender-related, and economic forces described above that encourage large families. This resistance to change is aided by Africa's general lack of resources. Raising Somalia's female literacy rate (6 percent) to South Korea's (88 percent) to produce a demographic transition sounds fine until one considers how so ambitious a reform could be implemented and paid for. Unfortunately, as noted above, the projections suggest that, as Africa's population almost trebles over the next few decades, the only development curtailing it could be the rapid growth of AIDS.[80]

In many parts of Latin America, the demographic explosion will also affect the capacity to handle globally driven forces for change. While wide differences in total fertility rates exist between the moderate-climate countries and those in the tropics, the overall picture is that Latin America's population, which was roughly equal to that of United States and Canada in 1960, is increasing so swiftly that it will be more than double the latter in 2025.[81] Even if birth-rates are now declining in the larger countries, there will still be enormous increases: Mexico's population will leap to 150 million by 2025 and Brazil's to 245 million.[82] This implies a very high incidence of child poverty and malnutrition, further strain upon already inadequate health-care and educational services, the crowding of millions of human beings into a dozen or more "mega-cities," pollution, the degradation of grazing land, forests, and other natural resources. In Mexico, for example, 44 million people are without sewers and 21 million without potable water, which means that when disease (e.g., cholera) strikes, it spreads swiftly.[83] These are not strong foundations upon which to improve the region's relative standing in an increasingly competitive international economic order.

In this regard, many Muslim states are in a similar or worse position; in no Arab country is the population increasing by less than 2 percent a year,[84] and in most the rate is considerably higher. The region's total population of more than 200 million will double in less than twenty-five years and city populations are growing twice as fast as national averages. This puts enormous pressures upon scarce food, water, and land resources, and produces unbalanced populations. Already, in most Arab countries at least four out of every ten people are under the age of fifteen—the classic recipe for subsequent social unrest and political revolution. One in five Egyptian workers is jobless, as is one in four Algerian workers.[85] In what is widely regarded as the most turbulent part of the world, therefore, demography is contributing to the prospects of future unrest year by year. Even the Israeli-Palestine quarrel has become an issue of demography, with the influx of Soviet Jews seen as countering the greater fertility of the Palestinians.

There is, moreover, little likelihood that population growth will fall in the near future. Since infant mortality rates in many Muslim countries are still high, further improvements in prenatal care will produce rises in the numbers surviving, as is happening in the Gulf States and Saudi Arabia (see chart).

As elsewhere, politics intrudes; many regimes are deliberately encouraging women to have large families, arguing that this adds to the country's military strength. "Bear a child," posters in Iraq proclaim, "and you pierce an arrow in the enemy's eye."[87] Countries such as Iraq and Libya offer many incentives for larger families, as do the Gulf States and Saudi Arabia, anxious to fill their oil-rich lands with native-born rather than foreign workers. Only in Egypt are propaganda campaigns launched to curb family size, but even if that is successful—despite resistance from the Muslim Brotherhood—present numbers are disturbing. With a current population of over 55 million Egyptians, six out of ten of whom are under twenty, and with an additional one million being born every eight months, the country is in danger of bursting at the seams during the next few decades.

6.

For much the same reasons, we ought to expect a differentiated success rate among developing countries in handling environmental challenges, with the newly industrializing East Asian economies way ahead of the others. This is not to ignore significant local

COMPARATIVE INFANT MORTALITY RATES[86]		
(Infant deaths per 1,000 live births)		
	1965–1970	1985–1990
Algeria	150	74
Egypt	170	85
Sudan	156	108
Yemen Arab Republic	186	116
Saudi Arabi	140	71
Kuwait	55	19
Iraq	111	69
Japan	16	5
US	22	10
Sweden	13	6

schemes to improve the ecology that are springing up in Africa and the interesting proposals for "sustainable development" elsewhere in the developing world,[88] or to forget that industrialization has caused environmental damage in East Asia, from choked roads to diminished forests. Yet the fact is that nations with lots of resources (capital, scientists, engineers, technology, a per capita GNP of over US $4,000) are better able to deal with environmental threats than those without money, tools, or personnel. By contrast, it is the poorer societies (Egypt, Bangladesh, Ethiopia) that, lacking financial and personnel resources, find it difficult to respond to cyclones, floods, drought, and other natural disasters—with their devastated populations augmenting the millions of refugees and migrants. Should global warming produce sea-level rises and heightened storm surges, teeming island populations from the Caribbean to the Pacific are in danger of being washed away.[89]

Finally, it is the population explosion in Latin America and South Asia and Africa that is the major cause for the overgrazing, soil erosion, salinization, and clearing of the tropical rain forests, which, while contributing to global warming, also hurts the local populations and exacerbates regional struggles for power. Elsewhere, in the Middle East for example, supplies of

water are the greatest concern, especially in view of growing demographic pressures. The average Jordanian now uses only one third the amount of domestic water consumed in Israel and has little hope of increasing the supply, yet Jordan's population, which is now roughly equal to Israel's, is expected to double during the next twenty years.[90]

With all governments in the region striving to boost agricultural output and highly sensitive to famine and unrest among their peasant farmers, the search for secure water influences domestic politics, international relations, and spending priorities. Egypt worries that either the Sudan or Ethiopia might dam the Nile in order to increase irrigation. Syria and Iraq have taken alarm at Turkey's new Ataturk dam, which can interrupt the flow of the Euphrates. Jordan, Syria, and Israel quarrel over water rights in the Litani, Yarmuk, and Jordan river valleys, as do Arabs and Jews over well supplies in the occupied West Bank. Saudi Arabia's ambition to grow wheat is draining its aquifers, and the same will occur with Libya's gigantic scheme to tap water from under the Sahara.[91] As more and more people struggle for the same—or diminishing—amounts of water, grand ideas about preparing for the twenty-first century look increasingly irrelevant; surviving *this* century becomes the order of the day.

1. A CLASH OF VIEWS

What are the implications for these societies of the new technologies being developed by Western scientists? The revolution in biotech farming, for example, is of great relevance to developing countries, even if the consequences will be mixed. Improved strains of plants and more sophisticated pesticides and fertilizers could, potentially, enhance yields in the developing world, reduce pressures upon marginal lands, restore agricultural self-sufficiency, improve the balance of payments, and raise standards of living. Since much biotech does not involve expensive enterprise, we could witness farmers' groups experimenting with new seeds, improved breeding techniques, cultivation of gene tissue, regional gene-banks, and other developments.

Yet it is also possible that giant pharmaceutical and agro-chemical firms in the "first" world may monopolize much of the knowledge—and the profits—that this transformation implies. Surpluses in global foodstuffs caused by the biotech revolution could be used to counter malnutrition. They could also undermine commodity prices and hurt societies in which most inhabitants were employed in agriculture. Removing food production from the farm to the laboratory—which is what is implied by recent breakthroughs in biotech agriculture—would undercut agrarian societies, which is why some biotech experts in the development field call for serious planning in "agricultural conversion," that is, conversion into other economic activities.[92]

While the uses of biotechnology are relatively diverse, that is not the case with robotics and automated manufacture. The requirements for an indigenous robotics industry—capital, an advanced electronics sector, design engineers, a dearth of skilled labor—suggest that countries like Taiwan and Korea may follow Japan's example out of concern that Japan's automation will make their own products uncompetitive. On the other hand, automated factories assembling goods more swiftly, regularly, and economically than human beings pose a challenge to *middle-income* economies (Malaysia, Mexico), whose comparative advantage would be undercut. As for countries without a manufacturing base, it is difficult to see how the robotics revolution would have any meaning—except to further devalue the resource which they possess in abundance, masses of impoverished and under-educated human beings.

Finally, the global financial and communications revolution, and the emergence of multinational corporations, threatens to increase the gap between richer and poorer countries, even in the developing world. The industrial conglomerates of Korea are now positioning themselves to become multinational, and the East Asian NIEs in general are able to exploit the world economy (as can be seen in their trade balances, stock-markets, electronics industries, strategic marketing alliances, and so on). Furthermore, if the increasingly borderless world rewards en-trepreneurs, designers, brokers, patent-owners, lawyers, and dealers in high value-added services, then East Asia's commitment to education, science, and technology can only increase its lead over other developing economies.

By contrast, the relative lack of capital, high-technology, scientists, skilled workers, and export industries in the poorer countries makes it difficult for them to take part in the communications and financial revolution, although several countries (Brazil, India) clearly hope to do so. Some grimmer forecasts suggest the poorer parts of the developing world may become more marginalized, partly because of the reduced economic importance of labor, raw materials, and foodstuffs, partly because the advanced economies may concentrate upon greater knowledge-based commerce among themselves.

7.

Is there any way of turning these trends around? Obviously, a society strongly influenced by fundamentalist mullahs with a dislike of "modernization" is unlikely to join the international economy; and it does not *have* to enter the borderless world if its people believe that it would be healthier, spiritually if not economically, to remain outside. Nor ought we to expect that countries dominated by selfish, authoritarian elites bent upon enhancing their military power—developing world countries spent almost $150 billion on weapons and armies in 1988 alone—will rush to imitate Japan and Singapore.

But what about those societies that wish to improve themselves yet find that they are hampered by circumstances? There are, after all, many developing countries, the vast majority of which depend upon exporting food and raw materials. With dozens of poor countries seeking desperately to sell their cane sugar or bananas or timber or coffee in the global market, prices fall and they are made more desperate.[93] Moreover, although much international aid goes to the developing world, in fact far more money flows out of impoverished countries of Africa, Asia, and Latin America and *into* the richer economies of Europe, North America, and Japan—to the tune of at least $43 billion each year.[94] This outward flow of interest repayments, repatriated profits, capital flight, royalties, fees for patents and information services, makes it difficult for poorer countries to get to their feet; and even if they were able to increase their industrial output, the result might be a large rise in "the costs of technological dependence."[95] Like their increasing reliance upon Northern suppliers for food and medical aid, this has created another dependency relationship for poorer nations.

In sum, as we move into the next century the developed economies appear to have all the trump cards in their hands—capital, technology, control of communications, surplus foodstuffs, powerful multinational companies[96]—and, if anything, their advantages are growing because technology is eroding the value of labor and materials, the chief assets of developing countries. Although nominally independent since decolonization, these countries are probably more dependent upon Europe and the United States than they were a century ago.

Ironically, three or four decades of efforts by developing countries to gain control of their own destinies—nationalizing Western companies, setting up commodity-exporting cartels, subsidizing indigenous manufacturing to achieve import substitution, campaigning for a new world order based upon redistribution of the existing imbalances of wealth—have all failed. The "market," backed by governments of the developed economies, has proved too strong, and the struggle against it has weakened developing economies still further—except those (like Korea and Taiwan) which decided to join.

While the gap between rich and poor in today's world is disturbing, those who have argued that this gap is unjust have all too often supported heavy-handed state interventionism and a retreat from open competition, which preserved indigenous production in the short term but rendered it less efficient against those stimulated by market forces. "Scientific socialism for Africa" may still appeal to some intellectuals,[97] but by encouraging societies to look inward it made them less well equipped to move to newer technologies in order to make goods of greater sophistication and value. And a new "world communications order," as proposed a few years ago by UNESCO to balance the West's dominance, sounds superficially attractive but would in all likelihood become the pawn of bureaucratic and ideological interests rather than function as an objective source of news reporting.

On the other hand, the advocates of free market forces often ignore the vast political difficulties which governments in developing countries would encounter in abolishing price controls, selling off national industries, and reducing food subsidies. They also forget that the spectacular commercial expansion of Japan and the East Asian NIEs was carried out by strong states which eschewed laissez faire. Instead of copying either socialist or free market systems, therefore, the developing countries might imitate East Asia's "mixed strategies" which combine official controls and private enterprise.[98]

Although the idea of a mixed strategy is intriguing, how can West or Central African countries imitate East Asia without a "strong state" apparatus, and while having a weak tradition of cooperation between government and firms, far lower educational achievements, and a different set of cultural attitudes toward family size or international economics? With the global scene less welcoming to industrializing newcomers, how likely are they to achieve the same degree of success as the East Asian NIEs did, when they "took off" a quarter-century ago?[99] Even if, by an economic miracle, the world's poorest fifty nations did adopt the Korean style of export-led growth in manufactures, would they not create the same crisis of overproduction as exists in the commodity markets today?

How many developing nations will be able to follow East Asia's growth is impossible to tell. The latest *World Development Report* optimistically forecast significant progress across the globe, provided that poorer nations adopted "market friendly" policies and richer nations eschewed protectionism.[100] Were Taiwan and Korea to be followed by the larger states of Southeast Asia such as Malaysia and Thailand, then by South Asia and a number of Latin American countries, that would blur the North-South divide and make international economic alignments altogether more variegated. Moreover, sustained manufacturing success among developing countries *outside* East Asia might stimulate imitation elsewhere.

At the moment, however, the usual cluster of factors influencing relative economic performance—cultural attitudes, education, political stability, capacity to carry out long-term plans—suggests that while a small but growing number of countries is moving from a "have-not" to a "have" status, many more remain behind. The story of winners and losers in history will continue, therefore, only this time modern communications will remind us all of the growing disparity among the world's nations and regions.

NOTES

[1] Discussed further in my new book, *Preparing For the Twenty-First Century* (Random House, 1993).

[2] For reasons of size and organization, China and India (containing around 37 percent of the world's population) are not treated here: for coverage, see Chapter 9, "India and China," of *Preparing For the Twenty-First Century*.

[3] *World Tables 1991* (Washington, DC: World Bank, 1991), pp. 268–269, 352–353.

[4] *World Tables 1991*, pp. 268–269, 352–353.

[5] See the World Bank publication *Trends in Developing Economies*, 1990, pp. 299–303, for Korea.

[6] For descriptions, see F. Braudel, *Civilization and Capitalism: Vol. 3, The Perspective of the World* (Harper and Row, 1986), pp. 506–511.

[7] See P. Lyon, "Emergence of the Third World," in H. Bull and A. Watson, editors, *The Expansion of International Society* (Oxford University Press, 1983), p. 229 ff.; G. Barraclough, *An Introduction to Contemporary History* (Penguin, 1967), chapter 6, "The Revolt Against the West."

[8] J. Ravenhill, "The North-South Balance of Power," *International Affairs*, Vol. 66, No. 4 (1990), pp. 745–746. See also, J. Cruickshank, "The Rise and Fall of the Third World: A Concept Whose Time Has Passed," *World Review*, February 1991, pp. 28–29. Ravenhill's divisions are high-income oil-exporting countries; industrializing economies with strong states and relatively low levels of indebtedness (Taiwan, etc.); industrializing economies with the state apparatus under challenge and/or with debt problems (Argentina, Poland); potential newly industrializing countries (Malaysia, Thailand); primary commodity producers (in sub-Saharan Africa, Central America).

[9] Ravenhill, "The North-South Balance of Power," p. 732.

[10] S. Fardoust and A. Dhareshwan, *Long-Term Outlook for the World Economy: Issues and Projections for the 1990s*, a World Bank report (February 1990), p. 9, Table 3.

[11] W. L. M. Adriaansen and J. G. Waardensburg, editors, *A Dual World Economy* (Groningen: Wolters-Noordhoff, 1989).

[12] P. Drysdale, "The Pacific Basin and Its Economic Vitality," in J. W. Morley, editor, *The Pacific Basin: New Challenges for the United States* (Academy of Political Science with the

East Asian Institute and the Center on Japanese Economy and Business, 1986), p. 11.

[13]While Korea has a population of around 43 million and Taiwan about 20 million, Hong Kong possesses 5.7 million and Singapore only 2.7 million.

[14]See especially, "Taiwan and Korea: Two Paths to Prosperity," *The Economist*, July 14, 1990, pp. 19–21; also "South Korea" (survey), *The Economist*, August 18, 1990. There is a useful comparative survey in L. A. Veit, "Time of the New Asian Tigers," *Challenge*, July–August 1987, pp. 49–55.

[15]N. D. Kristof, "In Taiwan, Only the Strong Get US Degrees," *The New York Times*, March 26, 1989, p. 11.

[16]Figures taken, respectively, from J. Paxton, editor, *The Statesman's Year-book 1990–1991* (St. Martin's Press, 1990); and from R. N. Gwynne, *New Horizons? Third World Industrialization in an International Framework* (New York/London: Wiley, 1990), p. 199.

[17]Lest this 1987 figure appear too distant, note that Korea's sixth Five-Year Plan calls for a national savings rate of 33.5 percent in the early 1990s: see *Trends in Developing Economies*, p. 300. This table is taken from p. 31 (Table 10) of T. Fukuchi and M. Kagami, editors, *Perspectives on the Pacific Basin Economy: A Comparison of Asia and Latin America* (Tokyo: Asian Club Foundation, Institute of Developing Economics, 1990).

[18]The table on p. 4 (Table 1) of Fukuchi and Kagami shows the different rates of growth, and of export's share of total GDP, of the Asian Pacific nations compared with those of Latin America. See also H. Hughes, "Catching Up: The Asian Newly Industrializing Economies in the 1990s," *Asian Development Review*, Vol. 7, No. 2 (1989), p. 132 (and Table 3).

[19]"The Yen Block" (Survey), *The Economist*, July 15, 1989; "Japan Builds A New Power Base," *Business Week*, March 20, 1989, pp. 18–25.

[20]"Taiwan and Korea: Two Paths to Prosperity," *The Economist*, p. 19; "South Korea: A New Society," *The Economist*, April 15, 1989, pp. 23–25.

[21]"Development Brief," *The Economist*, May 26, 1990, p. 81, for the first two columns; the GNP per capita comes from *World Development Report*, 1990, pp. 178–179.

[22]"When a Miracle Stalls," *The Economist*, October 6, 1990, pp. 33–34

(on Taiwan); *Trends in Developing Economies*, 1990, pp. 299–300 (Korea); R. A. Scalapino, "Asia and the United States: The Challenges Ahead," *Foreign Affairs*, Vol. 69, No. 1 (1989–1990), especially pp. 107–112; "Hong Kong, In China's Sweaty Palm," *The Economist*, November 5, 1988, pp. 19–22.

[23]See the detailed forecasts in "Asia 2010: The Power of People," *Far Eastern Economist Review*, May 17, 1990, pp. 27–58. On industrial retooling, see pp. 8–9 of "South Korea" (Survey), *The Economist*, August 18, 1990.

[24]N. Sadik, editor, *Population: The UNFPA Experience*, (New York University Press, 1984), chapter 4, "Latin America and the Caribbean," pp. 51–52.

[25]A. F. Lowenthal, "Rediscovering Latin America," *Foreign Affairs*, Vol. 69, No. 4 (Fall 1990), p. 34.

[26]Figure from "Latin America's Hope," *The Economist*, December 9, 1989, p. 14.

[27]Taken from page 5 of G. W. Landau et al., *Latin America at a Crossroads*, (The Trilateral Commission, 1990), which reports the source as being *Economic and Social Progress in Latin America: 1989 Report* (Washington, DC: Inter-American Development Bank, 1989), Table B1, p. 463.

[28]As mentioned earlier, Japan and its East Asian emulators also sought to protect fledgling domestic industries, but that was in order to create a strong base from which to mount an export offensive—*not* to establish an economic bastion within which their industries would be content to remain.

[29]For details, see the various national entries in *The Statesman's Year-Book 1990–91*; and *The Economist World Atlas and Almanac* (Prentice Hall, 1989), pp. 131–157. R. N. Gwynne's *New Horizons?* has useful comments on Latin America's "inward-oriented industrialization" (chapter 11), which he then contrasts with East Asia's "outward orientation" (chapter 12).

[30]World Resources Institute, *World Resources 1990–91* (Oxford University Press, 1990), p. 39.

[31]*World Resources 1990–91*, p. 246.

[32]In 1989, the net transfer of capital leaving Latin America was around $25 billion.

[33]For the above, see pp. 33–48 of *World Resources 1990–91*: "Latin America At a Crossroads," B.J. McCormick, *The World Economy: Patterns of Growth and Change* (Oxford University Press, 1988), chapter 13;

"Latin American debt: The banks' great escape," *The Economist*, February 11, 1989, pp. 73–74.

[34]For educational details, see *The Statesman's Year-Book 1990–91*, pp. 95, 236; for literacy rates, see especially those of Uruguay, Costa Rica, Argentina, and Venezuela in the table "Development Brief," *The Economist*, May 26, 1990, p. 81.

[35]T. E. Martinez, "Argentina: Living with Hyperinflation," *The Atlantic Monthly*, December 1990, p. 36.

[36]*The Statesman's Year-Book 1990–91*, pp. 584, 605.

[37]T. Kamm, "Latin America Edges Toward Free Trade," *The Wall Street Journal*, November 30, 1990, p. A10.

[38]C. Farnsworth, "Latin American Economies Given Brighter Assessments," *The New York Times*, October 30, 1990; "Latin America's New Start," *The Economist*, June 9, 1990, p. 11; N.C. Nash, "A Breath of Fresh Economic Air Brings Change to Latin America," *The New York Times*, November 13, 1991, pp. A1, D5.

[39]"Latin America's Hope," *The Economist*, December 9, 1989, p. 15; Nash, "A Breath of Fresh Economic Air Brings Change to Latin America."

[40]J. Brooke, "Debt and Democracy," *The New York Times*, December 5, 1990, p. A16; P. Truell, "As the U.S. Slumps, Latin America Suffers," *The Wall Street Journal*, November 19, 1990, p. 1.

[41]For these arguments, see especially Lowenthal's fine summary, "Rediscovering Latin America," in *Foreign Affairs*; also G.A. Fauriol, "The Shadow of Latin American Affairs," *Foreign Affairs*, Vol. 69, No. 1 (1989–1990), pp. 116–134; and M.D. Hayes, "The U.S. and Latin America: A Lost Decade?" *Foreign Affairs*, Vol. 68, No. 1 (1988–1989), pp. 180–198.

[42]This is the subdivision preferred by *The Economist World Atlas and Almanac*, pp. 256–271, which discusses the North African states (except Egypt) in a later section, under "Africa."

[43]"The Arab World" (survey), *The Economist*, May 12, 1990.

[44]See "Religions," p. 21 of the *Hammond Comparative World Atlas* (Hammond, Inc., 1993 edition).

[45]The few oil-producing countries in Africa, such as Gabon and Nigeria, still have relatively low per capita GNPs compared with the Arab Gulf states.

46G. Brooks and T. Horwitz, "Shaken Sheiks," *The Wall Street Journal*, December 28, 1990, pp. A1, A4.

47"The Arab World," *The Economist*, p. 12.

48In 1985, adult female literacy in the Yemen Arab Republic was a mere 3 percent, in Saudi Arabia 12 percent, in Iran 39 percent. On the other hand, many women from the middle and upper-middle classes in Muslim countries are educated, which suggests that poverty, as much as culture, plays a role.

49M. A. Heller, "The Middle East: Out of Step with History," *Foreign Affairs* Vol. 69, No. 1 (1989–1990), pp. 153–171.

50See also the remarks by S. F. Wells and M. A. Bruzonsky, editors, *Security in the Middle East: Regional Change and Great Power Strategies* (Westview Press, 1986), pp. 1–3.

51D. E. Duncan, "Africa: The Long Good-bye," *The Atlantic Monthly*, July 1990, p. 20.

52J. A. Marcum, "Africa: A Continent Adrift," *Foreign Affairs*, Vol. 68, No. 1 (1988–1989), p. 177. See also the penetrating article by K. R. Richburg, "Why Is Black Africa Overwhelmed While East Asia Overcomes?" *The International Herald Tribune*, July 14, 1992, pp. 1, 6.

53C. H. Farnsworth, "Report by World Bank Sees Poverty Lessening by 2000 Except in Africa," *The New York Times*, July 16, 1990, p. A3; Marcum, "Africa: A Continent Adrift"; Duncan, "Africa: The Long Good-bye"; and "The bleak continent," *The Economist*, December 9, 1989, pp. 80–81.

54B. Fischer, "Developing Countries in the Process of Economic Globalisation," *Intereconomics* (March/April 1990), p. 55.

55J.S. Whitaker, *How Can Africa Survive?* (Council on Foreign Relations Press, 1988).

56As will be clear from the text, this discussion excludes the Republic of South Africa.

57T. J. Goliber, "Africa's Expanding Population: Old Problems, New Policies," *Population Bulletin*, Vol. 44, No. 3 (November 1989), pp. 4–49, an outstandingly good article.

58*World Resources 1990–91*, p. 254.

59*World Resources 1990–91*, p. 254 (overall population growth to 2025), and p. 258 (infant mortality). L.K. Alt-
man, "W.H.O Says 40 Million Will Be Infected With AIDS by 2000," *The New York Times*, June 18, 1991, p. C3 (for percentage of GNP devoted to health care).

60L.K. Altman, "W.H.O. Says 40 Million Will Be Infected With AIDS Virus by 2000"; and for further figures, see Kennedy, *Preparing For the Twenty First Century*, chapter 3.

61K.H. Hunt, "Scenes From a Nightmare," *The New York Times Magazine*, August 12, 1990, pp. 26, 50–51.

62See Whitaker, *How Can Africa Survive?*, especially chapter 4, "The Blessings of Children," for a fuller analysis; and J.C. Caldwell and P. Caldwell, "High Fertility in Sub-Saharan Africa," *Scientific American*, May 1990, pp. 118–125.

63"The bleak continent," *The Economist*; Whitaker, *How Can Africa Survive?*, chapters 1 and 2; Goliber, "Africa's Expanding Population," pp. 12–13.

64Whitaker, *How Can Africa Survive?*; Duncan, "Africa: The Long Good-bye."

65"Fruits of Containment" (op-ed), *The Wall Street Journal*, December 18, 1990, p. A14, for the Africa-Belgium comparison; H. McRae, "Visions of tomorrow's world," *The Independent* (London), November 26, 1991, for Africa's share of world GDP.

66"Aid to Africa," *The Economist*, December 8, 1990, p. 48.

67In this regard, East Asian nations like Taiwan and Korea, possessing coherent indigenous populations, are once again more favorably situated.

68*The Economist World Atlas and Almanac* (Prentice Hall, 1989), p. 293.

69Apart from the country by country comments in *The Economist World Atlas and Almanac*, see also K. Ingham, *Politics in Modern Africa: The Uneven Tribal Dimension* (Routledge, 1990); "Africa's Internal Wars of the 1980s—Contours and Prospects," United States Institute of Peace, *In Brief*, No. 18 (May 1990).

70T. R. Odhiambo, "Human resources development: problems and prospects in developing countries," *Impact of Science on Society*, No. 155 (1989), p. 214.

71*The Statesman's Yearbook 1989*, p. 84; Goliber, "Africa's Expanding Population," p. 15.

72*The Statesman's Yearbook 1989*, pp. 1,159–1,160 (certain smaller groups of students are excluded from these totals).
73P. Lewis, "Nyere and Tanzania: No Regrets at Socialism," *The New York Times*, October 24, 1990.

74"Wind of change, but a different one," *The Economist*, July 14, 1990, p. 44. See also the encouraging noises made—on a country by country basis—in the World Bank's own *Trends in Developing Economies*, 1990, as well as in its 1989 publication *Sub-Saharan Africa: From Crisis to Sustainable Growth* (summarized in "The bleak continent," *The Economist*, pp. 80–81).

75See especially P. Pradervand, *Listening to Africa: Developing Africa from the Grassroots* (Greenwood, 1989); B. Schneider, *The Barefoot Revolution* (London: I. T. Publications, 1988); K. McAfee, "Why The Third World Goes Hungry," *Commonweal* June 15, 1990, pp. 384–385.

76See Edward Sheehan's article "In the Heart of Somalia," *The New York Review*, January 14, 1993. See also Duncan, "Africa: The Long Good-bye," p. 24; G. Hancock, *Lords of Poverty: The Power, Prestige, and Corruption of the International Aid* (Atlantic Monthly Press, 1989); G.B.N. Ayittey, "No More Aid for Africa," *The Wall Street Journal*, October 18, 1991 (op-ed), p. A14.

77Whitaker, *How Can Africa Survive?* p. 231.

78See, for example, the conclusions in B. Fischer, "Developing Countries in the Process of Economic Globalisation," pp. 55–63.

79Caldwell and Caldwell, "High Fertility in Sub-Saharan Africa," *Scientific American*, p. 88.

80"AIDS in Africa," *The Economist*, November 24, 1989, p. 1B; E. Eckholm and J. Tierney, "AIDS in Africa: A Killer Rages On," *The New York Times*, September 16, 1990, pp. 1, 4; C.M. Becker, "The Demo-Economic Impact of the AIDS Pandemic in Sub-Saharan Africa," *World Development*, Vol. 18, No. 12 (1990), pp. 1,599–1,619.

81*World Resources 1990–91*, p. 254. The US-Canada total in 1960 was 217 million to Latin America's 210 million; by 2025 it is estimated to be 332 million to 762 million.

82*World Resources 1990–91*, p. 254.

83Apart from chapters 2 and 4 above, see again *World Resources 1990–91*, pp. 33–48; T. Wicker, "Bush Ventures South," *The New York Times*, December 9, 1990, p. E17; T. Golden, "Mexico Fights Cholera But Hates to Say Its

Name," *The New York Times*, September 14, 1991, p. 2.

[84]"The Arab World," *The Economist*, p. 4.

[85]"The Arab World," p. 6; Y. F. Ibrahim, "In Algeria, Hope for Democracy But Not Economy," *The New York Times*, July 26, 1991, pp. A1, A6.

[86]*World Resources 1990–91*, pp. 258–259.

[87]As quoted in "The Arab World," p. 5.

[88]See again Pradervand, *Listening to Africa*. Also important is D. Pearce et al., *Sustainable Development: Economics and Environment in the Third World* (Gower, 1990).

[89]F. Gable, "Changing Climate and Caribbean Coastlines," *Oceanus*, Vol. 30, No. 4 (Winter 1987–1988), pp. 53–56; G. Gable and D.G. Aubrey, "Changing Climate and the Pacific,"

Oceanus, Vol. 32, No. 4 (Winter 1989–1990), pp. 71–73.

[90]"The Arab World," p. 12.

[91]*World Resources 1990–91*, pp. 176–177; *State of the World 1990*, pp. 48–49.

[92]C. Juma, *The Gene Hunters: Biotechnology and the Scramble for Seeds* (Princeton University Press, 1989).

[93]D. Pirages, *Global Technopolitics: The International Politics of Technology and Resources* (Brooks-Cole, 1989), p. 152.

[94]McAfee, "Why the Third World goes Hungry," p. 380.

[95]See P. K Ghosh, editor, *Technology Policy and Development: A Third World Perspective* (Greenwood, 1984), p. 109.

[96]C. J. Dixon et al., editors, *Multina-*

tional Corporations and the Third World (Croom Helm, 1986).

[97]For a good example, B. Onimode, *A Political Economy of the African Crisis* (Humanities Press International, 1988), especially p. 310 ff.

[98]M. Clash, "Development Policy, Technology Assessment and the New Technologies," *Futures,* November 1990, p. 916.

[99]L. Cuyvers and D. Van den Bulcke, "Some Reflections on the 'Outward-oriented' Development Strategy of the Far Eastern Newly Industrialising Countries," especially pp. 196–197, in Adriaansen and Waardenburg, *A Dual World Economy.*

[100]*World Development Report 1991: The Challenge of Development*, a World Bank report (Oxford University Press, 1991). See also the World Bank's *Global Economic Prospects and the Developing Countries* (1991).

Global Change

INCREASING ECONOMIC INTEGRATION AND ERODING POLITICAL SOVEREIGNTY

RALPH C. BRYANT

Ralph C. Bryant is a senior fellow in the Brookings Economic Studies program. His book, International Coordination of National Stabilization Policies *(forthcoming), is one of the studies for the Integrating National Economies project.*

Two fundamental facts characterize the political and economic structure of the world at the end of the 20th century. First, the world is, and for the foreseeable future will be, organized politically into nation-states with sovereign governments. Second, increasing economic integration among nations has been eroding the differences among national economies and undermining the autonomy of national governments, a trend that also shows no sign of stopping.

International economic interdependence has significantly improved standards of living for most nations and promises further sizable benefits. Yet the heightened competition between national political sovereignty and increased cross-border economic integration could cause major trouble if national policies and international cooperation are poorly managed.

Increasing World Economic Integration

Profound technological, social, and cultural changes have bound the world's nations more closely together by reducing the effective economic distances among them. The same transportation and communication wizardry that makes it easier and cheaper for compa-

The opportunities and tensions arising from the competition between cross-border economic integration and national political sovereignty are the focus of a major Brookings project, entitled Integrating National Economies. Scholars from a variety of disciplines have produced 22 studies for the project, to be published over the course of the next year. In this article Ralph C. Bryant identifies some important themes and issues common to all these studies. For a complete list of the studies, contact the Brookings Marketing Department or call toll-free 1-800-275-1447.

nies in Ohio to ship goods to California, for residents of Marseilles to visit relatives in Paris, and for investors in Hokkaido to buy and sell shares on the Tokyo Stock Exchange also speeds trade, migration, and capital movements among nations and continents. Technology has, in effect, shrunk the planet.

Consumers and producers are increasingly aware of potentially profitable international exchanges and of economic opportunities abroad. Foreign goods, foreign vacations, and foreign financial investments were once exotic but are now virtually commonplace.

Communications technology has especially boosted financial activity. Computers, switching devices, and telecommunications satellites have slashed the cost of transmitting information internationally, of confirming transactions, and of paying for transactions. Forty years ago foreign exchange could be bought and sold only during business hours in the initiating party's time zone. Now large banks pass the management of their worldwide foreign-exchange positions around the globe from one branch to another, staying continuously ahead of the setting sun.

Government policies have reinforced the effects of technology. Before World War II nations routinely erected "separation fences" at their borders—taxing goods moving in international trade, directly restricting imports and exports, and curbing financial exchanges between domestic and foreign residents. The effect was to reduce cross-border transactions, sometimes even to eliminate them. The particularly zealous use of these policies during the 1930s is now believed to have deepened and lengthened the Great Depression.

After the war, most national governments began, sometimes unilaterally, more often collaboratively, to lower these fences, to poke holes in them, or sometimes even to jettison parts of them altogether. The international negotiations under the auspices of the General Agreement on Trade and Tariffs (GATT)—for example, the Kennedy Round in the 1960s, the Tokyo Round in the 1970s, and most recently the protracted negotiations of the Uruguay Round, formally signed only last April—stand out as the most prominent examples of fence lowering for trade in goods. Though contentious and only partially successful, the GATT negotiations sharply reduced at-the-border restrictions on trade in goods and services.

The fences barring financial transactions were lowered later and to less dramatic effect. Nonetheless, by the 1990s curbs on capital flows, especially among the industrial countries, were much less important and widespread than they had been during the 1950s.

The recent strides in technology alone would have substantially integrated the world economy—as would the lower trade fences alone. But together, the two have reinforced each other and profoundly transformed the world economy.

Changes in the Government of Nations
As the world's nations have grown together economically, the world's political structure has also changed markedly. Since World War II the number of nation-states has grown rapidly, and political power has been diffused more broadly among them. Rising nationalism and, in some areas, heightened ethnic tensions have accompanied that increasing political pluralism.

Only 44 nations participated in the July 1944 Bretton Woods conference that gave birth to the International Monetary Fund. By the end of 1970, the IMF had 118 member nations; by the mid-1980s, 150; by December 1993, 178. Much of this growth reflects the collapse of colonial empires. While many nations today are small and carry little individual weight in the global economy, their combined influence is considerable and their interests can no longer be as easily ignored.

Over the years the United States gradually lost its political and economic hegemony. Immediately after World War II, the United States alone accounted for more than a third of world production. By the early 1990s, the U.S. share had fallen to about one fifth. The political and economic influence of the European colonial powers also waned while the economic significance of nations such as Japan, Korea, Indonesia, China, Brazil, and Mexico grew. A world once dominated by one or a few nations has yielded to one in which economic power and influence are widely shared.

Turmoil and prospects for fundamental changes in the formerly centrally planned economies have been still other forces radically transforming world politics. Governments that for years tried to isolate their economies are now trying to adopt reforms modeled on Western capitalist principles. To the extent they succeed, those nations' economies will increasingly become integrated with the global economy. Political and economic alignments among Western industrialized nations will be forced to adapt.

Dilemmas for National Policies
Unfortunately for the peace of mind of nations' policymakers, the interplay between the trends of enhanced economic integration and increasing political pluralism tends to generate discord. Each trend has ex-

acerbated a mismatch between the economic and political structures of the world. The effective domains of economic markets have come to coincide less and less well with national governmental jurisdictions.

When the separation fences at nations' borders were high, governments and citizens could easily distinguish "international" from "domestic" policies. International policies dealt with at-the-border barriers (for example, tariffs) or events abroad. Domestic policies involved everything behind the nation's borders—for example, competition and antitrust rules, corporate governance, product standards, worker safety, regulation and supervision of financial institutions, environmental protection, tax codes, and the government's budget. Domestic policies were treated as a sovereign preserve, to be determined by the preferences of the nation's citizens and its political institutions, without regard for effects on other nations.

With economic integration, however, the differences in nations' domestic policies, formerly neglected, have increasingly been exposed to international scrutiny. Accordingly, national governments and international negotiations have been confronted with numerous issues of deeper, behind-the-border integration. For example, if country A permits manufacturers to emit air and water pollutants whereas country B does not, companies that use pollution-generating methods of production will find it cheaper to produce in country A. Manufacturers in country B that compete worldwide with those in country A are likely to complain and to press for international pollution standards.

Many issues of this type have already complicated negotiations over the evolution of the European Community, the GATT Uruguay Round, and the North American Free Trade Agreement. As time goes on, debates about behind-the-border policies will occur more and more often and prove at least as complex and contentious as past negotiations over at-the-border barriers.

Cross-Border Spillovers and Diminished National Autonomy
A chief source of tensions is activities in one nation whose economic consequences spill across borders and affect other nations. Such spillovers in turn make it more difficult for governments to control events within their borders.

Illustrations abound. Lax banking and securities regulations in one nation undermine the ability of all to enforce their regulations and deal with fraudulent transactions. When one nation pollutes the air or water that other nations breathe or drink, it becomes a matter for international negotiation. Spillovers between national financial markets erode the power of any one nation's central bank to maintain monetary conditions different from those in other countries.

The tensions resulting from cross-border spillovers and diminished autonomy can be particularly vexing when national policies are alleged to be competitively unfair, as in a dispute where manufacturers in country A emit pollutants and those in country B do not. Likewise, if country C requires all goods, whether produced at home or abroad, to meet safety or labor standards that foreign competitors find too expensive to meet, C's standards effectively limit or even eliminate foreign competition for its own producers. Citing examples of this sort, producers or governments in individual nations often complain that business is not conducted on a "level playing field." Typically, the complaining nations proposes that *other* nations adjust their policies to moderate or remove the competitive inequities.

Yet international trade exists precisely because of differences among nations—in resource endowments, labor skills, and consumer tastes. Nations produce goods and services in which they are relatively most efficient. In a fundamental sense, cross-border trade is valuable because the playing field is *not* level. When David Ricardo first developed the theory of comparative advantage early in the 19th century, he focused on national differences in technology or climate. Today the "climatic" differences are often social, not physical. But the theory of comparative advantage, taking all differences into account, continues to argue validly that free trade among nations will typically maximize global welfare.

It is unrealistic, even pernicious, to suppose that all nations can be made homogeneous in every important respect. Suppose country A decides that it is too poor to afford a clean environment and that it will permit production of goods that pollute local air and water supplies—or that it cannot afford stringent safety standards. It will then argue that other nations should not impute to it the high value they place on a clean environment and stringent safety standards (just as A should not impose its valuations on other nations). The essence of political sovereignty is that national residents be able to order their lives and property in accord with their own preferences.

Which perspective is more compelling? Is country A merely exercising its national preferences and appropriately exploiting its comparative advantage in goods that are dirty or dangerous to produce? Or does a legitimate problem exist that justifies pressure from other nations urging country A to change its policies (thus curbing its national sovereignty)?

Challenges to Political Sovereignty

In today's world political system, a nation's residents are presumed free to select their own political arrangements without interference from outsiders. Property rights, too, are allocated by nation. (The "global commons," such as outer space and the deep seabed, are the sole exception.) A nation is assumed to have the sovereign right to choose how to use its own property.

Although some nations have had sovereignty wrested from them by force in times of war, until recently few people have questioned the premises of political sovereignty. Today, however, more and more people and groups—occasionally even national governments—are claiming that, under certain circumstances, a more universal or international set of values should override the preferences or policies of particular nations.

Environmental groups from many nations, for exam-

ple, characterize tropical rain forests as the lungs of the world and as the genetic repository for numerous species of plants and animals. Regarding those forests as the heritage of all mankind, Americans, Europeans, and Japanese challenge the timber-cutting policies of Brazilians and Indonesians. Likewise, many citizens worldwide found South Africa's apartheid policies an affront to universal values and denied that the government legitimately represented the majority of the nation's people. Many national governments thus banded together to apply economic sanctions against South Africa.

A common feature of cases of this type is the presence, real or alleged, of what can be termed "psychological externalities" or "political failures." Those who challenge conventional national politics from these perspectives insist on the international community's right to constrain the exercise of individual nations' sovereignties through negotiations or, if necessary, even stronger intervention.

Options for Managing International Convergence

For issues where cross-border spillovers are weak and psychological externalities or political failures may be minor (for example, education and road-building expenditures), national governments encounter few problems stemming from the increasing integration of the global economy. Diversity across nations may persist rel-

DOMESTIC POLITICAL INSTITU-

TIONS MUST EVOLVE IN WAYS

THAT ARE RESPONSIVE

TO THE WORLD'S PERVASIVE

DRIFT TOWARD BEHIND-

THE-BORDER INTEGRATION.

atively easily. But at the other extreme, for issues where spillovers are strong and political sensitivities are asserted powerfully, diversity in nations' policies will be contentious and may even be impossible. For such issues national policies and behaviors may eventually have to converge to common, worldwide patterns. Whether such convergence proves harmful (national policies and practices being driven to a least common denominator, in effect a "race to the bottom") or mutually beneficial ("survival of the fittest and the best") will depend on how governments manage the transition.

1. A CLASH OF VIEWS

Economic convergence could be managed in a variety of ways. At one extreme of a continuum—the traditional practice for most of this century—national governments could persist in making decisions unilaterally, relying solely on market competition to guide convergence. A more cooperative approach, known as mutual recognition, assumes that governments make separate decisions, but exchange information and consult with each other to constrain formation of national regulations and policies. Each member state of the European Union, for example, agrees to accept, in many policy areas, the regulations, standards, and certification procedures of other EU members. Wine or liquor produced in any EU country can be sold in all 12 member countries despite differing production standards. Doctors licensed in France are permitted to practice in Germany, and vice versa, even if licensing procedures in the two countries differ.

Going further in the direction of cooperation, governments could mutually monitor each other's behavior (as happens in the Group of Seven finance ministers meetings) and agree on guidelines or rules that restrict their freedom to set independent policies. More ambitiously, governments could "coordinate" by jointly designing and mutually adjusting policies, as for example in the World Health Organization's procedures for controlling communicable diseases and the 1987 Montreal Protocol for protecting stratospheric ozone by reducing emissions of chlorofluorocarbons.

Harmonized "regional standards" or "world standards," as in the 1988 agreement among major central banks to set minimum ratios for the required capital positions of commercial banks, require still higher levels of intergovernmental cooperation. Finally, at the other extreme of the continuum, governments could engage in continuous bargaining and joint, centralized decision-making. This last approach to managing economic convergence, however, is of only theoretical interest for now, and can be imagined only for the middle or late decades of the 21st century.

Political Challenges for the Future

Clearly, economic integration poses many challenges for national governments. All the issues have complex economic dimensions, and governments must better understand the economic costs and benefits involved before they can choose sound national policies and the most appropriate management options for cooperating with other governments.

Nonetheless, the most profound challenges are political. Existing political institutions within nations and the nascent international institutions cannot plausibly stand still: "business as usual" will not be viable.

To be sure, the useful concept of "subsidiarity"— the presumption that decentralized allocations and exercises of political power are to be preferred absent compelling reasons for centralization—provides a solid foundation for retaining many governmental decisions at the national (and even local) level. For many functional issues, the option of mutual recognition of separately decided national policies is an appealing first-recourse approach to managing international convergence. In effect, national governments would choose decentralized decisions and mutual recognition where possible, would coordinate decisions when necessary, and would centralize decisions or delegate authority to an international institution only when mutual recognition and coordination were shown to be unworkable.

Even with a heavy emphasis on subsidiarity, however, national governments must develop and nurture many varieties of cooperation. Still more important, domestic political institutions must evolve in ways that are responsive to the world's pervasive drift toward behind-the-border integration. The rapid pace at which economic behavior has become internationalized has far outstripped the adaptation of political institutions. This gap—in effect, a burgeoning political deficit—will have to be narrowed if the world economy and polity are to evolve satisfactorily in the 21st century.

The two axial principles of our age—tribalism and globalism—clash at every point except one: they may both be threatening to democracy

JIHAD VS. McWORLD

BENJAMIN R. BARBER

Benjamin R. Barber is the Whitman Professor of Political Science at Rutgers University. Barber's most recent books are Strong Democracy *(1984),* The Conquest of Politics *(1988), and* An Aristocracy of Everyone *(1992).*

Just beyond the horizon of current events lie two possible political figures—both bleak, neither democratic. The first is a retribalization of large swaths of humankind by war and bloodshed: a threatened Lebanonization of national states in which culture is pitted against culture, people against people, tribe against tribe—a Jihad in the name of a hundred narrowly conceived faiths against every kind of interdependence, every kind of artificial social cooperation and civic mutuality. The second is being borne in on us by the onrush of economic and ecological forces that demand integration and uniformity and that mesmerize the world with fast music, fast computers, and fast food—with MTV, Macintosh, and McDonald's, pressing nations into one commercially homogenous global network: one McWorld tied together by technology, ecology, communications, and commerce. The planet is falling precipitantly apart *and* coming reluctantly together at the very same moment.

These two tendencies are sometimes visible in the same countries at the same instant: thus Yugoslavia, clamoring just recently to join the New Europe, is exploding into fragments; India is trying to live up to its reputation as the world's largest integral democracy while powerful new fundamentalist parties like the Hindu nationalist Bharatiya Janata Party, along with nationalist assassins, are imperiling its hard-won unity. States are breaking up or joining up: the Soviet Union has disappeared almost overnight, its parts forming new unions with one another or with like-minded nationalities in neighboring states. The old interwar national state based on territory and political sovereignty looks to be a mere transitional development.

The tendencies of what I am here calling the forces of Jihad and the forces of McWorld operate with equal strength in opposite directions, the one driven by parochial hatreds, the other by universalizing markets, the one re-creating ancient subnational and ethnic borders from within, the other making national borders porous from without. They have

one thing in common: neither offers much hope to citizens looking for practical ways to govern themselves democratically. If the global future is to put Jihad's centrifugal whirlwind against McWorld's centripetal black hole, the outcome is unlikely to be democratic—or so I will argue.

McWorld, or the Globalization of Politics

FOUR IMPERATIVES MAKE UP THE DYNAMIC OF McWorld: a market imperative, a resource imperative, an information-technology imperative, and an ecological imperative. By shrinking the world and diminishing the salience of national borders, these imperatives have in combination achieved a considerable victory over factiousness and particularism, and not least of all over their most virulent traditional form—nationalism. It is the realists who are now Europeans, the utopians who dream nostalgically of a resurgent England or Germany, perhaps even a resurgent Wales or Saxony. Yesterday's wishful cry for one world has yielded to the reality of McWorld.

The market imperative. Marxist and Leninist theories of imperialism assumed that the quest for ever-expanding markets would in time compel nation-based capitalist economies to push against national boundaries in search of an international economic imperium. Whatever else has happened to the scientistic predictions of Marxism, in this domain they have proved farsighted. All national economies are now vulnerable to the inroads of larger, transnational markets within which trade is free, currencies are convertible, access to banking is open, and contracts are enforceable under law. In Europe, Asia, Africa, the South Pacific, and the Americas such markets are eroding national sovereignty and giving rise to entities—international banks, trade associations, transnational lobbies like OPEC and Greenpeace, world news services like CNN and the BBC, and multinational corporations that increasingly lack a meaningful national identity—that neither reflect nor respect nationhood as an organizing or regulative principle.

The market imperative has also reinforced the quest

for international peace and stability, requisites of an efficient international economy. Markets are enemies of parochialism, isolation, fractiousness, war. Market psychology attenuates the psychology of ideological and religious cleavages and assumes a concord among producers and consumers—categories that ill fit narrowly conceived national or religious cultures. Shopping has little tolerance for blue laws, whether dictated by pub-closing British paternalism, Sabbath-observing Jewish Orthodox fundamentalism, or no-Sunday-liquor-sales Massachusetts puritanism. In the context of common markets, international law ceases to be a vision of justice and becomes a workaday framework for getting things done—enforcing contracts, ensuring that governments abide by deals, regulating trade and currency relations, and so forth.

Common markets demand a common language, as well as a common currency, and they produce common behaviors of the kind bred by cosmopolitan city life everywhere. Commercial pilots, computer programmers, international bankers, media specialists, oil riggers, entertainment celebrities, ecology experts, demographers, accountants, professors, athletes—these compose a new breed of men and women for whom religion, culture, and nationality can seem only marginal elements in a working identity. Although sociologists of everyday life will no doubt continue to distinguish a Japanese from an American mode, shopping has a common signature throughout the world. Cynics might even say that some of the recent revolutions in Eastern Europe have had as their true goal not liberty and the right to vote but well-paying jobs and the right to shop (although the vote is proving easier to acquire than consumer goods). The market imperative is, then, plenty powerful; but, notwithstanding some of the claims made for "democratic capitalism," it is not identical with the democratic imperative.

Every nation, it turns out, needs something another nation has; some nations have almost nothing they need.

The resource imperative. Democrats once dreamed of societies whose political autonomy rested firmly on economic independence. The Athenians idealized what they called autarky, and tried for a while to create a way of life simple and austere enough to make the polis genuinely self-sufficient. To be free meant to be independent of any other community or polis. Not even the Athenians were able to achieve autarky, however: human nature, it turns out, is dependency. By the time of Pericles, Athenian politics was inextricably bound up with a flowering empire held together by naval power and commerce—an empire that, even as it appeared to enhance Athenian might, ate away at Athenian independence and autarky.

Master and slave, it turned out, were bound together by mutual insufficiency.

The dream of autarky briefly engrossed nineteenth-century America as well, for the underpopulated, endlessly bountiful land, the cornucopia of natural resources, and the natural barriers of a continent walled in by two great seas led many to believe that America could be a world unto itself. Given this past, it has been harder for Americans than for most to accept the inevitability of interdependence. But the rapid depletion of resources even in a country like ours, where they once seemed inexhaustible, and the maldistribution of arable soil and mineral resources on the planet, leave even the wealthiest societies ever more resource-dependent and many other nations in permanently desperate straits.

Every nation, it turns out, needs something another nation has; some nations have almost nothing they need.

The information-technology imperative. Enlightenment science and the technologies derived from it are inherently universalizing. They entail a quest for descriptive principles of general application, a search for universal solutions to particular problems, and an unswerving embrace of objectivity and impartiality.

Scientific progress embodies and depends on open communication, a common discourse rooted in rationality, collaboration, and an easy and regular flow and exchange of information. Such ideals can be hypocritical covers for power-mongering by elites, and they may be shown to be wanting in many other ways, but they are entailed by the very idea of science and they make science and globalization practical allies.

Business, banking, and commerce all depend on information flow and are facilitated by new communication technologies. The hardware of these technologies tends to be systemic and integrated—computer, television, cable, satellite, laser, fiber-optic, and microchip technologies combining to create a vast interactive communications and information network that can potentially give every person on earth access to every other person, and make every datum, every byte, available to every set of eyes. If the automobile was, as George Ball once said (when he gave his blessing to a Fiat factory in the Soviet Union during the Cold War), "an ideology on four wheels," then electronic telecommunication and information systems are an ideology at 186,000 miles per second—which makes for a very small planet in a very big hurry. Individual cultures speak particular languages; commerce and science increasingly speak English; the whole world speaks logarithms and binary mathematics.

Moreover, the pursuit of science and technology asks for, even compels, open societies. Satellite footprints do not respect national borders; telephone wires penetrate the most closed societies. With photocopying and then fax machines having infiltrated Soviet universities and *samizdat* literary circles in the eighties, and computer modems having multiplied like rabbits in communism's bureaucratic warrens thereafter, *glasnost* could not be far behind.

In their social requisites, secrecy and science are enemies.

The new technology's software is perhaps even more globalizing than its hardware. The information arm of international commerce's sprawling body reaches out and touches distinct nations and parochial cultures, and gives them a common face chiseled in Hollywood, on Madison Avenue, and in Silicon Valley. Throughout the 1980s one of the most-watched television programs in South Africa was *The Cosby Show*. The demise of apartheid was already in production. Exhibitors at the 1991 Cannes film festival expressed growing anxiety over the "homogenization" and "Americanization" of the global film industry when, for the third year running, American films dominated the awards ceremonies. America has dominated the world's popular culture for much longer, and much more decisively. In November of 1991 Switzerland's once insular culture boasted best-seller lists featuring *Terminator 2* as the No. 1 movie, *Scarlett* as the No. 1 book, and Prince's *Diamonds and Pearls* as the No. 1 record album. No wonder the Japanese are buying Hollywood film studios even faster than Americans are buying Japanese television sets. This kind of software supremacy may in the long term be far more important than hardware superiority, because culture has become more potent than armaments. What is the power of the Pentagon compared with Disneyland? Can the Sixth Fleet keep up with CNN? McDonald's in Moscow and Coke in China will do more to create a global culture than military colonization ever could. It is less the goods than the brand names that do the work, for they convey life-style images that alter perception and challenge behavior. They make up the seductive software of McWorld's common (at times much too common) soul.

Nationalism was once a force of integration and unification, but today, it is more often a reactionary and divisive force, pulverizing the very nations it once helped cement together.

Yet in all this high-tech commercial world there is nothing that looks particularly democratic. It lends itself to surveillance as well as liberty, to new forms of manipulation and covert control as well as new kinds of participation, to skewed, unjust market outcomes as well as greater productivity. The consumer society and the open society are not quite synonymous. Capitalism and democracy have a relationship, but it is something less than a marriage. An efficient free market after all requires that consumers be free to vote their dollars on competing goods, not that citizens be free to vote their values and beliefs on competing political candidates and programs. The free market flourished in junta-run Chile, in mili-

tary-governed Taiwan and Korea, and, earlier, in a variety of autocratic European empires as well as their colonial possessions.

The ecological imperative. The impact of globalization on ecology is a cliché even to world leaders who ignore it. We know well enough that the German forests can be destroyed by Swiss and Italians driving gas-guzzlers fueled by leaded gas. We also know that the planet can be asphyxiated by greenhouse gases because Brazilian farmers want to be part of the twentieth century and are burning down tropical rain forests to clear a little land to plough, and because Indonesians make a living out of converting their lush jungle into toothpicks for fastidious Japanese diners, upsetting the delicate oxygen balance and in effect puncturing our global lungs. Yet this ecological consciousness has meant not only greater awareness but also greater inequality, as modernized nations try to slam the door behind them, saying to developing nations, "The world cannot afford *your* modernization; ours has wrung it dry!"

Each of the four imperatives just cited is transnational, transideological, and transcultural. Each applies impartially to Catholics, Jews, Muslims, Hindus, and Buddhists; to democrats and totalitarians; to capitalists and socialists. The Enlightenment dream of a universal rational society has to a remarkable degree been realized—but in a form that is commercialized, homogenized, depoliticized, bureaucratized, and, of course, radically incomplete, for the movement toward McWorld is in competition with forces of global breakdown, national dissolution, and centrifugal corruption. These forces, working in the opposite direction, are the essence of what I call Jihad.

Jihad, or the Lebanonization of the World

OPEC, THE WORLD BANK, THE UNITED NATIONS, the International Red Cross, the multinational corporation . . . there are scores of institutions that reflect globalization. But they often appear as ineffective reactors to the world's real actors: national states and, to an ever greater degree, subnational factions in permanent rebellion against uniformity and integration—even the kind represented by universal law and justice. The headlines feature these players regularly: they are cultures, not countries; parts, not wholes; sects, not religions; rebellious factions and dissenting minorities at war not just with globalism but with the traditional nation-state. Kurds, Basques, Puerto Ricans, Ossetians, East Timoreans, Quebecois, the Catholics of Northern Ireland, Abkhasians, Kurile Islander Japanese, the Zulus of Inkatha, Catalonians, Tamils, and, of course, Palestinians—people without countries, inhabiting nations not their own, seeking smaller worlds within borders that will seal them off from modernity.

A powerful irony is at work here. Nationalism was once a force of integration and unification, a movement aimed at bringing together disparate clans, tribes, and cultural fragments under new, assimilationist flags. But as Ortega y Gasset noted more than sixty years ago, having won its victories, nationalism changed its strategy. In the 1920s, and again today, it is more often a reactionary and divisive force, pulverizing the very nations it once helped cement together. The force that creates nations is "inclusive," Ortega wrote in *The Revolt of the Masses*. "In periods of consolidation, nationalism has a positive value, and is a lofty standard. But in Europe everything is more than consolidated, and nationalism is nothing but a mania. . . ."

This mania has left the post–Cold War world smoldering with hot wars; the international scene is little more unified than it was at the end of the Great War, in Ortega's own time. There were more than thirty wars in progress last year, most of them ethnic, racial, tribal, or religious in character, and the list of unsafe regions doesn't seem to be getting any shorter. Some new world order!

The aim of many of these small-scale wars is to redraw boundaries, to implode states and resecure parochial identities: to escape McWorld's dully insistent imperatives. The mood is that of Jihad: war not as an instrument of policy but as an emblem of identity, an expression of community, an end in itself. Even where there is no shooting war, there is fractiousness, secession, and the quest for ever smaller communities. Add to the list of dangerous countries those at risk: In Switzerland and Spain, Jurassian and Basque separatists still argue the virtues of ancient identities, sometimes in the language of bombs. Hyperdisintegration in the former Soviet Union may well continue unabated—not just a Ukraine independent from the Soviet Union but a Bessarabian Ukraine independent from the Ukrainian republic; not just Russia severed from the defunct union but Tatarstan severed from Russia. Yugoslavia makes even the disunited, ex-Soviet, nonsocialist republics that were once the Soviet Union look integrated, its sectarian fatherlands springing up within factional motherlands like weeds within weeds within weeds. Kurdish independence would threaten the territorial integrity of four Middle Eastern nations. Well before the current cataclysm Soviet Georgia made a claim for autonomy from the Soviet Union, only to be faced with its Ossetians (164,000 in a republic of 5.5 million) demanding their own self-determination within Georgia. The Abkhasian minority in Georgia has followed suit. Even the good will established by Canada's once promising Meech Lake protocols is in danger, with Francophone Quebec again threatening the dissolution of the federation. In South Africa the emergence from apartheid was hardly achieved when friction between Inkatha's Zulus and the African National Congress's tribally identified members threatened to replace Europeans' racism with an indigenous tribal war. After thirty years of attempted integration using the colonial language (English) as a unifier, Nigeria is now playing with the idea of linguistic multiculturalism—which could mean the cultural breakup of the nation into hundreds of tribal fragments. Even Saddam Hussein has benefited from the threat of internal Jihad, having used renewed tribal and religious warfare to turn last season's mortal enemies into reluctant allies of an Iraqi nationhood that he nearly destroyed.

The passing of communism has torn away the thin veneer of internationalism (workers of the world unite!) to reveal ethnic prejudices that are not only ugly and deep-seated but increasingly murderous. Europe's old scourge, anti-Semitism, is back with a vengeance, but it is only one of many antagonisms. It appears all too easy to throw the historical gears into reverse and pass from a Communist dictatorship back into a tribal state.

Among the tribes, religion is also a battlefield. ("Jihad" is a rich word whose generic meaning is "struggle"—usually the struggle of the soul to avert evil. Strictly applied to religious war, it is used only in reference to battles where the faith is under assault, or battles against a government that denies the practice of Islam. My use here is rhetorical, but does follow both journalistic practice and history.) Remember the Thirty Years War? Whatever forms of Enlightenment universalism might once have come to grace such historically related forms of monotheism as Judaism, Christianity, and Islam, in many of their modern incarnations they are parochial rather than cosmopolitan, angry rather than loving, proselytizing rather than ecumenical, zealous rather than rationalist, sectarian rather than deistic, ethnocentric rather than universalizing. As a result, like the new forms of hypernationalism, the new expressions of religious fundamentalism are fractious and pulverizing, never integrating. This is religion as the Crusaders knew it: a battle to the death for souls that if not saved will be forever lost.

The atmospherics of Jihad have resulted in a breakdown of civility in the name of identity, of comity in the name of community. International relations have sometimes taken on the aspect of gang war—cultural turf battles featuring tribal factions that were supposed to be sublimated as integral parts of large national, economic, postcolonial, and constitutional entities.

The Darkening Future of Democracy

THESE RATHER MELODRAMATIC TABLEAUX VIvants do not tell the whole story, however. For all their defects, Jihad and McWorld have their attractions. Yet, to repeat and insist, the attractions are unrelated to democracy. Neither McWorld nor Jihad is remotely democratic in impulse. Neither needs democracy; neither promotes democracy.

McWorld does manage to look pretty seductive in a world obsessed with Jihad. It delivers peace, prosperity, and relative unity—if at the cost of independence, community, and identity (which is generally based on difference). The primary political values required by the global market are order and tranquillity, and freedom—as in the phrases "free trade," "free press," and "free love." Human rights are needed to a degree, but not citizenship or participation—and no more social justice and equality than are necessary to promote efficient economic production and consumption. Multinational corporations sometimes seem to prefer doing business with local oligarchs, inasmuch as they can take confidence from dealing with the boss on all crucial matters. Despots who slaughter their own populations are no problem, so long as they leave markets in place and refrain from making war on their neighbors (Saddam Hussein's fatal mistake). In trading partners, predictability is of more value than justice.

The Eastern European revolutions that seemed to arise out of concern for global democratic values quickly deteriorated into a stampede in the general direction of free markets and their ubiquitous, television-promoted shopping malls. East Germany's Neues Forum, that courageous gathering of intellectuals, students, and workers which overturned the Stalinist regime in Berlin in 1989, lasted only six months in Germany's mini-version of McWorld. Then it gave way to money and markets and monopolies from the West. By the time of the first all-German elections, it could scarcely manage to secure

---

Where new democratic experiments have been conducted in retribalizing societies the result has often been anarchy, repression, persecution, and the coming of new, noncommunist forms of very old kinds of despotism.

---

three percent of the vote. Elsewhere there is growing evidence that *glasnost* will go and *perestroika*—defined as privatization and an opening of markets to Western bidders—will stay. So understandably anxious are the new rulers of Eastern Europe and whatever entities are forged from the residues of the Soviet Union to gain access to credit and markets and technology—McWorld's flourishing new currencies—that they have shown themselves willing to trade away democratic prospects in pursuit of them: not just old totalitarian ideologies and command-economy production models but some possible indigenous experiments with a third way between capitalism and socialism, such as economic cooperatives and employee stock-ownership plans, both of which have their ardent supporters in the East.

Jihad delivers a different set of virtues: a vibrant local identity, a sense of community, solidarity among kinsmen, neighbors, and countrymen, narrowly conceived. But it also guarantees parochialism and is grounded in exclusion. Solidarity is secured through war against outsiders. And solidarity often means obedience to a hierarchy in governance, fanaticism in beliefs, and the obliteration of individual selves in the name of the group. Deference to leaders and intolerance toward outsiders (and toward "enemies within") are hallmarks of tribalism—hardly the attitudes required for the cultivation of new democratic women and men capable of governing themselves. Where new democratic experiments have been conducted in retribalizing societies, in both Europe and the Third World, the result has often been anarchy, repression, persecution, and the coming of new, noncommunist forms of very old kinds of despotism. During the past year, Havel's velvet revolution in Czechoslovakia was imperiled by partisans of "Czechland" and of Slovakia as independent entities. India seemed little less rent by Sikh, Hindu, Muslim, and Tamil infighting than it was immediately after the British pulled out, more than forty years ago.

To the extent that either McWorld or Jihad has a *natural* politics, it has turned out to be more of an antipolitics. For McWorld, it is the antipolitics of globalism: bureaucratic, technocratic, and meritocratic, focused (as Marx predicted it would be) on the administration of things—with people, however, among the chief things to be administered. In its politico-economic imperatives McWorld has been guided by laissez-faire market principles that privilege efficiency, productivity, and beneficence at the expense of civic liberty and self-government.

For Jihad, the antipolitics of tribalization has been explicitly antidemocratic: one-party dictatorship, government by military junta, theocratic fundamentalism—often associated with a version of the *Führerprinzip* that empowers an individual to rule on behalf of a people. Even the government of India, struggling for decades to model democracy for a people who will soon number a billion, longs for great leaders; and for every Mahatma Gandhi, Indira Gandhi, or Rajiv Gandhi taken from them by zealous assassins, the Indians appear to seek a replacement who will deliver them from the lengthy travail of their freedom.

The Confederal Option

HOW CAN DEMOCRACY BE SECURED AND SPREAD in a world whose primary tendencies are at best indifferent to it (McWorld) and at worst deeply antithetical to it (Jihad)? My guess is that globalization will eventually vanquish retribalization. The ethos of material "civilization" has not yet encountered an obstacle it has been unable to thrust aside. Ortega may have grasped in the 1920s a clue to our own future in the coming millennium.

Everyone sees the need of a new principle of life. But as always happens in similar crises—some people attempt to save the situation by an artificial intensification of the very principle which has led to decay. This is the meaning of the "nationalist" outburst of recent years. . . . things have always gone that way. The last flare, the longest; the last sigh, the deepest. On the very eve of their disappearance there is an intensification of frontiers—military and economic.

Jihad may be a last deep sigh before the eternal yawn of McWorld. On the other hand, Ortega was not exactly prescient; his prophecy of peace and internationalism came just before blitzkrieg, world war, and the Holocaust tore the old order to bits. Yet democracy is how we remonstrate with reality, the rebuke our aspirations offer to history. And if retribalization is inhospitable to democracy, there is nonetheless a form of democratic government that can accommodate parochialism and communitarianism, one that can even save them from their defects and make them more tolerant and participatory: decentralized participatory democracy. And if McWorld is indifferent to democracy, there is nonetheless a form of democratic government that suits global markets passably well—representative government in its federal or, better still, confederal variation.

Democracy will continue to be obstructed by the undemocratic and antidemocratic trends as the movement toward uniformitarian globalism continues.

With its concern for accountability, the protection of minorities, and the universal rule of law, a confederalized representative system would serve the political needs of McWorld as well as oligarchic bureaucratism or meritocratic elitism is currently doing. As we are already beginning to see, many nations may survive in the long term only as confederations that afford local regions smaller than "nations" extensive jurisdiction. Recommended reading for democrats of the twenty-first century is not the U.S. Constitution or the French Declaration of Rights of Man and Citizen but the Articles of Confederation, that suddenly pertinent document that stitched together the thirteen American colonies into what then seemed a too loose confederation of independent states but now appears a new form of political realism, as veterans of Yeltsin's new Russia and the new Europe created at Maastricht will attest.

By the same token, the participatory and direct form of democracy that engages citizens in civic activity and civic judgment and goes well beyond just voting and accountability—the system I have called "strong democracy"—suits the political needs of decentralized communities as well as theocratic and nationalist party dictatorships have done. Local neighborhoods need not be democratic, but they can be. Real democracy has flourished in diminutive settings: the spirit of liberty, Tocqueville said, is local. Participatory democracy, if not naturally apposite to tribalism, has an undeniable attractiveness under conditions of parochialism.

Democracy in any of these variations will, however, continue to be obstructed by the undemocratic and antidemocratic trends toward uniformitarian globalism and intolerant retribalization which I have portrayed here. For democracy to persist in our brave new McWorld, we will have to commit acts of conscious political will—a possibility, but hardly a probability, under these conditions. Political will requires much more than the quick fix of the transfer of institutions. Like technology transfer, institution transfer rests on foolish assumptions about a uniform world of the kind that once fired the imagination of colonial administrators. Spread English justice to the colonies by exporting wigs. Let an East Indian trading company act as the vanguard to Britain's free parliamentary institutions. Today's well-intentioned quick-fixers in the National Endowment for Democracy and the Kennedy School of Government, in the unions and foundations and universities zealously nurturing contacts in Eastern Europe and the Third World, are hoping to democratize by long distance. Post Bulgaria a parliament by first-class mail. Fed Ex the Bill of Rights to Sri Lanka. Cable Cambodia some common law.

Yet Eastern Europe has already demonstrated that importing free political parties, parliaments, and presses cannot establish a democratic civil society; imposing a free market may even have the opposite effect. Democracy grows from the bottom up and cannot be imposed from the top down. Civil society has to be built from the inside out. The institutional superstructure comes last. Poland may become democratic, but then again it may heed the Pope, and prefer to found its politics on its Catholicism, with uncertain consequences for democracy. Bulgaria may become democratic, but it may prefer tribal war. The former Soviet Union may become a democratic confederation, or it may just grow into an anarchic and weak conglomeration of markets for other nations' goods and services.

Democrats need to seek out indigenous democratic impulses. There is always a desire for self-government, always some expression of participation, accountability, consent, and representation, even in traditional hierarchical societies. These need to be identified, tapped, modified, and incorporated into new democratic practices with an indigenous flavor. The tortoises among the democratizers may ultimately outlive or outpace the hares, for they will have the time and patience to explore conditions along the way, and to adapt their gait to changing circumstances. Tragically, democracy in a hurry often looks something like France in 1794 or China in 1989.

It certainly seems possible that the most attractive democratic ideal in the face of the brutal realities of Jihad and the dull realities of McWorld will be a confederal union of semi-autonomous communities smaller than nation-states, tied together into regional economic associations and markets larger than nation-states—participatory and self-determining in local matters at the bottom, representative and accountable at the top. The nation-state would play a diminished role, and sovereignty would lose some of its political potency. The Green movement adage "Think globally, act locally" would actually come to describe the conduct of politics.

This vision reflects only an ideal, however—one that is not terribly likely to be realized. Freedom, Jean-Jacques Rousseau once wrote, is a food easy to eat but hard to digest. Still, democracy has always played itself out against the odds. And democracy remains both a form of coherence as binding as McWorld and a secular faith potentially as inspiriting as Jihad.

Population

The world's population situation is not restricted to rapid growth and too many people. In some areas, governments do not believe there are enough people. In the oil-rich Gulf states (e.g., Saudi Arabia), governments pursue a high birthrate policy. Large numbers of foreign workers have immigrated to these countries to work in the oil fields and at other, related projects. Consequently, the governments are pursuing policies that encourage large families so that eventually their own population will be able to replace the foreign workers.

Population demographics also vary a great deal from nonindustrial countries to the industrially developed nations. In North America and Western Europe, women, on the average, are having two children or less. Population in the United States is growing primarily because people are immigrating into the country, not because people are having large families.

The global population reached 5.3 billion in 1990, a gain of 2.3 billion in just 30 years. The lead article in the section provides an overview of the dynamics of demography. Explosive population growth and massive migration from the countryside are creating cities that dwarf the great capitals of the past. By 2000 there will be several "megacities" with populations of 10 million or more. Most of these will be in developing countries.

The section continues with a discussion of contending perspectives on the implications of population growth. Some experts view population growth as the major problem facing the world, while others see it as secondary to social, economic, and political problems. This theme of contending views, in short, has been carried forward from the introductory section of the book to the more specific discussion of population.

This broad discussion is followed by a series of articles that examine specific issues such as the movement of people from developing world countries to industrial nations. Much of contemporary international trade policy and the movement toward regional trading blocs has at its foundation a concern about this migration. The European Community's 1992 market integration and the North American Free Trade Agreement are both responses in varying degrees to this issue. In addition, the migration issue raises many questions that go beyond purely economic considerations. How does a culture maintain its identity when it must absorb large numbers of new people? Where will a government obtain the resources necessary to integrate these new members into the mainstream of society?

As the world approaches the next century, there are many population issues that transcend numerical and economic issues. The future of indigenous people is a good example of the pressures of population growth and the future of people who live on the margins of modern society. Finally, while demographers develop various scenarios forecasting population growth, it is important to remember that there are circumstances that could lead, not to growth, but to significant decline in global population. The spread of AIDS and other infectious diseases reveals that confidence in modern medicine's ability to control these age-old scourges may be premature. Nature has its own checks and balances to the population dynamic that are not policy instruments of some governmental organization. This factor is often overlooked.

Making predictions about the future of the world's population is a complicated matter, for there are a variety of forces at work and considerable variation from region to region. The danger of oversimplification must be overcome if governments and international organizations are going to respond with meaningful positions and policies.

Looking Ahead: Challenge Questions

What are the basic characteristics of the global population situation? How many people are there? How fast is the population growing?

How do population dynamics vary from one region to the next?

What regions of the world are attracting large numbers of international immigrants?

How does rapid population growth affect the environment, social structures, and the ways in which humanity views itself?

How does a rapidly growing population affect a developing world country's development plans?

How can economic and social policies be changed to reduce the impact of population growth on the quality of the environment?

In an era of global interdependence, is it possible for individual governments to have much impact on demographic changes?

What would be the political implications if the United States decided to end immigration?

The ICPD Programme of Action

Three years of what in the United Nations vernacular is called consensus-building—a painstaking and sometimes acrimonious process of debate, consultation, negotiation, and revision involving governments, non-governmental organizations, development agencies, scientists, and experts at national, regional, and international levels—culminated in the adoption on 13 September of the Programme of Action of the International Conference on Population and Development (ICPD).

Delegations from 179 states and seven observers took part in the official Conference. Their 16-chapter Programme of Action sets out a series of general pinciples as well as specific recommendations to guide future population policy-making and programmes.

As POPULI goes to print, the Programme of Action is being edited and printed for public distribution. What follows is a chapter-by-chapter description based on an unedited version of the document dated 19 September 1994, official ICPD press releases, and working summaries prepared by the United Nations.

Chapter 1: Preamble

The Preamble provides an overview of the main issues covered in the ICPD Programme of Action and sets the context for action in the field of population and development. It stresses that the ICPD is not an isolated event and that the Programme of Action builds on the considerable international consensus that had developed since the 1974 World Population Conference in Bucharest and the 1984 Mexico City International Conference on Population. The ICPD's broader mandate on development issues reflects the growing awareness that population, poverty, patterns of production and consumption, and other threats to the environment are so closely interconnected that none of them can be considered in isolation. The Conference follows and builds on other recent international activities, and the Programme of Action will make significant contributions to upcoming conferences, including the World Summit for Social Development and the Fourth World Conference on Women, both scheduled for 1995, and Habitat II, the Second UN Conference on Human Settlements, scheduled for 1996.

Chapter 2: Principles

This chapter lays out the document's guiding principles, and starts with a chapeau which states, in part, that

the implementation of the Programme of Action is the sovereign right of each country, consistent with national laws and development priorities, with full respect for the various religious and ethical values and cultural backgrounds of its people, and in conformity with universally recognized human rights.

Principle 1 states that all human beings are born free and equal in dignity and rights, including all the rights and freedoms of the Universal Declaration of Human Rights, and have the right to life, liberty, and security of person.

Principle 2 calls on all nations to ensure that all individuals are given the opportunity to make the most of their potential.

Principle 3 states that the right to development is a universal and inalienable right and an integral part of fundamental human rights, and that the human person is the central subject of development.

Principle 4 calls for advanced gender equality and equity and the empowerment of women, and the elimination of all kinds of violence against women.

Principle 5 says that population-related goals and policies are integral parts of cultural, economic, and social development, the main aim of which is to improve the quality of life of all people.

Principle 6 indentifies sustainable development as a means to ensure human well-being and calls on states to

From *Populi*, October 1994, pp. 6-11. Reprinted by permission of *Populi* magazine, United Nations Population Fund.

pursue development which meets the needs of current generations without compromising the ability of future generations to meet their own needs.

Principle 7 calls on states to work together to eradicate poverty.

Principle 8 says that everyone has the right to enjoy the highest attainable standard of physcial and mental health and that states should ensure universal access to health-care services, including those dealing with reproductive and sexual health and family planning.

Principle 9 states that the family, which exists in various forms, is the basic unit of society and therefore should be strengthened.

Principle 10 says that all people—and particularly women—have the right to education, which should focus on the full development of human resources, dignity, and potential.

Principle 11 calls on states and families to give the highest priority to children, especially as regards their right to health and education.

Principle 12 calls on countries receiving documented migrants to provide adquate health and social welfare services and to ensure their physical safety.

Principle 13 states that everyone has the right to seek asylum, and that states have responsibilities toward refugees, as stated in the Geneva Convention on the Status of Refugees.

Principle 14 calls on states to consider the population and development needs of indigenous people, to recognize and support their identity, culture, and interests, and enable them to participate fully in the economic, political, and social life of the country.

Principle 15 requires that in the context of sustainable development and social progress, sustained economic growth be broadly based, offering equal opportunities to all people, within and between countries.

Chapter 3: Interrelationships between Population, Sustained Economic Growth, and Sustainable Development

This chapter reflects general agreement that persistent, widespread poverty and serious social and gender inequality have significant effect on, and are in turn affected by, demographic factors such as population growth, structure, and distribution. Governments must give priority to investment in human resource development in their population and development strategies and budgets. Programmes should seek to increase people's—especially women's—access to information, education, skill development, employment, and high-quality health services. Meeting the basic needs of growing populations is dependent on a healthy environment, however, hence the emphasis on sustainable development, which

includes environmentalism. The chapter includes a call for a supportive economic environment for developing countries and countries with economies in transition.

Chapter 4: Gender Equality, Equity, and Empowerment of Women

This chapter calls on countries to empower women and eliminate inequality between men and women; eliminate all forms of discrimination against the girl child and the root causes of son preference; increase public awareness of the value of girl children, beyond their potential for childbearing; and promote equal participation of women and men in all areas of family and household responsibilities.

Chapter 5: The Family, Its Roles, Rights, Composition, and Structure

This chapter describes the family as the basic unit of society. It calls for policies and laws that support the family, contribute to its stability, and take into account its various forms, particularly the growing number of single-parent families. It calls for equality of opportunity for family members, especially the rights of women and children in the family, with particular emphasis on protecting families, and individual family members, from the ravages of extreme poverty, chronic unemployment, and domestic and sexual violence.

Chapter 6: Population Growth and Structure

This chapter has five sections: fertility, mortality, and population growth rates; children and youth; elderly people; indigenous people; and persons with disabilities. It urges governments to: give greater attention to the importance of population trends for development; promote the health, well-being, and potential of all children, adolescents, and youth and enforce laws against their economic exploitation, physical and mental abuse, and neglect; develop social security systems that ensure greater equity and solidarity between and within generations and that provide support to elderly people; incorporate the perspectives and needs of indigenous communities at every step into population, development, and environmental programmes that affect them and address social and economic factors that serve to disadvantage them; and develop the infrastructure to address the needs of persons with disabilities, in particular with regard to their education, training, and rehabilitation, and eliminate discrimination against them.

Chapter 7: Reproductive Rights and Reproductive Health

This chapter covers some of the issues considered most controversial during the negotiating process; it begins by invoking the qualifying chapeau to Chapter 2. Chapter 7 contains five sections: reproductive rights and reproductive health; family planning; sexually transmitted diseases (STDs) and HIV (human immunodeficiency virus) prevention;

human sexuality and gender relations; and adolescents. It defines reproductive health as "a state of complete physical, mental, and social well-being and not merely the absence of disease or infirmity, in all matters relating to the reproductive system and to its functions and processes. Reproductive health therefore implies that people are able to have a satisfying and safe sex life and that they have the capability to reproduce and the freedome to decide if, when, and how to do so. Implicit in this last condition are the right of men and women to be informed and to have access to safe, effective, affordable, and acceptable methods of family planning of their choice, as well as other methods of their choice for regulation of fertitlity which are not against the law…"

And "reproductive rights embrace certain human rights that are already recognized in national laws, international human rights documents, and other relevant United Nations consensus documents. These rights rest on the recognition of the basic right of all couples and individuals to decide freely and responsibly the number, spacing, and timing of their children and to have information and means to do so, and the right to attain the highest standard of sexual and reproductive health. It also includes the right of all to make decisions concerning reproduction free of discrimination, coercion, and violence as expressed in human rights documents."

The chapter also states that "appropriate services" for adolescents "must safeguard [their] rights…to privacy, confidentiality, respect, and informed consent, respecting cultural values and religious beliefs. In this context countries should, where appropriate, remove legal, regulatory, and social barriers to reproductive health information and care for adolescents."

Chapter 8: Health, Morbidity, and Mortality

This chapter contains sections on: primary health care and the health-care sector; child survival and health; women's health and safe motherhood; and HIV/AIDS. It contains the paragraph that was subject to perhaps the most lengthy and heated debate, paragraph 8.25, which now states: "In no case should abortion be promoted as a method of family planning. All governments and relevant intergovernmental and non-governmental organizations are urged to strengthen their commitment to women's health, to deal with the health impact of unsafe abortion*** as a major public health concern and to reduce the recourse to abortion through expanded and improved family planning services. Prevention of unwanted pregnancies must always be given the highest priority and all attempts should be made to eliminate the need for abortion. Women who have unwanted pregnancies should have ready access to reliable information and compassionate counselling. Any measures or changes related to abortion within the health system can

only be determined at the national or local level according to the national legislative process. In circumstances in which abortion is not against the law, such abortion should be safe. In all cases women should have access to quality services for the management of complications arising from abortion. Post-abortion counselling, education, and family planning services should be offered promptly which will also help to avoid repeat abortions." The footnote, which cites the World Health Organization, reads: "***Unsafe abortion is defined as a procedure for terminating an unwanted pregnancy either by persons lacking necessary skills or in an environment lacking the minimal medical standards or both."

The chapter also urges countries to strive to achieve specific goals, such as:

■ reducing infant and under-five mortality rates by one third, or to 50-70 per 1,000 live births, whichever is less, by the year 2000;

■ reducing infant mortality to below 35 per 1,000 live births, and under-five mortality to below 45, by 2015; and

■ reducing maternal mortality to half its 1990 level by 2000 and halving it again by 2015.

Chapter 9: Population Distribution, Urbanization, and Internal Migration

This chapter describes urbanization as "intrinsic" to economic and social development and calls on countries to adopt strategies that encourage the growth of small or medium-sized urban centres and to seek to develop rural areas while shoring up efforts to develop large municipalities' capacity to meet their own needs. It also states that "measures should be taken, at the national level with international cooperation, as appropriate, in accordance with the United Nations Charter, to find lasting solutions to questions related to internally displaced persons, including their right to voluntary and safe return to their home of origin."

Chapter 10: International Migration

This chapter states that poverty and environmental degradation, combined with the absence of peace and security, and human rights violations are all factors affecting international migration. It examines the specific circumstances of documented and undocumented migrants, refugees, asylum-seekers, and displaced persons. It urges governments to: address the root causes of migration, especially those related to poverty; encourage cooperation between sending and receiving countries; facilitate the integration of returning migrants; prevent the exploitation of undocumented migrants and ensure that their basic human rights are protected; protect migrants from racism and xenophobia; find durable solutions to the plight of refugees and displaced persons; and prevent the erosion of the right to asylum.

On the issue of family reunification, which was the subject of some debate at the Conference, the document states: "Consistent with Article 10 of the Convention on the Rights of the Child and all other relevant universally recognized human rights instruments, all governments, particularly those of receiving countries, must recognize the vital importance of family reunification and promote its integration into their national legislation in order to ensure the protection of the unity of families of documented migrants." And: "Governments are urged to promote, through family reunion, the normalization of the family life of legal migrants who have the right to long-term residence."

Chapter 11: Population, Development, and Education

This chapter describes education as a key factor in sustainable development and recommends providing universal access to quality education, especially primary and technical education and job training; eradicating illiteracy; eliminating gender inequality in educational opportunties and support; promoting non-formal education for young people; and introducing and improving the content of the curriculum so as to promote greater responsibility towards, and awareness of, the interrelationships between population and sustainable development, health issues, responsible parenthood, and gender equity.

Chapter 12: Technology, Research, and Development

This chapter stresses the importance of valid, reliable, timely, and internationally comparable data on all aspects of policies and programmes. It acknowledges that reproductive health research, especially biomedical research, has been instrumental in giving increasing numbers of people greater access to a wider range of safe and effective modern contraceptives. It adds that social and economic research is needed to enable programmes to take into account the views of their intended beneficiaries, especially women, the young, and other less empowered groups.

Chapter 13: National Action

This is the first of four chapters dedicated to implementation of the Programme of Action, and includes estimates of the funding levels required to meet the needs of developing countries and countries with economies in transition in the period 2000-2015 for basic reproductive health services including family planning and prevention of STDs and HIV/AIDS; population data collection, analysis, and dissemination; policy formulation; and research. The price tag: US$17.0 billion in 2000; US$18.5 billion in 2005; US$20.5 in 2010; and US$21.7 billion in 2015.

The chapter states that national legislators can have a major role to play in enacting domestic legislation to implement the Programme of Action, allocating appropriate financial resources, ensuring accountability of expenditure, and raising public awareness of population issues. It encourages governments to improve the skills and accountability of managers and others involved in national population and development strategies, policies, plans, and programmes.

Chapter 14: International Cooperation

This chapter urges the international community to fulfil the target, agreed upon for years, of committing 0.7 per cent of gross national product for overall official development assistance (ODA), and increasing the proportion of ODA dedicated to population to the levels necessary to implement the Programme of Action. Given the estimates laid out in Chapter 13, and assuming that developing countries and economies in transition will be able to generate sufficient increases in domestic resources, the need for complementary resources from "donor" countries would be roughly US$5.7 billion in 2000; US$6.1 billion in 2005; US$6.8 billion in 2010; and US$7.2 billion in 2015.

The chapter also takes note of an initiative to mobilize resources to give all people access to basic social services, known as the 20/20 Initiative, which will be studied further by the World Summit for Social Development.

Chapter 15: Partnership with the Non-Governmental Sector

This chapter acknowledges the vital roles of two sets of players in population and development: local, national, and international non-governmental organizations (NGOs); and the private sector. It calls on governments and development agencies to integrate NGOs into their decision-making and facilitate the contributions NGOs can make in implementing the Programme of Action. It also urges governments in the North and South to respect and help preserve NGOs' autonomy.

Chapter 16: Follow-up to the Conference

This chapter reiterates some of the points made in the preceding three chapters and adds that all interested individuals and organizations should be involved in the Conference follow-up; that they should publicize the Programme of Action as widely as possible and seek public support for it; that the international community, UN system, and anyone else in a position to provide financial and technical assistance should do so; and that South-South cooperation should play an important role in helping countries to implement the Programme of Action.

This article is a summary description of the ICPD Programme of Action, and is not an official version of the document. For more information, contact: ICPD Secretariat, 220 East 42nd Street, 22nd floor, New York, NY 10017, USA.

Damping the World's Population

Birthrates are falling now, but more needs to be done in the long term

Boyce Rensberger

Washington Post *Staff Writer*

Birthrates are plummeting in almost every country on Earth and are expected to continue falling for decades. And yet the number of people on the planet is now growing faster than ever and is likely to continue climbing for at least a hundred years.

Those trends may seem contradictory, but they are not. In fact, they inspire the two feelings that have driven the nine-day United Nations world population and development conference that opened Sept. 5 in Cairo.

First, there is confidence that human numbers are well on the way to leveling off in the foreseeable future, largely as a result of population stabilization initiatives already made. But, at the same time, there is fear that if efforts to bring down birthrates are not redoubled, human numbers will plateau later rather than

sooner, and at a much higher total. If such action is not taken, experts say, human suffering and environmental degradation may become catastrophic in larger parts of the world than otherwise would be the case.

Many population specialists say the wide-ranging plan of action being considered by the conference could have a dramatic effect. If nothing more is done, the world's current population of 5.6 billion could rise to between 10 billion and 12.5 billion by the year 2050, according to U.N. projections. But if the Cairo plan is implemented, there may be only 7.8 billion human beings by then.

"This conference," says Nafis Sadik, a Pakistani woman who is executive director of the U.N. Population Fund and secretary general of the Cairo meeting, "is about choices and responsibilities—for the individual, the community, the nation and the world. Its aim is to widen our freedom of choice—choice in the matter of family size, choice in population policy and programs, choice in development philosophy and practice."

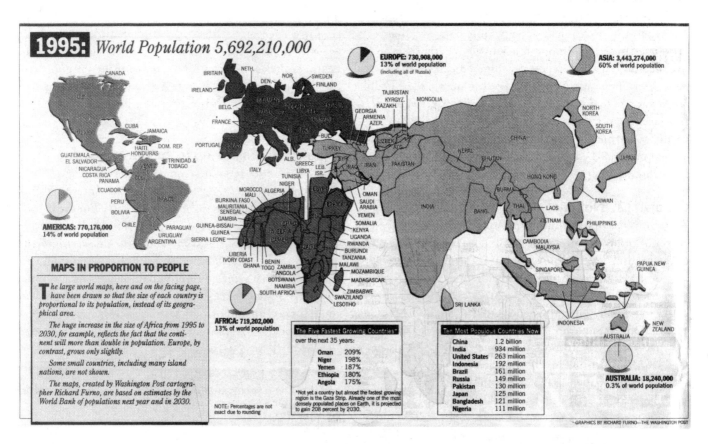

1995: *World Population 5,692,210,000*

EUROPE: 730,908,000
13% of world population
(including all of Russia)

ASIA: 3,443,274,000
60% of world population

AMERICAS: 770,176,000
14% of world population

AFRICA: 719,202,000
13% of world population

AUSTRALIA: 18,240,000
0.3% of world population

MAPS IN PROPORTION TO PEOPLE

The large world maps, here and on the facing page, have been drawn so that the size of each country is proportional to its population, instead of its geographical area.

The huge increase in the size of Africa from 1995 to 2030, for example, reflects the fact that the continent will more than double in population. Europe, by contrast, grows only slightly.

Some small countries, including many island nations, are not shown.

The maps, created by Washington Post cartographer Richard Furno, are based on estimates by the World Bank of populations next year and in 2030.

NOTE: Percentages are not exact due to rounding

The Five Fastest Growing Countries*
over the next 35 years:

Oman	209%
Niger	198%
Yemen	187%
Ethiopia	180%
Angola	175%

*Not yet a country but almost the fastest growing region is the Gaza Strip. Already one of the most densely populated places on Earth, it is projected to gain 208 percent by 2030.

Ten Most Populous Countries Now

China	1.2 billion
India	934 million
United States	263 million
Indonesia	192 million
Brazil	161 million
Russia	149 million
Pakistan	130 million
Japan	125 million
Bangladesh	121 million
Nigeria	111 million

GRAPHICS BY RICHARD FURNO—THE WASHINGTON POST

From the *Washington Post National Weekly Edition*, September 12–18, 1994, pp. 10-11. © 1994 by the Washington Post. Reprinted by permission.

The 113-page draft of the plan of action, details of which have been debated by delegations from about 170 countries, calls on governments not just to make family planning services available to all, but also to take measures to reduce illness and poverty, improve educational opportunity and work toward environmentally sustainable economic development.

Prominent in the plan is a call to improve health, education and economic opportunity for girls and women, who as a group suffer much more than men from the effects of rapid population growth and frequent pregnancy.

The Cairo meeting is the third of the major U.N.-sponsored world population conferences that have come to be held every 10 years. But it is the first in which virtually all the delegations, from rich countries and poor, are agreed on a plan. Only the Vatican, which has observer status because it is an independent state, and a handful of countries have dissented.

"We're moving. The whole world is moving and the political will is getting stronger to make population stabilization happen," says Timothy E. Wirth, undersecretary of State for global affairs and a leader of the U.S. delegation to what formally is called the International Conference on Population and Development.

Wirth and others from the United States have played a major role in shaping the proposed plan of action. "There's an extraordinary level of agreement among leaders all over the world on recognizing the problem and on how to go about solving it," Wirth says.

It was not always so.

When the first such conference was held in 1974 in Bucharest, Romania, rich and poor countries clashed over whether there was a population problem at all.

The rich brandished warnings of a "population bomb" and said the poor were having too many babies. The poor said the rich were advocating genocide and, in any case, that it was the rich world's industry and heavy consumption of natural resources that were degrading the planet. The poor countries said that what they really needed was help in developing their economies.

At the second conference, in Mexico City 10 years later, the climate shifted dramatically. By then, the poor countries had recognized that their populations were growing too fast and that the growth rate was frustrating efforts to develop economically. The developing countries sought help in making modern family planning services more widely available.

But the United States, under President Ronald Reagan, who then was courting the antiabortion vote in his reelection bid, reversed its 1974 stance, allied itself with the Vatican, and proclaimed that population growth was not a problem. The United States, long the major supporter of Third World family planning programs, abruptly withdrew aid from those that provided abortion counseling or services.

So threatening was the U.S. position, recalls Joseph Spiedel, head of Population Action International, that once when officials in Bangladesh were confronted with a woman dying of a botched, illegal abortion, they refused to take her to a clinic because they feared it might jeopardize the clinic's access to American foreign aid.

This time around, however, an extraordinary amount of preconference planning and preparatory meetings—and a major effort to involve hundreds of private educational, advocacy and service organizations—has led to a remarkable degree of international consensus. Only the Vatican-led faction comprising a

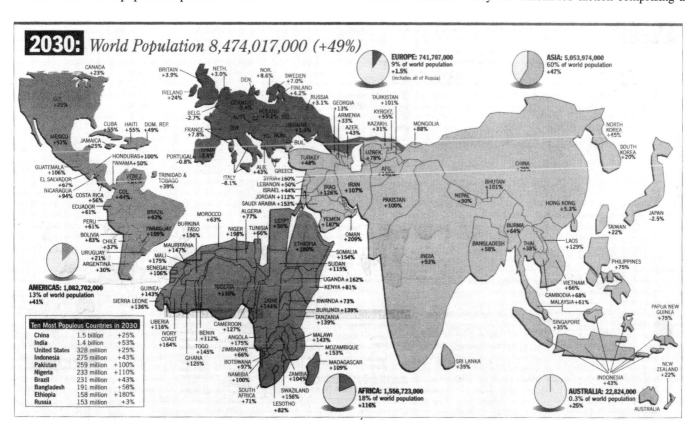

When More Education Means Fewer Children

Perhaps the most distinctive element of the Cairo plan of action is its emphasis on improving the rights, opportunities and economic status of girls and women. Population experts say there are two reasons to do so. One is that females suffer more than males from the effects of high population growth rates. The other is that there is growing evidence that one of the most effective ways of bringing down the number of unwanted pregnancies and increasing the use of modern contraceptives is to improve the lot of girls and women.

"The clearest evidence of negative effects of population growth under high fertility are at the individual and household levels," says Robert Cassen, a University of Oxford economist. "Mothers exposed to a large number of pregnancies have a high risk of dying. Children with large numbers of brothers and sisters will be more likely to be deprived in various ways. Girls suffer in particular, and once they fail to be educated, the scene is set for intergenerational transmission of poverty and high fertility."

Among the chief causes of poor health among women of reproductive age are having one's first pregnancy at too young an age and having too many pregnancies too close together. Children born less than two years after a previous birth are more likely to be underweight and ill and more likely to die in childhood. These and other reasons account for the extremely high infant and child death rates in poor countries. The best way to increase the survival of children, many experts like to say, is to have fewer of them.

Every year, according to United Nations figures, an estimated 500,000 women die of pregnancy-related causes, more than 90 percent of them in developing countries. An African woman, for example, is 200 times more likely to die in childbirth than a European women. In addition, more than 100,000 women die each year from unsafe abortions, almost all of them in Third World countries.

In many parts of the world, according to a statement by the State Department's Office of Global Affairs, "girls are fed less, given less medical care, withdrawn from school earlier and forced into hard labor sooner than boys. Women, who perform an estimated 60 percent of the world's work, own only 1 percent of the world's land and earn just 10 percent of the world's income." As a result, experts say, one of the few ways women can attain status and security is through bearing more children.

"The education of women stands out in study after study as the most consistent way to make an impact on reproductive behavior, on infant mortality, on family health, on individual productivity," says Timothy E. Wirth, undersecretary of State for global affairs. "Again and again, even a little education for women pays dividends in every recognized index of social progress and development."

STUDIES IN DOZENS OF countries have found that the more schooling a woman has, the fewer children she bears. In Botswana, for example, women with no formal education average 5.9 children each. Those with four to six years of school average 5.1 children and those with 10 or more years have just 3.1 children. In Senegal, women with no education average seven children, but the total drops to 3.6 if they have had 10 years. The story has been much the same in Asia and South America.

Many who have helped plan for the Cairo conference say it was the involvement of women's groups in particular that helped broaden the plan and, experts agree, make it more responsive to people's needs. In the past, family planning programs were designed by "experts" and more or less imposed from the top down as government leaders set arbitrary quotas for such things as the number of sterilizations or lower birthrates to be achieved.

"What we've learned is that the women of the Third World are a lot smarter than the demographers," World Bank demographer Thomas W. Merrick says. "You can get more progress by addressing their actual needs than by demanding it from the top down."

—*Boyce Rensberger*

few countries has dissented, objecting primarily to including abortion among a broad range of family planning services to be made available.

Some Muslim groups have joined with the pope in raising religious objections to the plan of action. But governments of the world's most populous Muslim countries—Indonesia, Pakistan and Egypt—are said to be squarely behind the plan of action.

For all the publicity given the Vatican's objections to some points, the church hierarchy does support the bulk of the plan. Some 92 percent of the language is agreed on by all parties.

By comparison, at the 1992 U.N. environment conference in Rio de Janeiro, only about 50 percent of that plan of action was accepted by all countries beforehand.

Moreover, Wirth and others say the church's longtime advo- cacy of economic and social advancement has helped shape the Cairo plan's recommendations to make development an important component of the overall effort.

One key to the unanimity is the plan's clear policy favoring only voluntary measures of family planning and economic development.

Coercive measures, including government sterilization quotas, for example, policies that ask people to violate personal moral codes, are plainly rejected.

In keeping with the emphasis on voluntary measures, Sadik says, "We must also recognize and accept responsibility. Men must take responsibility for contraception and fatherhood, communities for the weaker and most vulnerable members, nations for the well-being of their people, and the global community for the future of the environment on which all else depends."

MEGACITIES

By the millions they come, the ambitious and the downtrodden of the world drawn by the strange magnetism of urban life. For centuries the progress of civilization has been defined by the inexorable growth of cities. Now the world is about to pass a milestone: more people will live in urban ares than in the countryside. Does the growth of megacities portend an apocalypse of global epidemics and pollution? Or will the remarkable stirrings of self-reliance that can be found in some of them point the way to their salvation?

EUGENE LINDEN

KINSHASA, ZAIRE—HOME TO 4 million people—is no place to live. The city's social fabric has been fraying for years, but in September 1991 it started to unravel completely. The crisis began when a group of élite government troops, angry because they had not been paid for months, went on a looting spree that was quickly joined by civilians. During the next few days, nearly $1 billion worth of property, from clothes to computers, was pillaged. After the rampage, foreign businessmen—and foreign money—fled the city. The economy collapsed. Since the government now has almost no money to buy supplies and spare parts from abroad, all the services that make urban life bearable are breaking down. Buses and trains stall, fuel supplies are uncertain, electricity is unreliable and water quality is in jeopardy.

To the people of Kinshasa, the chaos brings much more than inconvenience and financial loss. The real threats are epidemics and starvation. Antibiotics and other medicines are scarce, and diseases such as malaria and tuberculosis are spreading rapidly. Strikes and sabotage by disgruntled workers hamper the flow of flour, vegetables and manioc to the city.

For Jonas Mutongi Kashama, whose well-kept, one-room home belies his desperate straits, the disintegration of Kinshasa means that for long periods his family must subsist on one meal every two days. Mutongi is actually one of the lucky ones, since, after six months of unemployment, he found work as an accountant. Even so, with the jobless rate at 80%, he must support out-of-work relatives on a tiny salary that is constantly eroded by an annual hyperinflation rate of more than 3,000%. "If things do not change, we will die," says Mutongi with quiet resignation.

"Is Kinshasa an aberration or rather a sign of things to come?" asks Timothy Weiskel, a Harvard anthropologist. His answer: Many of today's cities will go the way of Kinshasa. After all, he points out, the rise and fall of great cities has been part of civilization's cycle since humans first began to congregate in large numbers some 6,000 years ago.

Then there is Curitiba, Brazil, a surprisingly good place for 2.2 million people to live. It has slums and shantytowns, just like Kinshasa. But Curitiba's government has relied on imagination, commonsense planning and determination to deliver enviable services, including a bus system that quickly gets people where they want to go and public housing projects that are still immaculate 20 years after being built.

If Curitiba has a theme, it is self-reliance. The city is not rich, but it makes the most of the resources it has. Recycling, for example, is practically a religion. Jogging paths in the city's many parks are lit with lamps made from Fanta soda bottles, and the offices of Curitiba's environmental department were built in part with old telephone poles.

Most important, the government knows how to tap the energy of the people. In some communities of former squatters outside the routes of sanitation trucks, residents take their own garbage to designated sites and in exchange receive bags of surplus vegetables from the city. A woman named Lindamir Vas Floriano says that before this so-called green-exchange program, her hilly neighborhood was completely carpeted with trash and plagued by disease. Now the area is almost litter free, and the people are noticeably healthier.

Kinshasa or Curitiba: two visions of the future for most of the world's people. Which shall it be?

KINSHASA, ZAIRE

In a country blessed with gold, diamonds, copper, rich agricultural land, abundant clean water and inexpensive electric power, Kinshasa should be one of Africa's most prosperous capitals. Instead, the city has crumbled under corruption during the 27-year-reign of President Mobutu Sese Seko.

In this kleptocracy, looting sometimes exceeds even the anarchic standards of Somalia. On one occasion, officials pilfered all but 24 tons out of 369 tons of emergency food aid sent by the European Community. "It's not that officials do not know how to run ministries honestly," says a foreign diplomat, "but that there is no reason to do so."

The routine disappearance of fuel, manufactured goods, food and medical supplies has helped raise the price of almost everything. A sack of manioc that will barely feed a family for a month costs far more than the basic monthly salary of a clerk. If patients want operations at some public hospitals, they have to supply their own drugs.

Zaïrians have put their hopes in a national conference, which has chosen Mobutu's rival, Etienne Tshisekedi, as Prime Minister for a new government. Mobutu, however, continues to maneuver to keep control. Last December he dismissed the Tshisekedi government, though he had no power to do so, precipitating a crisis in the transition to democratic government. Even if Tshisekedi and Western pressure manage to inch Zaïre toward democracy, it could be several years before Kinshasa's economy recovers.

From *Time*, January 11, 1993, pp. 28-38. © 1993 by Time Inc. Magazine Company. Reprinted by permission.

THE DAWNING AGE OF MEGACITIES

In the coming years, the fate of humanity will be decided in places like Kinshasa and Curitiba. Faster than ever before, the human world is becoming an urban world. Near the end of this decade, mankind will pass a demographic milestone: for the first time in history, more people will live in and around cities than in rural areas.

Explosive population growth and a torrent of migration from the countryside are creating cities that dwarf the great capitals of the past. By the turn of the century, there will be 21 "megacities" with populations of 10 million or more. Of these, 18 will be in developing countries, including some of the poorest nations in the world. Mexico City already has 20 million people and Calcutta 12 million. According to the World Bank, some of Africa's cities are growing by 10% a year, the swiftest rate of urbanization ever recorded.

Is the trend good or bad? Can the cities cope? No one knows for sure. Without question, urbanization has produced miseries so ghastly that they are difficult to comprehend. In Cairo, children who elsewhere might be in kindergarten can be found digging through clots of ox dung, looking for undigested kernels of corn to eat. Young, homeless thieves in Papua New Guinea's Port Moresby may not know their last names or the names of the villages where they were born. In the inner cities of America, newspapers regularly report on newborn babies dropped into garbage bins by drug-addicted mothers.

But cities remain the cradle of civilization's creativity and ambition. To focus on the degradation is to miss the deep well of pride and determination that inspire the urban poor to better their lives. In Bombay, high school girls learn about sanitation, nutrition and immunization so that they can pass on this information to illiterate neighbors. In Bangkok a program called Magic Eyes has reduced street trash by 85% through the gentle method of encouraging children to hum a jingle about sloppiness when they see their parents litter. In Mexico City cash-starved peasants band together to form cooperatives that guarantee credit for people who might otherwise never be able to afford a home.

History issues grim warnings about the future of cities. Since the beginning of civilization, they have risen to greatness only to collapse because of epidemics, warfare, ecological calamities, shifts in trade or social disorder. Calah, Tikal and Angkor are among the fabled places that disappeared into the sands or jungles of time. Surviving cities have undergone wild swings of fortune. Alexandria, Egypt, may have housed several hundred thousand people at its peak in Roman times, but

---

CURITIBA, BRAZIL

While mayors around the world spend their time making excuses for crime, drugs and urban decay, Jaime Lerner of Curitiba, Brazil, has the enviable problem of trying to be modest about his city's success. "Curitiba is different from other Third World cities because it has made an effort to be different," says Lerner. Beginning in 1970 he launched low-cost programs to build parks, control garbage, house the poor and develop a mass-transit system. Two decades ago, Curitiba had 0.46 sq m (5 sq. ft.) of open space for every citizen; now it has 51 sq m (550 sq. ft.). New York City, by contrast, has 14.5 sq m (156 sq. ft.) of open space per capita. Most astonishing, Curitiba has added parks and plazas even as its population increased 164% since 1970.

"Services like parks and high-quality public transportation give dignity to the citizen," says Lerner, "and if people feel respected, they will assume responsibility to help solve other problems." Lerner has used his high public approval ratings to mobilize support for such initiatives as the establishment of 40 centers that feed street children and teach them simple skills.

Some of Lerner's innovations have caught the attention of the developed world. Last spring, for instance, New York City began experimenting with a low-cost bus system invented in Curitiba as an alternative to subways. Curitiba's "speedy line" uses express street lanes from which cars are banned and loading platforms where passengers pay their fare before boarding the bus. The buses travel through the city at an average speed of 32 km/h (20 m.p.h.) and can transport 3.2 times as many passengers as standard buses can during a given interval. The system was installed in six months. That, says Lerner, "means you don't have to waste a generation building a subway." People all over Brazil respect Lerner's commonsense approach. He has been mentioned as a candidate to succeed former President Fernando Collor de Mello.

---

when Napoleon entered it in 1798, it had shrunk to 4,000 souls. Since then, it has again boomed to nearly 3 million and faces grave ecological threats. The gleaming city that Arab poet Ibn Dukmak compared to "a golden crown, set with pearls, perfumed with musk and camphor, and shining from East to the West," is slowly sinking into the unstable, sewage-contaminated Nile Delta.

During earlier periods of urban collapse, the fact that human society was largely rural tempered the effects of catastrophes. When the black death wiped out 80% of Europe's urban population, more than 95% of the people lived in the country. But if the world enters a new age of epidemics, few will escape unaffected.

CITIES AND CIVILIZATION

Workers laying a new sewer line in a Cairo suburb uncover foundations of a 4,600-year-old working-class neighborhood; a subway project in Rome reveals a long-dead Pope's toothbrush; improvements in Red Square during the twilight of the Soviet empire unearth wooden homes built before Moscow had its first prince in the 13th century. In the next millennium, construction workers in Cairo, Rome and Moscow will no doubt be puzzling over traces of current cultures. As the triumphant remake the world's cities, the shards of the vanquished are literally trodden into the ground.

These layers of sediment become pages in urban history, which, in large measure, is the history of civilization. The need to preserve foods and seeds at trading centers in ancient Mesopotamia and Anatolia focused human ingenuity on the problem of storage and led eventually to the development of armories, banks and libraries. Along a treacherous path paved with bloodshed and pestilence, cities evolved as the repositories of humanity's collective intelligence: the record of culture and science that enables a civilization to benefit from the lessons of the past.

But the development of cities fostered competition among humans and alienation from nature. The price of a city's greatness is an uneasy balance between vitality and chaos, health and disease, enterprise and corruption, art and iniquity. The Elizabethan London that nurtured Shakespeare, after all, was a fetid dump cloaked with coal dust.

This delicate balance always threatens to tip, and when it does, cities can spiral into an anarchy that defies all attempts at reversal. From Belfast, where religious hatred spawns terror, to Los Angeles, where the acquittal of four white policemen accused of beating a black motorist triggered last April's rampage of looting and arson, city dwellers have paid a horrible price when ethnic and political tensions boiled to the surface. When fighting began in Beirut in 1974, merchants spoke confidently of a return to normality within months. Few Lebanese expected that strife would still rule their lives 18 years later.

Yet the catalytic mixing of people that fuels urban conflict also spurs the initiative, innovation and collaboration that move civilization forward. The late social critic Lewis Mumford once remarked that "the city is a place for multiplying happy chances and making the most of unplanned opportunities." Curitiba's mayor, Jaime Lerner, bases his whole approach to urban planning on this idea. "If life is the art of encounter, then the city is the setting for encounter," he says. Curitiba has multiplied the chances for encounters by providing its citizens with an abundance of pedestrian walks and parks. Even the bus terminals make cozy and comfortable meeting places. The mayor's public housing program mixes both low- and middle-income people in a largely successful effort to discourage ghettos.

Ironically, the very programs that have made Lerner one of the most popular mayors in Brazilian history threaten Curitiba's future. Says Ashok Khosla, president of the New Delhi–based Society for Development Alternatives: "Each city contains the seeds of its own destruction because the more attractive it becomes, the more it will attract overwhelming numbers of immigrants." Luciano Pizzato, a federal Deputy from Curitiba, notes that during the next 10 years, Brazil's population will grow by 40 million people—an increase the size of Argentina's population. "You cannot create facilities for a new Argentina in 10 years," says Pizzato, who fears that Brazil's poor will make Curitiba their destination of choice.

It is easy to understand why Brazilians would migrate to Curitiba, but why do people keep streaming into a Kinshasa or a Karachi, Pakistan? What is the irresistible lure of the megacity? To the outsider, a neatly swept native village in Africa, Asia or Latin America may look more inviting than a squalid urban squatter settlement. But until recently even the most wretched city slums have offered better access to paying jobs, more varied diets, better education and better health care than what was available in rural communities.

THE MEDICAL AND ENVIRONMENTAL TOLL

No one knows how big some cities are or how rapidly they are expanding. Estimates of Mexico City's population vary from 14 million to 20 million, depending on whether demographers calculate the figure according to the 1990 census (which some believe drastically undercounted), or whether the number is determined by estimates of water use. Still, the fastest urban growth is in those areas

NEW YORK CITY

Urban experts often say that inside every First World city is a Third World city. In the case of New York City, that could be construed as an insult to the Third World. After a series of editorials depicting the city as "the New Calcutta," the *New York Times* ran a rebuttal pointing out that the poorest neighborhoods of the Indian city had less crime and more community spirit than the Big Apple.

A walk through the South Bronx fulfills every outsider's vision of urban decline. With their cracked façades and broken windows, abandoned tenements stare vacantly, like blind sentinels over street corners and rubble-strewn lots where drug dealers congregate openly.

Amid this blight, however, is evidence of resilience. In the Hunts Point district, rows of neat homes built by urban homesteaders testify to the determination of the poor to reclaim the most degraded blocks of the city. Many of New York's bravest urban pioneers are immigrants who, with the American Dream firing their ambition, come from Haiti, Russia, Ethiopia, Korea, Poland, Guatemala, India and many other nations. As New York's middle-class professionals exit, this new blood could provide an infusion of taxpayers.

In the past, New York has risen from its ashes. It lost its pre-eminence as a port and a manufacturing center, but still discovered new roles to fill. Now, when it needs to reinvent itself once more, the city can call on the energy of its immigrants and its unsurpassed intellectual resources in the fields of finance, industry, the media, design, advertising and the arts.

that are poorest and least prepared.

Karachi, for instance, may be swelling by 6% a year. Estimates of its population range from 8.4 million to 11 million, a figure that could rise to 19 million by the year 2002. That increase would be the same as adding on New York City's population in a decade. But Karachi makes do with a central sewer system not significantly improved since 1962. The city provides 30% less water than needed, forcing the poor to drink from untreated supplies often contaminated with hepatitis virus. An epidemic of the disease has been raging for more than a year. Those taking medicines often get sicker because unscrupulous local manufacturers sometimes boost profits by adulterating pills and potions with motor oil, sawdust and tainted tap water. Says Mohammad Farooq Sattar, 32, the former mayor, who started his career as an M.D.: "Karachi is a city very much in need of a doctor."

So are many other cities. The era of the megacity could bring the triumphant return of microbes that have toppled empires throughout history. Says Harvard public-health expert Jonathan Mann: "We only have a truce with infectious disease, and if a city's infrastructure gets overloaded, the balance can tip back to microbes at any time." The cholera epidemic that hit Latin American cities last year, hospitalizing more than 400,000 people and killing at least 4,000 in a few months, shows how quickly a disease can move when it finds a foothold in crowded slums.

Large cities are breeding grounds for novel, antibiotic-resistant strains of old germs and for entirely new kinds of microbes. Not since the bubonic plague has the world encountered anything like the

AIDS virus, which has infected at least 10 million people. No one knows exactly where AIDS originated, but it has become an epidemic in the cities of Africa, Europe, Asia, Latin America and the U.S. In addition to its own deadly impact, AIDS fosters the spread of other diseases. The tuberculosis germ, for example, attacks weakened AIDS victims and uses them as a beachhead for invading healthy populations.

The possibility that AIDS evolved in the African rain forests has raised the nightmare prospect that as humans continue to cut back tropical forests, other opportunistic new viruses may emerge to fasten on human hosts. "Imagine a virus like AIDS that was transmitted by droplets in the air rather than sexually, and which led to death in months rather than years. In these circumstances we might not have time to study the disease before it ravaged cities," says Uwe Brinkmann, a Harvard epidemiologist.

Inadequate sanitation often provides new pathways for infectious agents. In Mexico cysticercosis, caused by a tapeworm that invades the human brain, used to be transmitted primarily by improperly cooked pork. Now people are getting the disease from vegetables grown in fields irrigated by water containing effluent that flows into the Tula River from Mexico City. Brinkmann estimates that more than half of the 300 million urban poor in the developing world are in a permanently weakened condition because they carry one or more parasites.

The threat of disease is heightened by urban pollution. Brinkmann notes that in industrial countries, as much as 50% of the population will suffer from a rash or other skin disease during the course of a year, compared with maybe 2% in the 1950s. "Is this an indication that pollutants have weakened human immune defenses, leaving city dwellers more vulnerable to otherwise benign diseases?" the epidemiologist asks. Many of the effects of environmental degradation are far from benign. In Upper Silesia, Poland, indiscriminate dumping of toxic wastes has so poisoned the land and water that 10% of the region's newborns have birth defects, from missing limbs to brain damage.

Nowhere is pollution more palpable than in Mexico City. When the wind is still, the fumes of 3 million cars and 35,000 industrial sites become trapped by the high ring of mountains that surrounds the city. Last February a cloud of smog pushed ozone readings above 0.35 parts per million on some days, severe enough to harm even healthy people and four times the level considered safe under, say, California law. In recent years Mexico City has started to shut down polluting factories, introduce lead-free fuels, get rid of diesel-powered buses, mandate emission controls on new cars, and even decree that vehicles be driven only six days a week. But with the number of cars growing 7% a year, ozone pollution still worsened 22% between 1990 and 1991. Today the city is looking at electric cars and new pollution controls for buses and industry. The situation is desperate enough that the ordinarily sensible mayor, Manuel Camacho Solis, has entertained daffy ideas such as the installation of 100 giant fan complexes, each 13.3 hectares (33 acres) in size, to blow pollution out of the area.

Even the best-managed cities have trouble coping with the crush of population growth. Tokyo is overwhelmed by its own trash—22,000 tons each day—despite massive recycling and incineration programs. Ironically, Japanese fastidiousness is a big part of the problem. In a city where taxi drivers wear spotless white gloves, Tokyo consumers want wrappers around virtually anything they buy.

At the present discard rate, Tokyo will run out of dump sites by 1995. The city has been building artificial islands in Tokyo Bay to hold garbage, but cannot continue to do so without threatening both the fishing and shipping industries. Some critics argue that in its obsession with technology, the government has chosen the wrong tack. Notes Keisuke Amagusa, editor of the journal *Technology and People*: "The government is focusing on garbage collected and not doing anything to reduce the garbage created."

The pell-mell expansion of cities creates risks not just for their residents but for every human being. As cities grow, so does the demand for standardized, easily transportable foods. Farmers in the coun-

MEGACITIES

Population of metropolitan areas*
in millions

	1992	2000
Tokyo	25.8	28.0
São Paulo, Brazil	19.2	22.6
New York City	16.2	16.6
Mexico City	15.3	16.2
Shanghai	14.1	17.4
Bombay	13.3	18.1
Los Angeles	11.9	13.2
Buenos Aires	11.8	12.8
Seoul	11.6	13.0
Beijing	11.4	14.4
Rio de Janeiro	11.3	12.2
Calcutta	11.1	12.7
Jakarta, Indonesia	10.0	13.4
Tianjin, China	9.8	12.5
Metro Manila	9.6	12.6
Cairo	9.0	10.8
New Delhi	8.8	11.7
Lagos, Nigeria	8.7	13.5
Karachi, Pakistan	8.6	11.9
Bangkok	7.6	9.9
Dacca, Bangladesh	7.4	11.5

* Urban area estimates vary widely, depending on area definitions and recency of census.
Source: Population Division of the U.N. Secretariat

tryside respond to this demand by planting a narrower range of crops, which in turn increases the likelihood of major disruptions of the food supply by pests and droughts. Particularly in the developing world, cities act as destructive parasites on the surrounding countryside. Urban thirst for fuel wood and building materials leads to deforestation, which can destroy an area's watershed and thus cause flooding and soil erosion. In many cases, the impact of urban centers extends across the seas. Demand for plywood building materials in Japanese cities drives the decimation of Borneo's forests.

With every kind of threat, the stakes are higher than ever before. A repeat of Tokyo's devastating 1923 earthquake today might cause worldwide economic stagnation as rebuilding the city soaked up hundreds of billions of dollars of Japanese capital. If global warming causes a sharp rise in sea levels during the next century, as many scientists predict, the coastal megacities may have to build giant dikes to prevent disastrous flooding, but only a few urban areas can afford such an undertaking.

Ideally, it might be better to disperse humanity more evenly around the countryside. But people have flocked to cities for thousands of years, and the lure of the bright lights runs so deep that it cannot easily be overcome by government policies. With the world's population growing by nearly 100 million a year, the forces driving urban expansion are irresistible.

WILL CITIES LOSE THEIR ALLURE?

Yet there are signs that urban growth can be slowed. Four decades ago, Mexico City was a relatively attractive place, with only 4 million people and not much traffic along its spacious boulevards. Since then the population has quadrupled, and the congestion has become stifling. In recent years the city's immigration rate has declined while the flow of people to smaller Mexican cities has increased. This trend suggests that the combination of crowding, poor sanitation, noise and pollution can eventually become intolerable.

In rich countries as well, many cities are not quite the magnets they used to be. In return for the highest combined city and state taxes in the U.S., residents of New York City get deteriorating bridges and roads, racial tension that frequently ignites violence, schools in which students must worry about gun battles erupting in the hallways, subway stations that double as public urinals, and streets full of panhandlers. Last summer one house in a middle-class neighborhood in Brooklyn was burglarized on five separate occasions, and the police did nothing to stop the robberies.

Not surprisingly, the city has been losing its middle class and is in danger of losing many of its professionals. A New York *Times* poll showed that 60% of the people sampled were thinking of leaving. "If the ability to believe in the future is what separates a growing from a dying civilization, then New York is in deep trouble," says Stephen Berger, a former executive director of the Port Authority of New York and New Jersey.

For all its problems, though, New York still has a superb infrastructure for housing, transporting and employing large numbers of people. "It's far easier to fix New York," says Berger, "than to rebuild it in Des Moines." More important, cities such as New York and Tokyo will never lose their role as marketplaces of ideas. Even as electronic communications increasingly link people over long distances, they still crave face-to-face encounters.

Kenzo Tange, the revered Japanese architect, points out that in his country there is no substitute for sizing up business associates in meetings and at social occasions. Tange thinks the Tokyo area, though choked with nearly 30 million people, will remain the focal point of Japan's economy simply because the city houses the headquarters of two-thirds of the country's major companies. In Japan and around the world, many of the most creative minds in business, finance, fashion, the arts and the media will keep wanting to brainstorm in the megacities.

THE REVIVAL OF SELF-RELIANCE

Experts began predicting the violent collapse of Third World megacities more than a decade ago. Urban planner Janice Perlman recalls the skepticism she encountered in the mid-1980s when she first proposed Mega-Cities, a project to promote the exchange of ideas and innovations among the world's biggest urban areas. She was told that her proposal was futile because such cities as Jakarta and Mexico City would be torn apart by disease and disorder within a few years.

The first modern urban apocalypse could easily have started at 7:18 a.m. on Sept. 19, 1985. That was when an earthquake measuring 8.1 on the Richter scale rocked Mexico City. Hundreds of thousands were left homeless, water mains broke, the threat of epidemics loomed, and the government fumbled helplessly in dealing with the crisis.

But instead of obliterating the city, the earthquake tapped a wellspring of self-reliance that astonished officials and outside observers alike. Neighborhoods and communities organized themselves to rescue those buried, clean up the rubble and restore services. Since then, a chastened government has tried to do a better job of harnessing local initiative. Says Mayor Camacho: "We have learned to take advantage of mass mobilization."

The awakening of self-reliance in the urban poor is a global phenomenon. In Karachi, architect Akhter Hameed Khan rallied the people of the Orangi district around a self-help initiative to upgrade their sanitation. With 800,000 residents from five of Pakistan's major ethnic groups, the neighborhood is periodically racked by violence. Still, working lane by lane, beginning in 1980, Hameed Khan and his co-workers in the Orangi Pilot Project proved to the district that with a tiny investment ($40 a house), it could install its own sewerage system. Since then, roughly 70% of the 6,347 lanes have been linked to the system. The people of Orangi can now see for themselves the difference between the neat lanes in the project and the garbage-strewn open sewers of neighboring alleys. Hameed Khan's programs, particularly initiatives to improve the role of women, have stirred some fundamentalist mullahs in this Islamic country to call for his death, but the 78-year-old social activist resolutely continues his efforts to make Karachi more livable.

The World Bank, which generally finances giant projects, increasingly supports small community-based initiatives. One such project is the Kampung Improvement Program in Jakarta. Its success grew out of a decision to give squatters title to plots of land. In return, the new landowners agreed to help build footpaths, improve drainage and reduce garbage. "Instead of thinking of themselves as temporary boarders, the poor began to look at their

MEXICO CITY

When Hernán Cortés gazed in 1519 on what is now called Mexico City, he saw a vast Aztec center of several hundred thousand souls that dwarfed any European city of his era. The city had grown by feeding on tribute from subdued tribes.

Though centuries have passed, Mexico City is still subsidized by the countryside. Its children, for instance, can ride to school for one-tenth the cost of a bus ticket in rural areas. Education, health care and jobs are much more available. No wonder several thousand peasants flocked to Mexico City each week

throughout the 1980s. Exequiel Ezcurra, chairman of the National University's Ecological Center, is concerned that the capital has exceeded its sustainable limits. "In a city this large," he says, "a catastrophe such as a rash of deaths caused by air pollution can go unnoticed."

The city's great assets are its homogeneity and the determination of its citizens. Profound devotion to community saved it from collapse after the 1985 earthquake. The question is whether this spirit can prevent an urban apocalypse as the population inexorably increases.

community as their home," says Josef Leitmann, a World Bank urban planner. "A simple change in psychology produced a change in physical surroundings."

The cities obviously need more money. In many countries the help that urban areas receive from the national government has dwindled steadily. Moreover, during the past decade, foreign aid shifted more and more to rural problems even as people moved to the cities. Now, with urban areas producing half the world's income, and governments nervous about restive urban populations, agencies such as the World Bank have begun to focus more on cities once again.

But money by itself will not prevent the collapse of megacities. The troubles of a Karachi or a Jakarta will not disappear if planners from the World Bank rush in to build housing projects and a freeway system. Humanitarian aid in the form of food and medicine can be a godsend, but it will not give a city prosperity.

Ultimately, the responsibility for making cities livable rests with their governments and their people. Too often those governments, whether in New York City or Kinshasa, become corrupt systems for dispensing benefits to agencies, employees and political supporters. If, as in Curitiba, governments can learn again how to serve the public, they can regain a mighty power—the power that comes from harnessing the combined imaginations and enterprise of millions of human beings.

The historical cycle of urban growth and collapse will be hard to break, but hope can be found in the stubborn self-reliance shown by people in some of the world's poorest cities. Like the cumbersome bumblebee that flies in the face of aerodynamic theory, the megacities will have to defy gravity and invent a sustainable future for themselves. Since the fate of the world is entwined with the fate of its cities, humanity has no other choice.

TOKYO

During Japan's imperial era, Tokyo's planners built unexpected curves and dead ends into streets to confuse any invader who dared enter the capital. These mystifying turns still befuddle taxi drivers and lend a rare whimsical touch to a city that has evolved into a sprawling technopolis. There is nothing whimsical, however, about the problems that have accompanied Tokyo's metamorphosis into a colossus: traffic-choked streets, housing costs beyond the reach of young families and the overwhelming waste generated by 30 million people.

Still, the Japanese obsession with efficiency and technological wizardry may generate solutions. One scheme makes use of Tokyo's vast waste stream. Called the Urban Heat system, it extracts heat from sewage and then uses the energy to regulate temperatures in several Tokyo buildings, including the monumental new city hall. If such innovations were matched by programs that encouraged ordinary people to reduce waste, Tokyo's governor, Shunichi Suzuki, might yet live up to his commitment to make the capital an earth-friendly city.

Part 1

Must It Be
THE REST
Against
THE WEST?

"Now, stretching over that empty sea, aground some fifty yards out, [lay] the incredible fleet from the other

side of the globe, the rusty, creaking fleet that the old professor had been eyeing since morning. . . .

He pressed his eye to the glass, and the first things he saw were arms. . . . Then he started to count. Calm and

unhurried. But it was like trying to count all the trees in the forest, those arms raised high in the air, waving

and shaking together, all outstretched toward the nearby shore. Scraggy branches, brown and black, quickened

by a breath of hope. All bare, those fleshless Gandhi-arms. . . . thirty thousand creatures on a single ship!"

—THE CAMP OF THE SAINTS

MATTHEW CONNELLY
AND PAUL KENNEDY

*Matthew Connelly ("Must It Be the Rest Against the West?")
is a Ph.D. candidate in the Department of History at Yale
University. He is now in Paris doing research for his
dissertation, on the diplomatic history of the Algerian war of
independence.*

*Paul Kennedy ("Must It Be the Rest Against the West?") is
the J. Richardson Dilworth Professor of History and the
director of international security studies at Yale University.
He is internationally known for his writings and commentary
on global political, economic, and strategic issues. Kennedy
is the author of* The Rise and Fall of the Great Powers
(1988), among many other books, the most recent being
Preparing for the Twenty-first Century *(1993).*

Absent major changes in North-South relations, the wretched should inherit the earth by about 2025

WELCOME to the 300-page narrative of Jean Raspail's disturbing, chilling, futuristic novel *The Camp of the Saints*, first published in Paris twenty-one years ago and translated into English a short while later. Set at some vague time—perhaps fifteen or twenty years—in the fu-ture, the novel describes the pilgrimage of a million desperate Indians who, forsaking the ghastly conditions of downtown Calcutta and surrounding villages, commandeer an armada of decrepit ships and set off for the French Riviera. The catalyst for this irruption is simple enough. Moved by accounts of widespread famine across an Indian subcontinent collapsing under the sheer weight of its fast-growing population, the Belgian government has decided to admit and adopt a number of young children; but the policy is reversed when tens of thousands of mothers begin to push their babies against the Belgian consul general's gates in Calcutta. After mobbing the building in disgust at Belgium's change of mind, the crowd is further inflamed by a messianic speech from one of their number, an untouchable, a gaunt, eye-catching "turd eater," who calls for the poor and wretched of the world to advance upon the Western paradise: "The nations are rising from the four corners of the earth," Raspail has the man say, "and their number is like the sand of the sea. They will march up over the broad earth and surround the camp of the saints and the beloved city. . . ." Storming on board every ship within range, the crowds force the crews to take them on a lengthy, horrific voyage, around Africa and through the Strait of Gibraltar to the southern shores of France.

But it is not the huddled mass of Indians, with their "fleshless Gandhi-arms," that is the focus of Raspail's attention so much as the varied responses of the French and the other privileged members of "the camp of the saints" as they debate how to deal with the inexorably advancing multitude. Raspail is particularly effective here in capturing the platitudes of official announcements, the voices of ordinary people, the tone of statements by concerned bishops, and so on. The book also seems realistic in its recounting of the crumbling away of resolve by French sailors and soldiers when they are given the order to repel physically—to shoot or torpedo—this armada of helpless yet menacing people. It would be much easier, clearly, to confront a military foe, such as a Warsaw Pact nation. The fifty-one (short) chapters are skillfully arranged so that the reader's attention is switched back and forth, within a two-month time frame, between the anxious debates in Paris and events attending the slow and grisly voyage of the Calcutta masses. The denouement, with the French population fleeing their southern regions and army units deserting in droves, is especially dramatic.

THE VOYAGE OF
THE *GOLDEN VENTURE*

WHY revisit this controversial and nowadays hard-to-obtain novel? The recovery of this neglected work helps us to call attention to the key global problem of the final years of the twentieth century: unbalanced wealth and resources, unbalanced demographic trends, and the relationship between the two. Many members of the more prosperous economies are beginning to agree with Raspail's vision: a world of two "camps," North and South, separate and unequal, in which the rich will have to fight and the poor will have to die if mass migration is not to overwhelm us all. Migration is the third part of the problem. If we do not act now to counteract tendencies toward global apartheid, they will only hurry the day when we may indeed see Raspail's vision made real.

One of us (Kennedy) first heard *The Camp of the Saints* referred to at various times during discussions of illegal migration. One such occasion was in the summer of 1991, following media reports about the thousands of desperate Albanians who commandeered ships to take them to the Italian ports of Bari and Brindisi, where they were locked in soccer stadiums by the local police before being forcibly returned to a homeland so poor that it is one of the few parts of Europe sometimes categorized as "developing" countries. Apparently, one reason for this exodus was that the Albanians had been watching Italian television—including commercials for consumer goods, cat food shown being served on a silver platter, and the like. More than a few colleagues mentioned that the incident struck them as a small-scale version of Raspail's grim scenario.

If a short trip across the Adriatic seems a far cry from a passage from Calcutta to Provence, the voyage of the *Golden Venture* was even more fantastic than anything imagined by Raspail. This 150-foot rust-streaked freighter left Bangkok, Thailand, in February of 1993 carrying ninety Chinese refugees, mostly from the impoverished Fujian province. Two hundred more Chinese boarded in Mombasa, Kenya. When they finally came ashore, on June 6, in the darkness and pounding surf off Rockaway, Queens, in New York City (eight drowned trying to swim to land), all had traveled a much greater distance than Raspail's fictional refugees.

What was remarkable about the *Golden Venture* was not that Chinese refugees tried to smuggle themselves into the United States—some experts estimate that 10,000 to 30,000 manage to do so each year—but that in traveling west rather than east, they were taking a new route to America. In the past most Chinese illegal immigrants came ashore on the West Coast or crossed into California after landing in Mexico. But the *Golden Venture* rounded the Cape of Good Hope and thus crossed some of the same waters as Raspail's imaginary armada.

The Camp of the Saints was also to some extent recalled in a special report of October 18, 1992, by the *New York Times* correspondent Alan Riding, about the remarkable increase in illegal immigration across the Strait of Gibraltar, the narrowest gap between Africa and Europe. The most startling fact in the report was not that ambitious, unemployed North Africans were heading to Europe to find jobs but that such traffic has now become pan-continental or even global. Of the 1,547 immigrants detained by the Spanish authorities in the first ten months of the year of Riding's report, 258 were from Ethiopia, 193 from Liberia, seventy-two from South Africa, and sixty-four from Somalia. Seventy-two from South Africa! Did they walk, hitchhike, or take buses across the entire continent? Even a journey that long pales beside Riding's further point that "word of the new route had spread far beyond Morocco, with not only Algerians and growing numbers of sub-Saharan Africans, but also Filipinos, Chinese and even the occasional Eastern Europeans among those detained." Take a look at an atlas and pose the question, Just how does a desperate citizen of, say, Bulgaria get to Morocco *without* going through western Europe?

THE DOOM
OF THE WHITE RACE

JEAN Raspail, born in 1925, has been writing works of travel and fiction since the 1950s. Many of his books recount his experiences in Alaska, the Caribbean, the Andes; he is not ignorant of foreign lands and cultures. Raspail won prizes from the Académie Française, and last year only narrowly failed to be elected to that august body. *The Camp of the Saints* is different from his other writings. In the preface, written a decade after the book, he states that one morning in 1972, at home by the shore of the Mediterranean, he had this vision:

> A million poor wretches, armed only with their weakness and their numbers, overwhelmed by misery, encumbered with starving brown and black children, ready to disembark on our soil, the vanguard of the multitudes pressing hard against every part of the tired and overfed West. I literally saw *them*, saw the major problem they presented, a problem absolutely insoluble by our present moral standards. To let them in would destroy us. To reject them would destroy them.
>
> During the ten months I spent writing this book, the vision never left me. That is why *The Camp of the Saints*, with all its imperfections, was a kind of emotional outpouring.

Is this simply a work of imagination or, as Raspail's critics charge, a racist tract dressed up as fiction? In some parts of the novel Raspail appears to be resigned, fatalistic, *not* taking sides: "The Good are at war with the Bad, true enough," he says at one point. "But one man's 'Bad' is another man's 'Good,' and vice versa. It's a question of sides." And he has the President of France, puzzling over the question of inequality among races, attribute to the Grand Mufti of Paris the idea that it is "just a question of rotation," with "different ones on top at different times"—as if to imply that it is quite natural for Europe, having expanded outward for the past 500 years, to be overwhelmed in turn by non-Western peoples. Indeed, Raspail claims that in depicting the French armed forces fleeing from confrontation rather than bloodily repulsing the armada, he shows he is no racist, for "I denied to the white Occident, at least in my novel, its last chance for salvation."

Yet for much of the rest of the novel Raspail makes plain where his cultural and political preferences lie. Whereas the Europeans all have characters and identities, from the Belgian consul in Calcutta, trampled to death by the crowd, to the French politicians paralyzed by their impending fate, the peoples of the Third World, whether already laboring in the slums of Paris or advancing upon the high seas, are unrelentingly disparaged.

> All the kinky-haired, swarthy-skinned, long-despised phantoms; all the teeming ants toiling for the white man's comfort; all the swill men and sweepers, the troglodytes, the stinking drudges, the swivel-hipped menials, the womanless wretches, the lung-spewing hackers; all the numberless, nameless, tortured, tormented, indispensable mass. . . . They don't say much. But they know their strength, and they'll never forget it. If they have an objection, they simply growl, and it soon becomes clear that

their growls run the show. After all, five billion growling human beings, rising over the length and breadth of the earth, can make a lot of noise!

> Meanwhile, along with Josiane and Marcel, seven hundred million whites sit shutting their eyes and plugging their ears.

If anything, Raspail's contempt for sympathizers and fellow travelers in the West is even more extreme. The collection of churchmen who plead for tolerance of the approaching armada; the intellectuals and media stars who think this is a great event; the hippies, radicals, and counterculture people who swarm south to greet the Indians as the panic-stricken Provençois are rushing north—all these get their comeuppance in Raspail's bitter, powerful prose. In one of the most dramatic events, close to the book's end, the leader of the French radicals is portrayed as rushing forward to welcome the "surging mob" of Indians, only to find himself "swept up in turn, carried off by the horde. Struggling to breathe. All around him, the press of sweaty, clammy bodies, elbows nudging madly in a frantic push forward, every man for himself, in a scramble to reach the streams of milk and honey." The message is clear: race, not class or ideology, determines everything, and the wretched of the earth will see no distinction between unfriendly, fascistic Frenchmen on the one hand and liberal-minded bishops and yuppies on the other. All have enjoyed too large a share of the world's wealth for too long, and their common fate is now at hand.

It is not just the people of France who suffer that fate. Near the end of Raspail's novel the mayor of New York is made to share Gracie Mansion with three families from Harlem, the Queen of England must marry her son to a Pakistani, and just one drunken Russian general stands in the way of the Chinese as they swarm into Siberia. "In the Philippines, in all the stifling Third World ports—Jakarta, Karachi, Conakry, and again in Calcutta—other huge armadas were ready to weigh anchor, bound for Australia, New Zealand, Europe. . . . Many a civilization, victim of the selfsame fate, sits tucked in our museums, under glass, neatly labeled."

To describe *The Camp of the Saints* as an apocalyptic novel would be a truism. The very title of the book comes, of course, from Saint John's Apocalypse, the lines of which are uttered almost exactly by the messianic untouchable early on in the book. The work is studded with references to much earlier clashes between "the West" and "the Rest": to Charles Martel, to the fall of Constantinople, to Don John of Austria, to Kitchener at Omdurman—all to fortify the suggestion that what is unfolding is just part of a millennium-old international Kulturkampf that is always resolved by power and numbers. When Europe dominated the globe, the Caucasian race's relative share of world population achieved its high point; as the proportion shrinks, Raspail argues, so the race dooms itself. In his 1982 preface he spells it out again: "Our hypersensitive and totally blind West . . . has not yet understood that whites, in a world become too small for its inhabitants, are now a minority and that the proliferation of other races dooms our race, my race, irretrievably to extinction in the century to come, if we hold fast to our present moral principles."

"NOT SINCE GENGHIS KHAN"

WHEN *The Camp of the Saints* first appeared, in 1973, it was, to put it mildly, not well received. Sixties radicalism still prevailed in Paris; a century of capitalist imperialism was blamed for the problems of the Third World, though the feeling was that Africans and Asians now at least had control of their own destinies; and French intellectuals and bureaucrats believed that they had a special rapport with non-European cultures, unlike the insensitive Anglo-Saxons. Besides being shocking in its contents, Raspail's book was also offensive: it insulted almost everything that Sorbonne professors held dear. *The Camp* was swiftly dismissed as a racist tract. As for Raspail, he went off to write other novels and travel books. But in late 1985 he offended again, by joining forces with the demographer Gérard Dumont to write an article in *Le Figaro Magazine* claiming that the fast-growing non-European immigrant component of France's population would endanger the survival of traditional French culture, values, and identity. By this time the immigration issue had become much more contentious in French politics, and only a year earlier Jacques Chirac, then the mayor of Paris, had publicly warned, "When you compare Europe with the other continents, it's terrifying. In demographic terms, Europe is disappearing. Twenty or so years from now our countries will be empty, and no matter what our technological power, we shall be incapable of putting it to use." The Raspail-Dumont article was highly embarrassing to the French Socialist government, which, though pledged to crack down on illegal immigrants, was deeply disturbed by the potential political fallout from such a controversial piece. No fewer than three Cabinet Ministers, including Prime Minister Laurent Fabius, attacked it as "racist propaganda" and "reminiscent of the wildest Nazi theories." It was no consolation to them that Jean-Marie Le Pen, the head of the fast-growing National Front, was making immigration the leading issue as he campaigned among the discontented French electorate.

Despite attempts by centrist politicians to ignore this touchy topic, it refuses to go away. For example, although the early 1990s were supposed to mark the culmination of the decades-long drive toward the European Union's integration, an increasing number of Europeans were looking over their shoulders, especially after the British Broadcasting Corporation raised the specter of a "march" on Europe in a 1990 made-for-TV movie of that name. In the program a band of Sudanese refugees decide to walk straight across the Sahara rather than slowly starve on the paltry rations of Western relief agencies. With timely assistance from the Libyan government, which calls them the "spirit of suffering Africa," a throng swollen to 250,000 finally arrives at the Strait of Gibraltar. "We've traveled almost as far as Columbus," says their leader, now called the Mahdi. "We have no power but this: to choose where we die," he proclaims before embarking for the European shore. "All we ask of you is, watch us die." On the advice of a media-savvy African-American congressman, the flotilla washes ashore in the glare of flashbulbs and prime-time TV broadcasts—and a large force of EU soldiers. The movie ends there, and what happens next is left to the viewer's imagination. But its production was enough to provoke Raspail to complain. The producers insisted that when they began the project they had been unaware of the earlier work—an insistence that only confirmed that the themes of *The Camp* continue to resonate. *The March* has itself become something of a cult classic. Though rejected by the Public Broadcasting System as "not suitable to their programming" (nobody actually said it was

 revisit Jean Raspail's controversial and hard-to-obtain novel? Many members of the more prosperous economies are beginning to agree with his vision: a world of two "camps," North and South, separate and unequal, in which the rich will have to fight and the poor will have to die if mass migration is not to overwhelm us.

too hot to handle), after four years it continues to be shown to audiences throughout Europe.

All of which brings us to the present day. Raspail may have written the most politically incorrect book in France in the second half of the twentieth century, but the national mood concerning immigration is nowadays much less liberal than it was two decades ago. In fact, France's tough new Conservative government began this year by announcing a series of crackdowns on illegal immigrants, including mass deportation. "When we have sent home several planeloads, even boatloads and trainloads, the world will get the message," claimed Charles Pasqua, the hardline Cabinet Minister in charge of security and immigration affairs. "We will close our frontiers." Last year he announced that France would become a "zero immigration" country, a stunning reversal of its 200-year-old policy of offering asylum to those in need. That Pasqua believed it was in fact possible to halt immigration was called into doubt when he later remarked, "The problems of immigration are ahead of us and not behind us." By the year 2000, he asserted, there will be 60 million people in Algeria, Morocco, and Tunisia under the age of twenty and "without a future." Where else to go but France, whose television programs they can view every evening, much as Albanians goggle at Italian cat-food commercials?

The Camp of the Saints is not well known in the United States, but it has attracted some attention in predictable circles. The only English-language edition we could find came from the American Immigration Control Foundation, which, as its name suggests, campaigns for stricter policies. That is an aim also expressed by the Federation for American Immigration Reform (FAIR) in its recent publication *Crowding Out the Future: World Population Growth, U.S. Immigration, and Pressures on Natural Resources*, which presents the following argument very early on:

> A traditional moralist may object, asserting, "I am my brother's keeper." We must ask him: "And what about your children? And your children's children? What about the children of your neighbor next door? Must we subdivide and distribute our patrimony among the children of all the world?" Americans are already outnumbered twenty-to-one by the rest of the world. Our grandchildren will be outnumbered even more. Must we condemn them to the poverty of an absolutely equal distribution? How would that benefit them or the descendants of other people?
>
> Total poverty can be avoided only if people agree that the ancient admonition "Charity begins at home" is still the best guide to philanthropic action.

The Washington Times is also strongly in the "let's regain control of our borders" camp, and its staff writers and op-ed contributors find reference to Raspail particularly useful in attacking the United States' liberal immigration policy. Illegal immigrants caught coming by boat—Chinese, Haitians —make for especially neat comparisons, and nowadays the language is as blunt as Raspail's own. "Not since Genghis Khan rode out of the Asian steppes has the West—Europe as well as the United States—encountered such an alien invasion," the *Washington Times* columnist Samuel Francis has written. His fellow columnist Paul Craig Roberts predicts "a cataclysmic future." Roberts has written, "Not since the Roman Empire was overrun by illegal aliens in the fifth century has the world experienced the massive population movements of recent years." Both writers posit what others have called a growing "Third-World-ization" of America's cities, with a privileged minority increasingly besieged by a disgruntled, polyglot lumpenproletariat. (Raspail had carefully built such a situation into *The Camp of the Saints*: the night came when the "black tide," learning what had happened in Provence, rose up and overwhelmed the elegant apartments around Central Park.)

Readers made uncomfortable by all this nativist and racist opinion will no doubt find it easy to counterattack. Migrants are not usually the poorest of the poor—instead they are the ones best informed about opportunities elsewhere and able to act on them. Paul Craig Roberts's figure of an "estimated" three million illegal aliens who find their way into the United States *each year* is much higher than other guesses we've seen. And historically, the greatest population migrations of all consisted of the tens of millions of "illegal aliens" who sailed from Europe to the Americas, Africa, and Australasia during the past 250 years; in the face of them the aboriginal inhabitants could do little but submit or be annihilated. In pointing to the reversal of that flow, Raspail was at least willing to concede that "different ones [are] on top at different times." Moreover, many economists—Julian Simon, at the University of Maryland, is one—argue that immigration gives a net boost to the United States, a position also held by the free-market paper *The Wall Street Journal*. Those who predict that immigration will become one of the hottest political issues of the 1990s may be correct; what is less certain is that Fortress America attitudes will win the day. Yet if the United States maintains a liberal policy while every other rich nation decides, like France, to do the opposite, will that not simply increase the pressures on this country's borders?

CORNUCOPIAN HOPES

LET us now get to the heart of the matter. Readers may well find Raspail's vision uncomfortable and his language vicious and repulsive, but the central message is clear: we are heading into the twenty-first century in a world consisting for the most part of a relatively small number of rich, satiated, demographically stagnant societies and a large number of poverty-stricken, resource-depleted nations whose populations are doubling every twenty-five years or less. The demographic imbalances are exacerbated by grotesque disparities of wealth between rich and poor countries. Despite the easy references that are made to our common humanity, it is difficult to believe that Switzerland, with an annual average per capita income of about $35,000, and Mali, with an average per capita income of less than $300, are on the same planet—but Raspail's point is that *they are*, and that a combination of push and pull factors will entice desperate, ambitious Third World peasants to approach the portals of the First World in ever-increasing numbers. The pressures are now much greater than they were when Raspail wrote, not only because we've added 1.5 billion people to our planet since the early 1970s, but also, ironically, because of the global communications revolution, which projects images of Western lifestyles, consumer goods, and youth culture across the globe. Ambitious peasants no longer need a messianic untouchable to urge them to leave by boat for Europe; they see the inducements every day on their small black-and-white television sets.

Is all this gloom and doom justified? What about rosier visions of the future? What about the good news? The apocalyptic literature appears to be at odds with an equally large array of writings, chiefly by free-market economists and consultants, that proclaim a brave new world of ever-greater production, trade, wealth, and standards of living for all. In these portrayals of "the coming global boom," a combination of market forces, diminished government interference, ingenious technologies, and the creation of a truly universal customer base will allow our planet to double or treble its income levels during the next few decades. In the view of those who believe that the global technological and communications revolution is making the world more integrated, rather than more envious, the constant modernization of the world economy is leading to a steady convergence of standards of production and living. As more and more countries open up to a borderless world, the prospects for humankind—or, at least, for those able to adapt—are steadily improving.

Yet a closer look at this cornucopian literature reveals that its focus is overwhelmingly upon the world's winners—the well-educated lawyers, management consultants, software engineers, and other "symbolic analysts" analyzed by Secretary of Labor Robert Reich—who sell their expertise at handsome prices to clients in other rich societies. To the extent that they consider the situation in the Third World, the cornucopian writers typically point to the model minority of global politics—the East Asians. The techno-liberals pay hardly any attention to the mounting human distress in Calcutta or Nicaragua or Liberia, and no wonder: were they to consider the desperate plight of the poor-

est two *billion* beings on our planet, their upbeat messages would sound less plausible.

Our global optimists might consider Robert D. Kaplan's horrific analysis, in the February, 1994, *Atlantic Monthly*, of the collapse of entire societies across West Africa. With governments losing control of any areas they cannot intimidate through their armies and police, groups of unemployed young men plundering travelers, AIDS and tuberculosis joining malaria to kill people in their prime, forests cut down and topsoil washed away, the region increasingly looks like strife-torn, plague-ridden medieval Europe. Even *The Economist*, claiming to detect "a flicker of light" in Africa amid the gloom, admits that if the sub-Saharan countries did grow at the (overoptimistic) rates recently predicted by the World Bank, "Africans would have to wait another 40 years to clamber back to the incomes they had in the mid-1970s. Exclude Nigeria, and the wait would last a century." What *The Economist* did not ask was whether the more than a billion and a half Africans likely to be living in 2035 will be content to watch the Northern Hemisphere grow and prosper while they themselves struggle to attain the same standard of living their great-grandparents had.

It is often argued that Africa is a special case (the Third World's Third World, as the saying goes), although Kaplan's more general point is that the same combination of rapid population growth, mass unemployment among youth, environmental devastation, and social collapse is to be seen, in a less acute form, everywhere from central China to the Euphrates Valley. Reportedly the State Department has sent copies of Kaplan's article to many embassies and missions abroad; the Pentagon prefers Martin Van Creveld's grim portrayal of future chaos and ethnic conflict, *The Transformation of War* (1991)—to which Kaplan's article pays tribute—as recommended reading for its service officers. Perhaps the most significant thing about these writings is their assumption that the demographically driven breakdown of order will not be confined to one continent but will be global in its manifestations—precisely what Raspail sought to convey in his stark account of swarms of immigrants moving out of Jakarta, Karachi, and Conakry.

If the problem is global, it is not all of a piece. There is a world of difference between, say, Mexican immigrants searching for a better life and Rwandan refugees fleeing a grisly death. But the most relevant divide is not between migrants and refugees—we will be seeing a lot more of both—but rather between what they lack and what we have to offer. Regardless of whether it is in an increasingly resentful American labor market or an overcrowded relief camp, the West will be hard put to provide answers to this burgeoning problem.

The techno-liberals are right to draw attention to the fact that virtually all the factors of production—capital, assembly, knowledge, management—have become globalized, moving across national boundaries in the form of investments, consulting expertise, new plants, patents, and so on. What they ignore is that one factor of production has not been similarly liberated: labor. Even the most outré proponent of free-market principles shrinks from arguing that any number of people should be free to go anywhere they like on the planet. This irony—or, better, this double standard—is not unnoticed by the spokespeople of poorer countries, who charge that while the North presses for the unshackling of capital flows, assembly, goods, and services, it firmly resists the liberalization of the global labor market, and that behind the ostensible philanthropic concern about world demographic trends lies a deep fear that the white races of the world will be steadily overwhelmed by everyone else.

NUMBERS COUNT

IT is impossible to isolate population growth from the economy, environment, politics, and culture of each country to prove that it causes external migration—though it is suggestive that Haiti and Rwanda have about the highest fertility rates in Latin America and Africa. What cannot be contested is that the sheer size of other countries that are "at risk" will make international migration a problem of ever greater magnitude. Similarly, in broad figures the future pattern of global population increases is not in dispute. At present the earth contains approximately 5.7 billion people and is adding to that total by approximately 93 million a year. It is possible to estimate the rough totals of world population as the next century unfolds: by 2025 the planet will contain approximately 8.5 billion people. The pace of growth is expected to taper off, so the total population may stabilize at around 10 or 11 billion people by perhaps 2050, although some estimates are much larger. By the second quarter of the coming century India may well rival China as the world's most populous country—with 1.4 billion to China's 1.5 billion inhabitants—and many other countries in the Third World are also expected to contain vastly expanded numbers of people: Indonesia 286 million, Nigeria 281 million, Pakistan 267 million, Brazil 246 million, Mexico 150 million, and so on.

Of the many implications of this global trend, four stand out—at least with respect to our inquiry. The first and most important is that 95 percent of the twofold increase in the world's population expected before the middle of the next century will occur in poor countries, especially those least equipped to take the strain. Second, although globally the relative share of human beings in poverty is expected to shrink, in absolute numbers there will be far more poor people on earth in the early twenty-first century than ever before, unless serious intervention occurs. Third, within the Third World a greater and greater percentage of the population is drifting from the countryside into gigantic shantycities. Even by the end of this decade São Paulo is expected to contain 22.6 million people, Bombay 18.1 million, Shanghai 17.4 million, Mexico City 16.2 million, and Calcutta 12.7 million—all cities that run the risk of becoming centers of mass poverty and social collapse. (Right now there are 143,000 people per square mile in Lagos and 130,000 per square mile in Jakarta, as compared with 23,700 per square mile in the five boroughs of New York.) And fourth, these societies are increasingly adolescent in composition—in Kenya in 1985, to take an extreme case, 52 percent of the population was under fifteen—and the chances that their resource-poor governments will be able to provide education and jobs for hundreds of millions of teenagers are remote. In many North African cities unemployment rates among youth range from 40 to 70 percent, providing highly combustible levels of frustration among young men who turn with interest to the anti-Northern messages of fundamentalist mullahs or, equally significant, to tempting televised portrayals of European lifestyles.

Regardless of the rosy prospects for East Asia, the gaps between rich and poor countries—between Europe and Africa, between North America and Central America—are widening, not closing; and, as Raspail bluntly put it, numbers do count. The southern European states of Spain, Portugal, France, Italy, and Greece, whose combined populations, it is estimated, will increase by a mere 4.5 million between 1990 and 2025, lie close to North African countries—Morocco, Algeria, Tunisia, Libya, Egypt—whose populations are expected to grow by 107 million in the same period. The population of the United States is expected to rise by 29 percent by 2025, while its southern neighbors Mexico and Guatemala may grow by 63 percent and 135 percent respectively. Together Europe and North America, which contained more than 22 percent of the world's population in 1950, will contain less than 10 percent by 2025.

In any case, even if tremendous economic progress were to be made over the next few decades in some of the poor regions of the globe, the result, ironically, would also challenge the West, as the economic and political balances of power swung toward countries that, on current evidence (the 1993 human-rights conference in Vienna, the Singapore caning), will actively resist cultural homogenization. Kishore Mahbubani, the deputy secretary of Singapore's Foreign Ministry, recently suggested as much when he pointed to a "siege mentality" in the West, affirming that "power is shifting among civilizations." "Simple arithmetic demonstrates Western folly," he wrote. "The West has 800 million people; the rest make up almost 4.7 billion. . . . no Western society would accept a situation where 15 percent of its population legislated for the remaining 85 percent." Westerners' "fatal

 only solution is to persuade our political leaders to recognize the colossal, interconnected nature of our global problem and to strain every element of our human ingenuity, resourcefulness, and energy to slow down, or if possible reverse, the buildup of worldwide demographic and environmental pressures.

flaw," according to Mahbubani, is "an inability to conceive that the West may have developed structural weaknesses in its core value systems and institutions." He added, "The West is bringing about its relative decline by its own hand." It is probably still premature to predict when China will overtake the United States as the world's largest economy, but it is undeniable that a shift in material power toward Asia is under way. Raspail's "seven hundred million whites" may well confront two very different challenges by early next century: Africa's collapse and Asia's rise.

Perhaps the global problem of the early twenty-first century is basically this: that across our planet a number of what might be termed demographic-technological fault lines are emerging, between fast-growing, adolescent, resource-poor, undercapitalized, and undereducated populations on one side and technologically inventive, demographically moribund, and increasingly nervous rich societies on the other. The fault line central to *The Camp of the Saints* lies along the Mediterranean, but it is easy to point to several others, from the Rio Grande to central Asia. One of the most interesting lines of all runs right through China, dividing most of the coastal provinces from the interior. How those on the two sides of these widening regional or intercontinental fissures are to relate to each other early in the next century dwarfs every other issue in global affairs.

If one accepts that this is our biggest long-term challenge, then the inadequacies of simplistic, knee-jerk responses assume great importance. The zero-immigration policies of France and Japan do nothing to affect tilting population balances and probably increase the resentment of these countries' poorer neighbors, but denying that migration is an international problem, as some American liberals do, invites the possibility that a continuing (and growing) flow of immigrants will place even greater strains on this country's social and cultural politics.

Yet what are the alternatives? Even if we wished to alter demographic balances, is there any acceptable prospect of doing so? When Raspail said, obliquely, that our "present moral principles" were dooming the West, was he really getting at the idea that rich societies could expect to preserve the status quo only if they were prepared to use any means necessary to cut global population? It is easy to see where that logic leads. To take but one of the more extreme examples, a Finnish philosopher has become a best-selling writer in his country by arguing that the world can continue to be habitable only if a few billion human beings are eliminated; another world war would therefore be "a happy occasion for the planet."

Some would argue that we must reverse the decline of Western populations, and that any people that falls below the replacement fertility rate (2.1 children per woman) is committing demographic suicide. This is a sensitive topic. Quite apart from environment-oriented objections to a rise in the birth rates of rich societies (the average American or European baby will consume in its lifetime hundreds of times as many resources as the average Chadian or Haitian baby), there are simply too many social and cultural obstacles to reversing a declining national birth rate. Japanese and American politicians who bemoan the failure of "bright, well-educated women" to bear enough children have been noticeably unsuccessful in their campaigns. Perhaps, then, we should just accept that the global demographic imbalances are so huge that nothing can be done to affect them, and, like the old professor in Raspail's book, simply hunker down and survey the impending invasion through a spyglass.

The only serious alternative, it seems to us, is simultaneously to persuade our political leaders to recognize the colossal, interconnected nature of our global problem and to strain every element of our human ingenuity, resourcefulness, and energy to slow down, or if possible reverse, the buildup of worldwide demographic and environmental pressures. Such an effort cannot rest upon a single policy, such as urging Third World countries to reduce their population growth; it must instead be part of a major North-South package wherein all parties, in accepting changes to their present policies, are persuaded to see that a comprehensive and coordinated response is the only way forward. If political leaders and their advisers cannot come up with some sort of win-win solution, in which every country can see benefits for itself, serious reforms are unlikely and humankind's prospects by 2025 may indeed be bleak.

A NEW
(NORTH-SOUTH) DEAL

WHAT elements should be included in such a package? In offering some answers to that question, it is important to stress that nothing that follows is either new or impossible. In theory, there are lots of things that the global community could do to improve its condition, and such ideas have been around for decades, if not longer. The real problem has been the lack of political commitment to change, or, to put it more charitably, the tendency of national leaders and delegates to see only the elements of the package that call for sacrifices on their part—the North to contribute more money, the South to accept environmental monitoring—and to ignore both the individual and the collective gains that could flow from a linked set of agreements between developed and developing countries. If that mindset can be changed, so can everything else.

• What if, for example, the rich Organization for Economic Cooperation and Development countries actually fulfilled their quarter-century-old promise to allocate 0.7 percent of gross domestic product annually to development aid, instead of (for the most part) falling far short of that target? The United States, with one of the poorest records of all, now contributes less than 0.2 percent of GDP each year. What if the OECD countries were bold enough to contribute one percent of GDP each year? As a kind of global insurance premium—protecting not only poorer countries but also ourselves from the worst consequences of mismatched demographics and development—this is not very much. In fact, if viewed more positively, as an investment in the future of the people of our planet, it is a modest sum indeed.

• What if this money could actually be spent efficiently and appropriately, instead of falling into the wrong hands and being devoted to the wrong purposes? For the fact is that international-aid agencies have (again for the most part) acquired a reputation for investing in ambitious, technologically inappropriate schemes, channeling funds to highly paid consultants and local leaders and ignoring the ideas of in-

digenous inhabitants, while poor countries themselves have provided far too many examples of corrupt, oppressive, or simply inefficient regimes that have squandered their treasuries and their resources for years. Extra development aid has no chance of succeeding unless it is accompanied by vastly improved accounting and supervisory techniques. However, the failings of present regimes and of previous aid programs are no reason not to continue to try to assist development; if anything, these provide compelling reasons to redouble—and reform—our efforts.

• What if we were able to use some of this money to employ the tens of thousands of scientists and engineers now released from Cold War–related research to seek solutions to our global environmental problems? Such solutions might include a truly dramatic breakthrough in solar or photovoltaic energy production, achieving such a drop in the cost of sun-powered energy that it could be made available to the peoples of Asia and Africa, and could wean them from their reliance on wood, oil, coal, and other fossil fuels. The enhanced technology might also include the mass production of small solar ovens, sufficient to cook a village's meals without a daily search for firewood. The results of breakthroughs in biotech agriculture (new disease-resistant and heat-resistant crop strains) might be shared without requiring large patent and user fees from poor nations.

• What if it were possible to respond to the desire of hundreds of millions of women in Third World countries for access to safe and inexpensive contraceptives, to allow them to stabilize family size and concentrate on nurturing their existing children? The costs involved are not enormous—a few billions of dollars rather than hundreds of billions—and when such programs are administered through women's groups and supported by enlightened governments, they can have a dramatic effect on fertility rates, as has recently been demonstrated in Kenya and Egypt. (Such programs ought to be kept apart from the issue of abortion, which is much more problematic politically and which, in any case, is used disproportionately in many Third World countries to prevent the birth of girls.)

• Since order is the precondition of social betterment, what if, instead of the nations of the world having to respond to or rebuff the United Nations Secretary General's pleas to send troops for peacekeeping purposes to one crisis spot after another, some of the more useful schemes to improve the UN's capacities—from creating a military staff to establishing "ready-to-go" units—were agreed upon by the Security Council nations and implemented in the next year or two?

• And what if, as a separate yet parallel measure to reduce violence, a much more serious effort were made to stem the flow of arms (simple guns as well as sophisticated systems) into Third World countries—arms that are manufactured primarily by the five permanent members of the Security Council?

• What if, as a contribution to reducing the forecast clash of civilizations, the United Nations strove to promote agreement not just in the important sphere of human rights but also on the equally important issue of recognizing cultural diversity, both within countries and between technologically dominant cultures and the rest of the globe? This is not a call for a revival of the crude and ideologically inept UNESCO programs of the early 1980s. We would, however, argue that a genuine North-South entente is unlikely unless Third World countries grow less fearful that their cultures will be swallowed up by the technologies and material way of life of richer nations, especially the United States. Cultural arrogance bedevils our planet and gives rise to many conflicts and antagonisms, just as it suffuses *The Camp of the Saints*. If the relationship between North and South is to be improved significantly, a set of norms (and agreements to disagree) must be established that all or at least most nations can abide by.

Various other matters—from measures to enhance the status of women in Third World countries to improved coordination between UN agencies and the Bretton Woods institutions—might also be incorporated into a North-South package of linked agreements. As it is, any one of the aforementioned elements—more aid more efficiently allocated, appropriate and accessible technological advances, reduced fertility rates, enhanced peacekeeping powers, acceptance of cultural diversity—might by itself make all the difference, though we cannot know which one that might be.

DONNE'S ISLAND

HOW likely are any of these changes to come about during the next few years? This is the critical period if we hope to change the socio-economic condition of humankind in the early decades of the twenty-first century. A global idealist could point to some promising indicators even in the midst of our present woes. There is a growing awareness in at least a few rich societies (the Scandinavian countries, Germany, the Netherlands, Canada) that a serious effort has to be made to improve the lot of poorer countries and protect their environments. There are the impressive economic successes of most of the nations of East Asia, which are raising the quality of life of hundreds of millions of people and which, provided that further environmental damage can be avoided (a big proviso, admittedly), offer a possible model to Third World countries. The end of the Cold War, while certainly not signaling the start of any new world order, has at least permitted the UN Security Council to function as it was designed to. International agencies, especially those within the UN but also innumerable nongovernmental ones, are actively pursuing policies that not only are more realistic than those of previous decades (for example, no more World Bank loans for giant dam projects) but also reveal a greater awareness of the interconnectedness of agendas for real improvement: economic growth, environmental protection, population control, the status of women, migration, jobs, investment, education, human rights, and democracy are all related considerations in any serious effort to improve the condition of the poorer half of humanity. And at least some commentators are openly arguing that the need for concerted action ought to be presented no longer in humanitarian-response terms (because, for example, after the fifth or sixth Ethiopian famine "aid fatigue" sets in) but in terms of a global ethic that recognizes our common human destiny and the necessity for shared stewardship of our delicate global ecosystem.

But can these sporadic signs of promise really prevail against the lack of effective political leadership, the turning inward of so many rich societies, the problem of global structural unemployment in an age of intensified modernization, the resistance to many programs to encourage the limitation of family size (even when the thorny issue of abortion is excluded), and the widespread lassitude and even downright hostility that exist in many quarters toward the idea of helping the world's two billion poorest? As Zaire, Rwanda, and Yemen follow Somalia, Sudan, Bosnia, Georgia, and Tajikistan into bloody chaos and ethnic wars, while Boutros Boutros-Ghali finds fewer and fewer nations willing to contribute peacekeeping forces, can one seriously expect significant reforms soon? With the political leadership of the world's most powerful nation deeply divided over scandals and parochial issues, with its public evincing exhaustion in respect to international problems, and with irresponsible though powerful senators blaming the United Nations for every peacekeeping mishap (such as the deaths of U.S. Rangers in Somalia), is it not naive and unrealistic to hope for a North-South package of reforms along the lines suggested above?

Perhaps it is. Perhaps, as some observers fear, we shall have to observe truly awful and widespread societal destruction—the collapse of continents rather than single states; oceans of dead rather than mere rivers—with repercussions that significantly affect rich countries as well as poor before our public and our political leadership finally appreciate that an intelligent and far-reaching response is unavoidable, and that, tempting though it is to turn away from the world, too large a proportion of humankind is heading into the twenty-first century in too distressed a condition for any nation to imagine that it can avoid the larger consequences. We will have to convince a suspicious public and cynical politicians that a serious package of reform measures is not fuzzy liberal idealism but a truer form of realism. It is simply a matter of perspective—or of timing. Doing little or nothing at present seems the more practical course; yet given the pace and intensity of global change, the richer societies need to recognize that John Donne's reasoning applies on an international scale. "No man is an island, entire of itself"—with massacres, social collapse, and migrations occurring across our planet on a weekly basis, do not ask "for whom the bell tolls; it tolls for thee."

These are, of course, idealistic arguments, and just how many Americans, Europeans, and citizens of other privileged countries will heed the tocsin is unclear. For the remainder of this century, we suspect, the debate will rage over what and how much should be done to improve the condition of humankind in the face of the mounting pressures described here and in other analyses. One thing seems to us fairly certain. However the debate unfolds, it is, alas, likely that a large part of it—on issues of population, migration, rich versus poor, race against race—will have advanced little beyond the considerations and themes that are at the heart of one of the most disturbing novels of the late twentieth century, Jean Raspail's *The Camp of the Saints*. It will take more than talk to prove the prophet wrong.

SECOND OPINION

OPTIMISM AND OVERPOPULATION

Well, yes, the West must pay attention to the population problems of the Third World. But what sort of attention? The conventional wisdom holds that economic development—and thus economic aid from the West— is the key to curbing population growth in poor nations. Not true, says **VIRGINIA ABERNETHY**

Virginia Abernethy ("Optimism and Overpopulation") is a professor of psychiatry and anthropology at Vanderbilt University and the editor of the journal Population and Environment. *She is the author of* Population Pressure and Cultural Adjustment *(1979) and* Population Politics: The Choices That Shape Our Future *(1993).*

OVERPOPULATION afflicts most countries but remains primarily a local problem—an idea that this article will seek to explain. Reproductive restraint, the solution, is also primarily local; it grows out of a sense that resources are shrinking. Under these circumstances individuals and couples often see limitation of family size as the most likely path to success.

Many scholars, ancient and modern, have known that actual family size is very closely linked to the number of children people want. Paul Demeny, of The Population Council, is exceptionally clear on this, and the World Bank economist Lant Pritchett asserts that 85–95 percent of actual fertility rates are explained by parents' desires—not by mere availability of contraceptives. Pritchett writes that "the impressive declines in fertility observed in the contemporary world are due almost entirely to equally impressive declines in desired fertility." Of Paul Kennedy's contention, in his book *Preparing for the Twenty-first Century*, that "the only practical way to ensure a decrease in fertility rates, and thus in population growth, is to introduce cheap and reliable forms of birth control," Pritchett says, "We could not have invented a clearer and more articulate statement of the view we argue is wrong."

PROGRESS AND POPULATION

CROSS-CULTURAL and historical data suggest that people have usually limited their families to a size consistent with living comfortably in stable communities. If left undisturbed, traditional societies survive over long periods in balance with local resources. A society lasts in part because it maintains itself within the carrying capacity of its environment.

However, the perception of limits that derive from the local environment is easily neutralized by signals that promise prosperity. Quoting the late Georg Borgstrom, a renowned food scientist and a much-decorated specialist in Third World economies who died five years ago, a 1971 Population Reference Bureau publication explains,

> A number of civilizations, including India and Indonesia, "had a clear picture of the limitations of their villages or communities" before foreign intervention disrupted the traditional patterns. Technical aid programs . . . "made them believe that the adoption of certain technical advances [was] going to free them of this bondage and of dependence on such restrictions."

Economic expansion, especially if it is introduced from outside the society and is also broad-based, encourages the belief that formerly recognized limits can be discounted, that everyone can look forward to prosperity, and, as in recent instances, that the West can be counted upon to provide assistance, rescue, and an escape valve for excess population.

The perception of new opportunity, whether due to technological advance, expanded trade, political change, foreign aid, moving to a richer land, or the disappearance of competitors (who move away or die), encourages larger family size. Families eagerly fill any apparently larger niche, and the extra births and consequent population growth often overshoot actual opportunity.

Increase beyond a sustainable number is an ever-present threat, because human beings take their cue from the opportunity that is apparent *today*, and are easily fooled by change. Relying on what is near in space or time, we calculate with difficulty the long-term momentum of population growth, the limits to future technological advance, and the inexorable progression of resource depletion.

The appearance (and short-term reality) of expanding opportunity takes various guises. In the 1950s land redistribution in Turkey led formerly landless peasants to increase significantly the size of their families. Among African Sahel pastoralists, deep-water wells drilled by donor countries in the 1950s and 1960s prompted larger herds of cattle and goats, earlier marriage (because bride-prices are paid in animals and the required number became easier to accumulate), and higher fertility. Similarly, Ireland's widespread cultivation of the potato in the early eighteenth century increased agricultural productivity and encouraged peasants to subdivide portions of their farms into plots for their sons, which in turn promoted younger marriage and a baby boom. Still earlier, between the sixth and ninth centuries, the introduction in Europe of the stirrup, the rigid-collar harness, and nailed horseshoes greatly enhanced the agricultural output of Europe's northern plains. Better nutrition helped lead Europe out of the Dark Ages to economic recovery and thence, from about 1050 to 1350, to a tripling of population size in countries such as England and France.

India offers another example. Its population was nearly stable from 400 B.C. to about A.D. 1600. After the end of the Mogul invasions, and with the advent of new trade opportunities, the population began to grow (at about half the European rate). Later, European trade offered India further opportunity, and population growth accelerated. It took off for the skies shortly after the country shed its colonial status, in 1947; assistance from the USSR, the World Bank, and the International Monetary Fund bolstered perceptions of a prosperous future, and the rate of population growth accelerated up until about 1980.

Successful independence movements and populist coups are prominent among the kinds of changes that carry the message that times are good and getting better. China commenced its euphoric interlude with the expulsion of the Nationalists, in 1949. Communism triumphed, and its philosophy held that a greater nation required more people. The fertility rate and population size rocketed upward. A mainland-China population that was estimated to be 559 million in 1949 grew to 654 million in 1959, whereas in the preceding 100 years of political turmoil and war the average growth rate of the Chinese population had been just 0.3 percent a year. Both lower mortality and higher fertility contributed to the increase. Judith Banister writes in *China's Changing Population*, "Fertility began rising in the late 1940s, and was near or above 6 births per woman during the years 1952-57, higher fertility than had been customary" in prior decades. Banister attributes China's baby boom to war's end and to government policy: "Land reform of 1950-51 redistributed land to landless peasants and tenant farmers."

Cuba experienced a baby boom when Fidel Castro displaced Fulgencio Batista, in 1959. Castro explicitly promised a redistribution of wealth, and according to the demographers S. Díaz-Briquets and L. Pérez, fertility rose in response. Díaz-Briquets and Pérez write, "The main factor was the real income rise among the most disadvantaged groups brought about by the redistribution measures of the revo-

THE encounters with scarcity that are currently being forced upon billions of people by the natural limits of their environment are beginning to correct the consequences of decades of misperception. Now, as it has done many times in human history, the rediscovery of limits is awakening the motivation to limit family size.

lutionary government. The fertility rises in almost every age group suggest that couples viewed the future as more promising and felt they could now afford more children."

The populations of Algeria, Zimbabwe, and Rwanda grew rapidly around the time colonial powers left. Algeria, for example, achieved independence in 1962, and thirty years later 70 percent of its population was under thirty years of age. Zimbabwe gained independence in 1980, and soon achieved one of the highest population-growth rates in the world; the growth was encouraged by the Health Minister, who attacked family planning as a "white colonialist plot" to limit black power.

Because of their effect on family size, development programs entailing large transfers of technology and funds to the Third World have been especially pernicious. This kind of aid is inappropriate because it sends the signal that wealth and opportunity can grow without effort and without limit. That rapid population growth ensues should surprise no one. Africa, which in recent decades has received three times as much foreign aid per capita as any other continent, now also has the highest fertility rates. During the 1950s and 1960s the African fertility rate rose—to almost seven children per woman—at the same time that infant mortality was dramatically reduced, health-care availability grew, literacy for women and men became more widespread, and economic optimism pervaded more and more sectors of society. Extraordinarily high rates of population growth were new to Africa; during the 1950s the Latin American rate had been higher.

Even immigration can affect total world population. Studies of nineteenth-century England and Wales and modern Caribbean societies show that in communities already in the throes of rapid population growth, fertility stays high as long as the option to emigrate exists, whereas fertility falls rapidly in communities that lack such an escape valve. And while fertility rates are falling in most African countries, the rate remains high in Ghana (6.2 births per woman in 1993), perhaps because an established pattern of emigration (one per 1,000 in the population) provides a safety valve for excess numbers. This effect on fertility is consistent with independent reports that emigration raises incomes both among emigrants and among those they leave behind.

In sum, it is true, if awkward, that efforts to alleviate poverty often spur population growth, as does leaving open the door to immigration. Subsidies, windfalls, and the prospect of economic opportunity remove the immediacy of needing to conserve. The mantras of democracy, redistribution, and economic development raise expectations and fertility rates, fostering population growth and thereby steepening a downward environmental and economic spiral.

Despite this fact, certain experts and the public they inform nevertheless wish to believe that fertility rates have traditionally been high worldwide and have declined only in industrialized countries or in countries where modern contraception is available, and that the post–Second World War population explosion is explained mostly by better health and nutrition, which led to rapidly declining mortality rates and slight, involuntary increases in fertility. The possibility that larger family size resulted from wanting more children continues to be denied.

Experts in population studies were the first to be fooled. In the 1930s many demographers predicted a steady decline in population, because the low fertility of Western industrialized countries was attributed to development and modernization rather than to the endemic pessimism brought on by the Great Depression. Still missing the point, many failed to see that the high fertility after the Second World War was a response to the perception of expanding economic opportunity. The U.S. Baby Boom (1947–1961) and the slightly later booms in Western Europe took most demographers by surprise.

THE MESSAGE OF SCARCITY

As it happens, the encounters with scarcity that are currently being forced upon literally billions of people by the natural limits of their environment are beginning to correct the consequences of decades of misperception. The rhetoric of modernization, international development, and egalitarianism is losing its power to mislead. As Europe is revealed to be incapable of alleviating the suffering of the former Yugoslavia, as rich countries in general prove nearly powerless to help the countless distant multitudes, it becomes difficult to believe in rescue. Now, as it has done many times in human history, the rediscovery of limits is awakening the motivation to limit family size.

In Ireland land became scarce relative to the rapidly growing population in the early nineteenth century, whereupon fertility began a retreat to its low, pre-potato level. By 1830 only about two thirds of women married before age twenty-five. Ten percent married this young in 1851—a drastic postponement of marriage in response to the 1846–1851 potato famine. Following a brief recovery, as few as 12 percent married before age twenty-five. The pattern of late marriage persisted from about 1890 through the Second World War. In the United States the Baby Boom ended at about the time the jobs pipeline began to fill; the fertility rate dropped below replacement level after the 1973 oil shock occurred and many Americans' real income stopped rising. In post-revolutionary China population momentum built until famine, unrelieved by Western aid, forced a confrontation with limits. In 1979, mindful of severe food shortages, the government instituted a one-child-per-family policy, thus completing the evolution of incentives and controls that returned the country to the pre-Communist pattern of marital and reproductive restraint. In Cuba the Castro-inspired baby boom gave way to below-replacement-level fertility when communism's inability to deliver prosperity became manifest. In Eastern-bloc countries, including Russia, economic restructuring, the dissipation of government consumption subsidies, and the public perception of rising infant mortality have promoted lower fertility rates and created demand for the avoidance of pregnancy.

In Zimbabwe, prodded by the international economic retrenchment of the late 1980s, the government began to support family planning. According to *The Economist*, "The hefty cost of supporting a large family has helped persuade some men of the value of limiting its size." The fertility rate is falling among the Yoruba in Nigeria, owing to a combination of delayed marriage and increasing acceptance of modern contraception. Two thirds of the women who responded to a recent survey said that "the major force behind marriage postponement and the use of contraception to achieve it was the present hard economic conditions."

Elsewhere the demand for modern contraception is also rising, and again the reason seems to be that couples view early marriage and large families as unaffordable. In his new book, *Critical Masses*, the journalist George D. Moffett reports that a mother of two in Mexico defended her use of contraception before a village priest by explaining, "Things are difficult here. A majority of people are having hard times. Jobs are hard to come by." Similarly, a day laborer in Thailand, in the words of Moffett, "would like to have one more child, but he understands that that is beyond his means."

Without the motivation to limit family size, access to modern contraception is nearly irrelevant. For six years in the 1950s a project directed by the British researcher John Wyon provided several villages in northern India with family-planning education, access to contraception, and medical care. The villagers had positive attitudes toward the health-care providers and toward family planning, and infant mortality had fallen way down. But the fertility rate stayed way up.

Wyon's group soon figured out why: the villagers liked large families. They were delighted that now, with lower infant mortality, they could have the six surviving children they had always wanted. The well-funded Wyon project may even have reinforced the preference for large families, by playing a part in making extra children affordable.

THINK LOCALLY

MISCALCULATION about the *cause* of the population explosion has led to irrelevant and even counterproductive strategies for helping the Third World to balance its population size and its resources. In the late 1940s and the heady decades that followed, trade, independence movements, populist revolutions, foreign aid, and new technology made people in all walks of life believe in abundance and an end to the natural limits imposed by the environments with which they were familiar.

Now it is a step forward for industrial nations, their wealth much diminished, to be retrenching and targeting aid more narrowly. Their remaining wealth must not be squandered on arming opposing factions, reckless foreign assistance, or support for international migrations that rob and ultimately enrage—to the point of violence and possibly civil war—resident populations. This retrenchment saddens many, but the former liberality did a disservice to every country targeted for development.

With a new, informed understanding of human responses, certain kinds of aid remain appropriate: microloans that foster grassroots enterprise, where success is substantially related to effort; and assistance with family-planning services, not because contraception is a solution in and of itself but because modern contraception is a humane way of achieving small family size when small family size is desired. This modest agenda remains within the means of industrialized countries even as they look to the needs of the growing ranks of their own poor. And it does not mislead and unintentionally harm intended beneficiaries.

The idea that economic development is the key to curbing world population growth rests on assumptions and assertions that have influenced international aid policy for some fifty years. These assumptions do not stand up to historical or anthropological scrutiny, however, and the policies they have spawned have contributed to runaway population growth.

The human capacity for adaptive response evolved in face-to-face interactions. Humanity's strong suit is quick response to environmental cues—a response more likely to be appropriate when the relevant environment is immediate and local. The mind's horizon is here and now. Our ancestors evolved and had to succeed in small groups that moved around relatively small territories. They had to succeed one day at a time—or not be anyone's ancestors. So, unsurprisingly, signals that come from the local environment are powerfully motivating.

Let the globalists step aside. One-world solutions do not work. Local solutions will. Everywhere people act in accord with their perception of their best interests. People are adept at interpreting *local* signs to find the *next* move needed. In many countries and communities today, where social, economic, and environmental conditions are indubitably worsening, the demand for modern contraception is rising, marriage and sexual initiation are delayed, and family size is contracting. Individuals responding with low fertility to signs of limits are the local solution. One prays that the hucksters of inappropriate development do not mess this up.

Vicious Circles

African Demographic History as a Warning

Timothy C. Weiskel

Timothy C. Weiskel is Director of the Harvard Seminar on Environmental Values at Harvard Divinity School.

The terms of debate on global population issues have changed significantly in the last several decades. Theories which tried to isolate simple causes and define simple solutions have been discarded; we have come to recognize that the causes of population growth can only be found in the complexities of the international political economy and the ways it affects the cities and villages of the Third World. The "Developing World" is not developing along Western lines, nor does its demographic history mirror Europe's. Intelligent population policies must be informed by a thorough understanding of population dynamics and of the complex historical, cultural and economic circumstances within which they operate.

Human population growth was identified as a contemporary problem in the 1950s, with the advent of the post-World War II population surge. Initially, the use of birth control pills, condoms and other contraceptive techniques was thought to be the key to slowing population growth. Attention was thus focused on making these new technologies more widely available, especially in the Third World. Contraceptive technologies, however, proved less effective than originally promised. They were difficult to deliver and were resisted by local populations, who considered limits on their reproductive behavior to be limits on their potential livelihood. Rural populations in many parts of the Third World had come to depend upon large families to supply labor, create wealth and provide for the elderly. Thus, attempts to limit family size were regarded with mistrust and suspicion.

Attention eventually shifted to development and economic growth. The general correlation between higher levels of economic prosperity and lower birth rates seemed clear from analyses of global economic and demographic data—poverty appeared to cause excessive population growth. The strategic conclusion was that the population problem would solve itself if significant economic development occurred. With economists in the lead, population experts intoned in mantra-like fashion, "Development is the best contraceptive."

This thinking was guided by the model of "the demographic transition," a phenomenon observed in Europe as it underwent industrialization. One country after another moved from a pattern of high mortality and high birth rates to one of lower mortality and lower birth rates. This same demographic transition, it was thought, would occur throughout the world. The popularity of this model caused the goal of population stabilization to be subsumed by that of economic development. The problem with this approach, however, soon became clear: industrial development according to the European model was not inevitable or even probable in the Third World. Instead, many regions, particularly in Africa, experienced a decline in real GDP per capita. Unless unforseeable rates of economic growth were to spring forth miraculously in these regions, this demographic transition could not occur.

Furthermore, researchers have begun to notice that the presumed correlation between economic growth and declining birth rates is not as absolute as originally believed. Recent studies indicate that, despite a lack of economic growth, selected regions of India and Kenya have witnessed a marked decline in fertility. These studies challenge the idea that economic development is the primary cause of population stabilization. Women's status and education now appear to be far more significant than overall economic growth as a correlate of declining fertility. Many population experts have now embraced this insight, and it is likely to join economic development as a guiding

Patterns of production based on cash crops impoverish developing nations.

principle in the formulation of population policy at the International Conference on Population and Development in Cairo this September.

Years of research and debate on population issues have failed to produce convincing mono-causal explanations or successful, unidimensional interventionist strategies; it is finally being accepted that there is no silver bullet. Neither birth control technologies nor development programs alone promise a solution to the population problem. Even programs aimed at improving women's education are not sufficient in themselves; they must be combined with sensitively designed family planning services and facilities.

The case of Bangladesh is instructive: in a poor, male-dominated society that deprives women of access to education, birth rates have been significantly slowed by family planning efforts. This led Jessica Tuckman Mathews of the Council on Foreign Relations to conclude in the *Washington Post* that, "the debate over which is more important, economic development or family planning, can finally be laid to rest. The slogan 'Development is the best contraceptive' stands exposed as the mindless rallying cry of people whose real agenda is opposition to family planning." It is now clear that more attention needs to be devoted to voluntary programs that address the reproductive needs of women.

Population growth is a bio-social problem embedded in the particular history and culture of a society. This realization leads to the awareness that simple mechanical models of causation ("A" causes "B") are inadequate tools

for devising population policy. Such models posit that in order to effect a change in "B" one must attempt to change "A." This logic dominated both the contraceptive technology phase and the economic development phase of population policy discussion, but it is fundamentally unsuited to the problem.

We are coming to realize that population dynamics are not based on such simple relationships; their causality is cumulative, reciprocal and nested. It is *cumulative* in the sense that cultures are strongly bound to tradition. Accepted habits and norms of behavior change slowly and are influenced by the past at least as strongly as by prevailing contemporary circumstances. The causation of population growth is also *reciprocal*: while "A" may cause "B," it is equally true that, over time, "B" causes "A." For example, while having many children may reduce a family's welfare, declining family income may lead to a decision to have more children in an attempt to gain labor and eventually expand household income. Finally, this causation is *nested* because patterns of micro-behavior are conditioned by, and in turn, affect shifts in macro-behavior; local conditions are shaped by global circumstances and vice versa.

Population Growth in Africa: A Case Study

African demographic history provides an illustration of this three-fold framework for examining population dynamics. The magnitude of Africa's population expansion in recent decades is staggering. In 1950, the entire continent had an estimated population of 199 million.

2. POPULATION

By 1992, this figure had reached 682 million. The United Nations projects that by the year 2000 the continent will be home to 856 million people, and by the year 2025, 1.583 billion. How we account for this remarkable population surge will clarify some of the complexities of the population dilemma confronting us today.

At least five historical components have fueled African population growth. First, Africa's population grew during the slave-trade period. Very little is known about African demographics before the era of the European slave trade, but there is no doubt that the slave trade itself was a significant impulse for population expansion. The warfare and disorder involved in slave acquisition led to a state of generalized conflict in which maximum reproductive performance was highly valued and rewarded. All else being equal, larger families, villages and kingdoms survived more successfully in this state of insecurity than smaller ones.

We have blithely ignored the global patterns of economic integration, urbanization and migration that have conditioned and shaped local reproductive norms for the last five hundred years.

A further consequence of Europe's trade with the Americas was the introduction of foodstuff crops from the New World, like maize, groundnuts and cassava to West Africa. This new food supply made possible the growth of families and villages that, for reasons of self-defense, had become a necessity. Thus, the slave trade launched a fertility boom in Africa. But the fertility boom did not manifest itself as a population boom at the time for two reasons: mortality rates increased during the warfare engendered by the slave trade, and much of the added population was exported as slaves in what became known to demographers as "the largest non-voluntary migration in human history."

The slave trade and the warfare that it fueled lasted from roughly 1500 to 1850, establishing a pattern of large families; however, the impulse to have many children did not end with the close of the slave trade. Rather, European and American interactions with Africa in the latter half of the 19th century placed new demands on the continent's economy. These burdens motivated the second phase of African population growth. The "legitimate commerce" in palm oil, groundnuts, wild rubber and other tropical products put a premium on families that could mobilize large numbers of dependents in order to increase their household production. Thus, the cash-cropping boom of the 19th century—prior to formal colonial rule—maintained and extended the cultural logic that rewarded maximum reproductive performance.

The period of colonial conquest, from approximately 1885 to 1910, generated a third major component in Africa's population history. Much of this conquest was accomplished through destructive warfare. Moreover, in the wake of military intervention, African populations experienced a measurable decline from famine and epidemic disease. As is generally the case with catastrophes caused by famine, disease and warfare, Africa experienced a quick demographic rebound from these early colonial traumas. Thus, in many regions during the 1910s and 1920s a "baby boom" occurred which restored local populations to their pre-colonial numbers. International trade catalyzed this recovery. Based on the labor-intensive export of agricultural commodities, colonial cash-crop regimes—which continue to dominate African economies today, decades after the demise of colonial rule—gave even more support to the well-ingrained cultural preference for large families.

A fourth factor in Africa's population surge involved the gradual expansion of access to elementary hygiene and rudimentary medicine. Infant mortality rates were brought down by the investment in wells and sanitary water supplies for emerging African cities and the instruction in the use of that clean water. Large families (which, over the previous 400 years, had become culturally valued and economically rewarded) were now easier to maintain, since fewer infants died from childhood diseases.

The fifth historical factor contributing to Africa's contemporary population expansion was a remarkable period of urbanization. Whereas fewer than 12 percent of Africa's population lived in cities in 1950, nearly 25 percent did in 1980. This trend has continued; United Nations demographic indicators project that by the year 2010 more than 45 percent of Africa's population (440.9 million people) will be living in cities. In many parts of the world, urbanization is linked to declining fertility rates in the cities, but the impact upon the remaining rural populations is quite different. Many rural households view the loss of young adults to the cities as a "death," or at least as an export of labor. The net effect is to motivate rural households further to expand their dependent labor force by having more children.

Thus, a pattern of significant rural "out-migration" to the cities has actually served to motivate increased reproductive performance in rural areas. The growth of cities with their incessant demands for land, food, fuel and fodder has in turn accelerated the degradation of surrounding rural regions, driving more people off the land and into the cities, and further encouraging the rise of rural fertility rates. In Africa and elsewhere in the Third World, the growth of cities has had a very different impact on the demographics of society than it had in Europe. European urbanization, accompanied by industrialization, has led to marked *declines* in fertility on a society-wide basis. In the contemporary Third World, however, rapid urbanization may actually serve to stimulate society-wide *increases* in fertility, as rural areas seek to replace "lost" labor with more children.

Africa finds itself in what ecologists would call a massive "positive feedback loop." Having more children creates a vicious circle, the only perceived solution for which is to have even more children. Mobilizing greater amounts of dependent labor appears to be the only means households have to work their way out of poverty. The apparent solution is thus the source of the problem in the first place, and the vicious circle manifests itself as a cycle of decline.

African Demographics and the Global Economy

From an analytical perspective, Africa's contemporary population dynamics are best understood within the larger context of the continent's relation to the global economy. Mono-causal explanations do not account for Africa's population dynamics, and neither can these issues be adequately regarded as simply Africa's problem. Responsibility for Africa's population growth may be traced back hundreds of years; it is shared and should be acknowledged by those nations in Europe and the Western hemisphere whose economies have benefited from Africa's demographic history.

Once rural populations were drawn into this pattern of primary production, the local calculus of reproduction became intimately linked to the dynamics of the global economy.

Europe's expansion into Asia and the New World triggered massive demographic dislocations. The New World's population collapse, caused by the disease, famine and warfare engendered by early European encounters, created resource-rich but labor-scarce economies. Slaves from Africa supplied these economies with the means to build prosperity, and Africa became the specialized source for the production of human labor over a period of several hundred years. People were its most valued export commodity.

As European economies stopped demanding unskilled plantation labor and started demanding natural resource inputs for a growing industrial structure, Africa's expanding labor force was put to work in a succession of cash-crop booms. While the objects of this commerce may have changed from palm oil to wild rubber to coffee and cocoa, the underlying logic of expanding the household to expand prosperity was constantly reinforced.

In a broader sense, this pattern came to characterize the entire Third World, even those areas that were not formally absorbed into European colonial empires. While no other region became as involved in the export of labor as Africa did during the slave trade, cash-crop export economies linked to European industrial demand spread throughout Latin America, Asia and the Pacific. Once rural populations were drawn into this pattern of primary production, the local calculus of reproduction became intimately linked to the dynamics of the global economy.

Ironically, the very success of household production units has pressured them to expand their size. The Third World has produced surpluses of coffee, cocoa, tea, so high that the international glut of these commodities has led to a decline in their unit value. The result is what economists call "the primary producer's squeeze." The "squeeze" is simply this: in the face of the declining unit value of its commodity, the surest means available for a peasant household to maintain its income is to expand its production of that same commodity. This requires more labor, hence larger families. Yet, by expanding production in this manner, the primary producer contributes to an even greater glut of their particular commodity on world markets, which, in turn, leads to a further decline in its unit value. Receiving still less for the same volume of production, the peasant household is "squeezed" into expanding its production still further, and the vicious circle of population growth and subsequent emmiseration starts once again.

Urbanization and Population Growth

It is now becoming apparent that global patterns of urbanization are echoing those already manifest in Africa. Urban populations are increasing at rates that exceed average population growth. On a global scale, populations are continuing to grow, but, at an even faster pace, they are agglomerating in massive urban concentrations.

The evidence from Asia is the most dramatic in this regard. A recent report of the United Nations Economic and Social Council for Asia and the Pacific claimed that "by the year 2000, the population of Dhaka is expected to double to 12.2 million; Bombay, Calcutta, Delhi, Jakarta, Karachi, Manila and Shanghai [will] each gain four million people; and Bangkok, Bangalore and Beijing [will each gain] three million." There will be 21 cities with populations in excess of 10 million by the turn of the century, with 13 of these in the Asia-Pacific region. By the year 2020, the report estimates that 1.5 billion more people will be living in Asian cities: the equivalent of creating a new city of 140,000 people every day for the next thirty years.

In a similar vein, recent studies conducted by the Peace and Conflict Studies Program at the University of Toronto in cooperation with the American Academy of Arts and Sciences have drawn attention to rural out-migration in China. Citing Dr. Thomas Homer-Dixon, the author of one of these studies, the *New York Times* reported, "tens of millions of people are already trying to migrate to coastal cities from the country's rural north and interior which...cannot possibly support the next few decades' booming population." The result is the growth of these cities in a locally unsustainable manner; China's growing urban population will have to be supported by 25 percent less arable land per capita by the year 2010.

Chinese cities may therefore become dependent upon an international trade in surplus grains produced in Europe and the United States, as many African cities are today. Any sudden interruption of supply to these cities or continued environmental decline in rural areas could well rekindle age-old regional tensions or trigger ethnic conflict in Asia, as it already has in Africa. Dr. Homer-Dixon's

2. POPULATION

Are growing cities one cause of rural population growth?

study suggests the emergence of a global pattern characterized by "falling grain prices and regional food surpluses in Western countries occurring simultaneously with scarcity-induced civil strife in parts of Africa and Asia." Recently reported rural strife in China is particularly troubling in this regard.

A newly published report of the International Food Policy Research Institute delivers another sobering message to population planners: "Over the next 20 to 30 years, farmers and policy-makers in developing countries will be challenged to provide food at affordable prices for almost 100 million [new] people every year—the largest annual population increase in history." Dr. Per Pinstrup-Anderson, the author of the Institute's study, *World Food Trends and Future Food Security*, quite bluntly claims, "Failure to significantly reduce population growth, particularly in sub-Saharan Africa, [within] the next 20 years will render all other development efforts insufficient to avoid greater human misery in the future." The report suggests that unless immediate commitments are made to undertake accelerated agricultural research, food production will not keep pace with population growth.

The problem we as population analysts face is our failure to develop a global understanding of population dynamics. Instead, we proceed with country-by-country demographic studies, expecting in each case that demographic change will mimic Europe's experience. We have blithely ignored the global patterns of economic integration, urbanization and migration that have conditioned and shaped local reproductive norms for the last five hundred years. In other words, we divide the world into the "West" and the rest—all those other people who are just waiting to pursue economic and social development on the West's terms.

However, Europe's "demographic transition" may prove to be the exception, not the rule. Similarly, while cities in the Western world have generally stabilized, this is surely not the trend in Third World areas. In the next twenty years 97 percent of world population growth will occur in what we now call the Third World—but perhaps should more accurately name the "Nine-Tenths" World.

Effective population policy can only emerge from a new understanding of the cumulative, reciprocal and nested character of population dynamics on a planetary scale. This expanded understanding of causation necessarily entails an enlarged sense of responsibility and a renewed sense of commitment to this issue on the part of all peoples and all nations. In effect, we face a global population problem without a global understanding of it. We persist in thinking that Africa or Asia have population problems—someone else, somewhere else, not us, not here. In reality, the world now has a human population problem that is most dramatically apparent in its weakest economies and most vulnerable ecosystems.

If we wish to survive as a global species, we must begin to think of ourselves as global citizens. In this context, who is "we"? Who is "they"? What is in our "national self-interest"? These are all concepts that will need to be re-cast as we struggle to forge a morally responsible world community.

U.N. High Commissioner for Refugees/P. Moumtzis

No Refuge

DICK KIRSCHTEN

From Cuba to Bosnia to Rwanda, a surging tide of refugees is creating a global crisis. During the Cold War, refugees often were welcomed as pawns in propaganda battles. But now most nations seem inclined to pull up the drawbridges.

With the Cold War over and America proclaimed the sole remaining superpower, U.S. foreign policy is increasingly being shaped by the plight of the powerless. A global epidemic of civil strife has exacted a grisly toll in human lives and ruined economies, and it has loosed a torrent of refugees whose needs and demands dominate a crisis-driven international agenda.

"The new strategic enemy is not a single nation or government; it is the tumult of chaos that failed states are leaving in their wake," said J. Brian Atwood, the much-traveled administrator of the Agency for International Development (AID).

Whether at sea in frail craft in the Caribbean, trapped in misnamed "safe havens" in Bosnia or dying of disease and dehydration in overcrowded camps in Central Africa, refugees are the leading indicator of the chaos about which Atwood speaks.

It is an indicator that President Clinton, despite his passion for domestic poli-

cy, has been unable to ignore. His inaugural preparations were disrupted by the need to hatch a plan to ward off an expected exodus of Haitian boat people. Now, in a sudden reversal of long-standing U.S. policy, he's trying to repel a new Cuban boatlift.

In the meantime, Clinton has dithered over the travail of displaced Bosnians and has been embarrassed by a U.S. humanitarian mission gone awry in Somalia. Yet he has launched a major military relief mission in Rwanda. *(See box, p. 71.)*

Welcome to the new world disorder. Since the mid-1970s, the number of people driven from their homes by war or famine has increased nearly tenfold. *(See chart, p.70.)* In addition to 23 million people uprooted into exile, the United Nations reports that another 26 million are "internally displaced" within their own countries.

And new refugee-related crises can be expected to crop up at any time. "To know that the number of rural poor has doubled since 1950, that per capita incomes have fallen steadily in a number of regions and that malnutrition has risen is to know that the stage is set for continuing floods of refugees," said Kathleen Newland, author of a U.N. report on refugees.

It's little wonder that Clinton's foreign policy agenda has been so dominated by responses to humanitarian disasters. "In the past, refugee policy has always been a handmaiden of U.S. foreign policy," Newland said during a recent interview at the Carnegie Endowment for International Peace, where she is a senior associate. "But now the tail is wagging the dog in several very high-profile areas."

Although decision makers in high places are focusing more closely on refugees, it doesn't necessarily follow that things are looking up for the dispossessed millions. Clinton's response to the Cubans and Haitians fits with a general tendency around the globe to pull up the drawbridges and keep refugees out.

In Washington, refugees no longer are viewed as useful pawns in the propaganda battles of the Cold War. The cruel fact is that since the collapse of a global Communist threat, the United States has become a lot less interested in providing haven to victims of political persecution.

"The effort now is not to help protect them or accommodate them as refugees, but rather to figure out how to prevent the refugee flows," said Bill Frelick, a senior analyst for the U.S. Committee for Refugees, a private advocacy group. "It's an irony," he said, that politicians who now regard refugees as "less of a value" are being forced to devote so much energy to refugee issues.

"During the Cold War, when refugees were lauded for 'voting with their feet' [against Communism], they were seen as the victims," Frelick added. "Now they are viewed as a burden or even a security threat." Instead of being seen as "the fallout from a larger problem, they are seen as the problem."

SANCTIONS THAT BACKFIRE

Nothing dramatizes the change in thinking more than Clinton's about-face on Cuba. For more than 30 years, refugees from Fidel Castro's regime generally received red-carpet treatment, including financial assistance for resettlement and virtually automatic eligibility for U.S. citizenship. Benefits for Cuban defectors are codified by the 1966 Cuban Adjustment Act.

But this summer, with Castro threatening a repeat of the disruptive Mariel boatlift of 1980, the Administration found itself under pressure to rethink the Cuban refugee calculus. For one thing, it was having a difficult time justifying its disparate treatment of Haitian boat peo-

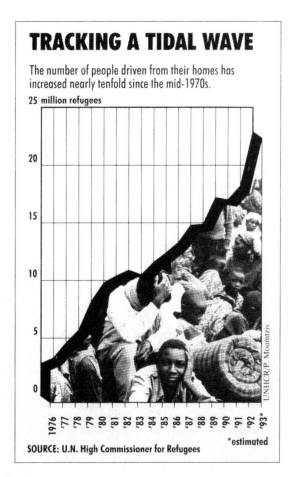

TRACKING A TIDAL WAVE

The number of people driven from their homes has increased nearly tenfold since the mid-1970s.

SOURCE: U.N. High Commissioner for Refugees

*estimated

ple, who initially were forcibly turned back and now are being detained in camps outside the United States. For another, domestic political opinion—especially in Florida—has grown sour toward immigrants, viewing them as an unwelcome economic burden.

Although Clinton was loath to offend Cuban-American leaders, he was taking heat from American black politicians who contended that Haitians were being discriminated against. In addition, Frelick noted, conservatives who hailed Cuban refugees as foes of Communism in the 1960s are now more likely to rail against unregulated immigration and to point out that many of the "Marielitos" had criminal records.

For Haitians and Cubans, the Administration finally has a refugee policy that is consistent:

Boaters from either country who are intercepted at sea by U.S. Coast Guard and naval vessels will not be forcibly returned, but neither will they be granted admission to the United States. Both groups are being provided safe haven in camps at the U.S. Naval Base at Guantanamo Bay, Cuba, or perhaps in third countries such as Honduras, Panama or Turks and Caicos.

Cubans who make it to U.S. shores no longer are granted instant political asylum, but instead are detained—just like Haitians—in stateside facilities run by the Immigration and Naturalization Service.

At first blush, Clinton's new strategy of refugee deterrence seems consistent and simple. It satisfies the domestic political imperative to crack down on uninvited immigrants, and it meets international humanitarian standards. Safe haven is offered to those in danger of death or persecution, but for those whose primary objective is to seek their fortune in the United States, there is the unattractive prospect of prolonged detention in a camp outside the United States.

Clinton has learned, however, that it's not sufficient to simply discourage refugees from coming. To provide moral justification for the exclusion of Haitians and Cubans, he has pledged to end human rights abuses in those countries by working to bring down their dictatorial rulers. Toward that end, he has applied harsh economic sanctions designed to undercut the offending regimes.

The Administration's refugee policy, however, has run into a glaring catch-22. Instead of raising hopes that democracy will soon be restored, reducing pressure to emigrate, economic sanctions often have exactly the opposite effect.

For example, following Clinton's Aug. 20 announcement that he will bar Cuban-Americans from sending money to relatives in Cuba—an annual cash flow estimated at $500 million—the Coast Guard reported that more, not fewer, Cubans were braving the perilous waters of the Florida Straits.

Although economic embargoes appeal to an Administration that seeks to avoid more-forceful foreign intervention, they are a weak weapon. They usually prove too porous to inflict unbearable pain on ruling elites, but bite quickly and painfully among the poor and oppressed. As a strategy to keep refugees away from America's doorstep, they seem destined to backfire.

And Clinton's use of economic exclusion in the Caribbean makes it trickier for him to explain his approach to Communist China, which holds that the best way to foster human rights and democracy there is to liberalize trade relationships.

OUR KIND OF REFUGEES

What separates refugees from other migrants is their vulnerability to ill treatment at the hands of their own governments. Under international conventions established after the end of World War II, refugee tides have flowed through two channels—one orderly and one much less so.

Refugee groups selected for resettlement by willing host nations are carefully processed in advance—usually in so-called countries of first asylum—and then admitted in accordance with preset annual quotas.

But individuals who flee independently are entitled under international law to apply for political asylum upon arrival in a foreign land. If such refugees can prove a legitimate fear of persecution in their home country, the receiving nation is obliged to ensure that they are not sent back to face the peril from which they fled.

For most of the Cold War period, the dual system worked well for the United States. Refugees who could escape from behind the Iron Curtain were not only welcomed but sought after, especially Soviet Jews whose inability to emigrate freely became a major bone of contention in U.S.-Soviet relations. Third World refugees, who lacked U.S. sponsors or the wherewithal to get themselves to the United States, were never much of a factor.

After Vietnam, the Cold War calculus dictated that America offer safe haven to victims of oppression by Southeast Asia's victorious Communist regimes. The U.S. response was generous but, by now, has just about run its course.

A CRISIS THEY COULDN'T IGNORE

Seldom has the refugee tail wagged the foreign policy dog more insistently than in late July, when J. Brian Atwood returned from a visit to the camps in Zaire, where hundreds of thousands of Rwandan refugees were facing imminent death.

Atwood, administrator of the Agency for International Development (AID), was headed home from a trip to the Middle East on July 15 when he received an urgent request from President Clinton to check out the plight of the Rwandan refugees.

Traveling as Clinton's special envoy, Atwood visited camps in Goma and Bakuvu in Zaire, met with officials in Bujumbura, the capital of neighboring Burundi, and compared notes with French leaders in Paris. He arrived back in Washington the evening of July 20, expecting to report to the President the next morning and testify that afternoon on Capitol Hill.

But Atwood was informed that Clinton could not meet with him until July 22, forcing a 24-hour postponement of his scheduled appearance before the House Foreign Affairs Subcommittee on Africa.

The delay outraged humanitarian aid advocates. At a July 21 breakfast meeting with reporters, refugee advocate Lionel A. Rosenblatt, also just back from Goma, said that the Rwandans were on "a refugee death march" and that an immediate military relief effort was needed to avert a monumental tragedy. As for the Clinton Administration, "the people at the top still don't get it," fumed Rosenblatt, head of the nonprofit organization Refugees International.

Before the day was out, however, the White House had found time for Clinton to see Atwood. After an early-afternoon meeting with the AID administrator, the President used a speech to Girls' Nation delegates to announce that U.S. assistance would be stepped up to help stem the cholera epidemic spreading through the refugee camps in Zaire. Atwood then briefed the White House press corps, explaining that an additional $41.4 million had been committed.

The next day, Clinton and his top foreign policy advisers, along with Atwood, met to hammer out details of a rapidly unfolding plan to send more than 2,000 troops to take part in the relief effort. The first U.S. units landed at the airport in Goma the next morning, and a staging base for relief supplies was quickly established at Entebbe, in neighboring Uganda.

Among those taking part in the July 22 session were Vice President Albert Gore Jr., national security adviser Anthony Lake, deputy Defense secretary John M. Deutch and Gen. John M. Shalikashvili, the chairman of the Joint Chiefs of Staff.

In a week's time, the ante was raised considerably. On July 29, Clinton announced that the scope of the mission was being enlarged to include the opening of a new airport for relief supplies at Kigali, the Rwandan capital. And he asked Congress for an additional $320 million, which he said would bring total humanitarian aid for Rwanda since April to "almost a half-billion dollars."

Since then, according to an Atwood aide, there have been thrice-weekly meetings with White House national security advisers to monitor the situation in Rwanda, as well as in Burundi, where the threat of intertribal violence remains high. Such is the way that foreign policy is being made on the fly in the new and chaotic post-Cold War era.

In the meantime, refugees from other-than-Communist persecution have had a hard time getting in the door. Haitians fleeing the Duvalier dictatorship in the late 1970s encountered obstacles. So did the droves of refugees who came from El Salvador in the 1980s seeking haven from the "death squads" linked to the country's U.S.-supported government.

Unlike prior flights of Cold War refugees, the exodus of the Salvadorans gave a black eye not to Communism, but to U.S. foreign policy. Predictably, the Reagan Administration resisted their appeals for asylum and held many of them in detention camps along the U.S.-Mexican border.

To this day, U.S. refugee quotas—which average roughly 120,000 a year—primarily are reserved for escapees from what once was the Communist Bloc. Of those admitted in 1993, 85 per cent came from either Southeast Asia (50,000), the former Soviet Union (49,000), Cuba

UNHCR/B. Press

An Ethiopian woman and her children—among the millions of Africans who have fled their homes—travel to a camp in Kenya.

(2,800) or Eastern Europe (2,700). Similar admission ceilings are in effect for 1994.

But that pattern is unlikely to continue. The refugee camps of Southeast Asia at long last are beginning to empty. Most of Cambodia's nearly 400,000 refugees have been voluntarily repatriated since U.N.-supervised elections were successfully conducted there last year.

Refugees no longer are fleeing Laos and Vietnam in significant numbers, and the United States's Comprehensive Plan of Action for resettling Southeast Asians is scheduled for termination at the end of 1995.

In the former Soviet Union, where upsurges in ultra-nationalist and anti-Semitic sentiment have been reported, Jews and other traditionally oppressed religious minorities are expected to continue to seek—and be granted—the right to resettle in the United States. "Yet even here the pool of eligible applicants . . . will have been largely taken up by the end of this decade," the U.S. Committee for Refugees reports.

"We thus are at a major policy decision point in the U.S. refugee resettlement program," said Ralston Deffenbaugh, executive director of the New York City-

based Lutheran Immigration and Refugee Service. If restricted to the currently welcomed groups, U.S. refugee admissions will soon dwindle to roughly half the current level.

Deffenbaugh, who notes that the U.S. resettlement program already is out of kilter with "the international community's determination of who needs protection most urgently," would like to see those 60,000 unused slots made available to refugees from different places. But given the current climate of anti-immigrant sentiment, that's an unlikely outcome.

ERECTING BARRIERS

In today's world, refugees no longer are neatly tagged with East Bloc and West Bloc labels. Even if they were, it might not matter much because in an era of exponential population increases and rising international migration, traditional host countries are rolling in their welcome mats.

Nor does it help that racially tinged xenophobia is on the rise in predominantly white Western industrial nations, most notably France, Germany and the United States. More than four of every five refugees, according to a 1994 survey, are peo-

ple of color from Africa, Asia or the Near East.

"We have witnessed a major shift in the world's approach toward persons who are forced out of their homes because of potential ethnic violence and the threat of persecution," Frelick of the U.S. Committee on Refugees wrote in a review of the past year. "The international community is now generally committed to keeping would-be refugees at home."

A prime example is the treatment of the estimated 1.3 million Bosnians who've been displaced in the "ethnic cleansing" campaign carried out by Serb militia units. Despite a death toll of close to a quarter-million, the West declined to take sides in the bloodletting that followed the splintering of Yugoslavia. (U.S. reluctance to arm Bosnia's beleaguered Muslims stems in part from a post-Cold War shift that finds America courting Russia, a historic ally of the Serbs.)

Western European governments were already in the process—as is the United States—of tightening their political asylum laws to prevent perceived abuses. Bosnian citizens attempting to flee the carnage in their homeland were not recognized as victims of persecution who were entitled to protection as refugees.

PRINCIPAL SOURCES OF THE WORLD'S REFUGEES

Even before the headline-grabbing events of recent months, the world was awash in refugees. At the end of 1993, according to U.N. officials, nearly 23 million people were in flight from persecution or violence in their homelands and in need of international protection.

That total does not include refugees who've been offered permanent residence or citizenship in host countries, including tens of thousands of Southeast Asians and Soviet Jews who have resettled in the United States. Nor does it include the more than 20,000 Cuban boat people who in recent weeks have joined roughly 14,000 Haitian refugees who are being detained by U.S. authorities.

The biggest surge in the world refugee total this year resulted from genocidal intertribal warfare in the tiny, overpopulated Central African nation of Rwanda. At the height of the crisis, more than a fourth of Rwanda's 8 million citizens had fled the country and another 2.5 million were displaced internally. More than 500,000 were killed.

The sources of the largest refugee flows as of Dec. 31, 1993, are shown at right.

SOURCE: U.S. Committee for Refugees

Former Yugoslavia 1,319,650
Azerbaijan 290,000
Palestinians 2,801,300
Afghanistan 3,429,800
Myanmar 289,500
Vietnam 303,500
Sudan 373,000
Eritrea 421,500
Somalia 491,200
Liberia 701,000
Burundi 780,000
Angola 335,000
Mozambique 1,332,000

"One European country after another imposed visa requirements on Bosnians during 1993, erecting legal barriers to match the physical barriers created around the [safe haven] enclaves in Bosnia itself," Frelick noted. "Relatively few Bosnians managed to escape during the year."

As a result, the office of the U.N. High Commissioner for Refugees, which originally was established as a temporary agency to tend to the needs of out-of-country refugees, was forced to shift gears. The commissioner, Sadako Ogata, "has taken on a role that goes far beyond the normal mandate" of the agency, the Carnegie Endowment's Newland said. "She's dealing with hundreds of thousands of internally displaced people and working with U.N. peacekeeping forces to run convoys of humanitarian supplies all over the country."

But it wasn't just Bosnians who were affected by legislative changes that, in Frelick's words, "simply defined refugees out of existence." Support for the concept of political asylum was on the wane around the world. In Germany, where hate crimes against Turks and other immigrant workers were creating embarrassing headlines, the parliament in May 1993 enacted sweeping restrictions to replace what previously had been an unqualified right to apply for asylum in that country.

In the United States, a package of asylum reforms was proposed by the Administration last year with much hoopla, but until recently it remained bottled up in Congress pending an assessment of administrative steps that have been taken to speed up the disposition of asylum requests and limit appeals.

This year, the Administration amended its proposed "Expedited Exclusion and Alien Smuggling Enhanced Penalties Act." The revised legislation would give the Attorney General sweeping powers to suspend the customary rights of asylum applicants by declaring an immigration emergency. During such an "extraordinary immigration situation," laws guaranteeing due process for refugees seeking asylum would be suspended. The measure was approved on Aug. 11 by the Senate Judiciary Committee and awaits floor action.

According to Newland, the changes in attitudes and laws affecting political asylum are already having a major effect. After rising precipitously from about 100,000 in 1983, applications for asylum in Australia, Canada, Western Europe and the United States peaked at 825,400 in 1992, then declined last year to 725,000. Preliminary estimates indicate that they'll dip even more sharply this year to about 425,000.

Western industrialized nations are not the only ones erecting barriers against the rising flood of refugees. Pakistan, which for more than a decade harbored hundreds of thousands of Afghans uprooted by the Soviet invasion of their country, has closed its borders to prevent a new flood of Afghan refugees threatened by internecine warfare among the Muslim factions that ousted the Soviets.

And in northern Iraq, an estimated 700,000 Kurds remain displaced in the safety zone created in the aftermath of the Persian Gulf war. The zone was created in the spring of 1991 by U.S. forces and their allies who were called in after Saddam Hussein's army had forced 1.5 million Kurds into temporary refugee camps in Iran and Turkey.

A POLICY VACUUM

U.S. military units have mostly won plaudits for the execution of the humanitarian missions that are becoming part of their post-Cold War role. In responding to the emergencies of the Iraqi Kurds and Rwanda's fleeing Hutu tribe, they've demonstrated that they have the equipment, the transport capacity and the know-how to arrive in a hurry and provide quick relief.

Even in Somalia, which strictly speaking was not a refugee crisis, the U.S. troops of Operation Restore Hope performed admirably in distributing food to a population that had been driven from its land or looted of its grain stores by warring militia factions. It was only when the mission turned from peaceful to belligerent that U.S. forces withdrew under a cloud of confusion over policy and adverse public reaction back home.

The humanitarian interventions in Iraq, Rwanda and Somalia have a common thread. They were ad hoc reactions to disasters that had gotten out of hand and had become the subject of heart-rending news reports on American television screens.

"The level of human suffering in Rwanda was greater at the time of the [mass killings of Tutsis by Hutus] that precipitated the refugee crisis than it was in the camps" in neighboring Tanzania and Zaire to which the Hutus later fled, said David Smock, coordinator of Africa programs at the federally financed U.S. Institute of Peace in Washington.

But, Smock said, "the press often has easier access to the refugee camps than to the fighting situations." And the political will to respond is closely linked to the "manipulation" that occurs when the public sees that "people have been uprooted from their homes and are suffering because the country that has received them isn't ready for them."

The refugee stage of a crisis, although it comes late in the game, also satisfies another apparent criterion for post-Cold War intervention. It usually occurs after the shooting has stopped, when it appears that the delivery of humanitarian aid will be "a safe expedition," Smock said. One of the lessons drawn from Somalia, he noted, is that "we shouldn't get involved in the middle of a civil war and have our troops shot at."

Newland agreed that televised images of emaciated refugees seem to be dictating foreign policy. "There is a really strong humanitarian impulse abroad in this country," she said. "People want to see their government doing something to help those poor starving people."

Reacting to television coverage is a poor substitute for a coherent foreign policy, Administration critics say. They note that U.S. interest in pressing for NATO strikes in Bosnia seems to rise and fall in rhythm with the intensity of news coverage of besieged Muslim enclaves such as Sarajevo and Gorazde. At the same time, the plight of some 380,000 refugees from Sudan who are scattered in

UNHCR/A. Hollmann

Displaced Bosnians, denied admittance to most European nations, take refuge at a school.

Ethiopia, Kenya, Uganda and Zaire apparently is less compelling to assignment editors—and thus is a low priority for government decision makers.

From the outset, the Clinton Administration has given lip service to a major reorientation of foreign policy that would stress sustainable development: a long-term program of economic, environmental and democracy-building assistance designed to head off refugee-producing catastrophes.

AID's Atwood has spoken frequently and fervently about the need for such a strategy of preventive diplomacy. This year, he spearheaded an international effort to put food stocks in place in the Horn of Africa before an expected drought.

Newland cites the conspicuousness of Atwood's role as evidence of the "vacuum that has occurred in the part of the bureaucracy that you would expect this thinking to be coming from." She said she has seen "no imprint of creative thinking about this kind of thing in the State Department." (At State, refugee issues

this year were folded into a new Bureau of Population, Refugees and Migration. The bureau and its recently confirmed chief, Phyllis E. Oakley, had been enmeshed in preparations for participation in the U.N. International Conference on Population and Development in Cairo that began on Sept. 5.)

Smock warned, however, that there are fiscal and diplomatic limits to what can be done to prevent man-made and natural calamities around the globe. Preventive diplomacy, he said, is "a great phrase, and I'm all for it, but in practice it can be hard to pull off."

In Smock's view, excessive optimism and a failure to openly define the mission's goals in advance led to the embarrassing U.S. withdrawal from Somalia. When the Bush Administration decided to launch the operation in late 1992, he said, "the thinking seemed to be: 'Now this is a new day in which the United Nations and the United States, in collaboration with each other, can right the wrongs of the Third World and set things straight.'"

The tragedy of the experience, Smock said, is that the Clinton Administration overreacted to the deaths of U.S. servicemen there and adopted overly restrictive rules of engagement for future missions. In cases where the President identifies a clear strategic objective and explains it to the public, he said, it should be acceptable to send the military into harm's way. "The killing of 18 American soldiers—if you have a sound policy and a sound strategy—may not be an excessive cost for saving hundreds of thousands of lives in Africa."

Newland argues that early intervention often is far less expensive than waiting to come in and sweep up after a calamity. In Rwanda, the international community faces the staggering task of restoring order to a society in which more than half of its eight million people have been routed from their homes or killed.

U.S. officials are "talking about spending a half-billion dollars now [to resettle Rwandan refugees], when we failed to find $10 million in April and May" to support U.N. proposals to send in peacekeeping forces to try to prevent the impending bloodletting, she said. Relatively simple steps, such as jamming the radio broadcasts that were inciting the killing, could have been taken but weren't, she added.

If a post-Cold War refugee policy is to emerge, Newland contends, preventive intervention will have to be the first pillar. The second will be to maintain the capacity for emergency response; the third, and perhaps most important, will be a willingness to help failed nations rebuild institutions of governance so that their refugees can be peacefully repatriated.

Newland's recipe is a tall order. And in a world where the prevailing political response to refugees is to shut the doors, it may be an overly optimistic one.

THE KILLERS ALL AROUND

New viruses and drug-resistant bacteria are reversing human victories over infectious disease

Michael D. Lemonick

THEY CAN STRIKE ANYWHERE, anytime. On a cruise ship, in the corner restaurant, in the grass just outside the back door. And anyone can be a carrier: the stranger coughing in the next seat on the bus, the college classmate from a far-off place, even the sweetheart who seems perfect in every way. For wherever we go and whatever we do, we are accosted by invaders from an unseen world. Protozoans, bacteria, viruses—a whole menagerie of microscopic pests constantly assaults every part of our body, looking for a way inside. Many are harmless or easy to fight off. Others—as we are now so often reminded—are merciless killers.

Humanity once had the hubris to think it could control or even conquer all these microbes. But anyone who reads today's headlines knows how vain that hope turned out to be. New scourges are emerging—AIDS is not the only one—and older diseases like tuberculosis are rapidly evolving into forms that are resistant to antibiotics, the main weapon in the doctor's arsenal. The danger is greatest, of course, in the underdeveloped world, where epidemics of cholera, dysentery and malaria are spawned by war, poverty, overcrowding and poor sanitation. But the microbial world knows no boundaries. For all the vaunted power of modern medicine, deadly infections are a growing threat to everyone, everywhere. Hardly a week goes by without reports of outbreaks in the U.S. and other developed nations. Some of the latest examples:

■ A Royal Caribbean cruise ship on a trip to Baja California returned early to Los Angeles last week after more than 400 pas-sengers came down with an unidentified intestinal ailment. It may have been the reason one elderly man died. And just a few weeks ago, 1,200 disgruntled passengers were evacuated from the ocean liner *Horizon* in Bermuda because of the threat of Legionnaires' disease. Among customers on previous *Horizon* voyages this summer, there have been 11 confirmed cases of the potentially fatal pneumonia-like illness and 24 suspected cases. At least one victim died.

■ A Yale School of Medicine researcher is recovering from a rare and potentially lethal disease called Sabiá virus. Before 1990, the illness was unknown to medicine. Then a

---

When bacteria began to outwit antibiotics, doctors found themselves retreating in the battle against the germs

---

woman in the town of Sabiá, Brazil, died from a mysterious virus that had evidently been circulating in local rodents for years before making an assault on humans. Brazilian doctors sent samples to Yale, and a month ago the scientist became infected when he accidentally broke a container holding the virus. Health officials point out that it is not easily passed between humans, but some 80 people who came into contact with the man have been under observation.

■ More than 850 people have come down with cholera in southern Russia, and officials fear the disease could erupt into an epidemic. Cholera outbreaks were rare in that part of the world before the breakup of the Soviet Union, but collapsing health services and worsening sanitary conditions have fostered the disease. Shortages of vaccines, meanwhile, have led to an upsurge in diphtheria in Russia, and health experts have encountered cases of typhoid, hepatitis, anthrax and salmonella in neighboring Ukraine.

■ The notorious flare-up in Gloucestershire, England, of what the press dubbed flesh-eating bacteria alerted people to the dangers of streptococcus-A infections. The common bacteria that cause strep throat generally produce no lasting harm if properly treated, but certain virulent strains can turn lethal. Strep-A infections claim thousands of lives each year in the U.S. and Europe alone.

■ Newspaper accounts publicized a startling flare-up of tuberculosis that was first detected last year at a high school in Westminster, California, a middle-class suburb of Los Angeles. The disease was apparently brought in by a 16-year-old Vietnamese immigrant who contracted it in her native country. Nearly 400 young people, or 30% of the school's students, have tested positive for the infection, and at least 12 have a variety of the TB bacterium that is resistant to standard antibiotic treatment. One student has lost part of her lung.

■ The *New England Journal of Medicine* reported that the children of Cincinnati suffered an epidemic of pertussis (whooping cough) last year. There were 352 cases (none fatal), compared with 542 cases in the 13 years from 1979 to 1992. The alarming part was that most of the children had been properly vaccinated, suggesting that an unusually hardy strain of the pertussis bacterium might be emerging. Another disturbing statistic: there were more than 6,500 cases nationwide, the largest number in more than 26 years.

■ In many parts of the U.S., especially the Northeast, people are already leery of strolling in wooded areas for fear of encountering ticks carrying Lyme disease, a potentially chronic, arthritis-like condition. Now the *Journal of the American Medical Association* has reported on another tick-borne disease, which struck 25 people in Wisconsin and Minnesota, killing two. It is caused by a new variety of the *Ehrlichia* bacterium, which was first detected in humans in 1954. Doctors are concerned because life-threatening *Ehrlichia* infections may be misdiagnosed as Lyme disease or even a bad cold.

A GENERATION AGO, NO ONE HAD ever heard of Lyme or Legionnaires' disease, much less AIDS. Back in the 1970s, medical researchers were even boasting that humanity's victory against infectious disease was just a matter of time. The polio virus had been tamed by the Salk and Sabin vaccines; the smallpox virus was virtually gone; the parasite that causes malaria was in retreat; once deadly illnesses, including diphtheria, pertussis and tetanus, seemed like quaint reminders of a bygone era, like Model T Fords or silent movies.

The first widespread use of antibiotics in the years following World War II had transformed the most terrifying diseases known to humanity—tuberculosis, syphilis, pneumonia, bacterial meningitis and even bubonic plague—into mere inconveniences that if caught in time could be cured with pills or shots. Like many who went through medical school in the 1960s, Dr. Bernard Fields, a Harvard microbiologist, remembers being told, "Don't bother going into infectious diseases." It was a declining specialty, his mentors advised—better to concentrate on real problems like cancer and heart disease.

The advent of AIDS demolished that thinking. The sight of tens of thousands of young people wasting away from a virus that no one had known about and no one knew how to fight was a sobering experience—especially when drugs proved powerless to stop the virus and efforts to develop a vaccine proved extraordinarily difficult. Faced with AIDS, and with an ever increasing number of antibiotic-resistant bacteria, doctors were forced to admit that the medical profession was actually retreating in the battle against germs.

The question ceased to be, When will infectious diseases be wiped out? and became, Where will the next deadly new plague appear? Scientists are keeping a nervous watch on such lethal agents as the Marburg and Ebola viruses in Africa and the Junin, Machupo and Sabiá viruses in South America. And there are uncountable

---

The question ceased to be, when will diseases be gone? and became, Where will the next deadly virus appear?

---

threats that haven't even been named: a virus known only as "X" emerged from the rain forest in southern Sudan last year, killed thousands and disappeared. No one knows when it might arise again.

A U.S. Army lab in Frederick, Maryland, faced a terrifying situation in 1989 when imported monkeys started dying from a strain of the Ebola virus. After destroying 500 monkeys and quarantining the lab and everyone in it, officials found that this particular strain was harmless to humans. But the episode was dramatic enough to inspire an article in the *New Yorker* magazine—now expanded into a soon-to-be released book called *The Hot Zone*—and work on two competing movies (one of which seems to have collapsed before production).

The Ebola affair and the emergence of AIDS illustrate how modern travel and global commerce can quickly spread disease. Germs once confined to certain regions may now pick up rides to all parts of the world. For example, the cholera plague that is currently sweeping Latin America arrived in the ballast tanks of a ship that brought tainted water from Asia. And the *New England Journal of Medicine* has reported two cases of malaria in New Jersey that were transmitted by local mosquitoes. The mosquitoes were probably infected when they bit human malaria victims who had immigrated from Latin America or Asia. Writes author Laurie Garrett in a book to be published next month called *The Coming Plague:* "AIDS does not stand alone; it may well be just the first of the modern, large-scale epidemics of infectious disease."

The latest bulletins from the germ front come on top of a long series of horror stories. For years now people have been reading about—and suffering from—all sorts of new and resurgent diseases. As if AIDS were not enough to worry about, there was a rise in other sexually transmitted infections, including herpes, syphilis and gonorrhea. People heard about the victims who died in the Northwest from eating undercooked Jack in the Box hamburgers tainted with a hazardous strain of *E. coli* bacteria. They were told to cook their chicken thoroughly to avoid food poisoning from salmonella bacteria. And last year they saw how the rare hantavirus, once unknown in the U.S., emerged from mice to kill 30 people in as many as 20 states.

All this bad news is undoubtedly having a cumulative impact on the human psyche. The age of antibiotics is giving way to an age of anxiety about disease. It's getting harder to enjoy a meal, make love or even take a walk in the woods without a bit of fear in the back of the mind. No wonder people pay an unreasonable amount of attention when tabloids trumpet headlines about "flesh-eating bacteria." And no wonder Stephen King's *The Stand*, a TV mini-series based on his novel about a "superflu" that ravages the world's population, earned some of the year's highest ratings.

The odds of contracting a life-threatening infectious disease are still very low—at least in the developed world. But the threats are real and frightening enough to spur medical researchers to redouble efforts to learn more about how the many kinds of microbes cause disease—and how they can be kept at bay.

MICROORGANISMS

IT IS TEMPTING TO THINK OF the tiny pathogens that produce such diseases as malaria, dysentery, TB, cholera, staph and strep as malevolent little beasts, out to destroy higher forms of life. In fact, all they're trying to do is survive and reproduce, just as we are. Human suffering and death are merely unfortunate by-products.

Plasmodium, a protozoan responsible for malaria, flourishes in the human body, growing inside red blood cells until the cells burst. And without enough red cells to carry oxygen through the body, humans become anemic and can die from renal failure or convulsions. Bacteria, which are considerably smaller than protozoans, generally do their damage indirectly, producing toxins that stimulate the body to mount an immune response. Ideally the immune cells kill the bacteria. But if the bacteria get out of control, their poisons can either kill cells or generate a huge immune reaction that is itself toxic.

In an illness like tuberculosis, the immune system kills the body's own cells in the localized areas where TB germs have taken hold, including the lungs or the bones. With staph or strep, the sheer volume of disease-fighting immune cells can overload blood vessels, ripping tiny tears in the vessel linings; toxins can also damage the vessels directly. Plasma begins to leak out of the bloodstream; blood pressure drops, organs fail, and the body falls into a state of shock. In cholera, bacterial toxins attack intestinal cells, triggering diarrhea, catastrophic dehydration and death.

Before the coming of penicillin and other antibiotics, bacterial diseases simply ran their courses. Either the immune system fought them off and the patient survived or the battle was lost. But antibiotics changed the contest radically: they selectively killed bacteria without harming the body's cells. For the first time, potentially lethal infections could be stopped before they got a foothold.

Unfortunately, as Columbia University's Dr. Harold Neu observed in the journal *Science*, "bacteria are cleverer than men." Just as they have adapted to nearly every environmental niche on the planet, they have now begun adjusting to a world laced with antibiotics. It didn't take long. Just a year or two after penicillin went into widespread use, the first resistant strain of staph appeared. As other antibiotics came along, microbes found ways to resist them as well, through changes in genetic makeup. In some cases, for example, the bacteria gained the ability to manufacture an enzyme that destroys the antibiotic.

BY NOW NEARLY EVERY DISEASE organism known to medicine has become resistant to at least one antibiotic, and several are immune to more than one. One of the most alarming things about the cholera epidemic that has killed as many as 50,000 people in Rwandan refugee camps is that it involves a strain of bacterium that can't be treated with standard antibiotics. Relief agencies had to scramble for the right medicines, which gave the disease a head start in its lethal rampage.

Tuberculosis, too, has learned how to outwit the doctors. TB is an unusually tough microbe, so the standard therapy calls for several antibiotics, given together over six months. The length and complexity of the treatment have kept underdeveloped nations from making much progress against even ordinary TB. But now several strains have emerged in the U.S. and other developed countries that can't be treated with common antibiotics.

Even such seemingly prosaic but once deadly infections as staph and strep have become much harder to treat as they've acquired resistance to many standard antibiotics. Both microbes are commonly transmitted from patient to patient in the cleanest of hospitals, and they are usually cured routinely. But one strain of hospital-dwelling staph can now be treated with only a single antibiotic—and public health officials have no doubt that the germ will soon become

The World's Deadliest Scourges		
Infectious disease	Cause	Annual deaths
Acute Respiratory Infections (mostly Pneumonia)	Bacterial or Viral	4,300,000
Diarrheal Diseases	Bacterial or Viral	3,200,000
Tuberculosis	Bacterial	3,000,000
Hepatitis B	Viral	1,000,000 to 2,000,000
Malaria	Protozoan	1,000,000
Measles	Viral	880,000
Neonatal Tetanus	Bacterial	600,000
AIDS	Viral	550,000
Pertussis (Whooping Cough)	Bacterial	360,000

Sources: World Health Organization, Harvard School of Public Health, 1990 figures

impervious to that one too. Hospitals could become very dangerous places to go—and even more so if strep also develops universal resistance.

One of medicine's worst nightmares is the development of a drug-resistant strain of severe invasive strep A, the infamous flesh-eating bacteria. What appears to make this variant of strep such a quick and vicious killer is that the bacterium itself is infected with a virus, which spurs the germ to produce especially powerful toxins. (It was severe, invasive strep A that killed Muppeteer Jim Henson in 1990.) If strep A is on the rise, as some believe, it will be dosed with antibiotics, and may well become resistant to some or all of the drugs.

Microbes' extraordinary ability to adapt, observes Harvard microbiologist Fields, "is a fact of life. It's written into evolution." Indeed, the end run that many organisms are making around modern antibiotics is a textbook case of Darwin's theory in action (anti-evolutionists, take note). In its simplest form, the theory states that new traits will spontaneously appear in individual members of a given species—in modern terms, mutations will arise in the organisms' genetic material. Usually the traits will be either useless or debilitating, but once in a while they'll confer a survival advantage, allowing the individual to live longer and bear more offspring. Over time, the new survival trait—camouflage stripes on a zebra, antibiotic resistance in a bacterium—will become more and more common in the population until it's universal.

The big difference between animals and bacteria is that a new generation comes along every few years in large beasts—but as often as every 20 minutes in microbes. That speeds up the evolutionary process considerably. Germs have a second

advantage as well: they're a lot more promiscuous than people are. Even though bacteria can reproduce asexually by splitting in two, they often link up with other microbes of the same species or even a different species. In those cases, the bacteria often swap bits of genetic material (their DNA) before reproducing.

They have many other ways of picking up genes as well. The DNA can come from viruses, which have acquired it while infecting other microbes. Some types of pneumococcus, which causes a form of pneumonia, even indulge in a microbial version of necrophilia by soaking up DNA that spills out of dead or dying bacteria. This versatility means bacteria can acquire useful traits without having to wait for mutations in the immediate family.

The process is even faster with antibiotic resistance than it is for other traits because the drugs wipe out the resistant bacterium's competition. Microbes that would ordinarily have to fight their fellows for space and nourishment suddenly find the way clear to multiply. Says Dr. George Curlin of the National Institute of Allergy and Infectious Diseases: "The more you use antibiotics, the more rapidly Mother Nature adapts to them."

HUMAN BEHAVIOR JUST MAKES the situation worse. Patients frequently stop taking antibiotics when their symptoms go away but before an infection is entirely cleared up. That suppresses susceptible microbes but allows partially resistant ones to flourish. People with viral infections sometimes demand antibiotics, even though the drugs are useless against viruses. This, too, weeds out whatever suscepti-

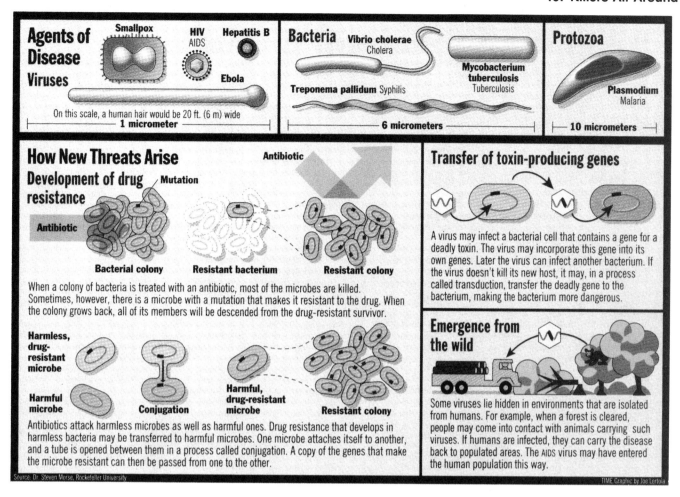

Agents of Disease

Viruses

Smallpox · HIV AIDS · Hepatitis B · Ebola

On this scale, a human hair would be 20 ft. (6 m) wide
1 micrometer

Bacteria

Vibrio cholerae Cholera · Treponema pallidum Syphilis · Mycobacterium tuberculosis Tuberculosis

6 micrometers

Protozoa

Plasmodium Malaria

10 micrometers

How New Threats Arise

Development of drug resistance

Antibiotic · Mutation · Antibiotic

Bacterial colony · Resistant bacterium · Resistant colony

When a colony of bacteria is treated with an antibiotic, most of the microbes are killed. Sometimes, however, there is a microbe with a mutation that makes it resistant to the drug. When the colony grows back, all of its members will be descended from the drug-resistant survivor.

Harmless, drug-resistant microbe · Harmful microbe · Conjugation · Harmful, drug-resistant microbe · Resistant colony

Antibiotics attack harmless microbes as well as harmful ones. Drug resistance that develops in harmless bacteria may be transferred to harmful microbes. One microbe attaches itself to another, and a tube is opened between them in a process called conjugation. A copy of the genes that make the microbe resistant can then be passed from one to the other.

Transfer of toxin-producing genes

A virus may infect a bacterial cell that contains a gene for a deadly toxin. The virus may incorporate this gene into its own genes. Later the virus can infect another bacterium. If the virus doesn't kill its new host, it may, in a process called transduction, transfer the deadly gene to the bacterium, making the bacterium more dangerous.

Emergence from the wild

Some viruses lie hidden in environments that are isolated from humans. For example, when a forest is cleared, people may come into contact with animals carrying such viruses. If humans are infected, they can carry the disease back to populated areas. The AIDS virus may have entered the human population this way.

Source: Dr. Steven Morse, Rockefeller University

TIME Graphic by Joe Lertola

ble bacteria are lurking in their bodies and promotes the growth of their hardier brethren. In many countries, antibiotics are available over the counter, which lets patients diagnose and dose themselves, often inappropriately. And high-tech farmers have learned that mixing low doses of antibiotics into cattle feed makes the animals grow larger. (Reason: energy they would otherwise put into fighting infections goes into gaining weight instead.) Bacteria in the cattle become resistant to the drugs, and when people drink milk or eat meat, this immunity may be transferred to human bacteria.

Because microbial infections keep finding ways to outsmart antibiotics, doctors are convinced that vaccines are a better way to combat bacterial disease. A vaccine is usually made from a harmless fragment of microbe that trains the body's immune system to recognize and fight the real thing. Each person's immune system is chemically different from everyone else's, so it's very difficult for a bacterium to develop a shield that offers universal protection. Diphtheria and tetanus can be prevented by vaccines if they are used properly. A vaccine against the pneumococcus bacterium has recently come out of the lab as well, and scientists ex-

pect to test one that targets streptococcus A within a year.

VIRUSES

UNLIKE BACTERIA AND PROTOZOANS, WHICH are full-fledged living cells, capable of taking in nourishment and reproducing on their own, viruses are only half alive at best. They consist of little more than a shell of protein and a bit of genetic material (DNA or its chemical cousin RNA), which contains instructions for making more viruses—but no machinery to do the job. In order to reproduce, a virus has to invade a cell, coopting the cell's own DNA to create a virus factory. The cell—in an animal, a plant or even a bacterium—can be physically destroyed by the viruses it is now helplessly producing. Or it may die as the accumulation of viruses interferes with its ability to take in food.

It is by killing individual cells in the body's all-important immune system that

---

Some microbes can reproduce in just 20 minutes

---

the AIDS virus wreaks its terrible havoc. The virus itself isn't deadly, but it leaves the body defenseless against all sorts of diseases that are. Other viruses, like Ebola, kill immune cells too, but very quickly; the dead cells form massive, deadly blood clots. Still others, hantavirus, for example, trigger a powerful reaction in which immune cells attack both the invading virus and the host's healthy cells.

Unlike bacteria and protozoans, viruses are tough to fight once an infection starts. Most things that will kill a virus will also harm its host cells; thus there are only a few antiviral drugs in existence. Medicine's great weapon against viruses has always been the preventive vaccine. Starting with smallpox in the late 1700s, diseases including rabies, polio, measles and influenza were all tamed by immunization.

But new viruses keep arising to challenge the vaccine makers. They may have gone undetected for centuries, inhabiting animal populations that have no contact with mankind. If people eventually encounter the animals—by settling a new part of the rain forest, for example—the virus can have the opportunity to infect a different sort of host.

Scientists believe Ebola virus made

Counterattack: How Drugmakers Are Fighting Back

By Leon Jaroff

Doctors and the public were not alone in feeling cocky about infectious disease a decade ago. The drug companies did too. More than 100 antibiotics were on the market, and they had most bacterial disease on the run, if not on the verge of eradication. So rosy was the outlook that U.S. government funding for antibiotic research was declining, and many pharmaceutical firms were focusing on cancer and viral diseases, especially AIDS.

Observes George Miller, a microbiologist at the Schering-Plough Research Institute in Kenilworth, New Jersey: "What we in the pharmaceutical industry had been doing was to take existing classes of antibiotics and modify them to stay one step ahead of the bacteria." But that approach seems no longer able to stem the spread of drug-resistant bacteria.

Instead, researchers are employing several new strategies that they hope will put medicine ahead, at least temporarily, in the battle against the bugs. One approach is "rational" drug design, based on new understanding of how bacteria function at the molecular level. Using the techniques of biochemistry and crystallography, scientists are identifying bacterial genes and enzymes that confer drug resistance, and are creating antibiotics that will act specifically against a targeted microbe.

By discerning the molecular structure of an enzyme used by a drug-resistant bacterium to fight off that drug, for example, scientists can design a molecule that fits precisely into the active site of the enzyme. That neutralizes the enzyme, depriving the bacterium of a crucial element of its defense and making it susceptible once more to the original drug. "It's like sticking a wad of gum into a keyhole and binding it up," says Fred Cohen, professor of pharmacology at the University of California, San Francisco.

Scientists are pursuing a similar line of attack against viral diseases. In their AIDS research, for example, some are concentrating on a protein called CD-4, which resides on the surface of immune-system T cells where the AIDS virus attacks. Before the virus can enter T cells, it must join with a receptor site on the CD-4 protein. Here, too, a properly designed molecule might block that site and protect the T cell.

Some companies are delving into "combinatorial" chemistry, which involves making Lego-like blocks of chemicals that can be joined in hundreds of thousands of combinations, one or a few of which might create molecular havoc with a particular bacterium.

"Chemists have conceived of ways to build vast libraries of these wonderful combinations of building blocks, concepts that did not exist five or 10 years ago," says Barry Eisenstein, a vice president of the Eli Lilly research labs in Indianapolis, Indiana. Roboticized testing has helped make this approach practical by enabling researchers to screen hundreds of thousands of compounds in just a few months.

Prevention is even better than cure, and scientists are also experimenting with new vaccines that will ward off infections by alerting and arming the body's immune system against the invaders. One such vaccine is already on the market. It is designed to prevent the ills brought on by pneumococcus, which include sinusitis and ear infections as well as pneumonia.

Scientists are sanguine about regaining the upper hand against infectious disease but now realize that no strategy will work forever. As long as microbes have the ability to neutralize medicine's weapons, the drug companies will have to keep adding to the arsenal.

—Reported by Lawrence Mondi/New York

---

just that kind of jump, from monkeys into humans; so did other African viruses such as Marburg and the mysterious X that broke out in Sudan. And many more are likely to emerge. "In the Brazilian rain forest," says Dr. Robert Shope, a Yale epidemiologist, "we know of at least 50 different viruses that have the capacity of making people sick. There are probably hundreds more that we haven't found yet."

Viruses like Ebola and X are scary, but they're too deadly to be much of a threat to the world. Their victims don't have much of a chance to infect others before dying. In contrast, HIV, the AIDS virus—which may have come from African primates as early as the 1950s—is a more subtle killing machine, and thus more of an evolutionary success. An infected person will typically carry HIV for years before symptoms appear. Thus, even though HIV doesn't move easily from one human to another, it has many chances to try. Since the first cases were reported in the late 1970s, HIV has spread around the world to kill perhaps a million people and infect an estimated 17 million.

The price of doing nothing will be millions of lives

It isn't just new viruses that have doctors worried. Perhaps the most ominous prospect of all is a virulent strain of influenza. Even garden-variety flu can be deadly to the very old, the very young and those with weak immune systems. But every so often, a highly lethal strain emerges—usually from domesticated swine in Asia. Unlike HIV, flu moves through the air and is highly contagious. The last killer strain showed up in 1918 and claimed 20 million lives—more than all the combat deaths in World War I. And that was before global air travel; the next outbreak could be even more devastating.

Vaccines should, in theory, work just as well for new varieties of disease as they do for old ones. In practice, they often don't. An HIV vaccine has proved difficult to develop because the virus is prone to rapid mutations. These don't affect its deadliness

but do change its chemistry enough to keep the immune system from recognizing the pathogen.

Creating a vaccine for each strain of flu isn't exactly simple either. "First," says Yale's Shope, "we have to discover something new is happening. Then we have to find a manufacturer willing to make a vaccine. Then the experts have to meet and decide what goes into the vaccine. Then the factory has to find enough hens' eggs in which to grow the vaccine. There are just a lot of logistical concerns."

People are partly to blame for letting new viruses enter human populations. Says Dr. Peter Jahrling, senior research scientist at the U.S. Army Medical Research Institute of Infectious Diseases: "If you're a monkey imported from the Philippines, your first stop when you hit this country is a quarantine facility. If you're a free-ranging adult human being, you just go through the metal detector and you're on your way."

Sometimes environmental changes help microbes move from animals to humans. Lyme disease, a bacterial infection, was largely confined to deer and wild mice until people began converting farmland into wooded suburbs—which provided equally good habitats for the animals and the bacteria-infested ticks they carry and also brought them into contact with large numbers of people. The mice that transmit the hantavirus often take refuge in farmers' fields, barns and even homes. Air-conditioning ducts create a perfect breeding ground for Legionnaires' disease bacteria. Irrigation ditches and piles of discarded tires are ideal nesting spots for the *Aedes aegypti* mosquito, carrier of dengue and yellow fevers; imported used tires have already brought the Asian tiger mosquito, also a carrier of dengue, into the U.S.

Clearly there is no way to prevent human exposure to microbes. But the risks can be reduced. To minimize bacterial re-sistance, for example, doctors can be stingier with antibiotics. "We've been careless," says Dr. Robert Daum, a University of Chicago pediatrician. "Every childhood fever does not require antibiotics." Nor does a healthy farm animal.

Most important is increased vigilance by public-health authorities. The faster a new microbe can be identified and its transmission slowed, the less likely a small outbreak will turn into an epidemic. Unfortunately, the trend has been in the other direction. "Even in the U.S.," says Thomson Prentice of the World Health Organization in Geneva, "disease-monitoring expertise has been lost, either through cost-cutting or reduced diligence. If some of the edge has been lost in the U.S., just imagine how poorer countries have reacted."

American health officials are convinced that their information-gathering network must be strengthened. That has begun to happen under a new program that will, among other things, increase the surveillance of new microbes and educate both health workers and the public about how to deal with emerging diseases.

An all-out effort to monitor diseases, vaccinate susceptible groups, improve health conditions around the world, develop new drugs and get information to the public would be enormously expensive. But the price of doing nothing may be measured in millions of lost lives. Doctors are still hopeful but no longer overconfident. "I do believe that we're intelligent enough to keep ahead of things," says epidemiologist Shope. Nonetheless, neither he nor any of his colleagues will ever again be foolish enough to declare victory in the war against the microbes. —*Reported by J. Madeleine Nash/Chicago, Alice Park/New York, Mia Schmiedeskamp/Washington and Andrew Purvis/Nairobi, with other bureaus*

Natural Resources

- **International Dimensions (Articles 11–15)**
- **Raw Materials (Articles 16–18)**
- **Food and Hunger (Articles 19–21)**
- **Energy (Articles 22–24)**

In the eighteenth, nineteenth, and early twentieth centuries, the idea of the modern nation-state was developed and expanded. These legal entities were conceived of as separate, self-contained units, which independently pursued their national interests. Scholars envisioned the world as an international political community of independent units, which "bounced off" each other (a concept that has often been described as a billiard ball model).

This concept of self-contained and self-directed units, however, has undergone major rethinking in the past 20 years, primarily because of the international dimensions of the demands being placed on natural resources. National boundaries are becoming less and less valid. The Middle East, for example, contains a majority of the world's known oil reserves, yet Western Europe and Japan are very dependent on this source of energy. Neither resource dependency nor such problems as air

pollution recognize political boundaries on a map. Therefore, the concept that independent political units control their own destiny is becoming outdated. In order to understand why it is so, one must look at how Earth's natural resources are being utilized today.

The articles in the first subsection of this unit discuss the international dimensions of the uses and abuses of natural resources. The central issue has to do with whether or not human activity is bringing about basic changes in the functioning of the biosphere. The lead article explores this issue and the debate within the scientific community about the likely impact on the climate resulting from the buildup of greenhouse gases. Central to this analysis is the fact that these problems transcend national boundaries. Global changes in the climate will affect everyone, and international efforts will be required to respond to these changes. A single country or even a few countries cannot have a significant impact on these problems.

The following articles examine other transnational dimensions of natural resources utilization. The collapse of Communism in Central Europe has revealed a region-wide pollution problem that creates all kinds of social questions regarding economic and environmental priorities.

Many environmental problems are truly international in scope. The consequences of human activity are profound and no one country or even a small group of countries can remedy these problems by themselves. Solutions will have to be conceived that are truly global in scope. Just as there are shortages of natural resources, there are also shortages of new ideas for solving many of these problems.

The second subsection begins with a discussion of the issues involved in moving from a perspective of the environment as simply an economic resource to be consumed to a perspective that has been defined as "sustainable development." This change is easily called for, but in fact it goes to the core of social values and basic economic activities. Implementing it, therefore, will be a challenge of great magnitude. This broad discussion is then followed by a case study that illustrates this challenge. "Facing a Future of Water Scarcity" looks at water resources and how wasteful practices need to be changed in order to encourage conservation and greater efficiency.

The third subsection focuses on the most fundamental relationship between society and nature: food production and hunger. Included is a description of how environmental problems such as deforestation negatively affect food production. In addition, an overview is provided on the ability of the world's population to feed itself.

Another critical relationship between social structures and the environment is the subject of the final subsection of this unit: the production and consumption of energy. Since 1973, the fluctuations in the price and supply of energy in general and oil in particular have had a major impact on everyone. The initial price shocks of 1973 (which resulted from an Arab oil boycott of Israel's political allies) have been followed by many ups and downs. At one point, the Organization of Petroleum Exporting Countries (OPEC) was perceived to be a major new force in the international political arena. In the mid-1980s OPEC's control of global oil markets dramatically declined. This was a result of new sources coming onstream along with the lack of discipline among the different factions within OPEC in terms of keeping their production at prescribed quotas. Those with the most oil (such as Kuwait) wanted to keep prices low so the industrial nations would have no

incentive to develop alternatives to oil. As a result, Kuwait and a couple of other Gulf producers produced well beyond their quotas, leading to an oil glut. Iraq, on the other hand, wanted higher oil prices. Increased revenues were necessary to pay for its imports, debts, and the damage incurred in its 8-year war with Iran. Iraq wanted the quotas to be observed in order to raise prices. Its gamble to quickly solve many of its economic problems by annexing Kuwait led first to dramatic increases in oil prices and then to war. These events once again demonstrated that the supply and price of oil remain at the core of the global political economy. However, many predict that the heavy dependence on oil will change as supplies dwindle and new technologies are developed. This prospect creates special problems for developing countries, for they will have to develop alternative energy sources and more efficient technologies than what is currently available.

Nature is not some object "out there" to be visited at a national park. It is the food we eat and the energy we consume. Human beings are joined in the most intimate of relationships with the natural world in order to survive from one day to the next. It is ironic how little time is spent thinking about this relationship. The pressures that rapidly growing numbers of people are placing on Earth's carrying capacity suggest that this oversight will not continue much longer.

Looking Ahead: Challenge Questions

How is the availability of natural resources affected by population growth?

In what ways has the international community responded to problems of pollution and threats to the common heritage?

What is the natural resource picture going to look like 30 years from now?

How is society, in general, likely to respond to the conflicts between economic necessity and resource conservation?

How is agricultural production a function of many different aspects of a society's economic and political structure?

Are there any similarities between the global energy shortages and food shortages?

What is the likely future of energy supplies in both the industrial world and the developing world?

What transformations will societies that are heavy users of fossil fuels have to undergo in order to meet future energy needs?

THE GREENHOUSE EFFECT:
APOCALYPSE NOW
OR CHICKEN LITTLE?

Is Earth's complex climate machine on the blink—or is it just having a bad century?

Robert Silverberg

The world's temperature has been rising lately, just as apocalypse-minded "greenhouse effect" scientists have predicted. And there's no doubt that the levels of carbon dioxide, methane, and other heat-retaining "greenhouse gases" in our atmosphere are also climbing. We seem to be well along our way toward the torrid, sultry, terrifying future that the climatologists say is coming—a world of melting polar ice caps, drowned coastal cities, and vast migrations as new patterns of drought and heat make great sections of the globe uninhabitable.

Or are we? Some scientists are not so sure that the recent doomsday scenarios ought to be taken so readily at face value. They call for cautious examination of the whole greenhouse concept before we plunge into any sort of crash program for purifying our atmosphere—a program that the congressional Office of Technology Assessment estimates could cost as much as $150 billion a year over the next 25 years, simply to reduce carbon dioxide emissions to about 65 percent of today's levels.

While the scientists bicker, what's the public to make of the baffling mass of seemingly conflicting data on global warming? History provides few clues; our climate records have proved an imperfect tool for prediction at best. It's enough to tempt even the most scientifically savvy among us to dismiss the issue altogether.

But that's just what we cannot afford to do. Crisis or not, it's time for a rational approach to unveiling the mysteries of the global climate machine. Whether

the greenhouse effect foreshadows a cataclysmic event or a mere blip on the climatic time line, the current debate deserves close attention.

The greenhouse-effect theory of climate is nothing new. The concept dates back to 1822, when the French mathematician Jean Fourier likened the earth's atmosphere to the glass walls of a plant conservatory. A greenhouse's walls allow solar energy to enter, then trap its component of heat by blocking the outward radiation of infrared waves. Later in the nineteenth century scientists discovered that the heat-trapping component of our atmosphere is carbon dioxide (CO_2); and in 1897 the Swedish chemist S. A. Arrhenius, studying the relationship between global temperatures and the quantity of CO_2 in the atmosphere, calculated that a doubling of the present amount of atmospheric CO_2 would produce a mean global warming of 4° to 6°C or 7° to 11°F— with accompanying catastrophic environmental changes.

The amount of CO_2 in the atmosphere is minute: a little more than 300 parts per million, or one thirtieth of one percent. But that percentage has been growing rapidly in the century since Arrhenius. Vast quantities of CO_2 were locked up long ago in the "fossil fuels"—coal, oil, natural gas—that were created by the decay of organic matter at a time when the earth's climate was much warmer than it is today. We are now busily unlicking that treasure house of energy and our rate of consumption is rising from year to year,

with the liberation of CO_2 rising in proportion as well.

Between 1860 and 1959 the combustion of coal and other fossil fuels released an amount of CO_2 equal to 14 percent of the total already in the atmosphere. Some of this was absorbed by the oceans; the rest remained in the air. By 1960 the quantity of atmospheric CO_2 was about 7 percent greater than it had been in the middle of the nineteenth century.

But that was only the beginning. Between 1958 and 1962 alone, the CO_2 content of the atmosphere grew by 1.15 percent. In those five years, the burning of fossil fuels released 53 billion tons of CO_2, and 26 billion tons of that accumulated in the atmosphere. And the CO_2 level has risen in each year since: In the past 30 years it has gone from 315 parts per million to 355, an increase of more than 20 percent in the past century and more than 10 percent in a single generation.

Nor is CO_2 the only gas that produces the greenhouse effect. Methane (CH_4), which is released by decaying matter in marshes and tundra, the actions of termites, and cattle breaking wind, has some 20 times the heat-trapping quality of CO_2. Methane is increasing in our atmosphere at a rate of about 1 percent a year. So, too, are the various nitrogen oxides thrown off by factory smokestacks, automobile exhausts, and the breakdown of agricultural fertilizers. Then there are the sinister chlorofluorocarbons (CFCs) emitted by refrigerators, air conditioners, aerosol devices, and other products of twentieth-century inge-

> **WHAT ARE WE TO MAKE OF THE MASS OF CONFLICTING DATA? THE CURRENT DEBATE WARRANTS OUR ATTENTION AND STUDY.**

nuity. Neither methane nor nitrogen oxide nor CFCs played any part in Arrhenius's original greenhouse-effect calculations.

With all four kinds of greenhouse gases piling up in the atmosphere at a rate unprecedented in the planet's history, then we must be right on course for the catastrophic warming that the Arrhenius data indicate. A rise of 7° to 11°F in the mean global temperature may not sound like very much. But in fact just such a drop, some 25,000 years ago, sent glaciers down across Europe and North America and plunged the world into an ice age lasting thousands of years. An increase of little more than that magnitude 200 million years ago created the muggy, swampy, tropical world in which the dinosaurs flourished.

If a temperature increase of the Arrhenius magnitude were to happen now, floods caused by the melting of the polar ice caps would submerge thousands of miles of low-lying coastline within a matter of 40 or 50 years. The rising oceans would cover all of Florida south of Lake Okeechobee, and Washington, DC, would be covered almost to the White House and the Capitol steps. Low-lying islands throughout the world would disappear. Rainfall patterns would shift, turning the grain-belt districts in the interiors of our continents into dust bowls and bringing devastating torrential deluges elsewhere. Some rivers would become virtually dry; others would rise to the point of becoming unnavigable. Millions would starve.

The climate crisis would disrupt the living habits of entire nations. No wonder that Roger Revelle and Hans Suess of the Scripps Institution of Oceanography, contemplating the steady increase in atmospheric CO_2 levels, declared as far back as 1957 that humanity is performing a "great geophysical experiment"—with the entire planet as its lab.

And all the evidence indicates that the globe is warming just as the theory predicts. 1987 and 1988 were the two warmest years since reliable record-keeping began in the late nineteenth century, and the summer of 1988 saw not only scorching temperatures almost everywhere but a horrendous drought in most agricultural regions. "We can state with ninety-nine percent confidence," James Hansen of NASA's Goddard Institute told the U.S. Senate during testimony that fierce summer, "that current temperatures represent a real global warming trend, rather than a chance fluctuation. We will surely have many more years like this—more droughts and many more days above a hundred degrees [F]—in the Nineties." Indeed the average temperature for 1989 was warmer than that of record-breaking 1988; and 1990 was hotter still, coming in with a mean global temperature of just under 60°F.

Hansen's dire warnings set off a political uproar. Environmental-minded legislators called for immediate cutbacks in fossil fuel usage, changes in agricultural practices, restrictions on CFCs beyond those already agreed to for minimizing ozone layer damage, a halt to the destruction of the world's forests, a worldwide treaty covering atmospheric pollution, and a host of other drastic corrective measures. World leaders issued statements and urged action. Petitions were signed; placards were waved; considerable panic was generated among ordinary citizens.

But very little of a substantive nature has been done so far to ward off the coming environmental catastrophe. Mainly, two big conferences have been held in Washington, DC, one in April 1990 and a second in February 1991 at which scientists and government officials from 130 nations got together to discuss the problem of global warming. What came out of both conferences were the expectable expressions of deep concern—an "action agenda" but no real action—and resolutions calling for continued study, plus plans for four more conferences, culminating with a June 1992 conference in Rio de Janeiro at which representatives would sign an international treaty.

Meanwhile, greenhouse gases continue to pour into the atmosphere every day. But while environmentalists, their dismay growing hour by hour, continue to call for strict and immediate regulatory action, climatologists argue over whether there is a crisis at all. The austere pages of *Science,* the nation's foremost scientific journal, have rung with accusations that the advocates of a crash antigreenhouse program are practicing "junk science" and "science by consensus." The more conservative scientists claim that their apocalyptic-minded colleagues have succumbed to a Chicken Little syndrome, crying out that the sky is falling when in fact nothing of the sort seems to be taking place. They say that what greenhouse alarmists are doing is sorting through the evidence looking for data that will advance their own research agendas.

"There is a selective use of facts," said S. Fred Singer, an atmospheric and space physicist with the Washington Institute, at the global-warming conference last winter. "Nobody tells an untruth, but nobody tells the whole truth, either. It all depends on the ideological outlook. . . . My nuclear friends are happy to promote the greenhouse effect. My natural gas friends are happy to promote the greenhouse effect. A lot of scientists promote the greenhouse effect because of increased funding." *Forbes* magazine ran a cover story entitled "The Global Warming Panic: A Classic Case of Overreaction."

What's going on? Are we doomed or aren't we?

There are three points to bear in mind as we contemplate the possibility of a world transformed by rising temperatures:

• Changes in greenhouse-gas levels aren't the only factor involved in worldwide temperature fluctuations.

• Feedback processes that we barely understand today may serve to counteract the worst of the greenhouse-effect problems caused by rising atmospheric gas content.

• Warmer global temperatures don't necessarily spell doom, especially if upward changes turn out to be less severe than some climatologists predicted.

Scientists, moreover, need to place the unquestionable statistics on global warming in the Eighties in a larger historical context. The world indeed saw a general pattern of warming temperatures around 1890, just as the modern era of industrial expansion was hitting its first great peak and greenhouse gas emissions began to climb. A steady pattern of rising temperatures was recorded over the succeeding decades.

But the rate of temperature increase between 1920 and 1940 exceeded the level that could be accounted for by greenhouse-effect calculations alone. And then in 1940 global temperatures began to turn *cooler* again—precisely at the time when World War II was spurring another tremendous expansion in industrial activity. For the next thirty years, *as atmospheric pollution increased year by year,* mean world temperatures dropped steadily. The winter of 1962–63, for instance, brought England its coldest winter since 1740, averaging 32°F for three consecutive months. Not until 1970 did temperatures start climbing again, a rise that so far has gone on unchecked.

Climatological history reveals all manner of sharp temperature fluctuations during eras utterly unaffected by human environmental meddling. The ice ages that periodically afflict this planet are the most spectacular examples. The temperature increase during the era of the dinosaurs constitutes another. Prehistoric shifts in rainfall distribution stimulated the development of extraordinary human cultures in prehistoric Egypt and Mesopotamia and wiped out one in the Sahara. More recently, a period of climate cooling lasting from the fifteenth to the eighteenth century brought a "little ice age" to preindustrial Europe that killed the rich vineyards of England and destroyed the colonies that the Norsemen had planted in Greenland. In Queen Elizabeth's time, people skated on the frozen Thames in winter. By 1800 the climate was turning warmer again; the Thames has not frozen over since 1814. And so it has gone, up and down, through all the billions of years of our planet's existence.

Many forces affect Earth's climate, not all of which we understand. The chief climatic factor is the energy we receive from the sun. But the amount of solar radiation we get is not necessarily consistent throughout time. The sun has undergone many changes in size and radiative power in the last few billion years. Its output seems to vary, furthermore, in relation to the 11-year sunspot cycle—the low-temperature points of the "little ice age" period in medieval and Renaissance Europe coincided with prolonged periods of low sunspot activity recorded in 1280–1350, 1450–1550, and 1645–1715. Larger changes in solar activity, the result of forces we don't really comprehend (and certainly could never hope to control), may correlate with the severe glacial periods in the remote past and with periods of above-average warmth during the icy interludes.

Volcanic activity, moreover, can produce cooling phases. The giant eruption of Krakatoa, near Java, in 1883, spewed 13 cubic miles of debris into the air and reduced the sunlight falling on distant European observatories from 10 to 20 percent for the following three years. Other great eruptions in 1902 (in the West Indies) and 1912 (in Alaska) had the same effect. An almost total absence of major volcanic blasts between 1920 and 1940 may have been responsible for the period of unusually rapid warming that was recorded then, rather than the increase in atmospheric greenhouse-gas levels that was going on at the same time. We just don't know.

Changes in the earth's position relative to the sun, movements of the earth along its own axis, and the migration of the continents over long periods of time, must all be considered possible causes of the great temperature shifts that are evident in the geological and fossil records. Against such immense geophysical upheavals, a rise in the level of greenhouse gases may turn out to be a very small factor indeed.

Then, too, we have no assurance that the undeniable increase in atmospheric CO_2 and the other greenhouse gases will have the predicted severe consequences. Large-scale feedback processes may protect us against the folly of our own pollutions.

Atmospheric CO_2, for example, stimulates plant growth. Plants absorb CO_2 in the course of the process of photosynthesis. The more plants there are, the more CO_2 they will take in, thereby helping to reduce the atmospheric oversupply. This is *negative feedback*—a self-correcting mechanism in which a problem generates its own solution.

Another kind of negative feedback that may ease our greenhouse problem: Clouds reflect sunlight back to space, thus cooling the climate. Increased ocean evaporation caused by rising temperatures may enhance cloud cover, helping to bring temperatures back down. (On the other hand, clouds can also serve as traps for infrared radiation; thus an increase in cloud cover could strengthen the warming trend. This would be an example of *positive* feedback, which amplifies a situation rather than correcting it.)

What's more, warmer temperatures hasten the breakdown of methane into the less damaging CO_2, a beneficial process. But a rise in ocean temperature might foster the release of oceanic methane into the atmosphere, further heating it—another positive-feedback event. The warming of the seas would also reduce their capacity to absorb CO_2, making more trouble for us, since the ocean swallows up much of the CO_2 we put into the atmosphere now. This is balanced, however, by the likelihood that the oceans—which are vast thermal sinks that keep planetary temperatures stable—would absorb much of the increase in heat produced by greenhouse effects, thereby minimizing or even canceling out any global warming that might occur. Similarly, the emergence of immense forests in areas now too cold for vegetation—particularly the Arctic and subarctic tundra—might lead to a net planetary gain in the amount of CO_2 absorbed during photosynthesis. Or the warming of the frigid tundra could release the CO_2 and methane now stored in its soil in the form of peat, making matters worse.

Adding to the general perplexity is the argument raised by University of East Anglia climatologist T. M. Wigley in the British scientific journal *Nature* last winter. Wigley points out that the burning of fossil fuels releases not only the dreaded greenhouse gases, but also sulfur dioxide particles, or "aerosols," which serve to reflect sunlight and moderate the temperature of the planet. A sudden and radical reduction in fossil fuel consumption, Wigley maintains, would diminish the cooling effect of the aerosols that the fossil fuels produce. And so a cutback in the use of greenhouse-effect fuels might actually *increase* the global warming trend.

The consequent rise in temperature could more than compensate for any cooling that a reduction in greenhouse gases would create, leaving us in even bigger trouble than we might be heading for otherwise. Robert Charlson, an atmospheric chemist at the University of Washington, calls this problem "a sleeping giant of a sort" and "something that has been missed, and the consequences are not trivial. It is going to complicate matters in setting policy."

These feedback forces illustrate just how tricky the whole problem is, and just how uncertain our climatologists really are about what is likely to happen. Even after two centuries of serious study, we have only an approximate understanding of the forces that drive our climate. In many cases, we are not sure which is the cause and which the effect. During a 10,000-year warm spell in the last ice age, for instance, atmospheric CO_2 and methane levels were far higher than they were in the surrounding colder periods. But did that increase in greenhouse gases create the warm spell, or was it the other way around? No one can say. And a study of the Alaskan permafrost conducted by the U.S. Geological Survey shows a thawing of several degrees in the past 100 years but a drop in temperature of more than a degree for the period 1984–87 alone. One suggested explanation is that the shrinkage of the Arctic snow cover during the warming period of the Eighties has reduced the amount of insulation that the snow provides, allowing greater radiation of heat from the permafrost. So a warming produces a cooling: negative feedback at work again.

Whether all these intricate processes will cancel each other out, leaving our climate more or less unscathed, is something that only time is going to tell. We are indeed conducting a geophysical experiment with the planet as our laboratory, and the outcome is far from certain, despite the confidence that various theorists express. At the moment there are no facts, only speculations, when we talk about global warming. We have had no experience with greenhouse effects from which we can predict what's ahead.

Computer simulations alone won't give us the answers, nor are our meteorological records accurate enough over a long period of time to provide us with a clear view of what has actually been going on. Scientists can measure CO_2 concentrations in ancient times by looking at ice cores brought up from polar depths, but the weather bureau records of 1850 and 1900 and even 1950 are statistically unreliable because the samplings tended to be too small, and the methods of measurement often had built-in inaccuracies that make comparisons with today's weather misleading. If we aren't sure where we have been, how can we be certain about where we are going?

The middle-of-the-road scientific position, though, seems to be that *some* climatic warming will happen during the first half of the twenty-first century as a result of the changes in the atmosphere that we have already brought about—though it may be a mean increase of only a degree or so, rather than the 5° to 10° that the most extreme environmentalists are predicting.

A minor warming of that sort would require some local readjustments. Low-lying coastal settlements in marginal areas where flooding has traditionally been a problem might have to be abandoned. Rainfall patterns would probably change to some extent, and some of today's productive agricultural regions may experience water shortages.

Middle-latitude zones might become too warm for efficient farming.

But these negatives would be balanced by corresponding positive changes elsewhere. Vast areas in Canada, the Soviet Union, and the northern United States, their development now hampered by cold weather much of the year, would experience a beneficial access of warmth. What farmers in Arkansas might lose, those in Saskatchewan would gain.

The same with rainfall patterns: Regions now blighted by chronic drought would become fertile. All over the planet, the increase in CO_2 levels would make plant growth more vigorous. Seas now blocked by ice much of the year would be open to navigation. And so forth: not catastrophe but change. And we are an adaptable species.

Part of the problem of knowing whether global warming will be good or bad is our geophysical ignorance. "We don't even know within a factor of ten how much total biomass there is on Earth," said NASA scientist Gerald Soffen at a greenhouse effect discussion at the 1991 meeting of the American Association for the Advancement of Science. "Is life expanding or not? We can't say." Another AAAS panelist, botanist Lynn Margulis of the University of Massachusetts, added, "We have millions of species, each processing carbon differently, and we don't understand any of them perfectly. If we try to guess how life will respond [to global warming] we'd really be fools rushing in."

We should not, of course, rule out the possibility that we are indeed heading for catastrophic climatic events. But the conservative climatologists, who deny that these events will be apocalyptic, hold that it's unwise to launch crash programs of industrial cutback that might well have economic consequences for many countries far more serious than any climatic change that's in the cards. We need to wait for further evidence that a severe global warming is actually coming.

Meanwhile, as we await that further evidence, what can we do to ward off the worst-case scenarios? One smart move would be to try—within the limits of economic realities—to reduce industrial emissions and the use of fossil fuels in general. Not in any panicky way, with visions of the oceans covering our

coasts and our forests turning into tropical jungles, but with a calm, clear-eyed resolve, based on the understanding that it's a dumb idea for any creature to foul its own nest. The junk we've been putting into the atmosphere can't possibly do us any good, and there's a reasonable chance that it can do us great harm. Therefore we should clean up our act, not by closing down the factories and switching overnight from cars to bicycles, but by zeroing in on the chief causes of pollution and finding rational ways of eliminating them, and by putting programs of energy conservation into use.

A halt in the indiscriminate destruction of forests in Third World countries would help, too. Those trees—the lungs of the planet—are one of the most powerful climatic moderators we have, and once they're gone, implacable deserts will replace them; tropical soils are surprisingly infertile and undergo dismaying changes once their forest cover is stripped away.

Another wise move would be systematic reforestation of areas already denuded. It isn't just that trees are pretty. They soak up CO_2—a forest the size of Alaska would take in a billion tons of it a year—and give off oxygen. Having them around is a fundamentally good idea.

These conservation measures, none of them so stringent that they will unsettle any nation's economy, may of themselves succeed in stabilizing our atmosphere. The worst-case greenhouse world isn't necessarily on the way. Prudent planetary housekeeping is in order right now. Hysteria isn't.

Because even now many of the processes that rule our climate are mysteries to us, many scientists are uncomfortable with the recent outcries for radical environmental reform. "Whenever you try to do this quickly, you run up against our ignorance and the quality of the data," says Michael Schlesinger, a climatologist at the University of Illinois, and his caution is echoed in many other quarters. We have greatly changed the face of our planet; but whether those changes have set a devastating climatic change in motion is something we simply don't know. For once, more studies really *are* needed. What we have to do now is to watch and wait.

Trouble on, in, and around the oceans...

CAN WE SAVE OUR SEAS?

Ron Chepesiuk

Ron Chepesiuk, a free-lance writer and member of the faculty of Winthrop College, Rock Hill, South Carolina, U.S.A., writes regularly about international political and environmental topics.

The pattern is worldwide and disturbing.

On 5 January 1993, the oil tanker *Braer* loses power off Scotland's Shetland Islands. Gale-force winds drive the ship aground, then batter it for more than a week, breaking the ship apart, and spilling its 98 million litres (26 million gallons) of light crude oil into the ecologically fragile waters and blowing a sheen of oil for long distances inland.

• In April 1992, the Maltese-registered ship *Katina P* grounds on a sandbar off the coast of Mozambique. The ship is carrying 73.4 million litres (19.4 million gallons) of oil, almost double the amount spilled from the *Exxon Valdez* into Alaska's Prince William Sound in 1989. Leaking oil from the tanker fouls Mozambique's unspoiled beaches.

• In the Gulf of Mexico, sea turtles mistake floating plastic bags for jellyfish, their natural prey. The bags twist in the turtles' stomachs, catch in their throats, or block their digestive tracts. The sea turtles suffocate.

• In the North Pacific, seals and otters seek food among plastic debris like beverage holders and discarded fishing nets and become entangled. The animals strangle and die.

• Near Corpus Christi, Texas, U.S.A., Atlantic bottlenose dolphins are dying at an unprecedented rate. In March 1992 more than 79 were found dead. Environmentalists believe the dolphins died because of changes in their habitat.

• Meanwhile, off the coast of New Jersey, U.S.A., the population of several of the most popular species of edible fish, including fluke, weakfish, and bluefish tuna, are so depleted that the state government and national agencies are drafting regulations to reduce the size of the catch for commercial and recreational

fishermen. National Marine Fisheries Service statistics show that while commercial fluke catches generated between 1.8 and 3.1 million kilograms (four and 6.8 million pounds) in New Jersey from 1980 to 1988, the catches had declined to 681,000 kilos (1.5 million pounds) by 1990.

"Before the end of the decade, every fish species in New Jersey will have some kind of regulation on it," says Thomas P. Fote, president of the 25,000-member New Jersey Coast Anglers Association, a group of recreational fishermen.

As these globe-spanning incidents show, something is going wrong with the oceans. Just a few years ago, the planet's oceans and seas were thought of as limitless resources, impervious to human abuse. Stretching over 70 percent of the Earth's surface, they contain an endless variety of plants, fish, and other animals that scientists say can be harvested for the world's needs. The oceans hold the promise of keeping mankind prosperous, of feeding desperately poor developing countries, and helping to propel them into the modern world.

But because they are vast, mankind has also considered them a bottomless garbage pit for sludge, trash, chemicals, and debris. As Anne W. Simon, author of "Neptune's Revenge: The Oceans of Tomorrow," says: "Our concept of the ocean has always been: Use it, enjoy it, take what you want from it."

Today, no part of the oceans is free from pollution. James A. Coe of the U.S. National Oceanic and Atmospheric Administration has calculated that Styrofoam alone litters the middle of the Pacific Ocean in concentrations of 50,000 particles per square kilometre (0.39 square mile). "It's true some parts of the oceans are more polluted than others," says Rod Fujita, staff scientist at the Environmental Defense Fund (EDF). "But pristine parts, as in the South Pacific, which don't have many people, are starting to have problems, too. That is scary."

Marine debris has no geographical boundaries. As famed ocean explorer Jacques Cousteau explains, "Water moves. That's why pollutants like DDT are found in the livers of penguins in Antarctica, where there's no pollution. To show how water moves: In 90 years there will not be one drop of water in the Mediterranean that is there today. The pollutants in that sea will finally come to pollute the rest of the oceans. The same is true of the Caribbean, the North Sea, the Gulf of Finland, and so on."

The deterioration of the oceans, which interact with the rest of the planet's ecology, is a serious threat to human survival. The oceans serve as the world's lungs and profoundly influence climatic change, both because they can moderate concentrations of atmospheric constituents believed to control average global temperatures.

Pollution can have an effect not only on fish and other sea animals, but on plankton as well. Plankton is a single-celled ocean plant that feeds higher forms of life. Through conversion of carbon dioxide, plankton may provide the world with as much oxygen as all land plants combined. If water-borne pollution kills the plankton, much of the oxygen we rely on will be depleted.

Ninety percent of all pollutants reaching the ocean come from land-based sources flowing through ground water and rivers into seashore water. Some of it is unintentionally discharged. For instance, when it rains, gutters and sewers fill up with oil, grease, litter, fertilizers, and pesticides, all of which eventually make their way into the ocean.

Most land-based ocean pollution, however, is intentional, created by sanitary sewage and industrial waste water and urban runoff either passing through sewage treatment plants or conveyed directly into coastal systems through "combined sewer overflows" (CSOs). These waste streams often contain toxic pollutants and sewage sludge that make their way to coastal areas, contaminating the water and killing the aquatic life.

In the U.S., thousands of CSOs line coastal areas, into which they discharge untreated waste every time it rains. "CSOs represent uncontrollable sources of water pollution that are preventing coastal areas from attaining even marginal water quality," says EDF's Tod Fujita. "They are the single most important reason why shellfish beds remain closed, why beaches are closed due to high bacterial counts after summer storms, and why 'floatable' items like tampons and plastic debris wash up on beaches."

A concerted effort to conserve water and develop new means of treating sanitary waste water is urgently needed to accommodate increasing population growth along the coasts of most countries. Some demographers project that by the year 2010, a fourth of the U.S. population will live within an hour's drive of the coast.

In addition to land-based sources of ocean pollution, an estimated 6.4 billion kilos (14 billion pounds) of garbage and waste is purposely dumped into the sea each year. "You name it, and we have dumped it into the oceans," says Suzanne Iudicello, program counsel for the Washington, D.C.-based U.S. Center for Marine Conservation (CMC).

This offshore dumping often has unpredictable consequences. Between 1946 and 1970, the U.S. dumped 90,000 concrete-lined drums of low-level radioactive waste off San Francisco, California, and Sandy Hook, New Jersey. Recent searches located only a few hundred of the drums. Some had collapsed; others were leaking.

But of all the items dumped into the oceans, plastics are the most destructive. Radioactive waste sinks, but plastic floats and can stay around for centuries, killing sea life and washing up on beaches. A typical plastic holder for beer and soft drink cans will not degrade for about 450 years. Each year, 44.9 million kilos (99 million pounds) of plastic is dumped from oceangoing vessels or flows from storm sewers into the sea.

Some experts estimate the annual death toll from plastics may exceed two million seabirds and 100,000 sea mammals. A recent U.S. Office of Technology report warned that plastic pollution is a greater threat to marine mammals and birds than are pesticides, oil spills, or even contaminated runoff from the land.

The estimated 135 million kilos (298 million pounds) of plastic nets and lines let loose on the high seas each year highlights the problem that overfishing poses for the oceans. Fish stocks—from the haddock off the eastern seaboard of the U.S. to the cod in the North Sea, from the pilchard off the Namibian coast to the ice fish around Antarctica—are in decline worldwide. The Food and Agriculture Organization, the international body monitoring world fisheries, reports that at least 40 percent of the world's fish stocks are considered to be in a declining state. The reason: High technology has revolutionized fishing methods.

Today, enormous fishing factories equipped with kilometre-long nets, vast holds and freezers, and sophisticated instruments are taking fish from the ocean much faster than the fish can reproduce. A net called the "purse seine" is one example of the ruthlessly efficient modern fishing methods. The net is pulled into a circle and "purse strings" are drawn to enclose the catch. Entire shoals of oceanic fish (herring, pollack, sardine, tuna) can be scooped up after detection by sonar. The drift net, another high-tech method used to catch tuna, squid, and salmon mainly in the Pacific, is nicknamed "the wall of death" because it accidentally traps and suffocates seals, dolphins, porpoises, and turtles. (A number of major U.S. tuna-packing corporations have banned the use of this net since 1991.)

"Many countries see the oceans as something to be mined rather than conserved for long-term sustainability," says Andy Palmer of the American Oceans Campaign, based in Santa Monica, California, and Washington, D.C. "We can't keep building fishing fleets that operate well beyond the capacity of the oceans to sustain such frenetic effort."

The human population growth, expected to double by the next century, will certainly put further pressure on the ocean's resources. But the problem of overfishing is more immediate, given that, today, fishing is the only source of protein for a billion people worldwide.

Oil spills also pose a threat, for oil is a potent toxin that can kill zooplankton and phytoplankton, the source of the food chain and most of the world's oxygen. And as the Valdez spill dramatized, oil can kill mammals and sea birds in large numbers. The American Oceans Campaign says that more oil was spilled in the oceans in 1991 than ever before. "Oil spills represent a small percentage of the totality of ocean pollution, but we shouldn't ignore them," Andy Palmer explains. "They tend to concentrate in specific areas, and ecologically, can completely destroy those places."

Land-based pollutants, dumping, overfishing, and oil spills have all taken a toll on the oceans, but fortunately, the problems of ocean abuse and pollution are preventable. "There is a lot of hope that we can get the problem under control," says Tod Fujita. "It appears that damage inflicted on the oceans is decreasing; however, we can't be satisfied with that."

Some evidence of improvement:
• On 1 January 1989, an international law called MARPOL V (for marine pollution) made it illegal to dump plastics in the ocean. More than 29 countries, representing half the gross tonnage of the world's merchant fleet, have signed the agreement. Public vessels are exempt from the treaty, but the U.S. Congress has decided to restrict all navy vessels as well. Congress voted that by 1993, the U.S. Navy will not be allowed to throw plastics overboard. Instead, Navy vessels will be equipped with shipboard trash compactors and sterilizers.
• Also in 1989, the United Nations adopted a resolution banning drift-net fishing, worldwide, starting in 1993. Japan, Taiwan, and South Korea, which opposed such a ban in the past, agreed to abide by the resolution.
• A number of major oil companies are building a new generation of double-hulled oil tankers, to decrease the likelihood of spills.
• Researchers are finding new technologies to replace plastics or make them biodegradable. Giant corporations like Dow Chemical and Du Pont now market plastics for beverage packs that degrade after 60 days of exposure to sunlight.

Another turning point is the move toward increased regional cooperation. Some environmentalists consider this a necessary and positive step that will help control ocean dumping and pollution—but add that the trash will still have to go somewhere. Moreover, such cooperation doesn't usually address the major cause of marine pollution—the land-based sources like CSOs and river discharges laden with excess nutrients and floatable debris.

"Rather than figure how much mistreatment the ocean can take before we wreck it entirely, governments and scientific and environmental groups are now saying: 'Let's start reducing toxins and pollutants in the first place,'" says Suzanne Iudicello. "That approach is real pollution prevention." She suggests recycling, reducing waste, and reclaiming sewage and upgrading and routinely inspecting sewage treatment plant infrastructure as important ways to reduce ocean pollution at the source.

Citizen participation and education are also important. "The ocean debris problem stems from old habits," explains marine biologist Kathryn J. O'Hara, who directs the marine debris and entanglement program at the CMC Chesapeake Bay Field Office. "That is why education is essential. People need to realize that tossing trash over the rail is no longer acceptable."

Environmental groups have organized community projects to get people involved in cleaning up beaches and teach them about ocean pollution. The Sea Grant Program at the Massachusetts Institute of Technology calculates that volunteers collect 77.2 kilos (170 pounds) of trash per person on clean-up days along Massachusetts beaches.

Each year dozens of such cleanups are held in U.S. coastal states. The CMC has a program called National Beach Cleanup, which in 1990 had 108,749 cleanup volunteers worldwide—including Rotary clubs. The volunteers removed at least 25,000 metric tons (about 28,000 U.S. tons) of trash from beaches. In 1992, Canadian members of the International Fellowship of Canoeing Rotarians cleaned debris from waterways in Ontario. The Fellowship hopes to expand the program to other countries in 1993.

Environmentalists are encouraged by both the heightened public awareness of the plight of the oceans and other waterways and efforts by industry and governments to improve the situation. Cautious optimism is a common attitude. "We have enough time to take action," says Andy Palmer of the American Oceans Campaign. "We will never be able to get the oceans to where they were, say, 1,000 years ago. They are changed systems now, but they *can* be made sustainable."

Sacrificed to the Superpower

The Soviet drive to achieve nuclear dominance left lives and the land in ruins

Michael Dobbs

Washington Post Foreign Service

SEMIPALATINSK, Kazakhstan
It was the happiest day of Sergei Davydov's life: Aug. 29, 1949. The retired engineer still remembers the blinding flash and his "feverish joy" at the sight of a huge, mushroom-shaped cloud erupting over the desert of northern Kazakhstan. The Soviet Union, the world's first Communist state, had become a nuclear superpower—and he had pressed the button.

In a squalid wooden hut 600 miles away in southern Russia, by the bank of the Techa River, Mavzhida Valeyeva remembers 1949 for a different reason. It was the year her health began to deteriorate dramatically. Along with practically all her neighbors, she now suffers from violent headaches and constant nosebleeds. Her blood is anemic. Her four children and five surviving grandchildren are all invalids.

It took Valeyeva more than four decades to make a connection between her family's devastating health problems and the Soviet Union's nuclear bomb project. In 1990, the Soviet government finally acknowledged that millions of tons of highly toxic radioactive waste had been secretly dumped in the Techa by a plutonium plant 49 miles upstream from Valeyeva's village, Muslyumovo. The river the villagers saw as a source of life was in fact a source of death.

"It would be better if they had never discovered this nuclear energy," says Valeyeva, who visited the river daily to collect drinking water and wash her family's clothes. "It would be better to be poorer, but at least to be healthy and give our children and grandchildren a chance of living a normal life."

The Communist politicians who launched the Soviet Union on a program of breakneck industrialization and transformed the country into a military and political rival of the United States, believed that the natural resources under their control were inexhaustible. Yet future generations of Russians and Tatars, Balts and Ukrainians, Czechs and Poles will pay a heavy price for the hubris of their leaders. There came a point when nature simply rebelled.

A two-month journey from the center of Europe to the Russian Far East to review the legacy of Marx, Engels, Lenin and Stalin revealed the destructive impact that communism had on the environment in Russia—one of the scars left by the combination of totalitarian rule and socialist economics that will almost certainly take generations to heal.

The environmental catastrophe left behind by 70 years of Communist rule is visible in poisoned rivers, devastated forests, dried-up lakes and smog-polluted cities. Some of these disasters, such as the evaporation of the Aral Sea after the diversion of rivers for an irrigation project, have permanently changed the contours of the vast Eurasian landmass. But, according to Russian scientists and ecologists, the most lasting physical damage will probably have been caused by the unleashing of nuclear power.

"Radioactive contamination is the number one environmental problem in this country. Air and water pollution come next," says Alexei Yablokov, a biologist who serves as President Boris Yeltsin's chief adviser on environmental matters. "The way we have dealt with the whole issue of nuclear power, and particularly the problem of nuclear waste, was irresponsible and immoral."

The scale of nuclear contamination in the former Soviet Union has only become clear over the last few years, with the advent of free speech and the lifting of censorship restrictions. In the wake of the 1986 Chernobyl catastrophe, Russians learned about other disasters, including a series of accidents at a plutonium-producing plant near the southern Urals city of Chelyabinsk between 1948 and 1967. They also learned about dozens of ad hoc nuclear dumps, some of which could begin seeping radioactivity at any moment. The seas around Russia—from the Baltic to the Pacific—are littered with decaying hulks of nuclear submarines and rusting metal containers with tens of millions of tons of nuclear waste. Russia itself is dotted with dozens of once secret cities with names like Chelyabinsk-70, Tomsk-7 and Krasnoyarsk-26, where nuclear materials have been stockpiled. Unmarked on any map, they hit the headlines only when there is an accident. Vast areas of the country have been treated as a nuclear dump, the result of four decades of testing.

"We were turned into human guinea pigs for these experiments," says Bakhit Tumyenova, a senior health official in the Semipalatinsk region, the main Soviet nuclear test site until 1989. "They kept on telling us that it was for the good of the people, the Communist Party, the future. The individual never counted for anything in this system."

The testing of the Soviet Union's first atomic bomb in 1949 represented a huge achievement for a backward, semi-Asiatic country. It had mobilized vast economic and human resources, from the team of elite scientists who designed the bomb to the army of slave laborers who mined the uranium and disposed of the nuclear waste.

The two sides of the Soviet nuclear project—the epic achievements and the disregard for human life—are symbolized by the man initially in charge of it. Lavrenti Beria, the chief of Stalin's secret police, was a great organizer. But he was also a great destroyer, willing to obliterate any obstacle to achieve his goal.

"It was a heroic epoch," recalls Igor Golovin, a leading scientist and biographer of Igor Kurchatov, the head of the nuclear project. "We worked days and nights and really believed in what we were doing. The propaganda instilled the idea that the United States had the bomb and wanted to enslave us, so it was vital that we acquired our own nuclear weapons as soon as possible, whatever the cost."

Few of the scientists and engineers working on the project gave much thought to the dangers of radioactive fallout. After pushing the button that triggered the first nuclear device, Davydov rushed to the site of the explosion without any protective clothing or gas mask. He was later sick with leukemia for about 20 years.

"They gave me special injections, and it somehow stabilized. Now I feel all right," says the 76-year-old pensioner, proudly displaying a chestful of medals. "Personally, I think that all those people who demand privileges from the government because their health suffered as a result of these tests are just crooks and swindlers."

The idea that any sacrifice was justified in the effort to turn the Soviet Union into a superpower was a fundamental part of the Communist ethos. ("You can't make an omelette without cracking eggs," Lenin liked to remark.) It permeated the nuclear project right from the start, and still exists to some extent among older people. The system elevated the state above ordinary individuals—and this was its basic flaw.

"The postwar generation was brought up with the idea that they should be ready to sacrifice themselves for the state. This was the philosophy of the time. It was a pernicious philosophy because it prevented any thought being given to ecological problems," says Natalya Mironova, an environmental activist in Chelyabinsk. "For many years we were unable even to discuss such matters."

Little attention was paid to such issues as nuclear safety and the training of responsible personnel. The manager of the Chernobyl plant at the time of the 1986 disaster had previously been in charge of a heating plant. According to officials, roughly 50 percent of the accidents in nuclear power stations and 75 percent of accidents on nuclear submarines are due to "human error."

This year alone, there have been at least three accidents at nuclear facilities in Russia involving the release of radioactivity. The government has been inundated with dozens of letters from scientists at both military and civilian nuclear facilities warning of "further Chernobyls" because of rapidly deteriorating working conditions and the departure of many highly qualified workers.

For the 1,000 inhabitants of Muslyumovo in the southern Urals, the Soviet Union's experiments with the atom are a curse that will blight the lives of many generations. According to the local doctor, Gulfarida Galimova, four of every five villagers are "chronically sick." She says the effects of radiation have altered the genetic code of the local Tatar population, with the result that babies are often sick from birth.

"We do not have a future," says Galimova. "We have been so genetically harmed that our descendants will not be able to escape this curse. Patients come to me, and I know I can never cure them. Radiation has entered the food chain. Our cows eat radiated grass. The potatoes we grow in our back yards are poisoned. The only solution is to close this entire region off—and not let anyone come here for 3,000 years. But they won't do that, because there isn't enough money."

The 2.75 million curies of radioactive waste flushed into the shallow Techa was equivalent to half the fallout from the bomb that fell on Hiroshima, but nobody bothered to inform local inhabitants. In the late 1950s, signs were posted along the Techa warning people not to bathe in the river. The nature of the danger was never explained, so most villagers paid little attention.

In the early 1980s, Galimova first started noticing that something was terribly amiss with the health of Muslyumova residents. Nearly 10 percent of births in the village were premature. Many of her patients were anemic. There was a high incidence of cancer. When she reported her findings to her superiors in Chelyabinsk, the problems were blamed on bad food and a lack of hemoglobin. She was accused of being a bad doctor.

What local people refer to as "the river illness" is now affecting the third and even fourth generation of Muslyumovo residents. Valeyeva's eldest son, Ural, 33, is mentally retarded. His three children—aged 6, 4 and 18 months—can barely summon up the energy to get out of bed. Another daughter, Sazhida, 29, has a chronic craving for chalk that has destroyed all her teeth. Her oldest son, Vadim, 11, has been sick from birth. Timur, 6, has chronic bronchitis and anemia.

It was not until April 1986 that Galimova finally guessed what was the matter. Chernobyl played a crucial role in convincing Mikhail Gorbachev and other Soviet leaders that the country's problems could not be solved without *glasnost*, openness. Discussion of ecological problems was no longer taboo.

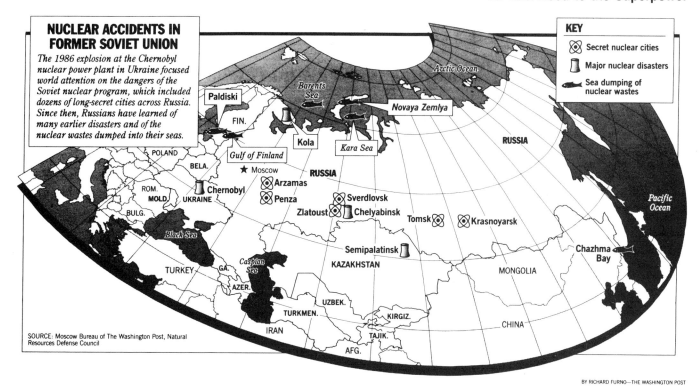

NUCLEAR ACCIDENTS IN FORMER SOVIET UNION

The 1986 explosion at the Chernobyl nuclear power plant in Ukraine focused world attention on the dangers of the Soviet nuclear program, which included dozens of long-secret cities across Russia. Since then, Russians have learned of many earlier disasters and of the nuclear wastes dumped into their seas.

KEY
- Secret nuclear cities
- Major nuclear disasters
- Sea dumping of nuclear wastes

SOURCE: Moscow Bureau of The Washington Post, Natural Resources Defense Council

BY RICHARD FURNO—THE WASHINGTON POST

When they finally came clean about the contamination of the Techa, the authorities also admitted two disasters involving the Mayak plutonium-producing plant at Kyshtym, about 60 miles northwest of Chelyabinsk. In 1957, a waste storage tank exploded at the plant, releasing 20 million curies of radiation. A decade later, a drought dried up nearby Lake Karachai, which had been used as a storage tank for 120 million curies of waste products from Mayak. High winds scattered radioactive dust over a wide area.

According to an official Russian government report released earlier this year, the three disasters at Mayak affected 450,000 people living in a contaminated region roughly the size of Maryland. The amount of radioactivity still stored at Mayak—much of it in insecure conditions—is equivalent to the fallout from 20 Chernobyl disasters.

Nearly 20,000 residents of the Chelyabinsk region were evacuated from their homes. By a tragic twist of fate, some of these people were moved from one high-risk region to another.

Valentina Lazareva, for example, was evacuated from a village near Mayak in 1957 as a 9-year-old orphan. There were rumors of an "explosion" at the plant, but nobody knew anything for sure. She spent the rest of her childhood in an orphanage in Brodokalmak, a village a few miles downriver from Muslyumovo. The children crossed the Techa every day on their way to school and drank water from a nearby well. In the summer, they would swim in the village.

"Now we are all sick," says Lazareva, who is 46 but looks much older. "There were 32 people in my class. We have already buried five of my classmates. Another 10 are dying. But all are invalids, in one way or another."

Today, there is no shortage of glasnost about the man-made environmental disaster confronting the former Soviet Union. But there is a desperate shortage of resources to do much about it. The amount of money the government has earmarked to clean up the Chelyabinsk region—roughly $20 million—is minuscule compared to the $40 billion to $60 billion cost the United States has projected for the cleanup of its main plutonium-producing facility, the Hanford nuclear reservation in Washington state.

In Kazakhstan, which declared itself an independent state in December 1991 after the breakup of the Soviet Union, health officials say they are unable to provide even basic medical care to villages exposed to four decades of nuclear tests. The lack of basic health services has encouraged many people to turn to charlatans and faith healers for help. In Semipalatinsk—the site of 470 nuclear explosions, including 116 in the atmosphere, between 1949 and 1989—a Muslim preacher named Sary-Aulie has been attracting crowds of 10,000 with his promise to cure aches and pains through "vibrations."

"We can't do much for these people, so it's not surprising that they put their trust in charlatans," says Tumyenova, the regional health administrator. "The Semipalatinsk test site served the entire Soviet Union. Now the other republics have gone their own way—and we have been left alone, sitting on top of a gigantic nuclear rubbish heap."

SHAPING THE NEXT
INDUSTRIAL REVOLUTION

*Companies must learn how to save energy and
preserve the environment without losing profits.*

**Christopher Flavin
and John Young**

*The authors are, respectively, vice president
for research and a senior researcher, Worldwatch Institute, Washington, D.C.*

THE NEED to achieve an environmentally sustainable world is shaping the evolution of the global economy. Ecological pressures increasingly will influence economic decisions, making some industries obsolete while opening up a host of new investment opportunities. Companies and nations that fail to invest strategically in the new technologies, products, and processes will fall behind economically and miss out on the jobs these new industries provide.

The size of the world economy has quintupled since 1950, bringing unprecedented, though unevenly distributed, prosperity to many nations, but much of the affluence has been borrowed from future generations. Destruction and degradation of natural assets—air, land, water, forests, and plant and animal species—have subsidized the profits of many businesses in the late 20th century. For industries around the globe, the debts are coming due.

Sulfur dioxide, hydrocarbons, and other pollutants flow in immense quantity from smokestacks, fouling the air and shortening lives. Billions of tons of greenhouse gases that enter the atmosphere each year are expected to make the Earth warmer during the next century than it has been for the last 100,000 years. Heavy metals, PCBs, and thousands of other chemicals find their way into the rivers, lakes, and seas, while chlorofluorocarbons have damaged the protective layer of ozone in the upper atmosphere. The relentless search for new sources of timber, fuels, and minerals is bringing destructive development to the far corners of the planet, disturbing the remaining storehouses of biological and cultural diversity.

Laws enacted by some countries to address these environmental threats have yielded many gains, from lower sulfur emissions to reduced water pollution levels. However, the challenge ahead is more fundamental—going beyond pollution controls and better management to reshape industries in order to make them environmentally sustainable. Responding to problems such as global warming and the loss of biological diversity will require the revamping of today's enterprises, such as chemicals and paper, and the creation of entirely new industries.

Primary responsibility for creating an environmentally sustainable economic system lies with elected governments, which represent the interests of society as a whole. Governments set the rules for environmental improvement, while consumers and local communities create the pressure for change. The challenge is to adopt policies that make economic and ecological imperatives converge, redirecting market forces to achieve the environmental goals. Since private businesses focused on earning profits, it is up to governments to ensure that the most profitable investments are the ones that are environmentally sustainable. Policies ranging from well-crafted regulations to taxes can be used to attain these goals.

In a world where private industry controls the bulk of capital investment, accounts for the preponderance of jobs, and provides trillions of dollars worth of goods and services each year, its role in damaging the environment—or ultimately in sustaining it—is central. In the end, it is industry that has the technological capacity, management skills, and investment capital to achieve an environmentally sustainable economy. Many large, diversified corporations—some with annual revenues that exceed the gross national products of many nations—now have the power to shift investments among continents as well as industries and to determine, in large part, the health of the environment. Small businesses also play a big role. While many have worse environmental records than large corporations do, they also contribute disproportionately to technical innovation in many industries.

Without the active participation of businesses of all sizes, there is little hope of achieving a sustainable global economy. In order to move forward, they will have to embark on extensive internal reforms that better equip them to respond to fast-moving environmental issues and opportunities. In a competitive global economy, corporations that allow themselves to fall behind will face serious financial risks. In short, those that fail to invest in the future may find they do not have one.

As the number of environmental concerns has multiplied in recent years, it has become clear that no corner of the Earth is unscathed and no industry free of responsibility for the dilemma that today's and future generations face. Gradually, focus has broadened from simple air and water pollution to sweeping problems of land use such as deforestation and soil erosion, and then to the long-range threats of ozone depletion and global warming. In the 1970s, it seemed that environmental issues could be solved one at a time through simple, focused solutions mandated by governments. Today, fundamental changes are inarguably necessary and, in some cases, already being pursued.

Once seen as a distraction to the real business of business, ecological awareness is becoming an engine of the next Industrial Revolution. It now is pervasive in traditional "dirty" industries, such as chemical manufacturing and metals processing, as well as high-tech and service industries, such as computer manufacturing and food companies. Businesses are likely to prosper in the future not by selling massive quantities of identical products—the traditional route to economic success—but by meeting consumer needs in the most efficient way possible. They will have to supply energy "services," rather than electricity; "information," rather than a newspaper; and crop protection, rather than pesticides. The challenge of the coming environmental revolution is likely to include alterations in manufacturing processes, the adoption of new agricultural techniques, and the development of alternatives to fossil fuels. Hardly an industry will go untouched.

Environmental protection already is a major industry. The Organisation for Economic Co-operation and Development estimates that the worldwide market of environmental goods and services was around $200,000,000,000 in 1990, and projects it will grow 50% by 2000. These figures are defined narrowly, however, only including such items as the market for sewage treatment equipment and the cost of cleaning up toxic wastes. The much larger demands of redesigning basic manufacturing equipment or creating new industries likely will be measured in trillions of dollars. The biggest areas of potential business growth lie in the most fundamental areas: finding alternatives to the internal combustion engine, substituting lightweight synthetics for steel, making solar electricity competitive with coal-fired power, substituting aquaculture for deep-sea fishing, etc.

Pressure on industries

The far-reaching economic consequences of ecological issues are apparent even for relatively simple areas like air pollution. In the early 1970s, scientists and policymakers believed that the solution lay in putting pollution control devices in factories and automobiles. Two decades of this approach have created a multi-billion-dollar market for catalytic converters and flue gas scrubbers. Although these efforts have improved air quality in some countries such as Japan and the U.S., few cities have genuinely clean air yet, and some have worse air pollution than ever.

The impact of environmental rules has ricocheted through the global automotive industry. Since 1990, prototype electric cars have been developed by General Motors and BMW, and work on hydrogen-powered vehicles has been announced by Mercedes and Mazda. Some of these models will be on the market by the late 1990s. It appears that automotive technology is about to undergo some of the most rapid change since Henry Ford introduced the Model T. The gasoline-powered internal combustion engine, which has dominated transportation for most of this century and which survived the oil crises of the 1970s unscathed, finally may be on the way out. Nissan and several European automakers are addressing another environmental issue—wasted materials. They have announced plans to build cars that will be nearly 100% recyclable.

Among the industries slated for rapid change, basic extractive and material processing enterprises are near the top of the list. Operations such as mining and logging are among the most ecologically destructive human activities, playing important roles in the rapid loss of old-growth forests and wetlands. Such losses of often-irreplaceable habitats are diminishing the Earth's storehouse of biological diversity. Scientists estimate that the planet is losing approximately 50,000 species annually, or about 140 each day.

The logging industry is under heavy pressure to clean up its act. Government regulations have pushed foresters in the northwestern U.S. to develop techniques known as new forestry, intended to cut valuable trees selectively while maintaining the integrity and diversity of the forest ecosystem. In addition, many trees are being grown as an agricultural product on managed plantations, although such practices are sustainable only if sufficient diversity is maintained to prevent serious blights and other problems.

Improved management can cut the environmental impacts of raw materials production, but even greater benefits will be gained through basic changes in other industries that reduce needs for timber and virgin minerals. The efficient use of recycled materials is likely to reduce the size of the mining and logging industries substantially. The per capita use of some virgin materials appears to have peaked in wealthy nations—which have built most of their materials-intensive infrastructure—while recycling is increasing at double-digit rates. There are enormous opportunities for more efficient use of wood. U.S. consumption could be cut in half through increased recycling and reduced waste in wood processing, consumer products, and construction.

Governmental mandates, consumers' pressure, and the rapid proliferation of recycling programs have caused paper manufacturers to convert a number of mills to the use of recycled pulp, and at the same time to eliminate the use of dioxin-producing chlorine bleaches. Manufacturers that once claimed recycled paper was only good for low-grade paper products now are making high-grade magazine stock at least partially from recycled fibers. Such developments have set off a technology race that could help determine winners and losers in the paper industry in the next decade. Over time, the industry may move away from the forested areas where it is centered to the outskirts of large cities, where its major future resource—discarded paper—and its markets lie.

The steel industry is undergoing a similar transformation. Under pressure of higher energy prices, declining grades of iron ore, and environmental concerns, it has been replacing its older, less efficient, more polluting mills. The most rapid area of growth is in modular minimills that rely on electric arc furnaces. They are far more energy-efficient and rely heavily on scrap steel, rather than iron ore. Because they do not need to be near iron and coal resources, minimills are likely to be decentralized and can be a center of economic development even in a small city.

The chemical industry is among those most affected by environmental concerns, having grown at a staggering pace in recent decades, as has the number of its products. Complex organic compounds, many of them toxic, find their way into virtually every product and production process. Government figures show that more than 700,000 tons of toxic pollutants are released each year by the U.S. chemical industry. Many of these are long-lived and contaminate lakes, groundwater, and the air people breathe.

Concerns over toxic emissions mushroomed after the catastrophic release of methyl isocyanate gas from a Union Carbide plant in India in 1984, killing almost 5,000 people and injuring 200,000 more. Governments gradually have cracked down on toxic releases—first into water, then onto land, and finally to the air. Many companies have been faced with the costly cleanup of decades' worth of negligent waste disposal. Others have been hit with massive lawsuits filed by those injured by exposure to toxic materials.

Early on, it became clear that end-of-pipe pollution controls were not always the most cost-effective way to deal with these toxic chemicals. In the U.S., 3M pioneered a different approach. Its "Pollution Prevention Pays" program, established in 1975, encourages employees to find ways to reduce or eliminate use of dangerous chemicals—and save money—through redesign of products and manufacturing processes. The corporation estimates it has prevented more than 1,000,000,000 pounds of emissions since then and saved over $500,000,000. The company planned to cut its releases to the air another 70% by the end of 1993.

Many other firms began to emulate the 3M approach. Dow Chemical reports that its pollution reduction program has cut its U.S. air emissions in half since 1985. The British chemical giant ICI has designed a new terephthalic acid plant in Taiwan that it claims produces virtually no chemical waste. The new, redesigned production processes usually are simpler and cheaper, and investments are repaid quickly. Some chemical companies have made process redesign an important part of corporate strategy.

An even greater challenge is to find substitutes for products that are hazardous or can not be manufactured without using toxic ingredients. The agricultural chemical business is one industry where cleanup efforts extend well beyond the factory wall. Agriculture has been transformed in recent decades by the massive use of herbicides and insecticides intended to boost yields. Pests have become immune to numerous chemicals, however, and many toxic substances have leached into groundwater. A number of farmers are turning to alternative forms of pest control, including integrated pest management (IPM). Combining small, targeted applications of pesticides with careful monitoring of field conditions and protection of predator insects, IPM often saves farmers money through reduced chemical bills. It is likely to have far-reaching consequences for agribusiness, giving rise to new firms offering IPM services. Companies may find they do better marketing "pest management" than pesticides alone.

Water conservation is another burgeoning enterprise. In contrast to the large dams and diversion projects of the past, improving the efficiency of water use will rely on a diverse array of manufacturing and service companies. Water shortages in many regions have led to government conservation programs. The market for low-flow toilets and showerheads is growing, and many industries are altering their production processes to cut water use by 75% or more. Agriculture, the largest user, is turning to drip irrigation and other forms of water management to deliver water more efficiently. Depletion of natural resources also may help create entirely new industries—supplying for profit what nature once provided free. Growth in the world fish catch, which has proceeded steadily for most of this century, is slowing and may not increase much more in the years ahead. With the world's population surging upward and demand for protein increasing, it is not surprising that fish prices are up. One response lies in fish farming. Although aquaculture is constrained by the availability of natural resources—such as clean water, energy, and space—commercial fish farming now is a growing enterprise. It currently contributes 10-15% of the world's fish, from the high-cost salmon farming practiced in the fjords of Norway to the prolific carp and tilapia farms now common in China.

Reforming corporations

The environmental revolution began with grassroots activism in the 1960s and was joined by active government policymaking in the 1970s and 1980s. Now, industry itself is being swept up in the process. During the past few years, business policies and practices have begun to undergo sweeping reforms that in the end may yield not only a cleaner environment, but a different kind of company. Industry as a whole, however, only has taken the first steps in a long

journey. In the years ahead, business executives will have to spur the process of reform, and governments will meet to cooperate in making the new approaches work.

A broad spectrum of ecological philosophies and practices is existent among businesses today. At the most primitive level, some still are in "attack mode"—lobbying tooth and nail against any environmental legislation and telling the public that such laws will cost jobs and add to the price of consumer goods. Top executives at auto companies devote more effort to fighting new fuel economy standards than toward developing more fuel-efficient engines. Such attitudes not only slow the evolution of public policy, they poison the corporate atmosphere—giving employees the notion that environmental improvement is something to be feared, rather than encouraged.

Another strategy popular among companies looking to resist change is to run glossy ads that exaggerate their environmental achievements. Mitsubishi, a major cutter of old-growth forests in Southeast Asia, claims it practices "sustainable forestry"; Solvay, a leading European manufacturer of plastics, has taken credit for recycling energy and materials within its normal production process, although much of the "recycling" involves potentially hazardous incineration. Others allow industry groups to do their "greenwashing" for them. Sometimes the group's name provides all the distortion needed. For instance, the Global Climate Coalition is a coal-industry-led group that fought the 1992 climate treaty signed in Rio de Janeiro and opposes efforts to reduce dependence on fossil fuels.

The contradictory signals stem not merely from hypocrisy, but from ongoing struggles within companies and industries over ecological issues. A growing number of executives see that such efforts can backfire—both in the form of attacks from groups such as Greenpeace and by slowing the internal process of reform. Yet, they often face stiff in-house opposition from those who vainly yearn for "the way things used to be."

For companies ready to change, it usually begins with better management—an area in which Japanese companies have lessons to offer. Their corporate culture of "quality management"—wherein waste is avoided, materials are managed as carefully as possible, and processes constantly are improved—is a key ingredient of Japan's economic miracle. Beginning in the 1970s, that nation's companies effectively turned this philosophy to environmental cleanup, thus allowing them to make steady gains. Although these concepts are not easy to transfer to Western corporate culture, many European and American firms are working to adapt them. In some industries, better

management alone can yield rich ecological rewards while adding to profits.

Sony established a high-level Global Environmental Council in 1990 that coordinates policy throughout the company. In more than one-third of major U.S. corporations, the senior environmental official reports directly to the chief executive officer and, in many cases, the CEO has taken a personal and public interest in environmental matters. At BankAmerica, for example, the CEO personally announced the company's new environmental strategy in 1990 and actively has led it since.

Since businesses are run by human beings, motivated by the usual mixtures of ambition, fear, compassion, and greed, there often are psychological reasons for a company's performance. Beyond their concern about the bottom line, executives have an obvious interest in their personal reputations—which sometimes are sullied by environmental disasters. Some report that criticism over the dinner table from their spouses or children has spurred them to action. As ecological issues have gained public attention, many businesses report a change in the corporate culture toward heightened sensitivity. Often, this occurs as part of a generational shift, as younger executives inherit the reins of power. New leadership frequently leads to revamping a company's culture and opens new opportunities for reform.

Another essential element of corporate environmental reform is refocusing on the long run. It is easier to be concerned about the environment if a company is not obsessed with quarterly profit figures, as many are today, particularly in North America. In 1985, for instance, Wall Street raider Charles Hurwitz gained control of Pacific Lumber Co., a California firm with a policy of cutting its forests no faster than they could grow back. To pay off his takeover debts, Hurwitz doubled the company's cutting rates—selling off 1,000-year-old trees for quick cash.

German and Japanese firms are less susceptible to pressures for short-term profit. In Japan, the boards of most companies mostly are controlled by executives who rise through the company's ranks and are more loyal to other employees than to the firm's shareholders. Free of the tyranny of the stock market, these executives are able to focus more on the long-term prospects of the company and are in a better position to consider ecological concerns.

Employees deliver better environmental results when they know their company will reward them for doing so. Today's most successful corporate pollution-prevention programs share several principles, among them formal recognition of employee environmental achievements, high-level responsibility for ecological issues, and a strong commitment from top management. Linking environmental performance with pay and promotion can offer strong incentives for innovation; 3M includes such considerations in employee performance reviews. Unlike some firms, it avoids giving cash awards for environmental ideas to individual employees, in the belief that this would discourage cooperation.

Environmental auditing

One of the keys to progress is to develop systems for routine measurement of performance—so-called environmental auditing. Until recently, companies rarely collected the comprehensive information needed for these evaluations, such as materials and energy consumption, emissions levels, and studies of the impacts of their products. Increasingly, though, companies are tracking emissions, and several accounting firms are offering assistance in identifying and monitoring environmental performance. British Petroleum now audits its compliance with regulations, record at individual plant sites, and over-all corporate performance.

Environmental auditing is growing in popularity, and the information it yields often spurs businesses to make changes that go beyond legal requirements. While these practices are evolving, lack of standardization and public access may limit the value of many auditing programs. Audits usually are done by company personnel according to their own criteria—and often for management's eyes only. Sometimes, even the board of directors is denied access. The next step will be for third-party environmental audits to become routine, with the results made available to shareholders and the public at large. Standardized, public audits would provide real accountability and lead to far-reaching changes in procedures.

Comprehensive tracking of materials and energy use can help companies get a handle on the economic and ecological implications of their production processes. Energy audits are becoming common practice in a number of firms, and some are moving toward accounting for the inputs and fate of all the materials used in business operations—allowing managers to identify inefficiencies quickly. Massachusetts now

requires companies to report information on inputs of toxic materials as well as emissions, which is likely to spur closer examination of industrial processes and alternatives for cleaner production.

The U.S. government does not require environmental audits, but it has established the world's most advanced pollution reporting system—the Toxics Release Inventory (TRI). Set up in 1986, TRI collects information on toxic chemicals released from about 24,000 U.S. industrial facilities each year. When first proposed, the inventory was assailed by industry groups as a paperwork nightmare. In practice, it has provided a powerful stimulus for emissions reduction. The CEO of Monsanto "reacted with shock," according to a company case history, when presented with the firm's first report to TRI. He then set an ambitious goal for emissions reduction. In addition, environmental organizations have used TRI data to put pressure on major polluters, assembling more than 150 reports on local, state, and national pollution problems during the last three years.

Armed with such evidence, other groups with a stake in corporate environmental performance are exerting pressure for change. It is increasingly difficult for firms to borrow money, obtain insurance, negotiate labor contracts, offer new stock, site facilities, or sell products without first demonstrating that their operations are ecologically sound. Many of these companies—recalling the precipitous stock decline that followed Union Carbide's Bhopal accident or the nearly 17,000 lawsuits by asbestos disease victims that led to Manville Corp.'s bankruptcy—are concerned not just with the direct cost of environmental problems, but with the risk of being stuck with an unintended financial burden. The liability clause in the U.S. hazardous-waste cleanup law, for instance, has spurred lenders and insurers to insist on site audits prior to virtually all industrial real estate transactions so as to preclude an expensive waste disposal problem.

A growing number of investors now seek out "green investments"—motivated by the potential financial rewards of such a portfolio and by the desire not to finance morally objectionable activities. This movement includes many pension funds, universities, and other institutional investors. Some are

choosing to invest only in firms they believe are ecologically progressive; others use their position as stockholders to demand reform, employing information provided by groups such as the Council on Economic Priorities in New York, the Investor Responsibility Research Center in Washington, and Environmental Data Services in London. In addition, environmentally focused investment firms and funds have emerged to serve the individual investor, including the Calvert Group mutual funds and the Global Environment Fund in the U.S. and British unit trusts, such as the Merlin Ecology Fund.

Although banks are somewhat less at risk in the companies they lend to, many have established environmental policies in recent years. At the simplest level, these include scrutinizing borrowers for potential environmental problems that could make it difficult to repay their loans. Germany's Deutsche Bank has established a European environmental data base that is available to its borrowers—most of whom are small businesses—in order to help them clean up their acts. For Deutsche Bank, this service appears to be intended in part as a way to attract business.

Although the process of corporate reform is in its early stages, there can be little doubt about the sweeping nature of the transition that lies ahead for many companies. The necessary changes will reach deep into business management and culture. The cornerstones of more environmentally responsible corporate practice—openness, accountability, taking a longer-term view—potentially offer corporations, and the societies in which they function, far-reaching benefits.

The transition to an environmentally sound economy is as great a challenge as business has encountered. While the costs may be high and the danger of missteps real, most companies will face greater risks if they ignore the need for change. Those that do not learn how to earn profits in an ecologically sound way may find they have no profits to worry about. At the national level, those that try to force a false choice between jobs and the environment may end up with neither. In the end, the health of the global economy will depend on the health of the global environmental base on which it stands.

GREEN JUSTICE: THE FACTS

THE EARTH DEVOURED

**Who is polluting the world and consuming its resources?
The New Internationalist tots up the environmental bill
per head, North and South.**

IN THE SOUTH:[1]

LIVE THREE QUARTERS OF THE WORLD'S PEOPLE

WHO CONSUME JUST ONE SIXTH OF THE WORLD'S RESOURCES

WITH AVERAGE INCOMES 18 TIMES LOWER THAN THOSE IN THE NORTH.

Throw-away energy

Australians and Bangladeshis both live in relatively warm climates, but Australians get through one hundred times more energy than Bangladeshis.
Western industrialized countries use roughly half the world's energy, while the Third World uses just one sixth.

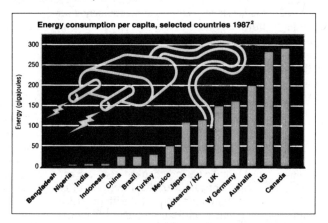

Energy consumption per capita, selected countries 1987[2]

Tree pulp

From diapers to doors, from wrapping to writing paper, the average Canadian gets through 100 times more trees than the average Indian – and recycles less.

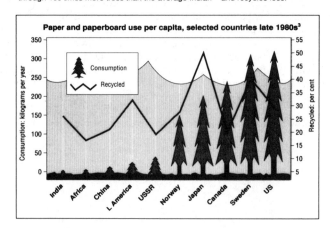

Paper and paperboard use per capita, selected countries late 1980s[3]

1 *Environment and Development: Towards a Common Strategy for the South in the UNCED Negotiations and Beyond,* South Centre – the Follow-up Office of the South Commission, Geneva, 1991. **2** *World Resources 1990-91,* World Resources Institute. **3** *State of the World 1990,* Worldwatch Institute. **4** *Human Development Report 1991,* UNDP. **5** 'Toxic waste for a small planet' by David Weir in *Consumer Lifelines,* IOCU, April 1989. **6** *State of the World 1991,* Worldwatch Institute. **7** US Department of Agriculture, 1989 figures. **8** Australian Board of Statistics 1989 figures. **9** New Zealand Meat Board 1989 figures. **10** Statistics Canada 1989 figures. **11** UK Meat Livestock Commission 1990 figures.

Unfair exchange

Between 1983 and 1989 a net total of $241 billion was transferred from South to North, mostly in the form of repayments on debts.

Trade protectionism in the North costs the South an estimated $100 billion a year in lost revenue from agricultural products and a further $50 billion a year for textiles.[2]

About 125,000 tons of toxic waste are sent to the Third World from Europe each year, and this is likely to increase with attempts to clean up Eastern Europe.[5]

IN THE NORTH:[4]

LIVE ONE QUARTER OF THE WORLD'S PEOPLE

WHO PUMP OUT FOUR FIFTHS OF THE WORLD'S GREENHOUSE GASES

WITH FACTORIES, CARS, AIR CONDITIONERS AND AEROSOL SPRAYS

THAT ALSO RELEASE ALMOST 90 PER CENT OF THE CFC GASES THAT

DESTROY THE OZONE LAYER.

Greenhouse greed

The average US citizen produces 170 times more pollution from burning fossil fuels like oil and coal (which causes 'global warming') than the average citizen of Zaire.

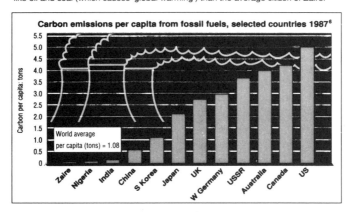

Carbon emissions per capita from fossil fuels, selected countries 1987[6]

Carbon per capita: tons

World average per capita (tons) = 1.08

Zaire, Nigeria, India, China, S Korea, Japan, UK, W Germany, USSR, Australia, Canada, US

Animal fat

There are three rungs on the ladder of the world's food consumption: at the bottom, 630 million people do not have enough to eat; in the middle, 3.4 billion grain eaters get most of their protein from plants; at the top, 1.25 billion meat eaters consume three times as much animal fat per person as the remaining four billion – and use 40 per cent of the world's grain to fatten the livestock they eat.

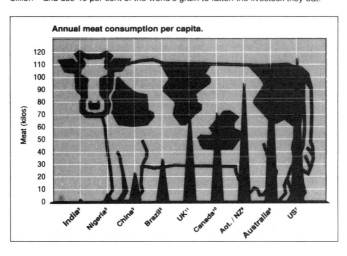

Annual meat consumption per capita.

Meat (kilos)

India[9], Nigeria[2], China[8], Brazil[8], UK[11], Canada[10], Aot. / NZ[8], Australia[8], US[7]

A Planet in Jeopardy

Despite increased attention to the environment, the health of the earth is deteriorating at an unprecedented rate. Time itself is our scarcest resource as we struggle to create a sustainable society.

Lester R. Brown, Christopher Flavin, and Sandra Postel

Lester R. Brown is president of the World-watch Institute, and Christopher Flavin and Sandra Postel are vice presidents for research with the Institute. Their address is 1776 Massachusetts Avenue, N.W., Washington, D.C. 20036.

Bruce Wallace, a biology professor at Virginia Polytechnic Institute and State University, offers this story from the past that reflects on our own times: "Five days after departing from Southhampton, England, the *Titanic* grazed an iceberg in the North Atlantic. The incident passed unnoticed by most passengers—a mere trembling, according to one.

"Having heard reports of water entering the hold, Captain Edward J. Smith and Mr. Thomas Andrews, a ship designer who was aboard representing the *Titanic*'s builders, went below to conduct an inspection. Upon returning to the bridge, Mr. Andrews made some rapid calculations, then broke the news to the captain: 'The ship is doomed; at best you have one and a half hours before she goes down.' An immediate order was issued: Uncover the lifeboats!

"The *Titanic*'s passengers were not seasoned sailors. The ship was large and reassuring; it had been their home for the better part of a week. Bankers still intent upon returning to their New York offices continued to plan upcoming business deals. Professors

returning from sabbatical leaves still mulled over lesson plans. Eventually, many preferred to stay on board rather than disembark on a tiny lifeboat.

"Grasp of an altered reality comes slowly, not as much the result of denial as of not comprehending. When the truth could no longer be denied, the passengers exhibited the entire range of human qualities—from bravery and heroism to cowardice. Some panicked and gave up hope entirely. Others achieved comfort by maintaining the status quo: Third-class passengers were prevented by many crew members from leaving the flooded steerage quarters for the temporary haven of the upper, higher-priced decks.

"In the end, reality could not be denied. Early on the morning of April 15, 1912, the *Titanic* sank with a loss of over 1,500 lives."

As the twentieth century nears a close, the tale of the *Titanic* comes uncomfortably close to describing the perceptual gap we now face: our inability to comprehend the scale of the ongoing degradation of the planet and how it will affect our future. Few understand the magnitude of the poten-

tial tragedy; fewer still have a good idea of what to do about it.

The *Titanic*'s passengers were mainly innocent victims, but the dilemma now facing society is largely of our own making. And for us, there is still hope. But saving Planet Earth—and its human passengers—will require going beyond the denial of reality that still characterizes many of our political and business leaders. It also hinges on the collective capacity and will to quickly make the transition from perception to policy change—an unprecedented challenge.

Success Stories Are Few

The first step—waking up to the dimensions of the world's environmental problems—has in a sense been under way for more than two decades. At the global level, a milestone was the U.N. Conference on the Human Environment held in Stockholm, Sweden, in 1972. The 20 years since that meeting have seen the birth of a worldwide environmental movement, the emergence of thousands of grass-roots environmental organizations, and the proliferation of environmental laws and regulations in nations around the world.

Now, as the world prepares for another global environmental summit, this time in Rio de Janeiro, Brazil, major speeches of prime ministers and presidents are incomplete without mention of the environment. Dozens of corporate executives have declared themselves committed environmentalists. And more than 115 nations have established environment agencies or ministries since 1972.

Laws and ministries are one thing. Real environmental progress is another. The two decades since the Stockholm conference have seen only scattered success stories. The Cuyahoga River in Cleveland, Ohio, no longer catches fire, and swimming has resumed in some of the Great Lakes. Air quality has improved in Tokyo and in many northern European cities as well. Soil erosion has slowed on U.S. cropland.

But outside of the "post-industrial" North, progress is rarer: Some regions of eastern Europe now face virtual epidemics of environmental disease, misuse of water resources is reducing the agricultural potential of wide sections of South Asia, and soil erosion is undermining the food prospects of much of Africa. Peru's inability to provide clean water for its people became evident when it was struck in 1991 by the world's worst cholera epidemic in decades. In Mexico City, coin-operated oxygen stations are being planned to help people cope with air pollution that has become life threatening.

At the global level, almost all of the indicators are negative. Each year now, the level of greenhouse gases in the atmosphere reaches a new high, and the ozone layer grows thinner. These fundamental assaults on the atmosphere are caused almost entirely by rich nations that use most of the fossil fuels and ozone-depleting chemicals. Yet, the long-term costs will be borne by humanity as a whole. Ozone depletion may cause skin cancer among Andean peasants who never used aerosol spray cans, while global warming could flood the homelands of Bangladeshis who have never used electricity.

Environmental concerns were viewed by many Third World leaders in 1972 as "luxury problems" that

only rich nations could afford to deal with. Although this view is still espoused by some, it has a thoroughly unconvincing ring. In the wattle-and-daub villages and urban shantytowns where most Third World people live, environmental quality is more than a question of the quality of life; it is often a matter of life or death. In many nations, environmental degradation is now recognized as a key barrier to governments' ability to meet basic needs and sustain living standards.

Winning Battles, but Losing the War?

But despite increased awareness, the health of the planet has deteriorated at an unprecedented rate. Since 1972, the world has lost nearly 200 million hectares of trees, an area the size of the United States east of the Mississippi. Deserts have expanded by 120 million hectares, claiming more land than is planted to crops in China and Nigeria combined. The world's farmers lost about 480 million tons of topsoil, roughly equal to that which covers the agricultural land of India and France. And thousands of plant and animal species with which we shared the planet in 1972 no longer exist.

In the past 20 years, human numbers have grown by 1.6 billion—the same number of people that inhabited the planet in 1900. Each year now, the annual addition of more than 90 million people is equivalent to the combined populations of Denmark, Finland, the Netherlands, Norway, Sweden, and the United Kingdom. Meanwhile, world economic output, which historically has paralleled demands on the earth's resources, has increased by nearly 75% over the same two decades.

Denis Hayes, chairman of Earth Day 1990, raised the essential paradox when he asked, "How could we have fought so hard, and won so many battles, only to find ourselves now on the verge of losing the war?" Part of the answer lies in the failure to alter the basic patterns of human activity that cause environmental deterioration—from our reproductive behavior to our dependence on fossil fuels. Like the *Titanic*'s passengers, most of whom were unable to grasp the fundamental nature of their

predicament, we are still struggling to understand the dimensions of the changes we are causing.

National governments have focused on building water-treatment facilities, controlling air pollutants from power plants, cleaning up toxic-waste sites, and trying to find new places to put their garbage. While much of this is necessary, such efforts cannot by themselves restore the planet's environmental health. Stabilizing the climate, for example, depends on restructuring national energy policies. Getting the brakes on population growth requires fundamental changes in social values and services. So far, only a handful of countries have undertaken such initiatives.

Economists vs. Ecologists

The still widely held belief that the global economy can continue along the path it has been following stems in part from a narrow economic view of the world. Anyone who regularly reads the financial papers or business weeklies would conclude that the world is in reasonably good shape and that long-term economic prospects are promising. Even the apparent problems—the U.S. budget deficit, Third World debt, and gyrating oil prices—are considered minor by most economic planners. They call for marginal course corrections as they pursue business as usual. To the extent that constraints on economic expansion are discussed on the business pages, it is in terms of inadequate demand growth rather than limits imposed by the earth's resources.

Lacking an understanding of the carrying capacity of ecological systems, economic planners are unable to relate demand levels to the health of the natural world. If they regularly read the leading scientific journals, their faith might be shaken. Every major indicator shows deterioration in natural systems.

These different views of the world have their roots in economics and ecology—disciplines with intellectual frameworks that contrast starkly. From an economist's perspective, ecological concerns are but a minor subdiscipline of economics—to be "internalized" in economic models and dealt with at the margins of economic planning. But to an ecologist, the economy is a narrow subset of the global ecosystem. Humanity's expanding economic activities cannot be separated from the natural systems and resources from which they ultimately derive, and any activity that undermines the global ecosystem cannot continue indefinitely. Modern societies, even with their technological sophistication, ignore dependence on nature at their own peril.

Environment and Development

The health of the planet is ultimately about the health of its people, and from this perspective as well, disturbing trends emerged during the past two decades. Despite soaring economic output, the ranks of the world's poor have increased. Some 1.2 billion people now meet former World Bank President Robert McNamara's 1978 definition of absolute poverty: "a condition of life so limited by malnutrition, illiteracy, disease, squalid surroundings, high infant mortality, and low life expectancy as to be beneath any reasonable definition of human decency."

In the 1980s, average incomes fell by 10% in most of Latin America; in sub-Saharan Africa, they were down by 20%. Economic "development" is simply not occurring in many countries. And even a large portion of the industrial world is no longer moving forward. In the former Soviet Union, the economy is in a state that economists describe as "free fall." Real income dropped 2% in 1990 and an estimated 10%–15% in 1991.

The ranks of the poor are concentrated among the rapidly growing populations of sub-Saharan Africa, Latin America, the Middle East, and South Asia. The growth in Third World jobs has fallen short of population growth, leaving tens of millions unemployed and hundreds of millions underemployed. Even more people lack access to clean water, adequate health care, and a full and balanced diet.

The rising tide of world poverty has many roots. Rapid population growth is one; another is the failure of many governments to reform their economic and political systems. Meanwhile, foreign-aid donations have stagnated since the mid-1980s,

and $1.2 trillion worth of foreign debt has accumulated, sapping financial earnings and undermining the credit-worthiness of low-income countries. The $950 billion spent on the military in 1990 was the biggest drain on resources of all.

The once separate issues of environment and development are now inextricably linked. Environmental degradation is driving a growing number of people into poverty. And poverty itself has become an agent of ecological degradation, as desperate people consume the resource bases on which they depend. Rather than a choice between the alleviation of poverty and the reversal of environmental decline, world leaders now face the reality that neither goal is achievable unless the other is pursued as well.

Unsustainable Economies

Our economies are engaged in a disguised form of deficit financing: Processes such as deforestation and overpumping of groundwater inflate current output at the expense of long-term productivity. In sector after sector, we violate fundamental principles of environmental sustainability. Relying on an incomplete accounting system, one that does not measure the destruction of natural capital associated with gains in economic output, we deplete our productive assets, satisfying our needs today at the expense of our children. As economist Herman Daly puts it, "there is something fundamentally wrong in treating the earth as if it were a business in liquidation."

To extend the analogy, it is as though a vast industrial corporation quietly sold off a few of its factories each year, using an accounting system that did not reflect these sales. As a result, its cash flow would be strong and profits would rise. Stockholders would be pleased with the annual reports, not realizing that the profits were coming at the expense of the corporation's assets. But once all the factories were sold off, corporate officers would have to inform stockholders that their shares were worthless.

To reverse this process, industries and governments will need to alter their world views—focusing less on

the short-term financial bottom line and more on the long-term sustainability of the economies they invest in. If we do not change our ways, we may find that the lifeboats are rapidly filling up and that it is too late for many to get aboard. While the rich may congregate on the upper decks and protect themselves for a while, they too are ultimately threatened.

The effort required to create a sustainable society is more like mobilizing for war than any other human experience. Time itself is the scarcest resource as we begin preparing for the struggle that will unfold in this decade and beyond. Indeed, we have only a few short years to overcome the political, social, and economic impediments to real progress—to lay the foundations for a fundamentally improved society. Once the self-reinforcing trends of environmental degradation and deepening poverty are too deeply established, only a superhuman effort could break the cycle and reverse the trend.

If the struggle for a sustainable society is to succeed, we must have some vision of what we are aiming for. If not fossil fuels to power society, then what? If forests are no longer to be cleared to grow food, then how is a larger population to be fed? If a throwaway culture leads inevitably to pollution and resource depletion, how can we satisfy our material needs? In sum, if the present path is so obviously unsound, what vision of the future can we use to guide our actions toward a global community that can endure?

A sustainable society is one that satisfies its needs without jeopardizing the prospects of future generations. Just as any technology of flight, no matter how primitive or advanced, must abide by the basic principles of aerodynamics, so must a lasting society satisfy basic ecological principles. At least two preconditions are undeniable: If population growth is not slowed and climate stabilized, there may not be an ecosystem on Earth we can save.

The 1990s will be the environmental decade—whether we want it to be or not. Already, it is a lost decade for many ecosystems and people, but it is also a last chance to begin turning things around.

Facing a Future of WATER SCARCITY

Enormous savings of the precious liquid are being thwarted by policies and laws that encourage wastefulness and misuse, rather than efficiency and conservation.

Rampant river pollution is wiping out millions of fish in Brazil.

Sandra Postel

Ms. Postel, vice president for research, Worldwatch Institute, Washington, D.C., is the author of Last Oasis: Facing Water Scarcity.

BENJAMIN FRANKLIN once pointed out that, "When the well's dry, we know the worth of water." Much of the world is in danger of learning Franklin's lesson the hard way. For decades, water has been wasted, mismanaged, and overused— and the consequences are beginning to hit home.

Water scarcity typically conjures up visions of drought, the temporary dry spells that nature inflicts from time to time. Yet, while droughts capture headlines, the far greater threat posed by escalating water consumption goes largely unnoticed. Despite 1993's floods, water tables are falling, lakes are shrinking, and wetlands are disappearing. Around water-short cities, competition is brewing between city-dwellers and farmers who lay claim to the same limited supply.

In each major area of water use— agriculture, industry, and cities—demands have increased rapidly. Global water use has more than tripled since 1950, and what is removed from rivers, lakes, and ground-water amounts to 30% of the world's stable renewable supply. People actually rely on a far larger share since water bodies dilute pollution, generate electricity, and support fisheries and wildlife. Because of improved living standards, demand has been growing faster than population—per capita use is nearly 50% higher than it was in 1950 and continues to climb in most of the world.

For decades, planners have met this rising demand by turning to ever more and larger water development projects, particularly to dams and river diversions. Engineers have built more than 36,000 large dams around the globe to control floods and provide hydroelectric power, irrigation, industrial supplies, and drinking water to an expanding population and economy. Rare is the river that now runs freely toward the sea, and many that still do are slated to come under control soon.

Limits to this ever-expanding supply are swiftly coming to light, however. Engineers naturally first selected the easiest and least-costly sites for water development. Over time, water projects have become increasingly complex, expensive to build, and more damaging to the environment. Fewer dams and diversion projects are making it off the drawing boards, and most that do will deliver water at a far higher price than in the past.

Meeting human needs while facing up to water's limits—economic, ecological, and political—entails developing an entirely new relationship to the precious liquid. Historically, it has been managed with a frontier philosophy, manipulating natural systems to whatever degree engineering know-how would permit. Modern society has come to view water as a resource that is there for the taking, rather than a life-support system that underpins the natural world humans depend on. Instead of continuously reaching out for more, people must begin to look within their regions, communities, homes, and themselves for ways to meet their needs while respecting water's life-sustaining functions.

Although water is a renewable resource, it also is a finite one. The water cycle makes available only so much each year in a given location. That means supplies per person, a first-order indicator of water security, drop as population grows. Thus, per capita water supplies worldwide are one-third lower than in 1970, due to the 1,800,000,000 people added to the planet since then.

One of the clearest signs of scarcity is the increasing number of countries in which population has surpassed the level that can be sustained comfortably with the water available. As a rule of thumb, hydrologists designate water-stressed countries as those with annual supplies of about 725-1,450 gallons per person a day. When the figure drops below 725 gallons, nations are considered water-scarce—its lack becomes a severe constraint on food production, economic development, and protection of natural systems. Today, 26 countries— collectively home to 232,000,000 people— fall into the water-scarce category. As many of them have very high population growth rates, their problems are deepening fast. Africa has the largest number of water-scarce countries, 11; by 2010, six others will join the list. At that time, the total number of Africans living in water-scarce nations will climb to 400,000,000, approximately 37% of the continent's projected population.

From *USA Today Magazine*, September 1993, pp. 68-71. © 1993 by the Society for the Advancement of Education. Reprinted by permission.

Nine of the 14 countries in the Middle East face water-short conditions, making this the most concentrated region of scarcity in the world. With populations in several of them projected to double within 25 years, a rapid tightening of supplies is inevitable. Since virtually all Middle East rivers are shared by several nations, tensions over water rights are a potent political force throughout the region and could ignite before the end of the century.

Although the population-water equation suggests where to expect trouble, numerous physical symptoms of stress already exist—not just in water-scarce areas, but in parts of water-wealthy ones as well. Among the most pervasive problems is that of declining water tables, which results when groundwater is used faster than nature replenishes it. If pumping is not brought into balance with recharging, the underground supply eventually becomes too expensive to keep tapping, too salty to use as it is pulled up from greater depths, or simply too depleted to serve as a supply. Overuse of groundwater is now ubiquitous in parts of China, India, Mexico, Thailand, the western U.S., North Africa, and the Middle East.

Some of the most troubling cases of unsustainable groundwater use involve "fossil" aquifers, underground reservoirs that hold water hundreds or thousands of years old and receive little replenishment from rainfall. Like oil reserves, these aquifers essentially are nonrenewable—pumping water from them depletes the supply in the same way that extractions from an oil well do. Farms and cities that depend on this water eventually will face the dilemma of what to do when the well runs dry.

Shrinking groundwater reserves, falling water tables, and projected demands that far exceed available supplies are clear signals of water stress. Perhaps the most worrying sign of trouble comes from examining the health of aquatic environments. The damming, diverting, and polluting of watercourses with little regard for the environmental services they provide and the species they support has wreaked havoc on the planet's wetlands, deltas, lakes, and riverine habitats. Of all the different forms of biological diversity on Earth, aquatic life may be the most in jeopardy.

A distressing conflict has emerged over two of water's roles—as a commodity serving the economic aims of greater agricultural productivity, industrial expansion, and urban growth, and as a key life support for all species and natural communities. Mounting scarcity has thrown this friction into sharp relief. More water devoted to human needs means less for sustenance of ecosystems—and, in many areas, nature is losing out fast.

The infamous shrinking Aral Sea in central Asia is the most dramatic in a long list of natural areas destroyed, degraded, or at grave risk from human use and abuse of water. Among them are many unique wild places—including California's Mono Lake, south Florida's Everglades, Spain's Donaña wetlands, and Sudan's Sudd swamps—that are home to astounding numbers and varieties of bird and wildlife species.

In many areas, there is a tug-of-war between the demands of conventional economic development and those of aquatic ecosystems. A more pervasive sign of the severely compromised health of the water environment is the number of aquatic species now in jeopardy. In North America, for example, the American Fisheries Society lists 364 species of fish as endangered, threatened, or of special concern—the vast majority of them at risk because of habitat destruction. An estimated one-third of the continent's fish, two-thirds of its crayfish, and nearly three-fourths of its mussels are rare or imperiled. They often reach such status by way of incremental human actions that end up undermining their basic habitat requirements—be it the timing, quantity, or quality of water's flow.

Of the many varieties of native fish species at risk in North America, perhaps the most notable for their cultural and recreational values are several species of salmon in the western U.S. The winter run of the chinook salmon in California's Sacramento River declined from 120,000 in the 1960s to 400 today, and the species was added to the Federal endangered list in 1989. In 1991, just four adult sockeye salmon made it from the Pacific Ocean past eight Federal dams in the Columbia River basin to their primordial spawning ground at Idaho's Redfish Lake. On the brink of extinction, the Snake River sockeye was listed as endangered in November, 1991.

Each wetland, lake, or aquatic species at risk presents a crucial test of whether a region's people and economy can adapt to the ecological needs of a healthy aquatic system. Only in rare instances are public values and future generations winning out over private rights to dam and divert natural watercourses. A growing movement to protect property rights from government actions to safeguard the environment could tip this balance even further away from ecosystem protection. Unfortunately for the future, protecting aquatic environments and their species still often is viewed as a luxury that can be traded off against pressing economic goals, rather than as essential to preserving the environmental foundation all else rests upon.

Water-thrifty food production

With agriculture claiming two-thirds of all the water removed from rivers, lakes, streams, and aquifers, making irrigation more efficient is a top priority in moving toward more sustainable use. The possible savings—ranging from 10 to 50%—constitute a large and mostly unexploited new source of supply. Reducing irrigation needs by 10%, for instance, would free up enough water roughly to double domestic water use worldwide.

A wide variety of measures exist to boost agriculture's water productivity, including new and improved irrigation technologies, better management practices by farmers and water managers, and changes in the institutions that govern the distribution and use of irrigation water. While gains have been made in each area, there remains a vast untapped potential.

Some of the biggest technological successes in improving irrigation efficiency have occurred where water scarcity poses serious threats to farming. In Texas, for example, many farmers have adapted old-fashioned furrow systems to a new surge technique that reduces percolation losses at the head of the field and distributes water more uniformly. This has cut their water use by 15-50% while reducing their pumping costs. For those in the Texas Plains, where savings have averaged 25%, the initial investment of about $30 per hectare (2.47 acres) normally is recouped within the first year.

Many irrigators in northwest Texas have moved from high-pressure sprinklers, which typically register efficiencies of 60-70%, to low-pressure ones that boost efficiency to around 80%. A relatively new sprinkler design, known as low-energy precision application (LEPA), offers even greater savings. LEPA sprinklers deliver water closer to crops by means of drop tubes extending vertically from the sprinkler arm. When used with water-conserving land preparation methods, LEPA can achieve efficiencies as high as 95%. Adapting an existing sprinkler for LEPA costs Texas farmers $60-160 per hectare; the water, energy, and yield gains typically pay back the initial investment in two to four years.

Elsewhere, Israel has brought about what widely is perceived as an agricultural miracle over the last three decades. Although it remains to be seen whether that nation's success in making the desert bloom will prove sustainable, Israel has developed technologies, methods, and scientific capabilities in irrigation that could prove invaluable to much of the world as the era of water constraints unfolds.

Among the most heralded of its accomplishments is the development of drip irrigation, whereby water is delivered directly to crops' roots through a network of porous or perforated piping installed on or below the soil surface. This keeps evaporation and seepage losses extremely low. Because water is applied frequently at low doses, optimal moisture conditions are maintained for the crop, boosting yields, and salt does not accumulate in the root zone. Modern Israeli farms often have highly automated drip systems, with computers and monitors sensing when and how much water to apply and determining the precise amount of nutrients to add. Israeli farmers liken their irrigation practices to "feeding the plant with a teaspoon."

New technologies that build efficiency into their designs—such as surge, LEPA, and drip irrigation—can help make crop production less demanding of the world's water supply. Equally important is raising the efficiency of the extensive surface canal systems that dominate the world's irrigated lands. Much land slated for irrigation, and often counted as receiving it, gets insufficient water or none at all because irrigation works are poorly maintained and operated.

Many problems with large canal systems arise because irrigation officials rarely have any incentive to improve the performance of projects they administer. Their operating budget may come from a state or national treasury and bear no relation to how well the system functions. Irrigation fees collected from farmers may go back into a general treasury, rather than being used to operate and maintain the local system. Since farmers have little say in how their projects are managed and are not charged for water according to their use, they, too, have few incentives to use water wisely. In short, there is barely any accountability of those in control, and little control by those who are supposed to benefit.

Especially in government-run projects, some form of "water users association" is necessary for farmers to have a say in management decisions. Such an organization also provides a mechanism for collecting fees to cover operation and maintenance costs and involving farmers directly in maintenance activities. Many studies have shown that, when farmers actively participate in projects and have some responsibility for the operation, canals and other infrastructure function better, a greater proportion of the project area gets irrigated, and crop yields rise.

Another way to stretch freshwater supplies is to use treated municipal wastewater for irrigation. Farmers worldwide spend heavily on chemical fertilizers to give their crops the nitrogen, phosphorus, and potassium that domestic wastewater contains in large amounts. By using municipal water supplies twice—once for domestic use and again for irrigation—would-be pollutants become valuable fertilizers, rivers and lakes are protected from contamination, the irrigated land boosts crop production, and the reclaimed water becomes a reliable, local supply.

By not making wastewater reuse a part of water planning and management, developing countries put their urban and rural populations at risk. As World Bank wastewater specialists Carl Bartone and Saul Arlosoroff note, "Examples abound of local farmers breaking into sewer interceptors both within and on the outskirts of urban areas to steal the effluents for watering their crops. These are often

vegetable crops destined for local markets that will be consumed raw. In addition . . . highly polluted rivers serve as major water sources for large-scale irrigation projects."

When designed and operated properly, waste stabilization ponds that biologically treat wastewater offer a low-cost way to keep sewage out of rivers and streams, safeguard human health from disease-causing organisms, and produce a nutrient-rich source of irrigation water. Studies have shown them capable of treating wastewater up to the World Health Organization's standards for irrigation of crops not eaten raw. Care always must be taken to prevent heavy metals from getting into wastewater destined for irrigation. Cadmium, copper, nickel, zinc, and other heavy metals can accumulate in crops and soils or percolate to groundwater and contaminate a drinking supply. A key to safe reuse is preventing untreated industrial effluent—often containing heavy metals—from mixing with domestic wastewater.

Finally, producing enough food for the world's expanding population while economizing on water will require boosting yields on the 84% of the planet's cropland watered only by rainfall. The drylands of Africa, western India, north-central China, and southwestern Latin America present formidable challenges to crop production. Altogether, arid and semi-arid lands cover about one-third of the Earth's land surface and are home to 600,000,000 people, including many of the world's poorest farmers. For them, conservation and more efficient use of scarce water quite literally is a matter of life and death.

Attention is turning to the potential of smaller-scale projects—micro dams, shallow wells, low-cost pumps, moisture-conserving land techniques, and a wide variety of rainwater harvesting methods—to make food production more secure for dryland dwellers. Many of these efforts have proved more cost-effective and less disruptive to local communities than the massive schemes that dominated development efforts during the past few decades. Their smaller size and use of local resources tend to make them less damaging to the environment.

Industrial recycling

Collectively, industries account for nearly one-quarter of the world's water use. In most industrial countries, they are the biggest user—frequently accounting for 50-80% of total demand, compared with 10-30% in much of the Third World. As developing countries industrialize, however, their water demands for electric power generation, manufacturing, mining, and materials processing are rising rapidly.

In contrast to that used in agriculture, only a small fraction of industrial water actually is consumed. Most of it is utilized

for cooling, processing, and other activities that may heat or pollute water, but do not use it up. This allows a factory to recycle its supplies. American steelmakers, for example, have reduced their water intake to 14 tons per ton of steel, securing the remainder from recycling.

So far, the main impetus for industrial water recycling has come from pollution control laws. Most of the world's wealthier countries now mandate that industries meet specific water quality standards before releasing wastewater into the environment. The most effective and economical way to comply with these requirements often is to treat and recycle water, thereby discharging less. Pollution control laws, therefore, not only have helped clean up rivers, lakes, and streams, they have promoted conservation and more efficient water use.

Given the proper incentives, industries of many types have shown they can cut their water needs 40-90% with available technologies and practices, while at the same time protecting water from pollution. Industrial conservation offers cities facing shortages a large untapped new supply. Ensuring that new factories incorporate conservation and recycling from the outset would help delay costly investments in urban water supplies, reduce overpumping of aquifers, lessen competition for water, and help prevent pollution from reaching levels hazardous to people and wildlife. Closing the industrial water and wastewater cycle not only is technically possible, it increasingly makes good economic and environmental sense.

Homes, apartments, small businesses, and other municipal enterprises account for less than one-tenth of the world's total water use. However, their demands are concentrated in relatively small geographic areas, and in many cases are escalating rapidly. As cities expand, they strain the capacity of local water bodies and force engineers to reach out to ever more distant sources.

In addition, the reservoirs, canals, pumping stations, pipes, sewers, and treatment plants that constitute a modern water and wastewater system require huge sums of money to build and maintain. Collecting and treating water and wastewater also takes large amounts of energy and chemicals, adding to environmental pollution and the over-all costs of a community's water system. Under such constraints, many cities are having difficulty meeting the needs of their residents, and large numbers of low-income households in developing countries get no service at all.

Conservation, once viewed as just an emergency response to drought, has been transformed in recent years into a sophisticated package of measures that offers one of the most cost-effective and environmentally sound ways of balancing urban water budgets. Just as energy planners have discovered that it often is cheaper to save energy than to build more power plants, water planners are realizing that an assortment of efficiency measures can yield permanent savings and thereby delay or avert the need for expensive new dams and reservoirs, groundwater wells, and treatment plants. The idea slowly is spreading that managing demand, rather than continuously striving to meet it, is a surer path to water security while saving money and protecting the environment at the same time.

Raising the price of water to reflect its true cost better is one of the most important steps any city can take. Water consistently is undervalued and, as a result, chronically is overused. The water rate structure of many utilities actually reward waste by charging less the more that is consumed.

Many residences in both industrial and Third World cities are not equipped with water meters, making it impossible to charge people appropriately for their water use. Metering not only is a prerequisite to the success of most conservation measures, it encourages savings in and of itself simply by tying the water bill to the amount used.

Raising water prices often can be politically difficult to do. Yet, if accompanied by public outreach explaining the need for the hike and steps consumers can take to keep bills down, higher prices can have a strong positive effect. When faced with dire water supply conditions in the mid 1970s, for instance, officials in Tucson, Ariz., raised rates sharply to make them reflect the true cost of service better. They also ran a public education campaign called "Beat the Peak" with a goal of curbing water use on hot summer afternoons, when the supply was most in danger of running short. The result was a 16% drop in per capita use within a few years, which, along with the lowered peak demand, allowed the Tucson water utility to cut its expansion expenses by $75,000,000.

Since economic incentives and public outreach will not motivate everyone to conserve, setting water-efficiency standards for common fixtures—toilets, showerheads, and faucets—can be a critical component of a reliable conservation strategy. Legislation that would set national standards passed Congress in October, 1992, as part of a broad energy bill. It requires that all new homes and major remodeling nationwide incorporate water-efficient fixtures and appliances.

Effective pricing, regulations, and public outreach also can help curb water use outdoors. In many dry regions, the sprinkling of lawns accounts for one-third to half of residential water demand. Many communities in the U.S. have turned to Xeriscape landscaping that draws on a wide variety of indigenous and drought-tolerant plants, shrubs, and ground cover to replace the thirsty green lawns found in most suburbs. A Xeriscape yard typically requires 30-80%

less water than a conventional one and can reduce fertilizer and herbicide use as well.

In addition to cutting indoor and outdoor use, a comprehensive urban conservation effort will curb waste in the water distribution system itself. As urban water systems deteriorate because of age or lack of maintenance, large amounts can be lost through broken pipes and faults in the distribution network. In most cases, finding and fixing leaks rewards a city not only with water savings, but with a quick payback on the investment. At a cost of $2,100,000, the Massachusetts Water Resources Authority's leak detection program cut system-wide demand in the greater Boston area by about 10%, making it one of the most cost-effective measures in a successful conservation strategy.

What does water cost?

Many of the shortages cropping up around the world stem from the widespread failure to value water at anything close to its true worth. Pricing it properly is especially important in agriculture because wasteful irrigation constitutes the single largest untapped new supply. Yet, water subsidies are larger and more pervasive in agriculture than in any other sector. Governments often build, maintain, and operate irrigation systems with public funds, then charge farmers next to nothing for these expensive services.

Undercharging not only fosters waste and the planting of water-intensive crops, it also deprives government agencies of the funds needed to maintain canals and other irrigation works adequately. Correcting the situation requires bucking deeply entrenched and politically influential special interests, instilling irrigation bureaucracies with a broader sense of mission, and decentralizing water management so that local water suppliers and users have more responsibility and accountability for the performance of their operations.

With the pace of development slowing and supplies no longer expanding in places, new demands increasingly must be met by shifting water among different users—irrigators, industries, cities, and the natural environment. In the western U.S., competition for scarce supplies has spawned an active water market. During 1991, 127 water transactions of various kinds were reported in 12 western states. Almost all the water sold or leased came from irrigation, and two-thirds of the trades resulted in cities getting more water for immediate or future use.

Exactly how far U.S. water trading ultimately will go in reallocating supplies remains unclear. According to some estimates, redirecting seven percent of western agriculture's water to cities could meet the growth in urban demand projected for the end of the decade. After that, larger shifts would be needed. Unless cities

stabilize their water use through conservation, reuse, and, where necessary, limits on the size of their populations and economies, agriculture ultimately could lose more water—and land—than is socially desirable, given the challenge that lies ahead of feeding a much larger world population.

Wherever pricing and marketing fail to take into account the full social, environmental, and intergenerational costs of water use, some additional correction is necessary. In areas with declining groundwater levels, for instance, governments can limit the total amount pumped to the average rate of aquifer recharge. In the case of fossil aquifers, a depletion tax might be levied on all groundwater extractions. In this way, those profiting from draining one-time reserves at least partially would compensate society.

Public action also is required to ensure that ecological systems get the water they need to remain healthy. One option is to limit the total amount that can be diverted from a river, lake, or stream. Protecting water systems also depends on regulating the use of those critical areas of land that help moderate its cycling through the environment. Degradation of the watershed —the sloping land that collects, directs, and controls the flow of rainwater in a river basin—is a pervasive problem in rich and poor countries alike. Besides contributing to flash floods and loss of groundwater recharge, which can exacerbate the effects of drought, it leads to soil erosion that prematurely fills downstream reservoirs with silt, shortening the useful life of expensive water projects.

Many of the measures that can help safeguard water supplies enhance crop production in upland areas. Terracing, mulching, agroforestry (the combined production of crops and trees), and planting vegetative barriers on the contour are a few of the ways soil and water can be conserved while improving agricultural output. On lands unsuitable for cultivation, the menu of options for watershed protection includes revegetating deforested slopes, reducing grazing pressures, and altering timber practices. The challenge for governments is to plan the use of watershed lands with soil and water conservation in mind, recognizing that the way uplands are managed greatly affects the livelihoods of people and the integrity of water systems downstream.

The idea is to devote as much human ingenuity to learning to live in balance with water as has been put into controlling and manipulating it. Conservation, efficiency, recycling, and re-use can generate a new supply large enough to get mankind through many of the shortages on the horizon. However, the pace of this transition needs to quicken if the planet is to avert severe ecological damage, economic setbacks, food shortages, and international conflicts. In the end, the time available to adjust may prove as precious as water itself.

GREENWATCH

RED ALERT FOR THE EARTH'S GREEN BELT

FRANCE BEQUETTE

France Bequette is a Franco-American journalist specializing in environmental questions. Since 1985 she has been associated with the WANAD-UNESCO training programme for African news agency journalists.

"TROPICAL forest" is the common name for what specialists call "rainforest", a term coined in 1898 by the botanist Andreas Schimper to designate forests that grow in a perpetually humid environment, receiving more than 2,000 millimetres of rain per year. In these conditions trees with smooth trunks can grow to more than sixty metres high. Their tops join together in what is known as the canopy, a roof of thick vegetation that keeps out the light.

Like a scarf girdling the equator, rainforests cover about 9.5 million square kilometres. The largest single tropical forest zone is in South America. Only five million square kilometres of rainforest now exist in tropical Asia and central Africa. A report published by UNESCO in 1991 reveals that Côte d'Ivoire has lost 75 per cent of its forest since 1960, and Ghana 80 per cent. In 25 years the Philippines have lost 15 out of 16 million hectares. By the year 2000 the forests of Viet Nam may well be no more than a fond memory. As British ecologist Edward Goldsmith noted in his *Report on Planet Earth*,

published in 1990, the Food and Agriculture Organization of the United Nations (FAO) estimated in the early 1980s that 100,000 square kilometres of rain forest were being lost each year. The American Academy of Sciences was far more pessimistic, deploring the loss of twice that area. The situation in Brazil seems to support the Academy's claim, since Brazil lost 48,000 square kilometres in 1988 alone.

Lowland forests, by far the biggest and the most easily accessible, have suffered most from human exploitation. Although less developed because of lower temperatures, rainfall variability and poorer soil, highland forests still play a very important role in preventing soil erosion and lowland flooding. Mangroves are a kind of rainforest growing in the salt-water and silt-rich coastal regions and along the banks of rivers flowing through forests. The mangrove forests in the Sundarbans region of the Ganges delta are the world's largest.

WHO IS TO BLAME?

Although they cover only 7 per cent of the earth's surface, rainforests are the home of more than half of the planet's plant species. With massive media support, international organizations are rightly insisting on the

need to preserve biodiversity, which is threatened from all sides, most notably by competition from agriculture. Again according to FAO, some 250 million farmers live in rainforests around the world. In search of land for crop-growing and livestock-raising, they occupy forest areas owned by the state, which is often unable to control access to it. These farmers have no recognized right to the areas they occupy. Alain Karsenty and Henri-Félix Maître of the forestry department of France's Centre for International Co-operation in Agronomic Research for Development (CIRAD) in a report to the XIth Directorate of the Commission of the European Communities published in 1993 stress that "recognition of property rights (not necessarily in the Western sense of the term 'property') for local communities is one of the necessary (but not sufficient) conditions for joint management of the forest with those who live in it."

Peoples who have lived for a long period in these zones are well adapted to their environment, but this is not the case with the new arrivals who grow cash crops such as cocoa and coffee. They follow the roads and trails gouged out by the loggers, thereby infiltrating the dense forest where, mainly by using fire, they create "frontiers" which push back the forest. "This interrelationship between exploitation

Reprinted with permission from *The Unesco Courier,* November 1994, pp. 41-43.

W O R L D

THE DIMINISHING OZONE LAYER

The World Meteorological Organization (WMO) reports that in 1993 low ozone levels were measured over most of South America. Ozone concentrations fell by 7% above Sao Paulo and by 3 to 4% above Rio de Janeiro. In March and April 1994 the depletion of the ozone layer above Europe, Siberia and the adjacent polar-ocean areas was more than 10% below long-term mean values. ■

FUEL FOR KANGWANE'S FIRES

An American reader, Suzy Liebenberg, former co-ordinator of Ecolink's environmental community development programme, has written to tell us about an interesting project in the eastern Transvaal lowveld of South Africa, where members of the rural community of Kangwane are growing Leucaena trees around their homes and in their vegetable gardens. The species grows quickly and produces many stems from ground level rather than a single trunk. This makes it ideal for coppicing, which involves cutting a few stems from each tree annually, thus ensuring renewable supplies of wood. Tree seedlings are provided at a reasonable cost to the villagers and are planted to act as windbreaks and to provide shade and slow down evaporation in vegetable gardens. Leucaena is a legume, and its root nodules contain bacteria that extract nitrogen from the atmosphere and improve soil fertility by producing nitrates. Community members are encouraged to plant 52 seedlings because in a 3-to-5-year period, 52 trees would supply enough fuel for a year. It also relieves women of having to carry heavy loads for great distances. ■

ON THE SCENT OF THE MUSK DEER

The musk deer (*Moschus moschiferus*), a small hornless ruminant that lives in mountainous regions of Central Asia, China, eastern Korea and Siberia, is out of luck. The musk gland of the male is coveted both by Asian medicine and the Western perfume industry. Consisting of sexual hormones, cholesterol and a waxy substance, musk gives out a strong odour. Although musk can be collected from farm-reared specimens without killing the animal, as is done in China, poachers do not hesitate to defy measures to protect the musk deer. According to World Wide Fund for Nature (WWF) estimates, there are no more than 100,000 musk deer left in the world. ■

SHRIMP IN CAGES

Since 1992, France's Research Institute for Exploitation of the Sea (IFREMER) has been co-operating with Brazil on a pilot project for farming shrimp in cages. The project is designed to increase production and to study the impact of aquaculture on the environment. In Ecuador, IFREMER is co-operating with the National Centre for Aquaculture and Marine Research (CENAIM) on the immunology and pathology of shrimp grown on farms. But while the cage technique is simple, the high-tech facilities being used in Ecuador have been strongly criticized by the British ecologist Edward Goldsmith on the grounds that their products are too expensive for the needy. ■

FIRE-LOVING FLOWERS

A rare flowering plant, the Peter's Mountain mallow (*Iliamna corei*), has made a remarkable comeback thanks to a prescribed burning programme in a Nature Conservancy Preserve in Virginia (U.S.A.). Only four such plants were known to exist when scientists discovered a large amount of dormant but viable seeds surrounding the plants. The fire-dependent plant was brought back from the brink of extinction when over 500 seeds sprouted after a controlled burn was conducted in the preserve. ■

THE GREEN BUSES OF BRUSSELS

Last March, Belgium's Ministry of Public Works and Communications and World Wildlife Fund (WWF) Belgium launched 20 new buses in Brussels that run on compressed natural gas (CNG). Although they cost almost $30,000 more than diesel buses to buy, maintenance costs are halved and a ministry subsidy keeps CNG prices even with those of diesel fuel. New York, Toronto and several other European cities including Utrecht (Netherlands) and Ravenna (Italy) already power public transport vehicles with natural gas. WWF-Belgium has sent education packs explaining the link between transportation and urban pollution to all secondary schools in Brussels. While the world waits for a miracle-fuel, CNG remains the least polluting of all. ■

and agricultural colonization," says Alain Karsenty, "makes it difficult to apportion the responsibility borne by each activity in deforestation processes."

Edward Goldsmith has no time for those who condemn farmers for clearing land by fire, for this process has always been used, even in Europe. Its disadvantages become apparent when the population grows and the land is not left fallow for long enough, thus preventing the forest from regenerating itself between two burnings.

Crops are greedy devourers of forest. In Ethiopia vast plantations have replaced trees: 60 per cent of the land is now given over to cotton-growing and 22 per cent to sugar cane. Central America has seen two-thirds of its forests sacrificed to livestock-raising. Numerous developing countries that once exported timber—Nigeria, for example, but above all the Philippines, once a major exporter—now import it. Of the last thirty exporters in the Third World today, only ten will still be exporting by the end of the century.

Another factor in deforestation is the timber industry. Until now Suriname on South America's northeastern coast has been 90 per cent covered by virgin rainforest. But the government has just granted a concession of 150,000 hectares to an Indonesian logging company and is considering throwing in two million hectares more. Ernie Brunings, a member of Suriname's National Assembly, was quoted by *Time* magazine as saying bluntly, "We cannot have these riches and keep them for their beauty if we have children dying of hunger, as we have here." This is the crux of the matter. The logging industry creates jobs, and however low the wages may be, they provide a basic minimum.

LAND-HUNGRY FARMERS

Sustainable management of rainforests on a planetary scale is essential. This is what the United Nations Environment Programme (UNEP), the World Bank and the World Resources Institute (WRI) are trying to achieve via an ongoing process known as the Tropical Forestry Action Plan (TFAP). This is not a new plan but it is still relevant, although there has been some criticism that state authorities and sources of finance have a bigger say in it than the populations directly concerned.

"Is it possible," Alain Karsenty wonders, "both to preserve vast multifunctional forest ecosystems (protectors of biodiversity, homes to local communities, bulwarks against erosion and regulators of climate) and to allow logging activities on an industrial scale?" He goes on to ask, "How can we reconcile a business rationale that thinks largely in the short term with natural forest regeneration, a process that extends over dozens of years?"

Forest space is in high demand. Not only by logging companies but—once the loggers have pulled out—by large-scale livestock-raisers and cacao and rubber planters, who are always ready to clear the land. Forms of exploitation vary from region to region. In Africa, where highly-prized wood like mahogany is found and logging is very selective, only one tree per hectare is felled on average. This may not be much, but to reach logging sites, trails have to be cut, sometimes as much as one hundred kilometres long, and this opens the way to land-hungry farmers. In tropical America, the opposite happens. The farmers go in first and are followed by loggers. Deforestation problems in southeast Asia result from intensive, often devastating, clear-cutting. The pockets of remaining forest are vulnerable to fires, as has been seen in Borneo.

SUSTAINABLE POSSIBILITIES

Several proposals for preserving the rainforest have been put forward. One is to limit the time period of concessions granted to logging companies and making their renewal dependent on "good behaviour". Logging companies might also be obliged by states to build on-site saw mills, as is done in Cameroon, to prevent them from clearing out once they have cut down all the valuable trees. The value of concessions could also be reassssed by taking account of their true commercial value and granting them on a competitive basis. Skid trails must also be laid down, for, according to the World Bank, from 15 to 35 per cent of the damage to forests is caused by tractors foraging randomly in search of felled trees. Felling techniques could also be improved so that falling trees cause less damage to their neighbours. If their operating costs could be brought down and their safety ensured for both men and forest, helicopters and blimps could eventually lift timber vertically out of the forest.

The preservation of the rainforest depends above all on the political determination of states. Either states tolerate tree-felling and impose taxes on it, or they define regulations for using and managing the forests that international organizations like the FAO and the World Bank are prepared to support.

Some states, such as Indonesia, prohibit the exporting of unprocessed wood. In the process of industrializing, they have sought to add value to their timber and create jobs. Is this a solution? In Indonesia there are 500,000 jobs in plywood mills and about three million jobs in the wood industry overall. To function, the industry requires 50 million m³ of unprocessed wood per year, but the country can no longer supply this amount. Wood must be obtained at any price—thus encouraging illicit practices—or the mills will have to be closed down, which is politically impossible.

German, Dutch and American ecologists have proposed that the developed countries should boycott tropical wood unless it carries the "green label" awarded to wood from forests that are exploited sustainably. Even this plan is not without drawbacks. What is to prevent timber companies from reaping maximum profits before the restriction becomes universal? It might also speed up the conversion of forests into huge cacao and coffee farms that are supposedly more profitable. Or states may simply cease to manage and develop their forests, in the belief they will not be able to make money out of them.

Preservation and exploitation are not incompatible. In the tropics as in Europe, a forest that is not taken care of is a dying forest. But in managing these renewable natural resources, we must be satisfied with reaping the interest without touching the capital.

FURTHER READING:

☛ *Tropical Forests, People and Food, Man and the Biosphere series*, UNESCO and Parthenon Publishing Group, 1993.
☛ *The Last Rain Forests*, Mark Collins, IUCN and Mitchell Beasley, 1990.
☛ *Tropical Forest Ecosystems* (UNESCO, UNEP and FAO), UNESCO, 1979.
☛ *The Disappearing Tropical Forests*, MAB and the International Hydrological Programme, UNESCO, 1991.
☛ *Etude des modalités d'exploitation du bois en liaison avec une gestion durable des forêts tropicales humides*, CIRAD-Forêts, the Commission of the European Communities, XI D.G.,1993.
☛ *Bois et forêts des tropiques*, revue n° 240, CIRAD, Nogent-sur-Marne, France1994.

THE LANDSCAPE

OF

HUNGER

We have seen the victims of mass starvation. We have shuddered at the images of millions of people arriving at remote camps for aid. Many of the world's famines result from wars or civil strife. But we rarely see that hunger also grows from environmental ruin.

BRUCE STUTZ

Bruce Stutz is features editor at Audubon. *He is the author of* Natural Lives, Modern Times.

The numbers alone are staggering: In 1990, 550 million people worldwide were hungry, 56 million more than in the early 1980s. During that time, the number of malnourished children in the developing world increased from 167 million to 188 million. And experts predict that the situation will only get worse as food production in the poorest countries continues to decline.

Deforestation, desertification, and soil erosion have devastating effects on food production. Where forests are cut down, the soils are washed or blown away. Where land is planted too often or grazed too long, it can no longer support crops or cattle.

Ironically, modern agriculture—the science of growing food—has had the greatest impact on the decline in the food supply. In the 1960s governments began encouraging nomads to settle in one place, to raise one cash crop instead of several, to herd only one kind of livestock, and the soils quickly became exhausted.

This "green revolution"—intensified farming of "improved crop varieties" with irrigation, chemicals, and pesticides—at first raised productivity, but the long-term results were just the opposite. According to Mostafa K. Tolba, former executive director of the United Nations' Environment Programme, the process "made agroecosystems increasingly artificial, unstable, and prone to rapid degradation."

Population growth and refugee migration add to the problems of environmental degradation. When the land becomes too crowded and the soil too exhausted to support life, farmers move into forests, slashing and burning new farms. As the land gives out, the people move on, again and again. Eventually, they find their way to the refugee camps.

At the 1972 United Nations Conference on the Human Environment in Stockholm, environmental issues were considered secondary to issues of economic development. But the 1968–74 drought in Ethiopia and the Sahel made it evident that the environmental costs of traditional economic development might be too high.

The Ethiopian government estimated that its highlands were then losing ap-

From *Audubon*, March/April 1993, pp. 54-63. © 1993 by the National Audubon Society. Reprinted by permission.

proximately 1 billion tons of soil a year through water and wind erosion. So when development experts convened at the United Nations Conference on Environment and Development (UNCED) last June, the agenda had changed. The environment had to be protected, it was decided. The diplomats finally recognized the simplest truth: The land that produces the food must be preserved.

The food web inextricably connects plants, animals, and people with the water, soil, and atmosphere of the planet; the hunger web begins as those connections are severed. Air and water pollution contaminate and ruin food sources. The predictions are that global warming will also have an effect, changing planting times, growing seasons, even the ability of crops to survive in their present ranges.

On the following pages *Audubon* examines the environmental causes of mass hunger and some possible solutions. Most do not involve high-tech, grand-scale megaprojects; the best of them are low-tech, local, modest in scale. The solutions may not be as dramatic as scenes of armies massing to feed millions. But they are sustainable—which means that in the future hunger may be defeated without the help of armies.

DEFORESTATION

Slash, Burn, Plow, Plant, Abandon

Forests now cover 27.7 percent of all ice-free land in the world. In 1990 wood was the main energy source for 9 out of 10 Africans, providing more than half of their fuel. By the end of this decade, according to Mostafa Tolba, 2.4 billion people will be unable to satisfy their minimum energy requirements without consuming wood faster than it is being grown.

As human beings encroach on the world's remaining woodlands, deforestation will exacerbate the problems of hunger. For when hillsides are denuded, soil erosion sets in.

In Haiti, where forests once covered most of the land, 40 to 50 million trees are cut each year to supply firewood, cropland, and charcoal. At the current rate of deforestation, Haiti's forests will cease to exist within two or three years.

Already, loss of forests has caused massive soil erosion, and when drought strikes, the quality of the remaining soil will decline. When rain finally *does* fall, runoff will be too rapid and farmers will be forced to abandon cultivation. Since the 1970s, food aid to Haiti has risen sevenfold.

In Bangladesh and India, deforestation has caused another kind of problem, increasing the frequency and force of floods. Bangladesh used to suffer a catastrophic flood every 50 years or so; by the 1980s the country was being hit with major floods—which wash away farms and rice paddies—every four years. Between the late 1960s and late 1980s, India's flood-prone areas grew from approximately 25 million hectares to 59 million. (One hectare equals 2.4 acres.)

PROTECT AND PRESERVE

Although some countries, notably Brazil and Costa Rica, have preserved tracts of their forested land, less than 5 percent of the world's remaining tropical forests are protected as sanctuaries, parks, or reserves.

Regenerating woodlands by replanting them would provide some measure of relief. Over the past 10 years, China has reforested some 70 million hectares of endangered landscape. The U.N. Food and Agriculture Organization estimates that 1.1 million hectares of trees are successfully planted each year worldwide.

Modifying wood stoves to make them more efficient and increasing use of solar cooking would slow the decline of forests by decreasing reliance on wood for fuel.

Using the forests sustainably—by tapping trees for rubber, for example, or developing environmentally sound tourism—would provide more revenue than slash-and-burn agriculture.

DESERTIFICATION
The Spreading Barrens

Every year nearly 6 million hectares of previously productive land becomes desert, losing its capacity to produce food. The United Nations defines desertification as "land degradation in arid, semiarid, and dry subhumid areas [drylands] resulting mainly from adverse human impact." Translated into human suffering, that phrase means that by 1977, 57 million people had seen their lands dry up. By 1984 the number had risen to 135 million worldwide. Today, one-sixth of the total world population is threatened with desertification.

When drylands—which make up about 43 percent of the total land area of the world—revert to desert, hunger follows almost axiomatically. Most crops can't survive in the parched land-scape, and harvests fail. Further, withered root systems can't hold the soil, and winds finally erode whatever topsoil remains.

Arid landscapes are so fragile that they break down quickly. A drought can mean catastrophe. In Mozambique, for instance, civil war combined with a worsening drought last year to leave 3.1 million people in need of food aid, 1.2 million more than in 1991.

But Africa is not the only place where food supplies are threatened by desertification. In Russia, annual desertification and sand encroachment northwest of the Caspian Sea were estimated to be as high as 10 percent. Around the drying Aral Sea, the desert has been growing at some 100,000 hectares per year for the last 25 years, an annual desertification rate of 4 percent.

STAVING OFF DISASTER

Agroforestry—planting trees as windbreaks and shade to protect pastureland—contributes to the maintenance of hard-used fields. In Kenya, for example, the Green Belt Movement has embarked on a large-scale tree-planting program.

Massive irrigation projects, such as those tried in Nigeria (see "Death of an Oasis," *Audubon* May-June 1992), are less practical, benefiting only a few at great cost to the environment. Small-scale projects, as low-tech and low-cost as collecting and managing rainwater, are often slow and laborious, but according to the Bread for the World Institute on Hunger and Development, they have succeeded in reclaiming hundreds of hectares of degraded land.

SOIL EROSION
A Worldwide Dust Bowl

Worldwide, erosion removes about 25.4 billion tons of soil each year. Deforestation and desertification both leave land open to erosion. In deforested areas, water washes down steep, naked slopes, taking the soil with it. In desertified regions, exposed soils, cleared for farming, building, or mining, or overgrazed by livestock, simply blow away. Wind erosion is most extensive in Africa and Asia. Blowing soil not only leaves a degraded area behind but can bury and kill vegetation where it settles. It will also fill drainage and irrigation ditches.

When high-tech farm practices are applied to poor lands, the result is often a combination of soil washing away and chemical pesticides and fertilizers polluting the runoff.

In Africa, soil erosion has reached critical levels, with farmers pushing farther onto deforested hillsides. In Ethiopia, for example, soil loss occurs at a rate of between 1.5 billion and 2 billion cubic meters a year, with some 4 million hectares of highlands considered "irreversibly degraded."

In Asia, in the eastern hills of Nepal, 38 percent of the land area consists of fields that have been abandoned because the topsoil has washed away. In the Western Hemisphere, Ecuador is losing soil at a rate 20 times what would be considered acceptable by the U.S. Soil and Conservation Service.

And even in the United States, 44 percent of cropland is affected by erosion.

DEFEATING THE ELEMENTS

According to the International Fund for Agricultural Development (IFAD), traditional labor-intensive, small-scale efforts at soil conservation—which combine maintenance of shrubs and trees with corp growing and cattle grazing—work best.

In the Barani area of Pakistan, a program begun by IFAD in 1980 to control rainfall runoff, erosion, and damage to rivers from siltation has resulted in a 20 to 30 percent increase in crop yields and livestock productivity.

POPULATION GROWTH
More Mouths to Feed

With a population growth rate of 1.7 percent, the world added almost 100 million people in 1992; an increase of some 3.7 billion is expected by 2030. Since 90 percent of the increase will occur in developing countries in Africa, Asia, and Latin America, the outlook is bleak: None of those countries can expect to produce enough food to feed a population increasing at such rates.

Population growth and environmental damage go hand in hand with poverty and hunger. In sub-Saharan Africa, for example, as colonial governments replaced pastoral lifestyles with sedentary farming, populations grew and farming and grazing intensified. Today, 80 percent of the region's pasture- and rangelands show signs of damage, and overall productivity is declining. Yet during the next 40 years the sub-Saharan population is expected to rise from 500 million to 1.5 billion.

Today only Bangladesh, South Korea, the Netherlands, and the island of Java have population densities greater than 400 people per square kilometer. (By comparison, the population density of the United States works out to 27 per square kilometer.)

By the middle of the next century, one-third of the world's population will probably live in overcrowded conditions. Bangladesh's population density could rise to 1,700 per square kilometer.

In Madagascar, population pressures have forced farmers to continuously clear new land. Virtually all the lowland forests in the country are gone. But cleared soil wears out quickly. Per capita calorie supply in Madagascar has fallen by 9 percent since the 1960s, probably the greatest decline anywhere in the world.

In Nepal, one of the world's poorest nations, increased population (700 people per square kilometer of cultivable land, the world's highest average) has forced villagers to expand their farm plots onto wooded hillsides. Marginal farmers rely on livestock, which they allow to graze in the remaining forests. Terraced soil once used for crop production has been abandoned for lack of nutrients, putting more pressure on ever-diminishing forest resources.

CHOOSING THE FUTURE

If a fertility rate of slightly more than two children per couple can be achieved by the year 2010, the world's population will stabilize at 7.7 billion by 2060. If that rate is not reached until 2065, world population will reach 14.2 billion by 2100.

According to a 1992 World Bank report, improving education for girls is an important long-term policy in the developing world. The more educated a woman is, the more likely she is to work outside the home and the smaller her family is likely to be. Choice also plays a role here: The United Nations' World Fertility Survey has found that women would have an average of 1.41 fewer children if they were able to choose the size of their family. Access to birth control methods could help lower the world's population by as many as 1.3 billion people over the next 35 years. During the Reagan-Bush years U.S. funding to programs offering such information was cut back; but President Bill Clinton has reversed that stand.

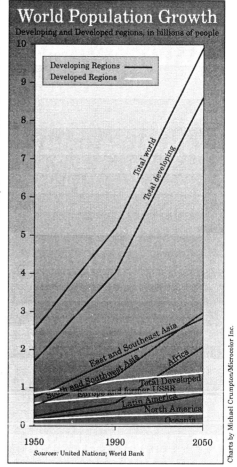

World Population Growth
Developing and Developed regions, in billions of people

Developing Regions
Developed Regions

Total world
Total developing
East and Southeast Asia
Africa
South and Southwest Asia
Europe and former USSR
Total Developed
Latin America
North America
Oceania

1950   1990   2050

Sources: United Nations; World Bank

Charts by Michael Crumpton/Microcolor Inc.

Somalia: An Ecopolitical Tragedy

Somalia's breakdown of law and order has created new waves of famine in recent months, but the groundwork for civil strife was laid by years of misuse of the nation's precious grazing lands and water resources.

Almost the entire country is categorized by the United Nations Environment Programme as susceptible to soil degradation, and most of the country is overgrazed.

Over the years the degradation was accelerated by the parceling out of communal grazing lands to private owners, which undermined traditional systems of land management. Private herds—which are generally larger than those owned communally—have stripped the hillsides bare, causing wind erosion during droughts and runoff during rains.

Building dams across valleys to halt water runoff in the north of the country has made matters worse by disrupting the natural drainage systems.

In the south the productivity of irrigated fields has been lessened by poor water management, which has created saline, waterlogged soils on the edge of the desert. There the salt will render the soil useless for food production in the decades to come.

—*Fred Pearce*

ENVIRONMENTAL REFUGEES
A Moveable Famine

The cycle of overpopulation, poverty, environmental ruin, and famine begins all over again when those trying to find a better life flee their ruined homelands. Land degradation is the largest cause of environmental-refugee movements.

According to Jodi L. Jacobson, a senior researcher at Worldwatch Institute, in Washington, D.C., 135 million people live in areas undergoing severe desertification.

But when those refugees move into areas that are already stressed by overpopulation or too intense agriculture, they place an added burden on the environment. Refugees need wood for fuel, water to drink, land on which to graze their livestock, and grain to eat—all of which are already scarce.

Jacobson estimates that some 10 million people worldwide are refugees from environmental ruin. "Competition for land and natural resources is driving more and more people to live in marginal, disaster-prone areas," she says, "leaving them more vulnerable to natural forces. Hence, millions of Bangladeshis live on *chars*, bars of silt and sand in the middle of the Bengal delta, some of which are washed away each year by ocean tides and monsoon floods."

CLIMATE CHANGE
Global Warning

Since 1800 atmospheric concentration of carbon dioxide (CO_2) has increased by about 25 percent and continues to rise each year. Over the same period atmospheric methane concentrations have doubled. Since the 1960s more than 100 separate studies have confirmed that a doubling of the CO_2 concentration would raise average surface temperatures by one to four degrees centigrade; three degrees is the figure used by the United Nations' Intergovernmental Panel on Climate Change.

Although a small number of scientists dispute these findings, weather and climate remain the biggest concern for farmers as warming begins to change growing seasons, irrigation needs, and land use. These changes will be especially serious in tropical regions, where farmland is already marginal and crops are growing near the limits of their temperature tolerance.

Those who live along shorelines will be hardest hit: The greenhouse effect could cause a global mean sea level rise of about six centimeters per decade. At that rate, many islands would become uninhabitable, and currently productive lowlands would be flooded. The developing countries that now experience the worst food shortages can expect to be hurt most by global warming. A study conducted by the University of Oxford and the Goddard Institute for Space Studies, funded by the U.S. Environmental Protection Agency, found that with an increase in average temperatures of three to four degrees centigrade, grain production in developing countries would decline by 9 to 11 percent by the year 2060, putting between 60 and 360 million people at risk from hunger—10 to 50 percent more than the currently predicted 640 million.

CLOSING THE GREENHOUSE

The use of renewable, or nonfossil, fuels—and more efficient use of all fuels—would go far to control the buildup of CO_2.

The World Bank recommends that governments remove energy subsidies and that they tax the use of carbon fuels. Maintenance of the world's large remaining forests would also help: Tropical deforestation accounts for 10 to 30 percent of the CO_2 released into the atmosphere.

The Oxford–Goddard Institute study found that slowing population increases could allow developing nations to cope more readily with the changing climate by changing land use and farming practices.

Hunger and the Ozone Hole

In early 1992 researchers from five U.S. marine-science institutes reported a drop of 6 to 12 percent in phytoplankton production under the Antarctic ozone hole. It appears that tiny marine organisms, which constitute more than half of all biomass on earth, may not be able to withstand harmful wavelengths of ultraviolet light—UV-B radiation—that penetrate the earth's thinning ozone layer.

When ozone holes form in the spring, most of the fish, shellfish, and crustaceans that humans harvest are in their larval, planktonic stages—floating in the topmost layer of the ocean. "Increasing intensities of UV-B radiation near the surface could negatively impact the reproductive potential of some of our most valuable marine resources, including tuna, pollock, cod, halibut, and flounder," wrote John Hardy, an associate professor at Huxley College, Western Washington University, in the November 1989 issue of *Oceanography*. Juvenile crabs, lobsters, shrimp, and anchovies are also vulnerable.

Just how such damage might move up the food chain is not known, but in Newport, Oregon, the Environmental Protection Agency's stratospheric ozone–depletion team found preliminary evidence of retarded growth in amphipods fed with phytoplankton that had been exposed to UV-B.

Although the leading industrial nations have agreed to halt production of the worst ozone-destroying compounds by 1996, ozone depletion is expected to continue for several decades as existing chemicals seep into the stratosphere. An ozone hole is likely to appear over the Northern Hemisphere, where ozone is dwindling at an estimated 1 percent per year. Each 1 percent decline in ozone is thought to increase exposure to biologically harmful ultraviolet light by at least 2 percent.

The United Nations Environment Programme warns that a 16 percent reduction in stratospheric ozone (which could occur in the next few years) would trigger a 6 to 9 percent drop in seafood production. Oceans now provide more than 30 percent of the animal protein eaten by humans.

—Brad Warren

Can the Growing Human Population Feed Itself?

*As human numbers surge toward
10 billion, some experts are alarmed,
others optimistic. Who is right?*

John Bongaarts

JOHN BONGAARTS has been vice president and director of the Research Division of the Population Council in New York City since 1989. He is currently a member of the Johns Hopkins Society of Scholars and the Royal Dutch Academy of Sciences. He won the Mindel Sheps Award in 1986 from the Population Association of America and the Research Career Development Award in 1980–85 from the National Institutes of Health.

Demographers now project that the world's population will double during the next half century, from 5.3 billion people in 1990 to more than 10 billion by 2050. How will the environment and humanity respond to this unprecedented growth? Expert opinion divides into two camps. Environmentalists and ecologists, whose views have widely been disseminated by the electronic and print media, regard the situation as a catastrophe in the making. They argue that in order to feed the growing population farmers must intensify agricultural practices that already cause grave ecological damage. Our natural resources and the environment, now burdened by past population growth, will simply collapse under the weight of this future demand.

The optimists, on the other hand, comprising many economists as well as some agricultural scientists, assert that the earth can readily produce more than enough food for the expected population in 2050. They contend that technological innovation and the continued investment of human capital will deliver high standards of living to much of the globe, even if the population grows much larger than the projected 10 billion. Which point of view will hold sway? What shape might the

future of our species and the environment actually take?

Many environmentalists fear that world food supply has reached a precarious state: "Human numbers are on a collision course with massive famines.... If humanity fails to act, nature will end the population explosion for us—in very unpleasant ways—well before 10 billion is reached," write Paul R. Ehrlich and Anne H. Ehrlich of Stanford University in their 1990 book *The Population Explosion.* In the long run, the Ehrlichs and like-minded experts consider substantial growth in food production to be absolutely impossible. "We are feeding ourselves at the expense of our children. By definition farmers can overplow and overpump only in the short run. For many farmers the short run is drawing to a close," states Lester R. Brown, president of the Worldwatch Institute, in a 1988 paper.

Over the past three decades, these authors point out, enormous efforts and resources have been pooled to amplify agricultural output. Indeed, the total quantity of harvested crops increased dramatically during this time. In the developing world, food production rose by an average of 117 percent in the quarter of a century between 1965 and 1990. Asia performed far better than other regions, which saw increases below average.

Because population has expanded rapidly as well, per capita food production has generally shown only modest change; in Africa it actually declined. As a consequence, the number of undernourished people is still rising in most parts of the developing world, although that number did fall from 844 million to 786 million during the 1980s. But this decline reflects improved nutritional conditions in Asia alone. During the

same period, the number of people having energy-deficient diets in Latin America, the Near East and Africa climbed.

Many social factors can bring about conditions of hunger, but the pessimists emphasize that population pressure on fragile ecosystems plays a significant role. One specific concern is that we seem to be running short on land suitable for cultivation. If so, current efforts to bolster per capita food production by clearing more fertile land will find fewer options. Between 1850 and 1950 the amount of arable land grew quickly to accommodate both larger populations and greater demand for better diets. This expansion then slowed and by the late 1980s ceased altogether. In the developed world, as well as in some developing countries (especially China), the amount of land under cultivation started to decline during the 1980s. This drop is largely because spreading urban centers have engulfed fertile land or, once the land is depleted, farmers have abandoned it. Farmers have also fled from irrigated land that has become unproductive because of salt accumulation.

Moreover, environmentalists insist that soil erosion is destroying much of the land that is left. The extent of the damage is the subject of controversy. A recent global assessment, sponsored by the United Nations Environment Program and reported by the World Resources Institute and others, offers some perspective. The study concludes that 17 percent of the land supporting plant life worldwide has lost value over the past 45 years. The estimate includes erosion caused by water and wind, as well as chemical and physical deterioration, and ranks the degree of soil degradation from light to severe. This degradation is least prevalent in North

Chronically Undernourished Individuals

Crop Yields Needed in 2050

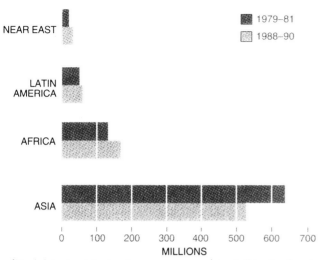

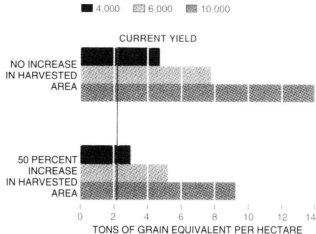

INCIDENCE OF CHRONIC UNDERNUTRITION fell in the developing world from an estimated 844 million sufferers in 1979 to 786 million in 1990, showing evidence of dramatic nutritional improvements in Asia (*left*). Agricultural productivity must improve to continue this trend (*right*). Even if more land is harvested in 2050, the average yield must rise sharply as well to offer the projected Third World population of 8.7 billion the current diet of 4,000 gross calories per day.

America (5.3 percent) and most widespread in Central America (25 percent), Europe (23 percent), Africa (22 percent) and Asia (20 percent). In most of these regions, the average farmer could not gather the resources necessary to restore moderate and severely affected soil regions to full productivity. Therefore, prospects for reversing the effects of soil erosion are not good, and it is likely that this problem will worsen.

Despite the loss and degradation of fertile land, the "green revolution" has promoted per capita food production by increasing the yield per hectare. The new, high-yielding strains of grains such as wheat and rice have proliferated since their introduction in the 1960s, especially in Asia. To reap full advantage from these new crop varieties, however, farmers must apply abundant quantities of fertilizer and water.

Environmentalists question whether further conversion to such crops can be achieved at reasonable cost, especially in the developing world, where the gain in production is most needed. At the moment, farmers in Asia, Latin America and Africa use fertilizer sparingly, if at all, because it is too expensive or unavailable. Fertilizer use in the developed world has recently waned. The reasons for the decline are complex and may be temporary, but clearly farmers in North America and Europe have decided that increasing their already heavy application of fertilizer will not further enhance crop yields.

Unfortunately, irrigation systems, which would enable many developing countries to join in the green revolu-

tion, are often too expensive to build. In most areas, irrigation is essential for generating higher yields. It also can make arid land cultivable and protect farmers from the vulnerability inherent in natural variations in the weather. Land brought into cultivation this way could be used for growing multiple crop varieties, thereby helping food production to increase.

Such advantages have been realized since the beginning of agriculture: the earliest irrigation systems are thousands of years old. Yet only a fraction of productive land in the developing world is now irrigated, and its expansion has been slower than population growth. Consequently, the amount of irrigated land per capita has been dwindling during recent decades. The trend, pessimists argue, will be hard to stop. Irrigation systems have been built in the most affordable sites, and the hope for extending them is curtailed by rising costs. Moreover, the accretion of silt in dams and reservoirs and of salt in already irrigated soil is increasingly costly to avoid or reverse.

Environmentalists Ehrlich and Ehrlich note that modern agriculture is by nature at risk wherever it is practiced. The genetic uniformity of single, high-yielding crop strains planted over large areas makes them highly productive but also renders them particularly vulnerable to insects and disease. Current preventive tactics, such as spraying pesticides and rotating crops, are only partial solutions. Rapidly evolving pathogens pose a continuous challenge. Plant breeders must maintain a broad

genetic arsenal of crops by collecting and storing natural varieties and by breeding new ones in the laboratory.

The optimists do not deny that many problems exist within the food supply system. But many of these authorities, including D. Gale Johnson, the late Herman Kahn, Walter R. Brown, L. Martel, the late Roger Revelle, Vaclav Smil and Julian L. Simon, believe the world's food supply can dramatically be expanded. Ironically, they draw their enthusiasm from extrapolation of the very trends that so alarm those experts who expect doom. In fact, statistics show that the average daily caloric intake per capita climbed by 21 percent (from 2,063 calories to 2,495 calories) between 1965 and 1990 in the developing countries. These higher calories have generally delivered greater amounts of protein. On average, the per capita consumption of protein rose from 52 grams per day to 61 grams per day between 1965 and 1990.

According to the optimists, not only has the world food situation improved significantly in recent decades, but further growth can be brought about in various ways. A detailed assessment of climate and soil conditions in 93 developing countries (excluding China) shows that nearly three times as much land as is currently farmed, or an additional 2.1 billion hectares, could be cultivated. Regional soil estimates indicate that sub-Saharan Africa and Latin America can exploit many more stretches of unused land than can Asia, the Near East and North Africa.

117

3. NATURAL RESOURCES: Food and Hunger

Even in regions where the amount of potentially arable land is limited, crops could be grown more times every year than is currently the case. This scenario is particularly true in the tropics and subtropics where conditions are such—relatively even temperature throughout the year and a consistent distribution of daylight hours—that more than one crop would thrive. Nearly twice as many crops are harvested every year in Asia than in Africa at present, but further increases are possible in all regions.

In addition to multicropping, higher yields per crop are attainable, especially in Africa and the Near East. Many more crops are currently harvested per hectare in the First World than elsewhere: cereal yields in North America and Europe averaged 4.2 tons per hectare, compared with 2.9 in the Far East (4.2 in China), 2.1 in Latin America, 1.7 in the Near East and only 1.0 in Africa.

Such yield improvements, the enthusiasts note, can be achieved by expanding the still limited use of high-yield crop varieties, fertilizer and irrigation.

The Potential Impact of Global Warming on Agriculture

The scientific evidence on the greenhouse effect indicates that slow but significant global warming is likely to occur if the emission of greenhouse gases, such as carbon dioxide, methane, nitrogen oxide and chlorofluorocarbons, continues to grow. Agriculture is directly or, at least in some cases, indirectly responsible for releasing a substantial proportion of these gases. Policy responses to the potentially adverse consequences of global climatic change now focus primarily on hindering emissions rather than on halting them. But considering the present need to improve living standards and produce more food for vast numbers of people, experts doubt that even a reduction in global emissions could occur in the near future.

In a 1990 study the Intergovernmental Panel on Climate Change estimated that over the next century the average global temperature will rise by three degrees Celsius. The study assumes that agriculture will expand considerably. This forecast of temperature change is uncertain, but there is now broad agreement that some global warming will take place. All the same, the effect that temperature rise will have on human society remains an open question.

Global warming could either enhance or impede agriculture, suggest Cynthia Rosenzweig of Columbia University and Martin L. Parry of the University of Oxford. Given sufficient water and light, increased ambient carbon dioxide concentrations absorbed during photosynthesis could act as a fertilizer and facilitate growth in certain plants. In addition, by extending the time between the last frost in the spring and the first frost in the fall, global warming will benefit agriculture in cold regions where the growing season is short, such as in Canada and northern areas of Europe and the former Soviet Union. Moreover, warmer air holds more water vapor, and so global warming will bring about more evaporation and precipitation. Areas where crop production is limited by arid conditions would benefit from a wetter climate.

If increased evaporation from soil and plants does not coincide with more rainfall in a region, however, more frequent dry spells and droughts would occur. And a further rise in temperature will reduce crop yields in tropical and subtropical areas, where certain crops are already grown near their limit of heat tolerance. Furthermore, some cereal crops need low winter temperatures to initiate flowering. Warmer winters in temperate regions could therefore stall growing periods and lead to reduced harvests. Finally, global warming will precipitate a thermal swelling of the oceans and melt polar ice. Higher sea levels may claim low-lying farmland and cause higher salt concentrations in the coastal groundwater.

Techniques used to model the climate are not sufficiently advanced to predict the balance of these effects in specific areas. The most recent analysis on the impact of climatic change on the world food supply, by Rosenzweig and Parry in 1992, concludes that average global food production will decline 5 percent by 2060. And they anticipate a somewhat larger drop in the developing world, thus exacerbating the problems expected to arise in attempts to feed growing populations. In contrast, their report predicts a slight rise in agricultural output in developed countries situated at middle and high latitudes.

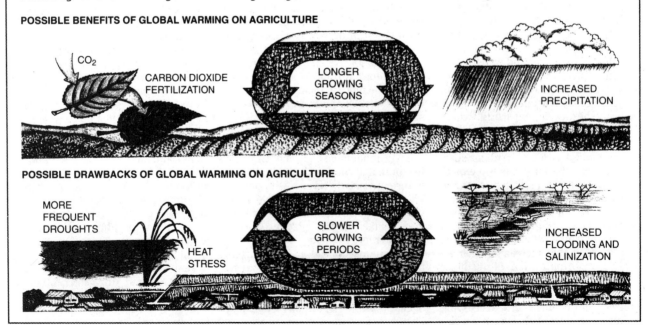

POSSIBLE BENEFITS OF GLOBAL WARMING ON AGRICULTURE

CO$_2$ — CARBON DIOXIDE FERTILIZATION — LONGER GROWING SEASONS — INCREASED PRECIPITATION

POSSIBLE DRAWBACKS OF GLOBAL WARMING ON AGRICULTURE

MORE FREQUENT DROUGHTS — HEAT STRESS — SLOWER GROWING PERIODS — INCREASED FLOODING AND SALINIZATION

Change in Food Production between 1965 and 1990

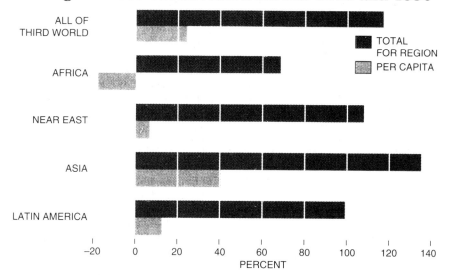

Soil Erosion of Vegetated Land

Arable Land

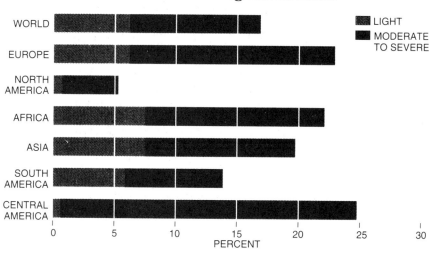

TOTAL FOOD PRODUCTION rose nearly 120 percent between 1965 and 1990 in the developing world. Per capita food production showed little change in regions outside Asia (*top*). Soil erosion has debased much of the land worldwide on which that food was produced (*middle*). But many Third World nations have vast holdings that could be farmed successfully if given more water and fertilizer (*bottom*).

In *World Agriculture: Toward 2000*, Nikos Alexandratos of the Food and Agriculture Organization (FAO) of the United Nations reports that only 34 percent of all seeds planted during the mid-1980s were high-yielding varieties. Statistics from the FAO show that at present only about one in five hectares of arable land is irrigated, and very little fertilizer is used. Pesticides are sparsely applied. Food output could drastically be increased simply by more widespread implementation of such technologies.

Aside from producing more food, many economists and agriculturalists point out, consumption levels in the developing world could be boosted by wasting fewer crops, as well as by cutting storage and distribution losses. How much of an increase would these measures yield? Robert W. Kates, director of the Alan Shawn Feinstein World Hunger Program at Brown University, writes in *The Hunger Report: 1988* that humans consume only 60 percent of all harvested crops, and some 25 to 30 percent is lost before reaching individual homes. The FAO, on the other hand, estimates lower distribution losses: 6 percent for cereals, 11 percent for roots and 5 percent for pulses. All the same, there is no doubt that improved storage and distribution systems would leave more food available for human nutrition, independent of future food production capabilities.

For optimists, the long-range trend in food prices constitutes the most convincing evidence for the correctness of their view. In 1992–93 the World Resources Institute reported that food prices dropped further than the price of most nonfuel commodities, all of which have declined in the past decade. Cereal prices in the international market fell by approximately one third between 1980 and 1989. Huge government subsidies for agriculture in North America and western Europe, and the resulting surpluses of agricultural products, have depressed prices. Obviously, the optimists assert, the supply already exceeds the demand of a global population that has doubled since 1950.

Taken together, this evidence leads many experts to see no significant obstacles to raising levels of nutrition for world populations exceeding 10 billion people. The potential for an enormous expansion of food production exists, but its realization depends of course on sensible governmental policies, increased domestic and international trade and large investments in infrastructure and agricultural extension. Such improvements can be achieved, the optimists believe, without incurring irreparable damage to global ecosystems.

Proponents of either of these conflicting perspectives have difficulty accepting the existence of other plausible points of view. Moreover, the polarity between the two sides of expert opinion shows that neither group can be completely correct. Finding some common ground between these seemingly irreconcilable positions is not as difficult as it at first appears if empirical issues are emphasized and important differences in value systems and political beliefs are ignored.

Both sides agree that the demand for food will swell rapidly over the next several decades. In 1990 a person living in the developing world ate on average 2,500 calories each day, taken from 4,000 gross calories of food crops made available within a household. The remaining 1,500 calories from this gross total not used to meet nutritional requirements were either lost, inedible or used as animal feed and plant seed. Most of this food was harvested from 0.7 billion hectares of land in the developing world. The remaining 5 percent of the total food supply came from imports. To sustain this 4,000-gross-calorie diet for more than twice as many residents, or 8.7 billion people, living in the developing world by 2050, agriculture must offer 112 percent more crops. To raise the average Third World diet to 6,000 gross calories per day, slightly above the 1990 world average, food production would need to increase by 218 percent. And to bring the average Third World diet to a level comparable with that currently found in the developed world, or 10,000 gross calories per day, food production would have to surge by 430 percent.

A more generous food supply will be achieved in the future through boosting crop yields, as it has been accomplished in the past. If the harvested area in the developing world remains at 0.7 billion hectares, then each hectare must more than double its yield to maintain an already inadequate diet for the future population of the developing world. Providing a diet equivalent to a First World diet in 1990 would require that each hectare increase its yield more than six times. Such an event in the developing world must be considered virtually impossible, barring a major breakthrough in the biotechnology of food production.

Instead farmers will no doubt plant more acres and grow more crops per year on the same land to help augment crop harvests. Extrapolation of past trends suggests that the total harvested area will increase by about 50 percent by the year 2050. Each hectare will then have to provide nearly 50 percent more tons of grain or its equivalent to keep up with current dietary levels. Improved diets could result only from much larger yields.

The technological optimists are correct in stating that overall world food production can substantially be increased over the next few decades. Current crop yields are well below their theoretical maxima, and only about 11 percent of the world's farmable land is now under cultivation. Moreover, the experience gained recently in a number of developing countries, such as China, holds important lessons on how to tap this potential elsewhere. Agricultural productivity responds to well-designed policies that assist farmers by supplying needed fertilizer and other inputs, building sound infrastructure and providing market access. Further investments in agricultural research will spawn new technologies that will fortify agriculture in the future. The vital question then is not how to grow more food but rather how to implement agricultural methods that may make possible a boost in food production.

A more troublesome problem is how to achieve this technological enhancement at acceptable environmental costs. It is here that the arguments of those experts who forecast a catastrophe carry considerable weight. There can be no doubt that the land now used for growing food crops is generally of better quality than unused, potentially cultivable land. Similarly, existing irrigation systems have been built on the most favorable sites. Consequently, each new measure applied to increase yields is becoming more expensive to implement, especially in the developed world and parts of the developing world such as China, where productivity is already high. In short, such constraints are raising the marginal cost of each additional ton of grain or its equivalent. This tax is even higher if one takes into account negative externalities—primarily environmental costs not reflected in the price of agricultural products.

The environmental price of what in the Ehrlichs' view amounts to "turning the earth into a giant human feedlot" could be severe. A large inflation of agriculture to provide growing populations with improved diets is likely to lead to widespread deforestation, loss of species, soil erosion and pollution from pesticides, and runoff of fertilizer as farming intensifies and new land is brought into production. Reducing or minimizing this environmental impact is possible but costly.

Given so many uncertainties, the course of future food prices is difficult to chart. At the very least, the rising marginal cost of food production will engender steeper prices on the international market than would be the case if there were no environmental constraints. Whether these higher costs can offset the historical decline in food prices remains to be seen. An upward trend in the price of food sometime in the near future is a distinct possibility. Such a hike will be mitigated by the continued development and application of new technology and by the likely recovery of agricultural production and exports in the former Soviet Union, eastern Europe and Latin America. Also, any future price increases could be lessened by taking advantage of the underutilized agricultural resources in North America, notes Per Pinstrup-Andersen of Cornell University in his 1992 paper "Global Perspectives for Food Production and Consumption." Rising prices will have little effect on high-income countries or on households possessing reasonable purchasing power, but the poor will suffer.

In reality, the future of global food production is neither as grim as the pessimists believe nor as rosy as the optimists claim. The most plausible outcome is that dietary intake will creep higher in most regions. Significant annual fluctuations in food availability and prices are, of course, likely; a variety of factors, including the weather, trade interruptions and the vulnerability of monocropping to pests, can alter food supply anywhere. The expansion of agriculture will be achieved by boosting crop yields and by using existing farmland more intensively, as well as by bringing arable land into cultivation where such action proves economical. Such events will transpire more slowly than in the past, however, because of environmental constraints. In addition, the demand for food in the developed world is approaching saturation levels. In the U.S., mounting concerns about health have caused the per capita consumption of calories from animal products to drop.

Still, progress will be far from uniform. Numerous countries will struggle to overcome unsatisfactory nutrition levels. These countries fall into three main categories. Some low-income countries have little or no reserves of fertile land or water. The absence of agricultural resources is in itself not an insurmountable problem, as is demonstrated by regions, such as Hong Kong and Kuwait, that can purchase their food on the international market. But many poor countries, such as Bangladesh, cannot afford to buy food from abroad and thereby compensate for insufficient natural resources. These countries will probably rely more on food aid in the future.

Low nutrition levels are also found in many countries, such as Zaire, that do possess large reserves of potentially cultivable land and water. Government neglect of agriculture and policy failures have typically caused poor diets in such countries. A recent World Bank report describes the damaging effects of direct and indirect taxation of agriculture, controls placed on prices and market access, and overvalued currencies, which discourage exports and encourage imports. Where agricultural production has suffered from misguided government intervention (as is particularly the case in Africa), the solution—policy reform—is clear.

Food aid will be needed as well in areas rife with political instability and civil strife. The most devastating famines of the past decade, known to television viewers around the world, have occurred in regions fighting prolonged civil wars, such as Ethiopia, Somalia and the Sudan. In many of these cases, drought was instrumental in stirring social and political disruption. The addition of violent conflict prevented the recuperation of agriculture and the distribution of food, thus turning bad but remediable situations into disasters. International military intervention, as in Somalia, provides only a short-term remedy. In the absence of sweeping political compromise, hunger and malnutrition will remain endemic in these war-torn regions.

Feeding a growing world population a diet that improves over time in quality and quantity is technologically feasible. But the economic and environmental costs incurred through bolstering food production may well prove too great for many poor countries. The course of events will depend crucially on their governments' ability to design and enforce effective policies that address the challenges posed by mounting human numbers, rising poverty and environmental degradation. Whatever the outcome, the task ahead will be made more difficult if population growth rates cannot be reduced.

FURTHER READING

POVERTY AND HUNGER: ISSUES AND OPTIONS FOR FOOD SECURITY IN DEVELOPING COUNTRIES. World Bank, 1986.

ENERGY, FOOD, ENVIRONMENT: REALITIES, MYTHS, OPTIONS. Vaclav Smil. Clarendon Press, 1987.

WORLD AGRICULTURE: TOWARD 2000. Nikos Alexandratos. New York University Press, 1988.

WORLD RESOURCES 1992-93. World Resources Institute. Oxford University Press, 1992.

Crowded out

Population-control advocates are often dismissed as racist and paranoid. But they increasingly have the facts on their side.

Will Nixon

Will Nixon is associate editor of E *Magazine.*

Americans always imagine that the disaster of overpopulation lies somewhere in the future, as in the 1973 science fiction movie *Soylent Green,* which envisioned a world so crowded that giant scoopers had to clear people like dirt from city squares. But we could just as easily look to the past. "Countryside hovels teemed with young children. . . . In the larger cities, a floating population of tens of thousands of unemployed slept on the ground overnight and poured into the streets the next day. Jails, pauper houses, foundling hospitals and lunatic asylums were packed with human casualties who had not yet arrived at their common grave," writes Yale historian Paul Kennedy in *Preparing for the Twenty-First Century.*

Kennedy is describing Europe in 1798, when the Caucasian population explosion was contributing to the social ferment of the French Revolution and inspiring Thomas Malthus to write *An Essay on the Principle of Population.* The Puritan professor was wrong about many things, such as failing to foresee the acceptance of contraception. But he was right to fear the potential gap between the exponential growth of human population and the linear growth of the food supply.

Malthus remains with us today mainly as an epithet cast at those who worry too publicly about the dangers of the world's rapidly growing population. Alexander Cockburn, in a series of columns in *The Nation* this year, has caricatured the new Malthusians as racist "overlords" eager to lock the gates against the world's poor and to promote sterilization as the cure for welfare. Cockburn writes in satirical

extremes, but many on the left still assume that "population" must be a code word for something sinister, masking the real issue of the distribution of wealth in the world. Once people in developing countries unshackle themselves from multinational capitalism and rise out of poverty, they will naturally have fewer children, or so the left claims. We should call for new economics, not new biology.

But the new Malthusians are hardly ogres—or even necessarily capitalists. In the debates over population, ideological lines are hardly so clear-cut; indeed, the most strident attacks on population control have come from Lyndon LaRouche. (In a recent full-page ad in the *Washington Post Weekly Edition,* LaRouche's Schiller Institute predicts "a new era of deliberate, global depopulation which will far surpass in savagery even Hitler's dreams.") Many on the right, only a little less stridently, dismiss concerns with population as disguised attempts to push an agenda of abortion and social control. Most capitalists, looking on people as potential customers, have no more interest in controlling population growth than Cockburn does.

The new Malthusians, often biologists by profession, simply do not share the common faith that humans are somehow exempt from the natural forces that lead other species to surge and collapse. At the least, they suggest that continued rapid population growth will add tremendous strains to the social problems we already have, from employment to ethnic strife to environmental degradation. The great spread of people is already causing the largest wave of extinctions since a meteor crash caused the death of the dinosaurs 65 million years ago. At the worst, the new Malthusians foresee a crash in the human population in the next century if we don't take steps right now

to change our reproductive behavior. It's this aura of apocalypse more than anything else, I think, that has made them pariahs. I don't care for the bleakness, either, especially if it comes tinged with misanthropy, but they are addressing one of the fundamental issues of our time.

The world today has 5.5 billion people, and the population grows by some 90 million each year. By the year 2000, the population of the world will likely top 6.2 billion. By the middle of the next century, according to United Nations estimates, population could reach 8 to 12 billion, depending on how quickly fertility rates drop. The International Conference on Population and Development, which is meeting in Cairo this month [Sept. 1994], has drafted a plan of action to steer us to the lower target. After 30 years of experience in the field, family planners believe we now know how to lower fertility rates. It doesn't require the redistribution of wealth so much as the empowerment of women—improved education for girls and women, better maternal health care, the freedom to choose the size of one's family. Only a decade ago, many feminists bristled at the concept of "population control"; now their ideas form the center of the debate. The major opposition to the conference now comes from the Vatican, which opposes abortion and birth control.

In the preparatory meetings for Cairo, the planners paid no attention to the neo-Malthusians. "The purpose of the conference is to bury Malthus, not to praise him," says Alex Marshall, who handles media for the United Nations Population Fund. The delegates have rejected the doomsday scenarios, dismissing "carrying capacity" and "optimum human populations" as fuzzy science at best, full of latent value judgments about how others should live. "In the Netherlands, people live comfortably with a density similar to that in Bangladesh," he says. And the population surge is not a spigot we can simply turn off because someone says the world would be a better place with 2 billion inhabitants. "No conceivable natural or human disaster is going to make much of a dent" in the growing wave toward 8 billion people, Marshall says, so conference delegates have focused on what the world can do to hold population growth to this level.

But the vital question that won't be debated at Cairo is whether the planet can even support 8 billion people. In the early '70s, Paul Ehrlich's book *The Population Bomb* galvanized the public by raising the specter of mass famine and impending scarcities of raw materials. His argument still thrives, albeit revised and refined, but the warning that struck a chord this year was Robert Kaplan's

"The Coming Anarchy" in the February *Atlantic Monthly*. Kaplan doesn't write about starvation or shortages; instead, he suggests that the environment will become "*the* national-security issue of the 21st century," because "surging populations, spreading disease, deforestation and soil erosion, water depletion [and] air pollution" will exacerbate the tensions between countries and between governments and their people. In West Africa, all too many people have egg-yolk eyes from repeated bouts of malaria, guards escort diners at restaurants across the sidewalk to their cars and bandits control the countryside. Kaplan foresees the same for much of the developing world. "We are entering a bifurcated world," he writes. "Part of the globe is inhabited by Hegel's and Fukuyama's Last Man, healthy, well fed and pampered by technology. The other,

larger, part is inhabited by Hobbes' First Man, condemned to a life that is 'nasty, brutish, and short.' Although both parts will be threatened by environmental stress, the Last Man will be able to master it; the First Man will not."

Overpopulation, Kaplan's article suggested, does not simply mean the starving children on UNICEF posters; it also means gun-wielding Somali teens dragging the bodies of their victims through the streets. "In the developing world," he writes, "environmental stress will present people with a choice that is increasingly among totalitarianism (as in Iraq), fascist-tending mini-states (as in Serb-held Bosnia) and road-warrior cultures (as in Somalia)." Two months after the article appeared, Rwanda, the most densely populated country in Africa, erupted in genocidal chaos, grisly coda to Kaplan's argument.

A sea change in U.S. policy

In what one leading advocate described as an "exceptionally important moment" in world population control, President Clinton recently announced a major shift in U.S. policy. At a State Department speech in July, the president declared that Washington—the world's leading contributor to population-control efforts—would no longer merely emphasize family planning.

Citing research showing that educated and empowered women have fewer babies, Clinton declared that "at the top of our agenda will be active support for the efforts to invest in the women of the world." He outlined a plan of action that called for equal education for girls, full rights of citizenship for women and the end of discrimination against women at home and in the workplace.

The speech didn't get Clinton much play in the American press; population control is generally considered too mushy for hard-nosed news editors. Nor did Clinton's bold new vision—endorsing prevention through universally available contraception and women's economic and social empowerment—endear him to powerful domestic lobbies, including the Roman Catholic Church, conservative Republicans and pro-life activists.

Much to their chagrin, Clinton expressed the hope that "new, high-quality, voluntary family planning and reproductive programs" would be available to

every person worldwide in just a few years. "Parents must have the right to decide freely and responsibly the number and spacing of their children," he claimed, endorsing the draft plan of action for this month's U.N. population conference in Cairo.

Many advocates in the field of sustainable development and population policy are pleased with the president's new policy. "I've been in this business 25 years, but in my entire career this was perhaps the most exceptionally important moment, says Adrienne Germain of the International Women's Health Coalition. "The president made clear the sea change in U.S. policy," "This field has never before dealt directly with the issues of sex and power relations."

But even some within the population community are concerned about Clinton's new approach, fearing that it strays too far afield from the concrete mechanics of family planning. They point out that the notion of full empowerment of women may seem abstract, even frivolous, when Third World women may be more concerned about feeding themselves and their families.

Still, Tim Wirth, a former Colorado senator who is now the State Department official in charge of formulating U.S. population-control policy, believes that empowerment of women is the necessary prerequisite to stabilizing population

growth. "In too many parts of the world, girls are fed less, given less medical care, withdrawn from school earlier and forced into hard labor sooner than boys," says Wirth. "And, although they perform an estimated 60 percent of the world's work, women own only 1 percent of the world's land and earn just 10 percent of the world's income."

The administration's makeover of U.S. population policy will have a ripple effect around the world. The United States is the single-largest contributor to population activities, earmarking $585 million in this year's budget for population stabilization. And the U.S. delegation to Cairo, led by Bella Abzug and comprised mostly of women, will loudly advocate the new themes of universally available contraception and the empowerment of women.

The developing world does want the United States' money. But lectures on stabilizing population irritate some leaders, who charge that the developed world's greedy consumption is more a threat to the Earth than Third World population booms. Notes another participant at the State Department event, Chief Bisi Ogunleye of Nigeria: "It is time for the rich to share their riches. If you don't, the poor will share their poverty."

—April Oliver (Sarah Colt contributed research to this article.)

3. NATURAL RESOURCES: Food and Hunger

Cockburn devoted two columns to calling Kaplan a racist, the U.N.'s Marshall wrote a letter to the *Atlantic* pointing out all the good that developing nations have accomplished, and many others read Kaplan as a dour traveller who looked upon all the countries he visited with a jaundiced eye. I'm not so sure. From Haiti to Somalia, from Chiapas to the Philippines, we see rural people in violent crises, with surging populations and declining natural resources. These people have been punished, too, by cruel politics and exploitative economics, but they still face the sheer crowding of the land. And, as Paul Kennedy has argued, these people don't really have the same options that Europeans had in Malthus' time: there's no undeveloped New World to which they can migrate.

The true pessimists in the debate are the naturalists watching the wild Earth vanish under the sprawl of people, who are consuming natural resources much faster than nature can possibly replenish them. "In the world where I spend my time—[among] thousands of people who are mostly scientists—there is no controversy," says Donella Meadows, who teaches environmental studies at Dartmouth College. "There is a hands-up-in-the-air helplessness. They expect a vast and terrible crash, and they can do nothing about it."

Meadows worked with the team that produced *The Limits to Growth* in 1972 and *Beyond the Limits* in 1992, two landmark studies that used computer models to predict future collisions over the next century between an economy geared to unlimited growth and a planet with limited resources. Since the industrial revolution, she notes, we have lost half of the world's wetlands and half of its tropical forests. Traditional economists have countered *Limits* by insisting that the

market can handle the problems of environmental overuse: as resources grow scarce, the economists argue, they grow more expensive, spurring technological innovations that allow us new alternatives. But rising prices can just as easily set off a feeding frenzy—as capitalists and poachers chase after the last rhinos and tigers, virgin redwoods and tropical teak trees.

So far, society has survived the shortages and the environmental stresses, but computer scenarios suggest that eventually our luck will run out: the various crises will come to a head all at once. "[T]he world system does not run out of land or food or resources or pollution absorption capability," Meadows warns, *"it runs out of the ability to cope."* And so, like any other species that exceeds the carrying capacity of its ecosystem, we face the prospect of a catastrophic population collapse—unless we can stabilize the world population at 8 billion or so.

David Pimental, an agricultural expert at Cornell University, dismisses 8 billion as a virtual sentence of poverty. His studies suggest that an "optimum human population" of 2 billion could be reached by 2100. "And I'm the optimist," he insists. "I've heard of three other studies that project 500 to 600 million." Pimental sees land as the ultimate limit. Each person needs about 0.5 hectares of cropland to provide themselves a nutritious diet of plants and animals, he notes. While some countries—such as the United States—have more than enough land to feed their current inhabitants, the world average is only about half this amount, which partly explains why 1.2 to 2 billion people live in poverty. To keep up with 90 million new mouths to feed each year and to replace the farmland spoiled by erosion, desertification or acidification, we will need to clear about 15

million hectares of forests a year for new cropland. We can't do that forever.

But the real crunch will come after we've run out of fossil fuels. We'll have to rely on biomass fuels from plants and trees, as well as on photovoltaic panels that directly generate electricity. Both technologies take up a great deal of room. A city of 100,000 people would need some 200,000 hectares of forests for fuel or 2,700 hectares for solar panels. Pimental suggests that the world population would have to drop to 2 billion in order for the planet to support all of its citizens at the standard of living now enjoyed by present-day Europeans. But he doubts that the world will take such drastic steps to lower its birthrates.

Some people in the family planning field dismiss Meadows and Pimental as academics with too much faith in their computer models. It's hard to treat 100-year forecasts as anything but intriguing exercises. And Paul Ehrlich made doomsday predictions in the early '70s that sound like howlers today. But why look ahead 100 years? The world already suffers from social injustice and environmental abuse. In 1993, the global grain harvest fell by 5 percent. Nine of the 17 major ocean fisheries are in serious decline. We lose topsoil 20 to 40 times faster than nature replenishes it. And yet we assume that we can simply outgrow these problems.

The truly radical idea, Meadows suggests, would be to meet our crises without counting on growth as the only answer. "The moment you recognize limits the question of sharing becomes absolutely foremost in your mind," she says. Sharing our wealth, sharing our resources, sharing our knowledge. The new Malthusians don't ask us to close the door against the world's poor, but to begin respecting them as neighbors.

OIL: THE STRATEGIC PRIZE

Daniel Yergin

Daniel Yergin is president of Cambridge Energy Research Associates, a leading energy consulting firm, and best-selling author of The Prize: The Epic Quest for Oil, Money, and Power. *This article is excerpted from Yergin's prologue to* The Prize.

Winston Churchill changes his mind almost overnight. Until the summer of 1911, the young Churchill, Home Secretary, was one of the leaders of the "economists," the members of the British Cabinet members critical of the increased military spending that was being promoted by some to keep ahead in the Anglo-German naval race. That competition had become the most rancorous element in the growing antagonism between the two nations. But Churchill argued emphatically that war with Germany was not inevitable, that Germany's intentions were not necessarily aggressive. The money would be better spent, he insisted, on domestic social programs than on extra battleships.

Then on July 1, 1911, Kaiser Wilhelm sent a German naval vessel, the *Panther*, steaming into the harbor at Agadir, on the Atlantic coast of Morocco. His aim was to check French influence in Africa and carve out a position for Germany. While the *Panther* was only a gunboat and Agadir was a port city of only secondary importance, the arrival of the ship ignited a severe international crisis. The buildup of the German Army was already causing unease among its European neighbors; now Germany, in its drive for its "place in the sun," seemed to be directly challenging France and Britain's global positions. For several weeks, war fear gripped Europe. By the end of July, however, the tension had eased—as Churchill declared, "the bully is climbing down." But the crisis had transformed Churchill's outlook. Contrary to his earlier assessment of German intentions, he was now convinced that Germany sought hegemony and would exert its military muscle to gain it. War, he now concluded, was virtually inevitable, only a matter of time.

Appointed First Lord of the Admiralty immediately after Agadir, Churchill vowed to do everything he could to prepare Britain militarily for the inescapable day of reckoning. His charge was to ensure that the Royal Navy, the symbol and very embodiment of Britain's imperial power, was ready to meet the German challenge on the high seas. One of the most important and contentious questions he faced was seemingly technical in nature, but would in fact have vast implications for the twentieth century. The issue was whether to convert the British Navy to oil for its power source, in place of coal, which was the traditional fuel. Many thought that such a conversion was pure folly, for it meant that the Navy could no longer rely on safe, secure Welsh coal, but rather would have to depend on distant and insecure oil supplies from Persia, as Iran was then known. "To commit the Navy irrevocably to oil was indeed 'to take arms against a sea of troubles,' " said Churchill. But the strategic benefits—greater speed and more efficient use of manpower—were so obvious to him that he did not dally. He decided that Britain would have to base its "naval supremacy upon oil" and, thereupon, committed himself, with all his driving energy and enthusiasm, to achieving that objective.

There was no choice—in Churchill's words, "Mastery itself was the prize of the venture."[1]

With that, Churchill, on the eve of World War I, had captured a fundamental truth, and one applicable not only to the conflagration that followed, but to the many decades ahead. For oil has meant mastery throughout the twentieth century.

At the beginning of the 1990s—almost eighty years after Churchill made the commitment to petroleum, after two World Wars and a long Cold War, and in what was supposed to be the beginning of a new, more peaceful era—oil once again became the focus of global conflict. On August 2, 1990, yet another of the century's dictators, Saddam Hussein of Iraq, invaded the neighboring country of Kuwait. His goal was not only conquest of a sovereign state, but also the capture of its riches. The prize was enormous. If successful, Iraq would become the world's leading oil power, and it would dominate both the Arab world and the Persian Gulf, where the bulk of the planet's oil reserves is concentrated. Its new strength and wealth and control of oil would force the rest of the world to pay court to the ambitions of Saddam Hussein. With the resources of Kuwait, it would be able to make itself into a formidable nuclear weapons state and, perhaps, even move down the road toward becoming a superpower. The result would be a dramatic shift in the international balance of power. In short, mastery itself was once more the prize.

But the stakes were so obviously large that the invasion of Kuwait was not accepted by the rest of the world as a fait accompli, as Saddam Hussein had expected. It was not received with the passivity that had met Hitler's militarization of the Rhineland and Mussolini's assault on Ethiopia. Instead, the United Nations instituted an embargo against Iraq, and many nations of the Western and Arab worlds dramatically mustered military force to defend neighboring Saudi Arabia against Iraq and to resist Saddam Hussein's ambitions. There was no precedent for either the cooperation between the United States and the Soviet Union or for the rapid and massive deployment of forces into the region. Over the previous several years, it had become almost fashionable to say that oil was no longer "important." Indeed, in the spring of 1990, just a few months before the Iraqi invasion, the senior officers of America's Central Command, which would be the linchpin of the U.S. mobilization, found themselves lectured to the effect that oil had lost its strategic significance. But the invasion of Kuwait stripped away the illusion. In early 1991, when peaceful means failed to secure an Iraqi withdrawal from Kuwait, a coalition of thirty-three nations, led by the United States, destroyed Iraq's offensive capability in a five-week air war and one hundred hours of ground battle, which forced Iraq out of Kuwait. At the end of the twentieth century, oil was still central to security, prosperity, and the very nature of civilization.

Though the modern history of oil begins in the latter half of the nineteenth century, it is the twentieth century that has been completely transformed by the advent of petroleum. In particular, three great themes underlie the story of oil.

The first is the rise and development of capitalism and modern business. Oil is the world's biggest and most pervasive business, the greatest of the great industries that arose in the last decades of the nineteenth century. Standard Oil, which thoroughly dominated the American petroleum industry by the end of that century, was among the world's very first and largest multinational enterprises. The expansion of the business in the twentieth century—encompassing everything from wildcat drillers, smooth-talking promoters, and domineering entrepreneurs to great corporate bureaucracies and state-owned companies—embodies the twentieth-century evolution of business, of corporate strategy, of technological change and market development, and indeed of both national and international economies. Throughout the history of oil, deals have been done and momentous decisions have been made—among men, companies, and nations—sometimes with great calculation and sometimes almost by accident. No other business so starkly and extremely defines the meaning of risk and reward—and the profound impact of chance and fate.

As we look toward the twenty-first century, it is clear that mastery will certainly come as much from a computer chip as from a barrel of oil. Yet the petroleum industry continues to have enormous impact. Of the top twenty companies in the Fortune 500, seven are oil companies. Until some alternative source of energy is found, oil will still have far-reaching effects on the global economy; major price movements can fuel economic growth or, contrarily, drive inflation and kick off recessions. Today, oil is the only commodity whose doings and controversies are to be found regularly not only on the business page but also on the front page. And, as in the past, it is a massive generator of wealth—for individuals, companies, and entire nations. In the words of one tycoon, "Oil *is* almost like Money."[2]

The second theme is that of oil as a commodity intimately intertwined with national strategies and global politics and power. The battlefields of World War I established the importance of petroleum as an element of national power when the internal combustion machine overtook the horse and the coal-powered locomotive. Petroleum was central to the course and outcome of World War II in both the Far East and Europe. The Japanese attacked Pearl Harbor to protect their flank as they grabbed for the petroleum resources of the East Indies. Among Hitler's most important strategic objectives in the invasion of the Soviet Union was the capture of the oil fields in the Caucasus. But America's predominance in oil proved decisive, and by the end of the war German and Japanese fuel tanks were empty. In the Cold War years, the battle for control of oil between international companies and developing countries was a major part of the great drama of decolonization and emergent nationalism. The Suez Crisis of 1956, which truly marked the end of the road for the old European imperial powers, was as much about oil as about anything else. "Oil power" loomed very large in the 1970s, catapulting states heretofore peripheral to international politics into positions of great wealth and influence, and creating a deep crisis of confidence in the industrial nations that had based their economic growth upon oil. And oil was at the heart of the first post-Cold War crisis of the 1990s—Iraq's invasion of Kuwait.

Yet oil has also proved that it can be fool's gold. The Shah of Iran was granted his most fervent wish, oil wealth, and it destroyed him. Oil built up Mexico's economy, only to undermine it. The Soviet Union—the world's second-largest exporter—squandered its enormous oil earnings in the 1970s and 1980s in a military buildup and a series of useless and, in some cases, disastrous international adventures. And the United States, once the world's largest producer and still its largest consumer, must import half of its oil supply, weakening its overall strategic position and adding greatly to an already burdensome trade deficit—a precarious position for a great power.

With the end of the Cold War, a new world order is taking shape. Economic competition, regional struggles, and ethnic rivalries may replace ideology as the focus of international—and national—conflict, aided and abetted by the proliferation of modern weaponry. But whatever the evolution of this new international order, oil will remain the strategic commodity, critical to national strategies and international politics.

A third theme in the history of oil illuminates how ours has become a "Hydrocarbon Society" and we, in the language of anthropologists, "Hydrocarbon Man." In its first decades, the oil business provided an industrializing world with a product called by the made-up name of "kerosene" and known as the "new light," which pushed back the night and extended the working day. At the end of the nineteenth century, John D. Rockefeller had become the richest man in the United States, mostly from the sale of kerosene. Gasoline was then only an almost useless by-product, which sometimes managed to be sold for as much as two cents a gallon, and, when it could not be sold at all, was run out into rivers at night. But just as the invention of the incandescent light bulb seemed to signal the obsolescence of the oil industry, a new era opened with the development of the internal combustion engine powered by gasoline. The oil industry had a new market, and a new civilization was born.

In the twentieth century, oil, supplemented by natural gas, toppled King Coal from his throne as the power source for the industrial world. Oil also became the basis of the great postwar suburbanization movement that transformed both the contemporary landscape and our modern way of life. Today, we are so dependent on oil, and oil is so embedded in our daily doings, that we hardly stop to comprehend its pervasive significance. It is oil that makes possible where we live, how we live, how we commute to work, how we travel—even where we conduct our courtships. It is the lifeblood of suburban communities. Oil (and natural gas) are the essential components in the fertilizer on which world agriculture depends; oil makes it possible to transport food to the totally non–self-sufficient megacities of the world. Oil also provides the plastics and chemicals that are the bricks and mortar of contemporary civilization, a civilization that would collapse if the world's oil wells suddenly went dry.

For most of this century, growing reliance on petroleum was almost universally celebrated as a good, a symbol of human progress. But no longer. With the rise of the environmental movement, the basic tenets of industrial society are being challenged; and the oil industry in all its dimensions is at the top of the list to be scrutinized, criticized, and opposed. Efforts are mounting around the world to curtail the combustion of all fossil fuels—oil, coal, and natural gas—because of the resultant smog and air pollution, acid rain, and ozone depletion, and because of the specter of climate change. Oil, which is so central a feature of the world as we know it, is now accused of fueling environmental degradation; and the oil industry, proud of its technological prowess and its contribution to shaping the modern world, finds itself on the defensive, charged with being a threat to present and future generations.

Yet Hydrocarbon Man shows little inclination to give up his cars, his suburban home, and what he takes to be not only the conveniences but the essentials of his way of life. The peoples of the developing world give no indication that they want to deny themselves the benefits of an oil-powered economy, whatever the environmental questions. And any notion of scaling back the world's consumption of oil will be influenced by the extraordinary population growth ahead. In the 1990s, the world's population is expected to grow by one billion people—20 percent more people at the end of this decade than at the beginning—with most of the world's people demanding the "right" to consume. The global environmental agendas of the industrial world will be measured against the magnitude of that growth. In the meantime, the stage has been set for one of the great and intractable clashes of the 1990s between, on the one hand, the powerful and increasing support for greater environmental protection and, on the other, a commitment to economic growth and the benefits of Hydrocarbon Society, and apprehensions about energy security.

These, then, are the three themes that animate the story that unfolds in these pages. The canvas is global. The story is a chronicle of epic events that have touched all our lives. It concerns itself both with the powerful, impersonal forces of economics and technology and with the strategies and cunning of businessmen and politicians. Populating its pages are the tycoons and entrepreneurs of the industry—Rockefeller, of course, but also Henri Deterding, Calouste Gulbenkian, J. Paul Getty, Armand Hammer, T. Boone Pickens, and many others. Yet no less important to the story are the likes of Churchill, Adolf Hitler, Joseph Stalin, Ibn Saud, Mohammed Mossadegh, Dwight Eisenhower, Anthony Eden, Henry Kissinger, George Bush, and Saddam Hussein.

The twentieth century rightly deserves the title "the century of oil." Yet for all its conflict and complexity, there has often been a "oneness" to the story of oil, a contemporary feel even to events that happened long ago and, simultaneously, profound echoes of the past in recent events. At one and the same time, this is a story of individual people, of powerful economic forces, of technological change, of political struggles, of international conflict and, indeed, of epic change. It is the author's hope that this exploration of the economic, social, political, and strategic consequences of our world's reliance on oil will illuminate the past, enable us better to understand the present, and help to anticipate the future.

1. Randolph S. Churchill, *Winston Churchill*, vol, 2, *Young Statesman, 1901–1914* (London: Heinemann, 1968), p. 529 ("bully"); Winston S. Churchill, *The World Crisis*, vol. 1 (New York: Scribners, 1928), pp. 130–36.
2. Interview with Robert O. Anderson.

Energy: The new prize

World energy markets will soon be roiled by surging demand from developing countries—with some distressing results, argues Edward Carr

I N 1973 the world suddenly woke up to the fact that control of oil, its main source of energy, had fallen into the hands of a bunch of desert sheikhs, tottering democracies and unpredictable dictators. Every link in the chain of energy supply and consumption reverberated to the shock. It took a decade, a second oil shock and a world recession for the rich economies to adjust. Wherever possible, coal, natural gas and nuclear power supplanted oil; conservation became an obsession.

Twenty years after that first shock, another huge shift is under way. The shape and size of world energy demand is increasingly being determined not by rich countries but by the fast-growing developing countries of Latin America and Asia. Just as the oil producers in OPEC achieved sudden prominence after more than a decade of obscurity, so the full effect of the shift among consuming countries will not be felt for many years. But it is equally inexorable; and no less far-reaching.

By 2010 the share of total energy consumption accounted for by the rich countries will have fallen below 50% for the first time in the industrial era. Eastern Europe and the former Soviet Union will consume a sixth. The share of developing countries will have climbed from 27% now to 40%, and be rushing upwards faster than ever. The growth in energy consumption in developing countries between 2000 and 2010 will be greater than today's consumption in Western Europe. By 2010 their emissions of carbon dioxide, the main contributor to global warming, will be almost as big as those of the whole world in 1970. So says the International Energy Agency (IEA), based in Paris, which in April published its latest "scenario" for world energy (after many energy buffs got things spectacularly wrong in the 1970s, issuing plain old "forecasts" is now seen as far too risky).

The World Energy Council (WEC), an umbrella organisation for diverse energy interests based in London, has published some scenarios too. These suggest that by 2020, in a "high-growth" case, annual world energy demand could be double today's level (see chart 1 on next page). More than 90m barrels a day (b/d) of oil will be consumed, an increase of 27m b/d—OPEC's entire output now. Coal output will almost double, approaching 7 billion tonnes, more than twice Britain's known reserves. Gas demand will more than double, reaching 4 trillion cubic metres, almost as much as America's current gas reserves. More electrical generating capacity will be built over the next 25 years than was built in the previous century.

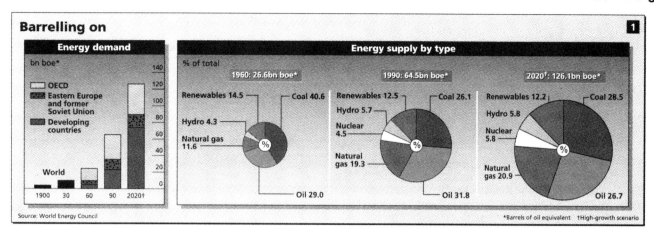

Barrelling on

Energy demand

bn boe*

☐ OECD
▨ Eastern Europe and former Soviet Union
▩ Developing countries

World

1900 30 60 90 2020†

Energy supply by type

% of total

1960: 26.6bn boe*

Renewables 14.5 — Coal 40.6
Hydro 4.3
Natural gas 11.6
Oil 29.0

1990: 64.5bn boe*

Renewables 12.5 — Coal 26.1
Hydro 5.7
Nuclear 4.5
Natural gas 19.3
Oil 31.8

2020†: 126.1bn boe*

Renewables 12.2 — Coal 28.5
Hydro 5.8
Nuclear 5.8
Natural gas 20.9
Oil 26.7

Source: World Energy Council

*Barrels of oil equivalent †High-growth scenario

The WEC's figures, like those of the IEA, are dominated by Latin America and especially Asia, which Daniel Yergin, the author of a history of oil, has called "the new prize". Under the council's high-growth scenario, demand in these countries will triple over the next 30 years. Demand in North America, on the other hand, will rise by only 13%. By 2020, energy use in the developing countries will account for as much as 60% of the world total, compared with 30% in the OECD.

So long as rich countries accounted for the lion's share of energy consumption, small changes in their economies swamped the relentless growth of demand in the developing world. That is one reason why improved energy efficiency and two recessions in the 1980s were able to keep the oil market slack, despite a rise in oil demand in developing Asia (ie, outside Japan, Australia and New Zealand) of more than 80% between 1982 and 1992. But this is about to change. "When you're 20% of world consumption, 6% growth doesn't matter," says Michael Grubb of the Royal Institute for International Affairs in London. "When you're 50%, it does."

Over the coming 25 years there will no doubt be enormous technological and regulatory changes in the OECD. Eastern Europe and Russia will rebuild their energy industries almost from scratch. But all this could be overshadowed by the growth of developing-country demand for energy. The capital needed to finance massive investments will force reform upon what has almost always been a state-run business. Asian countries that buy oil from abroad will have to buy more; its exporters will become importers. China, the world's sixth-biggest oil producer (ahead of Venezuela), became a net oil importer at the end of 1993. Fuel for its fleets of new vehicles will soon begin to arrive in supertankers from the Middle East. And the West's rather quaint efforts to restrain carbon emissions—its response to the dangers of unpredictable climatic change—will be overwhelmed by the billions of extra tonnes of coal that China and India are going to burn.

The numbers game

Perhaps all this sounds like an unthinking extrapolation into an unsustainable future. Think again. The world has seen periods of unbroken prosperity before. In the West after the second world war; in Japan from the late 1950s; and in the four tigers of South Korea, Taiwan, Hong Kong and Singapore.

Asia's cubs—Malaysia, Thailand and Indonesia—are thriving. Parts of Latin America are following suit. And then there are India and China.

With 40% of the world's people, India and China loom large in any analysis of energy's future. The WEC allocates "centrally planned Asia" (a category dominated by China) and "South Asia" (dominated by India) a quarter of world consumption by 2020. "If the future...is in Asia," says Lawrason Thomas, vice-chairman of Amoco, "then China will define the shape of that future."

Energy consumption in India has more than tripled since 1970. In China, consumption has increased 22-fold since 1952. And still there is huge suppressed demand in both countries. Even political turmoil has not dented demand for long. Chinese consumption halved after the Great Leap Forward in 1958-60. It grew at an average of 10% a year for the next decade. Later upheavals, such as the Tiananmen Square massacre, have had even less effect. Doubtless, political unrest in China or elsewhere would delay the shifts described by the IEA and the WEC. But it would not prevent them.

This is because the demand for energy in developing countries is being driven by irresistible forces. One is demography. The world's population will increase by 2.7 billion people, to over 8 billion, by 2020; over 60% of those extra people will be born in Asia and Latin America. A second is the process of early development. Consumers of non-commercial, scavenged fuel, usually firewood, animal dung and crop residues, gradually begin to consume kerosene, coal and other forms of commercial energy. As industrialisation takes off, farm workers leave the land for the cities. In 1955 all the power on Taiwanese farms was provided by humans or animals; by 1975 over half was mechanical, and the use of oil-based fertilisers was common.

New cities also need energy: to carry people to and from work; to bring raw materials to factories; to make and distribute things; to supply concrete and steel; to make plastic and iron to replace wood and leather; to build roads; to power the marble-clad offices in new financial districts. And still the squalid shanty towns are unlit. One study* concluded that if India and China were to double the proportion of their populations living in cities, something that the IEA believes will happen by

* "How Urbanisation Affects Energy-Use in Developing Countries". By Donald W. Jones. *Energy Policy*, September 1991.

2010, energy demand would be 45% higher than now even if their national incomes and populations remained the same.

Supposing that demand does follow these scenarios, the energy used by each inhabitant in developing countries will still be well below levels in the rich world today. Chart 2 shows the comparison in 1991. In the WEC's high-growth analysis, the consumption of a typical Chinese over the next quarter-century grows by 85%; and of an Indian, who starts off even poorer, by 145%. Both would then be using less than a fifth of the energy consumed by the average American today.

If anything, the scenarios look too cautious, not too bold. One planner working in Hong Kong for a big oil company is frustrated that colleagues back at head office routinely tell him that his Chinese forecasts are too big to be believable. Rates of economic growth and of car ownership, the efficiency of the car fleet, the distance each Chinese will drive, all are negotiated down to safer levels. What emerges certainly looks more plausible, but it may also be wrong. Even the "high-growth" scenario of the WEC assumes that world economic growth will be lower than in two of the past three decades.

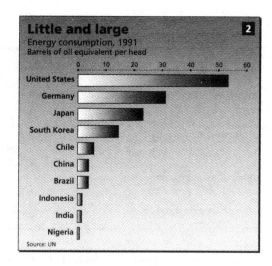

Little and large
Energy consumption, 1991
Barrels of oil equivalent per head

Source: UN

More controversially still, the WEC supposes that governments will be able to live up to their environmental rhetoric. It thus based its scenarios on the premise that the amount of energy used to generate a given level of income, known as energy intensity, will fall faster over the next 25 years than

Meanwhile . . .

ASIA and Latin America might be the fastest-changing markets for energy. But they are not yet the biggest. That accolade still belongs to the OECD. While developing countries strive merely to satisfy their needs, energy in rich countries revolves around the control of pollution, fears about a growing dependence on imports—and, perhaps, the beginning of the end of the fossil-fuel era.

The IEA suggests that energy use in the OECD will grow by 1.3% a year; and in the former Soviet Union and Eastern Europe by 0.3% a year, compared with 4.2% in developing countries. By 2010, the IEA expects the OECD to account for 45% of world energy demand and the former Soviet block for 15%, compared with 40% for the developing countries.

Both the IEA and the WEC expect oil and coal to become less important in OECD countries, although they disagree about how fast this will happen. Even with oil prices increasing to $28 a barrel, the IEA supposes that oil demand in the OECD will grow by almost 18%. Coal demand will grow by 1.3% a year. The WEC, however, sees both oil and coal demand shrinking in absolute terms in North America and Western Europe.

Whatever happens, natural gas will help to crowd out other fuels. It is clean, efficient and cheap (at least for now). When gas burns it releases less carbon than oil or coal; it contains virtually no sulphur; and with well-designed machinery, it also releases fewer nitrogen oxides.

When it comes to generating electric power, burning gas can be used to drive a turbine: the heat contained in the exhaust then makes steam that drives a second turbine. This arrangement, known as the combined-cycle, has raised the proportion of gas's heat that can be transformed into electricity from below 40% to above 50%. Only the higher gas prices expected early in the next century are likely to nudge gas from its charmed position.

Nobody doubts that renewable energy sources will one day take over from fossil fuels. But their prospects over the coming 20 years are mixed. A host of technologies are nearing commercialisation. Wind en-

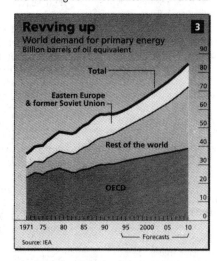

Revving up
World demand for primary energy
Billion barrels of oil equivalent

Total
Eastern Europe
& former Soviet Union
Rest of the world
OECD

1971 75   80   85   90   95   2000   05   10
Forecasts
Source: IEA

ergy and biomass, which comes from energy-rich crops such as eucalyptus, are commercially viable in some places. But although the use of these sources of renewable energy will probably grow fast, it will be from a pitifully small base. It will take decades before energy utilities have installed much capacity to handle such new technologies. And highly praised renewables have a nasty habit of running into green objections as soon as they show any promise of becoming profitable. Wind power is accused of being noisy and unsightly. Tidal power requires barrages that sacrifice prized habitats for birds. Biomass will doubtless be attacked for relying upon intensive farming.

Things that raise the cost of fossil fuels or lower that of renewable energy—environmental scares, say, scarcity, or technological breakthroughs—hold out the best hope that renewable energy can overcome the reservations of utilities and pressure groups. These have more or less stopped what was once a great white hope of energy buffs, nuclear power. Low rates of return and fierce resistance from green lobbies have between them created a famine of new nuclear projects everywhere in the OECD except Japan.

The world in 1994 seems to have come a long way from the obsessions of the Carter era in 1979-80, when the president pleaded with Americans to conserve energy and wage the "moral equivalent of war"—or MEOW, as it was cruelly called. By 2020, with higher prices, even more environmental worries and new technology, the meow could become a roar.

it has ever done before. Energy intensity is fiend-ishly hard to predict—especially in China, where it has fallen by 4% a year over the past decade. There is nothing odd in that: energy intensity normally falls as new technologies replace old, and services and light manufacturing outgrow heavy industry. But the speed of China's decline is remarkable.

The optimists maintain that China started as one of the world's least energy-efficient economies. There is thus plenty of scope for further savings and structural change, especially if China imports more steel and other energy-intensive products. If house-holders replaced smoky coal-fired stoves, they could get more useful energy without increasing overall consumption.

And yet it is easy to find pessimists. China ap-pears wasteful only if its economy is measured at market exchange rates. The IEA points out that, if comparisons are based on purchasing-power pari-ties instead, China's energy intensity is already rela-tively low, which would limit the future scope for saving energy. The country's knack for cutting en-ergy intensity could also have been overstated if economic growth has in fact been slower than the government thinks. This is more than just an ab-struse argument among energy boffins: if China's energy intensity had remained at its 1977 level, it would now consume 50% more energy than it does. If the intensity of oil use were similar to that of Western Europe in the 1960s, China would ulti-mately be consuming 40m barrels of oil a day—more than all OECD countries today.

The point is not that developing-country de-mand is bound to be larger than expected, but that most forecasters are already uncomfortably aware

of Malthus's shadow falling across their manu-scripts even before they go into print. In 1987 the WEC estimated that the developing countries would account for 26% of energy investment to 2010. Now it expects them to make well over half such investment by 2020. What will be the size of the estimate that it makes in 2000?

An IEA employee who worked on one of its sce-narios told Chris Cragg, editor of the FT Energy Economist, a newsletter, "We put in the $20 a bar-rel real-price scenario [compared with $16 a barrel today and $25 in the published scenario]... the numbers just went crazy. We all sat down and had a good laugh at them, because they were inconceiv-able in the real world." When it comes to scenarios, what you see is what their authors dare to think.

The demand is there. Even the reserves of oil, coal and gas are there. The main constraints, in-deed, may be that developing economies cannot get hold of enough capital to build the infrastruc-ture needed to supply and consume all this energy; and that their citizens might not tolerate the pollu-tion that it will cause. McKinsey, a management consultancy, has put the overall capital require-ments for power, oil, gas, coal, pipelines and refin-ing in Asia over the 1990s alone at $1.1 trillion.

So before considering what the noisy arrival of developing countries will mean for the world's oil market, its environment, and the formation of en-ergy policies, this survey will look first at the ques-tion of finance. Nowhere is this a bigger problem than in the generation of electric power, the most capital-intensive element of energy supply, and also the one most desperately in need of change.

Canada Is Ready to Exploit Huge Oil Reserves Locked in Sands

T. R. Stauffer

Special to The Christian Science Monitor

EDMONTON, ALBERTA

Alberta's tar sands, long recognized as a potential source of massive amounts of oil, may in a few years become a notable factor in the world oil market.

Recent tests of a new technique for exploiting the underground resource indicate costs can be brought down to a competitive level with recovery of deposits of liquid oil at present world prices, government experts say. The Athabasca tar sands are located in the flat, featureless terrain at the northern end of this province.

These deposits contain "greater volumes than the entire Middle East oil reserves," states the 1993 report of the Alberta Oil Sands Technology & Resource Authority, the agency mandated to promote exploitation of this vast energy resource. Official estimates record a volume of at least 1 trillion barrels of oil enmeshed in gritty, tarry masses of bitumen, sand, clay, and shale, equal to six times the reported reserves of Saudi Arabia.

To date, oil sand production is minor. Development has been disappointing because of the high costs of extracting the oil. One problem is weather. Winter temperatures drop well below zero degrees F., when tempered steel mining equipment can snap like dry noodles. Second, the oil does not flow. The tarry agglomerations must be mined and the bitumen separated from the sand. The tar then must be upgraded to a salable product.

Total costs for this process run about $20 per barrel (Canadian, US$15), leaving little margin for government royalties, federal taxes, or company profits. Even with royalty and tax breaks, the projects eke out a modest rate of return. Saudi oil can be produced for less than $2 a barrel.

"We are the Saudi Arabia of the North," says Dr. Rick Luhning, vice chairman of AOSTRA. "We now believe that we have developed the key to these riches." That key is a new mining/extraction process. It worked at the pilot stage and is now poised for commercial-scale development.

The tar sands are not new discoveries. Peter Pond, when first exploring the area more than 200 years ago, found Indians waterproofing canoes with bitumen from natural seeps.

Two multibillion-dollar "mega-projects" have been completed and produce almost 300,000 barrels per day (bpd)—as much as the smallest OPEC members. Four other follow-on schemes are on

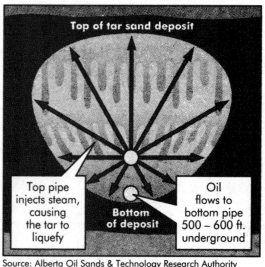

DAVE HERRING – STAFF

Extracting Oil From Tar Sands

By injecting steam through the top pipe, oil that is caught in sand, clay, or shale flows down into the bottom pipe. Recent tests show that extraction costs can be brought down to a competitive level with recovery of liquid oil at present world prices.

Top of tar sand deposit

Top pipe injects steam, causing the tar to liquefy

Bottom of deposit

Oil flows to bottom pipe 500 – 600 ft. underground

Source: Alberta Oil Sands & Technology Research Authority

hold. The technology, still too costly, leaves little scope for future refinement: The tarry masses are mined using oversize equipment including huge excavators and draglines. They are then frothed and centrifuged to separate the oil bitumen. The viscous residues are then upgraded to a low-sulphur "synthetic" crude oil in refinery-like plants. The process is capital intensive and promised savings from large-scale operations were not realized.

The new method reverses the conventional logic. First, it starts from the bottom up, rather than from the top down. Instead of surface mining the sands, the "steam-assisted gravity drainage" technique starts from mining shafts 500 to 600 feet down into hard rock underlying the tar beds. The surface is barely disturbed. Then pairs of parallel horizontal wells are drilled from the shaft into the sands. The top horizontal wells are pumped full of medium-pressure steam. That fluidizes the viscous tars, which flow into the lower horizontal well. The

tar is then easily pumped to the surface.

The second advantage of the new approach is its small scale: The optimal size is 30,000 bpd, a fraction of the size of the existing megaprojects.

The savings are dramatic. No overburden must be removed, no land reclamation costs whatsoever are incurred, and by far the bulk of the sand and waste rock is left undisturbed. Instead of excavating tons of sand and rock, the process pumps out tons of hot bitumen. The process is economically and environmentally much simpler.

The final technical breakthrough came as horizontal drilling techniques were perfected. The process only works if the pairs of pipes are properly positioned— about 8 to 14 vertical feet apart. If the pipes are too close, there is a "short-circuit," and the steam bypasses part of the sands. If too far apart, the yield is much reduced. Pipes now can be positioned within one to two feet of a target over almost 1,800 feet. This permits 50

percent to 60 percent of the contained oil to be recovered. These wells are prolific, flowing at 10 times the average for conventional ones in this area. The production cost for bitumen before upgrading to crude oil is US$6 per barrel, about $4 to $5 per barrel less than present projects and enough to make the process viable.

A consortium is mobilizing to launch the commercial project, although realization will take three to four years. The Alberta government has shared the costs and the technology with a clutch of North American oil companies, but two unexpected partners have recently joined. The Chinese National Petroleum Corporation hopes to use the techniques to exploit tar deposits in the eastern Gobi Desert.

The Japanese government is also represented. JAPEX, its agent, has spent billions of dollars searching for large-sized, reliable, and economic oil sources outside of the Middle East, a goal which has eluded them.

Development

- **Nonindustrial Nations (Articles 25–30)**
- **Industrial Nations (Articles 31–36)**

One of the terms most frequently used in descriptions of the world today is "development." Television talk shows, scholarly publications, political speeches, and countless other forums echo this term. Yet, if we gathered together a group of experts, it would soon be apparent that each one uses the word "development" in a somewhat different manner. To some, development means becoming industrialized—like the United States or Japan, for example. To others, development means having a growing economy; this is usually measured in terms of the expansion of Gross National Product (GNP). To still others, development is primarily a political phenomenon. They question how a society can change its economy if it cannot establish collective goals and successfully administer their implementation. And to still others, development means attaining a certain quality of life, based on the establishment of adequate health care, leisure time, and a system of public education, among other things. It is obvious, then, that the term must be defined before a discussion of the issue of development can begin.

Because this book includes both industrial and nonindustrial countries in its discussion of development, a broad definition will be used. Development will mean improvement in the basic aspects of life: lower infant mortality rates, greater life expectancy, lower disease rates, higher rates of literacy, healthier diets, and improved sanitation. While it is obvious that, judged by these standards, some groups of people are more developed than others, the process of development is an ongoing one for all nations. This unit, therefore, is divided into two parts. It looks first at the development process in nonindustrial countries, then focuses on the industrial countries of North America, Europe, and Japan. Although the economy of Russia differs from the consumer-oriented economies of the West, the structure of its industrial system is in the midst of a dramatic transformation. The outcomes of this historic change are difficult to predict, but the significance of these changes is recognized by all. This change, along with a variety of associated changes in the Russian social system, is likely to dominate much of the world news for the remainder of the 1990s.

Nonindustrial Nations. The decade of the 1980s was a period of considerable economic growth in the industrial nations of the world; but for the nonindustrial nations it was a period of stagnation and even decline. The gap between the rich and poor countries widened. Further-

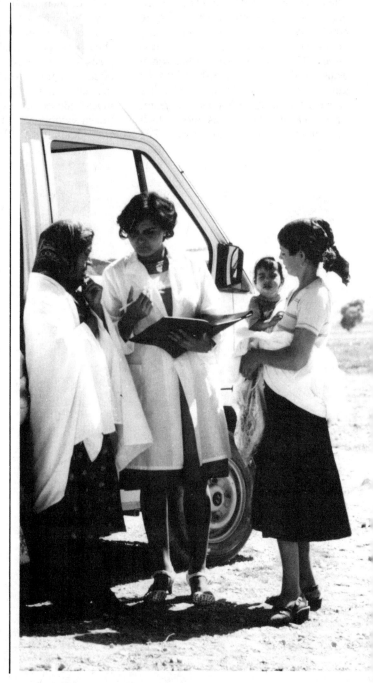

more, the burden of this growing inequality fell most heavily on women and children. Of the illiterate people in the nonindustrial nations, three out of every four are women. What is to be done about this situation is a question that is widely debated. The demise of the planned economies of the old Soviet Union and its allies no longer provides this approach as a model for development. There are also considerable doubts about the appropriateness of the capitalist model. Many argue that this system simply transfers wealth from the poor to the rich without any benefits flowing back to those who need the advantages of economic progress the most.

The articles in the nonindustrial nations section have been selected with the development debate as the focal point. The nature of the international economic system and how it rewards some and not others is examined from a number of perspectives, using numerous case studies.

Industrial Nations. Only a few years ago, industrialization was considered by many to be the end point of the development process. Industrialization, however, is not necessarily synonymous with improvement in the quality of life. When the industrial sector of the West's economy was thrown into deep recession after the oil price shocks of the 1970s, many experts joined the growing chorus of those calling for the development of industrial societies into a new, postindustrial structure, where knowledge, information, and space-age technologies would take over. Others believed that the "greening" of society, rather than a high-tech future, should become the new goal of development. This second group maintained that new, clean energy resources and an appreciation of the fragile nature of the environment would lead to a decentralized and sustainable economy. As yet, neither of these visions has come to pass. The industrial countries, like the nonindustrial countries, are in the midst of a development process with no single blueprint to guide them.

The articles in this subsection that focus on the development of industrial countries offer a variety of contending viewpoints. Some observers predict an increase in economic cooperation and further integration of national economies. Others warn that trading blocs are going to replace the flawed international trading system which was established after World War II. This economic system, they go on to say, is likely to be highly competitive, and not all will have an equal chance at being successful.

The United States, Japan, and the European Union are each viewed by various experts as the potential leader of the global economy in the next century. Each has problems as well as unique assets. Optimism and pessimism about these contenders tend to vary from year to year as they individually and collectively grapple with their own problems. However, if this contest for leadership is to be understood over the long run, it is essential to understand the core structural issues confronting each: increasing productivity, governmental reform, labor relations, political unrest, and sufficient investment in research and development, and so forth.

Finally, the future of the republics that comprised the former Soviet Union looms large on the horizon. There are no historical models for making the transition from planned economies to market economies. The former communist countries of Central Europe began this process a few years prior to Russia and the other members of the new Commonwealth of Independent States, but these various experiments in economic/political processes have not yielded a clear formula for success.

Industrial nations, like their nonindustrial counterparts, are in a period of transition. Many forces are at work, and as yet there is no widely accepted vision of where this is all going to lead. While much divides industrial and nonindustrial countries, uncertainty about the future and a lack of consensus about the policies necessary to improve the quality of life are two dimensions that they ironically have in common.

Looking Ahead: Challenge Questions

How are the social structures of traditional societies different from those of the consumer-oriented societies of the West?

How are the developing world countries dependent on the highly developed industrialized nations?

What are some of the barriers that make it difficult for nonindustrial countries to develop?

How has the role of the United States in the international economy changed in recent years?

The international economic system is faced with unprecedented problems. What are these, and what are some of the proposals for solving these problems?

How are the United States, Japan, and other industrial countries trying to alter their economies to meet new economic challenges? Are they likely to succeed?

SUCCESS: 1974–1994

The Boom

How Asians started the 'Pacific Century' early

John M. Leger

Asia's time has come.
> —Singapore Prime Minister
> **Goh Chok Tong**

What's all this talk about the imminent arrival of the "Pacific Century"? With America in decline, communism in retreat, and Europe suffering from one of its periodic bouts of "Eurosclerosis," it seems like the "Pacific Century" is already here and in full throttle.

In fact, maybe it's been the "Pacific Century" for the last 20 years, judging by Asia's incredible economic boom. And that boom has spawned at least one new industry—academics attempting to divine the "secrets" of Asia's success. Or "miracle," as so many like to say. They've published myriad studies, often with mathematical equations of mind-numbing complexity.

Forget all that. You only need to do some simple arithmetic to explain Asia's magnificent achievements of the last 20 years:

> **Hard Work**
> **+ Low Taxes**
> **+ High Savings Rates**
> **+ Minimal Government**
> ―――――――――――
> **= Economic Boom**

There's really no "miracle" here. In fact, the only "miracle" is that most governments outside of Asia haven't yet figured this out. While Asia powers into the 21st century, the United States and Europe impose ever greater regulations on business and higher taxes on their citizens. Based on the past two decades' experience in Asia, that's no recipé for success.

Let's take a closer look at what *really* leads to success.

HARD WORK

You think "hard-working Asians" is some cliché? Not at all. Check these numbers, courtesy of Union Bank of Switzerland:

City	Working hours per year	Paid holidays
Seoul	2,302	7.8
Bangkok	2,272	8.8
Hong Kong	2,222	12.1
Taipei	2,136	17.0
Singapore	2,044	17.7
Now, for a comparison:		
Copenhagen	1,669	25.0
Dusseldorf	1,682	30.5
Madrid	1,721	32.1
Frankfurt	1,725	31.2
London	1,880	22.1

REVIEW GRAPHIC/RINGO CHUNG

None of this will come as a surprise to Hong Kong's Catherine Yan. You don't have to tell her about hard work. The dynamic director of cleaning company Centuryan Services decided to forsake marriage "so that I could pay full attention to my work."

Then there's Taipei's Chen Chengchung. As a kid he delivered newspapers and worked at a banana-processing factory. He then took a job at a construction company at the ripe old age of 14. Today, at age 39, he runs a far-flung business empire.

Asia is full of success stories like Catherine Yan and Chen Chengchung. All these people have one thing in common: the will to succeed. They didn't sit around waiting for government handouts or make-work programmes or social "benefits" that destroy jobs in so many

Blistering Pace

Most Asian countries racked up breathtaking growth rates in the last 20 years. South Asian nations have lagged behind — but won't for long if they continue opening their economies

Newly industrialising economies — *Average GDP growth rate (1975-93)*

Taiwan	20.35
South Korea	17.74
Hong Kong	16.19
Singapore	15.14
China	19.54

Southeast Asia

Malaysia	13.42
Thailand	11.42
Indonesia	11.26
Philippines	3.41

South Asia

Pakistan	8.31
India	6.20
Nepal	5.87
Sri Lanka	3.98

Source: Asian Development Bank: Economics and Development Resource Centre

REVIEW GRAPHIC/RAY LEUNG

From *Far Eastern Economic Review*, November 24, 1994, pp. 43, 46, 48-49. © 1994 by Review Publishing Company, Ltd. Reprinted by permission of *Far Eastern Economic Review*, Hong Kong.

Western countries. No government tried to limit the hours they could work or the wages they could earn. No government mandated their hiring because they were the favoured ethnic group of the moment. They wanted to work. And they did.

Some may be tempted to attribute Asia's achievements to "Confucian values." While Confucius was certainly our kind of guy (an "enlightened conservative," according to the writer André Ryerson), we would be very cautious about ascribing Asia's success to Confucianism. After all, only 40 years ago, some academics had written off Asia, somehow predicting that Confucianism would hold back its development.

LOW TAXES

South Korea's An Byung Kyun is proud of the fact that he was identified as the country's top taxpayer in 1990. But at least he got something for his taxes: publicity for his Nasan clothing company.

Most people would rather keep their pay cheque than give it to the tax collector. And in Asia, they're far more likely to keep a larger share of their hard-earned money than in any other region of the world.

The REVIEW asked the international accounting firm Coopers &

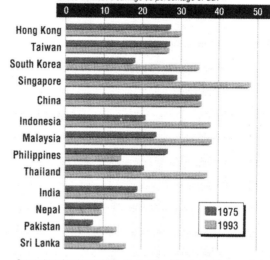

Rocket Fuel

High savings rates promote growth — and many Asian countries have sharply increased their savings rates in the last 20 years. The Philippines is a notable exception

Gross domestic savings as percentage of GDP

(Hong Kong, Taiwan, South Korea, Singapore, China, Indonesia, Malaysia, Philippines, Thailand, India, Nepal, Pakistan, Sri Lanka — 1975, 1993)

Source: Asian Development Bank, Economics and Development Resource Centre

Lybrand to prepare an analysis of the tax situation in Asia and in key countries outside the region (*see chart "Maybe There's a Connection"*). The results are striking.

For one thing, the maximum tax rates in Asia tend to be lower than in other parts of the world. For another, those rates often kick in at higher levels than in the industrialised world.

Yes, Japan has an exceptionally high maximum rate of 65%. But it doesn't bite until you've earned US$206,000. By contrast, France will grab nearly 57% of your income at the US$54,000 level. Japan should certainly lower its tax rates. But which country do you think offers the greater incentive to create wealth?

One other point: Don't be fooled by the 39.6% maximum in the U.S. That's the top federal rate. Americans also have to pay an infinity of state and local income taxes, property taxes and social-security taxes. They also get hit with capital-gains taxes. And woe be unto any American who tries to escape strangulating U.S. taxes by moving to, say, Hong Kong. Alone among countries in the

industrialised world, the U.S. chases down its citizens wherever they live and work, taxing them on their worldwide income.

Fortunately, the trend in Asia has been towards lower taxes. Malaysia, for example, recently announced cuts in personal-income taxes. In 1980, when Singapore announced reductions to its already low tax rates, the trade minister at the time noted: "Several advanced countries, like Britain, have been hypnotised by a soak-the-rich slogan, only to discover that by heavy taxes on personal incomes, they have stifled the drive to excel and succeed." That perceptive comment was made by Goh Chok Tong, who is now Singapore's prime minister.

Says George Gilder, the author of *Wealth and Poverty*: "Unlike Western leaders, the Asian capitalists understand the role of tax cuts in releasing enterprise." For instance, he notes that a series of tax cuts launched Taiwan's economic surge in the 1950s.

HIGH SAVINGS RATES

Low tax rates encourage savings. And Asia's savings rates have been

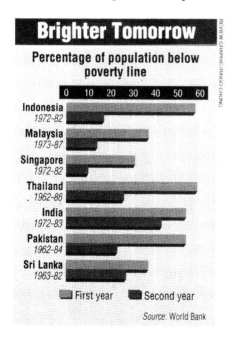

Brighter Tomorrow

Percentage of population below poverty line

Indonesia	1972-82
Malaysia	1973-87
Singapore	1972-82
Thailand	1962-86
India	1972-83
Pakistan	1962-84
Sri Lanka	1963-82

■ First year ■ Second year

Source: World Bank

nothing short of phenomenal, helping to power Asia's economic boom (*see chart "Rocket Fuel"*).

High savings allow countries to finance domestic investment—education, infrastructure and the like. In fact, that kind of investment is "crucial" for a country to grow, asserts Seiji Naya, professor of economics at the University of Hawaii.

As Naya notes, savings rates "have increased more rapidly in Asia than in other developing countries." Why? For one thing, the newly industrialised countries of Singapore, Hong Kong, South Korea and Taiwan generally maintained interest rates above the rate of inflation during the 1970s and 1980s. So, too, did Asean countries during the 1980s.

That's quite an incentive to save. In the case of Singapore, worker contributions to the Central Provident Fund have given the island republic the world's highest savings rate—currently a whopping 48% of GDP. Japan's rates have hovered around 30%.

In East Asia, there's one glaring exception to the impressive savings rates: the Philippines. Over the last 20 years, savings rates have actually

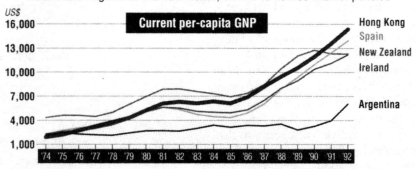

Getting Rich

Twenty years ago, Hong Kong was poorer than Spain, New Zealand, Ireland and Argentina. It's now richer, thanks to its free-market policies

Current per-capita GNP

Hong Kong
Spain
New Zealand
Ireland
Argentina

Source: World Bank

fallen. That one factor alone helps to explain why the Philippines' economic performance has lagged that of other Asian countries.

MINIMAL GOVERNMENT

In Lee Kuan Yew's Singapore, the state plays a significant economic role, but as servant not master.

—Jean-François Revel
Democracy Against Itself

Many academics and journalists studying the Asian boom have tried to discern the role of the state in contributing to the region's economic success. They ask: Did the state lead economic development? The experience in Asia suggests rephrasing the question. The more meaningful issue is this: Does the state promote the creation of wealth? Or does it destroy it?

In most of East and Southeast Asia, the state has clearly promoted the creation of wealth. Not by nationalising everything in sight, as in Africa, or by setting up huge state bureaucracies, as in much of the West. It did so by ensuring a stable, predictable economic environment—even if there was political upheaval. The state also actively promoted exports. It kept taxes low so that people could save and invest. Most of all, it let free-market forces flow. The state didn't try to pre-empt or overrule the market.

"Apart from the promotion of shipbuilding and steel in Korea and of a few strategic industries in Taiwan," says Bela Balassa of Johns Hopkins University, "the principal contribution of government in the newly industrialising countries has been to create a modern infrastructure, to provide a stable incentive system, and to ensure that government bureaucracy will help rather than hinder exports."

Does any country have a pure *laissez-faire* economy? Of course not. Not even Hong Kong, whose government interferes in the property market by restricting supply. Yet

Maybe There's a Connection

TAX

Fast-growing Asian countries tend to have lower tax rates than industrialised, slow-growing Western nations

	Maximum personal tax rate	Level at which maximum rate applies (US$)
Hong Kong		51,000
Singapore		272,000
Malaysia		59,000
Indonesia		23,000
Philippines		20,000
Thailand		160,000
Taiwan		128,000
South Korea		80,000
Japan		206,000
Sri Lanka		1,468
Pakistan		98,000
India		3,200
New Zealand		19,000
U.S.		250,000
Britain		39,000
Australia		37,000
France		54,000

Source: Coopers & Lybrand

most countries in East and Southeast Asia have a vigorous private sector that operates independently of the state. These countries also promote free trade. Says Helen Hughes, professor of economics at the Australian National University in Canberra: "If ill-advised countries wanted to dump goods in Hong Kong, Hong Kong consumers and producers were delighted."

What about Japan? Doesn't the Ministry of International Trade and Industry (MITI) call the shots in cahoots with an evil cabal of big businessmen? You'd think so, judging by all the Japan-bashing by American politicians and many U.S. businessmen.

But the truth is far different. As Charles Wolf Jr., dean of the Rand Graduate School, notes, Japan's domestic savings rate averaged 28% of GDP in the 1980s, double the American rate. Japan's annual rate of domestic investment averaged 24% of GDP in the 1980s, compared with 15–16% in the U.S. He also says: "Japan's work force is highly disciplined, trained, industrious and literate." For their part, Japanese

managers "strive continually to improve product quality and cut production costs."

No wonder Japanese growth rates have far outstripped American rates. Japan's success was not due to MITI, cabals, bent businessmen, "unfair trade practices" or any of the other excuses Westerners use to rationalise their own failures. Other countries' trade policies cannot simply be labelled "Made in Japan."

Then there's Singapore. It's true, as Professor Hughes notes, that Singapore "had a strongly interventionist outlook as it moved towards independence in 1959." Eventually, though, "the Singapore government gave up picking winners in favour of supporting market trends," she says. Indeed, Singapore now has an active programme of privatisation.

There you have it. Rather than trying to second-guess the market, Singapore and other governments around the region got out of the way and let the markets do what markets are supposed to do. In other words, governments acted to promote wealth. Not destroy it.

Indonesia, which didn't even have a stockmarket until 1992, is seeing an avalanche of companies raising capital to fuel further growth.

Some of the most exciting changes are taking place in India. Prime Minister P. V. Narasimha Rao and Finance Minister Manmohan Singh are busy dismantling the web of regulations that have helped to keep India mired in poverty. A recent Lehman Brothers report said it best: "The sub-continental giant's reform programme has not yet resulted in a bonfire of the country's past controls, but a healthy blaze has been kindled."

Some fret about the future of Hong Kong after the colony reverts to China in 1997. But maybe it's Hong Kong that's taking over China. Already, Hong Kong companies employ some 4 million people in neighbouring Guangdong province. As China continues to modernise and the provinces elude central-government control, it's possible that China will become more like Hong Kong.

There's no reason why Asia's success can't be duplicated in other parts of the world. But it means governments must lift the tax burdens on their citizens, reduce or eliminate the state's involvement in the economy, stop piling on regulations, and open their countries to free trade. Just as in Asia. . . .

Living Longer

Life expectancy is rising — and exceeds Western levels in Japan and Hong Kong

REVIEW GRAPHIC/RAY LEUNG

	0 10 20 30 40 50 60 70 80
Japan	*
Hong Kong	
Singapore	
Taiwan	**
South Korea	
Malaysia	
Thailand	
China	
Philippines	
Indonesia	
Sri Lanka	
India	
Pakistan	
Bangladesh	
U.S.	
Britain	
Germany	

★Japan: 1975 ★★Taiwan: 1993
■ 1992 ▨ 1977

Source: World Bank, Taiwan Department of Health

ECONOMIC BOOM

In the second quarter of the next century, China will almost certainly be the greatest economic power on earth, and Hong Kong the richest city, an amalgam of New York, London, Amsterdam and Venice at the height of their trading power, richer than any city on earth has ever been before.

—William Rees-Mogg, former editor, *The Times* of London

The boom will continue. All over Asia, governments are privatising industry, cutting taxes, welcoming foreign investment and developing their financial markets. China and Vietnam now have vigorous private sectors. The Philippines, buoyed by a flood of portfolio investment and a more open economy, will acquire the capital to leap into the 21st century.

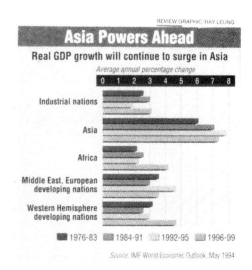

REVIEW GRAPHIC/RAY LEUNG

Asia Powers Ahead

Real GDP growth will continue to surge in Asia

Average annual percentage change

	0 1 2 3 4 5 6 7 8
Industrial nations	
Asia	
Africa	
Middle East, European developing nations	
Western Hemisphere developing nations	

■ 1976-83 ▨ 1984-91 ▨ 1992-95 ▨ 1996-99

Source: IMF World Economic Outlook, May 1994

INDIA GETS MOVING

Rahul Jacob

LINED UP AGAINST the wall of General Electric's medical equipment factory outside Bangalore are seven ultrasound machines covered in plastic. The $25,000 devices are headed for France, Wipro GE Medical Systems' first export destination in Europe. It is another triumph for this joint venture, which surprised even GE's managers by speeding in 12 months from breaking ground to its first shipment.

On the road outside, exhaust-spewing buses and trucks weave among carts pulled by oxen with brightly festooned horns. Within the sparkling factory, however, there is a laboratorylike calm as $250,000 to $400,000 CT scanners are tested by earnest technical workers. B.D. Vijaya, the plant manager, describes how cross-functional teams have brought down defects. He has just gotten off the phone with a colleague at Yokogawa Medical in Japan, an affiliate.

The plant sports Japanese, American, and Indian flags—and plenty of ambition. Annual sales are currently $25 million, but Wipro GE hopes they will rise to $200 million by the year 2000. To reach that target, exports will be critical. Says Vijaya, sounding decidedly Welchian: "It's not enough to be a quality manufacturer. We must be the low-cost producer as well."

After decades of disappointment, India is beginning to fulfill its economic promise. Along with China (see box), it is becoming a magnet for Western investment, especially from the U.S. India's program of economic liberalization, now three years old, has cleared a thicket of regulations. At the same time, the country's rapidly growing middle class, estimated at between 100 million and 300 million, is creating a vast consumer market. General Electric, the busiest new foreign investor in India, has joint ventures in

everything from financial services to household appliances, from lighting to industrial plastics.

American companies seem especially comfortable in India. Unlike in much of Asia, where U.S. investment trails that of Japan, about half the $3.3 billion of foreign proposals approved in the year ended last March was American. Says E. Neville Isdell, a senior vice president of Coca-Cola, which has invested $70 million since the reforms began: "We did not believe the government would move as rapidly as it has."

Problems remain, but foreign investment is welcome and Western companies are finding plenty of opportunity.

Indian companies aren't sitting back, either. Sundram Fasteners in Madras bought equipment from General Motors plants in England, shipped it to India, and has now become the primary supplier of metal radiator caps to GM North America. In the western Indian city of Ahmedabad, Arvind Mills is out to become one of the biggest denim manufacturers in the world. As its home markets become available to foreign competitors, India's once coddled companies are raising quality and looking overseas. Says C.K. Prahalad, a University of Michigan business school professor who lectured to 28 Indian CEOs in Bangalore last February: "Senior Indian managers are realizing that creating markets abroad is not different from defending markets in India."

The results are dramatic. India's exports rose 20% for the fiscal year ended in March, despite sluggish growth in the developed world. Foreign investment over the same period increased eightfold, to $4.7 billion. About $4 billion of that has been put into shares traded on Indian stock exchanges or global depositary receipts by institutional investors around the world.

Overseeing this monsoon of money is Indian Finance Minister Manmohan Singh, 61. A soft-spoken, self-deprecating Sikh, Singh looks like a cherub thrown among

PROMISING SIGNS

■ The world's fifth-largest economy based on purchasing-power parity is courting foreign investors.

■ American companies, who account for about half the foreign direct investment in India, are snapping up the best local companies as joint-venture partners.

■ Government approvals for new ventures that once took years now come in weeks.

■ The middle class, estimated at 100 million to 300 million, is eager for Western products.

cantankerous old men when he parries thrusts from diehard socialists on the opposition benches of India's Parliament.

Tariffs have been slashed from 200% to a maximum of 65% and are expected to come down to 25% in a few years. The rupee has depreciated by about 50% and been made convertible for trade transactions. Foreign investors can move money in and out at the

REPORTER ASSOCIATE *Meenakshi Ganguly*

INDIA OR CHINA: HOW TO CHOOSE

At first glance, China seems far ahead of India. China's per capita income grew at an annual rate of 8.5% between 1983 and 1993, while the figure for India was just 3.2%. The WEFA Group forecasts that China's GDP will be $451 billion in 1994, India's about $278 billion. Yet many major multinationals have started to speak of the two giants in the same breath.

Why? Though India's democracy has been accident-prone, its government seems the more stable of the two. India has long had a private sector that coexisted with inefficient state enterprises. That tradition of commerce means it has managers who know that the vitality of an enterprise is reflected in its profits rather than by the number of employees it has. India also has Western accounting and legal systems.

For different cultural reasons, doing business in both countries requires lots of patience. Says a senior executive at a major multinational that has large investments in both countries: "India did not invent bureaucracy but has made it an art form. In China, however, your business partner negotiates you to death. He feels that if there is a buck to be made and he makes 99 cents and you make a penny, that's okay. The concept of sharing profits is not well understood." Weighing the two countries, he offered this surprising conclusion: "We will make more on the top line in China but probably more on the bottom line in India." Neither will be easy money.

prevailing market rate. In February corporate tax rates were reduced to an effective rate of 46%, and income tax now has a ceiling of 40%. Foreign institutional investors are now allowed to trade on Indian stock exchanges.

Still smarting from 200 years of colonial rule, India until 1991 discouraged foreign direct investors by sitting on proposals for years. Now government officials make most decisions in a matter of weeks, and the answer is almost always yes. When Coca-Cola decided to go it alone in India after dissolving its joint venture with an overseas Indian partner, Coke got permission for a 100%-owned unit in India in eight weeks. Motorola recently received clearance in two days to add a new product line at its Bangalore factory—all over the fax. Companies as varied as Procter & Gamble and Enron, Daimler-Benz and Whirlpool, have rushed to take advantage of the new climate.

But it's not uniformly balmy. India is still an exceedingly underdeveloped country. By some measures, its infrastructure even lags behind that of China. The public sector continues to throw an imposing shadow across the economy, soaking up 50% of the country's capital while producing little more than a quarter of its output. And the zeal for reform is not as pronounced in many state governments as it is in New Delhi, nor has it percolated down to the mindlessly meddlesome lower echelons of the bureaucracy.

EVEN SO, investors' concerns have changed significantly over the past few years. The question is no longer whether the reforms might be reversed, but how fast they will go forward. That's no small matter when a country is just coming off the starting blocks and its competitors are halfway down the track. No wonder then that India's lively business press keeps demanding a faster pace, to the irritation of officials trying to provide it. Prime Minister P.V. Narasimha Rao told FORTUNE: "Each country has to find its own rhythm and pace. As a person trying to keep my finger on the pulse of the people, I am depending on sound judgment rather than induced fantasies."

For an indication of how much India is changing, leave behind the garish fast-food joints (McDonald's won't arrive until next year) with names like Hurry Curry and Hasty Tasty in the big cities to see the money being made in rural markets. Pooyransh Saini's 8-by-6-foot store is in the village of Kotputli in the northwestern state of Rajasthan. Rural consumers once made do with anything, but TV is making them brand conscious. Grumbles Saini, sitting cross-legged on the floor of his store: "If you don't stock what people see on television, you lose customers. It's a real nuisance."

Minutes later an elderly gentleman, his forehead smeared with ash in the manner of a devout Hindu, ambles up to the store. He asks for Surf, the detergent made by Unilever's subsidiary Hindustan Lever. Saini is deferential enough but brings back a one-kilogram pack of a cheaper, local brand called 555. When his customer insists on Surf, with some reluctance Saini produces a pack. Today, even in this Indian village where you compete for parking space with grouchy camels, brand loyalty is taking hold. Observes Titoo Ahluwalia, who heads India's largest market research firm, MARG: "Purchasing power is only partly a function of affluence. It is also a function of attitude."

American companies, reveling in an environment where business is conducted in English, have been especially adept at forming alliances with the best local firms to tap the Indian market. Says Paolo Fresco, GE's vice chairman: "We begin with the acknowledgement that we can learn as much from them as they from us." GE's appliances and industrial-plastics joint ventures are headed by managers from their partner companies.

A similar flexibility applies to brand names. Although GE's every move is breathlessly reported in India's financial press, the company is virtually unknown to the Indian consumer, while Godrej, its partner in appliances, is a household name. Says Scott Bayman, head of GE's Indian operations: "That brand has a 40% market share in refrigerators. Why would we change it?"

Intellectual capital—Wall Street smarts —was what Industrial Credit & Investment Corp. of India was after when it approached J.P. Morgan & Co. in the spring of 1992. The resulting investment-banking joint venture raised $2 billion in the primary markets last year and advised American clients on power projects and General Motors on its joint venture with the local Hindustan Motors. Charles Alexander, the tall Englishman who is deputy managing director of the joint venture, regards Indian financial markets as relatively well developed but sees a special need for Morgan's valuation skills as mergers and acquisitions bloom.

For all its recent progress, India is unlikely anytime soon to achieve the super growth rates of the Tigers of East Asia or of China. The government's reluctance to fully privatize India's huge, inefficient public sector, and the tortuous process by which it is opening up infrastructure development stand in the way of faster growth. For the next few years growth will average just above 6%, which is only a little ahead of the pace of the 1980s. India's population growth rate of 1.9% annually means that per capita incomes will increase only about 4% a year.

Still, India's overall GDP growth rate masks the dynamism of its corporate sector, which is growing at about 10% a year. Companies also benefit from the concealed purchasing power of India's underground economy. A legacy of the country's high taxes in the 1970s that made tax evasion a national pastime, the underground economy adds anywhere from 20% to 50% to the official GDP.

The bloated public sector will continue to hobble the economy, in part because it controls much of the country's inadequate infrastructure. Power shortages are widespread. Ports are pitifully slow. Says GE's Bayman, whose ambitious target of $2 billion in annual sales in India from $250 million today rests in part on a flurry of proposed private power projects: "We can build world-class products here, but will we be able to get them to our customers? The answer is privatization." The government seems to agree, but there is a notable lack of speed and cohesion. Typically, the Finance Ministry forges ahead while other ministries lag behind or throw up obstacles.

Given India's rowdy yet relatively resilient democracy, some businessmen seem satisfied, even supportive of the government's lumbering gait. Says Madhav Dhar of Morgan Stanley, which has 20% of its emerging-market portfolio invested in India: "It is difficult to do tough, antipopulist things in a country where nearly everyone is poor and everyone votes."

That about sums up the Sisyphean struggle India has ahead of it. Any investor must count on some harrowing lurches along the way. The ruling Congress Party now has a majority in Parliament and looks stronger than it has in the past three years. Should it be upset in general elections in 1996, the leading opposition party, the militant Hindu Bharatiya Janata Party, will be pro-business too, though it might prove less receptive to foreign investment. A recurrence of the kind of bloody religious rioting that brought Bombay to a standstill more than 18 months ago is a perennial risk. Even as a flood of foreign money helped push up the Bombay stock market last February, carpenters were finishing repairs as a result of a massive bomb blast 11 months earlier.

AT THE SOUTHERN END of the city is a pier where 16th-century travelers got their first glimpse of Bombay. After the Portuguese gave Bombay to Charles II as part of his bride's dowry, the tradition continued. The last British soldiers departed from the same pier when India became independent in 1947. Today, from the charming old hotel that overlooks the Arabian Sea, many foreign businessmen look out on an odd disarray of small yachts in the muddy water. Last spring the water was so brown and the tide so imperceptible that the boats looked as if they were mired in mud. This strangely static scene seemed a melancholy metaphor for the Indian economy, straining against its legacy of colonialism and socialism, heaving under the weight of a teeming population. Then a couple of boats cast off their mooring lines. Their sails caught the wind, and they quickly sailed into the morning sun. It was difficult not to feel hopeful, at least for the moment.

NAFTA is not alone

Latin American countries are already some way down the road to economic integration with each other—and now they are looking hard at NAFTA too

WHAT a change it has been. In the 1960s, when the first attempts at regional economic integration began, most Latin American countries were addicted to state intervention—indeed for many industries and most utilities, state ownership—and vigorous protection against the outside world. This week the Latin presidents meeting in the Colombian port town of Cartagena issued a paean of praise for the private sector, open markets, foreign investment and free trade.

Three of them set the ball rolling with a pact of their own. Given legislative approval, Mexico, Venezuela and Colombia—a market of 140m people—will now be formally linked in the free-trade Group of Three. It is just the newest of several such regional groupings. Nor do the Latins today

fancy these, as they used to, as inward-looking islands of self-sufficiency, but as first steps toward (and negotiating platforms with) the world at large. The one country that fights shy of such groupings, Chile, does so not because it wants to go slower but because it thinks it can go faster on its own.

Till now there have been three main groupings in Latin America: the Andean Group and the Central American Common Market, both born, none too happily, in the 1960s; plus, since 1991, Mercosur (*sur:* south), linking Argentina and Brazil with their small neighbours Paraguay and Uruguay. Besides these there are many bilateral agreements and one much bigger dream: that of a SAFTA, a free-trade area covering all of South America.

Started in 1969, the **Andean Group**—five countries and today about 100m people—had some early success, but soon became a sad specimen of how not to integrate economies. The idea was to keep out foreign goods and foreign multinationals. Instead, the five countries would lower tariffs among themselves, and launch local industries, deciding jointly which country should produce what. The result was predictable. In effect, says one Bolivian today, "We had agreed, You buy our overpriced goods and we'll buy yours." Soon country A began to feel that country B was getting the better of the bargain. All consumers meantime were getting the worst, paying high prices for low-quality regional products. The 1980s debt crisis was a further blow.

In 1988 the five relaunched the group in a very different spirit. Within the group, this has brought almost free trade since late 1992, and no more export subsidies; externally, lower tariffs, which will become a common tariff and customs union later this year, besides uniform "national" treatment for foreign investors and the like. Not all is perfect. Peru suspended its membership briefly in 1992, after President Alberto Fujimori's "coup", though it was reintegrated this spring. And disagreements have meant that the common external tariff is coming into operation six months late. There are still sundry "special cases". The big growth in trade—more due to bilateral efforts than group ones—has been between Venezuela and Colombia. But the show is on the road.

The **Central American Common Market** (all seven countries of the isthmus except Panama and Belize) had a rather similar history: early success in boosting intra-regional trade, then political instability, civil war—not to forget the 1969 "football war" between El Salvador and Honduras—and debt. Here too a relaunch followed, formalised by a new agreement (joined by Panama), in the new free-market spirit, last October. It works well—even travel is passport-

UNITED STATES
ATLANTIC OCEAN
MEXICO
HONDURAS
GUATEMALA
EL SALVADOR
COSTA RICA
NICARAGUA
VENEZUELA
COLOMBIA
ECUADOR
BRAZIL
PERU
PACIFIC OCEAN
BOLIVIA
PARAGUAY
URUGUAY
ARGENTINA

Trade areas
- NAFTA
- Central American Common Market
- Andean Group
- Mercosur
- ★ G-3

free—in the three northern countries, less so to the south.

The southern grouping, **Mercosur,** began with a mid-1980s deal between Argentina and Brazil and took its present shape in 1991. From the start it was a free-market idea. It has been cutting internal tariffs on an automatic schedule, to avoid pressures for delay. The last ones will go at the end of this year. The aim is a customs union and, in time, free movement of labour and capital.

Intra-regional trade growth has already been spectacular: it is up 2 ½ times since 1990. A deeper integration is also taking place: `for example, Mercedes will build gearboxes in Argentina for trucks that it assembles in Brazil. Problems are not lacking. Argentina has single-figure inflation and a stable exchange rate; Brazil's prices have been rising and its currency falling by 30–50% of each month. Argentina, its peso tied one-for-one to the dollar—too high, say exporters—has put a temporary 10% surcharge on Brazil's cheaper goods. But the embryo of something is not unlike Europe's common market is there.

The spirit, though, is overtly outward looking. Mercosur—representing about half of Latin America's GDP—is now seen as a step toward wider free trade. It was Brazil that launched the SAFTA scheme last October; in March its Mercosur allies formally gave their backing. The aim is free trade for not less than 80% of goods by 2005.

Overhanging all these plans is the issue of relations with the three NAFTA countries of North America. These matter less to South America than is often thought: Mercosur does more trade with Europe

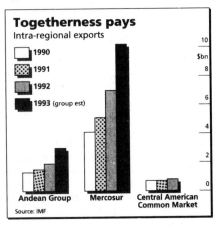

Togetherness pays
Intra-regional exports

- 1990
- 1991
- 1992
- 1993 (group est)

Andean Group   Mercosur   Central American Common Market

Source: IMF

than with NAFTA. But no Latin country can ignore the United States—still less now that Mexico has privileged access there.

How much is there in the vision expressed by Colombia's President Cesar Gaviria at Cartagena this week, of "the Americas integrated from north to south"? Chile quit the Andean Group in 1976 and is steering clear of Mercosur's customs union today. Instead it has a network of bilateral trade agreements (and wants one with Mercosur). But already it is talking of joining

NAFTA. Colombia could be next in line; already its new G3 grouping promises it and Venezuela free trade within ten years (13 for cars) with Mexico.

Most Central American (and Caribbean) products can in fact enter the United States tariff-free. Only—that is a big only—"sensitive" manufactures like textiles and clothing pay duty, as the Mexican equivalent does not, on the value added by the Latin manufacturer. But President Clinton is due soon to send Congress a bill extending NAFTA treatment to all goods.

There will be plenty of conditions—not least, yearly approval by Congress—and, even if the bill passes, real integration with the United States' "near abroad" is years away. Future links between NAFTA and the Andeans or Mercosur have barely been broached. Mr Gaviria's dreams—they go beyond trade to politics—are still on Cloud Nine. Yet already one thing is clear: any American who imagined that his country's NAFTA links were the end of a road is in for a series of uncomfortable shocks.

Iraq

Saddam bows, Clinton doesn't

ONE exception to the rule that sanctions usually work rather badly is Iraq, where they may be working too well. At considerable cost to ordinary Iraqis, they are close to achieving their stated aim of ensuring that Iraq shall not again be in a military position to threaten its neighbours. But they are still far from their unstated aim: getting rid of President Saddam Hussein. This is causing some awkwardness—and a split in the anti-Iraq coalition.

The UN ceasefire resolution passed in April 1991 says that the ban on the sale of Iraqi oil, which is the sanction that hurts, will be lifted when Iraq has destroyed all chemical and biological weapons, all missiles with a range of more than 150 kilometres (roughly 100 miles) and all material usable in nuclear weapons; and, still more important, when arrangements have been made to ensure that Iraq will not have the military wherewithal to offend again.

For the first two years of sanctions, Iraq gave the inspectors—from the UN Special Commission and the International Atomic Energy Agency—the runaround, cheating whenever it could. But a year ago, with its economy in grievous trouble, the regime started to co-operate. It agreed, formally, to the principle of long-term monitoring and it provided a list of suppliers, even if not a complete one.

The monitoring system is extraordinarily intrusive and on many levels. It in-

cludes high-flying aircraft keeping an eye on the whole country, daily helicopter patrols, ground inspectors, and tags and sensors attached to bits of sensitive equipment. The UN is on the watch for short-range missiles that could be transformed into long-range ones, for pesticides that could be turned into poison gas, for anything that could become a biological weapon. That covers what the Iraqis can make at home. As for imports, the special commission wants the Security Council to make it obligatory for countries to notify the UN of any dual-use equipment sold to Iraq—and for the UN to check such sales by having its own inspectors at Iraqi ports and airports.

Next month, Rolf Ekeus, the head of the special commission, has to give the Security Council an assessment of where things stand. With so much progress made, he will be embarrassed, he suggests, if the council does not at least show Iraq that there is light at the end of the tunnel. One condition, generally agreed on by the Security Council, has already been added to the original ones: Iraq must recognise Kuwait behind its new UN-demarcated frontiers. This makes sense—in the context of international security—though the Iraqi president still needs a lot of persuading.

To impose yet more conditions—not least, one requiring Mr Hussein to respect the human rights of his own subjects—would be nice. But it would strengthen his claim that the goalposts move so fast that it is not worth his while playing the game. Turkey is pushing for change; as a first step, it wants the Turkish-Iraqi pipeline unclogged from the 12m barrels of oil caught inside it. And 14 of the Security Council's 15 members tend to agree with Mr Ekeus's argument that the status quo cannot be maintained indefinitely. If his report is as favourable as expected, the debate should be turning—at latest by the beginning of next year—to the division of the money that Iraq will earn from renewed oil sales. There are many claimants who were hurt by the Gulf war, chief among them Kuwait.

The 15th member of the council, however, is the United States. And Bill Clinton has no desire at all to stand accused by American voters of giving away the battle that George Bush so bravely fought.

Jerusalem

Economical with the truth

JERUSALEM

HARBINGER of Yasser Arafat's own return to Palestine, Nabil Shaath, one of his top men, arrived in Gaza on June 12th. There was no definite arrival date for his boss, said Mr Shaath, but it could well be before the end of this month.

Meanwhile, rumours mount. Among them is the report in an Israeli Arabic newspaper this week that Mr Arafat wants the kings of Jordan and Morocco and the president of Egypt to pray with him at the mosque of al-Aqsa in Jerusalem. Israeli reporters quote Jericho merchants warning Mr Arafat against landing during an important World Cup soccer game. American television crews have already rented strategic rooftops around Jericho's main square.

Settlers are planning mass protests. Israel is ready to deploy 10,000 Israeli policemen to keep order in the West Bank and Jerusalem, in addition to soldiers, security agents, Palestinian policemen and Mr Arafat's own bodyguards. Several murder threats—including a leading rabbi's ruling (on religious grounds, sic) that Mr Arafat deserves death without trial—are being taken seriously.

If Mr Arafat visits Jerusalem—which, as the Israelis grudgingly concede, he is entitled to under the terms of the Gaza-Jericho agreement—he will face huge right-wing and religious demonstrations. The government will not be pleased either: it is constantly alert to anything done by the Palestinians that could make East Jerusalem look like their capital.

This week, though, Mr Arafat was doing what he could to calm the tension that has blown up over the future of the city. He informed Israel that he intends to transfer the bulk of the PLO's bureaucracy from Tunis to Jericho forthwith; a list of 1,200 officials has been submitted, as required under the agreement. Jericho, he said in letters to Israel's prime minister, Yitzhak Rabin, will indeed be the seat of the self-governing authority, as prescribed in the original declaration of principles last September.

At Mr Rabin's insistence, the declaration designated Jerusalem as one of the issues to be left for the "permanent status" talks which were supposedly to begin "as soon as possible", but could be left to start as late as in two years' time. Mr Arafat had to agree. But in return he got a letter from Israel's foreign minister, Shimon Peres, addressed to the late Johan Jorgen Holst (Norway's foreign minister, who acted as go-between), in which Israel undertook "not to hamper" and indeed "to encourage" the activities of "all the Palestinian institutions of East Jerusalem". That letter, signed last October 11th, was kept secret even from Israeli ministers and negotiators.

It has now come to light, provoking a political storm. The leak resulted from an intemperate speech by Mr Arafat in a Johannesburg mosque in mid-May in which he said, among other things, that he had a secret letter from the Israelis ensuring Palestinian rights in Jerusalem. Mr Arafat's details were not quite accurate, enabling

Messrs Rabin and Peres to issue straight-faced denials. But the truth came out in dribs and drabs, until eventually the two had no choice but to publish the full text, while resorting to heroic verbal contortions to defend their battered credibility.

They still profess not to understand why Mr Arafat saw fit to embarrass them in this way. They have themselves to blame. He spoke after a wave of threats and harassment by the Israeli authorities, national and municipal, against long-established Palestinian institutions in East Jerusalem. These include a cluster of research units headed by Faisal Husseini at Orient House, a stately building just outside the walls of the Old City that has become a focus of diplomatic activity.

The row that followed the publication of Mr Peres's letter caused the government to sound even tougher—at first. Mr Rabin told the government's draftsmen to prepare legislation empowering it to remove the Palestinian institutions. Even if he were not breaking his word, he would be breaking the law: since Israel sees East Jerusalem as part of its territory, these institutions enjoy full protection, including the right to freedom of association and freedom of speech, and cannot just be shut down. By this week Mr Rabin had indicated that no new legislation was contemplated, and that institutions operating at the time the letter was sent could continue to do so. Mr Arafat, for his part, is said to have signalled to his lieutenants in Jerusalem to avoid provocation.

The Jerusalem institutions are crucial to the Palestinians as a political toehold in the city, creating facts in anticipation of the eventual battle across the negotiating table. But such facts pale before the vigorous and massive expansion of Israeli settlement around the northern and eastern rim of the city. By the time the negotiations are due to begin, Israel will have completed a ring of Jewish suburbs right around Jerusalem.

Moderates in the government say privately that once that ring of concrete is shut tight, Israel will be better disposed to offer the Palestinians some symbolic concession on Jerusalem: say, extra-territorial status for the mosques and Muslim quarter in the Old City. That comes nowhere near the basic Palestinian demand, which is for an open, shared city that serves as the capital of both states, Israel and Palestine.

Angola

No relief

LUANDA

OUT of the world's sight, Angola continues to bleed. Fighting between the UNITA rebels and the government became so fierce this week that the United Nations' World Food Programme had to suspend all

relief flights to areas held by the rebels, cutting off a lifeline of food and medicine to some 1m Angolans.

Fighting intensified last month, when UNITA gunners began bombarding Kuito, a town in the central highlands. This was a town whose people were once sympathetic to the rebels: Jonas Savimbi, UNITA's leader, won a majority there in the country's 1992 election, though he lost nationally. That does not seem to worry the rebels, who have been shelling the town vigorously. Hundreds of civilians are said to have died.

The government's response was equally awful. Its Sukhoi and Mig jet aircraft dropped incendiary bombs which, say witnesses, smelled of petrol and exploded into fire on impact like napalm, into the centre of Huambo, the second-biggest city and UNITA's headquarters.

These attacks on civilian targets played havoc with the international relief effort. Food stocks in several big cities, such as Kuito, Huambo and Malanje, have been exhausted. When UNITA withdrew the security clearances it had given for World Food Programme and International Red Cross aircraft flying to areas it controls, whole cities were stranded without supplies.

Not that previous security clearances from either side guaranteed the safety of aid flights. Last month UNITA leaders in Huambo three times promised the UN they would allow aid planes to fly to Malanje, another city UNITA was shelling. The UN aircraft set off; but each time one tried to land, rebel gunners shelled the airport. The government, in return, played a similar trick: it launched a bombing raid on Huambo 15 minutes after a UN aircraft landed with governmental blessing.

Both the government and UNITA are reported to be spending lavishly on arms supplies: the government uses its massive oil revenues, UNITA the cash from sales of smuggled diamonds. Both sides have also launched forced recruitment drives to sign up teenagers to their cause; some of these unfortunates have been recruited after being fattened up in camps for displaced civilians run by foreign aid agencies.

The government's troops have made some headway on the ground. They captured N'dalatando, a provincial capital, in late April and have increased the pressure on Soyo, a strategically important oil enclave held by UNITA, and on the airstrip at Negage, near Uige. At least 100 foreign mercenaries fighting for the government have taken up positions in Saurimo, a town in the north-east. There, government planes have been deployed to strike at the diamond-rich region around Cafunfo, the source of UNITA's wealth.

It can be no coincidence that the renewed fighting has come at a time when government and rebel negotiators, under UN supervision, are reportedly on the brink

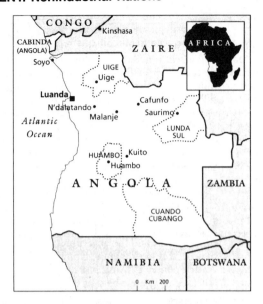

route from the airport at Kinshasa, the capital of Zaire, to rebel airstrips at Cafunfo and Huambo, remains open for business.

The UN's mission in Angola, at least, seems to be taking the prospect of peace seriously. Its mandate has been extended for another month. UN officials have been busy scouting for sites for camps to hold the 6,000 odd UN peacekeepers that would be deployed to oversee any deal. In Luanda the government has been drawing up plans to clear Angola's killing fields of mines and to demobilise the armies.

Officially, only one obstacle to peace remains: the role UNITA will play in a future power-sharing government. President Jose Eduardo dos Santos has offered the rebels four ministries, three governorships and various lesser posts, including control of dozens of municipalities. But the governorships on offer—Cuando Cubango, Uige and Lunda Sul—do not include Huambo, which UNITA, not unreasonably, wants. Mr Savimbi himself has said he does not want an official post, preferring to remain outside government—and, some suspect, well placed to return to war should the next peace not go his way.

of a deal after seven months of peace talks in Zambia. Each time the talks look close to agreement, the two sides try to strengthen their bargaining positions by making military gains. Government army officers are unlikely to agree to a ceasefire until they recapture Soyo and Uige, and manage at least to disrupt UNITA's sales of diamonds from the Cafunfo area. UNITA, meanwhile, looks ready to fight on. The critical supply

---

Nigeria
Clowning around

A YEAR ago, Nigerians went to the polls to elect a president. Their military rulers then annulled the result. On June 12th, exactly one year later, Chief Moshood Abiola, the winner of that poll, declared himself the rightful president, claimed he had set up a parallel government and demanded that the soldiers depart. A hundred policemen were hurriedly dispatched to Mr Abiola's house to arrest him. By the time they got there, he had disappeared, having snuck out, said reports, disguised as a woman.

His escape was wise. Nigeria's current ruling brass-hat, General Sani Abacha, had warned the pesky chief that he would be charged with treason if he went ahead with his plan for a rival government. He did so anyway. But when his allies urged Nigerians to demonstrate in the streets against the army, it was a flop. The police turned out in force, the democrats did not. A few hundred marched through Lagos, the capital, and in a couple of other south-western towns. Banks and businesses in the middle of Lagos stayed shut. Mr Abiola's whereabouts, meanwhile, remained a mystery.

The police have put 50,000 naira ($2,300) on Mr Abiola's head. How serious a threat does he pose? He is an odd figure, a millionaire Muslim Yoruba who owns a publishing business, an airline and a football club. Thanks to his sponsorship of sport, schooling and religion—he has built facilities for Yoruba, Hausa and Ibo, Muslim and Christian alike—he has been named chief of this and that (Bashorun of Ibadan and Magayaki Zazzau of Suleija are just two of some 235 titles). He has even sponsored the continent-wide African soccer cup, consequently claiming last year that he was better known in Africa than Nelson Mandela. Nigerians queuing to vote a year ago said they backed him because he was a rich man who gave people things.

Yet Mr Abiola has hardly proved the most dedicated of populist leaders. After the election result was annulled, he disappeared—to London. The weeks he spent there, while tension in Nigeria rose, lost him much support. Since returning home, he has uttered barely a political word.

In fact, his revival as a democratic symbol is largely the work of others: a group of politicians fed up with the army's broken promises to restore democracy. Last month they formed the National Coalition for Democracy, with support notably in the Yoruba south-west. Driving it are two veteran politicians, Anthony Enahoro, a 72-year-old former minister in Nigeria's first republic, and Michael Ajasin, a former state governor: old-timers not suspected of being interested in politics merely for the loot.

General Abacha insists he is taking democracy seriously: with no apparent irony, he took out a full-page advertisement in *Time* magazine last month to congratulate South Africa on getting there first. He has set up an "elected" conference to start discussing it on June 27th. The coalition is boycotting this as a stage-managed farce, and wants the general to negotiate with itself instead. The army's response has been to throw Mr Enahoro in a police cell for two days and arrest three former state governors. Two senators have been charged with treason. Also detained was Beko Ransome-Kuti, a human-rights campaigner, who this week began a hunger strike in his police cell.

General Abacha's trouble is that his conference will be an even greater farce without the participation of the Yoruba, one of the three big ethnic groups. Yet Mr Abiola himself, and the coalition more generally, can no more readily threaten General Abacha without support from across the country.

The result is stalemate—which is what many cynics suspect was the general's intention all along. Himself in power after forcing out an earlier general, he declared this week that he would not tolerate any "confrontation or subversion". Yet he cannot afford to be complacent. Some senior officers who do not share his agenda are busy manoeuvring. One such has just been posted to run military training in the Gambia.

The public treasury, meanwhile, continues to bleed. The government now appoints a special committee to allocate scarce foreign exchange at the official rate, leaving plenty of scope for political pickings. The reformist finance minister, Kalu Kalu, who many suspect was appointed in a vain attempt to give the soldiers a respectable gloss, is not even allowed to sit on this committee. The state oil company owes over $500m to the various foreign oil companies in (compulsory) joint ventures with it. The government itself is nearly $6 billion in arrears on its external debt; by the end of 1994 that figure could reach $9 billion.

Ordinary Nigerians, who put no trust in their soldier-politicians, have at least one temporary comfort: this week their soccer team set off for America to play in the World Cup. Unfortunately, they arrived in Dallas ten hours late. The crew of their Nigerian Airways flight had not got the right visas.

Canada

A gamble

VANCOUVER

EVERYONE likes easy money. No one more so than governments beset by deficits, unemployment and increasingly tight-fisted taxpayers. That is why Canada's provincial governments have turned to gambling in a big way. They have become the biggest promoters, backers and beneficiaries of gambling in the country—and they are getting bigger, with new ventures in Las Vegas-style casinos.

Last month Ontario opened a new casino operated by Caesar's World, in Windsor, supposedly to create jobs and attract tourists from the United States, just across the river. In fact, the provincial government sees it mostly as a cash cow which, with 62 tables and 1,680 slot-machines, will generate $200m a year in taxes and profits. It joins an earlier Manitoba-owned casino in Winnipeg and a Quebec-owned casino in Montreal. Quebec is planning new casinos for Quebec city and Hull; Nova Scotia has plans for Halifax and Cape Breton.

The glitziest government-backed casino so far is now proposed for Vancouver. The port corporation, a federal agency, has teamed up with Mirage Resorts, a Las Vegas casino operator, in a plan for a $750m cruise-ship-cum-hotel-cum-casino set-up on the harbour front. Some members of British Columbia's cabinet are slavering at the prospect of mega-money the easy way: a new cruise-ship dock—at no cost—for the port, and about $300m a year, one way and another, for the provincial government. But will the plan go through?

Earlier government expansions into casinos were launched without much public opposition (or indeed debate). But this plan has raised a storm. Many citizens fear that hidden costs—for the regulatory bureaucracy, for police to counter prostitution, loan-sharking, money-laun-dering and so on, and for the social impact of gambling addiction—will outweigh any gains in revenue. And many people in Vancouver believe the city does not need gambling to attract tourists. The provincial government has had to promise a serious review.

Provincial governments got hooked on gambling in the 1970s, when they began running lotteries, a business now taking in C$11 billion ($8 billion) a year, to finance social programmes. Then they started licensing small casinos raising funds for charity. And now the big time. Canada's criminal code was amended in 1985 to give the provinces sole jurisdiction over these forms of gambling.

Would the Vancouver venture open the floodgates? Charity-casino operators are already using it as an argument that they should be allowed to offer higher-stake gambling. Native Indians, in British Columbia and elsewhere, are eager to start casinos on their lands (as in the United States); many have tentative deals with international operators. This is a sensitive matter in British Columbia, whose government is eager for an amicable settlement with Indians of their land claims, and would find it difficult, politically and legally, to say No to their casino ambitions.

Beyond this, it is known that Mirage Resorts' real target in Vancouver is not tourists from cruise ships, but high-rollers from Asia. Some people in Vancouver fear an upsurge of money-laundering by Asian criminals. The government reckons it can keep control. But it is hardly a disinterested judge, not by $300m a year.

Chile's Economy Still Bustling

But some observers say growth has been no panacea to the worsening problem of a disparity in wealth

Jack Epstein

Special to The Christian Science Monitor

SANTIAGO, CHILE

In view of the snow-capped Andes mountains, shoppers at the Las Condes mall here buy Gucci bags and Calvin Klein sweaters and snack on Taco Bell burritos.

But across town, in the sprawling slum called La Piñata, dozens of residents hang out on street corners before lining up at one of the city's 124 soup kitchens.

Chile, a country with 14 million inhabitants, is known for its recent economic turnaround—thus, its nickname "Tiger of the Andes."

In the past nine years, the open-border, export-dependent model has produced average gross domestic product growth of 6 percent a year—the fastest clip of any economy in the Western Hemisphere. Inflation has plummeted from an annual rate of 505 percent in 1974 to about 10 percent in 1994.

Exports and foreign investment are surging, and the nation's stock market is up 62 percent in dollar terms so far this year, surpassed only by Brazil. As an auger of future success, Chile is expected to get the nod this week at the Summit of the Americas in Miami to begin negotiations to join the North American Free Trade Agreement.

Yet, economic growth hasn't been a panacea. The gap between the rich and poor has grown, prompting some observers here to refer to the "Two Chiles."

"There are two cultures emerging, one rich and one poor," says Hector Salazar, a human rights lawyer here. "Wealth is more concentrated now than ever."

The disparity in income, common throughout Latin America, is just one problem taking luster out of the new Chile. Mexico, which is on a similar economic path, is channeling private and public funds into infrastructure. But critics here hold that public highways and transportation, schools, and health facilities have deteriorated from the official policy of less government and more privatization.

In general, critics say, Chile is still recovering from the abrupt shift to free-market policies begun under the military dictatorship of Gen. Augusto Pinochet, who ruled from 1973 to 1990. General Pinochet slashed tariffs, ended price controls, and privatized hundreds of state-owned firms. And he spent more on the armed forces than on education, health, and other services. The transition away from a centralized, heavily subsidized economy hit many Chileans hard.

The poverty level more than doubled from 17 per 100 families in 1970 to a peak of at least 38 per 100 in 1987, according to one study by the United Nations Economic Commission for Latin America. Other studies put the poverty-level peak as high as 44 percent of the population. Unemployment soared to a record high of 30 percent in 1983. Soup kitchens appeared in city neighborhoods for the first time.

The latest United Nations and Inter-American Development figures show that the poverty level has fallen to 32 percent to 28 percent of the population. By Latin American standards, Chile is recovering well. But the widening income gap is a concern. The average income of the wealthiest 10 percent of the population is now more than 36 times greater than that of the poorest 10 percent.

The two Chiles are not only visible at shopping malls and soup kitchens. Sixty percent of the total school population attend overcrowded public schools, which lack both materials and qualified teachers.

President Eduardo Frei Ruiz-Tagle assumed power in March, promising to make further progress in the areas of poverty, education, and health. With widespread public and political consensus, he has created the National Committee to Overcome Poverty.

President Frei is following in the footsteps of ex-President Patricio Aylwin Azócar, who won Chile's first democratic election in 20 years in 1990. Mr. Aylwin, who promised "growth and equality," dramatically increased social spending.

Frei campaigned for a gentler capitalism and is expected to not only increase social spending from $1.7 billion in 1993 but spend more on education than defense for the first time since 1973.

"There's not a country in the world that has succeeded in crossing the threshold of development with one-third of its population in poverty," says presidential secretary Genaro Arriagada.

Nevertheless, Frei is getting a much rougher ride from public workers than his predecessor. Wage hikes still lag behind the rate of inflation.

In the past six months, his administration has been rocked by a series of strikes and work stoppages by miners, teachers, and health-care workers. In fact, doctors are threatening to continue with longer strikes every few weeks until they get a pay hike.

Economic growth has slowed in the past year; unemployment has risen to 6.7 percent, the highest rate since 1991. And the number of poor people appears to have leveled off at about 30 percent of the population.

Pro-free trade supporters say joining NAFTA should help keep Chile on the road to prosperity by providing easier access to the wealthy North American market.

But many economists argue that even a 6 percent growth rate won't resolve Chile's poverty problem. Most jobs available in the future, they say, will be in the service and commerce sectors that are traditionally low-paying.

"You can't call yourself a tiger for lowering inflation and having some macro economic successes," Alberto Etchegaray, the director of the government's anti-poverty commission, said recently. "We'll truly be tigers only when everyone feels [that] they are part of the same country."

Who, or what, can get it back on the right path?

The Continent That Lost Its Way

■ *Given the dire economic and social problems that beset Africa, many First World analyses of the continent no longer pull punches, as they once did for fear of blaming the victims or being labeled racist. While understandable jubilation in South Africa dominated recent media coverage—and its progress may indeed offer a sign of hope—Victoria Brittain, a veteran observer of Africa and the Third World, presents a hard look at Africa's real crises and its bleak prospects. Brittain wrote this essay for London's liberal weekly "New Statesman and Society" just before Rwanda's descent into hell this spring, a horror that underscores her warning.*

Across Africa, nation-states are disintegrating under the pressures of economic, environmental, political, and social stress more acute than at any time since the slave trade. Hundreds of thousands of people are on the move, even inside stable countries such as Ghana. In the chronically unstable states such as Sudan, Somalia, Zaire, and Sierra Leone, waves of desperate people pour over the borders into neighboring countries that lack the resources to feed or to care for them.

The Right Reverend Taban Paride, a Catholic bishop from Sudan, recently described the descent into barbarism that he has seen in southern Sudan. His people have been terrorized by the central government's bombing raids and offensives with mechanized artillery. "When a man, on the run since 1991, leaves his wife, or his child, to die beside the road, just putting a little earth on her head, or a woman gives birth on the road and then, in her flight, fords a river that the child cannot survive, . . . these are things too difficult to watch," he said quietly. A process of unraveling of ancient customs and complex civilizations is under way. It threatens vast areas of the continent with a future in which Joseph Conrad's *Heart of Darkness* will be read as a straightforward description.

Now marginalized, Africa's ongoing tragedies arouse only occasional interest outside the continent, when one of the waves of killings hits the TV screen with brief images of horror illuminated by a Western aid official handing out food. The stories of wholesale dispossession, rapes, and innumerable orphans remain the depersonalized tales of far away, evoking none of the media or public reaction that one sick European baby can generate.

In Burundi, Zaire, Somalia, Angola, Liberia, Sierra Leone, and Mozambique, as in Sudan, full-scale wars, fired by rivalry for power and economic resources and stoked by outsiders from Washington to Tehran, from Pretoria to Brussels, have destroyed the state, and none can say whether, or how, it can be reconstituted. In Algeria, Kenya, Senegal, Mali, Mauritania, Niger, and Zambia, economic crisis has fired violent political struggles and wiped out many of the fragile gains of independence.

Who could have imagined, 30 years ago, that, in Algeria—a country whose oil revenues allowed it to make a bid for industrialization unique in Africa—a civil war between Islamic fundamentalists and the army would reduce the government to impotence? Or that in the previously stable, wealthy Kenya, a president would organize a secret ethnic army to maintain his grip on power, turning tens of thousands of his citizens into dispossessed internal refugees? In the 1980s, 100,000 African professionals fled their continent for economic or political reasons, bleeding their countries of the talent, education, and energy that would offer a chance of reversing the trend of de-development.

Chronic underdevelopment was the legacy of nearly a century of colonialism in Africa. As the secretary-general of the Organization of African Unity, Salim Ahmed Salim, put it recently: "Colonial education, limited to training very low functionaries, did not prepare the African for the eventual assumption of leadership and management of the affairs of a modern state." It was a mark of those countries where the leadership itself was highly educated that education was the first priority after independence. In Ghana, Tanzania, and Mozambique—and, much later, Zimbabwe—the explosion of education became the basis for a proud nationalism that once characterized the continent.

Today, schools, dispensaries, even roads dating from the early years of independence have disappeared from huge areas. Local government and the rule of law have gone with them. Economies have collapsed. Corruption has become banal: Small, wealthy elites enjoy satellite TV, foreign travel, and the consumer tastes of Europe and America. They are more alienated from the majority than ever before. Africa is the poorest continent in the world and the only one getting poorer.

The core of the problem is economic. Africa is virtually excluded from the world economy, which revolves increasingly around the three dominant poles of Western Europe, North America, and the Pacific Rim. The North now has little need for Africa's primary products. In addition, competition from Asia and Latin America, encouraged by the World Bank, has taken the prices of African exports lower and lower.

R aw materials and commodities, which account for 94 percent of Africa's exports, have seen their prices crash on the world market. In a decade, coffee and cocoa prices have dropped by 34 and 46 percent, respectively. Many countries have economies virtually dependent on these commodities. In Burundi, 80 percent of revenue comes from coffee alone. Meanwhile, since 1960, the population of Africa has doubled, and food production has slipped back to a level 20 percent lower than that in 1970. This fall in food production stems partly from the agricultural policies, mainly suggested by Northern experts and institutions, that gave priority to the export crops that have served Africans so badly.

In the countries of the Sahel—Mauritania, Chad, Niger, Mali, Burkina Faso, Senegal, Sudan, Somalia, and Ethiopia—another factor in the vicious circle of instability is desertification. Water resources that used to satisfy great herds of elephants, as well as the camels and goats of the nomads, have partially dried up. Centuries-old forms of land use are under impossible pressures, and, like the Tuareg nomad women who beg on the streets of Accra or the former herdsmen who hustle in the markets of Dakar—both hundreds of miles south of their traditional homes—a new generation is giving up the battle against a hostile environment. Among those who remain, the competition for scarce resources sparks ethnic tensions such as expulsions of blacks from Mauritania and minor border wars between Burkina Faso and Mali. It is a major factor in the more devastating wars of the Horn of Africa and Sudan.

The wholesale destruction of primary rain forests in Sierra Leone, Guinea, and Ivory Coast is another strand of environmental degradation. In 30 years, Sierra Leone's rain forest has dwindled from 60 percent of the country to 6 percent. The erosion that follows deforestation is visible from the east to the west of Africa, as rivers run red-brown, carrying earth out to sea, and more peasants are forced off depleted land.

Uncounted thousands from the Sahel swell West Africa's urban slums. The new scourge of HIV is spreading faster in urban Africa than anywhere else in the world, and AIDS is already threatening to decimate the most productive age group in society, with devastating effects on the economy. In the next two decades, another 500 million people are expected to converge on the continent's urban areas, swamping whatever services still exist. Latin American-style, heavily protected ghettos where the rich live exist already. In a few years, they will need private armies to protect them.

Virtually no industrial investment comes to Africa's urban centers—there are no telecommunications, transportation infrastructure, or political or social stability to attract foreign business, despite the cheapness of African labor. In fact, it costs 50 percent more to run a business in Africa than in Asia, and the profits in Asia are nine times greater, according to a recent American report. In the 1980s, three quarters of all investment in developing countries went to just 10 countries—none in Africa. The 1990s will be no different.

The dream at independence was of freedom from colonialism. Today's dreams are more modest—personal ones born of the new mood of desperation: dreams of dignity, of education, health, employment, and land. Few of today's leaders articulate such goals at the grass-roots level.

In the mid-1980s, Thomas Sankara, the young president of the tiny, resourceless former French colony of Upper Volta, changed his country's name to Burkina Faso, which means "Land of Honest Men." He went to war on behalf of the poorest peasants against the privileged urban middle class. Sankara became a hero across the continent, because his every speech was an affirmation that change was possible—and that Africa was not condemned to a future as miserable as the present. More powerful than speeches were symbolic shifts of power: Government ministers, for example, saw their Mercedeses replaced with small Renaults. The budget was publicly debated in the national stadium for days and nights; rich and powerful men went to prison. But Sankara was killed in a coup mounted by his longtime friend, the current president, Blaise Compaoré, and Burkina Faso has reverted to the backwoods that Upper Volta was.

The death of Sankara was one symbol of the lost battle for national dignity. Another was the reversal of the politics of the post-independence period by the powerful ruling parties in such standard-bearers of the left as Algeria, Tanzania, Angola, and Mozambique. While the last two were victims of the special circumstances of a 30-year war with apartheid and its allies, the first two represent the failure of the best of one-party states under the external economic and political pressures of the 1970s and 1980s. Algeria and Tanzania once made the greatest contribution to the continent in terms of intellectual and practical leadership in key international policies.

B ut even before the full economic disaster of the 1980s hit, somewhere around the mid-1970s, the wave of pride and confidence in those policies failed at the most important point—the grass roots. The one-party states built into themselves a rigidity that prohibited democracy; a defensiveness that stifled debate, academic freedom, and the media. Increasingly, a divide developed between the elites in power and the people they had come to power to serve.

In reaction to years of political suffocation, an explosion of popular participation was seen in the late 1980s. Mass street protests culminated in national conferences; years of frustration with an ossified system were vented by a civil society previously kept invisible by repression. But the changes of regime were far less dramatic. Some parties, as in Zaire, Togo, and Kenya, simply stayed in place; other countries, such as Nigeria and Algeria, saw elections canceled. In those states where there was a change, as in Zambia, the incoming party was quickly bogged down in a crisis of disappointed expectations. The new leaders have no more economic leeway than their predecessors.

But at another level, a more hopeful legacy of the political failures is emerging in a new civil society. Modest new nongovernmental organizations are grappling with the urban problems of street children, drug addition, and unemployment. A new generation is fighting local battles with old community structures, independently of their discredited governments or advisers from the rich North. Battling to prevent what Robert Kaplan's apocalyptic article in the *Atlantic Monthly* forecasts as "the coming anarchy" in the Third World, Africa needs a reversal of current education policies to produce a new generation of leaders with the vision and confidence to speak for their people's dreams of a different Africa.

The Burden of Womanhood

Too often in the Third World, a female's life is hardly worth living

John Ward Anderson and Molly Moore

Washington Post Foreign Service

GANDHI NAGAR, India

When Rani returned home from the hospital cradling her newborn daughter, the men in the family slipped out of her mud hut while she and her mother-in-law mashed poisonous oleander seeds into a dollop of oil and forced it down the infant's throat. As soon as darkness fell, Rani crept into a nearby field and buried her baby girl in a shallow, unmarked grave next to a small stream.

"I never felt any sorrow," Rani, a farm laborer with a weather-beaten face, said through an interpreter. "There was a lot of bitterness in my heart toward the baby because the gods should have given me a son."

Each year hundreds and perhaps thousands of newborn girls in India are murdered by their mothers simply because they are female. Some women believe that sacrificing a daughter guarantees a son in the next pregnancy. In other cases, the family cannot afford the dowry that would eventually be demanded for a girl's marriage.

And for many mothers, sentencing a daughter to death is better than condemning her to life as a woman in the Third World, with cradle-to-grave discrimination, poverty, sickness and drudgery.

"In a culture that idolizes sons and dreads the birth of a daughter, to be born female comes perilously close to being born less than human," the Indian government conceded in a recent report by its Department of Women and Child Development.

While women in the United States and Europe—after decades of struggling for equal rights—often measure sex discrimination by pay scales and seats in corporate board rooms, women in the Third World gauge discrimination by mortality rates and poverty levels.

"Women are the most exploited among the oppressed," says Karuna Chanana Ahmed, a New Delhi anthropologist who has studied the role of women in developing countries. "I don't think it's even possible to eradicate discrimination, it's so deeply ingrained."

PHOTO BY JOHN WARD ANDERSON—THE WASHINGTON POST

Rani, 31, with Asha, 2, says she killed another daughter 3½ years ago. "I wanted to kill this child also . . . . Now I have killed, I still haven't had any sons."

From the *Washington Post National Weekly Edition*, March 22–28, 1993, pp. 6-7. © 1993 by the Washington Post. Reprinted by permission.

4. DEVELOPMENT: Nonindustrial Nations

This is the first in a series that will examine the lives of women in developing countries around the globe where culture, religion and the law often deprive women of basic human rights and sometimes relegate them to almost subhuman status. From South America to South Asia, women are often subjected to a lifetime of discrimination with little or no hope of relief.

As children, they are fed less, denied education and refused hospitalization. As teenagers, many are forced into marriage, sometimes bought and sold like animals for prostitution and slave labor. As wives and mothers, they are often treated little better than farmhands and baby machines. Should they outlive their husbands, they frequently are denied inheritance, banished from their homes and forced to live as beggars on the streets.

The scores of women interviewed for this series—from destitute villagers in Brazil and Bangladesh, to young professionals in Cairo, to factory workers in China—blamed centuries-old cultural and religious traditions for institutionalizing and giving legitimacy to gender discrimination.

Although, the forms of discrimination vary tremendously among regions, ethnic groups and age levels in the developing world, Shahla Zia, an attorney and women's activist in Islamabad, Pakistan, says there is a theme: "Overall, there is a social and cultural attitude where women are inferior—and discrimination tends to start at birth."

In many countries, a woman's greatest challenge is an elemental one: simply surviving through a normal life cycle. In South Asia and China, the perils begin at birth, with the threat of infanticide.

Like many rural Indian women, Rani, now 31, believed that killing her daughter 3 ½ years ago would guarantee that her next baby would be a boy. Instead, she had another daughter.

"I wanted to kill this child also," she says, brushing strands of hair from the face of the 2-year-old girl she named Asha, or Hope. "But my husband got scared because all these social workers came and said, 'Give us the child.'" Ultimately, Rani was allowed to keep her. She pauses. "Now I have killed, and I still haven't had any sons."

Amravati, who lives in a village near Rani in the Indian state of Tamil Nadu, says she killed two of her own day-old daughters by pouring scalding chicken soup down their throats, one of the most widely practiced methods of infanticide in southern India. She showed where she buried their bodies—under piles of cow dung in the tiny courtyard of her home.

"My mother-in-law and father-in-law are bedridden," says Amravati, who has two living daughters. "I have no land and no salary, and my husband met with an accident and can't work. Of course it was the right decision. I need

a boy. Even though I have to buy clothes and food for a son, he will grow on his own and take care of himself. I don't have to buy him jewelry or give him a 10,000-rupee [$350] dowry."

Sociologists and government officials began documenting sporadic examples of female infanticide in India about 10 years ago. The practice of killing newborn girls is largely a rural phenomenon in India; although its extent has not been documented, one indication came in a recent survey by the Community Services Guild of Madras, a city in Tamil Nadu. Of the 1,250 women questioned, the survey concluded that more than half had killed baby daughters.

In urban areas, easier access to modern medical technology enables women to act before birth. Through amniocentesis, women can learn the sex of a fetus and undergo sex-selective abortions. At one clinic in Bombay, of 8,000 abortions performed after amniocentesis, 7,999 were of female fetuses, according to a recent report by the Indian government. To be sure, female infanticide and sex-selective abortion are not unique to India. Social workers in other South Asian states believe that some communities also condone the practice. In China, one province has had so many cases of female infanticide that a half-million bachelors cannot find wives because they outnumber women their age by 10 to 1, according to the official New China News Agency.

The root problems, according to village women, sociologists and other experts, are cultural and economic. In India, a young woman is regarded as a temporary member of her natural family and a drain on its wealth. Her parents are considered caretakers whose main responsibility is to deliver a chaste daughter, along with a sizable dowry, to her husband's family.

"They say bringing up a girl is like watering a neighbor's plant," says R. Venkatachalam, director of the Community Services Guild of Madras. "From birth to death, the expenditure is there." The dowry, he says, often wipes out a family's life savings but is necessary to arrange a proper marriage and maintain the honor of the bride's family.

After giving birth to a daughter, village women "immediately start thinking, 'Do we have the money to support her through life?' and if they don't, they kill her," according to Vasanthai, 20, the mother of an 18-month-old girl and a resident of the village where Rani lives. "You definitely do it after two or three daughters. Why would you want more?"

Few activists or government officials in India see female infanticide as a law-and-order issue, viewing it instead as a social problem that should be eradicated through better education, family planning and job programs. Police officials say few cases are reported and witnesses seldom cooperate.

"There are more pressing issues," says a top police official in Madras. "Very few cases come to our attention. Very few people care."

Surviving childbirth is itself an achievement in South Asia for both mother and baby. One of every 18 women dies of a pregnancy-related cause, and more than one of every 10 babies dies during delivery.

For female children, the survival odds are even worse. Almost one in every five girls born in Nepal and Bangladesh dies before age 5. In India, about one-fourth of the 12 million girls born each year die by age 15.

The high death rates are not coincidental. Across the developing world, female children are fed less, pulled out of school earlier, forced into hard labor sooner and given less medical care than boys. According to numerous studies, girls are handicapped not only by the perception that they are temporary members of a family, but also by the belief that males are the chief breadwinners and therefore more deserving of scarce resources.

Boys are generally breast-fed longer. In many cultures, women and girls eat leftovers after the men and boys have finished their meals. According to a joint report by the United Nations Children's Fund and the government of Pakistan, some tribal groups do not feed high-protein foods such as eggs and meat to girls because of the fear it will lead to early puberty.

Women are often hospitalized only when they have reached a critical stage of illness, which is one reason so many mothers die in childbirth. Female children, on the other hand, often are not hospitalized at all. A 1990 study of patient records at Islamabad Children's Hospital in Pakistan found that 71 percent of the babies admitted under age 2 were boys. For all age groups, twice as many boys as girls were admitted to the hospital's surgery, pediatric intensive care and diarrhea units.

Mary Okumu, an official with the African Medical and Research Foundation in Nairobi, says that when a worker in drought-ravaged northern Kenya asked why only boys were lined up at a clinic, the worker was told that in times of drought, many families let their daughters die.

"Nobody will even take them to a clinic," Okumu says. "They prefer the boy to survive."

For most girls, however, the biggest barrier—and the one that locks generations of women into a cycle of discrimination—is lack of education.

Across the developing world, girls are withdrawn from school years before boys so they can remain at home and lug water, work the fields, raise younger siblings and help with other domestic chores. By the time girls are 10 or 12 years old, they may put in as much as an eight-hour work day, studies show. One survey found that a young girl in rural India spends 30 percent of her waking hours doing household work, 29 percent gathering fuel and 20 percent fetching water.

Statistics from Pakistan demonstrate the low priority given to female education: Only one-third of the country's schools—which are sexually segregated—are for women, and one-third of those have no building. Almost 90 percent of the women over age 25 are illiterate. In the predominantly rural state of Baluchistan, less than 2 percent of women can read and write.

In Islamic countries such as Pakistan and Bangladesh, religious concern about interaction with males adds further restrictions to females' mobility. Frequently, girls are taken out of school when they reach puberty to limit their contact with males—though there exists a strong impetus for early marriages. In Bangladesh, according to the United Nations, 73 percent of girls are married by age 15, and 21 percent have had at least one child.

Across South Asia, arranged marriages are the norm and can sometimes be the most demeaning rite of passage a woman endures. Two types are common—bride wealth, in which the bride's family essentially gives her to the highest bidder, and dowry, in which the bride's family pays exorbitant amounts to the husband's family.

In India, many men resort to killing their wives—often by setting them afire—if they are unhappy with the dowry. According to the country's Ministry of Human Resource Development, there were 5,157 dowry murders in 1991—one every hour and 42 minutes.

After being bartered off to a new family, with little education, limited access to health care and no knowledge of birth control, young brides soon become young mothers. A woman's adulthood is often spent in a near constant state of pregnancy, hoping for sons.

According to a 1988 report by India's Department of Women and Child Development: "The Indian woman on an average has eight to nine pregnancies, resulting in a little over six live births, of which four or five survive. She is estimated to spend 80 percent of her reproductive years in pregnancy and lactation." Because of poor nutrition and a hard workload, she puts on about nine pounds during pregnancy, compared with 22 pounds for a typical pregnant woman in a developed country.

A recent study of the small Himalayan village of Bemru by the New Delhi-based Center for Science and the Environment found that "birth in most cases takes place in the cattle shed," where villagers believe that holy cows protect the mother and newborn from evil spirits. Childbirth is considered unclean, and the mother and their newborn are treated as "untouchables" for about two weeks after delivery.

"It does not matter if the woman is young, old or pregnant, she has no rest, Sunday or otherwise," the study said, noting that women in the village did 59 percent of the work, often laboring 14 hours a day and lugging loads 1 1/2 times their body weight. "After two or three . . . pregnancies, their stamina gives up, they get weaker, and by the late thirties are spent out, old and tired, and soon die."

Studies show that in developing countries, women in remote areas can spend more than two hours a day carrying water for cooking, drinking, cleaning and bathing, and in some rural areas they spend the equivalent of more than 200 days a year gathering firewood. That presents an additional hazard: The International Labor Organization found that women using wood fuels in India inhaled carcinogenic pollutants that are the equivalent of smoking 20 packs of cigarettes a day.

Because of laws relegating them to a secondary status, women have few outlets for relaxation or recreation. In many Islamic countries, they are not allowed to drive cars, and their appearance in public is so restricted that they are banned from such recreational and athletic activities as swimming and gymnastics.

In Kenya and Tanzania, laws prohibit women from owning houses. In Pakistan, a daughter legally is entitled to half the inheritance a son gets when their parents die. In some criminal cases, testimony by women is legally given half the weight of a man's testimony, and compensation for the wrongful death of a woman is half that for the wrongful death of a man.

After a lifetime of brutal physical labor, multiple births, discrimination and sheer tedium, what should be a woman's golden years often hold the worst indignities. In India, a woman's identity is so intertwined and subservient to her husband's that if she outlives him, her years as a widow are spent as a virtual nonentity. In previous generations, many women were tied to their husband's funeral pyres and burned to death, a practice called *suttee* that now rarely occurs.

Today, some widows voluntarily shave their heads and withdraw from society, but more often a spartan lifestyle is forced upon them by families and a society that place no value on old, single women. Widowhood carries such a stigma that remarriage is extremely rare, even for women who are widowed as teenagers.

In some areas of the country, women are forced to marry their dead husband's brother to ensure that any property remains in the family. Often they cannot wear jewelry or a *bindi*—the beauty spot women put on their foreheads—or they must shave their heads and wear a white sari. Frequently, they cannot eat fish or meat, garlic or onions.

"The life of a widow is miserable," says Aparna Basu, general secretary of the All India Women's Conference, citing a recent study showing that more than half the women in India age 60 and older are widows, and their mortality rate is three times higher than that of married women of the same age.

In South Asia, women have few property or inheritance rights, and a husband's belongings usually go to sons and occasionally daughters. A widow must rely on the largess of her children, who often cast their mothers on the streets.

Thousands of destitute Indian widows make the pilgrimage to Vrindaban, a town on the outskirts of Agra where they hope to achieve salvation by praying to the god Krishna. About 1,500 widows show up each day at the Shri Bhagwan prayer house, where in exchange for singing "Hare Rama, Hare Krishna" for eight hours, they are given a handful of rice and beans and 1.5 rupees, or about 5 cents.

Some widows claim that when they stop singing, they are poked with sticks by monitors, and social workers allege that younger widows have been sexually assaulted by temple custodians and priests.

On a street there, an elderly woman with a *tilak* on her forehead—white chalk lines signifying that she is a devout Hindu widow—waves a begging cup at passing strangers.

"I have nobody," says Paddo Chowdhury, 65, who became a widow at 18 and has been in Vrindaban for 30 years. "I sit here, shed my tears and get enough food one way or another."

LAND MINES ON THE ROAD TO UTOPIA

Less menaced by doomsday than in the cold-war era, the world remains plagued by regional conflicts, environmental destruction, and overpopulation

If Emina, a Bosnian woman in her 40s, tried to look ahead to the 21st century, her view would be bleak. She's from Mostar, a centuries-old town on the Neretva River. It used to have one of Europe's most picturesque village centers. Now, after months of shelling, the damage is worse than in better-known Sarajevo, just 50 miles away. "I had everything, but it's all gone," says Emina, who now lives in a refugee camp in Croatia. "Two houses, a dishwasher, a video, a tractor. All gone." She doesn't mention incomparably greater losses: the deaths of all her menfolk in the fighting.

Of course, communism is dead and buried, and market capitalism is triumphing from Poland to Peru. Hundreds of millions of people are prospering, and billions may finally hope to escape from grinding poverty in a global economic bonanza unparalleled in human history. But Emina and her ruined Mostar are stark reminders of the possible setbacks and detours on the road to this better future.

CONSTANT THREAT. Governments, businesses, and international agencies will have to deal with these new uncertainties. In this transitional era, growth creates such hazards as pollution and overpopulation, global capital markets carry the potential for unprecedented instability, and old ethnic and nationalist hatreds can snuff out the gains of countries such as the former Yugoslavia.

Though the world will be more chaotic, it will also be less menaced by doomsday than the era that ended with the fall of the Berlin Wall. The four-decade face-off between the United States and the Soviet Union—the nuclear "balance of terror"—was a frightening chapter in human history. But the division of the world into two blocs, each led by a superpower with its allies and clients, at least brought a stable framework to big power relations. And the Iron and Bamboo curtains restricted the impact free-wheeling capitalism could have on undeveloped economies and markets.

Now geopolitical analysts, trying to discern the future's shape, see plenty of possible scenarios that if unchecked could slow the pace of global development and undermine the confidence many countries now have in market capitalism and its benefits. Interdependence—the flow of information, goods, money, and people—is magnifying the disruptive potential of events such as the outbreak of plague in India or the assassinations of Mexican political leaders and the Chiapas uprising. Too many such episodes could send investors retreating and drive governments to such measures as currency controls, trade barriers, and new isolationism.

War or the threat of war will pose a constant threat to global psychology. By one count, there are at least 30 "low-intensity" wars and insurgencies under way, from Angola to Peru and Turkey. Their number will increase, warns Martin van Creveld, a military historian at Israel's Hebrew University who has served as a consultant to the U.S., Canadian, and Swedish armed forces. "Large-scale interstate war is coming to an end," says Creveld. In its place he foresees "relatively smaller-scale conflicts."

Francis Fukuyama, a Rand senior researcher and former State Dept. official who coined the phrase "end of history" to describe the triumph of democratic capitalism over communism, says these wars afflict countries that remain trapped "in history." But many countries in Africa remain mired in economic stagnation and old conflicts. And with the removal of the blanket of Soviet power that dampened tribal, religious, and racial antagonisms, ethnic miniwars have erupted in the ex-Soviet republics of the Caucasus and Central Asia.

Despite such turmoil, Fukuyama argues there is no longer any credible alternative to the free market and democracy as the model for modern societies. All up-and-coming countries-those that will dominate the world-have adopted such a system or are moving toward it, in his view. That, he says, will lead to "a kind of democratic zone of peace."

But the advanced and advancing countries face their own threat from the market forces that bring them wealth. The impact is seen in the huge

From *Business Week*, Special Edition, October 1994, pp. 136-138, 140. © 1994 by McGraw Hill, Inc. Reprinted by special permission.

financial flows surging through the increasingly open global trading system. Today, a Singapore company backed by Taiwanese capital can use Israeli software to manufacture telecommunication devices in China for sale in the U.S. The company can hedge its U.S. dollar earnings for the next three years by simply taking options written on London's foreign exchange market.

LOSS OF CONTROL. Ten or 15 years ago, trade restrictions, currency regulations, political barriers, and the simple lack of electronic trading would have made this web of transactions unthinkable. If communism, as Lenin claimed, was Soviet political power plus electricity, today's global capitalism is free trade plus microprocessors.

Yet the ability of the Singaporean company to scour the world for the best technology, capital, and markets—the openness at the heart of today's free economies—has a potentially dangerous downside. That is the loss of control on the part of institutions that once policed the global marketplace. Everywhere, regulators are being bewildered by hybrid financial instruments from mortgage-backed securities to currency swaps and multibillion-dollar hedge funds. By some estimates, such dimly understood financial derivatives have a nominal value of $20 trillion—more than three times the size of the U.S. economy.

The investors of those funds have not panicked enough yet to overturn the system. Yet the potential shakiness of the markets is enormous. Just how little sway governments now exercise over globe-girdling money surges was revealed in June, when central bankers of the Group of Seven led a $4 billion coordinated intervention to support the dollar. Foreign exchange markets, which routinely trade $1 trillion a day, hardly noticed.

The message from that episode: Markets driven by short-term forces can override the will of nation-states to stop them. Indeed, in other areas of social life, the nation-state itself, the central institution in the West for 300 years, is in decline. Deregulation of

economies and downsizing of armed forces in most countries are diminishing governments' size and authority. Privatization, now a multibillion-a-year global business that frees up resources with sell-offs of everything from power monopolies to telephone companies, lessens state authority. Pensions, traditionally a basic government function, are being handed over rapidly to the private sector.

Such developments, spurring efficiency, are mostly positive. But as governments shrink, their ability to cushion the shocks of global change is also diminishing just when the pace and scale of changes are accelerating. Economic restructuring is causing vast job dislocations, from Chiapas to China, where as many as 100 million former rural workers have left their villages to seek work elsewhere, mostly on the booming east coast. The lowering of trade barriers is also removing protections for industries and workers that are often among the poorest and most vulnerable. And cheaper, faster transport and communications have triggered migrations that are eroding states' control over their borders. The result is rising social tensions and political backlash.

REBUILDING EFFORTS. To cope with this upheaval, some of the traditional functions of the nation-state are being taken over by plodding supranational institutions like the European Union and the U.N. But as civil war in Yugoslavia has shown, the EU and the U.N. are having great difficulty keeping the peace. And without a stable global-security system, the door is open to a variety of thugs, warlords, and maverick dictators, from Serbia's Slobodan Milosevic to Iraq's Saddam Hussein. To thwart Saddam's latest saber-rattling, President Clinton was able to reactivate mechanisms that were put in place by Desert Storm. But the U.S., though it is now the world's only superpower, is ill-equipped politically and militarily to cope with many of these challenges, from Somalia to Serbian warlords.

Part of the problem is setting priorities. The wealthy societies of Europe

and America can mobilize resources to combat the effects of disruption. They rebuilt Los Angeles' looted ghetto section, and Germany spent $450 billion to buy out the rundown German Democratic Republic. "It's the countries where you don't have the resources to take care of the inequalities that will be the biggest problems," says Harvard University's Richard B. Freeman, an expert on income distribution. That includes the roughly two-fifths of the globe where Marxism-Leninism once held sway. Freeman is worried about social strains in Russia itself, where male life expectancy is falling and gangsters live lavishly while government officials are paid just enough to survive.

"We have been living off [our] natural capital," says a State Dept. official, "and that's coming to an end"

The danger of instability in Russia is also a nightmare scenario for strategic planners. If President Boris Yeltsin is unable to keep a firm grip on the reins of power in the sprawling Russian federation, he could also lose control over its stockpile of some 50,000 nuclear warheads.

China, too, holds frightening possibilities. If Beijing's communist leaders can't hold together the increasingly disunited country, provincial bosses could become latter-day nuclear-armed warlords, or the central government could resort to throwing its political and military weight around. Such a threat could touch off a weapons race in East Asia. Says risk analyst Peter Schwartz, president of Global Business Networks in Emeryville, Calif.: "The greatest growth in arms spending in the world now is in Asia. There's a relatively high probability of conflict in the region."

On an increasingly crowded planet, the new surge of capitalist prosperity could also choke on its own success. Deforestation, loss of farmland, pollution of air and water supplies, depletion of fisheries, and proliferating streams of toxic waste are setting off alarm bells about the sustainability of economic growth. "We have been living off an enormous supply of natural capital," says U.S. Under Secretary of State for Global Affairs Timothy E. Wirth, "and that's coming to an end all over the world."

From tiny Haiti to giant China, environmental stresses and depletion are becoming acute. So thick is the smog over Benxi, a city of one million in northeastern China, that the city doesn't appear on satellite maps. In Tianjin, wells are draining groundwater so fast that the city is sinking 2.5 meters per year. Across China, soil erosion and urban sprawl are shrinking farmland in a country with 14 million new mouths to feed every year.

To boost income and head off discontent, Beijing's aging hierarchs believe they have only one choice: Go for growth, and worry about the environment later. But with roughly 1.2 billion people living on a limited resource base, swift environmental deterioration could put a sharp brake on growth. If China runs into an environmental wall, the shocks could reverberate around the world.

China's soaring energy demand, for example could trigger clashes with neighbors over oil in the South China Sea. And in the Middle East, water conflicts are bound to intensify. At the global level, Thomas Selden, an environmental economist at Syracuse University, thinks concentrations of carbon dioxide, a contributor to global warming, and other atmospheric pollutants will keep going up steeply. "We are engaged in an unparalleled experiment with the earth's atmosphere," he says.

SALVAGE JOB. At some stage of economic development—around $8,000 of gross domestic product a person, Selden figures—countries tend to feel wealthy enough to start trying to salvage their environments. But China, India, and Southeast Asian countries are nowhere near that point. While Taiwan and South Korea are now spending heavily on ecological repairs, one of the ways they are doing it is by going to other countries and taking resources from them. "It's a bit like an environmental chain letter—the Madagascars and Ecuadors get left at the bottom," maintains the U.S.'s Wirth.

The road to global prosperity through freer markets and democracy is probably studded with many such pitfalls, detours, and surprises. But at the least, the evident problems—pollution, overpopulation, poverty—will have to be dealt with soon. Otherwise, these obstacles may expand to such massive proportions they will block off the goal.

By John Rossant in Rome, with John Pearson in New York and bureau reports

THE TRIPLE REVOLUTION

Simultaneous upheavals in politics, technology, and economics could usher in an age of growth

Every once in a great while, the established order is overthrown. Within a span of decades, technological advances, organizational innovations, and new ways of thinking transform economies. From the 1760s to the 1830s, steam engines, textile mills, and the Enlightenment produced the Industrial Revolution. The years 1880 to 1930 were shaped by the spread of electric power, mass production, and democracy.

On the eve of the 21st century, the signs of monumental change are all around us. Chinese capitalists. Russian entrepreneurs. Nelson Mandela President of South Africa. Inflation at 7% in Argentina. Internet connections expanding by 15% a month. Fiber optics transmitting 40 billion bits of data per second. From government dictators to assembly-line workers, everyone seems aware that unfamiliar and unusually powerful forces are at work. Says Shimon Peres, Israel's Foreign Minister: "We are not entering a new century. We are entering a new era."

A great transformation in world history is creating a new economic, social, and political order. Communism's collapse and the embrace of freer markets by much of the developing world are driving huge increases in global commerce and international investment. The Information Revolution is forging strong links between nations, companies, and peoples. Improving education levels are creating a global middle class that shares "similar concepts of citizenship, similar ideas about economic progress, and a similar pic-

ture of human rights," says John Meyer, professor of sociology at Stanford University. Almost 150 years following the publication of the *Communist Manifesto,* and more than half a century after the rise of totalitarianism, the bourgeoisie has won.

PLUNGING POVERTY. Indeed, behind these simultaneous revolutions lies one powerful idea: openness. Governments everywhere are pursuing liberal economic policies. Multinational corporations are accelerating the exchange of innovations across open borders. Global investors are pressuring companies everywhere to open their books. Populations are demanding stronger political and civil rights.

Usual yardsticks may underestimate the chances for global prosperity

---

Already, signs of a payoff are apparent. The growth rate for developing Asia averaged a heady 7.8% a year from 1985 to 1990, and by the end of the decade, one-tenth of everything produced in the world will hail from developing Asia, according to DRI/McGraw-Hill, the economic consulting firm. In China, the percentage of people living below the poverty line has plunged from 33% in 1970 to 10% in 1990. Latin America, stagnant for much of the 1970s and 1980s, has been expanding at a 3% pace since 1991.

The traumatized economies of Eastern Europe appear ready to generate growth rates of 4% to 6% over the next several years. Even in sub-Saharan Africa, a region of the world experiencing severe economic problems, the global investment community has been taking a keen look at the new South Africa.

A growing number of governments in developing countries and emerging markets are struggling to get the fundamentals right: keep inflation low and fiscal policies prudent; maintain high savings and investment rates; improve the education level of the population; trade with the outside world and encourage foreign direct investment. In the 1990s, the 16 largest developing economies have all sharply reduced tariff, tax, and other barriers to foreign direct investment. And any country that runs the currency printing presses or walls out private foreign capital pays a steep price in economic welfare these days. "Most developing nations have turned away from self-sufficiency and hostility to the outside world, and see it is in their interests to connect [to it] as rapidly as they can," says Paul Romer, economist at the University of California at Berkeley.

What's more, the usual yardsticks may underestimate prospects for global prosperity. In the decades following the Bolshevik Revolution of 1917 and colonialism's end in the 1950s and 1960s, economic-development efforts largely focused on central planning and government-led investment. And the best and brightest people from Brazil to the

The Faces of Capitalism

CONSUMER CAPITALISM U.S., BRITAIN, CANADA, AUSTRALIA	PRODUCER CAPITALISM GERMANY, FRANCE, JAPAN, MEXICO	FAMILY CAPITALISM TAIWAN, MALAYSIA, THAILAND, INDONESIA	FRONTIER CAPITALISM CHINA, RUSSIA
TRAITS: Laissez-faire, open borders, small government, profit mentality	• Emphasizes production, employment, statist policies	• Created by Chinese diaspora, extended clans dominate business, and capital flows	• Government pursues for-profit business activities, entrepreneurial class sprouts
POTENTIAL PROBLEMS: Income inequality, low savings rates, weak central governments	• Fraying of social safety net, slowing innovation, consumer dissatisfaction	• Creating modern corporate organizations and money markets	• Must establish rule of law, open borders, curb criminal activity

Soviet Union joined the government bureaucracy, the military, or other economically unproductive institutions. When P. T. Bauer, the late development economist, lectured at a dozen or so Indian universities and research centers in 1970, teachers and students alike believed that central planning was indispensable for raising living standards. The only question was whether the Soviet or the Chinese model was the superior approach for development.

Today, the balance of power has decisively shifted away from government planners and toward markets. When markets are large and laws allow people to build companies and keep their profits, more and more talented citizens become entrepreneurs and wealth-creators. One study, covering many of the world's economies, by economists Andrei Schliefer, Kevin Murphy, and Robert Vishny, estimated that if an extra 10% of university students went into engineering, the growth rate of an economy would rise by 0.5% a year. "What were once called Third World countries are developing much faster than you would suppose if constrained by the traditional models of economic growth," says Donald N. McCloskey, economist at the University of Iowa.

Openness: It's the one powerful idea that lies behind all these upheavals

---

And over long periods of time, small differences loom large. For example, from 1870 to 1990, real per capita gross domestic product in the U.S. rose by 1.75% a year, to the world's highest level—from $2,224 to $18,258. Had the American growth rate been only one percentage point less a year—0.75%—then real per capita GDP in 1990 would have been $5,519, or about that of Mexico and Hungary, according to Robert J. Barro, economist at Harvard University.

ETHNIC CONFLICT. On a global scale, freer trade will spur growth by providing entrepreneurs from major economies access to bigger markets. Trade also encourages the spread of new technologies and manufacturing techniques. General Electric Co. is sinking tens of millions of dollars into building factories and power plants in Mexico and India. Microsoft Corp. gets more than 50% of its revenue from international sales. Toyota Motor Corp. is powering its way into Southeast Asia as is Volkswagen into China.

To be sure, revolutions are tumultuous. From the vast lands of the former Soviet Union to the Amazon forest in Brazil, frontier capitalism is brutal and very often criminal. In many developing countries, sweatshops and slums are commonplace, a bleak, Dickensian world of worker misery and raw social and political tensions. Fast growth in China and elsewhere creates dismaying environmental destruction. Corruption and sclerotic bureaucracies are deeply entrenched. Ethnic conflicts are flaring.

Still, the impact of global integration on growth could be staggering. Over the past two centuries, as national boundaries have shrunk in importance, the pace of economic development has quickened. Britain needed nearly 60 years to double its output per person beginning in 1780. It took Japan 34 years starting in the 1880s and South Korea only 11 years after 1966. "At the turn of the century, stellar growth meant 4% a year. Now, it means 10% plus," says Jeffrey D. Sachs, economist at Harvard University. Adds Henry S. Rowan, a professor at Stanford University's business school: "A process is under way that promises within a generation to make most of the world's population rich or much richer than it is today."

Take the three regions of the world where private enterprise is being unleashed: most of Asia, including India and China; Mexico and parts of Latin America; and several East European countries. These areas make up 50% of the world's population and about 20% of the GDP of the industrial nations. If these three regions achieve annual growth rates of 8% over the next 10 years—somewhat less than the sizzling performance of Asia's Four Tigers in the 1980s—then they would contribute almost as much to world growth as the industrial nations. Within several decades, a number of developing nations including Taiwan and Korea will join the club of wealthy nations. "Because the emerging markets' growth rates are much higher than those in the developed world, we are definitely seeing convergence," says Giles Keating, economist at CS First Boston in London.

Another benefit of global interdependence is lower inflation rates. True, industrial commodity prices will go up, especially with the new demand from the emerging economies. But heated international competition will keep wage demands moderate and put a lid on the ability of domestic producers to hike prices, especially in the developed

4. DEVELOPMENT: Industrial Nations

countries. Perhaps even more important, the policy actions of central bankers, the most powerful economic actors on the world stage, all share a similar anti-inflation ideology.

HOTBEDS OF TALENT. It's ironic, then, that at a time when prospects for global prosperity seem better than ever, gloom envelopes much of the industrial world. Japan's economic juggernaut is stalled. Unemployment is at 11% in Europe. Companies are still slashing payrolls in the relatively vibrant U.S. economy. At the same time, U.S., European, and Japanese multinationals have stepped up their investment spending in developing and former communist countries. It's no surprise that "ordinary citizens in most advanced industrial countries are confused and scared by what is happening to them," says Richard Lipsey, economist at the Canadian Institute for Advanced Research.

And there's much more to come. From Eastern Europe to Asia to Latin America, many countries are eager to compete with bountiful low-wage labor. Heightened international

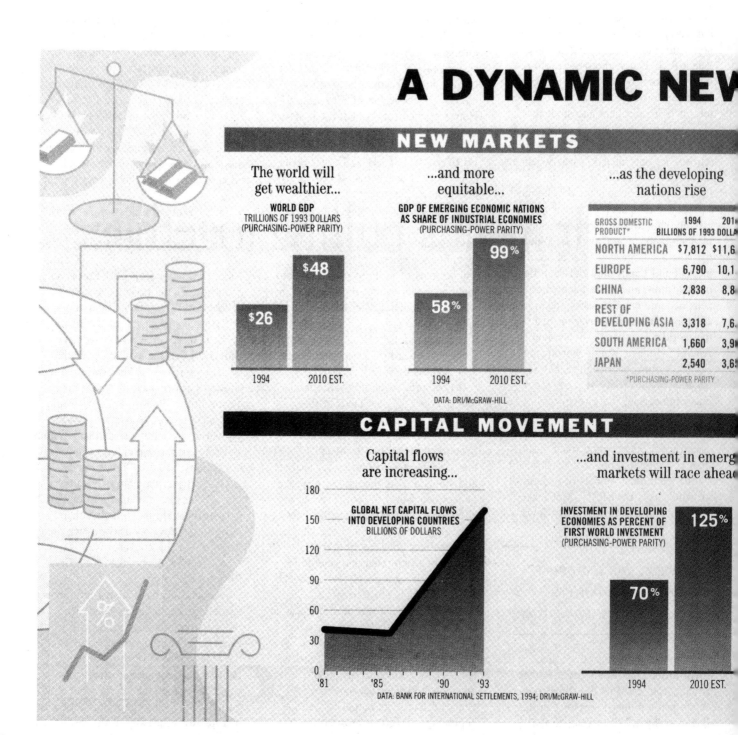

A DYNAMIC NEW

NEW MARKETS

The world will get wealthier...

WORLD GDP
TRILLIONS OF 1993 DOLLARS
(PURCHASING-POWER PARITY)

$48 (2010 EST.)
$26 (1994)

1994   2010 EST.

...and more equitable...

GDP OF EMERGING ECONOMIC NATIONS AS SHARE OF INDUSTRIAL ECONOMIES
(PURCHASING-POWER PARITY)

99% (2010 EST.)
58% (1994)

1994   2010 EST.

DATA: DRI/McGRAW-HILL

...as the developing nations rise

GROSS DOMESTIC PRODUCT*	1994 BILLIONS OF 1993 DOLLARS	201
NORTH AMERICA	$7,812	$11,6
EUROPE	6,790	10,1
CHINA	2,838	8,8
REST OF DEVELOPING ASIA	3,318	7,6
SOUTH AMERICA	1,660	3,9
JAPAN	2,540	3,6

*PURCHASING-POWER PARITY

CAPITAL MOVEMENT

Capital flows are increasing...

GLOBAL NET CAPITAL FLOWS INTO DEVELOPING COUNTRIES
BILLIONS OF DOLLARS

180
150
120
90
60
30
0

'81   '85   '90   '93

DATA: BANK FOR INTERNATIONAL SETTLEMENTS, 1994; DRI/McGRAW-HILL

...and investment in emerg markets will race ahea

INVESTMENT IN DEVELOPING ECONOMIES AS PERCENT OF FIRST WORLD INVESTMENT
(PURCHASING-POWER PARITY)

125% (2010 EST.)
70% (1994)

1994   2010 EST.

competition, along with rapid techno-logical change, largely accounts for the 22.5% plunge in real hourly wages for high school dropouts from 1973 to 1993 in the U.S. And in a sharp break with the past, German manufacturers are looking elsewhere when building new plants. After all, hourly wages of German manufacturing workers are 4.5 times higher than in Taiwan, 9 times greater than for Mexican workers, and 54 times the wages of Russian labor.

It isn't just cheap brawn, however. The competition is heating up for pro-ducing the kind of high-quality goods and sophisticated services in which the industrial nations have traditionally dominated. Cities such as Singapore, Penang in Malaysia, and Taipei in Tai-wan are hotbeds of engineering talent. India has millions of computer-literate workers. Central Europe is peppered with brilliant scientists. And when Hewlett-Packard Co. opened a research and development center in Guadalajara three years ago, it signaled Mexico's coming of high-tech age.

In the industrial world, protests against the new competition are start-

WORLD ECONOMY...

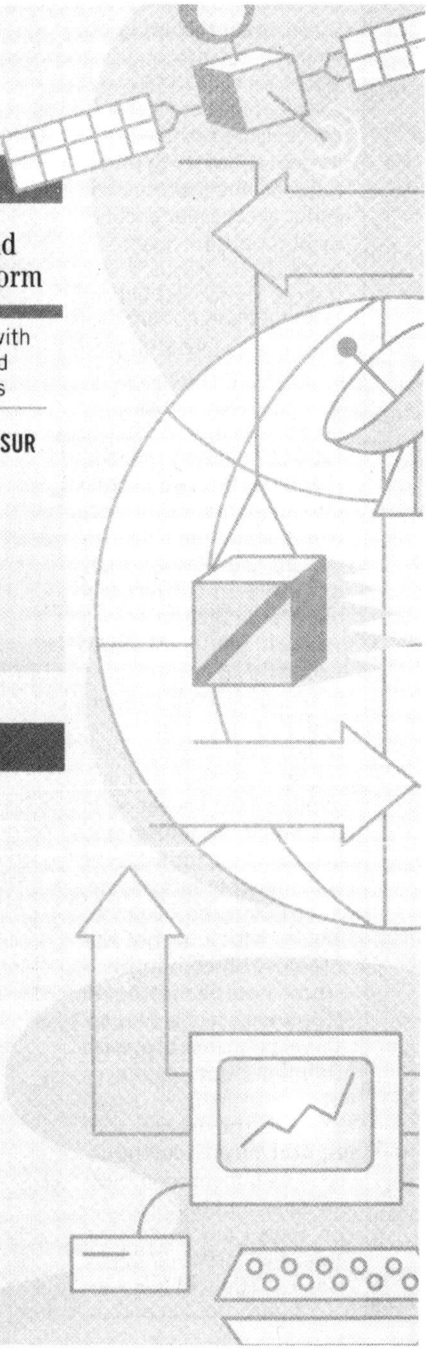

OPEN BORDERS

More people will cross the world's borders...

FOREIGN POPULATION AS PERCENT OF TOTAL POPULATION		
COUNTRY	1985	1991
AUSTRIA	3.6%	6.6%
BELGIUM	8.6	9.2
SWEDEN	4.6	5.7
SWITZERLAND	14.5	17.1
U.S.	7.0	8.0
AUSTRALIA*	20.8	22.7

*1986 FIGURE

...emerging markets will become powerful traders...

EMERGING MARKET EXPORTS AS A PERCENT OF TOTAL WORLD EXPORTS

35 — 30 — 25 — 20 — 15 — 0

'80   '90   2000   '10

...and new trade and political links may form

Megastates will emerge with open regional borders and similar economic systems

▶ NORTH AMERICA-MERCOSUR
▶ ASEAN
▶ TURKEY-CENTRAL ASIA
▶ NEW MIDDLE EAST
▶ GREATER EUROPE
▶ INDIAN OCEAN RIM

DATA: *WORLD INVESTMENT REPORT, 1994*; DRI/McGRAW-HILL, ORGANIZATION FOR ECONOMIC COOPERATION & DEVELOPMENT

TECHNOLOGY

Powerful catalysts for prosperity are technology...

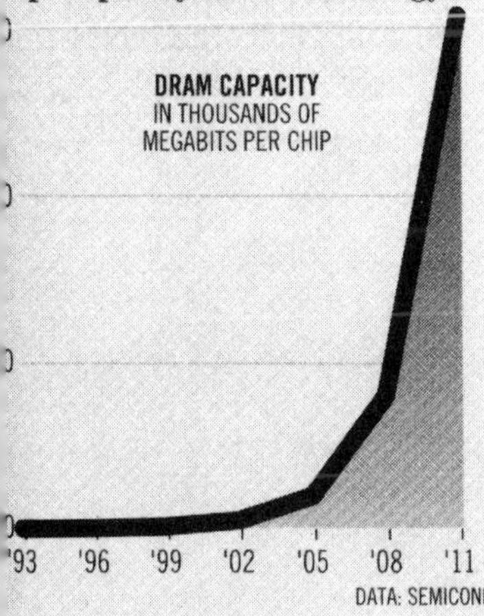

DRAM CAPACITY IN THOUSANDS OF MEGABITS PER CHIP

'93 '96 '99 '02 '05 '08 '11

...and exploding communications links

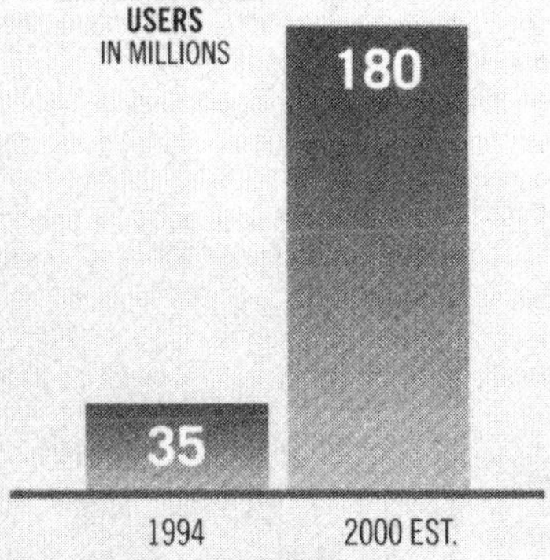

WORLD INTERNET USERS IN MILLIONS

180

35

1994   2000 EST.

DATA: SEMICONDUCTOR ASSN., COMPANY REPORTS, INTERNET SOCIETY, BUSINESS WEEK

ing to get louder and take on a nasty edge. Keep immigrants out. Bar low-wage imports from China and Hungary. Preserve our native culture. Frets André Lévy-Lang, chairman of the management board at Compagnie Financiére de Paribas, the big French investment bank: "The great temptation is going to be to say: 'Let's close the borders, and let's live happily ever after by ourselves.'"

Yet if policymakers succumb, it could lead to political and economic devastation. That, at least, seems to be the lesson of history. The period from 1870 to 1913, like this one, was a time of vast international capital flows. In 1913, the share of foreign securities traded in London was 59% of all traded securities; and by 1914, the stock value of foreign direct investment had reached an estimated $14 billion, or one-third of world investment. Some 36 million people left Europe; two-thirds of them emigrated to the U.S. and an even larger number of Chinese and Indians went to Burma, Indonesia, and elsewhere. Trade soared, technological innovation flourished, and economic growth surged. Yet beggar-thy-neighbor protectionist policies ended up contributing to two global wars and the Great Depression.

Today, international economic interdependence is once again generating a lot of discord. Nations are engaged in bitter international negotiations over cross-border pollution, intellectual-property rights, and differing workplace standards. Worse are the savage wars in Kuwait, the Balkans, Angola, and other hot spots. Military buildups and the spread of nuclear weapons in Asia and elsewhere offer the potential of even larger conflagrations.

Still, there's no gainsaying the geopolitical progress in the Middle East and in relations between the U.S. and Russia. And global economic integration isn't a zero-sum game. Worldwide trade has expanded by more than 6% a year since 1950, more than 50% faster than the growth in world GDP. The growing numbers of working-class and middle-class citizens in the emerging capitalist nations are demanding better housing, roads, water, and phones, as

well as more consumer goods. Rising demands will create bigger markets and new opportunities for profits for everyone including the industrial nations. "The forces of integration are so much more powerful than at the end of the 19th century," says David Hale, economist at Kemper Financial Cos.

Thanks largely to the Information Revolution, companies headquartered in the industrial nations will still have

a formidable edge in the global growth stakes. "Information technologies are the most powerful forces ever generated to make things cost-effective," says John S. Mayo, president of AT&T Bell Laboratories. It is the industrial nations, especially the U.S., that are behind the Internet boom and that are building the vast fiber-optic networks and web of new services of the Information Superhighway. The industrial

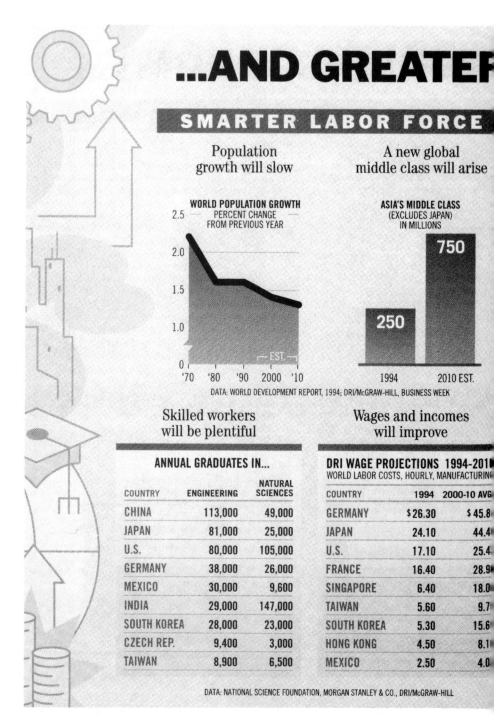

...AND GREATER

SMARTER LABOR FORCE

Population growth will slow

WORLD POPULATION GROWTH
PERCENT CHANGE FROM PREVIOUS YEAR

(Graph showing decline from ~2.5 in '70 to ~1.3 in '10, with EST. after 2000, axis '70 '80 '90 2000 '10)

A new global middle class will arise

ASIA'S MIDDLE CLASS
(EXCLUDES JAPAN)
IN MILLIONS

1994	2010 EST.
250	750

DATA: WORLD DEVELOPMENT REPORT, 1994; DRI/McGRAW-HILL, BUSINESS WEEK

Skilled workers will be plentiful

ANNUAL GRADUATES IN...

COUNTRY	ENGINEERING	NATURAL SCIENCES
CHINA	113,000	49,000
JAPAN	81,000	25,000
U.S.	80,000	105,000
GERMANY	38,000	26,000
MEXICO	30,000	9,600
INDIA	29,000	147,000
SOUTH KOREA	28,000	23,000
CZECH REP.	9,400	3,000
TAIWAN	8,900	6,500

Wages and incomes will improve

DRI WAGE PROJECTIONS 1994-201
WORLD LABOR COSTS, HOURLY, MANUFACTURING

COUNTRY	1994	2000-10 AVG
GERMANY	$26.30	$45.8
JAPAN	24.10	44.4
U.S.	17.10	25.4
FRANCE	16.40	28.9
SINGAPORE	6.40	18.0
TAIWAN	5.60	9.7
SOUTH KOREA	5.30	15.6
HONG KONG	4.50	8.1
MEXICO	2.50	4.0

DATA: NATIONAL SCIENCE FOUNDATION, MORGAN STANLEY & CO., DRI/McGRAW-HILL world is setting high standards for quality and manufacturing flexibility to produce low-cost goods, and its rich capital markets offer ample resources for financing new ventures or rejuvenating old ones.

WEALTHY ELITE. Of course, it's a market axiom that big returns come attached with greater risks—some fortunes will suffer spectacular declines even as others leap forward. It's a world where IBM can show a net income of $6.5 billion in 1984 and a loss of nearly $9 billion in 1993. And emerging-country stock markets are up an average of 20% in 1994 in dollar terms. But that spectacular return masks some huge setbacks, including a drop of 50% in the Turkish market, 48% in China, and more than 30% in Israel.

Such nerve-racking volatility is encouraging a lot of U.S., Japanese, and European multinationals to link up with foreign partners. It expands their presence in the world economy and hedges their investment risks at the same time. AT&T is forging broad alliances with a host of European telecommunications companies, and Mitsubishi has a cooperative relationship with Daimler Benz. Alliances are common in such knowledge-based and capital-intensive industries as information technologies and biotechnology. Says Paul A. Allaire, chief executive of Xerox Corp.: "You will see people working more closely than ever before."

There will be no shortage of consumers to buy products and services. Global capitalism is creating a wealthy international elite of cosmopolitan professionals comfortable working for companies headquartered in New York, Tokyo, or Buenos Aires. Millions more are joining the middle class in Asia, Latin America, and elsewhere. As in the U.S. or Japan, the middle class in the emerging capitalist nations is boosting its living standards by buying material goods. In Ho Chi Minh City, Vietnam, three Toyota dealerships are within a few miles of one another, and a Mercedes dealership is being built.

Consumers are demanding better services, too. Poorer countries will spend trillions of dollars on new roads, sewers, telephone systems, education, and health-care facilities in coming decades. Over the past 15 years, the share of households with access to clean water has increased by half, and power production and telephone lines per capita have doubled in developing nations. Still, 1 billion people lack clean water, electric power has yet to reach 2 billion people, and the demand for modern telecommunications networks far outstrips supply, according to the World Bank. To boost efficiency, many countries are privatizing their infrastructure. From 1988 to 1992, the value of developing-country privatizations in 25 countries totaled $61.6 billion. And infrastructure investment can propel giant leaps in economic activity.

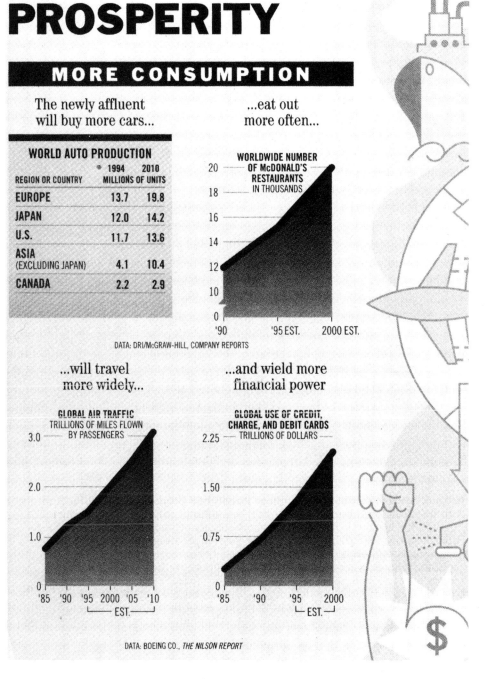

Clearly, global integration comes with enormous benefits. At the same time, pessimists proclaiming the decline of the industrial world often argue that global convergence is closer at hand than is the case. Even if all went smoothly, the inequalities between rich and poor nations are so vast that it will take decades for them to disappear. Much of the wage gap between manufacturing workers in rich and poor nations reflects large skill differences and exchange rates. According to Harvard economist Richard B. Freeman, some 43% of Mexican manufacturing laborers have less than six years of schooling, vs. 3% of American manufacturing workers.

Nor do economies grow in a straight line. At capitalism's frontier, including many of the Soviet Union's successor states and China, vicious cycles of reform and regression are probable in coming decades. Environmental problems and population pressures will worsen in many developing nations.

Policymakers worldwide also worry that rising social and economic pressures in a competitive global economy will spark "culture wars." Hinduism vs. Islam. Confucian values vs. Western values. "The fault lines between civilizations will be the battle lines of the future," wrote Harvard University professor Samuel P. Huntington in an influential 1993 *Foreign Affairs* article.

SIMILAR LOGIC. Cultural differences between economies are deep-rooted. Modern Japanese capitalism has been extremely successful in building large organizations, while American capitalism does better creating whole new industries, says Peter Berger, director of the Institute for the Study of Economic Culture at Boston University. Chinese capitalism is very different from French *dirigisme*. Yet the remarkable aspect of capitalism is the ability of citizens from around the world to strike deals with one another. Japanese, American, French, Chinese, and Russian capitalists can compete, negotiate alliances, and trade securities with the same goals and similar logic, according to economist Robert Heilbroner.

Indeed, capitalism is triumphant because it is multicultural. Unlike communism, it is open-ended and adaptive, and in the 21st century a range of capitalisms will evolve.

Ever since the Industrial Revolution began, the reality has been how much material wealth has grown in the modern nations of the industrial world. Given time, the triumph of the liberal ideas of the bourgeoisie, from free trade to democracy, coupled with the spread of technological innovations, should improve living standards throughout the world—bringing most people an opportunity for a better richer life.

Christopher Farrell in New York, with bureau reports

We're #1
And
It Hurts

The U.S. outruns the world, but some workers are left behind

GEORGE J. CHURCH

TO PROFESSIONAL ATHLETES—WHEN THEY are not on strike or locked out—and their adoring fans, there is nothing so exultant, as the chant of "We're No. 1!" American business executives are getting somewhat the same feeling. Finally, finally, they are beating their Japanese, German, South Korean, Taiwanese, name-the-country rivals—and in products like autos, machine tools and computer chips, where a few years ago they were being trounced. The U.S. firms are not only turning back an import invasion of American markets but also triumphing in so-called third-country export markets and even swiping some sales in Japan and other tormentor countries. The closest thing to an official world championship of business is top rank among the nations studied by the Swiss-based World Economic Forum, and last month the forum made the announcement: after eight years of Japanese domination, the U.S. in 1993 had the world's most competitive economy.

But many ordinary Americans, and even some corporate middle managers, might greet that news with a shrug and a "So what?"—or a skeptical obscenity. The price of beating overseas competition has been bitterly high: wave after wave of downsizing layoffs, wage increases limited or forgone, replacement of full-time workers by part-time or temporary hired hands. Even those who have hung on to regular jobs are often too exhausted by long hours of overtime and weekend work to enjoy the extra money they are earning.

The upshot, according to TIME's Board

of Economists, is this: the increases in productivity, or output per worker hour, that have helped make the U.S. No. 1 again have also laid the groundwork for an unprecedented period of steady growth in output and employment with little inflation. Says Stephen Roach, senior international economist at the investment firm of Morgan Stanley: "Ultimately, that could be translated into the long-awaited improvement in the standard of living of the American worker." But, as he and other board members note, it hasn't happened yet. Making it do so, says Roach, "is the real challenge" facing the economy.

Meanwhile, the public mood seems confused and contradictory. Among 800 people questioned last week in a TIME/CNN poll by Yankelovich Partners, 38% described the economy in general as either growing moderately or booming, versus only 9% who thought it was in recession. But in response to the question "Do you think the recession has ended in the area where you live?," 54% said it had not; only 40% thought it had. An even stranger contradiction: 81% thought their own family's finances were doing either fairly well (69%) or very well (12%). Yet when asked "Do you personally feel better off as a result of the recent improvement of the economy?," 58% answered no, 37% yes.

Even to experts, the economy displays two faces, both of which are on view in Flint, Michigan. It is the site of General Motors' Buick City works, which is central to all GM auto production because it makes parts for assembly plants throughout the

country. Buick City, in turn, was the scene in late September of a strike that, says Roach, "was symbolic of an issue that is really at the core of the debate right now: do workers get to reap the benefits of the improved efficiencies that they are delivering to employers?"

Eight years ago, after the closing of GM's Fisher Body plant, Michael Moore's sarcastic film *Roger & Me* portrayed Flint as a dying community. But since then U.S. automakers have turned themselves from the world's highest-cost producers to those with the lowest costs: only $42 in wages for each $100 in product turned out, about a third below Toyota or Mercedes-Benz. They have won back so many motorists who once bought foreign cars that the share of the U.S. market going to imported autos has fallen from 22% in 1991 to under 14% now. Profits are booming; GM turned a record $4.9 billion loss in 1991 to a profit of $2.5 billion in 1993 and $2.8 billion for the first half of this year. Buick City is running flat out to keep up with demand.

But workers complain that for them expansion spells exhaustion. Throughout American industry, companies are using overtime to wring the most out of the U.S. labor force: the factory workweek currently is averaging a near record 42 hours, including 4.6 hours of overtime. Americans, observes Audrey Freedman, a labor economist and member of TIME's board, "are the workingest people in the world." The big-three automakers have pushed this trend to an extreme. Their workers are putting in an average of 10 hours overtime a week and laboring an average of six eight-hour Saturdays a year.

WORSE STILL, THE BUICK City employees gripe, each is being asked to do what used to be several jobs. "If somebody retires, all they do is take the work and give it to other people" who already have their hands full, says one worker. That complaint is echoed by workers, blue collar and white collar, in varied industries all over the country.

"I'm doing the work of three people," says Joseph Kelterborn, 44, who works for the NYNEX telephone company in New York City. His department, which installs and maintains fiber-optic networks, has been reduced from 27 people to 20 in recent years, in part by combining what were once three separate positions—switchman, powerman and tester—into his job of carrier switchman. As a result, says Kelterborn, he often works up to four extra hours a day and one weekend in three. "By the time I get home," he complains, "all I have time for is a shower, dinner and a little sleep; then it's time to turn around and do it all over again."

In Chicago, Gamma, the city's largest commercial photo lab, has turned a loss into a profit within the past year partly by dismissing 25 employees and leaving the remaining 160 to carry the same workload. Says sales manager George Burns: "Everyone has to do everyone else's job in addition to their own. I sell, supervise and jump into the lab whenever that gets busy." His workdays have lengthened from eight or nine hours to 12 to 14, and "you feel it," he says. "I'm not burning out, but it's like a football player at the end of the season. You get out of bed a little slower. It gets a little tougher every day." Even those whose job it is to chart such trends tell similar stories. Allen Sinai, the chief global economist at the investment firm of Lehman Bros. and a member of TIME's board, notes that "I have many more responsibilities now. So much so I hardly have time to breathe."

For GM, and for other companies, the economics work out. Overtime is expensive, of course; many autoworkers are earning $65,000 to $70,000 a year, and electricians on plant-maintenance crews working seven-day weeks can push their take above $100,000. But the combined wage, fringe benefit and training costs of hiring new workers would be more expensive still. Consequently, GM has done no significant hiring since 1986, once more pushing to an extreme a common trend. Since the recovery from the last recession began in March 1991, the U.S. economy has

The productivity and skills of Americans are attracting foreign manufacturers

created almost 6 million new jobs, but in a sense that leaves it 2 million short; had companies hired at the pace of past expansions, the increase would have been 8 million jobs or more.

Finally, when it absolutely could not avoid adding workers, GM at Buick City and elsewhere turned to temporary-help agencies, which now supply blue-collar workers as well as stenographers, computer operators and other office hands. Once more the reason is economics: "temps" draw only wages, not health insurance and other expensive fringe benefits, and they can be used and let go as needed, without drawing the supplementary unemployment benefits GM and other companies must pay to laid-off regular workers.

Again, GM's strategy is typical of the auto industry and American companies generally. At the Ford Motor plant in St. Louis, Missouri, nearly 3,400 full-time employees make around $57,000 a year thanks to overtime pay. But the plant also uses 200 temporary employees who do essentially the same jobs but make only $20,000 annually because they work only two or three days a week. Economywide, the number of temps in the labor force has more than doubled in the past decade. Says Roach: "The [job-creating] leader in this recovery is not IBM, not Wal-Mart, not General Motors. It's Manpower, the company that offers you a job for a week without benefits, not knowing where you're going to be next Monday." About the only way in which the Buick City situation is untypical, in fact, is that the workers finally rebelled—and won. First, to hear them tell it, they literally worked themselves sick; by late September, more than 1,000 of the 11,500 workers were on sick leave. At that point, Local 599 of the United Auto Workers called them out, aiming to force GM to hire some permanent workers to relieve the overtime crush. Workers responded enthusiastically. ENOUGH MANPOWER FOR FIRST-AID CALLS, RESTROOM CALLS AND FAMILY NEEDS, demanded one picket sign. Said an assembly-line worker, a mother with four school-age children: "I never thought I'd see the day when I welcomed a strike for a few days off." GM settled after three days with a pledge to hire 779 more regular workers.

Whether that victory sets any kind of precedent remains to be seen. Not many other workers have been pressed as hard as those in Buick City, nor are many as strate-

gically placed to cripple their company's nationwide production by walking out. On the other hand, says Sinai, companies counting on their workers to be loyal may be in for a surprise: "Why would there be loyalty, given the way corporations have dealt with their workers over the past four or five years? At the first chance that workers have, they'll go looking for better jobs."

Nonetheless, Sinai notes, "the world is better than it was." The unemployment rate has dropped to a four-year low of 5.9%, and new claims for unemployment insurance—a measure of how many jobs are being lost—fell to an average of just over 300,000 for the most recent four weeks; that is a five-year low.

Sinai figures "we are generating this year 278,000 jobs a month." He concedes that "the character of those jobs really is questionable"; besides temps they include many low-paying service positions and not a little moonlighting. Freedman calculates that people holding two or more jobs constitute 6.1% of the labor force—more than the unemployment rate. Still, says Sinai, "some jobs are better than no jobs. Some income is better than no income."

Contrast even that lukewarm description with some of the doomsday prophecies of two years ago, when the loss of markets to foreign rivals seemed to haunt the presidential campaign. Paul Tsongas' basic campaign document in his run for the 1992 Democratic nomination foresaw "great economic peril [from] Europe and the Pacific Rim . . . cataclysmic erosion of our standards of living . . . a diminished economy of decline and defeat." Bill Clinton, in his acceptance speech to the Democratic Convention, intoned, "Our country is falling behind . . . we have an unpleasant economy stuck somewhere between Germany and Sri Lanka." That was calamity-howling, of course, but not too far out of touch with the popular mood.

In fact, though, by 1992 a number of American companies were already well into an aggressive counterattack on foreign competitors that has been reaping more and more success. Their methods vary, and in some cases seem contradictory. But they have some common elements: emphasis on high-tech prowess; ruthless concentration on marketing the products and techniques in which a company has a competitive advantage—plus the ubiquitous downsizing of plants and work force to get costs into line. Some examples:

▶ Compaq Computer Corp., with headquarters in Houston, was losing sales and profits so rapidly three years ago that directors fired founder Joseph ("Rod") Canion as chief executive and replaced him with Eckhard Pfeiffer. Under the new boss, sales have roughly tripled, to an expected $10 billion or so this year, and profits have increased even more, from $131

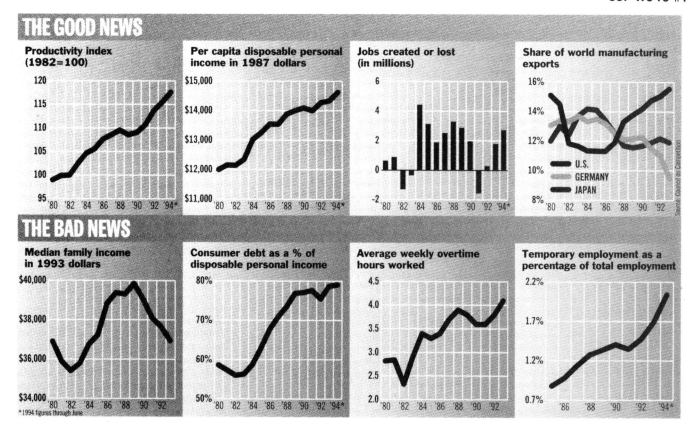

THE GOOD NEWS

Productivity index (1982=100)

Per capita disposable personal income in 1987 dollars

Jobs created or lost (in millions)

Share of world manufacturing exports
— U.S.
— GERMANY
— JAPAN

THE BAD NEWS

Median family income in 1993 dollars
*1994 figures through June

Consumer debt as a % of disposable personal income

Average weekly overtime hours worked

Temporary employment as a percentage of total employment

---

million in 1991 to $462 million last year and $423 million in just the first half of 1994—during which, several industry sources think, Compaq became the world's biggest maker of computers. Its strategy: shift from making a variety of high-end personal computers to mass-producing PCs, sold through extensive dealer networks in the U.S. and abroad, and cut, cut, cut—costs and especially prices. The company has slashed prices an average of almost 30% a year. Compaq is one of the few companies to fulfill the promise that downsizing would cut costs enough to expand business so rapidly as to produce more jobs in the end. Pfeiffer laid off 20% of the staff between 1991 and 1992, leaving around 9,000 workers, but then began selective hiring that has now boosted employment to more than 14,000.

▶ Intel in the past eight years has turned a $203 million loss into a $2 billion–plus profit and become, since 1992, the world's top producer of semiconductors, knocking Japan's NEC out of the No. 1 spot. Primarily it did so by picking out and pushing one product line: microprocessors, the tiny chips that serve as the brains of computers. It was a gutsy move, since microprocessors are harder to make and require far more research and development than the mass-produced memory chips that Japanese firms have been turning out at prices Intel could not match. But the timing was spectacular and the results self-evident. CEO

The U.S. now tops Japan in semiconductors

Andrew Grove's advice to companies eager to emulate that success: "You have to understand what it is that you are better at than anybody else and mercilessly focus your efforts on it."

▶ Electronic Data Systems, the company Ross Perot founded and later sold to General Motors, last November bagged a glittering international prize: a $1.5 billion, 10-year contract to overhaul and then manage the computer network of Inland Revenue, the British government's main tax-collecting agency. Again it was a case of American firms' specializing in a particular high-tech field. Other countries' firms may provide tough competition in making computer hardware and software, but nobody matches the Americans at the fine art of tying computers together into networks that do everything from running automated factories to sending out medical bills. On the Inland Revenue contract, for example, EDS' competition was all American. Only it and another U.S. company made it to the final bidding.

▶ Caterpillar took a more conventional, and controversial, lean-and-mean approach. In

the early 1980s, says Glen Barton, group president for construction and mining machinery, Caterpillar's "costs were out of line with what overseas markets were willing to pay for our products"; the company lost $1.5 billion cutting prices below cost to meet the competition of Japan's Komatsu and other rivals. But Caterpillar has slashed its work force 31% in the past dozen years, and that has lowered costs and raised productivity: from sales of $886,000 per employee to $2.3 million. Losses have turned to profits, and more than half its nearly $12 billion annual sales are made to overseas customers. The company has had to ride out a strike by about 28% of its employees that is now in its 16th week. It has kept production up partly by making supervisors work at line jobs, partly by luring some United Auto Workers members into crossing the picket lines, partly by turning out more machinery in overseas plants and by using 1,100 replacement workers.

There is another side to the overseas-success story. For all the triumphs of Compaq, Intel and other companies, Japan still dominates many high-tech fields. Its companies, for example, control 95% of the flat-screen-display market, a key area of computer technology, and Asian companies have pushed the U.S. out of the disk-drive business. At the same time, U.S. competitiveness has been vastly enhanced by a trend that could be reversed at a moment's notice—the cheapening of the exchange value of the dollar, which lowers the price of American goods to foreign buyers. Says General Electric's chief executive Jack Welch: "If the Japanese are prepared to complete at 90 yen to the dollar, the U.S. must be prepared to compete at 130 yen to the dollar. Until we are, we delude ourselves if we think we are in control of our own fate."

Also, though exports are now among the fastest-growing items in the U.S. economy, they are still running well behind imports, resulting in a gargantuan and growing trade deficit. That, however, comes about in part because the country must import such huge quantities of raw products, from coffee and bananas to crude oil, that it either cannot produce at all or not in the quantities it needs. The great fear of a few years ago was that foreign rivals would also take over manufacturing businesses, particularly high-tech firms, and reduce the U.S. work force to hamburger flipping. That fear is pretty much gone.

But, it might be asked, what's the difference? Corporate downsizing is wiping out high-paying manufacturing jobs almost as effectively as losses of sales to foreign rivals might. For example, in 1993 the top 100 U.S. electronics companies eliminated 480,000 jobs. Says John Stern, a vice president for the American Electronics Association: "The American life-style is supported by manufacturing jobs. They are the entry point into the middle class for women and minorities and anyone else climbing the ladder who doesn't have the contacts or education to become a software engineer. These people can't lead a middle-class life in the service jobs that are left over."

There is much evidence, in fact, that the U.S. is developing something of a two-tiered society. While corporate profits and executive salaries are rising rapidly, real wages (that is, discounted for inflation) are not growing at all. Indeed, the government has reported that last year real median household income in the U.S. fell by $312, while a million more people slipped into poverty; those official defined as poor were 15.1% of the U.S. population vs. 14.8% in 1992. Those were astonishing developments for the fourth year of a business recovery that is steadily gaining strength.

The intense drive for productivity is raising the rewards for training and education higher than ever. Between 1979 and 1989, calculates labor economist Freedman, median real income for year-round, full-time workers age 25 or more did not change significantly, but within that enormous group there were some dramatic shifts. College-educated women increased their earnings 16%, college-educated men slightly. Earnings of women with a high

Companies must go from cutting to rebuilding

school education or less held about even. The big losers were men who never got past high school. Their inflation-adjusted earnings fell 14%.

Freedman's analysis of the reasons for these wide disparities indicates that they may have widened further since 1989. Says she: "It's the blue-collar, production-worker jobs that were high-paying and secure and unionized that are much less available" to men with a high school education or less—a trend that corporate downsizing has accentuated still more. At the same time, "the jobs that are being created are computer-using jobs. They're service, white-collar types of work, and they are more likely to go to women. I think that's one of the reasons why women with a high school education or less haven't lost income while the men have."

Freedman identifies some other profound changes in job markets that tend to hold back wage growth. Full-time, full-year workers are no longer as dominant as they were. There is more self-employment, more part-time employment and the beginnings of what might be called task employment. Says Freedman: "I know one manufacturer who is opening a new location and is offering workers two years' employment and saying, 'After two years, you're not going to be employed any more.'"

Rigid wage structures have been broken up. Gone, for example, are the days when a raise for truck drivers would quickly be translated into raises for supervisors, warehousemen and trucking-company office employees to maintain standard differentials. Career-long service with a particular company, involving year-after-year raises for doing essentially the same work, is becoming a thing of the past too. The result: "You don't any longer have these internal spirals where a secretary at IBM will be making $75,000 a year with benefits, because spitting that secretary out onto the competitive labor market recalibrates the wage to maybe $25,000 or $30,000."

Fine for the companies. But in this environment, can gains in productivity and competitiveness be translated into enough wage hikes and additional employment to raise the average citizen's standard of living? There are some signs that such a turn might be coming. True, downsizing seems to have become a way of life. Among 713 companies polled by the American Management Association, 25% plan staff reductions in the next year—the largest propor-

tion in the eight-year history of this survey. But two-thirds of the companies reporting cutbacks are adding jobs. Roach predicts that "there will come a time" when downsizing companies will have increased productivity so much that they can "make the transition from cutting to rebuilding, and when market share is expanding, and the companies will have absolutely no choice but to reward their workers more equitably" because they will need a growing and contented labor force to realize those expansionary possibilities.

Perhaps, but there are tendencies that will have to be curbed for these happy possibilities to be reached. At some companies, at least, downsizing shows signs of turning into a fixation, an almost pathological urge to cut whatever the circumstances. While some cost-conscious companies like Compaq have avoided this so-called corporate anorexia and increased hiring after getting their costs down and their market share up, others are acting more like American Express. It is about to start another round of staff cuts, despite having turned a loss into a profit. Why? "Because we're doing so well," chairman Harvey Golub told the *Wall Street Journal*. "You can either cut costs when there is a clear and present danger, or you can do it when people feel good about the way things are going. But it's much harder when you're in trouble: the world is looking at you, and you don't have much time."

In the long run, continually cutting back is obviously no way to grow. Even in the short run, downsizing carried to an extreme can reduce the very productivity it first enhances. While Ford Motor Co. is working heavy overtime, chairman Alexander Trotman is worried about it. Says he: "You don't get real productivity by simply ramping up the line speed . . . In the beginning everyone enjoys the extra pay, but we all get tired, pressures build up, people get edgy and tensions break out." On the other hand, he says, hiring enough extra people to work everybody straight time "wouldn't make economic sense. The challenge to managements is to find the right balance."

Downsizing can also anger customers who find workers too busy to pay attention to them. U S West, a Baby Bell telephone company with headquarters in Englewood, Colorado, has announced a phasing out of 9,000 jobs, about one-seventh of its work force. Already, Lynn Schimmelfeder and Ben Rubin, two service representatives, have so few support staff members working under them that they are unable to chase down customer queries such as, "Why didn't the repair man get to my house today?" Phone operators like Carla West increasingly are having to listen to the gripes of irate callers who cannot reach the business office: the lines are always busy. West and other operators can't get through to repair people either. Customer complaints have been pouring in to public-utility commissions in U S West's 14-state operating area so heavily that several PUCs have scheduled a meeting in Seattle this week to discuss the problem.

Even professionals and middle managers, coping with the pervasive insecurity generated by wave after wave of cutbacks, may respond not by working harder but by adopting a to-hell-with-this-company attitude. A geologist for a Houston-based oil company relates how she lost all her onetime great enthusiasm for her job after successive waves of layoffs. The worry became so great, she says, that "I would come home and go to bed earlier and earlier just not to think about my job." She was briefly promoted to a manager's position, then returned to being a geologist again while still drawing a manager's salary, which she fears has increased her vulnerability. Currently, she says, she wants only to avoid attracting attention, and so she will not let her name be used: "I keep my head down so it doesn't get chopped off."

Such tension and turmoil do not have to continue. Year-to-year fluctuations aside, economists and executives generally agree that the U.S. has built the best-balanced, leanest, most efficient base for steady growth that it has had in decades. Workers can only add the fervent wish: after all the pain it has cost us to get here, don't blow it now. —*Reported by Bernard Baumohl/New York, Edward W. Desmond/Tokyo, William McWhirter/ Detroit, Richard Woodbury/Denver and Suneel Ratan/Washington*

THE FUTURE OF EUROPE

Beyond the Year 2000

Daniel Bell

For five hundred years, Europe has been the center of world civilization. In that time, it initiated—one can even say invented—the idea and the fact of sustained economic growth. Since Galileo, it has been the cradle of modern technology, particularly with navigation and scientific instruments. In philosophy, music, painting, and literature, it transformed our conceptions of perspective and perception, of tonality and the diatonic scale, and of the relation of fiction to reality. All this, in a sense, was the application of an idea of rationality unknown to the non-Western world.

And yet, in that same period of time, the plains of Europe saw some of the most devastating wars in the history of human civilization: from Napoleon's revolutionary army crossing to and retreating from Russia to the two world wars, involving all the major and minor powers, in which more than fifty million people were killed. The latter part of the nineteenth century saw the rapid spread of imperialism to almost all of Africa and Asia (with the exception of Japan), so that before World War II, 80 percent of the land mass of the world, and 80 percent of the world's peoples, were under Western domination. And the twentieth century saw the rise of the two most deadly ideologies in history, communism and fascism, which ended in the Gulag and the Holocausts of Stalin and Hitler.

Since the end of World War II, Western imperialism has almost completely disappeared, with a rapidity that future historians will find astonishing (though the legacies of tribalism, colonialism, and ill-fitting national boundaries remain, especially in Africa). Both communism and fascism have collapsed, their ideologies transformed into new nationalisms, especially in the old Soviet-dominated areas. War between the Great Powers—Great Britain, Germany, France, Italy—is entirely unlikely.

In the last decade and a half, Europe—and here I concentrate specifically on Western Europe—has begun an experiment that, from a historical perspective, is unparalleled—at least on such a scale. This is the effort of the twelve countries, now all democratic, to create a single harmonious community that would coordinate their economic and political institutions and by the year 2000—at least according to the original plan—create a unified currency and an integral political federation. The only parallel is Switzerland, which, after the Congress of Vienna in 1815, became a Federal Republic, half Catholic, half Protestant, with three different languages (German, French, and Italian), and twenty-six cantons, or local districts, with their own system of courts.

But beyond all this is the larger, more fateful, historical question—the role of Europe in a new and enlarged world society, with a global economy, and a great shift of power to the Pacific-rim nations in the twenty-first century. Even if there were a unified Europe, could it still play a major role in the economics, politics, and culture of world society in the next century?

The effort to create a "new Europe" can be identified in four steps, as follows.

This article is part of a larger study of the future of Europe, dealing with political, monetary, and cultural issues, and concentrates here largely on Europe's economy and welfare systems.

 From *Dissent*, Fall 1994, pp. 445-452. © 1994 by Daniel Bell. Reprinted by permission.

1. **The Common Market**, which is basically a customs union among the members, an area of free trade, and an external common tariff. This is now legally in effect.

2. **The Single Market** (a situation similar to that in the United States except for the currency), in which there would be complete free movement of capital and labor, the harmonization of welfare and labor policies, and the free establishment of services (financial, insurance, and legal) throughout the community. Here, in principle, the new freedoms are established, though there are many practical barriers.

3. **An Economic and Monetary Union.** This would mean a harmonization of economic policies, ceilings for public deficits, and, eventually, a single currency used by all members. But the first-step agreement to keep exchange-rate parities among members has broken down, because of actions last year by the German Bundesbank. (See my "Behind the European Currency Crisis," *Dissent*, Winter 1993.)

4. **A Political Federation.** A European Parliament now exists, with members elected from all nations. And there is a large administrative bureaucracy in Brussels. But the key to political federation was the Maastricht Treaty signed in December 1991, which adopted "convergence criteria" that would give the European Parliament veto power in several areas. Consumer protection, health, and education would come under community scrutiny, and steps would be taken to encourage a common foreign and defense policy. But Maastricht, and the fear of a central bureaucracy, has proven to be a stumbling block toward a united Europe.

The European Economic Arena, consisting of the twelve European Community countries (plus Scandinavia, Switzerland, and Austria, if they join), is now the largest trading bloc on earth, with more than 40 percent of the world's Gross Domestic Product (GDP) within its fold. Germany was considered to be the major powerhouse. The fall of the Berlin Wall and the reunification of Germany were going to create a two trillion dollar dream economy whose skilled workers and world-class manufacturers would make it the envy of the world.

Yet little has turned out that way. For the past three years, Europe has been in the midst of an agonizing economic recession. In 1992, real GDP growth in Europe was 0.5 percent. And in 1993, *every* country in Europe experienced *negative* growth. The German economy was hit the worst, experiencing a 2

percent drop in GDP, and industrial production in 1993 was 7 percent below that of 1992, reflecting the worst postwar recession. No one expects more than 1 percent growth in 1994.

Some of this is cyclical, reflecting the usual ups and downs of the business cycle, and the effects of the worldwide recession. But the more important question is how much is structural, likely to persist even in a recovery. One way to answer this question is to measure the budget deficits in each country as they widen or narrow. An OECD (Organization for Economic Cooperation and Development) study last year showed that in Europe the causes of the recession were largely structural. In Germany, the budget deficit as a percentage of GDP was 4.1 percent, of which 3 percent was structural. In Italy it was 9.5 percent, of which 7.4 was structural. And in France it was 5.7 percent, of which 3.1 was structural. The economies will probably turn up for cyclical reasons, but the deeper problems remain.

The structural question is central for understanding the long-term prospects of the economy. In Europe, the major structural problems are social welfare costs and aging, inefficient industries propped up by subsidies. These eat away at government revenues and reduce productive investment. A corollary factor is rigid labor markets (the costs of reducing a work force by benefit payments, and the unwillingness or inability of workers to move, for family reasons or because of cultural differences).

The most surprising issue is social welfare. Forty or so years ago, Marxist theory said that the capitalist state would spend for warfare, but not for welfare. But it is welfare that now may be strangling the capitalist state.

The modern welfare state was proposed fifty years ago in Great Britain by the famous "Beveridge Report" (though Germany had initiated some social insurance fifty years before, to "buy off" the growing socialist movement). Written during the war, the report proposed the end of hunger and poverty, and the use of the resources of the state to provide not only a "safety net" against the hazards of unemployment, but a framework of benefits that would guarantee an individual and a family the basis of self-respect. Beveridge proposed a comprehensive system of national insurance, financed by employer contributions, that would provide unemployment benefits, health services, and old-age pensions. In addition, there were family allowances for children, services for the disabled, and social-service counseling for family and mental health problems. The plan vastly increased the power of the state, which for the first time assumed responsibility for the relief of poverty and the welfare of the society. The Attlee Labour government in Great Britain initiated the program. And every country in Europe followed suit.

In Europe, public spending as a whole (government administrative expenses, subsidies to industry and farmers, and social welfare) amounts to about 49 percent of Gross Domestic Product (as against 37 percent twenty years ago). That compares with 37 percent in the United States and 32 percent in Japan. But social-security expenditures accounted for 25 percent of the total GDP in Europe, compared to 15 percent in the United States and 10 percent in Japan.

The welfare state has been most costly in Germany, with Italy second. One-third of German GDP goes for social spending, and social-insurance contributions (split 50-50 between employers and workers) amount to about 40 percent of gross pay. The average German manufacturing worker, the highest-paid in Europe, receives about $27 an hour in wages and benefits, of which $12.50 comes in the form of social benefits. Italian workers receive more in benefits than wages in their $21-an-hour compensation. (In contrast, in the U.S. a worker's $16 an hour has only $4.50 in benefits.) Hourly manufacturing labor costs in Germany are about 35 percent higher than in the United States, Japan, or even Great Britain.

Looking ahead, there are the rising costs of pensions. By the year 2015, the number of Germans over age sixty-five will rise by 50 percent, from twelve million to nearly eighteen million. By the year 2030, the number of Germans over age sixty will be double that under age twenty. According to the OECD, the present value of future pensions in Germany is 1.6 times current GDP.* In Italy, deficits in social programs accounted for half of the 1992 budget deficit, or a huge 10 percent of GDP. Italian old-age pensions are the most generous in Europe (and a person can retire, in many instances, at age 55, then seek another job) and about 40 percent of the members of the CGIL,

the largest trade-union movement in Italy, are today on retirement pensions. According to Luigi Spaventa, one of the most talented economists in Europe, and the minister of the budget in the caretaker "technocratic" government, pensions are the largest "fiscal drag" in the Italian budget.

Social spending has reached a limit in Europe for political, economic, and even moral reasons. Under the Maastricht agreement, setting up convergence criteria on public-sector debt and deficits, only Luxembourg, of the twelve European Community members, is in compliance. Economic costs have reduced industrial competitiveness, while the large social-insurance benefits reduce labor mobility, since workers often prefer to draw on unemployment compensation rather than move elsewhere. Assar Lindbeck, the Swedish economist, has argued that incentives to work and to produce are destroyed when the state takes away too much from those who are working and gives too much to those who are idle.

The other major structural problem is industrial. Europe led the way in the first two industrial revolutions. The first one was in England, where the invention of steam power by James Watt, and the application of energy to machines, began the transformation of the world. Steam power gave us locomotives and steamships. By applying steam power to machines, we began factory production. But there were other ways, equally important, unremarked in the textbooks. The most crucial was the creation of steam pumps, so that one could pump the water out of coal mines and dig deep down. England is an island that was bedded on coal, especially in the Midlands. By digging up the coal, one could create a steel industry. And with steel, the associated products in metals engineering, shipyards, and automobiles. Textiles and steel were the foundations of England's early wealth.

The second industrial revolution began in Germany around the 1880s. This was the creation of the large chemical and electrical industries. With chemicals, for the first time, humans could make things that were not found in nature, such as plastics, and with oil, the petrochemicals. With electricity we had both the new sources of amplified power and the transformation of night and day by light, as well as the ability to send coded messages and then voice on electrical lines, creating the telegraph and the telephone.

---

* Both Germany and Italy are increasing the retirement age to restrain expenditures. Germany's pension-law reform, which went into effect last January, provides that by 2001, the normal retirement age for men and women would be raised to 65.

All this is why Europe was able to lead the world in its industrial transformations. England and Germany were the sources of these transformations. One forgets that before World War II, France and Italy were not industrial societies. Theirs were small workshop industries run by family firms. After World War II, both were transformed. France opened a large new steel industry in Alsace-Lorraine and began the development of chemicals and electricity. Italy expanded its textile and chemical industries, as well as rubber. And all the major countries of Europe went in heavily for the manufacture of automobiles.

The major problem is that Europe has not made the transition, as have the United States and Japan, largely to the postindustrial sectors of information and knowledge (computers and telecommunications). There are some large individual firms in these sectors, such as NV Philips in the Netherlands, Erickson in Sweden, Siemens in Germany, Cable and Wireless in the United Kingdom, and Nokia in Finland. Yet in the crucial areas of microchip technology and software, there are no major players in Europe.

Europe is still struggling with the industrial society, particularly steel and automobiles. (The shipyard industry is gone almost completely.) The European Coal and Steel Commission (the forerunner of the European Community itself) was formed in 1951 to "rationalize" the industry. In the past twenty years it helped close down many mills and eliminate 500,000 jobs. But gluts and surplus capacity remain. The industry last year lost $4.5 billion, and it has sought to "dump" steel abroad to cover costs, prompting retaliation by the United States (which itself had lost 500,000 jobs). The European Commission wants to reduce capacity to about 80 percent of the current 190 million tons and cut 50,000 more jobs. But state-owned and subsidized steelmakers in Italy, Spain, and Germany have resisted. The European Commission, for example, wanted to reduce the tonnage of Ilva, a government-owned steel plant in Taranto, in southern Italy. But the government, which wanted to privatize part of the company, refused. And in Germany and other regions, local communities have bought the steel mills and continue to subsidize them to save jobs.

The same problem, only writ larger, exists in automobiles. There are now six major automobile companies in Europe—Fiat, Renault, Peugeot, Volkswagen, and the subsidiaries of Ford and General Motors. But the markets are now "mature," with little growth, and the intra-European competition will pit the major producers against each other. Fiat, which has been the major (if not the only) Italian firm, has concentrated its hopes on a new small car, the Punto. But European demand is estimated to grow by less than 400,000 cars a year, which is about half the decline in Fiat sales last year alone. BMW, the large luxury-car maker in Germany, has just taken over the English Rover (leaving England with no British-owned car manufacturer) and thus will increase the competition for mass sales. And Japanese factories in England are moving toward the production of a million cars a year by the year 2000, when all limits on Japanese imports into Europe are due to end.

Germany finds itself in increasing difficulty. Four big industries—autos, machinery and machine tools, electrical engineering, and chemicals—account for about 60 percent of Germany's $425 billion export trade. But increased competition has hurt Germany badly, especially in autos, which account for nearly 20 percent of German exports. Volkswagen, the highest-cost big-volume car producer in Europe, which last year made 3.5 million cars, did not earn a pfennig. The result is that it cut its work force by 15 percent. And all over Europe, manufacturing jobs are shrinking rapidly.

Europe can succeed only if it can make the transition to postindustrial sectors. Just as "motors" were the engines of industrial production, "microprocessors" are the engines of the postindustrial, information-based economies. Yet in the area of microchips, the United States produces 47 percent and Japan 41 percent of all micro-electronic units. Germany spends more on subsidies for its older "smokestack" industries, such as coalmining and shipbuilding ($6.4 billion), than for basic research ($5.6 billion).

Germany is today in the midst of a *techno-Angst*, and for good reason. It is losing out in computers, communication electronics, office technology, lasers, and energy technology. In the field of biotechnology and genetic engineering, which is predicted to be a $100 billion industry by the year 2000, German companies now spend an estimated 75 percent of their research-and-development budgets abroad, principally in the United States. Even more important, the revolution in materials technology, which is only now getting seriously under way, means that the older resource-based production becomes less important than technological substitutions (for example, fiber optics for copper). And it is the growth of "technology complexes" and "networking" that cross borders and favor regional developments that is now the source of economic growth. And that poses a challenge to the national state.

Can the transitions be made? All this, theoretically, is manageable in the cycle of industrial restructuring. Japan, from 1960 to 1990, was the world's shining example. It began with textiles and light industry, but when these were taken over by Hong Kong and cheaper producers, Japan moved into optics and instruments, and then to steel, shipbuilding, and automobiles. But after the oil shock of the 1970s, and the increasing costs of energy, it moved quickly into knowledge-based, and electronic and computer-based, industries. But where is Europe to go? The strong rigidities in the major industrial sectors have inhibited structural changes.

There are "rays of hope"—the growth of small-scale, cottage-type manufacturing areas, based on network-linked companies that share market information and allow workers to move about—as in the Prato and Veneto in northern Italy (making textiles and furniture, for example), or in southern Germany, with small machine-tools and parts, or in the Jutland area of Denmark. But these are not sizable enough to affect the major problems.

The single largest economic and social problem in Europe today is unemployment: about thirty-five million persons are without work. In France, Italy, Germany, Denmark, and Great Britain, more than 10 percent of the labor force is unemployed, and this figure may rise to 12 percent, as an average, by the end of 1994. (Spain is a special case, where 23 percent of the population is listed as unemployed, due largely to the delayed transition out of agriculture and the failure of industry to take up the slack.) All of this is politically explosive, especially since few political parties or the trade unions want to take the strong medicine necessary to reduce wage costs, increase labor mobility, or limit pensions and social spending.

In a remarkable report issued in December 1993, the European Commission proposed lowering the minimum wage and cutting social security payments in the hope of creating fifteen million jobs by the year 2000. In a statement presenting the report, Jacques Delors, the president of the commission and a French socialist, declared: "If we want to safeguard the current model of European society and its welfare state, we must adopt this program. *We are no longer in a world where everything is guaranteed.*" (Emphasis added.)

Western Europe, in the fifty years after World War II, was re-created on the model of social democracy. Eastern Europe was shaped on the model of communism or state socialism. The Eastern European model has collapsed. And now the model of social democracy faces an impasse. This is the basis for the coming political crisis of the left in Europe.

Japan's Non-Revolution

Karel van Wolferen

Karel van Wolferen, president of the Institute for Independent Japanese Studies, has lived in Japan since 1962. He is the author of The Engima of Japanese Power.

THE AGE OF UNCERTAINTY

The recent and ubiquitous speculation in the world's media that Japanese society has reached a watershed is based more on wishful thinking than on an understanding of the forces at work in the Japanese body politic. It is a curious phenomenon, indicative of Western apprehensions, that almost every time Japanese developments gain international attention they are accompanied by assertions that the Japanese people are making choices that will change the way they live and work. In reality, the saddest aspect of Japan is that the Japanese people are not in a position to make such choices.

It is true that Japan has entered what can properly be described as an age of uncertainty. The recent fracturing of the Liberal Democratic Party (LDP) and the parliamentary crisis are symptoms of a disorientation without precedent in postwar Japan. International reality has changed for Japan's elite administrators. Its dominant element, the relationship with the United States, has lost the underpinnings that kept it in place for over four decades. With the disappearance of Cold War certainties from American foreign policy, and Japan's emergence as a discomforting economic force, American indulgence toward Japan is shrinking to a point where the basic guarantees that Japan's political elite could count on for four decades have disappeared.

Changes in domestic reality have been less abrupt and are less easily singled out for analysis, but a pervasive sense of unease about Japan's economic future has left its elites disoriented. Although often deceived by their own propaganda, many of Japan's elite know that Japan's ability to export the costs of its postwar strategy of unlimited industrial expansion has been fundamental to that strategy's success. They doubt that Japan can much longer shift such costs as

unemployment, environmental degradation and industrial obsolescence to other countries. During the deflation of the "bubble economy" these past three years, the Ministry of Finance has again demonstrated its genius in disproving prophets of Japanese economic doom. But the officials are now confronting forces so enormous, and international hostility to Japan's "torrential exports" has made the future effectiveness of rescue actions so unpredictable, that continued confidence in their ability to control economic outcomes can no longer be taken for granted.

Japan's age of uncertainty reached an important moment on June 18 when two prominent members of the LDP joined non-LDP politicians in a routine no-confidence vote against Prime Minister Kiichi Miyazawa. Four days later 44 LDP members resigned, forming two new parties. Along with the year-and-a-half-old Japan New Party, they have overturned what Japanese political commentators called "the 1955 setup." This political system, crucial to the shaping of postwar Japan, rested on two pillars: the guaranteed incumbency of the LDP, and a Socialist Party that for 38 years was mired in internal squabbles and unrealistic priorities, guaranteed to keep it out of power.

Since the early 1960s Japan's politicians have not played a significant role in determining national policy.

For over a quarter of a century, informed Japanese and foreigners alike have readily expressed doubts about the authenticity of Japanese democracy. A vote in the countryside could be worth up to four times as much as one in the cities. The Supreme Court, although recognizing that this system violated the constitution, has refused to endorse corrective action that might "cause confusion." By the second half of the 1960s the urban electorate had by and large stopped supporting the LDP, and in successive elections switched what were widely understood to be "protest votes" from one minor party to another. The electorate outside the cities has to a large extent been bribed or subtly coerced into keeping the LDP in power. The Diet has hardly ever been used for genuine parliamentary debates on public issues because the socialist-led opposition indulged in utterly ritualistic politics, regular boycotts of Diet proceedings being its major weapon.

The July 18 elections to the House of Representatives have knocked over one pillar of the 1955 setup. The socialists have been punished for betraying the electorate for 38 years through the loss of half their seats. The politicians who now occupy those seats are not expected to follow the socialist example of marginalizing themselves, raising the possibility that the Diet will become less the rubber-stamp outfit than it has been. Japan's one-party system may well be dead.

POLITICIANS WITHOUT POWER

But the one-party aspect of the 1955 setup, on which doubts concerning Japanese democracy have usually centered, has obscured a more fundamental defect that is likely to remain even now that the 1955 setup is defunct. Since the early 1960s Japan's politicians have not played a significant role in determining national policy, with the sole exception, perhaps, of the brilliant and controversial Kakuei Tanaka. Despite periodic efforts by such talented politicians as Yasuhiro Nakasone, there has not been effective political oversight over bureaucratic decision-making. This bureaucratic decision-making has almost exclusively been restricted to administrative matters. A major shift in national priorities—the need for which is often conceded by independent members of the political elite—cannot come from the bureaucracy, because there is no single entity with the mandate to make decisions that are binding on the entire governing apparatus. The single most powerful entity, the Ministry of Finance, is ultimately guided by the course of action its institutional memory indicates will serve it best, which means that it continues to support the unlimited expansion of Japan's productive capacity.

It is unlikely that this arrangement could have continued for as long as it did without the strategic and diplomatic shield provided by the United States. As Japan concentrated solely on unlimited industrial expansion, there was almost no need to cope with a capricious world; no need to develop acrobatic skills in international diplomacy. These unusual conditions fulfilled the vision held by Japan's first important postwar prime minister, Shigeru Yoshida, of how the Japanese political elite could make the best of the unfortunate circumstances of the late 1940s.

In return for American protection, the LDP accommodated the United States in what Washington cared about most until the Berlin Wall collapsed. Security arrangements, giving the Pentagon unconditional use of whatever military bases it wished to maintain in Japan, were safe as long as the conservatives kept the socialists out of power. But the LDP failed the United States in a way that no one in Washington ever anticipated. By abdicating responsibility for the national agenda to the bureaucracy, the LDP deprived the American government (and that of any other country) of an effective means to discuss any major issue requiring Japanese action. It has not been possible for an American president to discuss the future with a representative of Japan whose mandate reaches further than adjusting technicalities. As things stand, no matter how often Bill Clinton talks with the Japanese prime minister, or how cordial their relationship may be, these two cannot even begin to come to grips with what is threatening to rupture their two countries' crucial relationship.

Japanese ministries come closer to being states unto themselves than any other government institution in the industrialized world.

For some time American trade representatives and other emissaries have been attempting to identify "the right people to talk with." And if there are not any individuals who could make a difference, so it is thought, there must be groups with access to "the right buttons." They do not exist. By leaving overall policymaking in the hands of an unelected and self-appointed group of officials, Japan's elected representatives turned over the core functions of government to men of great but limited competence. Since the 1950s, this bureaucracy has understood limitless industrial growth to be the unquestioned primary goal for Japan, a goal to which all other domestic concerns, such as education and general welfare, as well as international relations must remain subservient. Bureaucrats everywhere judge themselves by their efforts to gain prestige or power for their own institutions. Unless changes could conceivably bring further advantage to their own bureaus, bureaucrats will endeavor to work for the status quo. Japanese bureaucrats are no exception, which results in the institutional paralysis with which foreign negotiators have become familiar.

THE PERMANENT GOVERNMENT

The LDP's abdication of political responsibility fits in with previous forms of Japanese governance, and is connected with the major political flaw of twentieth-century Japan: the absence of a center of political accountability. This is fundamentally different from what has frequently been diagnosed as a "leadership problem," rooted in temporary weaknesses of political will on the part of Japan's highest elected officials. It must be understood that Japan's government agencies do not for practical purposes represent a real government – a core of the state entrusted with the right and duty of decision-making on behalf of the national interest, a core that Japanese citizens could get a grip on if they so desired. Japan poses major conceptual challenges to the West. Americans and Europeans, who take for granted that countries have centers of political accountability (as is clear from the frequent exhortations that "Japan should do this" or "Japan should accept that"), cannot easily understand the workings of a political system lacking a core that can explain to foreigners, to its own population and to the political elite itself what it is doing and why.

Japanese ministries come closer to being states unto themselves than any other government institutions in the industrialized world. Besides their responsibilities for administration, they also monopolize the lawmaking capacities and jurisdiction within their own bailiwicks. For all practical purposes they themselves are not subject to the rule of law. There exists no system of informal power in the world so vast as that of Japan. The system has, however, formal supports in laws that are purposely kept extremely vague to allow for the widest possible bureaucratic discretion. The only significant formal curb on the ministries would be the constitution, which is almost ignored by Japan's bureaucracy. This foreign document – bestowed upon Japan by General Douglas MacArthur – contains a number of articles designed to ward off, in one way or another, arbitrary bureaucratic rule, but these are consistently and systematically violated.

The Ministry of Finance is strongest among these semi-independent governing bodies, since the other government agencies depend on its budget bureau, which judges their annual requests. The banking law assumes that the banks will always follow the ministry's widely varying interpretations of the law. As the 1991 financial scandals demonstrated, ministry officials are not held accountable for violating the securities laws through their informal instructions. The ministry engineered a massive transfer of wealth from the household sector to the industrial sector during the "bubble economy" years, but no one thought to protest. Effective means for holding Ministry of Finance bureaucrats accountable do not exist. Japan's main financial and economic newspaper, the *Nihon Keizai Shimbun,* functions as an amplifier for what ministry officials want players in the Japanese economy to think and believe, preventing it from monitoring ministerial action with critical eyes.

Cabinet ministers are generally not even considered part of the ministries they ostensibly lead. Hence the actual coordination of the Japanese bureaucracy does not take place at cabinet level, and a prime minister's leverage over the entire governing apparatus is vir-

tually nonexistent. To ensure a measure of stability and coordination, and to minimize turf battles, ministries exchange personnel. These bureaucrats on loan double as diplomats and spies, and one of their main tasks is coordinating measures to keep at bay politicians with ambitions to make policy.

The changed circumstances that have ushered in Japan's age of uncertainty demand political adjustments from Japan that the bureaucracy cannot possibly deliver. This is understood by the main figures in the non-LDP ranks whose actions precipitated the recent political upheaval. Two of the new "reformers," now in the Japan Renaissance Party, Ichiro Ozawa and Tsutomo Hata, have for some years made clear that they are eager to apply their considerable political skills to national policymaking. They were protected by Shin Kanemaru, the single most powerful LDP boss, until an internal LDP power struggle one year ago resulted in his removal (with the help of the most recent political scandal in the press). Their loss of a solid political base inside the LDP and failure to get the LDP behind their program for electoral reform gave them an incentive to try their luck at establishing what the three had frequently mentioned as being good for Japan – a two-party system. The third major "reformer," Morihiro Osokawa, deserted the LDP the year before to form his own Japan New Party and has drawn attention with his advocacy of reviewing certain areas of bureaucratic power. The leader of a group of breakaway socialists, Satsuki Eda, also understands that new directions for Japan can only come from politicians.

An unknown number of senior officials in the ministries, as well as prominent retired bureaucrats, also believe in the need for political oversight. Some officials, understanding from personal experience their own ministries' limitations, privately worry that Japan will blunder into catastrophe, as it did in the 1930s, for lack of strong political guidance. But the flaw in Japan's political system is self-perpetuating. In the absence of a center of political accountability these concerned powerholders cannot take preventive action without losing their dignity and creating the impression that they are disloyal to the institutions in which they have made their careers.

A coalition government of reform-minded politicians fully intent on wresting political control from the bureaucracy would face phalanxes of the real powerholders in Japan who are highly skilled in sabotaging projects not to their liking. Drastic interference with bureaucratic personnel appointments would be required. Such steps would probably be followed by an uproar, with the activist politician pilloried among his colleagues and in the media as being un-Japanese for breaking the unwritten rules of Japanese "harmony." Ozawa, who is without a doubt the strongest of the politicians, has already gained a reputation as being too pushy for a Japanese politician. Someone of his caliber who takes a truly courageous stand in the face of bureaucratic opposition becomes very vulnerable, because it is not difficult to launch a scandal that can bring him down. As part of the new coalition parties, an ambitious group of "reformers" might actually assist officialdom in realizing bureaucratic schemes that would have been more difficult to accomplish under the old 1955 setup. It is entirely possible that the upheaval will eventually make the Japanese governmental system even less responsive to international interests and those of the Japanese citizenry. It is conceivable that future coalitions composed of the existing splitters of the LDP, new splitters, what is left of the LDP and the older, minor parties could become indistinguishable from what the LDP has been—a passive and secondary player in Japan's government.

THE SELF-CENSORING PRESS

Admiration for Japan's undoubted economic successes and for its putative supremacy in managerial skills has blinded many Westerners to the profound failures of the Japanese political system. The general assumption, which was again very much in evidence between the lines of most press commentary, assured us that when it really became necessary this political system would respond and repair itself. This may, of course, still happen. But there are good reasons for pessimism. Major obstacles to self-repair are not fully understood in the West, because they are entirely unexpected. But they could provide clues as to what the rest of the world, especially the United States, can do to help salvage what is salvageable of Japanese democracy.

The single biggest impediment to Japanese political reform is probably the Japanese press. It is monolithic, since the five large daily newspapers speak with one voice—their commentary on the issues of the day is almost indistinguishable, and their selection of what to report and what to ignore is virtually identical. The systematic and heavy self-censorship the newspapers engage in is without parallel in the industrialized world. Hence the press directly and decisively determines what others conceive of as political reality, and as such it should be considered Japan's most powerful political—as distinct from administrative—entity.

The vast informal Japanese power structure provides ample opportunity to flay politicians with corruption scandals. Almost any politician can be implicated in such scandals at any time, because gaining political stature in Japan requires raising large sums of money. The easiest means of raising this money stems from the discretionary licensing powers of the bureaucracy. Relatively new or rapidly expanding businesses must protect themselves against arbitrary treatment. Businesses turn to politicians and

offer them very lucrative roles as influence brokers. Without ever distinguishing between unethical bribery and generally accepted political funding, the newspapers consistently denigrate the motives and character of politicians, thus helping to keep alive a general sense that Japan's politicians should not be entrusted with more real power.

No newspaper doubts the need for political reform. But their standard preachings on this subject are placed safely in the context of alleged moral deficiencies of politicians and never concern the shortcomings and abuses of unchecked bureaucratic power. Senior Japanese newspaper editors view themselves as public guardians, entrusted to help maintain a disciplined society with a maximum of order and a minimum of conflict. Since politicians cause political disturbance, and cannot hide the fact that they want power—as opposed to bureaucrats, who are thought to be selfless and dedicated servants of the people—editors protect the bureaucrats and wage regular campaigns against politicians. The newspapers are effectively allied with the police, the public prosecutor, the ministries of finance, justice, education and the *Keidanren* (the umbrella organization of the business bureaucrats, a de facto public organization).

A very difficult aspect of Japanese political reality to fathom is the absence of public opinion. What passes for it is manufactured by the media, especially the five national dailies, and often bears little resemblance to what the Japanese people actually think. They are as capable as people anywhere of discussing a great variety of subjects with indignation and candor, but Japan lacks the institutions to turn these privately expressed opinions into a shared public opinion.

When, prompted by events, a "national debate" emerges concerning fundamental issues, it is immediately filtered by the press to conform to bureaucratic goals, in particular the overriding aim of preserving the status quo. It is therefore not surprising that the burning question in Japan's age of uncertainty, how to accomplish political direction over bureaucratic power, and the fact that this is central to the current parliamentary crisis, are not widely discussed.

Japanese civil society is extremely weak and politically ineffectual. In fact, the press can be said to have supplanted civil society. Genuine labor unions were crushed long ago and have a tradition of serving management. Japan's famous "company loyalty" precludes political activism (which would certainly destroy an employee's career in the company) and has prevented the emergence of a politically significant middle class. Political action and interest groups are not nationally coordinated and are invariably tied to single causes, making them unfit to serve as the foundation for sustained reasoned opposition to the status quo. The judiciary is not independent. With few exceptions, Japanese intellectuals are servants of the bureaucracy, indulging in a type of verbal political opposition that allows them to maintain an image of independence but is harmless because it remains unconnected with political reality.

Attributing Japan's parliamentary crisis to a Japanese public disgusted with political corruption, as the Western press has done, is therefore highly inaccurate. The widespread notion that the upheaval will lead to a shift from Japan's exclusive concern with producer interests to those of consumers is equally ill-conceived.

CAN JAPAN CHANGE?

Japan's true national interest cannot be discussed and served unless politicians gain ascendancy. If, instead, a succession of weak coalitions leads to the further consolidation of unaccountable bureaucratic and business-bureaucratic power, this would not only be tragic for the Japanese people, but highly problematic and perhaps even dangerous for the rest of the world.

As commentators such as R. Taggart Murphy and Christopher Wood have pointed out, endless additions to productive capacity without regard to profitability could create the conditions for global depression.[1] The gradual transformation of countries belonging to the Association of Southeast Asian Nations into "subcontracted economies" headquartered in Tokyo raises new questions about long-range Japanese security arrangements for the protection of these foreign assets.

Japan is today one of the world's most powerful political entities. Coping with it requires more than three days a year of the president's time and the attention of third- and fourth-rank American bureaucrats. Even though President Clinton has shown some understanding of the problem, there are very few people who understand how to deal with Japan effectively. They will be utterly overwhelmed with the magnitude of the task.

As experience shows, conventional diplomacy can achieve only limited goals in Japan. But the rest of the world does have levers to change Japan, while avoiding punitive sanctions. The greatest leverage comes from the desperate hankering on the part of Japan's elite administrators for acceptance of their country as a full political equal of the world's other major democratic states. The implied message from the American president and other governments should be that this is not possible unless Japan establishes a system of politi-

cal accountability. An appropriate context in which to send this message is Tokyo's ardent desire to be given permanent membership on the U.N. Security Council. The Security Council veto power should be made conditional on Japan demonstrating a functioning civilian control mechanism over its own security apparatus. The well-known apprehensions of Korea, Russia and the Southeast Asian countries will strengthen America's case in this matter.

Such concern will actually dovetail with latent and deep-seated fears of large segments of the Japanese political elite, notably the economic ministries. They continue to treat Japan's military (by budget allocation standards the third or fourth biggest in the world) as if it hardly existed—partly because they are unsure as to where in the scheme of Japan's informal power system a fully rehabilitated army and navy would come to rest.

A convincing civilian control mechanism over the defense bureaucracy would foster the development of control mechanisms over other powerful entities, particularly the Ministry of Finance and the business-bureaucratic establishment. Large Japanese companies are—in their behavior and incentive structure—effectively bureaucratic entities, not ultimately driven by considerations of profit making.

A well-informed, imaginative approach ready to engage in unconventional "diplomacy" can achieve much vis-à-vis Japan. Washington could start by urging the Japanese people to write their own constitution. The political/intellectual turbulence this would engender in Japan could only have a salutary effect on the growth of Japan's civil society. It would also end any lingering impression of the United States as postwar parole officer—a role Washington no longer cares to play or understands how to play in any case. Some of the "reformist" politicians, notably Ozawa, need no convincing that Japan needs a constitution giving it unambiguous sovereignty and legitimizing its armed forces.

Contrary to fashionable opinion, the way in which the Japanese have organized their sociopolitical system is very much the business of foreigners. Japanese journalists, many of them moved by feelings of guilt about their systematic self-censorship, frequently solicit and print opinions of foreigners on subjects they dare not touch themselves. Newspapers will prominently feature well-known Americans who direct themselves to the Japanese public with sympathy and genuine understanding. Constant reminders that the people of a great nation must wield power through their politicians and cannot leave fundamental questions of their lives undiscussed would have a far greater positive impact than Westerners now imagine.

R. Taggart Murphy, "Power Without Purpose: The Crisis of Japan's Global Financial Dominance," *Harvard Business Review*, March/April 1989; Christopher Wood, *The Bubble Economy*, New York: Atlantic Monthly Press, 1992.

Global Village or
Global Pillage?

JEREMY BRECHER

Jeremy Brecher is a historian and co-editor of Global Visions:
Beyond the New World Order *(South End).*

For most of the world's people, the "New World Economy" is a disaster that has already happened. Those it hurts can't escape it. But neither can they afford to accept it. So many are now seeking ways to reshape it.

When I first started writing about the destructive effects of globalization three years ago, The North American Free Trade Agreement was widely regarded as a done deal. The near defeat of NAFTA reveals pervasive popular doubt about the wisdom of an unregulated international market. The struggle against NAFTA represented the first major effort by Americans who have been hurt by global economic integration to do something about it. Like many mass movements, it included contradictory forces, such as the Mexico-bashing bigotry of Pat Buchanan, the populist grandstanding of Ross Perot and the nationalistic protectionism of some in the labor movement.

But other elements of the struggle against NAFTA prefigure a movement that could radically reshape the New World Economy. Out of their own experiences and observations, millions of Americans have constructed a new paradigm for understanding the global economy. Poor and working people in large numbers have recognized that NAFTA is not primarily about trade; it is about the ability of capital to move without regard to national borders. Capital mobility, not trade, is bringing about the "giant sucking sound" of jobs going south.

For the first time in many years, substantial numbers of people mobilized to act on broad class interests. I haven't seen a movement for years in which so many people at the grass roots took their own initiative. Typical was the unexpectedly large, predominantly blue-collar anti-NAFTA rally in New Haven, where a labor leader told me, "We didn't turn these people out."

The New Global Pillage

NAFTA became a symbol for an accumulation of fears and angers regarding the place of working people in the New World Economy. The North American economic integration that NAFTA was intended to facilitate is only one aspect of the rapid and momentous historical transformation from a system of national economies toward an integrated global economy. New information, communication, transportation and manufacturing technologies, combined with tariff reductions, have made it possible to coordinate production, commerce and finance on a world scale. Since 1983, the rate of

> **N**ational governments have lost much of their power to direct their own economies.

world foreign direct investment has grown four times as fast as world output.

This transformation has had devastating consequences. They may be summarized as the "seven danger signals" of cancerous, out-of-control globalization:

Race to the bottom. The recent quantum leap in the ability of transnational corporations to relocate their facilities around the world in effect makes all workers, communities and countries competitors for these corporations' favor. The consequence is a "race to the bottom" in which wages and social and environmental conditions tend to fall to the level of the most desperate. This dynamic underlies U.S. deindustrialization, declining real wages, eradication of job security, and

From *The Nation*, December 6, 1993, pp. 685-688. © 1993 by the Nation Company, Inc. Reprinted by permission.

downward pressure on social spending and investment; it is also largely responsible for the migration of low-wage, environmentally destructive industries to poor countries like Mexico and China.

Global stagnation. As each work force, community or country seeks to become more competitive by reducing its wages and its social and environmental overheads, the result is a general downward spiral in incomes and social and material infrastructures. Lower wages and reduced public spending mean less buying power, leading to stagnation, recession and unemployment. This dynamic is aggravated by the accumulation of debt; national economies in poor countries and even in the United States become geared to debt repayment at the expense of consumption, investment and development. The downward fall is reflected in the slowing of global GNP growth from almost 5 percent per year in the period 1948-1973 to only half that in the period 1974-89 and to a mere crawl since then.

Polarization of haves and have-nots. As a result of globalization, the gap between rich and poor is increasing both within and between countries around the world. Poor U.S. communities boast world-class unemployment and infant mortality. Meanwhile, tens of billions of dollars a year flow from poor to rich regions of the world, in the form of debt repayment and capital flight.

Loss of democratic control. National governments have lost much of their power to direct their own economies. The ability of countries to apply socialist or even Keynesian techniques in pursuit of development, full employment or other national economic goals has been undermined by the power of capital to pick up and leave. Governmental economic power has been further weakened throughout the world by neoliberal political movements that have dismantled government institutions for regulating national economies. Globalization has reduced the power of individuals and communities to shape their destinies.

Walter Wriston, former chairman of Citicorp, recently boasted of how "200,000 monitors in trading rooms all over the world" now conduct "a kind of global plebiscite on the monetary and fiscal policies of the governments issuing currency. . . . There is no way for a nation to opt out." Wriston recalls the election of "ardent socialist" François Mitterrand as French President in 1981. "The market took one look at his policies and within six months the capital flight forced him to reverse course."

Unfettered transnational corporations. Transnationals have become the world's most powerful economic actors, yet there are no international equivalents to national antitrust, consumer protection and other laws that provide a degree of corporate accountability.

Unaccountable global institutions. The loss of national economic control has been accompanied by a growing concentration of unaccountable power in international institutions like the International Monetary Fund, the World Bank and the General Agreement on Tariffs and Trade (GATT). For poor countries, foreign control has been formalized in the World Bank's "structural adjustment plans," but I.M.F. decisions and GATT rules affect the economic growth rates of all countries. The decisions of these institutions also have an enormous impact on the global ecology.

Those harmed by the New World Economy need not be passive victims.

Global conflict. Economic globalization is producing chaotic and destructive rivalries. In a swirl of self-contradictory strategies, major powers and transnationals use global institutions like GATT to impose open markets on their rivals; they pursue trade wars against one another; and they try to construct competing regional blocs like the European Community and NAFTA. In past eras, such rivalries have ultimately led to world war.

In sum, the result of unregulated globalization has been the pillage of the planet and its peoples.

Transnational Economic Programs

What are the alternatives to destructive globalization? The right offers racism and nationalism. Conventional protectionism offers no solution. Globalization has also intellectually disarmed the left and rendered national left programs counterproductive. Jimmy Carter's sharp turn to the right in 1978; François Mitterrand's rapid abandonment of his radical program; the acceptance of deregulation, privatization and trade liberalization by poor countries from India to Mexico; and even the decision of Eastern European elites to abandon Communism—all reflect in part the failure of national left policies.

But the beginnings of a new approach emerged from the anti-NAFTA movement itself. Rather than advocate protectionism—keeping foreign products out—many NAFTA opponents urged policies that would raise environmental, labor and social standards in Mexico, so that those standards would not drag down those in the United States and Canada. This approach implied that people in different countries have common interests in raising the conditions of those at the bottom.

Indeed, the struggle against NAFTA generated new transnational networks based on such common interests. A North American Worker-to-Worker Network links grass-roots labor activists in Mexico, the United States and Canada via conferences, tours, solidarity support and a newsletter. Mujer a Mujer similarly links women's groups. The Highlander Center, Southerners for Economic Justice, the Tennessee Industrial Renewal Network and a number of unions have organized meetings and tours to bring together Mexican and U.S. workers. There are similar networks in other parts of the world, such as People's Plan 21 in the Asian-Pacific and Central American regions and the Third World Network in Malaysia.

These new networks are developing transnational programs to counter the effects of global economic restructuring. Representatives from environmental, labor, religious, consumer and farm groups from Mexico, the United States and Canada have drawn up "A Just and Sustainable Trade and Development Initiative for North America." A parallel synthesis, "From Global Pillage to Global Village," has been endorsed by more than sixty grass-roots organizations. Related proposals by the Third World Network have recently been published as "Towards a New North-South Economic Dialogue."

Differing in emphasis and details, these emerging alternative programs are important not only because of the solutions they propose but also because those solutions have emerged from a dialogue rooted in such a diversity of groups and experiences. Some require implementation by national policy; some by international agreement; some can be implemented by transnational citizen action. Taken together, they provide what might be described as "seven prescriptions" for the seven danger signals of the unregulated global economy:

International rights and standards. To prevent competition from resulting in a race to the bottom, several of these groups want to establish minimum human, labor and environmental rights and standards, as the European Community's "social charter" was designed to do. The International Metalworkers Federation recently proposed a ten-point "World Social Charter," which could be incorporated into GATT.

"A Just and Sustainable Trade and Development Initiative for North America" spells out in some detail an alternative to NAFTA that would protect human and worker rights, encourage workers' incomes to rise in step with productivity and establish continental environmental rights, such as the right to a toxics-free workplace and community. Enforcement agencies would be accessible to citizens and could levy fines against parties guilty of violations. The initiative especially emphasizes the rights of immigrants. Activists from nongovernmental organizations in all three countries have proposed a citizens' commission to monitor the human, labor and environmental effects of trade and investment.

Upward spiral. In the past, government monetary and fiscal policy, combined with minimum wages, welfare state programs, collective bargaining and other means of raising the purchasing power of have-nots, did much to counter recession and stagnation within national economies. Similar measures are now required at international levels to counter the tendency toward a downward spiral of inadequate demand in the global economy. The Third World Network calls on the I.M.F. and World Bank to replace their ruinous structural adjustment plans with policies that "meet the broad goals of development . . . rather than the narrower goal of satisfying the needs of the creditors." It also demands a reduction of developing country debt. "A Just and Sustainable Trade and Development Initiative" proposes that the remaining debt service be paid in local currency into a democratically administered development fund. Reversing the downward spiral also ultimately requires a "global Keynesianism" in which international institutions support, rather than discourage, national full-employment policies.

An upward spiral also requires rising income for those at the bottom—something that can be encouraged by international labor solidarity. Experiments in cross-border organizing

by U.S. unions like the Amalgamated Clothing and Textile Workers and the United Electrical Workers, in cooperation with independent unions in Mexico, aim to defeat transnationals' whipsawing by improving the wages and conditions of Mexican workers.

Redistribution from haves to have-nots. "A Just and Sustainable Trade and Development Initiative" calls for "compensatory financing" to correct growing gaps between rich and poor. A model would be the European Community funds that promote development in its poorer members. The Third World Network calls for commodity agreements to correct the inequities in the South's terms of trade. It also stresses the need to continue preferential treatment for the South in GATT and in intellectual property protection rules.

Strengthened democracy. NAFTA, GATT and similar agreements should not be used—as they now can be—to preempt the right of localities, states, provinces and countries to establish effective labor, health, safety and environmental standards that are higher than the guaranteed minimum in international agreements. Above all, democratization requires a new opportunity for people at the bottom to participate in shaping their destiny.

Codes of conduct for transnational corporations. Several transnational grass-roots groups call for codes of conduct that would, for example, require corporations to report investment intentions; disclose the hazardous materials they import; ban employment of children; forbid discharge of pollutants; require advance notification and severance pay when operations are terminated; and prohibit company interference with union organizing. United Nations discussions of such a code, long stymied by U.S. hostility, should be revived.

While the ultimate goal is to have such codes implemented by agreements among governments, global public pressure and cross-border organizing can begin to enforce them. The Coalition for Justice in the Maquiladoras, for example, a group of religious, environmental, labor, Latino and women's organizations in Mexico and the United States, has issued a code of conduct for U.S. corporations in Mexico and has used "corporate campaign" techniques to pressure them to abide by its labor and environmental provisions.

Reform of international institutions. Citizens should call on the U.N. to convene a second Earth Summit focusing on democratizing the I.M.F. and the World Bank, and consider formation of new institutions to promote equitable, sustainable and participatory development. International citizen campaigns, perhaps modeled on the Nestlé boycott and the campaign against World Bank–funded destruction of the Amazon, could spotlight these institutions.

Multiple-level regulation. In place of rivalry among countries and regions, such programs imply a system of democratically controlled public institutions at every level, from global to local.

After NAFTA: Globalization From Below

These proposals provide no short-term panacea; they are objectives to organize around. The New World Economy is not going to vanish from the political agenda. Neither will the passions and political forces aroused by the NAFTA debate. Many of the same issues will resurface in connection with the Asia-Pacific Economic Cooperation Forum and with GATT. As the fiftieth anniversaries of the I.M.F. and World Bank approach, calls for their reform are being sounded all over the world.

The struggle against NAFTA has shown that those harmed by the New World Economy need not be passive victims. So many politicians were so unprepared for the strength of the anti-NAFTA movement because it represented an eruption into the political arena of people who have long been demobilized. But to influence their economic destinies effectively, they need a movement that provides an alternative to the Ross Perots and Pat Buchanans. Such a movement must act on the understanding that the unregulated globalization of capital is really a worldwide attack of the haves on the have-nots. And

it must bring that understanding to bear on every affected issue, from local layoffs to the world environment. "From Global Pillage to Global Village" suggests a vision to guide such a movement:

> The internationalization of capital, production and labor is now being followed by the internationalization of peoples' movements and organizations. Building peoples' international organizations and solidarity will be our revolution from within: a civil society without borders. This internationalism or "globalization from below" will be the foundation for turning the global pillage into a participatory and sustainable global village.

The organizations that have led the fight against NAFTA have a responsibility not to retreat to parochial concerns. They must regroup and begin addressing the broader impact of economic globalization on people and planet.

Conflict

In the international arena, governments are sometimes able to fulfill their goals by making mutually agreeable exchanges (i.e., giving up something in order to gain something they value more). This exchange process, however, often breaks down. When threats and punishments replace mutual exchanges, conflict ensues. Neither side benefits, and there are costs to both. Each side may hope the other will capitulate, but if efforts at coercion fail, the conflict may escalate into violent confrontation.

With the end of the cold war, the issues of national security are changing for the world's major powers. Old alliances are changing, not only in Europe but in the Middle East as well. These changes not only have major policy implications for the major powers but for participants in regional conflicts as well. Agreements between the leadership of the now-defunct Soviet Union and the United States led to the elimination of support for participants in low-intensity conflicts in Central America, Africa, and Southeast Asia. Fighting the cold war by proxy is now a thing of the past. Nevertheless, there is no shortage of conflicts in the world today.

The section begins with a broad overview of the major forces at work shaping the international politics of the twenty-first century. Included is a discussion of the types of conflicts that are likely to result and how these present new challenges to keeping them from escalating into warfare. This lead article is then followed with specific case studies: ethnic violence, terrorism, regional arms races, and the spread of nuclear weapons.

This unit concludes by examining one of the most important issues in history—the avoidance of nuclear war. Many experts initially predicted that the collapse of the Soviet Union would decrease the threat of nuclear war. However, many now believe that the threat has increased as control of nuclear weapons has become less centralized and the command structure less reliable. What these dramatically different circumstances mean for strategic weapons policy in the United States is also a topic of considerable debate. With this changing political context as the backdrop, the prospects for arms control and increased international cooperation are reviewed in the areas of nuclear and conventional weapons. Methods to reduce the risk of accidental nuclear war are also examined.

Like all the other global issues described in this anthology, international conflict is a dynamic problem. It is important to understand that it is not a random event, but there are patterns and trends. Forty-five years of cold war established a variety of patterns of international conflict as the superpowers contained each other with vast expenditures of money and technological know-how. The consequence of this stalemate was a shift to the developing world for the arena of conflict. With the end of the cold war, these patterns are already changing. Will there be more nuclear proliferation or will there be less? Will the emphasis be shifted to low-intensity conflicts related to the interdiction of drugs? Or will economic problems for the industrial world have them turn inward and allow a new round of ethnically motivated conflicts to turn brutally violent as we have seen in Yugoslavia? The answers to these and related questions will determine the patterns of conflict in the post–cold war era.

Looking Ahead: Challenge Questions

Is violent conflict and warfare increasing or decreasing today?

What changes have taken place in recent years in the types of conflicts that occur and in who participates?

How is military doctrine changing to reflect new political realities?

How is the role of the United States in global security likely to change?

Are nuclear weapons more or less likely to proliferate in the post–cold war era?

What institutional changes can be established to reduce the danger of nuclear war?

In this era, when keeping track of the number of times the superpowers can destroy the world is obsolete, attention has shifted to the number of brushfires cropping up in the world. As Michael Klare points out, it remains to be seen whether international organizations are up to the challenge of extinguishing them or whether they will be allowed to rage because of international inattention, inactivity, and indecision.

The New Challenges to Global Security

MICHAEL T. KLARE

MICHAEL T. KLARE *is the Five College Associate Professor of Peace and World Security Studies, a joint appointment at Amherst, Hampshire, Mount Holyoke, and Smith Colleges and the University of Massachusetts at Amherst. He is the author of* American Arms Supermarket *(Austin: University of Texas Press, 1984) and co-editor of* Low-Intensity Warfare *(New York: Pantheon, 1988) and* World Security: Trends and Challenges at Century's End, *2d ed.(New York: St. Martin's Press, 1993).*

For 45 years, from World War II's finish to the end of the cold war, most agreed that the greatest threat to global security was an all-out war between the two superpowers that would culminate in the use of nuclear weapons. Fearing this, government officials and concerned citizens sought to diminish the risk of nuclear conflict through intensive diplomacy, improved crisis management, arms control, and cultural and other exchanges. Because of these efforts and the reforms that Soviet President Mikhail Gorbachev set in motion in 1985, the risk of a superpower conflict has largely vanished, and the world no longer dreads a nuclear conflagration.

The post–cold war era, however, is by no means free of the threat of armed conflict, as demonstrated by continuing warfare in areas as diverse as Afghanistan, Angola, Burma, Indonesia, Kashmir, Liberia, Peru, Somalia, Sri Lanka, the Caucasus (Georgia, Armenia, and Azerbaijan), and the former Yugoslavia. While these conflicts do not have the potential to erupt into a nuclear holocaust, they do pose a threat of widespread regional fighting with fearsome death tolls and destruction. Moreover, as weapons of mass destruction be-

come more widely diffused, a growing number of these regional wars will entail a risk of chemical and even nuclear attack. Preventing, controlling, and resolving these conflicts, and impeding the spread of advanced weaponry will, therefore, constitute the principal world security tasks of the 1990s and beyond.

THE SHIFTING POLITICAL LANDSCAPE

A metaphor popular among analysts thinking about the current reshaping of the world is that of "tectonic motion," or the movement of the giant "plates" that make up the earth's rocky crust. Because this movement can reshape continents and alter climates—sometimes cataclysmically—through the earthquakes and volcanoes it produces, it serves as an apt analogy for the end of the cold war and other dramatic changes now occurring throughout the world.[1]

The geological metaphor conveys the scale of the changes now under way around the globe and illustrates how surface events are the product of deeper sociohistorical forces. Thus we sense that the drive for democracy and human rights in Russia and eastern Europe is related to similar pressures in Myanmar, Chile, China, Haiti, Mexico, the Philippines, and Thailand. The image of tectonic motion also suggests the havoc wreaked by the breakup of large empires and federations (notably the Soviet empire and the old Yugoslavia) and the fracturing of established alliances such as the Warsaw Pact and, to a lesser degree, NATO.

But to adequately describe the security environment of this era after the cold war, the tectonics metaphor must be supplemented by an additional image—one that captures the profusion of ethnic, tribal, religious, and national conflicts that we are witnessing today. Imagine a piece of glass laid over a map of the world and then struck by a large, heavy weight: the result would be an intricate web of cracks across the world, with heavier concentrations in some areas but with none left entirely unscathed.

These cracks represent the many fissures in our multiethnic, multiclass, and multilingual societies—

---

[1] As the historian John Lewis Gaddis has observed, "Like the tectonic forces that move continents around on the surface of the earth," the end of the cold war and other recent developments suggest a massive shift in the "historic tectonics" of human civilization. John Lewis Gaddis, "Tectonics, History, and the End of the Cold War" (Columbus, Ohio: Occasional Paper from the Mershon Center of the Ohio State University, 1992), p. 4.

the divisions between rich and poor, black and white, Hindu and Muslim, Muslim and Jew, Czech and Slovak, Serb and Croat, Azeri and Armenian, and so on. The fissures are stressed by the tectonic shifts occurring beneath the surface, but it is along their jagged lines that the battles of the post–cold war era are being fought.

The fractured-glass analogy suggests the multiplicity of conflictual relationships in the world. Just consider for a moment the situation in the Middle East, which is not just a conflict between the Arab states and Israel, or between Iran and Iraq, but rather a far more elaborate configuration of animosities. In Lebanon, for instance, it involves Maronite Christians, Sunni and Shiite Muslims, the Druze, and Palestinians; in Syria, the Alawites and other Muslims; and in Iraq, Kurds, Sunnis, and Shiites. A similar diversity in the conflictual pattern is found in the former Yugoslavia, and in the Caucasus region of what was once the Soviet Union.

Each of these images—tectonic motion and fractured glass—is helpful in identifying features of the current world security environment. However, to best describe this environment it is useful to combine the images: tectonic movements causing massive shifts beneath the surface that in turn accentuate and extend the cracks appearing on the surface. By assessing both the tectonic movements and networks of cracks, we can arrive at a comprehensive picture of current world security issues.

FIVE FORCES THAT SHAKE THE WORLD

It is risky, of course, to attempt an analysis while the world is still undergoing transformation. But enough has already occurred on the surface for us to be able to begin to understand what is happening below. Five tectonic shifts in particular are worthy of discussion:

The Pull of Economic Forces

There was a time, not so long ago, when the "fate of nations" was determined largely by political and military factors—most significantly, the ability of the state to marshal a country's resources for war, conquest, or defense. Today the state remains a major international actor, but its capacity to organize resources for its purposes has been circumscribed by what has been called "supranational capitalism." As the economist Robert Heilbroner sees it, the global nexus of multinational corporations and international financial institutions has accumulated vast power and influence at the expense of national capitalism and state agencies. This, Heilbroner notes, endows suprana-

tional capitalism with the ability "to rearrange the global division and distribution of political and economic power"—a capacity that, when exercised, is often "seismic" in its impact.[2]

Obviously it is impossible to establish a one-to-one correlation between broad economic phenomena and specific world events. But that the failure of the Soviet Union and its eastern European satellites to keep pace with economic growth in the West contributed to the debilitation of Communist regimes is certain. Unable to generate funds for investment in economic and social revitalization, these regimes stagnated and lost what remained of their political legitimacy. The eventual result was a rapid slide from power, with what had become a corrupt and demoralized ruling class putting up little resistance.

The same economic forces are now exacerbating intergroup conflicts around the globe. Because some groups and societies have adapted more successfully than others to the competitive pressures of global capitalism, socioeconomic divisions in multinational states are becoming more visible and pronounced, provoking increased conflict between those on opposite sides of these rifts. Thus, the dissolution of Yugoslavia can be partially attributed to the desire of the country's stronger economic units, Croatia and Slovenia, to break away from their less advantaged fellow republics and integrate more closely with the western European economies. Similarly, the breakup of Czechoslovakia can be explained in part by growing resentment in Slovakia over the faster pace of economic activity in the Czech Republic.

Perhaps even more destabilizing is the widening economic gap between the industrialized "North" and underdeveloped "South." Although some third world countries have in recent years managed to join the ranks of the more affluent nations—one thinks especially of the newly industrialized countries of the Pacific Rim—most of the less developed countries of Asia, Africa, and Latin America have seen the difference between their standard of living and that of the wealthier nations widen over the past decade. At the same time, the global spread of Western culture and consumption patterns via the mass media have inculcated an appetite for goods and services not attainable by the masses of the poor and unemployed. The result is increased North-South tensions ranging from the growing militancy of political and religious movements with anti-Western themes (movements, for example, like the Maoist Shining Path in Peru and the Islamic Jihad in Egypt) to more South-to-North drug smuggling. Depressed economies in the South are also behind the rise in migration to the nations of the North—itself a growing cause of violence in the destination countries.

---

[2] Robert L. Heilbroner, "The Future of Capitalism," in Nicholas X. Rizopoulus, ed., *Sea Changes: American Foreign Policy in a World Transformed* (New York: Council on Foreign Relations, 1990), pp. 114–115.

The Global Diffusion of Power

The rise of supranational capitalism has been accompanied by a diffusion of political, military, and economic power away from the United States and the Soviet Union, the two main poles of the cold war era, to other actors in the international order. This has been in progress since the 1950s and 1960s, when the western European countries and Japan began to recover from the devastating effects of World War II and many third world nations secured their independence; it gained further momentum in the 1970s and 1980s with the slowdown of economic growth in the United States and the Soviet Union and the acquisition of major military capabilities by emerging third world powers. The process culminated in 1989–1991 with the collapse of the Soviet Union, the dissolution of the Warsaw Pact, and the resulting disappearance of the bipolar world.

As of yet, no clearly defined system of power relationships has developed in place of the bipolar system and the tight alliances of the cold war period. Rather, a number of regional power centers—Japan in Asia, Germany in Europe, Russia in central Euroasia, the United States in North America—have emerged, each surrounded by a cluster of associated states. These centers cooperate with each other in some matters and compete in others; states not aligned with any of the principal clusters manage as best they can.

The diffusion of political and military power and the realignment of global power relationships have multiple implications for world security. With the erosion of superpower influence and the proliferation of modern weapons, newly strengthened regional powers see an opportunity to pursue their hegemonic ambitions, often provoking fierce conflict in the process (as in the case of Iraq's 1980 invasion of Iran and its 1990 invasion of Kuwait). Furthermore, the collapse of central control over the periphery of what was the Soviet Union has resulted in a series of ethnic and territorial clashes between former components of the empire. And the worldwide diffusion of nonnuclear weapons has contributed to the duration and intensity of insurgencies and civil and ethnic conflicts.

Increased Popular Assertiveness at the Grass-Roots Level

Paralleling the growth of globalized economic institutions and the diffusion of political power among international players is the increased assertion at the local and national level of "people power." Wherever we look in the world today, we find grass-roots citizens movements striving for fundamental change in key social, economic, and political structures. In some areas, including the Philippines, China, Haiti, eastern Europe, and the former Soviet Union, this assertiveness has entailed a drive for democratic rights; it has also, however, appeared as anti-foreigner sentiment in Germany and increased anti-Semitism in Russia.

By far the most potent manifestation of this grass-roots assertiveness is the militant expression of ethnic, national, linguistic, and religious affiliations by peoples who have previously lived peacefully in multinational, multicultural societies. This expression takes many forms: the calls for secession by the constituent nationalities of the former Soviet Union and Yugoslavia; the militant assertion of Hindu fundamentalism in India and Islamic fundamentalism in Egypt; the Kurdish rebellion in Iraq and the Tamil rebellion in Sri Lanka; and the Palestinian intifada. As suggested by Myron Weiner of the Massachusetts Institute of Technology, "Peoples'—however they identify themselves by race, religion, language, tribe, or shared history—want new political institutions or new relationships within existing institutions"; when accommodation is not forthcoming, they are likely to escalate their demands.

The growing assertion of populist claims, whether of a political or an ethnic nature, has significant implications for world security. At the very least it is jeopardizing the ability of current leaders from North and South, East and West, to hold on to power. In many areas it has led to violent clashes between members of opposing groups. And in Yugoslavia it has created a maelstrom of ethnic fury that threatens to engulf much of southeastern Europe.

The Diminishing Power and Authority of the Nation-State

Caught between ever more powerful supranational capitalism on one side and restive populations on the other is the modern nation-state. Although still among the actors with the most clout on the international stage, the state is steadily losing ground to international financial institutions and well-organized ethnic and religious constituencies. This is evident both in the ability of the International Monetary Fund to dictate government spending practices in many third world and eastern European countries, and in that of Muslim clerics to affect foreign policy in Iran and Saudi Arabia.

To a great extent, the decline in the power of the nation-state is a product of a global revolution of rising expectations at a time of increased international economic competition. As Stanley Hoffmann of Harvard University observes, people still "count on their state to play the game of wealth effectively," and thus attain or protect high standards of living. But state authorities have less control over their economies than ever before, and when they fail to satisfy popular expectations invite popular revolt—through electoral channels where that option exists, through rioting and civil strife where it does not.

The replacement of older, unrepresentative regimes by new, popularly backed governments in the Soviet bloc and elsewhere has not, unfortunately, always resulted in greater social stability. In many cases the new regimes have played the game of wealth with even less success than their predecessors, resulting in widespread discontent and a risk of coups and mob action. To retain their hold on power, some of these regimes—most notably that in Serbia—have turned to ultra-nationalism as a solution, thereby provoking fresh outbreaks of ethnic violence. In other cases, such as Afghanistan, Mozambique, and Peru, the state has lost control over wide areas, ceding authority to local warlords and sectarian forces; in extreme cases, the state has simply withered away, giving free rein to the sort of gang warfare seen in Liberia and Somalia.

Population Growth and Environmental Decline

The erosion of the state's power and authority has been accelerated, in many instances, by a fifth tectonic force: rapid population growth and the emergence of harsh environmental limits. Population growth is not by itself a cause of instability—historically, it has often contributed to the health and vigor of societies, as in the case of the United States. But when population increases exceed the rate of economic growth (as in many third world countries today), and when they contribute to the depletion of valuable resources (such as tropical forests and tillable soil), the ability of states to engage in long-term economic and social development is impaired—thus ensuring worse hardship and unrest in the future.

The world's population now stands at about 5.5 billion people, and this figure is expected to double by the middle of the twenty-first century. Such a jump could theoretically be sustained if the planet's resources were evenly distributed, and if new products were developed to replace those natural substances being depleted. But resources are not evenly distributed, and new products might not be available at an affordable price to all who need them. As things stand now, many states in Asia, Africa, and Latin America (where population growth rates are at an all-time high) are not able to provide for burgeoning numbers of young people, and will be even less able to do so in the future. The consequences include a rising incidence of hunger and malnutrition, increased migration from the impoverished countryside to urban shantytowns, soaring unemployment (especially among youths), and the growing appeal of extremist movements.

---

[3]These findings emerge from the Project on Environmental Change and Acute Conflict, a joint study of the American Academy of Arts and Sciences and the Program on Peace and Conflict Studies of the University of Toronto. See Thomas Homer-Dixon, Jeffrey Boutwell, and George Rathjens, "Environmental Change and Violent Conflict," *Scientific American,* February 1993, pp. 38–45; Homer-Dixon, "Environmental Scarcity and Intergroup Conflict," in Michael Klare and Daniel Thomas, *World Security,* 2d ed. (New York: St. Martin's Press, 1993).

Even if population growth is stabilized, the world must still contend with the problems arising from human-induced degradation of the environment. Much has been written about the long-term effects of global warming and the depletion of the atmosphere's ozone layer, and on their implications for human, plant, and animal populations; much less, however, is known about the impact of environmental decline on intergroup and interstate relations. Preliminary research suggests that environmental decline, especially when it occurs in environmentally stressed areas of the third world (deserts, rainforests, hillsides, coastal lowlands) will exacerbate intergroup competition and conflict and drive yet more people into crowded urban shantytowns where the prospects for meaningful employment are dim and the danger of unrest is high.[3]

BREAKUP, BREAKDOWN, AND BLOW-UP

These tectonic forces act on the peoples, states, and societies of the world in such a way as to exacerbate existing tensions between groups and in many cases to provoke or intensify conflict. The resulting struggles take several forms, all of which have become all-too-common features of the global environment.

One manifestation is the world's decomposing empires and superstates. By far the most striking products of the cold war's end and communism's demise have been the dissolution of the Soviet Union and Yugoslavia. The Soviet Union was both an empire, assembled through centuries of conquest by the Russian czars and their Communist successors, and a modern superstate, uniting many individual nations in one centrally administered, confederated system. Yugoslavia also possessed attributes of empire and confederation. Systems of this sort can survive only when the center possesses enough strength to subdue separatist pressures in the periphery, and when there are sufficient social, economic, and political links between the disparate parts to resist the centrifugal forces that inevitably tear at such an assemblage.

With the collapse of communism—the binding agent in both the Soviet Union and Yugoslavia—and the growing impact of tectonic forces, these two superstates broke up in 1991, and the individual groups that had constituted them sought to establish full sovereignty over (what they viewed as) their rightful territory. As suggested by past instances of imperial decomposition, such as the breakup of the Austro-Hungarian and Ottoman Empires after World War I, the process inevitably spawns discord and conflict. Pieces of the decomposing empire fight over the demarcation of new international boundaries (hence the fighting between Croatia and Serbia, and between Armenia and Azerbaijan), and ethnic minorities find themselves trapped within alien and inhospitable states (hence the struggles of the Abkhazians and South Ossetians in Georgia, the Ingush and Chechens in Russia, the ethnic Russians in Moldova, and the ethnic Albanians in the Kosovo region of Serbia).

Such struggles are not limited to the former Soviet Union and Yugoslavia; other multinational superstates are feeling the vibrations of tectonic forces. Hence the survival of Canada remains in doubt as the French-speaking people of Quebec continue to seek greater autonomy from the English-speaking provinces, while India has experienced significant separatist pressures in Kashmir, the Punjab, and Assam. Ethiopia, once an imperial kingdom, has long been troubled by armed separatist movements in the provinces of Eritrea and Tigre, and is likely to experience renewed conflict if these pressures are not relieved. Two other third world superstates, China and Indonesia, continue to encounter resistance on their peripheries (the former in Tibet, the latter in East Timor) and will likely come under intensified pressure from separatists in the future.

Accompanying the breakup of large multinational states has come a surge in ethnonationalist and irredentist struggles as ethnic groups that have been denied a state (or have had theirs submerged in a larger multinational entity) seek to establish one, and as other groups already in possession of a state seek to enlarge it so as to incorporate adjacent territories occupied by large numbers of their kinsmen. Such impulses have long sparked fighting, but seem to have gained renewed vigor in recent years as the bipolar system broke and the balance of power between state authorities and populist elements shifted in favor of the latter.

As has been noted, ethnonationalist forces are evident in the separatist struggles in the former Yugoslavia, Georgia, India, China, and Indonesia. Other groups engaged in like struggles include the Kurds in Iraq and Turkey, the Palestinians in the West Bank and Gaza Strip, the Tamils in Sri Lanka, the Shan and Karen peoples of Burma, and the Basques of France and Spain.

Major irredentist struggles include the Serbians' campaign to create a "Greater Serbia" out of the remnants of Yugoslavia, Armenia's push to gain control over Nagorno-Karabakh (now controlled by Azerbaijan), Russia's drive to repossess the Crimean peninsula (which was ceded to Ukraine in 1954 by Nikita Khrushchev), and China's continuing efforts to repossess Taiwan. Many fear that irredentists in Hungary will press for the incorporation of Hungarian-speaking regions of Slovakia, Romania, and the former Yugoslavia in a "Greater Hungary."

REGIONAL RIVALRIES

The rivalries engendered by the breakup of larger states will be paralleled by regional rivalry. The breakdown of the bipolar system and concomitant diffusion of political power have given added impetus to rivalries between regional states, especially in East Asia, South Asia, and the Middle East. Of particular concern are the ongoing rivalries between China and Taiwan, North Korea and South Korea, India and Pakistan, India and China, Iran and Iraq, Iran and Saudi Arabia, and Israel and Syria. These have all flared up periodically in the past, but they seem to have gained renewed intensity in recent years as the inhibiting influence of the superpowers declined and the regional power equation became more unsettled. Several of these contests could experience a fresh outbreak of fighting in the latter 1990s.

Factors that will come to bear on such rivalries include: the degree of progress (or lack of it) in regional peace negotiations, especially the Middle East peace talks; the degree to which these states are hobbled by internal power struggles; the ability of the United States—now the world's sole superpower—to discourage adventurism on the part of regional powers; and the impact of global economic conditions on these states' inclinations to engage in external conflict. No one can predict how these factors will play out in the years ahead, but it is reasonable to assume, for example, that a breakdown in the Mideast peace talks, coupled with a decline in United States influence and/or the emergence of aggressive-minded leaders in one or more states would increase the risk of a new regional conflagration.

Another key factor in all of this is the effect of weapons proliferation on the dynamics of conflict between regional rivals. All the states named above are engaged in major military buildups—in many cases involving weapons of mass destruction—and thus each has reason to fear the arms acquisition programs of its adversaries. Should any of these powers achieve a sudden and unexpected increase in its military capability—through, say, the acquisition of nuclear weapons or ballistic missiles—it could invite a preemptive strike by a rival. Such strikes have taken place before—for example, the 1981 Israeli attack on Iraq's Osirak reactor—and are all too likely to occur again.

REVOLUTIONARY AND FUNDAMENTALIST CRUSADES

Though the appeal of Soviet-style communism has largely dissipated, revolutionary and millenarian movements continue to hold an attraction for downtrodden and dispossessed peoples. Such movements promise not merely a change of leaders but a sweeping transformation of society, typically involving the elimination of existing institutions and their replacement by more "righteous" or egalitarian structures. Movements of this sort appear to be gaining strength in areas where economic conditions have worsened for the majority (or for particular groups) and where the capacity or inclination of state authorities to overcome widespread impoverishment and inequity has diminished. Revolutionary and millenarian groups in such areas appear increasingly willing to employ violence in their efforts to reform society.

At present two main types of revolutionary crusade can be discerned: ideological or political movements, usually attempting to end exploitation of the poor by the middle class and the rich; and religious fundamentalism, entailing a drive to subject all societal interactions to religious law and practice. Examples of the first type include the Shining Path in Peru, the Farabundo Martí National Liberation Front of El Salvador, Cambodia's Khmer Rouge, and the New People's Army in the Philippines; examples of the second category would be the Hindu fundamentalist Bharatiya Janata party in India, the Islamic Salvation Front in Algeria, the Islamic Jihad in Egypt, and the various Islamic fundamentalist forces in Afghanistan.

Finally, the world is confronted with an assortment of pro-democracy and anti-colonial movements, which tend to erupt periodically in strikes or civil disorders and/or to provoke repressive violence by the authorities. All these movements reflect the tectonic increase in grass-roots activism described earlier, and while they may experience setbacks in the short term are not likely to disappear anytime soon.

They include: popular drives for Western-style electoral democracy and human rights, as have been working themselves out in Burma, China, Haiti, the Philippines, South Korea, Thailand, and Zaire; struggles by disenfranchised minorities and majorities to abolish unrepresentative or discriminatory governments, from Northern Ireland to South Africa; and efforts by subject peoples to cast off what is viewed as colonial rule (even though the "colonizers" involved may be other third world countries), as in East Timor, Kashmir, the Western Sahara, and the West Bank and Gaza. Paralleling these movements are the increasingly vigorous efforts of indigenous people to reclaim rights and lands that have long been denied them by the dominant cultures.

WILL WEAPONS INHERIT THE EARTH?

Adding to the dangers posed by all the factors described above is the global proliferation of modern weapons and the technologies for producing them. Such proliferation entails not only the spread of nuclear, chemical, and biological weapons—the so-called weapons of mass destruction—but also a wide range of "conventional" arms—the tanks, planes, guns, and missiles used by regular military forces. Both sorts of weapons are finding their way into the arsenals of more and more nations, thereby stimulating local arms races and ensuring that future wars will be fought with ever-ascending lethality and destructiveness.

In the nuclear realm, the five declared nuclear weapons powers (the United States, Russia, Great Britain, France, and China) have been joined by three undeclared nuclear ones (Israel, India, and Pakistan), while Iran, Iraq, and North Korea continue their efforts to develop such weapons and Argentina, Brazil, South

Africa, South Korea, and Taiwan retain a capacity to do so in the future. (Belarus, Kazakhstan, and Ukraine inherited some nuclear weapons from the former Soviet Union, but have pledged to turn them over to Russian authorities. Still, many analysts worry about the possible spread of former Soviet nuclear materials and technology.)

As for chemical weapons, American intelligence officials have identified 14 third world countries believed to possess an offensive chemical warfare capability: Burma, China, Egypt, India, Iran, Iraq, Israel, Libya, North Korea, Pakistan, South Korea, Syria, Taiwan, and Vietnam. Many of these nations have also engaged in research on biological weapons, and have acquired ballistic missiles that can be used to deliver nuclear, chemical, and biological warheads. We have already witnessed the extensive use of chemical weapons in the Iran-Iraq war, and in Iraq's subsequent campaign to liquidate Kurdish villages in strategic border areas. Iraq also threatened chemical attacks against Israel in 1990 and 1991, and Israeli officials responded with threats of possible nuclear retaliation. Central Intelligence Agency officials have reported that India and Pakistan were prepared to use nuclear weapons in 1990, when it was feared the fighting in Kashmir would spark a full-scale conflict.

The proliferation of advanced conventional arms has proceeded apace with that of weapons of mass destruction. According to estimates by the Congressional Research Service, third world countries spent $339.5 billion on imported weapons from 1983 to 1990 (in constant 1990 US dollars)—which translates into (among other things) some 13,010 tanks and self-propelled guns, 27,430 pieces of heavy artillery, 2,920 supersonic combat planes, 38,430 surface-to-air missiles, and 53,790 surface-to-surface missiles. These weapons sustained the Iran-Iraq war of 1980–1988 and other regional conflicts, and swelled the arsenals of emerging powers in Africa, Asia, and Latin America.

Security analysts are also worried about the growing diffusion of advanced conventional weapons. As military spending in NATO and the former Warsaw Pact falls, arms manufacturers in these countries, whether state-owned or private, are increasingly disposed to export their products to the third world, where the demand for modern weapons is high and the likelihood of their being used in combat is growing. The stockpiles built up by the Soviet Union and its Warsaw Pact allies during the cold war era constitute a vast reservoir of surplus arms that are increasingly finding their way into the black market—and thence into the hands of terrorists, guerrillas, separatist forces, and other irregular formations that threaten the peace in many areas of the world.

Proliferation of arms of all types is certain to figure as a primary security concern in the 1990s and beyond because it helps increase the number, length, and duration of conventional conflicts and also increases the risk that future wars will involve the use of weapons of mass destruction, whether deliberate or accidental.

KEEPING THE PEACE

The tectonic forces currently in motion and the growing tempo of internal, local, and regional conflict have placed enormous strain on the international community, forcing world leaders to consider new and enhanced methods of conflict control. The development and application of these to actual conflicts are likely to remain a central issue in security affairs for the foreseeable future.

With the cold war over and the superpowers no longer assuming responsibility for maintaining peace and stability within their respective spheres of influence, a greater burden has naturally fallen on the United Nations, which has responded by greatly expanding its peacemaking and peacekeeping operations around the world. Between 1991 and 1992 the United Nations established 13 new peacekeeping operations—exactly the number initiated by the world body in the entire previous 42 years of its existence. At the start of 1993, United Nations peacekeeping forces were serving in Angola, Cambodia, Cyprus, El Salvador, the Golan Heights, Kashmir, along the Kuwait-Iraq border, in Lebanon, Mozambique, the Sinai, Somalia, the former Yugoslavia, and the Western Sahara; all told, some 60,000 military and police personnel were involved in these operations, with the number expected to increase substantially in the months ahead.

These operations have contributed to stability in many parts of the globe and given the United Nations enhanced international visibility and respectability. And while some of the operations have run into difficulties, most observers agree that conditions in these areas would probably be much worse without the presence of the blue helmets. Nevertheless, world leaders generally agree that the United Nations' current capabilities and methods are inadequate for the wide range of conflicts and security challenges expected in the years to come. The Security Council has called on Secretary General Boutros Boutros-Ghali and his staff to suggest ways in which the organization's peacemaking activities can be improved, and development and implementation of these suggestions is likely to be the organization's top priority in the mid-1990s.

To inform the discussion on peacemaking, Boutros-Ghali published *An Agenda for Peace* last June.[4] In this document, the secretary general identifies five key areas in need of improvement: preventive diplomacy, or the negotiated termination of conflicts; peacemaking; peacekeeping, or the use of United Nations forces to monitor cease-fires and to prevent the re-ignition of hostilities;

peace enforcement, or the use of force to prevent or resist aggression by a belligerent in violation of United Nations resolutions; and post-conflict peace-building designed to alleviate human suffering and thus eliminate conditions that might contribute to the renewal of fighting. Boutros-Ghali proposed a number of initiatives in each of these areas, and broke new ground by calling for the formation of a permanent peacekeeping force under United Nations control (the current system staffs such units with contingents drawn from national forces on an ad hoc basis).

The development of new approaches to local and regional conflict has also been a matter of great concern in the United States, which has been under great pressure to step in and resolve certain ongoing crises (notably those in Bosnia and Herzegovina and Somalia). While some American leaders would prefer to delegate all such activities to the United Nations, others, including both Presidents George Bush and Bill Clinton, contend that the United States has an obligation to act in certain cases where no other option appears viable. Thus in December Bush, with only six weeks left in his term, ordered United States forces to Somalia in order to restore order in a country torn by factional warfare and to protect the delivery of relief supplies to starving Somalis.

In announcing Operation Restore Hope, the president indicated that the United States cannot assume such responsibility in every instance of regional disorder, but that it must be prepared to act when the survival of many human beings is at stake and when no other entity is available to do the job. "I understand [that] the United States cannot right the world's wrongs, but we also know that some crises in the world cannot be resolved without American involvement [and that] American action is often necessary as a catalyst for broader involvement of the community of nations." These comments, and the dispatch of American troops to Somalia, have sparked a heated debate in the United States over where and under what circumstances United States forces should be employed in such operations abroad.

Whatever the outcome in the United States and at the United Nations on the use of force in humanitarian and peacekeeping operations, it is apparent that the problem of preventing and controlling local, ethnic, and regional conflict has become the premier world security concern of the post–cold war era. Because such conflicts are likely to proliferate in the years ahead, and because no single power or group is willing and able to guarantee global peace and stability, United States and world leaders will be forced to enhance existing peacemaking instruments and to develop new techniques along the lines suggested by Secretary General Boutros-Ghali. How peaceful a world we inhabit in the twenty-first century will depend to a great extent on these endeavors.

---

[4]Boutros Boutros-Ghali, *An Agenda for Peace* (New York: The United Nations, 1992), p. 28.

The disintegration of Yugoslavia has led to a reevaluation of the idea that a multi-ethnic state is a viable entity. The factors that led to the dismantling of such a state in Yugoslavia are many and are open to revision, but one of the lessons that can be drawn from the process is clear: "The wars in the former Yugoslavia [show] that the principles and practices that provided a stable framework for international security in the era of the cold war are no longer sufficient to preserve the peace."

Why Yugoslavia Fell Apart

STEVEN L. BURG

STEVEN L. BURG *is associate professor of politics at Brandeis University. This article is part of a larger project,* Nationalism and Democracy in Post-Communist Europe: Challenges to American Foreign Policy, *supported by The Twentieth Century Fund.*

The disintegration of the Yugoslav federation and its descent into atavistic interethnic violence cannot be attributed to any single factor. Internal political conflicts in the 1980s, and the effort by Serbian leader Slobodan Milosevic to mobilize Serb nationalism on behalf of a strengthened federation, destroyed the cohesion of the country's regional Communist leaderships and weakened their control over society. Deteriorating economic conditions—especially plummeting living standards—eroded the benefits of sustaining the Yugoslav state and stimulated the rise of mass nationalisms and interethnic hostilities. The conflicting nationalist aspirations of the Yugoslav peoples and their leaders' efforts to maximize power, led to conflict over the control of disputed territories.

The end of the cold war left both Soviet and Western policymakers believing that Yugoslavia no longer held the strategic significance, or merited the attention, it had enjoyed in a world divided between East and West. This mistaken belief, as well as the attention commanded by the Persian Gulf War, led to neglect of the brewing crisis in Yugoslavia until the cost of meaningful action had risen beyond the point acceptable to Western policymakers and their publics. Even when less costly but still effective action remained possible, Western policymakers were deterred from acting by the fear that the dissolution of Yugoslavia, even if achieved through peaceful negotiation, would hasten the disintegration of the Soviet Union.

The fall of Yugoslavia thus can be attributed to internal conflict and the international community's failure to respond to the crisis effectively. However, forceful action by either Yugoslav leaders or American and European administrations would have required innovative thinking about some of the most basic principles of the international system and the post–cold war security framework in the Euro-Atlantic community. No political leadership—Yugoslav, American, or European—was then ready to confront these tasks. The only positive outcome of the Yugoslav debacle, therefore, may be the stimulus it has provided for such new thinking.

THE DOMESTIC CONTEXT OF DISINTEGRATION

By the mid-1970s, Yugoslavia had become a highly decentralized federation in which the constituent republics dominated the central government. Regional leaderships carefully protected the interests of their territorial constituencies at the expense of other regions and the federation. The regional leaders shared a common interest in preserving the Communist political order that shielded them from responsibility and popular accountability but little else. Ethnic and political integration processes had only modest impact. The proportion of the population that declared itself to be "Yugoslav" rather than an ethnic identity in the national census, for example, increased from 1.3 percent in 1971 to 5.4 percent in 1981. For the vast majority of the population, distinct ethnic or national identities continued to command emotional loyalties and provide the most powerful bases for political mobilization.

The ethnically defined territorial structures of the Yugoslav system reinforced the political strength of ethnic identities and intensified political divisions in the leadership. Federal political bodies, including the collective state presidency and the Communist party leadership, were composed of representatives of the republics and provinces, selected by the regional leaderships. Individual positions in these bodies, including the country's prime ministership and presidency, rotated among the regions according to an explicit agreement. Only the army remained a unified, all-Yugoslav, organization.

5. CONFLICT

While the political regions of Yugoslavia were defined in ethnic terms, in most cases they were not ethnically homogeneous. With the exception of Slovenia, their leaderships could not mobilize ethnic nationalism in support of political ambition or fulfill the nationalist aspirations of their ethnic majorities without alienating substantial minority populations and raising the prospect of severe ethnic conflict. The vast majority of ethnic Slovenes were concentrated in Slovenia and made up the majority of the population. Efforts by ethnically Slovene regional leaders to advance Slovene national-cultural interests and to strengthen Slovenian autonomy effectively encompassed all Slovenes. At the same time, these efforts neither threatened the status of a large minority inside Slovenia nor challenged the power of any other group over its own republic by encouraging a large Slovene minority population outside the republic to demand autonomy.

In Croatia, however, Serbs constituted a large minority or even a majority of the population in several areas of the republic. Croat leaders thus could not pursue exclusionary nationalist ambitions inside the Croatian state without risking the alienation of a large and territorially compact Serb minority that enjoyed strong links to Serbs outside the republic's borders. At the same time, a nationalistic Croatian government would stimulate unrest among the large, territorially compact population of ethnic Croats in adjacent areas of neighboring Bosnia and Herzegovina.

No single group could claim the overall majority in Bosnia and Herzegovina. While Muslims constituted the largest group (about 44 percent of the population in the 1991 census), they did not represent a majority. Serbs (over 31 percent) and Croats (more than 17 percent) constituted large minorities in the republic's population. In many areas of Bosnia there was no single ethnic majority. In the larger cities, those who took the nonethnic "Yugoslav" identity constituted from 20 to 25 percent of the population. Thus the pattern of ethnic settlement in Bosnia was highly complex. No ethnic leadership could advance exclusionary nationalist ambitions on behalf of its ethnic constituency without alienating vast portions of the population—including substantial numbers of its own group who had adopted the multiethnic civic culture associated with "Yugoslavism."

By the mid-1980s, the collective leaderships of the country were divided between those who supported a looser association among the regions and those who continued to support a strengthened federal government. This division was reinforced by differences over the scope and pace of further economic and political reform. The Yugoslav economy had gone into sharp decline in the 1980s. Living standards fell and regional economic differences widened. In the 1960s and 1970s, for example, per capita national income in Slovenia had been about six times that in Kosovo province and about three times that in Macedonia and Bosnia and Herzegovina. Income in Croatia had been about four times that in Kosovo and about twice that in Macedonia and Bosnia. By 1988, income in Slovenia was more than eight times that in Kosovo and income in Croatia was approximately five times higher. The frictions introduced by these growing inequalities were intensified by the ethnic differences between the regions, and especially by the increasingly violent conflict between Serbs and ethnic Albanians in Kosovo.

KOSOVO AND MILOSEVIC

The 1980s began with the outbreak of nationalist demonstrations by the Albanian people in Kosovo.

THE NEW BALKAN STATES

⊕ National capitals
⊛ Yugoslav republic capitals
● Yugoslav autonomous regions capitals
• Other cities

0 25 50 75 100 Miles

© Current History, Inc.

THE BREAKUP OF YUGOSLAVIA

1990

Jan. 22—The Communist party votes to allow other parties to compete in a new system of "political pluralism."

Feb. 5—Slobodan Milosevic, president of the republic of Serbia, says he will send troops to take control of Kosovo, a province where ethnic violence has entered its 2d week.

April 8—The republic of Slovenia holds parliamentary elections—the 1st free elections since World War II.

April 22—The 1st free elections in more than 50 years are held in the republic of Croatia.

July 5—The parliament of the Serbian republic suspends the autonomous government of the Kosovo region. On July 2, ethnic Albanian members of the Kosovo legislature declared the region a separate territory within the Yugoslav federation.

July 6—The state president orders Slovenia's parliament to rescind its July 2 declaration that the republic's laws take precedence over those of the Yugoslav federation.

Sept. 3—In Kosovo, more than 100,000 ethnic Albanians strike, closing factories, offices, stores, and schools to protest Serbian takeovers of formerly Albanian-controlled enterprises and the dismissal of Albanian workers.

Sept 13—The Yugoslav press agency reports that ethnic Albanian members of the dissolved parliament of Kosovo have adopted an alternative constitution and have voted to extend the mandate of parliament until new elections are held. The Serbian government has called the alternative constitution illegal.

Nov. 11—The republic of Macedonia holds its 1st free elections since 1945.

Nov. 18—Parliamentary elections are held in the republic of Bosnia and Herzegovina.

Dec. 9—The 1st free parliamentary elections in Serbia since 1938 are held.

1991

Feb. 20—The Slovenian parliament approves laws allowing the republic to take over defense, banking, and other government functions from the central Yugoslav government; the parliament also approves a resolution to divide Yugoslavia into two separate states; Slovenia has warned that it will secede if the other republics do not approve the plan.

Feb. 21—The Croatian parliament adopts measures giving the republic government veto power over central government laws it considers threatening to the republic's sovereignty; the parliament also adopts resolutions that support the dissolution of the Yugoslav federation.

March 2—After reports of violent clashes between Serb villagers and Croatian security forces, Borisav Jovic, the leader of the collective presidency, orders federal army troops to the Croatian village of Pakrac.

March 16—Milosevic declares that he is refusing to recognize the authority of the collective presidency; with this act he effectively declares Serbia's secession from Yugoslavia.

March 17—Milosevic proclaims Krajina, an area in Croatia where 200,000 ethnic Serbs live, a "Serbian autonomous region."

June 25—The parliaments of Slovenia and Croatia pass declarations of independence. The federal parliament in Belgrade—the capital of Serbia as well as of Yugoslavia—asks the army to intervene to prevent the secessions.

June 27—Slovenian Defense Minister Janez Jansa says, "Slovenia is at war" with the federal government.

July 18—The federal presidency announces that it is ordering all federal army units to withdraw from Slovenia.

Sept. 8—Results of yesterday's referendum in Macedonia show that about 75% of voters favor independence; ethnic Albanians boycotted the referendum.

Oct. 1—Heavy fighting in Croatia between Croatian militia and rebel Serbs (aided by the federal army) continues near the Adriatic port city of Dubrovnik.

1992

March 1—A majority of voters approve a referendum on independence in Bosnia; Serb citizens, who comprise 32% of Bosnia's population but control 60% of the territory, have threatened to secede if the referendum is passed.

March 25—Fighting between Serb militias—backed by the federal army—and Bosnian government troops begins.

April 5—After the Bosnian government refuses to rescind a call-up of the national guard, Serb guerrillas shell Sarajevo, the Bosnian capital.

April 27—Serbia and Montenegro announce the establishment of a new Yugoslavia composed of the 2 republics.

May 19—At a news conference in Washington, D. C., Haris Silajdzic, the foreign minister of Bosnia, says his country is being subjected to "ethnic cleansing" by Serb forces.

May 24—In an election in Kosovo termed illegal by Belgrade, ethnic Albanians vote overwhelmingly to secede from the rump Yugoslav state.

July 2—Croat nationalists living in Bosnia declare an independent state that includes almost one-third of the territory of Bosnia; Mate Boban, head of the 30,000-strong Croatian Defense Council militia, says the name of the new republic is Herzeg-Bosna.

Nov. 3—*The New York Times* reports the Serbian-dominated Yugoslav army has quit the siege of Dubrovnik, Croatia, and has withdrawn its forces from the surrounding area.

1993

Jan. 22—Croatian army units attack Serb-held positions in Maslenica and the port city of Zadar; Ivan Milas, a Croatian vice president, says the attacks came after Serbs delayed returning the areas to Croatian control as called for in the January 1992 UN-sponsored cease-fire agreement; state radio in Belgrade says the self-declared Serbian Krajina Republic has declared war on Croatia.

April 7—The Security Council approves UN membership for Macedonia under the provisional name "the Former Yugoslav Republic of Macedonia" as a compromise with the Greek government; Greece has objected to the new country using the same name as Greece's northernmost province.

May 16—In the Bosnian town of Pale, Bosnian Serb leader Radovan Karadzic announces that in a 2-day referendum, at least 90% of Serb voters rejected the provisional peace plan put forward by UN mediator Cyrus Vance and EC mediator Lord Owen; the plan called for a UN-monitored cease-fire; the establishment of a central government composed of 3 Muslims, 3 Croats, and 3 Serbs; the creation of 10 partially autonomous provinces with proportional representation of ethnic groups in the provincial governments; and the return of forcibly transferred property. Karadzic says the world should now recognize that a new state—Republika Srpska—exists in the Serb-controlled territory in Bosnia.

Aug. 28—The mainly Muslim Bosnian parliament votes 65 to 0 to reject a peace plan devised by the UN and the EC that would divide the country into 3 separate republics based on ethnicity; in the mountain town of Grude, the parliament of the self-declared Croat state approves the plan and officially declares the Croat republic of Herzeg-Bosna; the self-declared Bosnian Serb parliament also accepts the plan.

Kosovo is viewed by Serbs as the "cradle" of their nation, but is populated by a demographically robust majority (over 80 percent in 1991) of ethnic Albanians. The demonstrations were initially suppressed by military force. But the decade saw almost continuous and often violent confrontations in the province between Serbs and Albanians. The Serbian leadership in Belgrade responded with increasingly repressive measures against the Albanians and their indigenous leaders.

Violence against Serbs in Kosovo contributed to the growth of nationalist sentiment among Serbs in Serbia and the other regions of Yugoslavia. But the movement received its most important support from Serbian Communist party President Slobodan Milosevic. Motivated at least in part by genuine personal outrage over the treatment of Serbs in Kosovo and by the failure of other Serbian leaders to defend them, Milosevic ousted a key proponent of interethnic accommodation with the Albanians of Kosovo and seized control of the Serbian leadership in September 1987. He then escalated his public defense of Serbian ethnic and political interests. He exploited the situation in Kosovo to further stimulate popular nationalism among Serbs all across Yugoslavia, and used that nationalism as leverage against the leaders of other republics and provinces. The intensity of popular emotions among Serbs was demonstrated by a series of large-scale, openly nationalist demonstrations across Vojvodina, Serbia, and Montenegro in the fall of 1988, and by a mass gathering of Serbs in Kosovo in June 1989.

The growing force of Serbian nationalism allowed Milosevic to oust independent leaders in Vojvodina and Montenegro, replacing them with more subservient ones, and to intensify repressive measures against the Albanians of Kosovo while placing that province, heretofore a relatively autonomous territory within the Serbian republic, under direct rule from Belgrade. These changes gave Milosevic effective control over four of the eight regional leaderships represented in the collective state presidency, the most authoritative executive body in the country. However, the disproportionate Serbian influence contributed to the de-legitimation of central authority and accelerated the political dissolution of the country.

Milosevic represented a powerful synthesis of Serbian nationalism, political conservatism, support for centralism, and resistance to meaningful economic reform. Developments in Serbia under his leadership stood in stark contrast to those in Slovenia, where the growth of popular nationalism took the form of demands for political democracy and rapid economic reform, the pluralization of group activity in the republic, and support for further confederalization of the Yugoslav regime. In Serbia the republic remained under the control of the unreformed Communist party. The Serbian Communists renamed themselves the Socialist party and co-opted some formerly dissident intellectuals into their leadership, but remained under Milosevic's control. The Slovenian Communist leadership, in contrast, cooperated with emergent social and political forces in their republic to move rapidly toward a more pluralistic order. The Slovenian leadership, rather than seeing organized popular pressure only as a threat, also viewed it as an important and necessary asset in its struggle for economic and political reform in Belgrade.

THE DISINTEGRATION BEGINS

Relations between Serbia and Slovenia began to grow tense at both the elite and mass levels. In October 1988 the Slovenian representative to the central party presidium resigned because of increasingly acrimonious relations with Milosevic. In February 1989 the use of federal militia to suppress a general strike in Kosovo raised widespread concern among Slovenes that, if such force could be used against more than 1 million Albanians, it could also be used against the 2 million Slovenes. This fear was not entirely unfounded. A year earlier an independent Slovenian journal, *Mladina,* revealed that federal Yugoslav military leaders had met to discuss emergency plans for the takeover of the republic.

After the suppression of the strike, the president of the Slovenian Communist party, Milan Kucan, publicly condemned the repression in Kosovo. This marked the beginning of open conflict between the Ljubljana and Belgrade leaderships—the former having embarked on a secessionist strategy calling for internal democratization, and the latter having begun an effort to re-centralize power and authority in the entire country while constructing a new, nationalist authoritarian regime in Serbia.

The escalation of conflict in Yugoslavia reached crisis proportions in the fall of 1989. The Slovenian leadership adopted constitutional amendments in September asserting the economic and political sovereignty of the republic, denying the right of the federation to intervene, and claiming the right to secede. In December it blocked an attempt by Serbian nationalists supported by Milosevic to pressure the Slovenian government into abandoning its strategy by bringing Serbs to Ljubljana for a mass demonstration. Milosevic responded to Slovene resistance by breaking off economic relations between the two republics. Democratic activist groups in Slovenia pressed for a complete break with Serbia. That move came the following month, at the January 1990 extraordinary congress of the ruling League of Communists of Yugoslavia.

Originally conceived by Milosevic and the Serbian leadership as a means of imposing greater central authority, the congress instead became the occasion for the collapse of the old regime. Unwilling and politically unable to support a draft platform calling for greater party unity, the Slovenian delegation walked out of the congress. The military and other regional party delegations, unwilling to surrender their own independence, refused to continue the congress. The congress then adjourned indefinitely, marking the de facto breakup of the nationwide party organization. This left each of the republic party organizations to respond independently to conditions in its own region. It also left the military (the Yugoslav People's Army, or JNA) the only organization still committed to, and dependent on, the continued survival of the federation.

The electoral victories of independence-oriented coalitions in Slovenia and Croatia in the spring of 1990, and the former Communists' victory in Serbia in December of that year, deepened political divisions among the regional leaderships of the Yugoslav federation. At the same time, political support for maintaining the federation evaporated almost completely. Federal Prime Minister Ante Markovic's attempt to create a countrywide political party committed to preserving the federation, for example, generated little support. And his effort to accelerate the holding of free elections for the federal parliament as a means of democratizing and legitimizing the federation failed completely.

In August 1990, Serbs in the central Dalmatian region of Croatia began an open insurrection against the Zagreb government. Already fearful of the nationalist campaign themes of the governing Croatian Democratic Community, and mindful of the violently anti-Serb character of the most recent episodes of extreme Croatian nationalism, the Serbs of Dalmatia viewed the government's effort to disarm ethnically Serb local police forces and replace them with special Croatian police units as a portent of further repression to come.

The Dalmatian Serbs declared their intention to remain part of a common Yugoslav state or, alternatively, to become an independent Serb republic. Their uprising should have been a clear warning to all concerned: the republic borders established by the Communist regime in the postwar period were extremely vulnerable to challenges from ethnic communities that did not share the identity on which new, nationalist post-Communist governments sought to legitimate themselves. Such communities were alienated or even threatened by the nationalistic legitimation of these new governments. If existing borders were to be preserved, substantial political guarantees had to be provided for the ethnic minority enclaves in the republics.

The overwhelming declaration of support for a sovereign and independent state by 88 percent of the Slovenian electorate in a December 23, 1990, referendum made the republic's secession look inevitable. The decision by Yugoslav leaders in February 1991 to begin determining how to divide the country's assets among the regions suggested still more clearly that the breakup of the country was at hand. But the threat by the Yugoslav minister of defense in December to use force to prevent Slovenia or Croatia from seceding signaled the possibility that a breakup of Yugoslavia would not be peaceful.

The most explosive conflict in Yugoslavia has been between the political aspirations of Croats and Serbs, whose historical and imagined national homelands and claims to sovereignty overlap. This is the conflict that destabilized the interwar regime and threatened to destabilize the Communist government in 1971. In December of that year, the Yugoslav leader, Josip Broz Tito, used the military to suppress the mass nationalist movement and to purge the leadership in Croatia. As a result, in the 1980s Croatian Communist leaders remained more conservative than their Slovenian counterparts. More important, because Croatian leaders traced their origins to the anti-nationalist purges of the early 1970s, they enjoyed little popular legitimacy. With the breakup of the Yugoslav Communist party in January 1990 and the onset of competitive elections in the republics, they were decisively defeated by the Croatian Democratic Union, a nationalist coalition led by Franjo Tudjman. The CDU's electoral victory polarized relations between Croats and Serbs in that republic and set the stage for a renewed confrontation between Croat and Serb nationalisms.

THE BATTLE OVER THE ETHNIC MAP

By 1990, definition of the emerging post-Communist order became the object of open conflict among several competing, and even mutually contradictory, nationalist visions. The Serbian vision allowed for two fundamentally different outcomes: either the federation would be sufficiently strengthened to assure the protection of Serb populations everywhere in the country, or the dissolution of the federation would be accompanied by the redrawing of boundaries to incorporate Serb populations in a single, independent Serb state. This did not preclude the accommodation of the Slovenian vision of an entirely independent Slovenian state, but it did contradict Croatian aspirations for an independent state defined by the borders inherited from the old regime.

Serb and Croat nationalist aspirations might both still have been accommodated by creating independent states that exercised sovereignty over their respective ethnic territories. But such a solution would have required the redrawing of existing borders that would call into question the continued existence of Bosnia as a multinational state of Muslims, Serbs, and Croats. Moreover, any agreement openly negotiated by Serbia that legitimated claims to self-determination based on the current ethnic composition of local populations would strengthen the Albanian case for an independent Kosovo, and raise the prospect for Serbia of either giving up that province peacefully or having to escalate the level of repression.

The increasing autonomy of the republics and the

growing interregional conflict stimulated fears among Serb nationalists that large portions of the Yugoslav Serb community might be "cut off" from Serbia. The repeated use of military force to suppress Albanian demonstrations in Kosovo in the 1980s, and changes in the Serbian constitution that revoked provincial autonomy, suggested that Milosevic and other Serb nationalists might take similar actions in retaliation for any effort to separate the Serb populations of either Croatia or Bosnia from Serbia. At the very least it suggested that any claim by Croats or Muslims to the right of national self-determination would lead to Serb demands for self-determination, and for the redrawing of internal borders to permit the consolidation of Serb-populated territories under the authority of a single Serbian national state.

Serbs, however, were not the only ethnic group in the former Yugoslavia that might exploit the redrawing of borders. Albanians in Kosovo had already declared their independence and adopted their own constitution in the summer and fall of 1990. Redrawing borders might lead them to claim several western counties of Macedonia where ethnic Albanians constituted the majority or a plurality of the local population. They might even lay claim to the bordering Serbian county of Presevo, where ethnic Albanians also constituted the majority. Radical nationalist elements in Kosovo had already called for the unification of all ethnically Albanian territories. Similarly, Muslim nationalists in Bosnia might lay claim to the several counties of the Sandzak region that lie across the Serbian-Montenegrin border in which Muslims make up the majority.

AN INEPT INTERNATIONAL RESPONSE

A narrow window of opportunity to negotiate a peaceful solution to the growing dispute among the republics and to address the demands raised by ethnic communities appeared to remain open until March 1991. The West's inaction in late 1990 and early 1991 can be partly attributed to preoccupation on the part of western European leaders with negotiations over European integration. Collective action through the European Community was further stymied by clear differences in perspective among the British, French, and Germans. United States policymakers, on the other hand, consciously chose to distance themselves from the issue. United States inaction may even have been due to a cynical calculation on the part of Secretary of State James Baker that this conflict should be left for the Europeans to handle, precisely because the difficulty of the issues and the internal divisions among them assured that they would fail, thus reaffirming the need for American leadership in Europe.

As noted earlier, the attention of Western policymakers was also diverted by two other issues: the military effort to reverse the Iraqi invasion of Kuwait, and the continuing political crisis in the Soviet Union. Any effort to facilitate the breakup of Yugoslavia appeared to have been precluded by fear that it might create an undesirable precedent for the Soviet Union. As a result, the political responses of the United States and other Western states to events in both the Soviet Union and Yugoslavia ignored the fundamental commitments to human rights for which they had pressed in meetings of the Commission on Security and Cooperation in Europe (CSCE) for more than a decade. Yugoslav policy was shaped almost entirely by the desire to preserve the territorial integrity of the Soviet Union.

Western states remained firmly committed to the status quo in Yugoslavia. No effort was made to encourage Yugoslav leaders to hold the federation together by devising new political arrangements that addressed the special interests and concerns of the territorially compact communities of ethnic minorities in the republics. Even more important, in an unprecedented and ill-advised extension of the Helsinki principles of territorial integrity and the inviolability of state borders, the West extended its political support to the borders between the republics of the Yugoslav federation. Neither the United States nor its European partners acknowledged that the growing nationalism of the various peoples of Yugoslavia not only called into question the survival of the federation—they also raised doubts about the political viability of multiethnic republics. The same principle of self-determination that the Slovenes and Croats might use to justify their independence could also be used to justify Dalmatian Serbs' demands for separation from Croatia. Moreover, any reference to the principles of sovereignty and territorial integrity to defend the Croats' claims to Croatia could be used just as easily by Serbs in Belgrade to justify defending the integrity of the former Yugoslavia. International actors made no attempt, however, to confront these issues. They failed to address the growing probability that the Serbian leadership in Belgrade and its Serb allies in the military would use the JNA either to prevent the secession of Slovenia and Croatia or to detach Serb-populated territories of Croatia and Bosnia and annex them to Serbia.

By taking a more comprehensive approach, the international community might have been able to mediate among the several contradictory values and goals of local actors. Extreme demands for the right to self-determination on the part of Serbs in Croatia and Bosnia might have been counterbalanced, for example, by Serbian concerns that adoption of the principle of the right to self-determination might lead to the loss of Kosovo. Croatian ambitions with respect to western Herzegovina might similarly have been moderated by the desire to hold on to the Krajina region.

Under these circumstances, it might have been possible to achieve an overall settlement based on trade-offs among the parties involved. But such an approach would have required the international community to place the peaceful settlement of conflicting demands for self-determination above the principle of territorial integrity of states. At the very least, it would have required the United States and the European Community to abandon their support for the borders of the republics as the basis for establishing new states within the boundaries of the former Yugoslavia. However, this approach stood the best chance of success before the cycle of interethnic violence had set in. By mid-1991 it already was too late.

THE LESSONS OF YUGOSLAVIA

The wars in the former Yugoslavia have made it clear that the principles and practices that provided a stable framework for international security in the era of the cold war are no longer sufficient to preserve the peace. The principles of state sovereignty, territorial integrity, human rights, and self-determination embedded in the United Nations Charter and other United Nations documents, and developed in detail in the documents of the CSCE, have proved contradictory, or at least subject to contradictory interpretation. Moreover, the mounting human tragedy in Bosnia has revealed the inadequacies of the decision-making principles, operational guidelines, and conflict-management capabilities of Euro-Atlantic institutions such as the CSCE, NATO, and the European Community, as well as the UN.

New diplomatic and political mechanisms must be developed to cope with demands for self-determination in ways that do not undermine the basic foundation of international stability—the system of sovereign states. The development of such mechanisms requires reconsideration of the meaning of self-determination in the contemporary era and the careful reconsideration of the indivisibility of state sovereignty. At the very least, it requires limiting the ability of states to use their claim to sovereignty to shield abuses from international inquiry. For any mechanisms to be effective, however, individual states and international organizations alike must become more proactive, undertaking preventive diplomatic and political efforts to solve interethnic and other conflicts before they threaten international peace.

International engagement in the Yugoslav crisis as early as 1990 would have remained futile if the Western states had continued to refuse to support the redrawing of borders as a possible path to a peacefully negotiated solution to the crisis. The declaration of independence by a territorially compact ethnic community, such as that of the Serbs in Croatia or any other group in Yugoslavia, could have been recognized as a legitimate demand for self-determination. By recognizing the equal rights of all peoples in the country to self-determination, international mediators might have been able to lead local actors toward mutual concessions. The key to such negotiations, however, lay in the recognition that international principles, and the rights derived from them, were equally applicable to all parties, as well as in a willingness to undertake the renegotiation of borders. This the international community failed to do.

Early insistence by outside powers on the democratic legitimation of existing borders might have encouraged greater concern for the protection of human rights and avoided the escalation of ethnic tensions in Croatia and Bosnia. The Communist order that held Yugoslavia together began to disintegrate as early as 1986. It entered into crisis in December 1989. This left sufficient opportunity for international actors to influence events. The importance in such a situation of clearly and forcefully articulating and enforcing the human rights standards to which states seeking recognition will be held cannot be overemphasized. By doing so international actors may affect popular perceptions and politics. In Yugoslavia, for example, the regional elections held in 1990 might have produced more moderate governments if the human rights standards of potential ruling parties had been at issue.

The existence of competing claims to territory complicated the Yugoslav crisis. But it does not by itself account for the magnitude of human destruction that has occurred. The extreme violence in Yugoslavia must also be attributed to the establishment of ethnically defined governments that failed to provide democratic safeguards for the human rights of minority communities. This reinforces the conclusion that if the international community is to facilitate the peaceful settlement of such conflicts elsewhere, it must devise the means to prevent ethnic domination and safeguard human rights. In short, the principles of sovereignty, territorial integrity, and national self-determination must be integrated into a single framework for determining the legitimacy of claims to political authority. And that framework must be based on the superiority of principles of human rights and democracy.

As the former Soviet republics of Central Asia struggle to define themselves, they face a fundamental question: "Is a single Central Asian identity possible? The new states require a national consensus about their place in the region. Do they lie basically with Russia? Asia? The Muslim world? The Turkic world? Or is each state fated to find its own destiny—a destiny quite distinct from that of its neighbors?"

Central Asia: The Quest for Identity

GRAHAM E. FULLER

GRAHAM E. FULLER *is a senior political scientist at* RAND *and author of the* RAND *study* Central Asia: The New Geopolitics *(Santa Monica, Calif.: RAND, 1993) and* The Democracy Trap: Perils of the Post–Cold War World *(New York: Dutton, 1992).*

The five new states of Central Asia—entities thrust onto the map as independent countries by factors far beyond their control or influence—are moving into their third year. The factors that will determine their future—some internal, some external—are slowly beginning to reveal themselves. These former Soviet republics have no past track record as independent states. Their borders are a colonial hodgepodge. Their economies have been hobbled by 70 years of enforced participation in the failed Soviet experiment with a command economy—and the transition into a market economy is an often uncharted path. They have sustained high levels of threatening ecological damage. They also offer a relatively well-educated population, bear a significant cultural legacy from Islam and Asia, are blessed with significant raw materials, and in principle should be able to evolve into productive states if they manage their affairs wisely and their international environment remains benign.

CENTRAL ASIA'S "IDENTITY"

Identity is a vague and abstract concept, yet it is essential to nations' solidity and substance. Like individuals, nations need to know who they are, their origins, their peculiarities, and how they resemble—and differ from—other peoples and states near them. Only when a nation has a sense of its place in history, geography, and culture can it begin to act with certitude. Central Asia itself has a rich history, but the individual states did not arise from national liberation struggles. Their leadership, mostly inherited from the Soviet period, was recycled to give it a more nationalist patina. Today, the states of Central Asia still seek their identities. Is a single Central Asian identity possible? The new states require a national consensus about their place in the region. Do they lie basically with Russia? Asia? The Muslim world? The Turkic world? Or is each state fated to find its own destiny—a destiny quite distinct from that of its neighbors?

The states' choices among all these possible and viable identities will reveal a great deal about the kind of course they will set for themselves. They will also indicate the political values nourished by the elite and the broader population, as well as whether the leadership is in tune with those values. Today, the Central Asian states seem quite uncertain about these identity questions, partly because identity includes ethnicity, which is a very contentious issue.

A look at the ethnic overlap of nationalities from one state to another suggests that ethnic issues are a potential crisis for nearly all Central Asian states. Will each state's titular nationality (the people after whom the former republic is named) seek to impose its own ethnic stamp and privilege upon large ethnic minorities? Since the titular nationalities are taking advantage of the opportunity to create new identities within new states, they are by definition less sensitive to the identity process of other major nationalities who share the same space. As the Kazakhs will point out, for example, there is only one homeland for the Kazakhs in the world; if they do not advance their own culture and language there, where else and how else can they develop? After all, this is the first time in history that any of these nationalities (Kyrgyz, Tajik, Uzbek, Turkmen, Kazakh) have been able to formulate state policies almost exclusively in their interests. It appears evident that local nationalism will be a growing, not diminishing, issue in the next decades.

And how is that nationality defined? There are, after all, at least two definitions of Kyrgyz: a native speaker of Kyrgyz who identifies him or herself as Kyrgyz, and a citizen of Kyrgyzstan of any ethnic background. The first, the linguistic-cultural definition, will receive dominant attention in the nation-building process of the next decade: given the suppression of nationalism under the Soviet system, how else could it be? Yet that tendency also militates against the creation of a more liberal and tolerant society in which all citizens of the state should, in principle, be accorded equal rights. But even a liberal Uzbek or Tajik society will feel an obligation to devote special attention and resources to the preservation and advancement of its native culture.

In this sense, the peoples of Central Asia are under special pressure to develop in contradictory directions: the titular nationalities must seize the first opportunity in history to build a sense of modern nationality and identity in an unrestricted environment, and at the same time evolve liberal, democratic, and tolerant processes of government to satisfy their multiethnic populations. How manageable will this process be? The heady forces of nationalism seem likely to predominate in the near future—even at the expense of building a liberal society. The Russian residents in these republics will be the first, but not the only, victims of this process, for they are former oppressors and the dominant ethnic-regional power, if not threat. Indeed, the care exercised by most regional leaders today regarding local Russians' rights is largely aimed at self-preservation from reprisals by Moscow rather than a commitment to a genuinely multinational state where all power is equally shared. The unreality of the process is reflected, for example, in the use of the term "Kazakhstani" instead of "Kazakh" to refer without ethnic discrimination to all citizens of the Kazakh state. Realistically, we will likely witness a long and gradual process towards the ethnic homogenization of each state—not necessarily to the good, but hopefully at least peaceful. Post-Communist states do not offer comfortable crucibles for the creation of the liberal state.

DEFINING THE STATE

What is the natural unit of identity for the Central Asian peoples who have for so long shared a common culture and close linguistic connections? The high degree of ethnic mixture and ethnic overlap of political borders complicate Central Asian state-building. For example, the only way the Tajik population within Uzbekistan, or the Uzbek population in Tajikistan will find fulfillment of national and cultural aspirations is as political-cultural entities inside a federated Uzbekistan or Tajikistan. Even more visionary would be a much broader federation that included all of Central Asia, subdivided into many smaller ethnic entities—somewhat like the much-abused Soviet concept of autonomous regions. In Central Asia this concept is called "Turkestan," a concept going back several hundred years. At the least it denotes the broad parts of the common cultural heritage of Central Asia before czarist Russia assumed control, and well before the Soviet authorities invented the "new" nationalities such as Uzbek, Kyrgyz, or Turkmen out of tribal names. While the imposed Soviet system could not ensure ethnic harmony except by force, federal relationships freely arrived at by constituent nationalities within a larger "Turkestan" framework would have a much better chance of avoiding ethnic rivalry and explosion.

Finally, the deeply complex regional problems of ecology and water management desperately suffer from an absence of central vision and control. The dwindling water resources of the region, the dying Aral Sea, and the sinking and polluted water table cry out for some regional approach that the present system of competitive states may not deliver.

In short, Central Asia faces daunting problems of how to create identity and translate it into concrete political form and policies. If Central Asia does not work its way back to the older vision of Turkestan, then the tensions inherent in the present system will prove crippling. With divisive national interests at play, authoritarianism provides a tempting solution as "the only way to keep the country together." That, of course, was the justification for the Soviet iron hand. It is dismaying to see a harsh authoritarian approach resuscitated by Uzbekistan's President Islam Karimov as the sole response to potential ethnic divisions within his republic—and as a rationalization for his own hold on power.

Today, the governance of Central Asia cannot be discussed without reference to its relationship with Russia. In the end, Moscow is likely to prefer authoritarian leadership in the new Central Asian states precisely because it does offer a chance to "keep the lid on" and avoid turmoil—at least in the short run. The last thing Russian President Boris Yeltsin needs right now is conflagration in the former Soviet republics, which only fuels the ambitions of neo-imperialists and Zhirinovsky. Authoritarian leaders in Central Asia are also likely to strike a deal with Moscow in order to strengthen their own positions, primarily by accession to joint agreements with Russia within the context of a reinvigorated Commonwealth of Independent States. Moscow wants the influence and dominant voice for Russia that the CIS structure provides; if Central Asian leaders join with Moscow on major economic and security issues, Moscow can lend support as well.

Indeed, those leaders who in 1992 avoided close membership in the CIS—Azerbaijan, Georgia, and

5. CONFLICT

Tajikistan—faced grim reminders of their need for Moscow's good will when disastrous ethnic strife and civil war broke out in each former republic. Moscow studiously avoided any active intervention on their side, forcing them to accept Moscow's conditions in return for help to end the convulsions. Indeed, many in these states believe that Russia not only refrained from assisting the besieged leaders, but actually helped provoke the internal rebellions themselves as a sign of its power (the evidence on this is questionable). In any case, the three former republics quickly returned to the fold in 1993. It remains to be seen whether Moscow will feel any compulsion to bring down the only democratic leader left in power, Kyrgyzstan's Askar Akayev; he has otherwise been cautious not to offend Moscow.

The present neo-Communist leadership in all the Central Asian states (and Muslim Azerbaijan) represents only a transitional phase in the political development of these states. The old and well-entrenched Communist elite did not perish during the Gorbachev period, even though perestroika cleared out the worst toadies and considerably modernized the political structure, placing greater emphasis on technocrats rather than pure party functionaries. After independence the neo-Communists reentrenched themselves, often with Moscow's help, especially in Azerbaijan, Turkmenistan, Uzbekistan, and Tajikistan. Only Kazakhstan, and even more so Kyrgyzstan, today represent more democratic and nationalist variants.

In this sense, then, much of the current Central Asian leadership does not represent the "nationalist future" that will ultimately emerge in nearly every state with the passage of time and deeper, more informed growth of nationalist sentiment. The newer nationalist forces are more suspicious of Russian intentions, wish to preserve their independence from excessive Russian influence and strengthen ties with the world beyond the CIS, and are intent on building a modern nationalist state on the basis of each state's dominant nationality and culture.

These nationalist elements so far are either weakly developed (as in the states with a nomad tradition—Kazakhstan, Kyrgyzstan, and Turkmenistan), or else have been suppressed, as in Uzbekistan, Tajikistan, and Azerbaijan. As they gain in strength, they will change the present internal, and especially external, orientation of the former Soviet republics in new directions. It is so far unclear whether they will remain devoted to the Soviet-period construct of individual Central Asian states, or will be attracted to the broader concept of Turkestan. Some indications suggest that the Turkestan idea is far from dead, but simply too much to think about now, given the day-to-day concerns of simply making the individual countries function effectively.

In a sense, then, we have not yet seen the "true face" of Central Asia, which will only emerge after nationalist elements come to the fore. Only in Azerbaijan and Georgia have we seen the emergence of nationalist leadership—both of which refrained from joining the CIS until internal rebellion forced them to reconsider. In these two states (especially Azerbaijan), a new nationalist agenda sought to move in quite new foreign policy directions and away from Moscow. The still indeterminate overall shape, character, and orientation of the Central Asian states thus have yet to be established and remain key determinants of the region's future.

The problem of Islamic fundamentalism (or Islamism) is part and parcel of this same issue, for the growth of political Islam hinges not just on ideology, but on the political character of the regimes now in power. Put simply, there is no reason to believe that Central Asia should not be subject to the same forces of political Islam that have affected the rest of the Muslim world. Political Islam flourishes under certain conditions: political repression; economic hardship and social grievance; regimes beholden to non-Muslim states to help maintain power; state suppression of Islamist political activity; and repression of all alternative political movements that might also express economic, political, and cultural grievances—thereby giving the Islamists a de facto monopoly on opposition and the sole voice of cultural-religious legitimacy.

These conditions may emerge in Uzbekistan, Tajikistan, and eventually Azerbaijan. Political Islam is a less likely threat in Turkmenistan, Kazakhstan, and Kyrgyzstan, where Islam has been less well developed. While traditional culture is a factor in the spread of political Islam, the type and effectiveness of governance is perhaps the key determinant in the future power of the Islamist movement in Central Asia. Russian intervention to help stave off the growth of Islamist power is likely to be highly counterproductive, and repressive regimes that benefit from such Russian intervention are likely to lose their legitimacy at an accelerated rate.

RUSSIA'S SHADOW

Russia, too, is undergoing sharp reassessment of the character of its new state, borders, and national interests in the wake of collapse of not only 70 years of communism, but of some 200 or more years of colonial empire. The Russian political scene displays many elements that openly seek to restore the empire, even if not in its old Communist form. Realistically speaking, any Russian government must concern itself deeply with relations with its former republics—in policy terms described as the "near abroad." The CIS mechanism perhaps represents the old colonial instinct in its most benign form: indeed it is unreasonable to expect that Russia would *not* seek a dominant sphere of influence in these regions—even within the framework of a voluntary and consensual body of states. The critical question at hand is the specific kind of great power influence to be exerted.

First, Russia's own security, and the security role of the states to its immediate south, depend heavily on Russia's own policies. An expansionist and nondemocratic Russia will disturb all states in the region, causing them to react defensively and seek their own independent security alliances in response—much as Poland, the Czech Republic, and Ukraine are doing today. This is, in a sense, a replay of the Soviet Union's old fear of "encirclement"—a self-fulfilling prophecy.

Second, Russia's policies toward the near abroad will be a powerful determinant of its policies toward the "far abroad." Russia's intentions and methods will be judged by these policies; Moscow will be perceived either as an expansionist threat or a responsible partner on the international scene. It is furthermore unlikely that Russia can aid in suppressing Muslims in Central Asia and at the same time become a trusted ally of most other Muslim countries farther away.

Third, almost any Russian government will be tempted to prefer authoritarian regimes in Central Asia that can guarantee stability rather than instability on its borders. Authoritarianism is a quick fix. Over the longer run, however, authoritarian suppression of natural political forces does not provide an answer. Only the normal political evolution of Central Asia toward the inevitably more nationalist and/or democratic policies—that by definition place greater distance between themselves and Russia—will guarantee genuine long-term stability. Furthermore, despotic rulers in Central Asia who are seen as having a cozy relationship with Moscow may not enjoy long-term popularity. Economic relationships too must inevitably expand beyond the artificial borders of the old Iron Curtain (or CIS) to embrace natural new partnerships to the east and south as well. None of this is inherently anti-Russian, but it suggests growth away from Moscow's former monopoly on influence.

ON THE BORDER OF INSTABILITY

As was noted, over the past two years Central Asia has established new sovereign relations with the states to its east, south, and west. These states will exert religious, ethnic, regional, and economic influence on Central Asia's own options. Several of these states also provide illustration of significant instability, or potential instability.

Afghanistan, whose own Tajik, Uzbek, and Turkmen populations directly affect Central Asian politics, is itself afflicted by separatist tendencies. With an Islamist-oriented government in place in Kabul, these influences are already slipping across the border into the civil war in Tajikistan—although they are not the cause of that conflict. Afghanistan's own civil war is far from

resolved and its outcome remains unclear. Its separatist tendencies spell the greatest threat to the former republics to its north. The governments of Central Asia clearly have resolved not to tolerate any irredentism or border changes among themselves—at least for the time being. But the situation is not entirely within their control, and is subject to drastic geopolitical change in an era when such drastic change is far more thinkable than five years ago. If Russian-dominated northern Kazakhstan should break away from Kazakhstan, for instance, a rump Kazakh state would probably play a more radicalized role in the region, affecting Uzbek, Turkmen, and Uighur populations in particular. A second example would be the breaking away of Uzbek-dominated northwestern Tajikistan. A truncated Tajik state would almost surely start looking south to Afghanistan to strengthen its demographic weight against Uzbekistan.

Iran's influence lies primarily with the Turkmen (due to proximity and ethnic spillover) and the Tajik (cultural and linguistic ties). In neither case is there evidence of enough serious Iranian meddling in Central Asian affairs to cause breakaway movements or even the radicalization of Islamic movements. Iran's interest in religious movements to its north will remain, but at present Iran's goal is simply to gain a presence and to counter the religious activities of Saudi Arabia and Turkey. Iran's influence in a crumbling Afghanistan would be extensive.

Turkey remains the primary cultural magnet for Central Asia as the most important and advanced Turkic state in the world. Turkey's influence is limited by its own modest economic and industrial resources, but a strengthening of nationalist forces in Central Asia will benefit Turkey. Over the longer run, Turkish influence will probably increase rather than decrease, even though Turkey's initial expectations from its "Central Asian brothers" have been disappointed—largely by neo-Communist leadership. For this reason Turkey can be expected to play a stronger role in support of democratization in the region in the expectation that it will lead to greater Turkish influence as nationalists have a chance to gain power.

China presents a major question mark. There is no reason to believe that China will remain immune to the forces of breakup that have affected nearly all post-Communist empires and multiethnic groups. True, Uighur-dominated Xinjiang province is economically booming, and it could greatly influence Central Asia's economy through Chinese (including overseas Chinese) investment, the sale of massive quantities of consumer goods, and other trade through Turkic Uighur middlemen. That indeed is Beijing's hope. Resurgent Uighur nationalists, however, are quite likely to seek separation from China. Few Muslim minorities ever remain happily contained within another state and culture, especially a Communist one.

5. CONFLICT

The model of political independence lies just over the border in former Soviet Central Asia. Religious sentiments are particularly strong in southern Xinjiang around Kashgar, a region culturally linked to Central Asia's Fergana Valley—and historically a center of Islamic fervor. Any struggle inside China will deeply affect Central Asia. Both the Uzbeks and the Kazakhs will contend for influence in Uighur affairs, especially the Kazakhs, who have historically feared Chinese culture's ability to swallow up a whole variety of Turko-Mongol cultures that once flourished in China.

Central Asia's role between Russia and China will also be complex. Which way will the states lean? Or will they divide, with Kazakhstan taking a more pro-Russian, anti-Chinese tilt versus an opposite tendency in Uzbekistan? Major geopolitical questions have yet to be resolved here and will surely emerge within the next decade as China faces the collapse of Communist rule and assertive new regionalisms.

The West itself, of course, poses new issues to Central Asia as well. First, United States interests in the region appear modest. Apart from investment in the potential energy resources of Kazakhstan and Turkmenistan, there are no unique economic opportunities there that will draw special United States focus. That is not to say that many Western firms will not have an interest in developing the region's mineral, agricultural, and hydroelectric resources. But the United States is more concerned that the region not become the breeding ground of civil war, nuclear proliferation, radical Islamic movements, a battleground for Asian geopolitics, an ecological wasteland, an economic basket case, or the target of a resurgent Russian imperial vision. The geopolitical centrality of Central Asia—its spokes radiating out in all directions across a vital continent—is of considerable importance.

Chances are that Central Asia today only dimly reflects the kind of Central Asia that we will see 50 years from now. To be sure, all regions of the world are changing, but few regions today step out into the world with so little experience as modern states. Central Asia's traditional civilizations make it an area that is capable of rapid and sophisticated growth, but its peoples are not yet accustomed to the radical new experience of encountering the world encumbered with the nominal ethnicities, borders, economic relationships, and problems bequeathed it by the Soviet era.

Above all else, not too much of the present should be taken as representative of too much of the future. What we witness today is but the beginning of a long-term process of settling down into new relationships and patterns of activity that will differ sharply from the Soviet period and even the present transitional period. It is important to look into the character of the internal and regional dynamics of the area in order to discern what might be the true outlines of this strategic region as we enter the next millennium.

ISLAM AND THE WEST

The next war, they say

THIS survey is different from most surveys in *The Economist*. It is not about a country, an industry, a financial organisation or anything else that can be described and measured with some degree of precision. It is about an idea: perhaps the only idea of its kind in today's world.

The idea, Islam, ignores the frontier that most people draw between man's inner life and his public actions, between religion and politics. It may be the last such idea the world will see. Or it may, on the contrary, prove to be the force that persuades other people to rediscover a connection between day-to-day life and a moral order. Either way, it denies turn-of-the-century western conventional wisdom. This survey is an exploration of the misty territory of religio-political conviction.

If that sounds dreamy, think again. One of the commonest prophecies of the mid-1990s is that the Muslim world is heading for a fight with other parts of the world that do not share its religio-political opinions: above all, worry nervous Europeans, a fight with Europe. On current evidence, this is by no means impossible.

In Europe, Bosnian Muslims have for more than two years been brutally harried by Serbs who are theoretically Christians. On the border between Europe and Asia, Christian Armenians have thumped Muslim Azeris, admittedly with rather more provocation, and Jews and Muslims still

Are Muslims and the people of the West doomed to perpetual confrontation? Not if they both see that this is a moment for change, says Brian Beedham

shoot each other in Palestine. Farther east, Muslims complain of the Indian army's brutality to them in Kashmir, and of Indian Hindus' destruction of the Ayodhya mosque in 1992. Such experiences tend to make Muslims think the world is against them. If it is, then they are against the world. Hence the xenophobia that gets foreigners murdered by Koran-quoting terrorists in Algeria and Egypt. Islam, as Samuel Huntington, a professor at Harvard University, has put it, has bloody borders.

It was Mr Huntington who provided the intellectual framework for the fear of a confrontation between Islam and the West. In a widely read article about a coming "clash of civilisations" in *Foreign Affairs* in the summer of 1993 he argued, correctly, that the nation-state is no longer the primary unit of international relations. Just as correctly, alas, he assumed that competition and conflict are not about to disappear from men's relations with each other. So the competition and the conflict will have to be worked out at another level—chiefly, says Mr Huntington, among the larger units known as cultures or civilisations, each consisting of groups of countries. Here comes the contest of the giants.

As a general thesis, this may be true enough; but, of the eight civilisations that Mr Huntington lists, four or five do not really fit his definition. Latin America is not fundamentally different from the western culture that brought it into being, as both

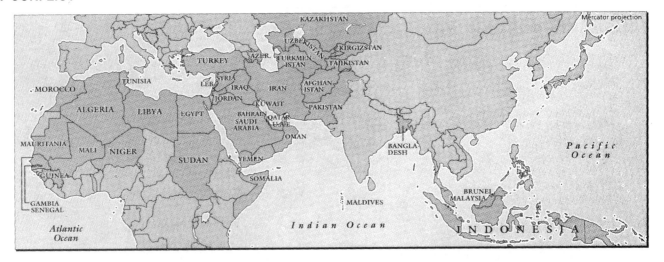

parts of its name suggest. The same can be said, with a little more hesitation, about the Slavs of the orthodox Christian tradition, who are admittedly different from the Protestant and Catholic West but probably not enough to be called a separate civilisation. With one more degree of hesitation, that also applies to Japan and its connection with the Chinese culture to its west. The culture of India's Hindus is indeed *sui generis,* but Hinduism is not—and probably never will be—a player on the world stage. And Africa, as Mr Huntington himself seems to admit, is not really in this league.

The three prime numbers

There are in fact only three reasonably clear contenders in Mr. Huntington's advertised clash of civilisations. The first is the West, the Euro-American culture that is the product of the Renaissance, the Reformation and the Enlightenment, and is the begetter of modern capitalism and democracy.

The second is the Confucian culture, the body of ideas that has grown up around the Chinese language and the habits of public life that are said to belong to the Chinese region. But this has its qualification. Those supposed Confucian habits of public life—a cheerful respect for authority on the part of the governed, based upon the assumption that Confucian governments honestly use their authority for the benefit of those they rule—may be no more than a polite fiction. The history of the Chinese-speaking world contains at least as much selfishness and brutality on the part of the rulers, and at least as much dumb suffering on the part of the ruled, as the history of any other part of the globe. The idea that there is today a special understanding between governors and governed in eastern Asia is largely self-protecting propaganda by the men in power in Beijing, Singapore, Kuala Lumpur and elsewhere.

The third contender is Islam. This does genuinely stand alone. There is good reason why the culture of the Muslim world is regarded by many people as the West's only real ideological competitor at the end of the 20th century. Unlike the Confucians—and even more unlike Latin Americans,

Ranks of Islam*

	Population		GNP per person		Debt†
	1992 m	1985-92 avg. % increase	1992 $	1985-92 avg. % change	1992 % of GDP
Indonesia	184.3	1.8	670	4.7	67.4
Pakistan	119.3	3.1	410	1.7	48.0
Bangladesh	112.8	2.2	220	1.7	55.7
Turkey	58.5	2.2	1,950	2.7	50.6
Iran	59.8	3.7	2,190	-1.4	12.8
Egypt	54.8	2.4	630	0.8	116.8
Sudan	26.6	2.8	125 est	2.6	na
Algeria	26.4	2.7	1,830	-2.0	61.0
Morocco	26.3	2.5	1,040	1.3	77.8
Afghanistan	21.6	2.5	**	-3.8	na
Iraq	19.2	3.3	1,000 est	na	311.3
Malaysia	18.6	2.5	2,790	5.7	36.1
Saudi Arabia	15.9	3.5	7,940	1.3	19.7
Yemen	13.1	4.4	400	na	86.2
Syria	13.0	3.3	1,170 (1991)	0.0	104.1
Mali	9.0	2.8	300	-1.9	93.2
Tunisia	8.4	2.0	1,740	2.1	55.5
Somalia	8.3	3.1	120 (1990)	-1.2	283.9
Niger	8.2	3.2	300	-1.5	73.9
Senegal	7.8	3.0	780	0.3	58.0
Guinea	6.0	2.8	510	0.8	86.0
Libya	4.9	3.6	5,100	-2.8	na
Jordan	3.9	5.8	1,120	-7.0	179.1
Lebanon	3.8	2.3	1,170	na	30.2
Mauritania	2.1	2.7	530	-0.1	205.6
UAE	1.7	3.1	22,220	0.0	na
Oman	1.6	3.8	6,490	1.0	27.6
Kuwait	1.4	-2.3	15,500	na	na

*All countries with over 50% Muslim population excluding ex-Soviet republics of Azerbaijan, Kazakhstan, Kirgizstan, Tajikistan, Turkmenistan, Uzbekistan; and countries with less than 1m population: Bahrain, Brunei, Gambia, Maldives and Qatar
Sources: World Bank, EIU   †Total external **Low income, below $675

Slavs and Japanese—Islam claims to be an idea based upon a transcendental certainty. The certainty is the word of God, revealed syllable by syllable to Muhammad in a dusty corner of Arabia 1,400 years ago and copied down by him into the Koran.

As a means of binding a civilisation together, there is no substitute for such a certainty. Moreover—and this is not happening anywhere else—new recruits are flocking to join this claim to certainty. Whether it is because of the repeated defeats inflicted upon Muslims by the outside world, or because of the corrupt incompetence of most of their own governments, the past 25 years have seen a huge growth in what outsiders call Islamic fundamentalism. Muslims themselves hate the phrase, but it is not inaccurate. A large number of people who feel ashamed of the past few centuries want to show they can do better. To do that, they need to rediscover a sense of identity. And to do that, they turn back to the Koran. You can call it a revival, or a resurgence; but it is also a return to the foundations.

This is what has set scalps tingling in other parts of the world, especially among Europeans. They see the Last Ideology on the march. A Muslim crescent curls threateningly around the southern and eastern edges of Europe. A new cold war could be on the way. And it may not stop at being a cold war.

The writer of this survey is not convinced. It is true that some Muslims are behaving ferociously these days, and that on the southern shore of the Mediterranean, in particular, some ugly things are taking shape. It is also true that Europe and Islam have had a rough time together in the past. That rough time included two penetrations by Muslim armies deep into Europe, the largely incompetent European counter-attacks called the crusades, and the absorption of virtually the whole Muslim world into various European empires in the 19th and early 20th centuries. It is not a good-neighbourly story. But past enmities and present bad temper need not be the premises of a syllogism that is bound to end: therefore, new war between Islam and the West.

For one thing, these two civilisations have more in common with each other than either has with the Confucian world or the Hindu one, or most of the rest of the Huntington culture collection. Both have their origins in religions that believe in a single God (and any westerner who asks what that has to do with modern life needs to think about what made the West as it is today). Few westerners believe that God dictated the Koran, and no Muslim believes that Jesus was the son of God. Those are important disagreements, but they sit alongside a large number of shared convictions. A Muslim and a westerner both believe, more clearly than most other people, in the idea of individual responsibility. They can exchange opinions about the nature of good and evil, or property rights, or the preservation of the environment, in something like a spirit of brotherhood.

It is even tempting to wonder whether Islam's bloody clashes with Europe in the past could have been avoided had geography and history been a little kinder. Of course, religion was one of the things that drove these two peoples into battle with each other, especially in the early days when the Arabs pushed up to Poitiers and the crusaders lumbered to Jerusalem. But religion was never the entire explanation for such clashes.

These were two young cultures, full of energy and eager to show what they could do; and in the world of that time, between Muhammad's death in 632AD and the capture of Louis IX of France in Egypt during the seventh crusade in 1250, they had nobody to unleash their zeal on but each other. The rest of the world was still largely a blank to them. Had they lived in today's many-

peopled world—or been separated from each other by sea or desert, so that they could not so readily march and counter-march—their religious differences might not have had such bloody results. But self-assertion and propinquity did their work, with the usual results.

The difficulty with neighbours

The trouble is that propinquity and self-assertion are still at work today. The proposition of this survey is that there is no insuperable reason why Muslims and westerners cannot live peaceably with each other. It will take sensible handling by both sides, and some re-examination by both of their present ideas about the world. In particular, Muslims will need to find a way of adjusting their habits to three specific requirements of modern life. There is no fatal obstacle to this; nothing in the essentials of either civilisation to make harmony impossible.

The hope contained in that proposition has even survived the Iranian revolution of 1979. Iran is the chief home of the Shias, the always quarrelsome 15% minority of Muslims who broke away from the Sunni majority way back in the early days of the faith. Iran's revolutionaries started out as snarling enemies of the West. They can still growl, and bite. But time, and the sobering experience of government, have made them noticeably milder in their foreign policy as well as in what they do at home. They do not destroy the belief that, in the long run, Islam and the West can co-exist.

Unfortunately, in the shorter run—meaning within the next year or so—something may happen in North Africa that could throw at least a temporary spanner into the works. This is the highly probable collapse of the present government of Algeria, and its replacement by a singularly intransigent bunch of Islamic rebels, fundamentalists of the most bloody-minded sort. A series of mistakes—first by the generals running Algeria, then by most of the West's governments—seems likely to bring to power in Algiers a group of men who will, for a time, be very hard to deal with. They are for good reason angry both with the corruptly authoritarian regime they will be replacing and with the West for having supported that regime, even when it had plainly been rejected by the Algerian people.

If this happens in Algeria, the effects will spill over into other parts of North Africa, and maybe even farther into the Islamic world; and a familiar cycle will begin all over again. Anti-western anger on one side of the Mediterranean will provoke anti-Muslim resentment on the other, which will further feed that anti-western anger. Europe and Islam will, for a period, be at it again.

Three articles later in the survey will look at the three things Muslims need to do (and in some countries are already doing) to move confidently into the 21st century. These are, in rising order of difficulty, coping with a modern economy, accepting the idea of sexual equality, and, hardest of all, learning to absorb the principle of democracy. But first a closer look at that swelling thunder-cloud on the southern coast of the Mediterranean.

Rogue States, Criminals and Terrorists Crash the Nuclear Club

Charles A. Cerami

When it was reported earlier this year that fuel rods were being removed from a nuclear reactor near Pyongyang, the North Korean capital, alarms rang in Washington. Since the spent fuel could be used as a source of plutonium and thus as fuel for nuclear weapons, strategists were worried that the communist nation was diverting it to a clandestine weapons-development program.

Western observers established in May that none of the rods had been diverted, but revelations by a North Korean defector that Pyongyang secretly removed 26 pounds of spent fuel in 1988 have kept North Korea's nuclear activities in the headlines — and heightened concern about whether other countries are pushing ahead with secret weapons-development efforts.

The problem of nuclear proliferation is serious and urgent, as Les Aspin noted in his last days as defense secretary. "First among the chief threats to the United States is a new danger posed by the increased threat of proliferation of nuclear weapons and other weapons of mass destruction," Aspin said in January. "The old nuclear danger we faced was thousands of warheads in the Soviet Union. The new nuclear danger is perhaps a

Despite existing treaties to control them, nuclear materials and know-how are spreading fast. No one knows how many weapons are out there, and it may already be too late to keep them out of dangerous hands.

handful of nuclear devices in the hands of rogue states or even terrorist groups."

There are, of course, constraints on the spread of nuclear weapons. Aside from the Nuclear Non-Proliferation Treaty, there are the safeguards of the International Atomic Energy Agency, which monitors nuclear facilities in more than 50 countries, and other controls on suppliers of nuclear materials. Yet, according to Aspin, more than 20 countries — many of them hostile to the United States and its allies — now have, or are developing, nuclear, biological and/or chemical weapons. More than 12 countries have operational ballistic missiles and others have programs to develop them. Such weapons, Aspin noted, could directly threaten U.S. forces in the field and keep them from being used effectively.

Nuclear weapons used to be "the equalizer" for the United States against the Soviets' huge superiority of conventional forces in Europe, said Aspin, but things have changed. Today, it is the United States that has unmatched conventional power — but violent regimes and potential adversaries now exist that, if armed with nuclear weapons, could nullify that power. "We're the ones who could wind up being the equalizee," he said.

While some knowledgeable military observers say that there probably will be 30 more nuclear nations in the next two decades, Jon Wolfsthal, a senior analyst with the Arms Control Association, notes that the numbers are unpredictable. "Some say, as if it were a settled thing, that Iran is seven or eight years from having nuclear weapons. That may or may not happen. A sudden, new alliance and new supply source could make it happen sooner; or, just as Taiwan dropped its plans under pressure from the United States, some internal political fact may cause Iran to back off. But one thing is clear: We have to act as though the worst could happen — or else it surely will."

Another observer, recently retired from the State Department's Office of Nuclear Technology and Safeguards, argues that there is nothing to prevent any number of nations from becoming nuclear powers. "Some people have been rattled into thinking a high school physics class could put a bomb together," says Stanley Ifshin. "It's not as easy as that. Just getting the critical materials is quite an undertaking. But for a country to do it is now simple enough to make it very frightening for the rest of us. The main question for any nation with such an ambition is, 'What political price will we have to pay? On top of the actual monetary cost — which is in the billions — what trade, financial and other pressures will the Americans and their allies bring to bear on us?' I'm sure a number of nations have thought about starting a nuclear program, put it on hold and finally thought better of it."

Viewed in that way, the rate at which nuclear weapons proliferate is, to a large extent, in the hands of the major powers and, to a lesser degree, of the United Nations. When they look weak-willed, they actually encourage the problem to spread. That fact will be

> **Washington has learned to mistrust even its own intelligence about which countries are trying to get around the rules and which are close to success.**

on the front burner in April 1995 when New York hosts a meeting (to which more than 160 of the world's nations have been invited) to discuss whether the 1970 Nuclear Non-Proliferation Treaty should be extended permanently or only for a fixed period after which it would expire. "An extension for a short fixed period would almost certainly mean the end of the nonproliferation treaty for good," says Thomas Graham Jr., acting deputy director of the U.S. Arms Control and Disarmament Agency, the top official with responsibility for keeping the agreement alive.

These days Graham is in almost constant motion around the globe, pushing the cause of nonproliferation. Since every country in the world sees the issue as the greatest of all foreign policy problems, he notes, it is natural to question why there should be any doubt about getting a heavy "yes" vote. "There are a variety of reasons given

for opposition," he says. "Some consider the treaty elitist because it allows the five declared nuclear nations to retain their weapons while denying them to all the rest. There are already a number of other countries which have acquired some degree of nuclear might and don't like agreeing to a treaty which would force them to roll back or be outlaws. Some countries may be reluctant to promise anything forever. 'You, the original five, should commit now to eventually disarm yourselves before asking us to agree,' some insist."

That, of course, is far more complex than it sounds. The political balance in each region of the world is based partially on the nuclear power of those five nations, and it would take years of adjustments to work out ways of balancing strengths by conventional arms alone.

"Bear in mind that next year's meeting will be a onetime opportunity," Graham stresses. "It's a once-in-history event when we'll either opt for law and order or for 'anything goes.' It's not as if we could revive or redo the treaty in another year or two. That would mean having to pass through a minimum of 82 governments and parliaments again in much harder circumstances. It's really inconceivable."

Why is pressure intensifying now to control the nuclear spread? One key reason is the breakup of the Soviet Union. Many Soviet nuclear missiles were based in what have become three new countries — Ukraine, Belarus and Kazakhstan — creating four nuclear nations where only one existed before. But that's a tangible problem that is being handled through diplomacy and negotiation.

More worrisome is the fact that controls over the weapons technology have been weakened, introducing the danger that Russian experts (whose status and incomes have been reduced drastically) might sell their services to outlaw nations. It also means that Russian workers are selling critical supplies and equipment to ill-intentioned nations — and possibly even to criminal elements. Indeed, FBI Director Louis Freeh told a Senate subcommittee in late May that Russian organized crime groups "may already have the capability to steal nuclear weapons, nuclear weapons components or weapons-grade nuclear materials."

It is only now becoming apparent how important were the old and often-ridiculed restrictions the United States and its allies placed on equipment and know-how believed to be even remotely usable in making advanced weapon-

ry. The memoirs of former Soviet spymasters tell how difficult it was to procure certain parts for constructing nuclear bombs and how badly their scientists were hampered by crude substitutes.

Iraq, for one, has benefited from looser controls. When a U.N. inspection team descended on Baghdad in late 1991, suspicions that the country had been developing a nuclear weapon — denied by Iraqi officials — proved correct. The inspectors came away with Iraqi documents detailing work on a variety of weapons which could have raised the Persian Gulf war into a nightmarish nuclear confrontation.

Fortunately, Baghdad was stopped in its tracks, and U.N. nuclear inspection team leader David Kay concluded that Saddam Hussein probably would have needed another 12 to 18 months to perfect both his bomb and a method by which to deliver it. But it was alarming to learn that such a major program had been transpiring undetected since 1988.

Iraq was able to move ahead with foreign help. Its nuclear program was beset by problems with centrifuges — high-speed spinning machines that separate uranium ores. A German centrifuge designer named Bruno Stemmler has told in detail of trips he made to two plants outside Baghdad to inspect the Iraqi designs in 1988 and 1989. He was paid about $75,000 for a few key suggestions about a new type of steel and a change in the size of certain parts. These suggestions helped Saddam make much faster progress than U.S. intelligence had thought possible. And Stemmler has insisted, successfully so far, that he is innocent of any wrongdoing because he broke no German law.

Later, Saddam made a further leap forward when his scientists adopted an electromagnetic process for separating ores — obtained from openly published U.S. documents. These two apparently minor breaks played a big part in bringing about the Iraqi progress.

"The general progress of technology spreads know-how, so what was once known by only a few top scientists becomes common knowledge," says the U.S. Arms Control and Disarmament Agency's Graham. "For instance, the operations performed by what used to be called supercomputers and closely controlled because their computations help in making bombs are now done by products that any one of us can buy in a store. Lots of private individuals have them. And of course, nearly all foreign governments. Just as it's said that a rising tide lifts all boats, a rising tide of knowledge causes many secrets to float into view."

As this has happened, a number of countries have been attracted to the profits of the nuclear trade. China, for example, has sold Pakistan missiles that give the country the means to use atomic weapons against India — even though by doing so, China facilitated an attack against itself. North Korea's current project to become a nuclear power has this potential commercial aspect, over and above the obvious threat to South Korea and the attempt to pry political and trade concessions from the United States.

"I wouldn't even try to dope out the mental processes of Kim [Il-sung] or his son," says Ifshin. "But a multiple threat certainly exists. The sale of any technology Kim develops is definitely one of them. Trying as he is to push his way into a stronger commercial position, we can't rule out the possibility that if we won't give him all he asks for, he would try for financial success by selling atomic equipment to the very nations or criminal elements that we are most anxious to keep it away from."

North Korea reportedly has been developing a 1,000-kilometer-range missile which the country is believed to have offered for sale to Iran. With countries such as China and North Korea as suppliers, about 25 countries, according to CIA Director James Woolsey, have missiles capable of carrying nuclear, chemical or biological warheads.

Wolfsthal of the Arms Control Association sees the United States using a strategy of cash or barter incentives to steer countries away from such aggressive transactions — in effect, paying them not to misbehave. "But this," he points out, "raises the danger of appearing to reward states that pursue nuclear weapons as a ruse to bargain for favors."

Espionage also has played a role in the spread of nuclear technology. Former Soviet spymaster Pavel Sudoplatov has described how his team of operatives in America subtly made nuclear scientists such as J. Robert Oppenheimer and Enrico Fermi believe it was noble to share atomic secrets with the Soviets. (Sudoplatov's allegations, however, are widely disputed.)

But sometimes key intelligence and materials are simply given away, as the case of Pakistan illustrates. Concern about Pakistan's nuclear ambitions date back to the late 1970s, when Washington pressured France to stop supplying Pakistan with nuclear reactors for supposed peaceful energy purposes and to cancel a reprocessing plant that gave Pakistan a way to separate plutonium, the key element in advanced nuclear weapons. But France was, and remains, an enthusiast for the use of reactors as an energy source. It paid no heed to the complaint.

Pakistan then asked the Netherlands if a Pakistani physicist could visit the laboratories of a Dutch-German company specializing in high-quality centrifuges. These machines have many industrial uses and are not necessarily related to weaponry. But they are critical to many atomic projects, since their high efficiency makes it possible for countries to quickly produce highly enriched, weapons-grade uranium or plutonium. The Dutch now say that they saw no reason to turn down the request, since they had friendly relations with Pakistan.

Abdul Qadar Khan, the scientist sent to the Netherlands by Pakistan, is said to have a fine sense of humor and a kindly personality. Even the scholarly *Bulletin of the Atomic Scientists* points out that employees at Khan's plants in Pakistan, who enjoy exceptional pay and working conditions, are devoted to him. So it is not surprising that he became well-liked in the Dutch labs, had many friendly talks over coffee and finally left on the best of terms — his pockets filled with the minute details of centrifuges. The Dutch government later filed a lawsuit against Khan, but it was too late — he had the information, and Pakistan, according

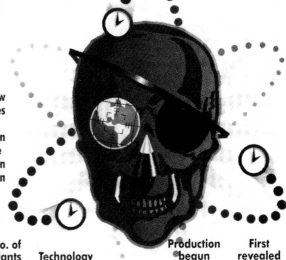

SECRET
Production Plants

Most of the smaller nations now possessing nuclear capabilities have been producing such weapons in secret. It has taken the efforts of U.S. intelligence agencies to discover the location and nature of these production plants. Even more secretive, however, are the motives of these countries for producing nuclear weapons.

	No. of plants	Technology	Production begun	First revealed
ARGENTINA	2	Gaseous diffusion, plutonium separation	1978	1983
BRAZIL	2	Centrifuge	1978	mid-1980s
INDIA	3	Centrifuge (2), plutonium separation	1950s	1950s
IRAQ	6	Calutrons (2), centrifuge (3), plutonium separation	early 1980s	1991
ISRAEL	2	Plutonium separation, reactor	mid-1950s	late 1950s
NORTH KOREA	3	Plutonium separation (2), reactor	before 1975	1984
PAKISTAN	1	Centrifuge	mid-1970s	late 1970s
SOUTH AFRICA	1	Aerodynamic separation	1970	1970

Source: Bulletin of the Atomic Scientists

DOUG STEVENS / INSIGHT

to many indications, soon had the bomb.

The number of atomic concerns on the horizon appears endless. Among them is the "Islamic Bomb." In his death cell awaiting his 1979 execution, former Pakistani Prime Minister Zulfikar Ali Bhutto said, "We know Israel and South Africa have full nuclear capability. Christian, Jewish and Hindu civilizations have this capability. The communist powers also. Only the Islamic civilization was without it. But that position is about to change."

Nevertheless, Pakistan is not in the vanguard of states pushing a pan-Islamic fundamentalist agenda. Some proliferation-watchers are concerned, however, about Algeria. Until just six years ago, Algeria was viewed favorably in America for its role as a go-between in the long negotiations to free U.S. hostages from Iran. But when the oil-price boom that had sustained its attempts to modernize collapsed in 1986, Algeria was left with huge debts.

Demonstrations by unemployed and angry urban youths started in 1988, and soon a group known as the Islamic Salvation Front began to make itself known. By mid-1990, this fundamentalist party scored a great upset in municipal elections. When the military cracked down, the Islamists started a terror campaign that has continued to worsen.

Algeria's embattled government faces a hostile takeover by radical Islamic elements, and such a regime would inherit many sophisticated weapons including Scud missiles, advanced fighter planes and a nuclear reactor secretly supplied by China and believed to be capable of producing weapons-grade plutonium. The amounts are estimated to be small, so it would take a long time to build up an arsenal under normal circumstances. But with a fundamentalist victory stimulating similar movements in Morocco, Tunisia and other parts of the Near East, no one can be sure what cooperative arrangements might be made among terrorist groups, especially at a time when nuclear materials are becoming available on the black market.

Washington has learned to mistrust even its own intelligence about which countries are trying to get around the rules and which are close to success. Most of the detection methods have been a bust so far, and inspections by the International Atomic Energy Agency have not been entirely effective, Ifshin says. "They work well when a nation being inspected is cooperative

and tells the inspectors, 'Here's where we're doing our project. Come have a look.' But when a country is hiding something, you've got to settle for methods such as air and water sampling. If there's bomb-making going on, you may detect traces of significant isotopes. But even then, since air and water are so fluid, you may be left merely with suspicions — little or nothing which pinpoints where the work is located. When it comes to finished bombs, it's almost impossible to discover them in a place the size of a country. They might be hidden in any barn or sewer. So it's like the problem of finding a pistol in a large school. The good kid will tell you if he sees a hidden one. But the ones you really need to catch are only discovered by a lucky accident."

That's one thing Aspin noted should be changed. "We face a bigger proliferation problem than we've ever faced before," he said. "Diplomacy alone cannot be counted on to curb it." Aspin also stated that Washington was tripling the number of Defense Department experts assigned to non-proliferation, adding, "We're looking for intelligence that is useful militarily, not only diplomatically. Many more scientists are being assigned to make practical use of the intelligence as soon as it's collected."

Meanwhile, President Clinton has been trying quietly to plug loopholes wherever possible. He recently ordered regional commanders to produce detailed plans to combat threats of proliferation and has been trying to buy as much enriched uranium as possible from Russia and other countries to keep it out of circulation. The FBI's Freeh has been asking for, and getting, broader jurisdiction in investigating anyone involved in proliferation, even if that has to be done across borders. He also has announced that the bureau will open a Moscow office this month.

The place where the whole nuclear era began — the Los Alamos National Laboratory — also maintains today's Nuclear Emergency Search Team, more than 600 people working to prevent nuclear terrorism. The lab's director, Dr. Siegfried Hecker, says: "What concerns me most right now is keeping track of all the nuclear weapons and the nuclear materials in the former Soviet Union. As soon as one nuke gets away or nuclear material is diverted, you lose the ability to judge the credibility of a terrorist's threat forever."

Regrettably, that concern keeps growing. Freeh confirms a long list of

cases documented by the German government, citing dates and quantities of radioactive materials found in the possession of, for example, "a Romanian technician," "workers in a St. Petersburg nuclear plant," "a Romanian-born German," "a Belgian and three Slovaks" and so on. Nobody pretends that the seized material accounts for everything. These are just a few lucky arrests that have been made—perhaps just the tip of an iceberg that could be for sale to Iran or the highest bidder.

The experts hope that most of the stolen goods consist of lesser radioactive materials, such as spent nuclear fuel, and do not include much plutonium or enriched uranium. It takes only 15 pounds of the former or 35 pounds of the latter to form the core of a bomb, so uncertainty is the dominant fact of today's atomic world.

Among the technical experts, diplomats and administrators there is a sense of urgency to:

●Extend the Nuclear Non-Proliferation Treaty to preserve at least minimal discipline.
●Restrict possession of nuclear arsenals to the original five nations.
●Offer incentives to countries that already have atomic weaponry to relinquish it (such as the current offer of advanced fighter planes to Pakistan).
●Mount a battery of all-out scientific and intelligence efforts to upgrade detection capability.
●Increase international police cooperation to stop black-market sales.

Is there any chance of disposing of all nuclear weapons?

Yes, according to former State Department member Ifshin. "It may be time to start working toward total denuclearization of the whole world," he says, adding that it would be one of the most difficult decisions an American president has ever been called upon to make. In fact, Ifshin explains, nuclear generation of electric power might become a necessity in the next century as oil and gas reserves run lower. "In the West, only France is pointing strongly that way, but in Asia they're planning reactors in great numbers. Wherever there are reactors, especially like Japan's new breeder reactors, materials that could be used to make nuclear weapons would be generated as by-products. But even if we talk of giving up just all the atomic arsenals, we run a great risk unless we first achieve foolproof detection methods."

CONTEST OVER ASIA
Search for Security In the Pacific

Clayton Jones

Staff writer of The Christian Science Monitor

SINGAPORE

Despite the diplomatic smiles at an unprecedented summit of Asia-Pacific leaders this month, an uneasy, cold peace hangs over the most economically dynamic area of the world.

From boardrooms to warrooms, the region is probing for a new stability after the cold war's demise, communism's decline, and the closing out of Western colonialism in Asia.

The once-menacing ships of the Soviet Pacific Fleet now rust in port. The 1991 retreat of the United States from its huge Subic Bay naval base in the Philippines has left a security vacuum. China's rush to riches has allowed it to flex new military muscle, and Japan's economic dominance has led it to search for a role as guardian of regional peace.

No longer convinced they can rely on Western partners, Asians are being forced to identify potential threats. Old suspicions of one another are reviving; large and small nations are stockpiling arms.

Why, its neighbors ask, did China test a nuclear bomb last month and why is it building a military airstrip on an island in the South China Sea? Why is Japan building a fast warship that could be converted to an aircraft carrier?

Smaller powers, too, from Thailand to North Korea, are adding formidable weapons to their arsenals. In 1991, Asia surpassed the Middle East as the top buyer of conventional arms, according to the Stockholm International Peace Research Institute. "There is a strategic contest for leadership in the Asia-Pacific," says Derek da Cunha, a Singaporean military analyst. "So far, [it's] a friendly arms race."

By 1999, Asia will have shaken off the last vestige of Western colonialism when tiny Portuguese-owned Macao reverts back to China, almost 500 years after Portuguese ships landed at Malacca port on the Malaysian peninsula in search of spices, converts, and gold, becoming the first Westerners to plant a flag on Asian soil. Their arrival inaugurated centuries of colonialism in Asia, with European powers carving up much of the region for economic gain.

But even with the departure of the outsiders, ideological differences persist. Four of the world's five remaining Communist-run nations are in Asia. "Asia is caught in a time warp," says Winston Lord, US assistant secretary of state for East Asian and Pacific affairs.

A number of latent issues and disputes could escalate into war in the absence of a security framework, concludes the London-based International Institute for Strategic Studies. Power is being redistributed between China, Japan, and the US, as well as between the medium-sized powers of Indonesia, Korea, and India, says Bilahari Kausikan, head of the East Asia and Pacific bureau in Singapore's Foreign Ministry.

"You have all these adjustments going on. A lot of them can't be predicted," he says. "The uncertainties are high even though military conflict is at its lowest. We have no precedents, no landmarks. Everyone is groping."

To cope with the new anxieties, many Asian nations are using preventive diplomacy, forming institutions for cooperation and "confidence-building" that, at the very least, keep historic and potential adversaries talking to each other.

One such group is called the Asia Pacific Economic Cooperation forum, or APEC, created just two years ago in an attempt to liberalize trade and investment. The group has shown only a little cohesion leading up to its Nov. 17–21 meeting in Seattle. Its formation has been sluggish because of political maneuvering among the region's leading nations. China, for example, had to be cajoled into accepting Taiwan and Hong Kong as APEC members.

Nonetheless, the region has "a much greater sense of community," than it once did, Mr. Lord says. "The outlines of a Pacific community are taking shape." President Clinton's request that a summit meeting be held was itself a bold move to re-exert US leadership in Asia.

A summit handshake between Mr. Clinton and Chinese President Jiang Zemin, coming four years after the Tiananmen massacre, could be regarded as either the start of a new US–China partnership or the onset of a post–cold-war contest for influence.

"The US sees the importance of its role in Asia, especially while China's intentions are still not clear and because millions of US jobs depend on maintaining stability [in Asia]," says a US diplomat in Singapore. "We are still worried about the disparity between what China says and what it is doing."

China's plans to build a far-reaching, "blue water" navy, its recent nuclear test, its forceful seizure of islands from Vietnam in 1988, and its reluctance to rule out a violent takeover of Taiwan have kept its neighbors on guard.

Few analysts say China is a threat now, as it races toward market wealth and appears to prefer regional stability. "After the cold war, the main issue in Asia is the absence of an overriding threat," says Zakaria Haji Ahmad, a security expert at the University of Malaya in Kuala Lumpur.

China's neighbors worry that it may want to reassert its historic role as the center of Asia, winning back what it thinks it has lost in wealth, territory, or influence.

Should China be estranged or engaged? The US is shifting toward engagement, while some nations, such as Malaysia, are not sure. "If you accept China as a military power, then you don't confront it," Dr. Ahmad says.

After the Tiananmen massacre, China looked for friends in Asia to side with it against the West. It found some backing in the Association of Southeast Asian Nations (ASEAN), a noncommunist group that includes Singapore, Malaysia, Thailand, Indonesia, Brunei, and the Philippines.

"We don't feel there is a threat from China—for many years," says Tommy Koh, a former Singaporean ambassador to the US. "But memories of China [under Mao Zedong] using the Chinese in Southeast Asia are still alive."

'There is a strategic contest for leadership in the Asia-Pacific. . . . So far, [it's] a friendly arms race.'

—Singaporean military analyst

Since 1977, ASEAN has debated how to rid Southeast Asia of any big-power influence by creating a "zone of peace, freedom, and neutrality." But it now realizes that the idea was a pipe dream. Sitting at the crossroads of two oceans, the region's geography is its destiny.

"We tried to deny that there would be a power vacuum if the US withdrew," says Kusuma Snitwongse, director of the Institute for Security and International Studies in Bangkok. "While it's old thinking to suggest that we should hang on to a US [military presence], in this uncertain period there's an ambivalence. If the US leaves, will Japan and China be more aggressive in the region?"

At present, Japan is seen as a very theoretical threat. Its military is constrained by a war-renouncing constitution and a dependence on US forces under a security treaty. The Japanese Army has

only 180,000 soldiers, and that number is shrinking. Japan's new prime minister, Morihiro Hosokawa, wants his country to lead the world in disarmament.

But what worries its neighbors is that Japan could turn its technological prowess into deadly weapons overnight or leave the American security umbrella. Some Japanese officials warn privately that Japan might build a nuclear bomb if North Korea does.

And a widespread feeling exists in the region that Japan has failed to learn from its occupation of Asia before and during World War II. "For Japan not to tell its children what happened in the war—it causes a lot of worry," Mr. Koh says.

Hoping to change that image, Japan made its first postwar overseas deployment of troops in 1992 by sending 600 soldiers to Cambodia to aid United Nations peacekeeping. But, Mr. Kusuma says, the deployment "didn't change perceptions of Japan. In fact, it reinforces the fear of Japan, because Southeast Asia insisted that Japan remain only under UN command."

Likewise, the threat of Russia's Pacific Fleet, while diminished, has not evaporated in the eyes of many Asians, especially since Moscow seeks to maintain some of its access to the warm-water port in Vietnam's Cam Ranh Bay.

Unlike Europe, where communism has gone to ashes, Asia still has remnants of the cold war, such as the standoff between North and South Korea, that make forming a security framework difficult.

In 1992, ASEAN decided to build on its 25-year success as a friendly regional group and invited Japan, China, Russia, as well as South Korea, Vietnam, Laos, Papua New Guinea, and Western nations to start a new group devoted to tackling security issues.

"The problem is not how to exclude anybody, but how to keep this happy state of affairs," Mr. Kausikan says. "It's a matter of a balance of big powers, not the vacuum of power."

The new group, known enigmatically as the ASEAN Regional Forum (ARF), met for a Sunday dinner last July in Singapore. Substantive talks are slated for next summer in Bangkok.

ARF has had a rough start. Japan did not want Russia and China to join. The US did not want Vietnam. "We have to go slowly," Kusuma says. "It's a meeting of the not-like-minded."

But, Koh says, "the takeoff of ARF has really surprised us. At a minimum, you

keep all the countries talking. The ASEAN way of doing things is very gradualist."

ARF's progress may be measured in inches. The first hurdle is how to convince each state to be more open about its military situation, especially arms purchases.

"We need to develop patterns of behavior that would lead people to resolve problems peacefully," the US diplomat says.

Even ASEAN, despite its members' successful track record of working together since 1967 on various issues, has failed to form its own security forum—until now.

For the first time, defense officials from all six ASEAN states will meet in coming months as a prelude to the ARF meeting. One of the first steps may be for each nation to issue a "white paper" describing military strategy and weapons.

"ASEAN is not and will not become a military pact," says Singaporean Prime Minister Goh Chok Tong. "But consultations among defense and military officials will help build an environment of confidence."

The move is risky. ASEAN does not want to appear to be an anti-China bloc. Vietnam, a historic enemy of China, wants to join the group, but ASEAN is wary.

"Once you form an ASEAN security forum, you have to ask, 'Who is the enemy?' " says Lee Tai To of the National University of Singapore. "ASEAN has already been a sort of secret security group—containing conflict with each other."

Indonesia's recent purchase of three former East German submarines has helped fuel concerns of an ASEAN arms race. So has Malaysia's plan to buy 18 Russian-built MIG-29 jet fighters and 8 US-made F-18 Hornets. Thailand plans to buy a Spanish-made helicopter carrier.

This nascent arms race in Asia must be kept in context, says Dr. da Cunha, a fellow at Singapore's Institute for Southeast Asian Studies. "Each nation buys weapons for a number of reasons, usually just for a matter of national pride. One of the lesser motives these days is to keep pace with potential adversaries."

Until now ASEAN nations have had only a spiderweb of bilateral military ties with each other, usually to conduct joint exercises. Singapore keeps a battalion in Brunei, primarily to help guard it against Malaysia. "They all still don't trust each other," Da Cunha says.

The US remains the glue among AS-EAN militaries. Since the Philippines closed the US bases on its soil in 1991, the US has had ready access to commercial ship-repair yards in Indonesia, Malaysia, and Singapore. Malaysia, despite its anti-US rhetoric, holds the most bilateral military exercises with the US.

"The withdrawal from the Philippines has allowed closer ties for the US with several Southeast Asian militaries," the US diplomat says. Singapore is now home to more than 100 US military personnel. Logistics and training exercises for the US Navy's 7th Fleet are managed here, and jets of the US Air Force 497th fighter squadron practice in Singapore at least six times a year.

The US presence, although small, serves as a "trip-wire," Da Cunha says. "No country wants to cross swords with America on day one of a conflict. The security of the US and Singapore are now one."

One US Navy commander in Singapore admits the US is here mainly for political reasons. "We could provide these services anyplace. But it allows Singapore to be a player in Southeast Asia, and it keeps the US more involved in the region."

"This is the most benign presence," the officer adds. "We have no combat capability. But we're right on the highway between two oceans."

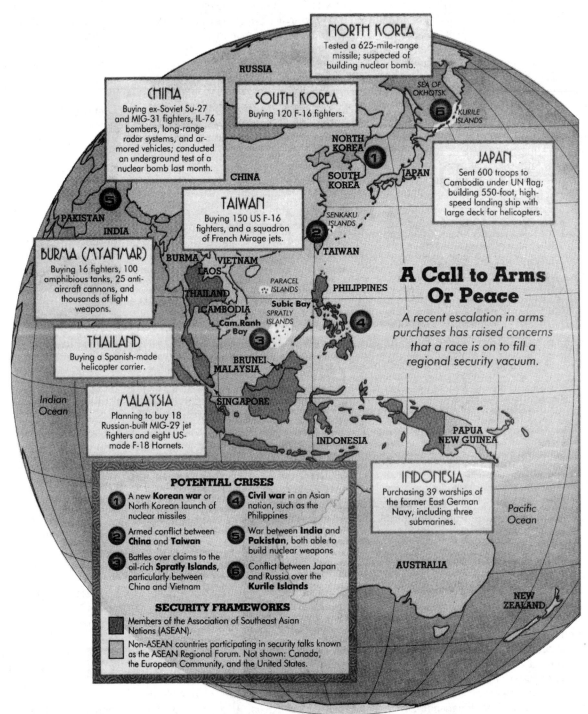

NORTH KOREA
Tested a 625-mile-range missile; suspected of building nuclear bomb.

CHINA
Buying ex-Soviet Su-27 and MIG-31 fighters, IL-76 bombers, long-range radar systems, and armored vehicles; conducted an underground test of a nuclear bomb last month.

SOUTH KOREA
Buying 120 F-16 fighters.

JAPAN
Sent 600 troops to Cambodia under UN flag; building 550-foot, high-speed landing ship with large deck for helicopters.

TAIWAN
Buying 150 US F-16 fighters, and a squadron of French Mirage jets.

BURMA (MYANMAR)
Buying 16 fighters, 100 amphibious tanks, 25 anti-aircraft cannons, and thousands of light weapons.

THAILAND
Buying a Spanish-made helicopter carrier.

MALAYSIA
Planning to buy 18 Russian-built MIG-29 jet fighters and eight US-made F-18 Hornets.

A Call to Arms Or Peace
A recent escalation in arms purchases has raised concerns that a race is on to fill a regional security vacuum.

INDONESIA
Purchasing 39 warships of the former East German Navy, including three submarines.

POTENTIAL CRISES

1 A new **Korean war** or North Korean launch of nuclear missiles

2 Armed conflict between **China** and **Taiwan**

3 Battles over claims to the oil-rich **Spratly Islands**, particularly between China and Vietnam

4 **Civil war** in an Asian nation, such as the Philippines

5 War between **India** and **Pakistan**, both able to build nuclear weapons

6 Conflict between Japan and Russia over the **Kurile Islands**

SECURITY FRAMEWORKS

■ Members of the Association of Southeast Asian Nations (ASEAN).

□ Non-ASEAN countries participating in security talks known as the ASEAN Regional Forum. Not shown: Canada, the European Community, and the United States.

DISMANTLING THE ARSENALS
Arms Control and the New World Agenda

Jack Mendelsohn

Jack Mendelsohn, a former State Department official, was a member of the U.S. SALT II and START delegations and served at the U.S. Mission to NATO. He is currently Deputy Director of the Arms Control Association in Washington, D.C.

The collapse of communism and the promise of a more cooperative East-West relationship have transformed the world of arms control. Goals that were once unthinkable—making enormous cuts in strategic forces or actually destroying nuclear warheads—are now at the top of the agenda. Developments that were always dangerous but of only secondary concern because of the primary East-West confrontation—the widespread deployment of short-range nuclear weapons or the spread of conventional weapons to the developing world—have now become urgent issues. And verification measures, originally born of deep distrust between East and West and intended to inform adversaries about each other's military programs, are now available to help monitor agreements, build trust, and reduce tensions.

Nuclear Weapons

Understandably, the most immediate concern of both the United States and Europe is the future of nuclear weapons in a disintegrating Soviet empire. For now, at least, the goals of the United States and Russia seem to be congruent: to ensure the centralized command and control of the nuclear forces of the newly formed Commonwealth of Independent States (CIS), to encourage the safe and secure withdrawal of tactical (and, eventually, strategic) nuclear weapons from the outlying republics to Russia, and to prevent the spread of nuclear hardware and brainpower to third countries. Programs to address these problems are already under way or un-

der consideration, although concern about their continued successful implementation will certainly persist.

In the longer term a different set of nuclear arms control issues will challenge policymakers. The end of the Cold War offers a unique opportunity to push the size of U.S. and Russian strategic nuclear forces down to considerably lower levels. As Soviet President Gorbachev suggested last October, and as President Bush proposed in his State of the Union speech in January, the United States and Russia could readily cut in half the number of strategic weapons permitted under the Strategic Arms Reduction Treaty (START).

How low strategic forces can ultimately be taken will depend on the actual role assigned to nuclear weapons. Most analysts agree that the United States can maintain its present "warfighting" strategy with as few as 3,000–4,000 nuclear weapons (see table 1). If, on the other hand, the United States were prepared to abandon its current warfighting strategy, which targets thousands of military, political, and economic sites, in favor of a purely deterrent one involving a very limited set of military-industrial targets, it would facilitate even steeper reductions in strategic warheads. This is apparently the strategy that underlies Russian President Boris Yeltsin's recent offer to reduce strategic arsenals to 2,000–2,500 warheads.

An essentially deterrent strategy would be based on the premise that relatively few warheads are required to dissuade an adversary from launching a deliberate nuclear attack. According to former Secretary of Defense Robert McNamara, during the 1962 Cuban missile crisis, when the United States had approximately 5,000 strategic warheads to the Soviet Union's 300, "President Kennedy and I were deterred from even considering a nuclear attack on the USSR by the knowledge that, although such a strike would destroy the Soviet Union, *tens* of their weapons would survive to be launched against the United States" (emphasis added). Nothing in the past 30 years has invalidated that conclusion or diminished the deterrent value of even a few nuclear weapons.

From *The Brookings Review*, Spring 1992, pp. 34-39. © 1992 by the Brookings Institution. Reprinted by permission.

5. CONFLICT

Preventing Inadvertent Conflict

With the end of the adversarial relationship between the United States and Russia and the prospect of large-scale reductions in existing nuclear arsenals, longstanding fears of deliberate attack have yielded to a new concern about inadvertent conflict. To respond to this concern, the two nations will need to make it as difficult as possible to launch their nuclear weapons. They will have to ensure that all nuclear weapons are subject to both physical safeguards and chain-of-command arrangements that cannot be defeated or circumvented. To this end, all deployed and nondeployed nuclear weapons should have the latest technology electronic locks to prevent unauthorized use. Both arming and release codes for all nuclear weapons should be held by the national command authority (on-board commanders have access to the codes for U.S. ballistic missile submarines).

Another way to reduce the risk of inadvertent war is to increase the overall confidence of both sides in the survivability of their nuclear forces. This can be done by some relatively simple measures. For example, the president has proposed that land-based ballistic missile systems be limited by agreement to one warhead. That is one way to eliminate the concern that a small number of land-based multiple-warhead missiles on one side could be used early in a crisis and, in theory at least, destroy large numbers of similar systems on the other side. Alternatively, land-based systems could be made mobile or dispersed among multiple protective shelters. Finally, overall warhead reductions, on the scale discussed above, would by themselves decrease the number of multiple warhead systems and increase survivability by making it difficult, if not impossible, to undertake a disarming strike against the nuclear forces of the other side.

As one confidence-building measure, warheads could be removed from a portion of the land-based missile force and the systems taken off high state of alert. Ballistic missile submarines could patrol out of range of their targets, and aggressive anti-submarine warfare training activities could be strictly limited. Strategic bombers should remain off alert and their weapons stored away from operational bases. The sides could also limit the size and frequency of large-scale exercises and enhance confidence by exchanging data and giving advance notice of strategic force tests or practice alerts.

Finally, the United States, Russia, and the relevant CIS countries should agree to destroy the existing stockpile of retired and surplus nuclear weapons, perhaps 15,000 to 18,000 warheads on each side. As the two sides reduce their tactical and strategic arsenals, the number of warheads in storage will increase dramatically—as will concern over their possible theft, sale, misappropriation, or rapid redeployment. The destruction of redundant warheads should be coupled with a ban on the further production of fissile material for weapons purposes, a monitored limit on the production of new warheads to replace existing systems, and the storage, under international safeguards, of fissile material withdrawn from retired weapons.

Table 1. Selected Proposals for Strategic Arms Reductions below Warhead Levels in START

NUMBER OF WARHEADS	PROPOSAL
600	Andrei Kokoshin, *Bulletin of the Atomic Scientists*, September 1988
1,000	Carl Kaysen, Robert S. McNamara, and George W. Rathjens, *Foreign Affairs*, Fall 1991
1,000–2,000	Committee on International Security and Arms Control, National Academy of Science, 1991 (second-stage cuts)
1,000–2,000	Jonathan Dean and Kurt Gottfried, Union of Concerned Scientists, 1991
Below 2,000	Harold A. Feiveson and Frank N. von Hippel, *International Security*, Summer 1990
2,000–2,500	Boris Yeltsin, United Nations, 1992
Below 3,000	Harold Brown, *Arms Control Today*, May 1990
3,000	John D. Steinbruner, Michael M. May, and George F. Bing, *International Security*, Summer 1988*
3,000–4,000	Committee on International Security and Arms Control, National Academy of Science, 1991 (first-stage cuts)
4,700	George Bush, State of the Union Speech, 1992
4,000–6,000	Reed Report, Strategic Air Command, 1991
6,000	START Treaty, 1991**

*Most proposals consider 3,000 warheads to be the level beneath which current targeting strategy must be revised and 2,000 to be the level beneath which third-country forces (United Kingdom, France, China) must become involved in negotiations.

**START permits 6,000 "accountable" strategic warheads on each side. Because of lenient counting rules on air-launched weapons, each side may in reality deploy several thousand additional warheads.

Strategic Defenses

Closely related to the question of nuclear force reductions and to the shift from preparing for deliberate war to preventing inadvertent war is the issue of preserving the Anti-Ballistic Missile (ABM) Treaty's strict limits on strategic defensive systems. Despite the boost given anti-missile systems by the Scud-Patriot encounters during the Gulf war, the United States will have to tread carefully in its approach to tactical and strategic ballistic missile defenses. Strategic defenses, by their nature, undercut confidence in the retaliatory capability of strategic offensive forces and could therefore lessen the willingness of one side or another to make big cuts in strategic offensive forces. In some cases, such as those involving the relatively small national deterrent forces of France and Britain, deploying even a low level of strategic defenses may actually stimulate an increase in arsenals in order to overcome these anti-missile systems.

Thus the Bush administration's interest in rewriting the ABM Treaty to permit large-scale deployment of its newest version of Star Wars, known as Global

Protection against Limited Strikes (GPALS), runs contrary to a fundamental U.S. interest: to reduce nuclear arsenals in the CIS to as low a level as possible. Moreover, the goal cited by the administration in support of GPALS—to protect the United States against threats from third world "nondeterrables"—is questionable. CIA Director Robert Gates has predicted that it will be at least a decade before any country other than China or the CIS could strike the United States with long-range ballistic missiles. And most observers believe that long-range ballistic missiles would not be the delivery system of choice for any third world nation attempting to threaten the United States.

Although Yeltsin proposed a joint SDI program, it is unlikely, given the economic situation in the CIS, that in the long run Russia will really pursue such a costly defensive project. The same should be true for the United States. If the United States nonetheless persists in its efforts to deploy defenses, and if the Russians acquiesce to a similar program, then it will be critically important that any eventual strategic defensive deployments be limited to very few fixed land-based interceptors only. Anti–tactical ballistic missile systems, which are likely to be of interest to both sides and which are not prohibited by the ABM Treaty, should be designed so that neither their capability nor their widespread deployment will erode confidence in either side's strategic offensive retaliatory capabilities.

Conventional Weapons

In the short term, U.S., European, and CIS arms control goals regarding conventional weapons are likely to be similar: to encourage the prompt adherence to, and implementation of, past and pending arms control obligations, especially the recently concluded Conventional Armed Forces in Europe (CFE) agreement, and to complete the Open Skies and CFE follow-on talks (the former to create an aerial inspection regime and the latter to establish politically binding limits on troop levels). A third goal, to ensure the orderly transfer of conventional military forces from Union control to the newly formed states, is certainly shared by the West and Russia. But tensions among the states of the new CIS may make it difficult, or even impossible, to distribute conventional forces quickly or smoothly (see table 2).

In the longer term, now that the fear of a massive land war in Europe has become, in the words of the CIA director, "virtually nonexistent," the conventional weapons arms control agenda is likely to be occupied with four principal issues. The first is greater openness, or transparency, in military programs and activities. After several decades of relying primarily on satellites and sensors to monitor military activities, and as the infatuation with on-site inspection fades, we are just now beginning to recognize and exploit the potential of relatively straightforward cooperative measures to provide intelligence. Through extensive and intensive multilateral exchange, nations can increase

Table 2. CFE-Limited Conventional Weapons in the States of the Former Soviet Union (February 1991)

REPUBLIC	TANKS	ARMORED COMBAT VEHICLES	ARTILLERY	HELI-COPTERS	AIRCRAFT
Armenia	258	641	357	7	0
Azerbaijan	391	1,285	463	24	124
Belarus	2,263	2,776	1,384	82	650
Estonia	184	201	29	10	153
Georgia	850	1,054	363	48	245
Latvia	138	100	81	23	183
Lithuania	184	1,591	253	0	46
Moldova	155	402	248	0	0
Russia	5,017	6,279	3,480	570	2,750
Ukraine	6,204	6,394	3,052	285	1,431
TOTAL	15,644	20,723	9,710	1,049	5,582
Soviet forces in Germany*	5,081	9,167	4,228	432	1,029
TOTAL**	20,725	29,890	13,938	1,481	6,611
TOTAL PERMITTED UNDER CFE	13,150	20,000	13,175	1,500	5,150

Source: Arms Control Association.

* All Soviet forces in Germany are scheduled to be withdrawn by 1994.

** Under CFE, the states of the former Soviet Union west of the Urals (with the exception of Estonia, Latvia, and Lithuania) must agree to allocate among themselves the total equipment permitted the former Soviet Union. Surplus equipment must be destroyed.

the information available on budgets, force size, production levels, research, development and modernization programs, deployment plans, arms transfers, and operational practices. As such openness improves our ability to predict the evolution of the overall security environment, it will enhance stability and reduce the risk of overreaction.

A second objective regarding conventional arms is to defuse the dangers of localized or ethnic strife in Europe. While the threat of a general war in Europe is minimal, numerous potential regional flash points, such as Croatia-Serbia or Armenia-Azerbaijan, still exist. Even if the CFE treaty enters into force, a concentrated effort will still have to be made to deal with these problem areas by subregional arms control. Subregional constraints might involve lowering force levels in geographically restricted areas (force allotments in Hungary and Romania, for example, could be 25 percent beneath CFE levels); establishing disengagement zones (Hungary and Romania could both agree

5. CONFLICT

not to deploy military forces within 50 kilometers of their common border); or instituting special monitoring measures such as intensive aerial overflights or third-party inspections.

A third issue, how to integrate large numbers of demobilized soldiers into civilian life and forestall a "black market" in conventional military hardware, will be one of the most challenging, albeit nontraditional, new arms control tasks. But it may also be the one most amenable to direct economic intervention. The United States has already offered the CIS $400 million to help dismantle its nuclear and chemical warheads. The United States and its European allies may wish to consider establishing a similar Conference on Security and Cooperation in Europe (CSCE) fund to help destroy, securely store, or ultimately buy up surplus war material from Eastern Europe and the CIS states to keep it from leaking into the black market (as apparently happened during the Croatian-Serbian conflict).

We may also wish to use an international fund to help train, house, employ, or provide severance pay to demobilized CIS soldiers to keep them from becoming a disruptive social or political force. Germany did as much to speed the evacuation of Soviet soldiers from its territory, and the current Russian military budget has designated all its capital investment for housing. We may also wish to institute programs to train soldiers who remain in uniform to work on disaster relief, environmental clean-up, and other civil support missions.

Finally, with or without U.S. participation, the European states will need to work toward creating European-based peacekeeping, peacemaking (that is, interventionary), and conflict-resolution institutions to deal with continent-wide security issues. The U.S. government does not now favor such institutions because it fears that they would undercut U.S. influence in European security issues. But, at some point, the tensions created by Yugoslavian-type crises, where the United States adopted a hands-off policy and Europe had very limited tools to manage the conflict, will force the empowerment of one or another of the Euro-based organizations (the Conference on Security and Cooperation in Europe, the Western European Union, or the North Atlantic Cooperation Council), the United Nations, or another specially created body to deal directly and forcefully with subregional challenges to European security. Once some international institution is designated as the executive forum, it will have to earmark multinational forces for the peacekeeping task, and the member states will have to devise a decisionmaking process that keeps the parties to the problem from blocking action.

Stemming the Spread of Weapons

As the enormous changes in Europe have eased concerns about East-West conflict, the United States and other developed nations have turned their attention to the challenges to international security posed by the spread of weapons in the developing world. Ironically,

Table 3. U.S. Arms Transfers to the Middle East since the Iraqi Invasion of Kuwait

MILLIONS OF DOLLARS

COUNTRY	VALUE	EQUIPMENT
Bahrain	$ 37	Tanks
Egypt	2,170	Aircraft, munitions
Israel	467	Patriot, aircraft, helicopters
Kuwait	350	Air base upgrades
Morocco	250	Aircraft
Oman	150	Armored personnel carriers
Saudi Arabia	14,800	Aircraft, tanks, helicopters
United Arab Emirates	737	Helicopters
TOTAL	$ 18,961	

Source: Arms Control Association. The table lists transfers of major conventional weapons notified to Congress between August 2, 1990, and January 1, 1992.

the problem is largely the result of the developed world's own policies during the Cold War, when arming the enemy of one's enemy was considered to be the height of sophisticated geopolitics. Meeting the proliferation challenge will require of the developed world a full and rare measure of political will and self-restraint.

To be sure, regimes to control several types of proliferation already exist or are under negotiation. The nuclear Non-Proliferation Treaty, with some 140 members, has been a highly successful example of international cooperation and common perspective for a quarter of a century. Negotiations on a Chemical Weapons Convention are far advanced and likely to be concluded in the not-too-distant future. And major supplier groups (to control nuclear technology, chemical and biological weapons, missile technology, and conventional arms transfers to the Middle East) have already been established and are expanding their scope.

Building on the existing nonproliferation structures, arms control can make several useful contributions. The first is to encourage stronger supplier restraint. Supplier states first must resist domestic political or economic pressures to sell arms, and then they will have to demonstrate a high level of political skill to balance the concerns of the developed world with objections from less advanced countries that nonproliferation regimes will spark. The nuclear supplier group clearly increased the time and cost of Iraq's nuclear weapons program. Nonetheless, the extent of Iraq's program surprised almost everyone, a fact that underscores the need to strengthen and expand nuclear export guidelines to include limits on "dual use" items—an effort already under way.

The United States and the other major arms exporters will also have to make more explicit efforts to limit sales of conventional weapons to areas of tension. For example, in conjunction with a supplier regime, "caps" might be placed on the value of arms exports approved by the supplier group to any one country in any one year (see table 3). That would require an international register of arms transfer and agreement among at least the "big five" exporters (the United States, the United Kingdom, France, the former Soviet Union, and China, which accounted for nearly 90 percent of the arms trade in 1990) to declare transfers and respect the cap. Pressure could also be applied to potential arms recipients by linking, directly or informally, U.S. aid, as well as aid from international lending institutions, to military spending levels.

As important as supplier restraint may be, regional arms control will undoubtedly remain the best long-term way to slow proliferation. Models already exist: the Treaty of Tlatelolco (establishing a nuclear-free zone in Latin America) and the Conventional Forces in Europe treaty are examples. Rallying the political will and muscle to apply these models to regions of the world where the underlying tension has not been directly eased by the new cooperative spirit in Europe will be a challenge. But easing these regional concerns is the key to taking the pressure off the "demand" side of proliferation. In fact, supplier restraint should only be a tool to buy time for regional efforts to work.

Regional arms control in areas such as the Middle East, South Asia, and Korea will have to involve major outside players. The United States, Russia, France, or Britain, depending on the region involved, will have to take an active interest and leading role in bringing about even a modest reconciliation. This reconciliation process would involve, first, political dialogue (as between the two Koreas and at the Middle East peace talks), then transparency (as in the Sinai and on the Golan Heights), supplier restraint, confidence-building measures, and, eventually, explicit arms control measures to limit forces and disengage (or separate) threatening forces.

Improved verification and monitoring would also strengthen nonproliferation efforts. Confidence in arms control regimes and regional security arrangements can, in general, be buttressed by increased transparency and predictability. In the proliferation arena, where one is dealing, almost by definition, with countries trying to acquire military capabilities by clandestine means, comprehensive intelligence, monitoring, and verification regimes are critical. First, as the Iraq experience has demonstrated, all agreements dealing with weapons of mass destruction must permit the right to challenge inspections of suspect sites. Second, nations with sophisticated intelligence capabilities, the United States in particular, will have to begin to share intelligence more widely. Making information more generally accessible will increase the stake of other participating states in the nonproliferation regime, enhance their confidence in its viability, and strengthen any eventual case against violators.

Finally, arms control by example is an important adjunct to specific nonproliferation treaties and cooperative measures. Although it cannot by itself stop states or leaders determined to violate an international agreement or tacit understanding, it can enhance the moral authority of the major powers. Evidence of serious intent to implement supplier restraint, to pursue deeper nuclear force reductions, to destroy conventional weapons and nuclear warheads, to stop fissionable materials production, and to cease nuclear testing would bolster the case for "demand" reduction in the proliferation arena. It would also strengthen the hand of the major powers in making the case for taking collective action—whether export controls, political and economic sanctions, or military measures—against any state that violates international agreements or standards.

Cooperation

An individual in just about any location on Earth can write a letter to another person just about anywhere else, and if it is properly addressed, the sender can be relatively certain that the letter will be delivered. This is true even though the sender pays for postage only in the country of origin and not in the country where it is delivered. A similar pattern of international cooperation is true when an individual boards an airplane in one country and never gives the issues of potential language and technical barriers another thought, even though the flight's destination is halfway around the world.

Many of the most basic activities of our lives are the result of international cooperation. The creation of international organizational structures to monitor public health on a global scale or scientifically evaluate changing weather conditions are additional examples where governments have recognized that their self-interest directly benefits from cooperation (i.e., the creation of international governmental organizations or IGOs).

These transnational activities, furthermore, are not limited to the governmental level. There are now literally tens of thousands of international nongovernmental organizations (INGOs). These organizations stage the Olympic Games or actively discourage the hunting of whales and seals, to illustrate just two of the diverse activities of INGOs. The number and influence of these international organizations, it is important to note, have grown tremendously in the past 40 years.

In the same time period in which we have witnessed the growth in importance of IGOs and INGOs, there has been a parallel expansion of corporate activity across international borders. Most consumers are as familiar with products with a Japanese brand name as they are with products made in the United States, Germany, or elsewhere. The multinational corporation (MNC) is an important nonstate actor in the world today. The value of goods and services produced by the biggest MNCs is far greater than the Gross National Product (GNP) of many countries. The international structures that make it possible to buy an Italian automobile in Sacramento or a Swiss watch in Singapore have been developed over many years. They are the result of governments negotiating treaties and creating IGOs to implement these agreements. The manufacturers engaged in these activities have created complex networks of sales, distribution, and service that grow more complex with each passing day.

These trends at a variety of levels indicate to many observers that the era of the nation-state as the dominant player in international politics is passing. Others have observed these trends and have concluded that the state system has a monopoly of power and the diverse variety of transnational organizations depend on the state system and in many ways perpetuate it.

In many of the articles that appear elsewhere in this book, the authors have concluded by calling for greater international cooperation to solve our world's most pressing problems. The articles in this section show examples of successful cooperation. In the midst of a lot of bad news in the world, it is easy to overlook the fact that we are surrounded by international cooperation and that basic aspects of our lives are often the result of it.

Looking Ahead: Challenge Questions

What products do you own that were manufactured in another country?

What contacts have you had with people from another country? How was it possible for you to have these contacts?

How can the conflict and rivalry between the United States and Russia be transformed into meaningful cooperation?

What are the prospects for international governance? Would a trend in this direction enhance or threaten American values and constitutional rights?

Unit 6

The United Nations and the New Global Challenges

Boutros Boutros-Ghali

Boutros Boutros-Ghali is Secretary-General of the United Nations.

Social Education 58(7), 1994, pp. 403-406   ©1994 National Council for the Social Studies

With the end of the Cold War, the world has entered a period of transition and turmoil. This situation requires new thinking, new actions, and new responses from the United Nations itself as it is increasingly called upon to meet the demands of change. As an educator who spent three decades teaching in colleges and universities in different parts of the world, I know how important it is for young people to learn of this great contemporary challenge and, through their reactions, contribute to the indispensable need for greater international cooperation.

Throughout history, powerful states have divided peoples and territories using power as the sole justification. With the creation of the World Organization, and the adoption of the United Nations Charter (1945) and the Universal Declaration of Human Rights (1948), the doctrine of "might makes right" was rejected. These documents provide a normative framework for cooperation between states, based on the rule of law, toward peace, justice, human rights, and development. In a world no longer torn by the great power conflict of the Cold War, these documents are more applicable and more needed than ever. The fundamental achievements reflected in these documents must be appreciated and reinforced within the new international context. To this end, teachers play an important role by ensuring that all citizens are familiar with UN activities under the UN Charter and the Universal Declaration of Human Rights, and by fostering greater understanding of the commitment the member states have made to the UN.

The challenge the UN is facing is of course no less than the challenge that our world is facing. As we who are committed to the UN understand, its capacities, achievements, shortcomings, and hopes are expressions of our joint achievements, failings, and ability to envision and promote new solutions as members of a shared international community. The UN represents us, in our global totality. We are more aware today than ever before that poverty, pollution, and disease affect all of humanity regardless of political differences. It is clear that the ills of our planet respect no borders. Multilateral cooperation is therefore necessary to find global solutions.

The Heads of State/Government at the Security Council Summit convened in January 1992 expressed optimism that—with the end of the Cold War and the relaxation of bilateral, ideological tensions within the World Organization—the member states could work together more freely to fulfill the original aims of the Charter. But expectations almost always carry the danger of turning into disillusions. We need to be patient in our expectations but rapid in our efforts toward progress. It is tragic, and I believe very serious, if criticism of the UN slows down the pace of reform or prevents mistakes from being transformed into constructive changes. The next Security Council Summit, scheduled for January 1995, can serve to maintain the momentum for positive change.

In this article, I would like to give you some examples of the achievements of the UN, of the difficulties that the UN faces in this new post-Cold War world, and of my efforts as Secretary-General to restructure and reform the Organization. Please keep these three realities in mind when discussing or reading about the Organization: the comprehensive nature of the global challenge, the indispensability of the UN in the new international context, and the gap that has been revealed as the demands of member states on the Organization are not matched by the resources provided.

United Nations Headquarters, New York City.

UN Photo 1047 1 3/Saw Lwin

International Peace and Security

For millions of people, the end of the Cold War did not bring peace, but war and conflicts inside the boundaries of their own societies. The UN has increasingly been called upon to alleviate the suffering of civilians and negotiate peaceful solutions. At the Security Council Summit meeting convened in January 1992, the attending Heads of State/Government asked me to present a position paper suggesting measures and ideas to increase the capacity of the UN to meet the new threats to peace.

Preventive Diplomacy

Once an elusive and undefined concept, preventive diplomacy is a vital field for practical action. New forms of preventive diplomacy have evolved in the course of the past years. Preventive diplomacy now incorporates efforts designed to prevent the occurrence of armed conflict, such as fact-finding, good offices, and goodwill missions, the dispatch of special envoys to tense areas, and efforts

An UNTAC soldier from Bangladesh (second from left) teaching Cambodians about water purification, Siem Reap, Cambodia, March 9, 1993.

to bring parties to a potential conflict to the negotiating table. Preventive diplomacy takes place continuously and can range from a brief telephone conversation to the movement of troops. Today, the variety of challenges faced by the UN has led to a more intensive and creative use of such familiar techniques. I find myself frequently engaged in preventive diplomacy. Because of the nature of this work, and the requirements of the parties, such diplomacy often takes place behind the scenes. When efforts fail, the results will be seen in public. When there is success, the story must often remain untold.

Peacekeeping

Peacekeeping is a UN invention. It was not envisaged by the founders of the Organization and is not mentioned in the Charter. Peacekeeping is, however, based on some fundamental principles such as the consent by all parties to a conflict, the neutrality of peacekeeping troops, and the use of force only in self-defense or to protect the mandate of the operation. The decision to deploy a peacekeeping operation rests within the Security Council. The Council determines the mandate and the size of the operation.

These fundamental principles of traditional peacekeeping have been challenged by recent developments on the ground in certain peacekeeping operations.

Today, peacekeepers perform a variety of complex tasks, such as protecting humanitarian aid convoys, supporting the supervision of elections, and monitoring human rights, in addition to their basic responsibility of keeping apart the warring parties. Keeping the peace is, therefore, only a step in the process of the peaceful resolution of conflicts. It should not be confused with conflict resolution. Putting a halt to armed hostilities is not in itself a solution to conflicts. Peacekeeping offers temporary respite from hostilities while the crisis is being resolved in the political, humanitarian, economic, and social spheres.

Peacekeeping operations today have a large civilian component, and attempt to address the underlying root causes of the conflict. The military, political, and humanitarian functions are integrated, and each component serves as a catalyst for the other. Just as political reconciliation is facilitated when people feel secure and have enough to eat, so security increases when political dialogue begins.

Peace Enforcement

UN peacekeepers have been sent to areas where there are frail cease-fire agreements, where governments do not exist or have limited effective authority, and where the consent and cooperation of the parties cannot be relied upon. All too frequently, the work of the peacekeepers is obstructed by well-armed irregular groups and warlords who defy both their national authorities, where these exist, and the international community.

Peace enforcement thus means using force when peaceful means fail. The Security Council defines what constitutes a threat to international peace and security and when to involve peace enforcement measures. In some recent cases such as in Somalia and Bosnia and Herzegovina, the Security Council has extended the original peacekeeping mandate to include certain peace enforcement tasks.

Humanitarian Assistance

Even in situations where peace operations are not underway, the UN provides large quantities of humanitarian relief. The UN is the major provider and coordinator of humanitarian assistance around the world. The number of displaced persons forced from their homes within their own countries is estimated to be more than 23 million today. The number of refugees fleeing across international borders is an additional 19 million people. In simple terms that means the UN has the responsibility to assist more than 40 million lives disrupted by war, repression, and natural disasters. And the number is increasing.

This places a huge demand on our resources and capacity to respond adequately. Increasingly, therefore, the UN has strengthened cooperation with other organizations. Today, non-governmental and intergovernmental organizations cooperate with the UN as implementing partners in many humanitarian emergencies.

Development

As the definition of security is expanding beyond questions of land and weapons to include economic well-being, environmental sustainability, and human rights protection, it has become

6. COOPERATION

especially clear that most of the root causes of conflicts and new threats to peace are underdevelopment and/or violations of human rights. Despite this undeniable relationship between development and international peace and security, many in the world community greet with indifference the shocking fact that the gap between the world's richest and poorest countries is widening. No task is greater or more urgent than to impress upon the economically leading nations that the world cannot ultimately prosper if the poorest continue to suffer and decline.

Furthermore, development is now understood to involve many dimensions: it is no longer merely a matter of economic policy and resources. Political, social, educational, and environmental factors must be part of an integrated approach to development. Without development on the widest scale, the young will be restless, resentful, and unproductive. People will understandably fight for resources, and creativity will be misdirected.

Eritreans celebrating the conclusion of the UN-supervised referendum, held from April 23-25, 1993.

World Conferences

Having long been the special voice of the world's poorest nations, and encompassing all dimensions of the development challenge in both mission and mandate, the UN continues to serve as a forum for discussion and awareness-raising, as a tool for cooperation and decision-making, and as a vehicle for promoting multilateral action on development issues.

Another important area of work for the UN has been the organization of a series of landmark global conferences. Over the last decades, the UN has organized such conferences on topics ranging from the environment to human rights, social development, population, and the situation of women. It is perhaps difficult to fully measure the gains of these global conferences, but I will nevertheless offer some examples of their possible long- and short-term significance.

First of all, these conferences place global issues on the agenda of member states. They increase the pressure on them to give priority in their domestic policy to spending more on education and health facilities for their citizens and less on the military.

Second, international conferences usually lead to the adoption of conventions or plans of action. Both states that are parties to these agreements and states that remain outside of them find it increasingly difficult to justify actions that go against these agreements, particularly to their own citizens.

Third, major global conferences are not merely meetings. They provide a focal point for consensus-building and action. They are also occasions that can educate us all.

Rio

The UN Conference on Environment and Development, held in Rio de Janeiro from 3 to 14 June 1992, challenged governments to adopt long-term policies on matters of the environment and sustainable development that affect human well-being and survival. It tested the willingness of nations to cooperate in developing global strategies for the sustainable use of resources. In the aftermath of the Rio Conference, it has become clear that Agenda 21 adopted at the Conference is the first international agreement expressing a global consensus and a political commitment at the highest levels to action on population, environment, and economic advance, encompassed in a program of sustainable development. The UN and its member states must work toward the full implementation of Agenda 21.

Vienna

The World Conference on Human Rights, which was held in Vienna from 14 to 25 June 1993, was a turning point in UN activities for the promotion and protection of human rights. The Vienna Conference was worldwide, in terms both of the subjects deal with and of participation. Long and careful exchanges of views revealed considerable common ground among the different participants. The Conference was therefore able to adopt, by consensus, a declaration and program of action for human rights of historic proportions, but of course differences of opinion were also candidly stated.

The Vienna Conference reaffirmed the universality of fundamental human rights and the principle that the human person is the central subject and the principal beneficiary of human rights. The Conference recognized the right to development as a human right, emphasized the mutually reinforcing interrelationship between democracy, development, and respect for human rights, and stressed the need to assist developing countries in their democratization process. The Conference also recognized the fundamental contribution from non-governmental organizations in the protection of human rights and stressed education as a crucial element in building future respect for human rights.

In the aftermath of the Vienna Conference, member states in the General Assembly decided to create a post of UN High Commissioner for Human Rights. Under the direction and authority of the Secretary-General, the new High Commissioner will promote and protect the effective enjoyment by all of all civil, cultural, economic, political, and social rights. These efforts on an international level will be enhanced and strengthened by local efforts in all countries to include human rights in teaching programs, both in schools and in non-school programs. These programs will help foster a greater understanding of human rights and the fundamental connections between human rights and peace, development, and democracy, thus laying the groundwork for future respect for human rights.

Cairo

The International Conference on Population and Development was held in Cairo, Egypt, in September 1994. Its goal was to foresee a new international consensus that places population concerns at the center of all development activities. Global population growth has reached almost 100 million new people a year, placing a considerable social and economic burden on most developing countries. An envisioned twenty-year plan of action will address issues of rapid population growth, international migration, and urban expansion in the context of fostering human-centered, environmentally sustainable development. A commitment by developing countries to reduce population growth must of course be coupled with a commitment by developed countries to reduce the strain of consumption patterns on the global environment.

Copenhagen

The World Summit for Social Development to be held in Copenhagen, Denmark, from 6-12 March 1995 will bring together world leaders in an effort to put social issues at the center of the agenda of national governments and international organizations, and identify ways of promoting the economic and social advancement of all peoples. The Summit will consider three themes: enhancement of social integration, alleviation and reduction of poverty, and expansion of productive employment. It is expected to adopt a Declaration and a number of key documents on social development.

Beijing

A broad array of issues related to the role of women in society will be the focus of the Fourth World Conference on Women, to be convened in Beijing in September 1995. The Conference will carry the spirit of the 1976-1985 UN Decade for Women into the next century and make proposals to overcome age-old barriers of gender discrimination. Women's rights, the impact of structural adjustment on women, and strategies to get more women into decision-making positions are among the topics for discussion.

Criticism of the United Nations

The events since the end of the Cold War impress upon us the need for a new realism. The UN, by undertaking a range of problems as wide as the globe itself, must be expected to achieve successes but also to experience failures. The failures cannot be put to one side; they require continuing commitment. And successes cannot be regarded as permanent; every positive outcome is likely to be a starting point for further effort.

International action that emerges from debate and decision in the General Assembly, the Security Council, and the other organs of the UN carries with it the full authority of the world community. The UN is now understood to be humanity's best hope in the pursuit of peace, development, and human rights.

Dedicated to the integrity of each individual, drawing legitimacy from all peoples, expressing the consensus of states, the UN Organization embodies, through its universality and dedication to life's basic tasks, a great potential for international peace and development. In a spirit of realism and new possibility, a synthesis of heretofore opposing concepts is conceivable: the UN as the instrument of the body of member states and the UN as more than the sum of its parts.

Let me end by inviting you to celebrate the fiftieth anniversary of the UN in 1995. History has bequeathed to us an Organization that is a proven instrument of international cooperation. I regard the anniversary as a milestone to be marked not only by celebration but also by programs of serious reflection, education, and communication. It coincides with a turning point in history, a time when the institutions of international relations are being re-thought and re-considered. The Fiftieth Anniversary will therefore be a time not only for reflection on what has been achieved, and for learning from the lessons of the past, but also for charting a course for the next century as the UN continues in its efforts to realize peace, justice, equality, and development as the highest aspirations of the world's peoples.

I believe that one of the fundamental changes in the relationship between states after the Cold War has been their increased capacity to engage in meaningful dialogue and to discuss the real issues regardless of ideological adherence. The Security Council Summit meeting convened in January 1992 is an example. The Summit gathered Heads of State who pledged their renewed commitment to the UN Charter and the Bill of Human Rights. I was asked to formulate an Agenda for Peace suggesting measures and ideas to increase the capacity of the UN to meet the new threats to peace.

Polio conquered in Western Hemisphere

Five-year-old Peruvian boy confirmed as last victim.

Mim Neal

• *Mim Neal is the manager of Rotary's Media Relations Section.*

It was only three years ago, in August 1991, when two-year-old Luis Fermín Tenorio of Pichanaqui, Junín, Peru, woke up with what appeared to be a summer cold. Twenty-four hours later, the boy's legs were paralyzed. He was taken to the capital city of Lima where a doctor pronounced the chilling diagnosis: polio.

At the time, the boy's case was notable only because polio was thought to be on the brink of eradication in the Western Hemisphere. Now, the case is historic: Luis, now five years old, was recently confirmed as the region's last polio victim.

Rotarians around the world can rejoice in an unprecedented announcement made on 29 September at Pan American Health Organization (PAHO) headquarters in Washington, D.C.: "Based on the impressive evidence presented, the International Commission concludes that wild polio virus transmission has been interrupted in the Americas."

It was a proud moment for Rotarians worldwide, who have raised U.S. $247 million to eradicate polio globally. In Latin America alone, Rotarians have contributed $40 million through PolioPlus grants—not just for vaccine, but also for surveillance and social mobilization. Rotarians have been instrumental in providing a massive volunteer force unprecedented in public-health history. Despite limited resources, political upheaval, and even war, Rotarians in the Americas have persevered—and won—in the fight against polio.

A distinguished delegation represented Rotary at the historic event at PAHO headquarters—R.I. President Bill Huntley and his wife, Audrey; Rotary Foundation Trustee Chairman and Past R.I. President Hugh Archer; 1990-91 R.I. President Paulo Costa and wife, Rita; and 1984-85 R.I. President Dr. Carlos Canseco.

Dr. Frederick C. Robbins, chairman of the International Commission for the Certification of Poliomyelitis Eradication, made the milestone announcement. Although he shared the 1954 Nobel Prize in Medicine for isolating the polio virus, he had not—until recently—believed it possible to eradicate the disease.

At the meeting, Dr. Robbins cited Rotary as one of the early leaders in supporting the fight against polio, underscoring the crucial role of nongovernmental organizations in the effort. "We have another illustration . . . namely Rotary International, which has raised money and contributed in many ways with people and assistance to this program. I think they deserve special commendation."

President Bill Huntley described PolioPlus as "the first corporate action the association has ever undertaken. Beginning in many cases as amateurs, we learned that we, 1.2 million men and women, were able to take on a global perspective and to work with others on this tremendous project. How much we have learned! We now know all about surveillance. We talk about social mobilization. And we talk about advocacy. But we not only talk about them; we are *doing* them at this very moment in many places in the world."

For many journalists at the meeting, the event was just another assignment. But to the members of the medical community, Rotary, and the other organizations present, the happy news was the climax of a long and difficult struggle. If they closed their eyes, they could see the haunting image of a small boy—Luis Fermín Tenorio—in a red shirt limping down a dusty road in a remote Peruvian village.

It may never be possible to acknowledge all the heroes of this superlative effort. A galaxy of organizations and governments provided both the funds and official endorsements needed for the effort's success in the region. International public-health experts, led by PAHO's Dr. Carlyle Guerra de Macedo and Dr. Ciro de Quadros, designed the strategies. Legions of underpaid public-health workers, inspired by the dream of polio eradication, persevered in their task, assisted by a gentle army of volunteers (including thousands of Rotarians from northern Mexico to the southern toe of Argentina).

Organizations key to the regional success include PAHO, UNICEF, the U.S. Agency for International Development, the Inter-American Development Bank, U.S. Centers for Disease Control and Prevention, and the Canadian Public Health Association. Through the region's innovative Interagency Coordinating Committee (ICC), these groups collaborated with national health authorities to supplement the massive government resources committed to immunization.

It was in May 1985—nearly a decade ago—that PAHO announced its Latin American initiative to wipe out polio. Dr. Carlos Canseco of Mexico, then Rotary International president, was invited to join the effort because the organization pledged to "help eliminate polio" globally. Rotary had already started polio immunization efforts in 1981 in Latin America, with projects in Haiti and Bolivia. By 1985, The Rotary Foundation of R.I. had approved more than $1.9 million for additional polio projects in Belize, Costa Rica, El Salvador, Honduras, Guatemala, Panama, and St. Lucia.

E arly on, there was considerable skepticism about the value of a community service organization such as Rotary assisting medical professionals in the public-health field. Past President Canseco remembers the tentative welcome Rotary received when the organization first announced its PolioPlus Program after being granted consultative status by the World Health Organization [WHO]. He recalls:

"They granted us a two-year period as a member of WHO, with full rights, but we were, I would say, on probation. To prove that we could really help, we needed some examples. We decided to go to Paraguay, a small country—not more than 600,000 children—and establish national immunization days. The result was tremendous. In one year, polio dropped from as many as 100 cases to practically zero. We

continued in that country for five years and now it's free of polio.

"But they [the international health community] were not convinced, so I proposed to go to Mexico, with more than 15 million children under five years of age. As president of Rotary International, I went to see the [national] president and he supported the idea. It took us about a year to prepare the national days of immunization in Mexico, but at the end of January 1986, 13 million children were immunized in one day. More than half a million volunteers participated in this endeavor . . . [it] ended with Mexico's last case of polio in October 1990."

Paraguay and Mexico became prototypes for the region. In one year—from 1986 to 1987—Rotary transformed its dream into an operational program. As the organization's fundraising campaign surged toward its goal of $120 million, Rotary created and trained an International PolioPlus Task Force. The five members worked with professional staff to create club and national immunization manuals to guide and inspire Rotarians around the world.

Rotary International acted out of a conviction that community volunteers—if properly trained, supported, and utilized—can measurably increase immunization coverage and strengthen national Expanded Programs on Immunization.

Peru's Rotarians ably proved this point. During three national immunization days (NIDs) in 1986, more than 2,000 of the country's 2,300 Rotarians helped vaccinate children, publicize immunization days, provide transportation and meals for vaccinators, and they contributed an estimated $440,000 in funds and in-kind donations.

R.I. Director Gustavo Gross, chairman of Peru's PolioPlus Committee since 1986, spearheaded efforts to fight polio despite guerrilla warfare and a cholera epidemic. His leadership resulted in an effective Rotary support network for public health officials.

"PolioPlus has been in my heart since I was a Rotary club president. I have met Luis Fermín [the last polio victim] and held him in my arms," he says.

This type of support had an enormous impact. In May 1988, the World Health Assembly, aware of the progress in Latin America and of Rotary's commitment, adopted a resolution to eradicate polio by the year 2000. Dr. Halfdan Mahler, director general of WHO, sent a video message to the R.I. Convention in Philadelphia, where the organization celebrated not only reaching its original fundraising goal of $120 million—but also surpassing it by more than $100 million.

Dr. Mahler stated, "As business and professional leaders you have helped to change attitudes toward immunization. And you have given Ministries of Health needed advice or stimulation in making their programs more effective."

Rotary's immunization effort has taken many forms, depending on the country. In the last 10 years, Latin American Rotarians have been at the forefront of a massive publicity blitz, printing at least one million posters, pamphlets, street banners, calendars, stickers, caps, and even tote bags promoting immunization. They have also provided basic supplies, such as thermoses, ice boxes, and ice for transporting the vaccine.

Rotarians have also been successful in bringing their management and negotiating skills to the PolioPlus effort. For example:

• In 1987, Bolivian Rotarians in La Paz convinced private clinics to conduct immunizations in coordination with the country's Ministry of Health. Prior to this development, there was little teamwork between the public and private health sectors.

• Following a disappointing turnout for Guatemala's 1988 NIDs, Rotarians refused to request an additional PolioPlus grant until the Ministry of Health completed its immunization plans and budgets for each of the country's departments. Subsequently, each Guatemalan Rotary club "adopted" a department, providing both support and monitoring.

• During a February 1990 containment immunization in Ecuador, a Rotary club persuaded local health workers to forego a threatened strike.

6. COOPERATION

As a non-governmental organization, Rotary has been especially effective in implementing cross-border immunization efforts in Colombia/Venezuela, and Ecuador/Peru, and in delivering vaccine during the civil disorders in El Salvador, Nicaragua, and Peru. In fact, Rotarians in Peru were often the only means of reaching children in wartorn areas. In many instances, they were allowed to cross combat zones when government health officials were not.

As polio cases disappear, Rotarians are refocusing their efforts on surveillance, again utilizing private sector innovation. For example, Rotary clubs in Ecuador are offering $1,000 rewards, through a manufacturer's national ad campaign, for finding and reporting cases that are later confirmed to be polio.

Brazilian Rotarians are using surveys to enlist more than 12,000 pediatricians and neurologists in reporting cases of acute flaccid paralysis. With UNICEF, Bolivian Rotarians have launched media campaigns to encourage the reporting of possible polio cases.

Even with diminishing grant funds, Latin American Rotarians continue their support of immunization efforts and public education. They are also investigating the possibility of other private sector resources to help sustain the momentum until polio is eradicated globally.

As the international health community learned in the case of The Netherlands, which suffered a polio outbreak in 1992-93, polio can be reintroduced even in polio-free countries if immunization levels are not sustained.

In order to keep polio from being reintroduced in the Western Hemisphere, Rotarians must stay vigilant. As President Bill Huntley stated at the PAHO meeting on 29 September:

"As long as there is one case of polio caused by the wild virus, then we are all at risk. We look forward in the hope that by the year 2000 we can have another meeting such as this [one]. Only then can we say we have achieved the goal. Only then will the medical authorities of the world be able to proclaim that, for the second time in history, a disease has been eradicated."

Only then will the image of a tiny boy in a red shirt, limping down a dusty road, be a distant memory.

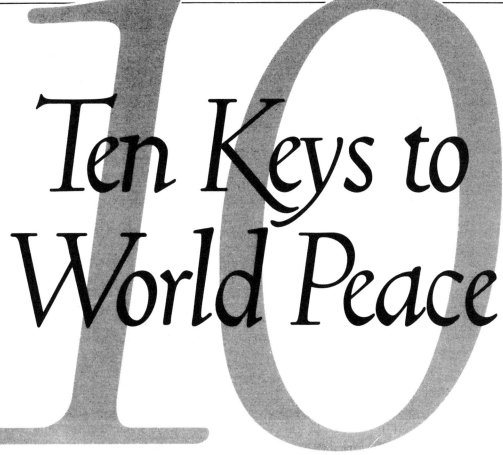

Ten Keys to World Peace

A "Club of Democracies" can maintain peace in a world torn by cultural diversity.
A noted diplomat and scholar presents guidelines for making it happen.

Harlan Cleveland

Harlan Cleveland, president of the World Academy of Art and Science, is a former U.S. assistant secretary of state and ambassador to NATO. He is the author of Birth of a New World: An Open Moment for International Leadership, *which is available from the Futurist Bookstore. His address is 1235 Yale Place, #802, Minneapolis, Minnesota 55403. Telephone 612/339-3589; fax 612/339-6230; e-mail address cleve004@maroon.tc.umn.edu.*

The author wishes to acknowledge that this article is based on work done with Lincoln P. Bloomfield for the "Reinventing International Governance" project, which resulted in the book Birth of a New World.

In a talk to the World Future Society in 1991, I voiced my worries about the global collision of cultural diversity—which President John F. Kennedy pledged to make the world safe for—with two other values on which the twenty-first century will also have to be built.

One of these collisions is clearly the clash of group rights, asserted by ambitious cultural and ethnic communities, with the contrasting ideology of individual and inalienable human rights—the idea that a person has rights not because he or she belongs to a nation, religion, gender, ethnic category, economic class, or even family, but by virtue of having been born into the human race.

The other collision with cultural diversity comes from the outward push of modern science and technology, which makes it possible, and therefore necessary, to think of the world as one—as a global market for goods, services, and money, as a biosphere to be monitored and protected, and as a community in which nuclear war might be outlawed and human hunger eliminated.

The community gives each of us part of our valued identities; it is an important component of reality. But so, too, is the value of each person as an individual, and so, too, is the need to shape more-inclusive communities and institutions that are made possible by modern knowledge.

So, while celebrating cultural diversity and the political change it's bringing about on four continents, we need to think hard about reconciling it with both individual human rights *and* global human opportunities. That's the triple dilemma—the trilemma—of the 1990s. How do we formulate the principles and fashion the institutions that will reconcile with each other these lively ambitions in the new world disorder?

A Third Try for Peaceful Change

There are many new opportunities for international leadership in this

6. COOPERATION

UNITED NATIONS

The United Nations will be an important force for peace in the future, but not the only one. Many nongovernmental organizations and various private corporations will also contribute toward the creation of a truly consultative world leadership.

time of world disorder. In the mid-1980s, 31 of my colleagues from 24 countries began doing what we called "postwar planning without having the war first."

Because there had already been two tries at world order in this century, our work together became a first draft of "the third try." But the aim of the third try cannot be "world order." That phrase has too often meant the defense of the status quo by those who were, temporarily, the most powerful. The object of this new try must be to ensure peaceful change in a world made safe for diversity. The future always has to be grafted onto the past. So for a third try, the United Nations Charter is the obvious starting point.

Years ago, a diplomat assigned to U.N. headquarters in New York gave me an important clue. "There's nothing wrong with the first five pages of the Charter," he said. "It's those following 50 pages that get in the way."

It is true that the elaborate procedural architecture of the United Na-

tions as an organization has often obstructed the pursuit of the common purposes set forth in the first few policy paragraphs. What's interesting and suggestive for the future is that, during the past half century, the agencies and processes that have worked pretty well in practice are those that remained loyal to the Charter's purposes and principles, but played fast and loose with its procedures.

For example, the United Nations' peacekeeping role (stepping in between belligerents) is not spelled out in the Charter's 50 pages of procedure. Yet, it has won a Nobel Peace Prize and is clearly consonant with the Charter's purposes to ensure, as the Preamble says, "that armed forces shall not be used, save in the common interest."

As another example, the Charter describes voting procedures but does not require voting. Most of the successful actions taken by agencies of the United Nations have been agreed on by consensus. When votes have been taken, it is mostly to confirm what has already been agreed on by consensus, or to record what hasn't yet been fully agreed upon—as in the Law of the Sea Treaty.

A third example is that the Charter's procedures describe an organization of governments and sees the parties to a dispute as being only governments. Not until the Charter drafters got to Article 71 did it occur to them that nongovernmental organizations might need to be consulted, and then only on matters of economic and social relevance. Even the chap-

TOYOTA MOTOR MANUFACTURING

Japanese and American work together at a Toyota plant. The global marketplace forces people to see the world as one in spite of cultural diversity.

ter on the secretary-general assumes that international staff work would be done only by U.N. employees.

Yet, the history of the last half century is replete with examples of nongovernmental organizations taking the lead in carrying out international policies, with the United Nations' official members catching up late, if at all.

Most of the systematic training for U.N. peacekeeping has been done by the nongovernmental International Peace Academy. Much of the mediation and conciliation efforts undertaken by the secretary-general have been done by people loaned to him or engaged by him outside the "international civil service," or even sometimes by volunteers with no formal U.N. affiliation. And most of the useful fact-finding and publishing on violations of human rights guaranteed by the Charter have been done by such nongovernmental gadflies as Amnesty International.

So strengthening the United Nations for the years ahead means taking its purposes and principles very seriously, but building fresh institutions within the framework of the Charter that reflect the probable real-

ities of the future. Viewed this way, the United Nations is needed more than ever, but new workways must be developed to bypass not the Charter's stated purposes but its outdated processes.

Uncentralizing Global Power

A clear distinction should be made between the two tiers of international cooperation: (1) the more centralized public-policy decisions with universal participation, where debate is encouraged and agreement reached on standards, norms, goals, and codes of ethics, and (2) the more operational, *uncentralized* processes, where many different enterprises and authorities "do their own thing," acting within the framework of the agreed standards and norms. In some cases, especially in the world economy, this operational level will be a market system

This distinction between the collective establishment of standards and the dispersed bargaining, sharing, and clearing is not well described by the much misused word "decentralization." In a decentralized system, the control is still in a

central office. It's the center that decides how partial controls will be exercised by subordinate authorities and keeps track of them through a central accounting system. This is why I use the word "uncentralized" for a system in which "many flowers" are encouraged to bloom, "many points of light" stimulated to shine. Learning works from the bottom up.

In such a two-tier system, setting norms and standards is everyone's business. That is not unrealistic. In practice, the world community has already made quite a lot of global policy.

Here are 10 guidelines for managing peace in a pluralistic world:

1. No nation, region, race, or creed is going to be in general charge.

2. Nations and their citizens, without homogenizing their cultural identities, can and will pool their collective learnings in win–win systems for shared purposes.

3. For much of what needs to be done, people can agree on next steps to be taken together without having to agree on *why* they are agreeing.

4. Some common norms are already widely accepted:

• Territorial integrity. Iraq's 1990 exception provoked a worldwide coalition in defense of this principle.

• The inviolability of diplomatic missions. The violations are dramatic because they are rare.

• The nonuse of nuclear, chemical, and biological weapons.

• The immunity of civilian aircraft and ships. A few brutal attacks and tragic accidents have served to strengthen norms against hijacking or firing on innocent craft.

• An international obligation to help refugees.

• The inadmissibility of colonial rule.

• The unacceptability of officially sanctioned racial discrimination.

• The undeniable equality of women.

• And the full menu of human rights described in the Universal Declaration of 1948, reinforced in the Helsinki Final Act of 1975.

5. In a third try, most of the world's people, and even their governments, might now agree on some even more far-reaching norms:

Collegial World Leadership

Creating a network of major nations could help the world solve international problems more effectively.

Raymond D. Gastil

Raymond D. Gastil is an independent consultant and policy analyst and is the director of studies for The Next Century Initiative. He is the author of numerous articles and books, including Progress: Critical Thinking about Historical Change, *which is available from the Futurist Bookstore. His address is 8 Frontier Road, Cos Cob, Connecticut 06807. Telephone 203/869-0872.*

The nations of the world need a more orderly and efficient means to address international problems. At the same time, the United States needs a more structured means of fulfilling its role of leadership—one that will serve both national and universal interests. If structured carefully, a "concert of major states" might serve both needs.

This *concert* would include states with a legitimate claim to a major international role. It should represent the majority of the world's peoples, military forces, and economic products and thus should at least include the United States, the United Kingdom, France, Germany, Italy, Russia, Japan, Brazil, and India.

Although the political systems in several of these countries remain shaky, all are functioning democracies. India and Brazil are on the list because they are the largest democracies in the developing world in terms of population, economic product, and geographical size. Russia must also be included as a leading member, unless it regresses decisively toward its repressive past.

China, however, should be left out of this concert until there is evidence that its leadership has accepted the understanding of human rights and democracy that is now regarded as the norm for the emerging world civilization. Since a principal goal of the concert would be to spread respect for modern human rights, it would be impossible to make China a "full member" of the concert in the near future due to its current human-rights violations. If respect for human rights were not maintained as a membership requirement, shaky democracies such as Russia or Brazil would feel they could return to authoritarianism without losing their position on the "management team."

The concert would, nevertheless, seek China's cooperation on many issues, for doing so will be in everyone's interest. Eventually, because younger Chinese are more in tune with the outside world and its standards, the next generation of leaders will change the way the country is ruled. China will then take its rightful place in the concert.

The concert would develop consultative relationships with the smaller countries of the world. These relationships would depend on how committed these countries are to democracy, human rights, and peace and on how directly involved they are in the issues at hand.

The concert of powers should not be regarded as replacing or supplanting other relationships among states, such as the European Union, the United Nations, the Organization for Economic Cooperation and Development, the General Agreement of Tariffs and Trade, and the World Bank. The concert should be open to change and expansion as new powers arise. For example, the European Union may gradually replace major countries such as France or Italy as members of the concert.

The concert should be structured this way for several reasons. First, the world needs a relatively small and manageable group of leaders who can effectively work together on major issues. Second, this group needs to be constituted so that it works against deepening the cleavages between East and West, North and South, rich and poor. Third, in order to preserve and extend the recent gains in democracy and world peace, the concert must institutionalize into "our world" those countries traditionally considered "outside." As these countries gradually gain power, the concert will expect of them more responsible and consistent engagement with world issues.

It is likely that Japan, Germany, Russia, India, and Brazil will soon emerge as leaders for regional groups of nations with special interests or natural geographical ties. It is also likely that these regional interests will often conflict with U.S. interests. But the experience that these five countries have in working with the United States and other powers on common world problems will enable them to resolve future conflicts with an increased awareness of mutual interests. India and Brazil, as models of democratic governance and performance in the developing world, could play a special role in the concert of major states, leading the movement toward democracy and respect for human rights in smaller countries.

The concert of major states will redefine what it means to be a world leader. Nations seeking acceptance into this informal, collegial club will realize the need for adherence to, or at least movement toward, universal democratic norms. It is hoped that association with the concert will strengthen and stabilize democracy in *all* member countries, but particularly in Russia and its neighboring states.

- A third World War is wholly impermissible.
- Nuclear weapons are militarily irrelevant—and should be made irrelevant to political conflict.
- Local conflicts should be insulated whenever possible from outside involvement to prevent any kind of escalation.

The United States can move toward this concert on a variety of diplomatic fronts. On one level, the United States should regard itself as the leader of a small network of responsible powers, dedicated to the upholding of human rights. As the United States relies more and more on such a network, consultations with other countries to resolve international problems should become more customary than in the past.

Developing the concert as described here would require little deviation from current U.S. foreign policy. That is one of its distinct advantages. Some of its purposes already have been achieved by informal groupings such as the Group of Seven and the Trilateral Commission.

The concert, unfortunately, may not always succeed. Tragedies such as Bosnia may still occur while the world wrings its hands. But, as the networking mechanism develops, the concert should improve the chance that the world will react effectively to the crises of the next century.

In the meantime, nations can work toward this collegial world leadership by developing the flexibility to deal with issues such as maintaining peace among peoples, strengthening democracy, expanding the commitment to human rights, improving social and economic conditions, enhancing the cultural and spiritual well-being of peoples, eliminating general threats to humanity (such as nuclear weapons), and improving the global environment.

If the nations of the world decide to pursue these steps, they will lay the basis for a future where greater independence and interdependence reign.

- Growth with fairness, not "equilibrium" or "balance," is the purpose of economic policy.
- The lives of innocent bystanders should not be used as political bludgeons.
- The quality of human life worldwide must be protected from catastrophic degradation of the atmosphere and the biosphere.
- And this above all: No child in the world should go to bed hungry.

6. A review of what works best in the new world disorder drives us to belated recognition of the crucial role played by major nongovernments. These include corporations whose decisions affect people's lives and fortunes, professional associations whose expertise educates and informs, religious movements with their unique capacities for love or hate, the distinctively international scientific community, and advocacy groups that mobilize people for behavioral change.

7. Some global issues require actions by millions of individuals, families, and small groups. There is an increasingly important role for the communications media in spreading the word and developing wide consensus as a basis for political cooperation.

8. When governments have to work together to make something different happen, they increasingly decide from the outset to act by consensus. In the many cultures accustomed to practicing decision making by "consensus," that word does not mean "unanimous consent." It means something more like *the acquiescence of those who care* about a particular decision, *supported by the apathy of those who don't.*

9. Almost nothing in world affairs needs to involve everyone. What's needed to handle each problem is a community of the concerned, what my MIT. colleague Lincoln Bloomfield was the first to call a "coalition of the willing." Those who can and will act have to take whatever action is to be taken. If a collective task is to be accomplished, it cannot be subject to acquiescence by the least relevant or least cooperative member of the world community— nor by the most apathetic one.

10. But in matters affecting the globe we all share, those who do act have an inescapable obligation to explain to the rest of the world what they are doing together and why. So we also need to open consultative forums where stakeholders not able or willing to act can nevertheless be heard.

The Club of Democracies

Who is both able and willing to work hard in this global workshop?

Troops dispose of munitions: Explosives experts from the U.S. Marine Corps prepare to detonate captured shells in a field near the Turkish-Iraqi border. Iraq's violation of Kuwait's territorial integrity led to a coalition of forces to defend Kuwait.

U.S. NAVY / JOC MARJIE J. SHAW

U.S. NAVY / JOC MARJIE J. SHAW

Providing aid to refugees: A U.S. Marine fills water jugs to give to Kurdish refugees fleeing from northern Iraq. The obligation to assist refugees, as well as supporting human rights in general, is widely accepted by nations everywhere.

Three of the leading clusters of advanced information societies are already closely associated as the nucleus of an emerging, open-ended "club of democracies": The United States and Canada, the European Union, and Japan. The parts of Europe outside the European Union and a good many of the larger or more successful developing countries will qualify as influential states and will join the club whether the more established democracies like it or not.

This expanding fellowship, acting in shifting patterns of cooperation and competition, will decide over the next generation what the formal organs of the United Nations will be empowered to do. They will decide what to do together within the U.N. Charter, but outside its procedures. They will decide how stability and fairness are to be reconciled in peacekeeping and peacemaking, economic growth and social development, and in using and protecting the global commons. In sum, this club of democracies will decide whether and how to work together worldwide for what the U.N. Charter called "better standards of life in larger freedom."

The politics of this club of democracies will be consultative. Writing about American local communities, public philosopher John Gardner described consultative politics in world affairs: "The play of conflicting interests in a framework of shared purposes is the drama of a free society. It is a robust exercise and a noisy one, not for the fainthearted or the tidyminded. . . . Wholeness incorporating diversity is the transcendental goal of our time."

Despite all their domestic troubles, an open-ended club of democracies

---

"Those who do act have an inescapable obligation to explain to the rest of the world what they are doing together and why."

is already forming. It is a consultative group of those willing and able to act together—in different guises, with differing leadership for different problems—on issues requiring an unusual degree of international cooperation to get anything done.

The club of democracies was at the core of the resistance to Iraqi aggression in the Persian Gulf. Its economic core is visible, if anemic, in the periodic summits of the "Group of Seven" on trade and money issues. It is the guts of U.N. peacekeeping, the determined majority in the U.N. Security Council, the main source of support for the World Bank and the International Monetary Fund, the moving force behind such disparate events as the treaties to protect the global ozone shield and the 1990 "children's summit."

The club of democracies is not a new organization, complete with secretariat and a permanent headquarters somewhere. It is a confederation of the concerned, a center of initiative, a habit of consultation. It coordinates government policies where governments are the main actors. And it will increasingly have to bring nongovernments into consultation where they, too, are major actors—as they obviously are on the world economy, international development, and the global environment.

If you bring together the nations that are now governed by consent and add those that are trying in their fashion to get that way, you have the bulk of the world's economic output, communication lines, science and technology, financial resources, and military power. Those who have a stake in a thoroughly democratic world have the resources, if they work together, to make change peaceful and prosperous, and thereby help democracy itself to flourish in its own diverse patterns.

Hunting for Africa's Wildlife Poachers

*Help for efforts in Tanzania is international, while pragmatism still allows
a lucrative game business*

W. Sean Roberts

Special to The Christian Science Monitor

DAR ES SALAAM, TANZANIA
For three hours under a glaring African sun, the anti-poaching patrol struggled through the dense Tanzania woodland, at times waist deep in flooded thickets, often forced to steer clear of the volatile Cape buffalo, and constantly at odds with the tsetse fly. Suddenly one scout gave a whistle, calling the six other men and one woman.

Pressed into a muddy highway of buffalo tracks were several sets of human footprints and a blood trail—tell-tale signs of poachers pursuing a wounded animal. After another 20 minutes, the game scouts were directly below a cloud of vultures and had run head on into a band of eight villagers hauling out their kill. The scouts gave chase, firing wildly over the poachers' heads as the melee stretched deeper into the bush.

Emerging without a single *jangili* (Swahili for poacher), these scouts patrolling Tanzania's sprawling 33,000 square-mile Selous Game Reserve will have ample opportunity to set the score straight in the days and weeks to come. With an estimated 700,000 animals illegally hunted in Tanzania per year, they have their hands full—but not their pockets.

As the prime protector of Tanzania's high-profile animals, such as the wild dog, cheetah, African elephant, and black rhinoceros, all of which have been drastically reduced in numbers during the last decade, a game scout averages about 39 cents a day or $12 per month—

not enough to make ends meet even in one of the world's least developed countries.

As low on morale as they are on funds, game scouts are often forced to poach wildlife to supplement their diets or to sell to villagers for cash. Many lack the motivation to apprehend poachers who may be relatives or friends. Logistical support is another problem, almost nonexistent in some cases. And those who persist in carrying out their duties despite the odds may find themselves fleeing from the very criminals they were hired to apprehend. Game-scout weaponry is archaic at best, while poachers may sport modern automatic weapons.

Riding to the scout's rescue, however, are a plethora of organizations intent on helping Tanzania preserve its natural environment. The Frankfurt Zoological Society, World Wildlife Fund for Nature, Friends of Conservation, and the Deutshe Gesellschaft für Technische Zusammenarbeit (GTZ), the German government's official aid organization, to name a few, have contributed to the cause.

POPULATION GROWTH
A THREAT

As a cofounder and the principal benefactor of the Selous Conservation Programme (SCP), GTZ has contributed well over $3 million during a five-year effort to insure the integrity of Africa's largest protected habitat.

One of the main tasks of the SCP has been to provide scouts with logistical support.

"The game scout is basically the pillar on whom the whole system in the bush rests," says Dr. Rolf Baldus, project coordinator for the SCP. "You have to get involved with management at higher levels, policy dialogue with the government, ecological monitoring and all that. But for me the first person to look at is always the game scout."

The battle to save Tanzania's ecosystems extends well beyond the scouts or even their government's capabilities. After 30 years of Marxism, which has kept the country's economy in the same primeval state as its natural habitats, poaching, runaway population growth, and development now threaten such showcase lands as the Serengeti, Kilimanjaro and Ngorongoro Crater wilderness areas with modern environmental problems.

As a result of its poor economic showing, Tanzania has sought to guarantee the sanctity of its protected areas by relying on international assistance in the form of aid, expertise, and mandates, as well as using the ability of wildlife to "pay for itself" through a lucrative tourist and sport hunting market.

One measure that continues to be of great assistance to the Tanzanian wildlife authorities in preserving the elephant is the 1990 international ban on ivory. By shutting down markets for ivory, the ban put an abrupt end to the blitzkrieg of poaching that slashed the African elephant population from 1.3 million to just over 600,000 animals during the 1980s alone.

Some southern African countries are currently crying out for a lifting of the ban, citing ivory as an important source of revenue. They claim that elephant herds have grown so large that they threaten the balance of the ecosystems. But if the ban were to go down, so too would the elephant, at least in Tanzania.

Edward Kishe, principal park warden in charge of law enforcement for Tanzania's national parks, doubts that his country could manage a responsible harvesting of ivory.

"I don't advocate that at all," Mr. Kishe says of a lifting of the ban. "We don't have the means to properly oversee this. Immediately if we started this ivory trade again, some people would poach and we could not stop all of them," he adds.

Agreeing with Kishe on the importance of the ivory ban is the Frankfurt Zoological Society's Representative for East Africa, Marjus Borner.

"I was against the ban on ivory in the beginning," Dr. Borner says, "because it didn't really make sense to me then. But looking at the results it has made a [great] difference. . . . I've been counting elephants here for the last 15 years and everywhere I went it was always down, down, down. It is in the last two or three years that there has been the same amount [of elephants] and at least in the Serengeti we have the first increase of any kind of elephant population anywhere."

HUNTING BRINGS INCOME

Another effective tactic that has greatly reduced poaching on otherwise unprotected lands, brought in much needed hard currency to conservation efforts, and is changing the way locals view wildlife is Tanzania's hunting enterprises.

Although the European and North American public, who have funded so much of the conservation effort in Tanzania today, may wince at the thought of the great white hunter on the savannas of the dark continent, Africa is a place that demands pragmatism.

Operating on "blocks" of land allotted to them by the government, professional hunting companies routinely and aggressively patrol their areas for poachers. Villages neighboring hunting blocks have been shown the value of preserving wildlife by companies donating meat or funding village projects, such as building schoolrooms or drilling wells in return for their support.

And with a 10-day safari averaging around $15,000 per client, hunting is a big business that few conservationists in Tanzania want to see nullified as long as

it continues to act as a benefit instead of a plague. It provides employment for local villagers and brings in much needed currency through licensing and other fees, which are pumped back into conservation.

"I do not hunt and I don't understand why people do," Borner says. "But you can't keep areas which are 10,000 square kilometers larger than Switzerland without any revenue coming out of them. Tanzania can't afford it. There are some protected areas that are completely dependent on hunting for revenue, and that is why they are still there. I think [hunting] is a very important contribution to conservation in this country."

But Tanzania's soaring population has long gone unaddressed by its government or aid organizations and may soon prove to be the most dire hazard to its natural habitats. With some villages near parks and reserves growing 10 percent a year, competition with wildlife has increased. And in a country that has traditionally viewed a large population as a benefit to its labor force, family planning has been slow in coming.

Although conservation organizations realize the threat Tanzania's population boom poses to wildlife, they have done very little in the way of addressing the problem.

Values and Visions

The final unit of this book considers how humanity's view of itself is changing. Values, like all other elements discussed in this anthology, are dynamic. Visionary people with new ideas can have a profound impact on how a society deals with problems and adapts to changing circumstances. Therefore, to understand the forces at work in the world today, values, visions, and new ideas must be examined.

Novelist Herman Wouk, in his book *War and Remembrance*, notes that there have been many institutions so embedded in the social fabric that the people of the time assumed they were part of human nature. Slavery and human sacrifice are two examples. However, forward-thinking people opposed these institutions. Many knew they would never see the abolition of these systems within their own lifetimes, but they pressed on in the hope that someday these institutions would be eliminated. Wouk believes the same is true for warfare. He states, "Either we are finished with war or war will finish us." Aspects of society such as warfare, slavery, racism, and the secondary status of women are creations of the human mind; history suggests that they can be changed by the human spirit.

The articles of this unit have been selected with the previous six units in mind. Each explores some aspect of world affairs from the perspective of values and alternative visions of the future. New ideas are critical to meeting these challenges. The examination of well-known issues from new perspectives can yield new insights into old problems.

It was feminist Susan B. Anthony who once remarked that "social change is never made by the masses, only by educated minorities." The redefinition of human values (which, by necessity, will accompany the successful confrontation of other global issues) is a task that few people take on willingly. Nevertheless, in order to deal with the dangers of nuclear war, overpopulation, and environmental degradation, educated people must take a broad view of history. This is going to require considerable effort and much personal sacrifice.

When people first begin to consider the challenges of contemporary global problems, they often become disheartened and depressed. They might ask: What can I do? What does it matter? Who cares? There are no easy answers to these questions, but people need only look around to see good news as well as bad. How individuals react to the world in which they live is not a function of that world but a reflection of themselves. Different people react differently to the same world. The study of global issues, therefore, is the study of people, and the study of people is the study of values. Ideally, people's reactions to these issues (and many others) will help provide them with some insight into themselves as well as the world at large.

Looking Ahead: Challenge Questions

Is it naive to speak of international politics and economics in terms of ethics? What role can governments, international organizations, and even the individual play in making the world a more ethical place in which to live?

Are the values of democracy easily transferred to new settings such as Russia?

What are the characteristics of leadership?

In addition to some of the ideas presented here, what other new ideas are being expressed and how likely are they to be widely accepted?

How do the contemporary arts reflect changes in how humanity views itself?

How will the world be different in the year 2030? What factors will contribute to these changes? What does your analysis reveal about your own value system?

Unit 7

UNIVERSAL HUMAN VALUES

Finding an Ethical Common Ground

Rushworth M. Kidder

Rushworth M. Kidder, former senior columnist for The Christian Science Monitor, *is president of the Institute for Global Ethics, Box 563, Camden, Maine 04843. Telephone 207/236-6658. He has spoken at several World Future Society conferences and at "Toward the New Millennium: Living, Learning, and Working," July 24–26, 1994, in Cambridge, Massachusetts.*

This article is excerpted with the publisher's permission from his new book, Shared Values for a Troubled World: Conversations with Men and Women of Conscience *(Jossey-Bass Publishers, Inc., 1994).*

In the remote New Zealand village of Panguru, tucked into the mountains at the end of a winding gravel road, a Maori woman nearly a century old pauses for a moment as she talks about the moral values of her people. "This is God's country!" says Dame Whina Cooper with great feeling, gesturing toward the flowers blooming among the bird songs outside her modest frame house. "Only, we the people running it must be doing something wrong."

Halfway around the world, in a United Nations office perched under the eaves of a fifteenth-century building in Florence, a leading journalist from Sri Lanka is asked what will happen if the world enters the twenty-first century with the ethics of the twentieth. "I feel it will be disastrous," Varindra Tarzie Vittachi replies simply.

Midway between, in his well-appointed residence in San Jose, Costa Rica, former president Oscar Arias explains that our global survival "will become more complicated and precarious than ever before, and the ethics required of us must be correspondingly sophisticated."

Turn where you will in the world and the refrain is the same. The ethical barometer is falling, and the consequences appear to be grave. That, at least, is one of the impressions to be drawn from the two dozen individuals from 16 nations interviewed over the past few years by the Institute for Global Ethics.

These interviews did not seek to discover the ethical failings of various nations, but rather to find the moral glue that will bind us together in the twenty-first century. These voices speak powerfully of an underlying moral presence shared by all humanity—a set of precepts so fundamental that they dissolve borders, transcend races, and outlast cultural traditions.

There is a pressing need for shared values in our age of global interdependence without consensus. But there is one very real question unanswered: Is there in fact a single set of values that wise, ethical people around the world might agree on? Can there be a global code of ethics? If there is a common core of values "out there" in the world, it ought to be identifiable through examination of contemporary modes of thought in various cultures around the world. Can it be found?

On that topic, the two dozen "men and women of conscience" interviewed had a clear point of view. "Yes," they said, "there is such a code, and it can be clearly articulated." These interviewees were chosen not because they necessarily know more about ethics than their peers—although some do, having made it a lifelong study. Nor were they chosen because they are the single most exemplary person of their nation or community—though some could easily be nominated for that honor. They are, however, ethical thought-leaders within their different cultures, each viewed by his or her peers as a kind of ethical standard-bearer, a keeper of the conscience of the community, a center of moral gravity.

Each of the interviews began with a common question: If you could help create a global code of ethics, what would be on it? What moral values, in other words, would you bring to the table from your own culture and background?

In an ideal world, one would have assembled all the interviewees around a table, had each talk for an hour, had each listen intently to all the others, and finally had them arrive at a consensus. If they could have done so, here's the core of moral values upon which they probably would have agreed:

LOVE

Despite the concern of foundation executive James A. Joseph in Washington that "the L-word, Love," is falling sadly into disuse, it figured prominently in these interviews. "Love, yes," said children's author Astrid Lindgren in Stockholm. "This is the main word for what we need—love on all stages and with all people."

"The base of moral behavior is first of all solidarity, love, and mutual assistance," said former first lady Graça Machel of Mozambique. Buddhist monk Shojun Bando in Tokyo agreed, detailing three different kinds of love and insisting that "it shouldn't be that *others* should tell you to love others: It should just come of its own will, spontaneously." Or, as author Nien Cheng from China put it, "You cannot guide without love."

For tribal chief Reuben Snake of Nebraska, the central word is *compassion*. "We have to be compassionate with one another and help one another, to hold each other up, support one another down the road of

life," he recalled his grandfather telling him. Thinking back on her dealings with a global spectrum of cultures at the United Nations, former ambassador Jeane Kirkpatrick in Washington noted that, no matter how severe the political differences, "there was a kind of assumption, on the part of almost everyone, that people would help one another at the personal level."

TRUTHFULNESS

Of the four theses that form Harvard University ex-president Derek Bok's code of ethics, two center on truth. "You should not obtain your ends through lying and deceitful practices," he said, and you have a "responsibility to keep [your] promises." Astrid Lindgren put it with equal clarity when she spoke of the need to "be honest, not lying, not afraid to say your opinion."

Looking through the lens of science, the late economist Kenneth Boulding of Colorado also put "a very high value on veracity—telling the truth. The thing that gets you run out of the scientific community is being caught out telling a lie." Fortunately, said Bangladeshi banker Muhammad Yunus, the spread of technology makes it increasingly difficult for the truth to be hidden. In the future, "people will be forced to reveal themselves," he said. "Nothing can be kept hidden or secret—not in computers, not in the halls of government, nothing. People will feel much more comfortable when they're dealing in truth. You converge around and in truth."

Here, however, as with many of these global values, there was also a residue of concern—a fear that trust, which is central to honesty and truthfulness, seems to be falling into abeyance. "The idea that you ought to be able to trust somebody is out of fashion," worried Katharine Whitehorn, columnist for *The Observer* of London. That's a point seconded by corporate executive James K. Baker of Indiana. "Little by little," he said, "if we let that trust go out of our personal dealings with one another, then I think the system really begins to have trouble."

FAIRNESS

Elevating the concept of justice to the top of his list, philosopher and author John W. Gardner of Stanford University said, "I consider that probably the number-one candidate

---

24 MEN AND WOMEN OF CONSCIENCE

Dame Whina Cooper: founding president of Maori Women's Welfare League in New Zealand; presented with the Order of Dame Commander of the British Empire by Queen Elizabeth.

"God wants us to be one people."

Varindra Tarzie Vittachi: Sri Lankan journalist and author; assistant secretary-general of the United Nations.

"One man in the twentieth century . . . led us back into morality as a practical thing and not as a cloud-cuckoo-land idea, and that was Mohandas Gandhi."

Oscar Arias: former president of Costa Rica; 1987 winner of the Nobel Peace Prize.

"The effect of one upright individual is incalculable."

James A. Joseph: former under-secretary of the U.S. Department of the Interior.

"I relate fairness to treating other people as I would want to be treated."

---

for your common ground." By *justice,* he meant "fair play, or some word for even-handedness."

"Here, one could get caught up in the very complicated theories of social justice," warned James A. Joseph. "Or one could simply look at the Golden Rule. I relate fairness to treating other people as I would want to be treated. I think that [rule] serves humanity well. It ought to be a part of any ethic for the future."

For many, the concern for fairness goes hand in hand with the concept of equality. "The pursuit of equality is basic," said columnist and editor Sergio Muñoz of Mexico City and

---

Astrid Lindgren: Swedish author of *Pippi Longstocking*.

"Love, yes. This is the main word for what we need—love on all stages and with all people."

Graça Machel: former first lady of Mozambique.

"The base of moral behavior is first of all solidarity, love, and mutual assistance."

Shojun Bando: Japanese Buddhist monk, studied under Zen scholar D. T. Suzuki.

"[Parents'] actions speak more than words. Their everyday doings teach the kids how to behave."

Nien Cheng: author of *Life and Death in Shanghai;* suffered over six years of solitary confinement and torture at the hands of Chinese Communists.

"You cannot guide without love."

Reuben Snake: former chairman of the American Indian Movement.

"The spirit that makes you stand up and walk and talk and see and hear and think is the same spirit that exists in me."

Los Angeles. "The people who come from Mexico and El Salvador have the same values, in my point of view, as the person who comes from Minnesota or from Alabama or from California—those basic principles that are common to all civilizations."

For some, like Joseph, the concept of fairness and equality focuses

strongly on racial issues. Others, like author Jill Ker Conway from Australia, see the need for "greater equity between the sexes." Still others, like UNESCO Director-General Federico Mayor of Spain, see the problem as one of international relations: Despite the groundswell of interest in democracy arising within the former East Bloc nations, Westerners "have not reacted as humans, but only as economic individuals. . . . Even equity—the most important value in all the world—has collapsed."

FREEDOM

Very early in human history, said John Gardner, "the concept of degrees of freedom of my action—as against excessive constraints on my action by a tyrant or by military conquerors—emerged." Even the earliest peoples "knew when they were subjugated"—and didn't like it. That desire for liberty, he said, persists to the present as one of the defining values of humanity.

But liberty requires a sense of individuality and the right of that individual to express ideas freely, many of the interviewees said. "Without the principle of individual conscience, every attempt to institutionalize ethics must necessarily collapse" said Oscar Arias. "The effect of one upright individual is incalculable. World leaders may see their effect in headlines, but the ultimate course of the globe will be determined by the efforts of innumerable individuals acting on their consciences."

Such action, for many of these thinkers, is synonymous with democracy. "I think democracy is a must for all over the world," said Salim El Hoss, former prime minister of Lebanon. He defined the ingredients of democracy as "freedom of expression plus accountability plus equal opportunity." While he worried that the latter two are lacking in many countries, he noted that the first condition, freedom of expression, is increasingly becoming available to "all peoples."

UNITY

As a counterbalance to the needs of individual conscience, however, stands the value that embraces the individual's role in a larger collective. Of the multitude of similar terms used for that concept in these interviews (*fraternity, solidarity, cooperation, community, group allegiance, oneness*) *unity* seems the most encompassing and the least open to misconstruction. For some, it is a simple *cri de coeur* in a world that seems close to coming undone. "I want unity," said Dame Whina Cooper of New Zealand, adding that "God wants us to be one people." For Tarzie Vittachi of Sri Lanka, the idea of unity embraces a global vision capable of moving humanity from "unbridled competition" to cooperation. "That is what is demanded of us now: putting our community first, meaning the earth first, and all living things."

The problem arises when the common good is interpreted "by seeing the relation between the individual and the common in individualistic terms," said Father Bernard Przewozny of Rome. Carried to the extreme, individualism is "destructive of social life, destructive of communal sharing, destructive of participation," he said, adding that "the earth and its natural goods are the inheritance of all peoples."

TOLERANCE

"If you're serious about values," said John Gardner, "then you have to add tolerance very early—*very* early. Because you have to have constraints. The more you say, 'Values are important,' the more you have to say, 'There are limits to which you can impose your values on me.'"

"It is a question of respect for the dignity of each of us," said Graça Machel. "If you have a different idea from mine, it's not because you're worse than me. You have the right to think differently." Agreeing, Derek Bok defined tolerance as "a decent respect for the right of other people to have ideas, an obligation or at least a strong desirability of listening to different points of view and attempting to understand why they are held."

"You have your own job, you eat your own food," said Vietnamese writer and activist Le Ly Hayslip. "How you make that food is up to you, and how I live my life is up to me."

Jeane Kirkpatrick: former U.S. ambassador to the United Nations.

"I don't think life is the supreme good. It's very nearly the supreme good, but quality of life matters a lot, too. And freedom matters a lot—prosperity, a decent standard of living, possibilities for self-development."

Derek Bok: president of Harvard University, 1971–1991.

"A decent respect for the right of other people to have ideas."

Kenneth Boulding: author of over 30 books; professor at the University of Colorado.

"[I put] a very high value on veracity—telling the truth."

Muhammad Yunus: managing director of the Grameen Bank, Dhaka, Bangladesh.

"The oneness of human beings is the basic ethical thread that holds us together."

Katharine Whitehorn: senior columnist for the London Sunday newspaper *The Observer*.

"I don't think that people habitually do anything unless they are programmed so that they are appalled with themselves when they don't."

Reuben Snake traced the idea of tolerance back to a religious basis. "The spirit that makes you stand up and walk and talk and see and hear and think is the same spirit that exists in me—there's no difference," he said. "So when you look at me, you're looking at yourself—and I'm seeing me in you."

Abstracting from the idea of tolerance the core principle of respect for variety, Kenneth Boulding linked it to the environmentalist's urgency over the depletion of species. "If the blue whale is endangered, we feel worried about this, because we love the variety of the world," he explained. "In some sense I feel about the Catholic Church the way I feel about the blue whale: I don't think I'll be one, but I would feel diminished if it became extinct."

RESPONSIBILITY

Oxford don A.H. Halsey placed the sense of responsibility high on his list of values because of its impact on our common future. "We are responsible for our grandchildren," he explained, "and we will make [the world] easier or more difficult for our grandchildren to be good people by what we do right here and now." This was a point made in a different way by Katharine Whitehorn, who noted that, while as a youth "it's fun to break away," it's very much harder to "grow up and have to put it together again."

For Nien Cheng, the spotlight falls not so much on the actions of the future as on the sense of self-respect in the present. "This is Confucius' teaching," she said. "You must take care of yourself. To rely on others is a great shame."

Responsibility also demands caring for others, Hayslip said. But, under the complex interactions of medicine, insurance, and law that exists in the West, "If you come into my house and see me lying here very sick, you don't dare move me, because you're not a doctor," she pointed out. "So where is your human obligation? Where is your human instinct to try to save me? You don't have it. You lost it, because there are too many rules."

Yet, paradoxically, "responsibility is not often mentioned in discussions of world politics or ethics," said Oscar Arias. "There, the talk is all of rights, demands, and desires." Human rights are "an unquestionable and critical priority for political societies and an indispensable lever for genuine development," he said. "But the impor-

tant thing is not just to assert rights, but to ensure that they be protected. Achieving this protection rests wholly on the principle of responsibility."

Chicago attorney Newton Minow agreed. "I believe the basic reason we got off the track was that rights became more important than respon-

---

James K. Baker: former president of U.S. Chamber of Commerce.

"There's only one 'ethics.' . . . Let's not think you've got to adhere to one standard at home and another standard at work."

John W. Gardner: philosopher; founder of Common Cause; author; Stanford University professor.

"[Even the earliest peoples] knew when they were subjugated."

Sergio Muñoz: executive editor, *La Opinion*, the largest Spanish-language daily newspaper in the United States.

"The pursuit of equality is basic."

Jill Ker Conway: Australian author of *The Road from Coorain*; feminist historian and former president of Smith College.

"Greater equality between the sexes."

Federico Mayor: director-general of UNESCO.

"There are a lot of fundamental values that are reflected in the Universal Declaration of Human Rights that nobody opposes."

---

sibilities, that individuals became more important than community interests. We've gotten to the point where everybody's got a right and nobody's got a responsibility."

At its ultimate, this sense of responsibility extends to the concept of the right use of force. "You shouldn't perpetrate violence," said Derek Bok simply, finding agreement with

Jeane Kirkpatrick's insistence that "war is always undesirable" and that "any resort to force should be a very late option, never a first option."

RESPECT FOR LIFE

Growing out of this idea of the responsible use of force, but separate from and extending beyond it, is a value known most widely in the West from the Ten Commandments: Thou shalt not kill. For Shojun Bando, it is an inflexible principle: Even if ordered in wartime to defend his homeland by killing, he said, "I would refuse. I would say, 'I cannot do this.'"

Such an idea, expressed in today's peaceable Japan, may seem almost naive when examined through the lens of such war-riddled areas as the Middle East. Yet, Salim El Hoss took much the same view. "I was a prime minister [of Lebanon] for seven and a half years. I can't imagine myself signing a death penalty for anybody in the world. I think that is completely illegitimate, and I think that is the kind of thing a code of ethics should deal with."

Reuben Snake, noting that the North American Indians have a warlike reputation, said, "Probably the most serious shortcoming of tribal governments is their inability to effectively resolve conflict within the tribe and externally." He described earlier Indian traditions, however, in which great efforts were made by the tribal elders to prevent killing. That's a point with which Tarzie Vittachi—himself from the much-bloodied nation of Sri Lanka—felt perfectly at home. The first element of the Buddhist "daily prayer" under which he was raised, he recalled, is "I shall not kill." It is also central to the Ten Commandments of the Jewish decalogue under which Newton Minow was raised and which he said he still feels form the basis for the world's code of ethics.

Salim El Hoss: former head of state of Lebanon.

"I can't imagine myself signing a death penalty for anybody in the world."

Bernard Przewozny: professor of Christology at the Pontifical Theological Faculty of St. Bonaventure in Rome.

"The earth and its natural goods are the inheritance of all peoples."

Le Ly Hayslip: survivor of Vietnam War; author; founder of the East Meets West Foundation.

"What are we here for? We're here so that we can help each other to grow."

A. H. Halsey: professor of social and administrative studies at Oxford University.

"We will make [the world] easier or more difficult for our grandchildren to be good people by what we do right here and now."

Newton Minow: chairman of the Federal Communications Commission; chairman of the board of the Carnegie Corporation.

"We've gotten to the point where everybody's got a right and nobody's got a responsibility."

OTHER SHARED VALUES

There were, of course, other significant values that surfaced in these interviews. Nien Cheng, for instance, pointed to *courage*. "One should basically know what is right and what is wrong," she said, "and, when you know that, be courageous enough to stand for what is right."

Figuring strongly in Shojun Bando's pantheon was *wisdom*, which he defined as "attaining detachment, getting away from being too attached to things."

Whina Cooper put *hospitality* high on her list, recalling that her father said, "If you see any strangers going past, you call them—*Kia Ora*—that means to call them to come here." Astrid Lindgren put an emphasis on *obedience*—a quality that runs throughout the life of her most famous character, Pippi Longstocking, though usually in reverse.

Kenneth Boulding pointed to *peace*, which he defined simply as "well-managed conflict." Thinking of peace brought Salim El Hoss to the concept of *stability*. "Peace is equivalent to stability," he said, adding that "stability means a long-term perspective of no problems." These and other values, while they don't find broad support, had firm proponents among those we interviewed and deserve serious attention.

Other values mentioned included the burning public concerns for racial harmony, respect for women's place, and the protection of the environment. Many of the interviewees touched on them, and some elevated them to high priority. Speaking of the need for racial harmony, James Joseph put at the top of his list a sense of "respect for the cultures of other communities, respect for the need to begin to integrate into our collective memory appreciation of the contributions and traditions of those who are different." Jill Conway topped her list with a warning about the "increasing exploitation of women" around the world. And of the many human rights identified by Father Bernard Przewozny, the one to which he has dedicated his life is the "right to a healthy environment."

So what good is this code of values? It gives us a foundation for building goals, plans, and tactics, where things really happen and the world really changes. It unifies us, giving us a home territory of consensus and agreement. And it gives us a way—not *the* way, but *a* way—to reply when we're asked, "Whose values will you teach?" Answering this last question, as we tumble into the twenty-first century with the twentieth's sense of ethics, may be one of the most valuable mental activities of our time.

Long Walk to
FREEDOM

RICHARD STENGEL

Richard Stengel, a contributor to TIME, *collaborated with Nelson Mandela on his autobiography.*

Prison steeled Nelson Mandela—what did not kill him made him stronger. He went to jail on Robben Island in 1964 as a self-described rabble-rouser and emerged as what André Malraux once described as that rarest thing in the world: a mature man. The 27 years behind bars formed the man we see today: measured, controlled, dignified, statesmanlike. While the sensitive herdboy from the Transkei never stopped feeling the lash of racism, prison taught him to hide his pain behind a mask of proud indifference. Yet the hard years on Robben Island also converted Mandela's youthful loathing of those who practiced apartheid to a purer, more abstract anger against the system itself. When he finally walked out of prison four years ago, nothing was going to stop Nelson Mandela from overturning the order that kept him behind bars for so many years.

Long Walk to Freedom, Nelson Mandela's account of his life, will be published later this month. Autobiography is traditionally a retrospective form: the protagonist looks back on a lifetime of highs and lows, the arc of achievement ending in retirement. What makes the autobiography of Nelson Mandela unusual is that it is being published at the summit of his career, just a few months after he became President of the country that had persecuted him for so long.

Mandela secretly began writing his memoirs in 1975, scribbling late at night on paper smuggled into his cell. One copy was spirited off the island by a released colleague; the other was buried in the prison courtyard. He wrote for reasons both practical and personal: if his memoirs were published, they would become an inspirational tale for future freedom fighters. But they were also a way for Mandela to hold on to the past—the past was all he had in prison, and his jailers were intent on erasing it.

Over the years, Mandela erected walls within walls, keeping his wounds hidden behind a shield of optimism. Throughout his life, he has seen himself not as a savior but as an ordinary man confronting extraordinary circumstances. The tale begins with a free-spirited boy, born to a royal Xhosa family in the Transkei, losing his father at an early age and being raised by a guardian who is the regent of the tribe. At 16, in Xhosa tradition, he becomes a man through an elaborate, public circumcision ceremony. When he is 21, he runs away to Johannesburg after his guardian tries to arrange a marriage for him. There the country boy in the big city resolves to become a lawyer.

He faces prejudice and repression at every turn, but he succeeds in becoming an attorney, undergoing a slow political awakening along the way. His refuge is the African National Congress, and he grows as a leader in the fight against apartheid; the struggle, as he says, became his life. That struggle was all-consuming, and his life as a family man collapses. He marries and divorces, and then meets the woman with whom he is destined to share great happiness and sadness, Nomzamo Winnie Madikizela. In 1960 he is forced underground by the authorities; he eludes the police for two years before he is captured and then tried with his A.N.C. comrades for high treason. Mandela risks—even courts—the death penalty by using the trial to make a statement of his principles, ending his testimony with the assertion that he would never stop fighting for his freedom and that of his people: "It is an ideal I hope to live for and achieve, but it is an ideal for which I am prepared to die." In a hushed courtroom on June 12, 1964, Mandela and his fellow defendants are sentenced to life imprisonment without possibility of parole.

In the following pages Mandela recounts his years on Robben Island, South Africa's Alcatraz, the outpost of last resort for political prisoners. In 1982 he was taken to Pollsmoor prison and then in 1988 to Victor Verster prison. There, living in a house that was halfway between detention and freedom, he began the negotiations that ended in his release in February 1990 and spurred the country's remarkable transition to a nonracial democracy. Today, as the first democratically elected President of South Africa, Nelson Mandela lives for more than six months a year in a stately house in Cape Town, only 10 miles from his island prison.

From *Time*, November 28, 1994, pp. 52-62. Adapted from *Long Walk to Freedom: The Autobiography of Nelson Mandela* by Nelson Rolihlahla Mandela. © 1994 by Nelson Rolihlahla Mandela. Reprinted by permission of Little, Brown and Company.

IT WAS A GRIM, OVERCAST DAY WHEN I STEPPED OUT OF the plane on Robben Island, and the cold winter wind whipped through our thin prison uniforms. My colleagues and I, sentenced at the Rivonia trial to life in prison for high treason, were met by guards with automatic weapons; the atmosphere was tense but quiet. We were driven to an isolated stone building, where we were ordered to strip while standing outside. One of the ritual indignities of prison life is that when you are transferred from one prison to another, the first thing that happens is that you change from the garb of the old prison to that of the new.

When we were undressed, we were thrown the plain khaki uniforms of Robben Island. Apartheid's regulations extended even to clothing. All of us, except Ahmed Kathrada, the one Indian among us, received short trousers, an insubstantial jersey and a canvas jacket. Kathy was given long trousers. Short trousers for Africans were meant to remind us that we were "boys." I put on the short trousers that day, but I vowed that I would not put up with them for long.

We were handcuffed and taken in a covered truck to a prison within a prison, isolated from the general prisoners. This was a one-story rectangular stone fortress with a flat dirt courtyard in the center, about 100 ft. by 30 ft. It had cells on three sides. The fourth side was a 20-ft. wall with a catwalk patrolled by guards with German shepherds. We were given cells on either side of a long corridor. Each cell had one window about a foot square, covered with iron bars, and two doors: a metal gate with iron bars on the inside, locked all day, and a thick wooden door outside of that, locked at night.

The cell walls were perpetually damp. Many mornings a small pool of water would have formed on the cold floor overnight. When I raised this with the commanding officer, he told me our bodies would absorb the moisture. We were each issued three blankets so flimsy and worn they were practically transparent. Our bedding consisted of a single sisal mat.

I could walk the length of my cell in three paces. When I lay down, I could feel the wall with my feet and my head grazed the concrete at the other side; the width was about 6 ft. Each cell had a white card posted outside of it with our name and our prison service number. Mine read, N MANDELA 466/64, which meant I was the 466th prisoner admitted to the island in 1964. I was 46 years old, a political prisoner with a life sentence, and that small cramped space was to be my home for I knew not how long.

Robben Island was without question

the harshest, most ironfisted outpost in the South African penal system. The warders were white and overwhelmingly Afrikaans-speaking, and they demanded a master-servant relationship. They ordered us to call them baas, which we refused. The island's isolation made it not simply another prison, but a world of its own, far removed from the one we had come from. We were face to face with the realization that our life would be unredeemably grim. We had the consolation of being with one another, but that was the only consolation. My dismay was quickly replaced by a sense that a new and different fight had begun.

From the first day, I had protested about being forced to wear short trousers. I demanded to see the head of the prison and made a list of complaints. The warders ignored my protests, but by the end of the second week, I found a pair of old khaki trousers unceremoniously dumped on the floor of my cell. No pinstripe three-piece suit has ever pleased me as much. But before putting them on, I checked to see if my comrades had been issued trousers as well. They had not, and I told the warder to take mine back. I insisted that all African prisoners must have long trousers. Finally, the commanding officer himself came to my cell to take them away. "Very well, Mandela," he said, "you are going to have the same clothing as everyone else."

Within a few months, our life settled into a pattern. Timepieces of any kind were barred, so we never knew precisely what time it was. With each week resembling the one before, one must make an effort to recall what day and month it is. One of the first things I did was to make a calendar on the wall of my cell. Losing a sense of time is an easy way to lose one's grip and even one's sanity.

Breakfast was delivered to us in the courtyard in old metal oil drums. We would help ourselves to pap—cereal made from corn—and we each received a mug of what was described as coffee, but which was in fact ground-up corn, baked until it was black and then brewed with hot water. Coloreds and Indians received a slightly better diet than Africans, but it was not much of a distinction. Food was the source of many of our protests, but in those early days the warders would say, "Ag, you kaffirs are eating better in prison than you ever ate at home!"

In the midst of breakfast, the guards would yell, "Fall in! Fall in!" and we would stand outside our cells for inspection. Each prisoner was required to have the three buttons of his khaki jacket properly buttoned. We were required to doff our hats as the warder walked by. If our buttons were undone, our hats unremoved or our cells untidy, we were charged with a violation of the prison code and punished with either solitary confinement or the loss of meals.

After inspection we would work in the courtyard hammering stones until noon. There were no breaks; if we slowed down, the warders would yell at us to speed up. At noon the bell would clang for lunch, and another metal drum of food would be wheeled into the courtyard. For Africans, lunch consisted of boiled mealies, coarse kernels of corn.

After lunch we worked until 4, when the guards blew shrill whistles and we once again lined up to be counted and inspected. We were then permitted half an hour to clean up. The bathroom at the end of our corridor had two seawater showers and three large galvanized-metal buckets, which were used as bathtubs. There was no hot water. We would stand or squat in these buckets, sometimes singing while washing, which made the water seem less icy. In those early days, this was one of the only times that we could converse.

Precisely at 4:30, there would be a loud knock on the wooden door at the end of our corridor, which meant that supper had been delivered. We again received mealie-pap porridge, sometimes with the odd carrot or piece of cabbage or beetroot thrown in, but one usually had to search for it. Every other day, we received a small piece of meat with our porridge. The meat was usually mostly gristle. Colored and Indian prisoners received a quarter of a loaf of bread and a slab of margarine. Africans, it was presumed, did not care for bread as it was a "European" type of food.

At 8 p.m., the night warder would lock himself in the corridor with us, passing the key through a small hole in the door to another warder outside. The warder would then walk up and down the corridor, ordering us to go to sleep. No cry of "Lights out!" was ever given on Robben Island because the single mesh-covered bulb in each cell burned day and night.

The challenge for every prisoner, particularly every political prisoner, is how to survive intact, how to emerge undiminished, how to conserve and even replenish one's beliefs. Our survival depended on understanding what the authorities were attempting to do to us, and sharing that understanding with one another. It would be very hard if not impossible for one man alone to resist. I do not know that I could have done it had I been alone. But the authorities' greatest mistake was keeping us together, for together our determination was reinforced. Whatever we learned we shared, and by sharing we multiplied whatever courage we had individually. The stronger ones raised up the weaker ones, and both became stronger in the process.

As a leader, one must sometimes take actions that are unpopular or whose results will not be known for years to come. There are victories whose glory lies only in the fact that they are known to those who win them. This is particularly true of prison, where one must find consolation in being true to one's ideals, even if no one else knows of it. I was now on the sidelines, but I also knew that I would not give up the fight. I was in a different and smaller arena, an arena in which the only audience was ourselves and our oppressors. We regarded the struggle in prison as a microcosm of the struggle as a whole. The racism and repression were the same; I would simply have to fight on different terms.

Prison and the authorities conspire to rob each man of his dignity. In and of itself, that assured that I would survive, for any man or institution that tries to rob me of my dignity will lose because I will not part with it at any price or under any pressure. I never seriously considered the possibility that I would not emerge from prison one day. I never thought that a life sentence truly meant life and that I would die behind bars. Perhaps I was denying this prospect because it was too unpleasant to contemplate. But I always knew that someday I would once again feel the grass under my feet and walk in the sunshine as a free man.

I am fundamentally an optimist. Whether that comes from nature or nurture, I cannot say. Part of being optimistic is keeping one's head pointed toward the sun, one's feet moving forward. There were many dark moments when my faith in humanity was sorely tested, but I would not give myself up to despair.

As a D Group prisoner, the lowest and

least privileged category, I was entitled to have only one visitor and to write and receive only one letter every six months. I found this one of the most inhumane restrictions. Visits and letters were limited to "first degree" relatives. To us this was not only irksome but racist. African family structures are larger and more inclusive; anyone who claims descent from a common ancestor is deemed part of the family.

When letters did arrive, they were cherished. A letter was like the summer rain that could make even the desert bloom. When I was handed one by the authorities, I would not rush forward and grab it, as I felt like doing. Though I yearned to tear it open on the spot, I would not give the authorities the satisfaction of seeing my eagerness. I would return slowly to my cell, as though I had many things to occupy me before opening a letter from my family.

At the end of August, after I had been on the island less than three months, I was told I would have a visitor the following day. They would not tell me who it was. I suspected, I hoped, I wished, I believed, that it would be a visit from Winnie.

I was called to the visitors' office in the late morning. I waited with some anxiety, and suddenly, filling out the glass on the other side of the window was Winnie's lovely face. She always liked to dress up for prison visits and tried to wear something new and elegant. It was tremendously frustrating not to be able to touch my wife, to speak tenderly to her, to have a private moment together.

I could see immediately that Winnie was under tremendous strain. Just getting to the island itself was difficult, and added to that were the harsh rituals of the prison. I later discovered she had recently received a second banning order [restricting her to Johannesburg and preventing her from attending meetings of any kind] and had been terminated from her job at the Child Welfare Office as a result. She loved her job as a social worker: it was the hands-on end of the struggle. The banning and harassment of my wife greatly troubled me. I could not look after her and the children, and the state was making it difficult for her to look after herself. My powerlessness gnawed at me.

I knew that Winnie was anxious about my health: she had heard stories that we were being physically abused. I quickly informed her that I was fine, and she could see that I was fit, though a bit thinner. She too was thinner, something I always attributed to stress. I inquired one by one about all the family. Suddenly, I heard the warder behind me say, "Time up! Time up!" I turned and looked at him with incredulity.

It was impossible that half an hour had passed. For all the years that I was in prison, I never failed to be surprised when the warder called, "Time up!" I always felt like lingering after Winnie left, just

to retain the sense of her presence, but I would not let the warders see such emotion. As I walked back to the cell, I reviewed in my head what we had talked about. Over the next months, I would return to that one visit again and again. As it turned out, Winnie was not able to visit me for another two years.

One morning, as we lined up to be

counted before beginning work in the courtyard, we were instead ordered into a covered truck. A few minutes later we arrived at a lime quarry. It looked like an enormous white crater cut into a rocky hillside.

We were met by the commanding officer, Colonel Wessels, a colorless fellow who cared only about strict adherence to regulations. We stood at attention as he told us that the work we would be doing would last six months, and afterward we would be given light tasks for the duration of our terms. His timing was considerably off. We remained at the quarry for the next 13 years.

We were handed picks and shovels and given rudimentary instructions as to the mining of lime. It is not a simple task. That first day we were clumsy with our new tools and extracted little. The lime itself is buried in layers of rock, and one had to break through to it with a pick and then extract the seam of lime with a shovel.

It was an attempt to crush our spirits. But those first few weeks at the quarry had the opposite effect on us. Despite blistered and bleeding hands, we were invigorated. I much preferred being outside in nature, being able to see grass and trees, to observe birds flitting overhead, to feel the wind blowing in from the sea. It felt good to use all of one's muscles, with the sun at one's back, and there was simple gratification in building up mounds of lime. Although some of the men regarded the march to the quarry as drudgery, I never did.

It was hot work, but worse was the light. The sun's rays would be reflected into our eyes by the lime. The glare hurt our eyes and, along with the dust, made it difficult to see. After a few days, we made an official request for sunglasses. The authorities refused. This was not unexpected, for we were then not even permitted reading glasses. We requested sunglasses again and again, but it was to take us almost three years before we were allowed to have them, and that was only after a sympathetic physician agreed that the glasses were necessary to preserve our eyesight. Even then, we had to purchase the glasses ourselves.

For us, such struggles—for sunglasses, long trousers, study privileges, equalized food—were corollaries to the struggle we waged outside prison. The campaign to improve conditions in prison was part of the apartheid struggle. It was all the same; we fought injustice wherever we found it, no matter how large or how small, to preserve our own humanity.

We were not allowed to have any news from outside, but one day that first year I noticed a newspaper lying on the bench. I plucked the paper off the bench, slipping it into my shirt. Normally, I would have hidden the newspaper in my cell and taken it out only after bedtime. But like a child who eats his sweet before his main course, I was so eager for news that I opened the paper immediately. I was so engrossed that I did not hear any footsteps. Suddenly, an officer appeared, and I did not even have time to slide the paper under my bed. "Mandela," the officer said, "we are charging you for possession of contraband, and you will pay for this." I offered no defense, and was sentenced to three days in isolation and deprivation of meals.

The first day in isolation was always the most painful. The body is not used to being deprived, but I found that by the second day I had more or less adjusted to the absence of food. Such deprivation was not uncommon among Africans in everyday life. I myself had gone without food for days at a time in my early years in Johannesburg.

But I found solitary confinement the most forbidding aspect of prison life. There is no end and no beginning; there is only one's own mind, which can begin to play tricks. One begins to question everything: Did I make the right decision; was my sacrifice worth it?

7. VALUES AND VISIONS

But I have found that one can bear the unbearable if one can keep one's spirits strong even when one's body is being tested. Strong convictions are the secret of surviving deprivation; your spirit can be full even when your stomach is empty.

Through a plastic-wrapped note hidden in our food drums, we learned in July 1966 that the criminal prisoners had embarked on a hunger strike to protest poor conditions. We did not know exactly what the strike was about, but we would support any strike of prisoners for whatever reason. We resolved to initiate a sympathetic strike beginning with our next meal.

During the first day, we were served our normal rations and refused to take them. On the second day, our portions were larger, with more vegetables. On the third day, juicy pieces of meat were served. By the fourth day, the porridge was glistening with fat, and great hunks of meat and vegetables were steaming on top—positively mouthwatering. The temptation was great, but we resisted.

The following day we learned of an extraordinary course of events: the warders had gone on their own food boycott. They had decided that if we could do such a thing, why couldn't they? They were demanding better food and improved living conditions. The combination of the two strikes was too much for the authorities. They settled with the warders, and then the general prisoners declared victory and called off the hunger strike. We followed suit a day later.

That was the first and most successful of the hunger strikes on the island. As a form of protest, they did not have a high success rate, and the rationale behind them always struck me as quixotic. For me, hunger strikes were altogether too passive. We who were already suffering were threatening our health, even courting death. I have always favored a more active, militant style of protest, such as work strikes, go-slow strikes or refusing to clean up—actions that punished the authorities, not ourselves. They wanted gravel, and we produced no gravel. They wanted the prison yard clean, and it was untidy. This kind of behavior distressed and exasperated them, whereas I think they secretly enjoyed watching us go hungry.

But when it came to a decision, I was often outvoted. Once the decision was taken, however, I would support it as wholeheartedly as any of its advocates. In fact, during the strikes I was often in the position of remonstrating with some of my wayward colleagues who did not want to abide by our agreement. Comrades would sometimes eat on the sly. We knew this for a simple reason: by the second day of a hunger strike no one needs to use the toilet, yet one morning you might see a fellow going to the toilet.

It would be hard to say what we did more of at the quarry: mine lime or talk. By 1966 the warders had adopted a laissez-faire attitude: we could talk as much as we wanted as long as we worked. We would cluster in small groups and talk all day long, about every subject under the sun, both solemn and trifling.

One issue that provoked much discussion was circumcision. Some among us maintained that circumcision as practiced by the Xhosa and other tribes was not only an unnecessary mutilation of the body but a reversion to the type of tribalism that the A.N.C. was seeking to overthrow. But the prevailing view, with which I agreed, was that circumcision was a cultural ritual that had not only a salutary health benefit but an important psychological effect. It was a rite that strengthened group identification and inculcated positive values.

The debate continued for years, and a number of men voted in favor of circumcision in a very direct way. A prisoner working in the hospital who had formerly practiced as an *ingcibi* (a man who performs circumcisions) set up a secret circumcision school. A number of the younger prisoners were circumcised there. Afterward, we would organize a small party of tea and biscuits for the men, and they would spend a day or two walking around in blankets, as was the custom.

We formed our own internal A.N.C. organization on the island. Known officially as the High Organ, it consisted of the most senior A.N.C. leaders on Robben Island, the men who had been members of the National Executive Committee and defendants at the Rivonia trial: Walter Sisulu, Govan Mbeki, Raymond Mhlaba and myself. I served as the head.

We decided the High Organ would not try to influence external A.N.C. policy. We had no reliable way of evaluating the situation in the country and concluded it would neither be fair nor wise for us to offer guidance on matters about which we were uninformed. Instead we made decisions about such matters as prisoners' complaints, strikes, mail, food—all of the day-to-day concerns of prison life. As large meetings were extremely dangerous and infrequent, the High Organ would often take decisions that were then communicated to all the other members.

I did not by any means dominate the High Organ, and in fact a number of proposals that I felt strongly about were rejected. This is as it should be, but I sometimes found it frustrating. There were two issues about which I could never persuade my colleagues. Prison regulations stated that prisoners must stand in the presence of a senior officer. I advocated that we should remain seated, as it was demeaning to have to recognize the enemy. My comrades believed this was trivial and that the consequences of resistance would outweigh any benefits.

The second issue was rejected by the High Organ on similar grounds. The warders called us by either our surnames or our Christian names. Each, I felt, was degrading, and I thought we should insist on the honorific "Mr." I pressed for this for many years, without success. It became a source of humor, as my colleagues would occasionally call me Mr. Mandela.

The graph of improvement in prison was never steady. We would push the rock up the hill, only to have it tumble down again. But conditions did improve. We had won a host of small battles that added up to a change in the atmosphere of the island. While we did not run the prison, the authorities could not run it without us, and our life became more tolerable.

Within our first three years on the island we were all given long trousers. By 1969 we received our own individual prison uniforms, instead of being issued a different set each week, and we were allowed to wash them ourselves. We were permitted out in the courtyard at all hours during the weekend. Although our food was not yet equalized, African prisoners would occasionally receive bread in the morning. We had been given board games and cards, which we often played on Saturdays and Sundays. We were allowed to study for degrees, and most of us did. At the quarry, our talk was rarely interrupted. If the commanding officer was coming, the warders on duty would blow a whistle to warn us to pick up our tools. We had neutralized the worst warders and befriended the more reasonable ones.

At Christmas, we were allowed to hold a chess and checkers tournament. Every year I competed in checkers, and some years I won the grand prize, usually a candy bar. My style of play was slow and deliberate, my strategy conservative. I carefully considered the ramifications of every option and took a long time between moves. I would ponder each possibility; when I was about to move I would call out, *"Qhipu!"*—which means "I strike!"—and move the piece. I resist such analogies, but it is my preferred mode of operating, not only in checkers but in politics.

In 1969 a young warder arrived who seemed particularly eager to get to know me. I had heard rumors that our people on the outside were organizing an escape for me, and had infiltrated a warder onto the island who would assist me. Gradually, this fellow communicated to me that he was planning my escape. In bits and pieces he explained the plan: one night he would drug the warders on duty at the lighthouse to allow for the landing of a boat. He would furnish me with a key to get out of our section so that I could meet the boat. On the boat I was to be equipped with underwater diving gear, which I would use to swim into the harbor at Cape Town; from there, I would be flown out of the country.

I listened to the plan and did not communicate to him how far-fetched it sounded. I consulted with Walter, and we agreed that this fellow was not to be trusted. I never told the warder that I would not do it, but I never took any of the actions required to implement the plan. He must have got the message, for he was soon transferred off the island.

As it turned out, my mistrust was justified, for we later learned that the warder was an agent of the Bureau of State Security, South Africa's secret intelligence agency. The plot was that I was to be successfully taken off the island, but killed in a dramatic shoot-out with security forces as I tried to leave the country. It was not the last time they would try to eliminate me.

One of the issues that always concerned us was how to keep the idea of the struggle before the people. One day, Kathy, Walter and I were talking in the courtyard when they suggested that I ought to write my memoirs. Kathy noted that the perfect time for such a book to be published would be on my 60th birthday. Walter said the story would serve to remind people of what we were fighting for, and could become a source of inspiration for young freedom fighters. The idea appealed to me, and I agreed to go ahead.

When I decide to do something, I like to start immediately, and I threw myself into this new project. I adopted a rather unorthodox work schedule: I would write most of the night and sleep during the day, except when I had to go to work at the quarry. After a few weeks of this, I notified the authorities that I was not feeling well and would not be going to the quarry. They did not seem to care, and from then on I was able to sleep most of the day.

We created an assembly line to process the manuscript. Each day I passed what I wrote to Kathy, who reviewed the manuscript and then read it to Walter. Walter and Kathy have never hesitated to criticize me, and I took their suggestions to heart, often incorporating their changes. This marked-up manuscript was then given to Laloo Chiba, a fellow political prisoner who spent the next night transferring my writing into his own almost microscopic shorthand, reducing 10 pages of foolscap to a single small piece of paper. It would be the job of Mac Maharaj, another A.N.C. prisoner, to smuggle the manuscript to the outside world.

I wrote rapidly, completing a draft in four months. I did not hesitate over choosing a word or phrase. I covered the period from my birth through the Rivonia trial and ended with some notes about Robben Island. Those nights, as I wrote in silence, I could once again experience the sights and sounds of my boyhood in the Transkei, the excitement and fear of coming to Johannesburg, the tempests of the Youth League, the endless delays of the treason trial. It was like a waking dream, and I attempted to transfer it to paper as simply and truthfully as I could.

Mac ingeniously hid the transcribed version of the manuscript inside the binding of notebooks he used for his studies. In this way he was able to safeguard the text from the authorities and smuggle it out when he was released in 1976. Mac would secretly communicate when the manuscript was safely out of the country; only then would we destroy the original. In the meantime, we still had to dispose of a 500-page manuscript. We did the only thing we could do: we buried it in the courtyard.

In order not to have to dig a great hole, we decided to bury the manuscript in three separate places. We divided it into segments, wrapped each in plastic and placed them inside empty cocoa containers. One morning after breakfast, Kathy, Walter and I drifted over to the garden, where we appeared to be having a political discussion. At a signal from me, we dropped down and began digging. I dug in the center, near a manhole cover that led to a drainpipe. When I reached the pipe, I carved out a space beneath it and deposited the largest of the three containers. The others dug two shallower holes for their portions.

A few weeks later, I heard the thud of picks and shovels in the courtyard. There at the south end was a work crew digging in the area where the manuscript was buried, to build a wall. The beginnings of the trench were already perilously close to the two smaller containers.

There was only one thing to do: when work halted, we began inconspicuously digging in the area where the two smaller pieces of manuscript would be and managed to unearth those containers rather quickly. To rescue the chunk of manuscript under the pipe would require more time, but we were confident that they would not find the manuscript because they would not dislodge the pipe in order to build the wall.

We hid the manuscript in our shirts as we walked back to our cells and then destroyed the two segments. When we returned from the quarry that afternoon, I strolled over to the far end of the courtyard. I attempted to appear as casual as possible, but I was alarmed by what I saw: the pipe had been removed from the trench altogether. They could not have helped uncovering the manuscript. I must have flinched or reacted in some way that was noticeable. Unbeknown to me, I was being watched by a number of warders who later said that my reaction confirmed that I knew a manuscript had been there.

Early the next morning, I was summoned to see the commanding officer. Without any greeting whatsoever, he announced, "Mandela, we have found your manuscript." I did not reply. The commanding officer then reached behind his desk and produced a sheaf of papers. "This is your handwriting, is it not?" he demanded. Again, I remained silent. "We do not need evidence," the commander said. "We have the evidence." For that offense, we lost study privileges for four years.

After Mac was released in December, he sent the notebooks overseas to England. He spent the next six months under house arrest in South Africa before slipping out of the country and going first to Lusaka to see Oliver Tambo and then to London. He stayed there for six months, reconstructing the manuscript and putting together a typescript. He returned to Lusaka and presented Oliver with a copy. From there, the trail grows cold. I heard nothing about the manuscript, and still do not know precisely what Oliver did with it. Although it was not published while I was in prison, it did survive and forms the spine of this memoir.

After the Soweto riots in August 1976, our section filled up with angry young men who had been arrested in the uprising. The new prisoners were appalled by what they considered the barbaric conditions of the island and said they could not understand how we could live in such a way. We told them that they should have seen the island in 1964. But they were almost as skeptical of us as they were of the authorities. They chose to ignore our calls for discipline and thought our advice feeble and unassertive. It was obvious that they regarded us as moderates. After so many years of being branded a radical revolutionary, to be perceived as a moderate was a novel and not altogether pleasant feeling. I knew that I could react in one of two ways: I could scold them for their impertinence, or I could listen to what they were saying. I chose the latter.

Though I was encouraged by their militancy, I thought that their philosophy, in its concentration on blackness, was exclusionary and represented an intermediate view that was not fully mature. I saw my role as an elder statesman who might help them move on to the more inclusive ideas of the Congress movement. I knew that these young men would eventually become frustrated, because the Black Consciousness movement offered no program of action.

In early 1977, the authorities announced the end of manual labor. This was liberating. I could now spend the day reading, writing letters, discussing issues with my comrades or formulating legal briefs. The free time allowed me to pursue what became two of my favorite hobbies on Robben Island: gardening and tennis.

To survive in prison, one must develop ways to take satisfaction in one's daily life. One can feel fulfilled by washing one's clothes so that they are particularly clean, by sweeping a hallway so that it is empty of dust, by organizing one's cell to conserve as much space as possible. The same pride one takes in more consequential tasks outside of prison one can find in doing small things inside prison.

Almost from my arrival on Robben Island, I asked the authorities for permission to start a garden in the courtyard. For years they refused without offering a reason. But eventually they relented, and we were able to cut out a small garden. The soil in the courtyard was dry, and I had to excavate a great many rocks: some of my comrades jested that I was a miner at heart, for I spent my days at the quarry and my free time digging in the courtyard.

The authorities supplied me with seeds. I initially planted tomatoes, chilies and onions, hardy plants that did not require rich earth or constant care. The early harvests were poor, but they soon improved. The authorities did not regret giving permission, for once the garden began to flourish, I often provided the warders with some of my best tomatoes and onions.

A garden was one of the few things in prison that one could control. To plant a seed, watch it grow, then harvest it offered a simple but enduring satisfaction. The sense of being the custodian of this small patch of earth offered a small taste of freedom. In some ways, I saw the garden as a metaphor for certain aspects of my life. A leader must also tend his garden; he too plants seeds and then watches, cultivates and harvests the result. Like the gardener, a leader must take responsibility for what he cultivates; he must mind his work, try to repel enemies, preserve what can be preserved and eliminate what cannot succeed.

I wrote Winnie two letters about a particularly beautiful tomato plant, how I coaxed it from a tender seedling to a robust plant that produced deep red fruit. But then, either through some mistake or lack of care, the plant began to wither and decline, and nothing I did would bring it back to health. When it finally died, I removed the roots from the soil, washed them and buried them in a corner of the garden.

I narrated this small story at great length. I do not know what she read into that letter, but when I wrote it I had a mixture of feelings: I did not want our relationship to go the way of that plant, and yet I felt that I had been unable to nourish many of the most important relationships in my life. Sometimes there is nothing one can do to save something that must die.

After I had been in prison for nearly 18

years, I began to wonder whether we had become stuck in a mind-set that was no longer revolutionary. The danger was that our ideas had become frozen in time. I had always attempted to remain open to new ideas, not to reject a position because it was new or different. During our years on the island we kept up a continuing dialogue about our beliefs and ideas; we debated them, questioned them and thereby refined them. I believe we had evolved.

In March 1982, I was visited by the commanding officer and a number of other prison officials. This was highly unusual; the commanding officer did not generally pay calls on prisoners. I stood up when they arrived, and the commander actually entered my cell. "Mandela," he said, "I want you to pack up your things." I asked him why. "We are transferring you," he said.

I was disturbed and unsettled. What did it mean? Where were we going? We had no warning, no preparation. We were each given several large cardboard boxes in which to pack our things. Everything that I had accumulated in nearly two decades could be fit in these few boxes. We packed in little more than half an hour. We had no time to say a proper goodbye to our comrades of many years. This is another one of the indignities of prison. The bonds of friendship and loyalty with other prisoners count for nothing.

Within minutes we were on board the ferry headed for Cape Town. I looked back at the island as the light was fading, not knowing whether I would ever see it again. A man can get used to anything, and I had grown used to Robben Island. I had lived there for almost two decades, and while it was never a home, it had become a place where I felt comfortable. I have always found change difficult, and leaving Robben Island, however grim it had been at times, was no exception. I had no idea what to look forward to.

Preparing Now for a Peaceful 21st Century

World order well may rest on the great powers' recognition of the need for cooperation to ensure mutual security.

Charles W. Kegley, Jr., and Gregory A. Raymond

Dr. Kegley is Associate American Thought Editor of USA Today *and Pearce Professor of International Relations, University of South Carolina, Columbia. Dr. Raymond is professor and chairman, Department of Political Science, Boise (Idaho) State University. They are co-authors of* A Multipolar Peace?: Great-Power Politics in the Twenty-First Century.

DESPITE the disruptions evident since the end of the Cold War, the great powers have yet to forge a clear, coherent strategy for promoting global security. Instead, confusion and conflicting impulses abound. From efforts to deal with the civil war in what was once Yugoslavia to coping with domestic turmoil in Somalia, their policies have been characterized by hesitation and false starts. The failure to prevent aggression stemming from long-suppressed ethnic hatreds, alongside percolating rivalries among themselves over trade issues, have heightened apprehensions about whether the great powers will be able to maintain peaceful relations in the long term.

To some extent, their struggles are understandable. Creating a global security policy for a chaotic and confusing post-Cold War world is a formidable challenge. The simple bipolar system of the recent past rapidly is giving way to a more complex configuration of strength, and the prevailing uncertainty surrounding the great powers' future intentions makes construction of a new security system difficult.

American Marines keep vigil during Operation Show Care while Somalis await their turn to see doctors. International intervention of this nature under United Nations auspices may play a greater future role in helping to maintain global security.

U.S. Navy photo by Ens. M.J. Lent

In today's cloudy global atmosphere, military and economic might are becoming increasingly diffused. In contrast to bipolarity, where two superstates held a preponderance of strength compared to all other countries, the multipolar system of the future appears destined to contain as many as five roughly equal great powers: the U.S., China, Russia, Japan, and either Germany or a European Union with a common defense policy. A "power transition" is well under way, and the changes provoked by this redistribution promise to be fundamental. The relative capabilities of the great powers are moving in the direction of approximate parity.

The diffusion of strength among the world's leading states demands attention because some previous forms of multipolarity have been more war-prone than others. For example, the multipolar system of antagonistic blocs that developed on the

From *USA Today Magazine,* September 1994, pp. 20-22. © 1994 by the Society for the Advancement of Education. Reprinted by permission.

eve of World War I proved particularly dangerous. When a world of many great powers splits into rival camps, there is little chance that competitors in one policy arena will emerge as partners somewhere else, so as to mitigate the competition. Rather, the gains made by one side will be seen as losses by the other, ultimately causing minor disagreements to grow into larger face-offs from which neither coalition is willing to retreat.

Since the international system of the early 21st century probably will include three or more extremely powerful states whose security interests are global, it is important that they do not become segregated into rival blocs. While the world can rejoice in the end of Cold War hostility, differences in the interests of the great powers have not disappeared, and there is no assurance that future disagreements will not culminate in intense conflict.

As former U.S. Secretary of State Lawrence S. Eagleburger warns, we are "returning to a more traditional and complicated time of multipolarity, with a growing number of countries increasingly able to affect the course of events." The primary issues are how well the U.S. and Russia can adjust to their unequal decline from overwhelming preponderance, and how well China, Japan, and the European Union will adapt to their newfound importance. "The change will not be easy for any of the players, as such shifts in power relationships have never been easy."

Can great-power cooperation, not renewed conflict, prevail? At issue is whether the security threats that collectively will face the world will be managed through multilateral great-power action instead of the unilateral pursuit of national advantage.

Great-power options in a multipolar future

As power in the international system becomes more diffused, what can be done to prevent the re-emergence of an unstable form of multipolarity? How can the great powers avoid the rivalries that historically have provoked the formation of polarized, antagonistic blocs? Three general courses of action exist: they can act unilaterally; develop specialized bilateral alliances with others; or engage in some form of broad collaboration with many nations. What matters for the stability of multipolar systems is the relative emphasis placed on "going it alone" vs. "going it with others," and whether joint action is defined in inclusive or exclusive terms.

Unilateral policies, though attractive because they symbolize the nostalgic pursuit of national autonomy, are unlikely to be viable in a multipolar future. The end of the Cold War has reduced public anxieties about foreign dangers and, in some countries, led to calls for a reduction in the scale of foreign commitments. A retreat from world affairs, however, would imperil efforts to deal with the many transnational threats to security that require active global engagement.

On the other hand, a surge of unilateral activism by any of the great powers would be equally harmful. None of them holds an unquestioned hegemonic status with enough power to override all others. Although the U.S. is unrivaled in military might, its offensive capability and unsurpassed military technology is not paralleled by unrivaled financial clout. Like others, the U.S. economy faces constraints that inhibit the projection of American power on a global scale.

Given the prohibitive costs of shouldering the economic burden of acting alone alongside the absence of a public mandate for international activism, and given the probability that other great powers would be unlikely to accept subordinate positions, unilateralism will be problematic in a multipolar future. As University of California political theorist Kenneth N. Waltz observes, major key nations such as Japan, Russia, and Germany thus "will have to relearn their old great-power roles, and the United States will have to learn a role it has never played before; namely, to coexist and interact with other great powers."

An alternative to acting unilaterally is joining with selected states in special partnerships. On the surface, this option also appears attractive. Yet, in a fluid balance-of-power system lacking stark simplicities, differentiating friend from foe is exceedingly difficult. It is exacerbated further when, as exists today, allies in the realm of military security also are the major trade competitors in a cutthroat global marketplace. Instead of adding predictability to international affairs, a network of special bilateral partnerships would foster a fear of ostracism among those who perceive themselves as the targets of these combinations.

Whether they entail informal understandings or formal treaties of alliance, all bilateral partnerships have a common drawback—they promote a politics of exclusion that can lead to dangerously polarized forms of multipolarity, whereby the competitors align by forming counter-coalitions. For example, a Russo-American alliance would concern many Western European leaders; similarly, a U.S.-Russian-European Union axis stretching from the Atlantic to the Urals would alarm both China and Japan. The problem with such potential partnerships in a freewheeling dance of balance-of-power politics is that it promotes much switching of partners, and those cast aside then are tempted to break up the entire dance.

Beyond forming special bilateral alliances, great powers have the option of establishing broad, multilateral associations. The most likely variants are concerts and collective security organizations. While unilateralism discourages mutual consultation and specialized bilateral relationships involve regularized consultation among a subset of powers at the top of the global hierarchy (to the exclusion of the rest), multilateral associations require full participation by all states. A concert offers the benefit of helping control the great-power rivalries that often spawn polarized blocs, though at the cost of ignoring the interests of those not belonging to the charmed circle.

Alternatively, the all-inclusive nature of a collective security system allows every voice to be heard, but hinders engineering a timely response to emergent threats. In past collective security experiments, consensus-building has proven both difficult and delayed, especially in identifying the culpable party, choosing an appropriate response, and implementing the selected course of action. Since a decision-making body can become unwieldy as its size expands, what is needed to make multilateralism a viable option for the multipolar future is a hybrid that combines elements of a great-power concert with those of collective security.

The key to the stability of any future multipolar system lies in the inclusiveness of multilateralism. It is not a panacea for all of the world's security problems, but offers humanity a chance to avoid the types of unilateral hegemonial pursuits and polarized alignments that have proven so destructive throughout history. Recall that every previous multipolar balance-of-power system has ended in a general war, and that each of these conflicts has been more destructive than its predecessors.

Creating a new security architecture seldom has proven easy. When seen from the perspective of the mid 1990s, all the existing institutions upon which a multilateral concert-based collective security system might be constructed have limitations. Consider first the potential role of the United Nations. After the Persian Gulf War, many people assumed that the UN at long last would be able "to take effective collective measures for the prevention and removal of threats to the peace," as originally proclaimed in its charter.

Whether this becomes a reality will depend on the political dynamics within the Security Council, which has "primary responsibility for the maintenance of international peace and security." Of the Security Council's 15 members, five hold permanent seats and possess the right to veto council actions—the U.S., Russia, Great Britain, France, and China. The harmonious veneer witnessed in the Cold War's wake could fade. Moreover, if, as proposed, the Security Council's permanent membership is expanded to include Germany, Japan, and such regional powers as Brazil, India, or Nigeria, reaching agreement for collective action will become even more challenging.

To complicate matters further, there is a pervasive fear among UN members that the organization has become a captive of its strongest member at the moment—the U.S. Although American influence is resented by many states, they still recognize the need for U.S. leadership if the UN is to play a peacekeeping and peacemaking role. This creates a dilemma, for, as political analyst Leslie H. Gelb explains, "Without U.S. leadership and power, the United Nations lacks muscle. With it, the United Nations loses its independent identity."

Thus, an invigorated, independent UN would need more resources to carry out its mandate for peacekeeping—a dim prospect since its members owe billions of dollars in back dues and appear unwilling to support financially the organization's new initiatives. Attempting to reform the United Nations to cope with the exploding demand for UN peacekeepers was described by Secretary-General Boutros Boutros-Ghali as "trying to repair a car while you are driving at a speed of 120 miles per hour." Nevertheless, he has lobbied for the creation of UN peace enforcement units to administer ceasefires between armed adversaries.

As with UN peacekeeping forces employed during the Cold War, Boutros-Ghali recommended that these rapid deployment units be established by the voluntary contribution of member states, act when authorized by the Security Council, and serve under the command of the Secretary-General. In contrast to traditional peacekeeping operations, their use could be ordered without the express consent of the disputants, and the UN's troops would be trained and equipped to use force if necessary.

Despite Boutros-Ghali's energetic quest, the creation of a large, easily mobilized multilateral UN contingency force positioned to manage disputes seems unlikely. The Clinton Administration, perhaps fearing a possible loss of control, vetoed in its 1994 Presidential Decision Directive 13 the contribution of U.S. military units to a permanent UN standby force. Without active enthusiasm in Washington, the other great powers appear unlikely to release command authority of their military units to the United Nations.

The Conference on Security and Cooperation in Europe (CSCE) offers a second multilateral option for a new concert-based security architecture. Although the Helsinki process has established principles that give the great powers incentives to

share costs and responsibilities for security without reducing the lesser powers to second-class citizens, the CSCE has not yet proven itself up to the challenge of operating as a global collective security institution. For that, the CSCE must transform itself from a regional security organization into a body that includes Japan, China, and other affected states. Furthermore, it must devise a decision-making formula grounded in majority rule, rather than in the unanimous consent among more than 50 diverse members.

The North Atlantic Treaty Organization represents a third possible multilateral mooring for international security. For many analysts, though, NATO is more an anachronism than an anchor. The utility of any alliance tends to diminish when the common external threat that brought it together disappears, and NATO is no exception. Without a Soviet or Russian threat to cement its unity, NATO must broaden its membership and the geographical definition of its responsibilities.

Yet, for all the optimistic speculation about a broadened, reconfigured NATO, until very recently there was little evidence that the alliance was prepared to take a bold step away from its original mission. With the creation of the North Atlantic Cooperation Council and the unveiling of the Clinton Administration's "Partnership for Peace" proposal, the security concerns of former Warsaw Pact members have received greater attention. Still, NATO's new Strategic Concept eschews leadership in favor of shared risks and roles. Unless NATO reconstitutes itself to deal directly with out-of-area operations and ethnic violence on its periphery, it likely will cease to exist.

To survive, NATO must redefine its mission. Even more critically in the long run, it must alleviate the fears of ostracism and encirclement by the other powers outside NATO's traditional zone of influence and operation. Russia, in particular, should not be excluded—a principle which Pres. Clinton recognized when, at the January, 1994, Brussels summit, he declared that his aim ultimately was "a security based not on Europe's division, but on the potential of its integration."

The Partnership for Peace must be extended and enlarged. Otherwise, the possibility that ultranationalist forces in Russia will seek to reassert their nation's imperial sway over its lost empire is likely to become a growing concern.

Similarly, an excluded China and Japan are unlikely to look favorably at an enlarged NATO that defines its purpose as their containment. Exclusion is the match that historically has ignited revanchist fires. Restricting security protection to only the 16 full-fledged members of NATO

effectively denies it to the others and thus does nothing to prevent the alliance from remaining a symbol of division.

NATO's enlargement is the best antidote to a return to the days of a world divided in separate blocs, each seeking to contain the expansion of the other. The U.S. solution of "separable but not separate" invites the very sort of polarization into competing alliances that it seeks to avoid. Filling the security vacuum around Russia (and China?) could revive the East-West division that followed Yalta—to no one's benefit.

Finally, some experts have suggested that the Group of Seven (G-7) should become the focal point for collective peacekeeping activities in the post-Cold War world. Two reasons typically underpin such arguments. First, G-7 members are democracies, and democracies almost never have waged war against each other to settle their disputes. Second, as countries connected by a web of economic linkages, there are material incentives for the G-7 to avoid policies that would rupture profitable business transactions.

These reasons notwithstanding, the drawback of the G-7 as a multilateral security mechanism is that it functions like an exclusive club whose formal membership does not include Russia or China. While shared democratic values may lay the groundwork for cooperation among members of the club, economic friction can limit the scope of its activities. Trading relationships involve both costs and benefits. The rewards of commercial exchange may be offset by fierce competition that breeds hostility.

In view of the differential growth rates among the great powers and their anxiety about trade competitiveness in an interdependent global marketplace, the major battles of the future may be clashes on the economic front, rather than armed combat among soldiers. Even in the event that political solidarity overrides economic rivalry, the G-7 is ill-equipped to orchestrate peacekeeping missions. Its business is managing business, not warfare.

Overcoming limitations

In sum, the United Nations, NATO, CSCE, and the G-7 all have limitations. Nevertheless, they will play prominent roles in the coming years if only because they are pre-existing structures. Because of this interdependence, for an efficacious concert-based collective security architecture to emerge, it must consist of an *ad hoc* combination of regional bodies tied together by an interlocking membership. For instance, the Eurasian land mass might have NATO or the CSCE anchoring its western flank and some type of a Conference on Security and Cooperation in the Pacific

7. VALUES AND VISIONS

devised for the eastern flank, with relevant great powers holding memberships in both organizations and meeting regularly under the auspices of the UN Security Council.

A full-fledged, comprehensive global collective security system, dedicated to containing aggression anywhere at any time, may be too ambitious and doomed to failure. Nevertheless, a restricted, concert-based collective security mechanism could bring a modicum of order in a fragile and disorderly new multipolar system.

The impending structural shift to multipolarity rivets the world's attention on the historical propensity of contending great powers to act as natural competitors by striving for position and pre-eminence. Whereas few powers seek to rule the world, all appear adamantly averse to subservient status—for no one wants equality with inferiors, only with superiors.

The diffusion of military and economic capabilities among powers that invariably have divergent interests presents serious obstacles for the preservation of world order. Multilateralism, with its emphasis on consultative, shared decision-making, provides an avenue for the great powers to recognize their convergent interest in avoiding the potentially bitter confrontations that otherwise might precipitate the formation of hostile blocs. Not all international conflict is amenable to multilateral resolution, but, by promoting mutual responsibility, multilateralism creates a legitimacy for concerted policy initiatives that is lacking in unilateralism and special bilateral partnerships.

Whether the great powers will seize the opportunity to create a concert-based collective security organization is problematic, however. The temptation to go it alone and compete, rather than cooperate to manage peaceful change, will remain strong. Yet, world order well may rest on the great powers' capacity to see their interests served by concerted multilateral initiatives at peacekeeping.

WOMEN'S ROLE IN POST-INDUSTRIAL DEMOCRACY

Eleanora Masini Barbieri

Italian sociologist, is the Director of the Executive Board of the World Futures Studies Federation and holds the Chair of Social Forecasting at the Gregorian University in Rome. Among her works published in English is Visions of Desirable Societies *(1983).*

ACCORDING to the American sociologist Elise Boulding, there are three areas in which the work of women has built what she calls a "civic society" based on mutual respect. The first is related to children and teaching. In almost all societies, women are responsible for the education of children up to their seventh year. Psychologists agree that these are the years in which the child's world-vision is formed.

The second is related to women's hidden economic role. Its arena may be the kitchen or the garden, the small production unit which played a crucial role in agricultural societies and has also often been, though less visibly, the salvation of the highly-industrialized societies of our time.

The third area has also been largely unnoticed. Women are and have been what Elise Boulding calls the "cement of society". They have fulfilled this role in private, in family life, and even in dynastic alliances between villages or towns over the centuries.

Boulding has described these areas, which belong to the "underside of history", as "society's green space, its visioning space, its bonding space. It is a space where minds can learn to grapple with complexities that are destroying the overside."

Women's efforts to build a viable society of respect and understanding also contribute to the creation of a democratic culture. Children learn respect, tolerance, and other principles of democratic behaviour at a very early stage, in their relations with other members of the family and the community. In this context, it is interesting to observe and compare the attitudes of families in different parts of the world: the strong community sense of the hierarchically organized extended family in Africa, the profound respect with which the elder members of the Chinese family are regarded, and the focus on younger family members in modern Western society. Women play a central role in the shaping of these attitudes through the way they behave and the example they set. It is because their public role has been invisible that they have learned respect for others—a respect that encourages democratic behaviour rather than the dominating behaviour often expected of men. Respect does not, however, mean accepting domination by others; it is coupled with the demand that women be respected in their turn.

Many examples could be cited of women's civic spirit. Polish women contributed to the rebuilding of Warsaw's schools after the Second World War; Japanese women organized

---

257

support systems after Hiroshima, as did the women of Mexico after the 1984 earthquake.

The concept of the democratic society developed in the industrial era. Today, industrial society appears to have reached its limits. The natural environment has been exploited, especially by the rich countries, in a way that certainly cannot be called democratic. Nor have people found happiness in material wealth, as is clearly evident among the young people of the wealthier countries of North America and Europe. We have reached both external and internal limits, to use a phrase coined by Aurelio Peccei, the founder of the Club of Rome. Our inner selves require answers that are far more profound than those industrial society has provided. In post-industrial society, whatever form it takes, a new mentality will be essential. We must use the many capacities of people, and especially the specific capacities of women, that are now untapped.

WOMEN CITIZENS OF TOMORROW

Post-industrial society will be a complex, uncertain society, in which such tools and methods of industrial society as specialization, separation of tasks, hierarchical structures, and mass production will no longer be relevant. Notable among its features will be decentralized networks of small units, diversified activities peformed by the same person or unit, and rapidity of action.

The society of the future will require people to be flexible. They will have to perform several tasks at the same time. They will need to possess a new sense of time. Production will be "personalized" rather than "standardized". As technology develops, people will have to learn new tasks and skills during their working lives, and in many cases to change jobs to keep pace with technological change.

In this society women are bound to play an increasingly important role, if only because in almost every country they have a higher life expectancy than men and head one-third of the world's households. The future of many major technological innovations, especially in biotechnology, will depend on whether women accept or reject them.

Women possess many of the capacities that will be needed in post-industrial society. Research in various countries has shown that they are particularly flexible and adaptable. Since their life-cycle forces them to stop and start work, often changing jobs, they are used to change. They have to be versatile. In addition to cooking, looking after the children, ironing and doing other household tasks, they may also have a job to do at home—sewing, perhaps, in developing countries, computer work in the industrialized world.

Women also tend to have a temporal rhythm which is closer to real time than to what Lewis Mumford called "clock time". This capacity too will be increasingly important in an overcrowded, unsynchronized society. Women find it difficult to standardize their production. In the society of the future, non-standardized production will become increasingly sought-after.

UNTAPPED POTENTIAL

In social life too, women seem to have capacities which will be important for the future—the capacity to create solidarity, to establish priorities, and to reject hierarchies.

Traditionally women have sought group solidarity. They exchange information about their children, their old people, matters of health and so on, as they collect water from the village well and as they meet in the supermarket. Whatever changes technology may bring, women will be unlikely to give up this exchange with each other. At moments of great distress—in time of war, revolution, natural catastrophe, during refugee movements—this capacity has been vital. The capacity of women to create solidarities and to understand and live with people from different cultures and backgrounds can make an enormous contribution to the building of a democratic culture.

Women have a strong sense of priorities. In times of need or stress, they make choices relating to their children and their future well-being, rather than to short-term benefits. In China, Canada, and in other countries with a large migrant population, research has shown that mothers faced with a range of choices put their children's education first. In developing countries, women's first priority might be water or food for their children rather than other economic benefits. There is also evidence that women are less inclined to accept hierarchical structures than men. This is important if, as the American futurologist Alvin Toffler believes, we are moving towards an increasingly egalitarian society.

Solidarity, the capacity to put first things first, and the rejection of hierarchies are traits that, if fostered rather than suppressed, may lead to a more democratic society, one that emerges from the behaviour of its citizens rather than from structures and laws.

If one accepts that the building of a democratic society depends more on citizens than on laws, institutions and structures, then women will have an essential contribution to make. And full use has not yet been made of their capacities.

We should be seeking to create democratic citizens, with the school working hand in hand with the family to foster democratic education. Although much has been accomplished already, much still remains to be done. The education system has undoubtedly changed for the better since the late 1960s, but in some countries there is plenty of room for improvement.

A democratic culture emerges from the sharing of values, however differently expressed, and from behaviour related to shared values. Only thus can a culture be built. There can be no democratic society without democratic citizens to construct it. Citizens rather than ideas, structures or institutions must be the starting-point.

The Post-Communist Nightmare

Václav Havel

President Havel gave the following speech on April 22, at George Washington University in Washington, DC, at a convocation honoring him with a presidential medal.

I remember a time when some of my friends and acquaintances used to go out of their way to avoid meeting me in the street. Though I certainly didn't intend it to be so, they saw me, in a way, as a voice of their conscience. They knew that if they stopped and talked with me, they would feel compelled to apologize for not openly defying the regime too, or to explain to me why they couldn't do it, or to defend themselves by claiming that dissent was pointless anyway. Conversations like this were usually quite an ordeal for both sides, and thus it was better to stay away from them altogether.

Another reason for their behavior was the fear that the police were following me, and that just talking to me would cause them complications. It was easier not to go near me. Thus they would avoid both an unpleasant conversation and the potential persecution that could follow. In short, I was, for those friends, an inconvenience, and inconveniences are best avoided.

For long decades, the chief nightmare of the democratic world was communism. Today—three years after it began to collapse like an avalanche—it would seem as though another nightmare has replaced it: postcommunism. There were many, not just in the West, but in the East as well, who had been looking forward for years to the fall of communism, and who had hoped that its collapse would mean that history had at last come to its senses. Today, these same people are seriously worried about the consequences of that fall. Some of

them may even feel a little nostalgic for a world that was, after all, slightly more transparent and understandable than the present one.

I do not share sentiments of that kind. I think we must not understand postcommunism merely as something that makes life difficult for the rest of the world. I certainly didn't understand communism that way. I saw it chiefly as a challenge, a challenge to thought and to action. To an even greater extent, postcommunism represents precisely that kind of challenge.

Anyone who understands a given historical phenomenon merely as an inconvenience will ultimately see many other things that way too: the warnings of ecologists, public opinion, the vagaries of voters, public morality. It is an easy, and therefore seductive, way of seeing the world and history. But it is extremely dangerous because we tend to remain aloof from things that inconvenience us and get in our way, just as some of my acquaintances avoided me during the Communist era. Any position based on the feeling that the world, or history, is merely an accumulation of inconveniences inevitably leads to a turning away from reality, and ultimately, to resigning oneself to it. It leads to appeasement, even to collaboration. The consequences of such a position may even be suicidal.

What in fact do we mean by postcommunism? Essentially it is a term for the state of affairs in all the countries that have rid themselves of communism. But it is a dangerous simplification to put all these countries in one basket. While it is true that they are all faced with essentially the same task—that is, to rid themselves of the disastrous legacy of communism, to

repair the damage it caused, and to create, or renew, democracy—at the same time, and for many reasons, there are great differences between them.

I will not go into all the problems encountered by post-Communist countries; experts are no doubt already writing books on the subject. I will mention only some of the root causes of the phenomena that are arousing the greatest concern in the democratic West, phenomena such as nationalism, xenophobia, and the poor moral and intellectual climate which—to a greater or lesser extent—go along with the creation of the new political and economic system.

The first of these causes I see in the fact that communism was far from being simply the dictatorship of one group of people over another. It was a genuinely totalitarian system, that is, it permeated every aspect of life and deformed everything it touched, including all the natural ways people had evolved of living together. It profoundly affected all forms of human behavior. For years, a specific structure of values and models of behavior was deliberately created in the consciousness of society. It was a perverted structure, one that went against all the natural tendencies of life, but society nevertheless internalized it, or rather was forced to internalize it.

When Communist power and its ideology collapsed, this structure collapsed along with it. But people couldn't simply absorb and internalize a new structure immediately, one that would correspond to the elementary principles of civic society and democracy. The human mind and human habits cannot be transformed overnight; to build a new system of living values and to identify with them takes time.

Address by President Václav Havel at George Washington University, April 22, 1993. Published in *The New York Review of Books* as "The Post-Communist Nightmare," May 27, 1993, pp. 8, 10. Reprinted by permission of Aurapont Literary Agency.

In a situation where one system has collapsed and a new one does not yet exist, many people feel empty and frustrated. This condition is fertile ground for radicalism of all kinds, for the hunt for scapegoats, and for the need to hide behind the anonymity of a group, be it socially or ethnically based. It encourages hatred of the world, self-affirmation at all costs, the feeling that everything is now permitted and the unparalleled flourishing of selfishness that goes along with it. It gives rise to the search for a common and easily identifiable enemy, to political extremism, to the most primitive cult of consumerism, to a carpetbagging morality, stimulated by the historically unprecedented restructuring of property relations, and so on and so on. Thanks to its former democratic traditions and to its unique intellectual and spiritual climate, the Czech Republic, the westernmost of the post-Communist countries, is relatively well off in this regard, compared with some of the other countries in the region. Nevertheless we too are going through the same great transformation that all the post-Communist countries are and we can therefore talk about it with the authority of insiders.

Another factor that must be considered in any analysis of post-Communist phenomena is the intrinsic tendency of communism to make everything the same. The greatest enemy of communism was always individuality, variety, difference—in a word, freedom. From Berlin to Vladivostok, the streets and buildings were decorated with the same red stars. Everywhere the same kind of celebratory parades were staged. Analogical state administrations were set up, along with the whole system of central direction for social and economic life. This vast shroud of uniformity, stifling all national, intellectual, spiritual, social, cultural, and religious variety, covered over any differences and created the monstrous illusion that we were all the same. The fall of communism destroyed this shroud of sameness, and the world was caught napping by an outburst of the many unanticipated differences concealed beneath it, each of which—after such a long time in the shadows—felt a natural need to draw attention to itself, to emphasize its uniqueness and its difference from others. This is the reason for the eruption of so many different kinds of old-fashioned patriotism, revivalist messianism, conservatism, and expressions of hatred toward all those who appeared to be betraying their roots or identifying with different ones.

The desire to renew and emphasize one's identity, one's uniqueness, is also behind the emergence of many new countries. Nations that have never had states of their own feel an understandable need to experience independence. It is no fault of theirs that the opportunity has come up decades or even centuries after it came to other nations.

This is related to yet another matter: for a long time, communism brought history, and with it all natural development, to a halt. While the Western democracies have had decades to create a civil society, to build internationally integrated structures, and to learn the arts of peaceful international coexistence and cooperation, the countries ruled by communism could not go through this creative process. National and cultural differences were driven into the subterranean areas of social life, where they were kept on ice and thus prevented from developing freely, from taking on modern forms in the fresh air, from creating, over time, the free space of unity in variety.

At the same time many of the nations suppressed by communism had never enjoyed freedom, not even before communism's advent, and thus had not a chance to resolve many of the basic questions of their existence as countries. Consequently thousands of unsolved problems have now suddenly burst forth into the light of day, problems left unsolved by history, problems we had wrongly supposed were long forgotten. It is truly astonishing to discover how, after decades of falsified history and ideological manipulation, nothing has been forgotten. Nations are now remembering their ancient achievements and their ancient suffering, their ancient suppressors and their allies, their ancient statehood and their former borders, their traditional animosities and affinities—in short, they are suddenly recalling a history that, until recently, had been carefully concealed or misrepresented.

Thus in many parts of the so-called post-Communist world, it is not just the regional order (sometimes referred to as the Yalta order) that is being corrected. There are also attempts to correct certain shortcomings in the Versailles order, and even to go farther back into history and exploit the greatest freedom some of them have ever had to make farther amends. It is an impossible desire, of course, but understandable all the same.

If we wish to understand the problems of the post-Communist world, or some of them at least, then we must continually remind ourselves of something else. It is easy to deny the latent problems, ambitions, and particularities of nations. It is easy to make everything the same by force, to destroy the complex and fragile social, cultural, and economic relationships and institutions built up over centuries, and to enforce a single, primitive model of central control in the spirit of a proud utopianism. It is as easy to do that as it is to smash a piece of antique, inlaid furniture with a single blow from a hammer. But it is infinitely more difficult to restore it all, or to create it directly.

The fall of the Communist empire is an event on the same scale of historical importance as the fall of the Roman empire. And it is having similar consequences, both good and extremely disturbing. It means a significant change in the countenance of today's world. The change is painful and will take a long time. To build a new world on the ruins of communism might be as extended and complex a process as the creation of a Christian Europe—after the great migrations—once was.

What are we to do if we don't wish to understand postcommunism simply as a new inconvenience that would be better avoided by sticking our heads in the sand and minding our own business?

I think the most important thing is not just to take account of external and more or less measurable phenomena like the gross national product, the progress of privatization, the stability of the political system, and the measurable degree to which human rights are observed. All of these things are important, of course, but something more is necessary. There must be an effort to understand the profound events taking place in the womb of post-Communist societies, to take note of their historical meaning and think about their global implications. The temptation must be resisted to adopt a disparaging and slightly astonished attitude, one based on a subconscious feeling of superiority on the part of observers who are better off. Just as Czechs should not sneer at the problems of Tadzhikistan, so no one should sneer at the problems of the Czech Republic. It is only against this background of understanding that meaningful ways of assistance can be sought.

It seems to me that the challenge offered by the post-Communist world is merely the current form of a broader and more profound challenge to discover a new type of self-understanding for man, and a new type of politics that should flow from that understanding. As we all know, today's planetary civilization is in serious danger. We are rationally capable of describing, in vivid detail, all the dangers that threaten the world: the deepening gulf between the rich and the poor parts of the world, the population explosion, the potential for dramatic confrontations between different racial and cultural groups, the arming of whom no one seems able to stop, the nuclear threat, the plundering of natural resources, the destruction of the natural variety of species, the creation of holes in the ozone layer, and the unstoppable global warming. What is unsettling is that the more we know about such dangers, the less able we seem to deal with them.

I see only one way out of this crisis: man must come to a new understanding of himself, of his limitations and his place in the world. He should grasp his responsibility in a new way, and reestablish a relationship with the things that transcend him. We must rehabilitate our sense of ourselves as active human subjects, and liberate ourselves from the captivity of a purely national perception of the world. Through this "subjecthood" and the individual conscience that goes with it, we must discover a new relationship to our neighbors, and to the universe and its metaphysical order, which is the source of the moral order.

We live in a world in which our destinies are tied to each other more closely than they ever have been before. It is a world with a single planetary civilization, yet it contains many cultures that, with increasing vigor and singlemindedness resist cultural unification, reject mutual understanding, and exist in what amounts to latent confrontation. It is a deeply dangerous state of affairs and it must be changed. The first step in this direction can be nothing less than a broad-based attempt by people from these cultures to understand one another, and to understand each other's right to existence. Only then can a kind of worldwide, pluralistic metaculture...evolve. It is only in the context of such a metaculture that a new sense of political responsibility—global responsibility—can come into being. And it is only with this newly born sense of responsibility that the instruments can be created that will enable humanity to confront all the dangers it has created for itself.

The new political self-understanding I am talking about means a clear departure from the understanding of the world that considers history, foreign cultures, foreign nations, and ultimately all those warnings about our future, as a mere agglomeration of annoying inconveniences that disturb our tranquility. A quiet life on the peak of a volcano is just as illusory as the notion I talked about at the beginning: that by avoiding an encounter with a dissident in the street, we can avoid the problem of communism and the question of how to deal with it.

Ultimately, I understand post-communism as one of many challenges to contemporary man—regardless of what part of the world he lives in—to awaken to his global responsibilities, and to awaken to them before it is too late.

This morning I had the honor of taking part in the opening of the Holocaust Memorial Museum.

On this occasion, as I have so often before, I asked myself how could this have happened? How could people in the twentieth century, aware of the theory of relativity, of quantum mechanics, who have penetrated to the heart of the atom and are exploring the reaches of outer space, have committed acts of horror so awful that to call them bestial would be to do an incredible disservice to all those creatures who happen not to be human. How could they have permitted it to happen?

In the context of what I have been talking about here, one aspect of a possible answer occurs to me. It was a failure of democracy, in which the politics of appeasement gave way to evil: what in my country we call the spirit of Munich. The inability of Europe and the world to recognize the emerging evil in time and stop it from growing to monstrous proportions is merely another form of what I have called here an understanding of the world as an agglomeration of inconveniences. The issue here is the absence of a wider sense of responsibility for the world.

Czechs remember well a remark made by a democratic statesman shortly before he signed the Munich agreement, the real beginning of all the horrors of the Second World War. He was appalled, he said then, that his country was digging trenches and trying on gas masks "because of a quarrel in a faraway country between people of whom we know nothing." It is a classic example of how suicidal it is to try to avoid inconveniences. This politician regarded Nazism as a problem that would go away if he stuck his head in the sand, or as it were crossed over to the other side of the street.

And so the chosen people were chosen by history to bear the brunt for all of us. The meaning of their sacrifice is to warn us against indifference to things we foolishly believe do not concern us.

In today's world, everything concerns everyone. Communism also concerned everyone. And it is also a matter of concern to everyone whether or not, and in what way, we manage to build a new zone of democracy, freedom, and prosperity on its ruins. Every intellectual and material investment in the post-Communist world that is not haphazard, but based on a deep understanding of what is happening there, will repay the whole world many times over.

And not only that: it will also be one more step on the thorny pilgrimage of the human race toward a new understanding of its responsibility for its destiny.

—translated from the Czech by Paul Wilson

The Global Village Finally Arrives

Pico Iyer

This is the typical day of a relatively typical soul in today's diversified world. I wake up to the sound of my Japanese clock radio, put on a T shirt sent me by an uncle in Nigeria and walk out into the street, past German cars, to my office. Around me are English-language students from Korea, Switzerland and Argentina—all on this Spanish-named road in this Mediterranean-style town. On TV, I find, the news is in Mandarin; today's baseball game is being broadcast in Korean. For lunch I can walk to a sushi bar, a tandoori palace, a Thai café or the newest burrito joint (run by an old Japanese lady). Who am I, I sometimes wonder, the son of Indian parents and a British citizen who spends much of his time in Japan (and is therefore—what else?—an American permanent resident)? And where am I?

I am, as it happens, in Southern California, in a quiet, relatively uninternational town, but I could as easily be in Vancouver or Sydney or London or Hong Kong. All the world's a rainbow coalition, more and more; the whole planet, you might say, is going global. When I fly to Toronto, or Paris, or Singapore, I disembark in a world as hyphenated as the one I left. More and more of the globe looks like America, but an America that is itself looking more and more like the rest of the globe. Los Angeles famously teaches 82 different languages in its schools. In this respect, the city seems only to bear out the old adage that what is in California today is in America tomorrow, and next week around the globe.

In ways that were hardly conceivable even a generation ago, the new world order is a version of the New World writ large: a wide-open frontier of polyglot terms and postnational trends. A common multiculturalism links us all—call it

Planet Hollywood, Planet Reebok or the United Colors of Benetton. *Taxi* and *hotel* and *disco* are universal terms now, but so too are *karaoke* and *yoga* and *pizza*. For the gourmet alone, there is *tiramisù* at the Burger King in Kyoto, echt angel-hair pasta in Saigon and enchiladas on every menu in Nepal.

But deeper than mere goods, it is souls that are mingling. In Brussels, a center of the new "unified Europe," 1 new baby in every 4 is Arab. Whole parts of the Paraguayan capital of Asunción are largely Korean. And when the prostitutes of Melbourne distributed some pro-condom pamphlets, one of the languages they used was Macedonian. Even Japan, which prides itself on its centuries-old socially engineered uniculture, swarms with Iranian illegals, Western executives, Pakistani laborers and Filipina hostesses.

> *The New World Order is a version of the New World writ large: a wide-open frontier of polyglot terms and post national trends*

The global village is defined, as we know, by an international youth culture that takes its cues from American pop culture. Kids in Perth and Prague and New Delhi are all tuning in to *Santa Barbara* on TV, and wriggling into 501 jeans, while singing along to Madonna's latest in English. CNN (which has grown 70-fold in 13 years) now reaches more than 140 countries; an American football championship pits London against Barcelona. As fast as the world comes to America, America goes round the world—but it is an America that is itself multi-tongued and many hued, an America of

Amy Tan and Janet Jackson and movies with dialogue in Lakota.

For far more than goods and artifacts, the one great influence being broadcast around the world in greater numbers and at greater speed than ever before is people. What were once clear divisions are now tangles of crossed lines: there are 40,000 "Canadians" resident in Hong Kong, many of whose first language is Cantonese. And with people come customs: while new immigrants from Taiwan and Vietnam and India—some of the so-called Asian Calvinists—import all-American values of hard work and family closeness and entrepreneurial energy to America, America is sending its values of upward mobility and individualism and melting-pot hopefulness to Taipei and Saigon and Bombay.

Values, in fact, travel at the speed of fax; by now, almost half the world's Mormons live outside the U.S. A diversity of one culture quickly becomes a diversity of many: the "typical American" who goes to Japan today may be a third-generation Japanese American, or the son of a Japanese woman married to a California serviceman, or the offspring of a Salvadoran father and an Italian mother from San Francisco. When he goes out with a Japanese woman, more than two cultures are brought into play.

None of this, of course, is new: Chinese silks were all the rage in Rome centuries ago, and Alexandria before the time of Christ was a paradigm of the modern universal city. Not even American eclecticism is new: many a small town has long known Chinese restaurants, Indian doctors and Lebanese grocers. But now all these cultures are crossing at the speed of light. And the rising diversity of the planet is something more than mere cosmopolitanism: it is a fundamental recoloring of the very complexion of societies. Cities like Paris, or Hong Kong, have always had a soigné, international air and served as magnets for exiles and émigrés, but now smaller places are multinational too. Marseilles speaks French with a distinctly North African twang. Islamic fundamentalism has one of its strongholds in Bradford, England. It is the sleepy coastal towns of Queensland, Australia, that print their menus in Japanese.

The dangers this internationalism presents are evident: not for nothing did the Tower of Babel collapse. As national borders fall, tribal alliances, and new manmade divisions, rise up, and the world learns every day terrible new meanings of the word Balkanization. And while some places are wired for international transmission, others (think of Iran or North Korea or Burma) remain as isolated as ever, widening the gap between the haves and the have-nots, or what Alvin Toffler has called the "fast" and the "slow" worlds. Tokyo has more telephones than the whole continent of Africa.

Nonetheless, whether we like it or not, the "transnational" future is upon us: as Kenichi Ohmae, the international economist, suggests with his talk of a "borderless economy," capitalism's allegiances are to products, not places. "Capital is now global," Robert Reich, the Secretary of Labor, has said, pointing out that when an Iowan buys a Pontiac from General Motors, 60% of his money goes to South Korea, Japan, West Germany, Taiwan, Singapore, Britain and Barbados. Culturally we are being reformed daily by the cadences of world music and world fiction: where the great Canadian writers of an older generation had names like Frye and Davies and Laurence, now they are called Ondaatje and Mistry and Skvorecky.

As space shrinks, moreover, time accelerates. This hip-hop mishmash is spreading overnight. When my parents were in college, there were all of seven foreigners living in Tibet, a country the size of Western Europe, and in its entire history the country had seen fewer than 2,000 Westerners. Now a Danish student in Lhasa is scarcely more surprising than a Tibetan in Copenhagen. Already a city like Miami is beyond the wildest dreams of 1968; how much more so will its face in 2018 defy our predictions of today?

It would be easier, seeing all this, to say that the world is moving toward the *Raza Cósmica* (Cosmic Race), predicted by the Mexican thinker José Vasconcelos in the '20s—a glorious blend of mongrels and mestizos. It may be more relevant to suppose that more and more of the world may come to resemble Hong Kong, a stateless special economic zone full of expats and exiles linked by the lingua franca of English and the global marketplace. Some urbanists already see the world as a grid of 30 or so highly advanced city-regions, or technopoles, all plugged into the same international circuit.

The world will not become America. Anyone who has been to a baseball game in Osaka, or a Pizza Hut in Moscow, knows instantly that she is not in Kansas. But America may still, if only symbolically, be a model for the world. *E Pluribus Unum,* after all, is on the dollar bill. As Federico Mayor Zaragoza, the director-general of UNESCO, has said, "America's main role in the new world order is not as a military superpower, but as a multicultural superpower."

The traditional metaphor for this is that of a mosaic. But Richard Rodriguez, the Mexican-American essayist who is a psalmist for our new hybrid forms, points out that the interaction is more fluid than that, more human, subject to daily revision. "I am Chinese," he says, "because I live in San Francisco, a Chinese city. I became Irish in America. I became Portuguese in America." And even as he announces this new truth, Portuguese women are becoming American, and Irishmen are becoming Portuguese, and Sydney (or is it Toronto?) is thinking to compare itself with the "Chinese city" we know as San Francisco.

This glossary contains primarily technical, economic, financial, and military terminology not usually defined in most textbooks.

— A —

Absolute poverty: The condition of people whose incomes are insufficient to keep them at a subsistence level.

Adjudication: The legal process of deciding an issue through the courts.

African, Caribbean, and Pacific Countries (ACP): Fifty-eight countries associated with the European Community.

African National Congress (ANC): South African organization founded in 1912 in response to the taking of land from Africans and the restrictions on their employment and movement. Following attempts at peaceful resistance, its leaders were tried for treason and imprisoned. In 1990, ANC de facto leader Nelson Mandela was released from prison, and a continued resistance against the apartheid state grew. The ANC was legalized in 1991.

Airborne Warning and Control System (AWACS): Flying radar stations that instantaneously identify all devices in the air within a radius of 240 miles and detect movement of land vehicles.

Air-Launched Cruise Missile (ALCM): A cruise missile carried by and launched from an aircraft.

Antiballistic missile (ABM): A missile that seeks out and destroys an incoming enemy missile in flight before the latter reaches its target. It is not effective against MIRVs.

Apartheid: A system of laws in the Republic of South Africa that segregates and politically and economically discriminates against non-European groups.

Appropriate technology: Also known as intermediate technology. It aims at using existing resources by making their usage more efficient or productive but adaptable to the local population.

Arms control: Any measure limiting or reducing forces, regulating armaments, and/or restricting the deployment of troops or weapons.

Arms race: The competitive or cumulative improvement of weapons stocks (qualitatively or quantitatively), or the buildup of armed forces based on the conviction of two or more actors that only by trying to stay ahead in military power can they avoid falling behind.

Association of Southeast Asian Nations (ASEAN): A regional regrouping made up of Indonesia, the Philippines, Singapore, and Thailand.

Atomic bomb: A weapon based on the rapid splitting of fissionable materials, thereby inducing an explosion with three deadly results: blast, heat, and radiation.

Autarky: Establishing economic independence.

— B —

Balance of payments: A figure that represents the net flow of money into and out of a country due to trade, tourist expenditures, sale of services (such as consulting), foreign aid, profits, and so forth.

Balance of trade: The relationship between imports and exports.

Ballistic missile: A payload propelled by a rocket, which assumes a free-fall trajectory when thrust is terminated. Ballistic missiles could be of short range (SRBM), intermediate range (IRBM), medium range (MRBM), and intercontinental (ICBM).

Bantustans: Ten designated geographical areas or "homelands" for each African ethnic group created under the apartheid government of South Africa. Beginning in the late 1970s, South Africa instituted a policy offering "independence" to the tribal leaders of these homelands. The leaders of four homeland governments accepted independent status, but no outside actors recognized these artificial entities as independent nation-states. Under the terms of the new constitution, all homeland citizens are now considered to be citizens of South Africa.

Barrel: A standard measure for petroleum, equivalent to 42 gallons or 158.86 liters.

Basic human needs: Adequate food intake (in terms of calories, proteins, and vitamins), drinking water free of disease-carrying organisms and toxins, minimum clothing and shelter, literacy, sanitation, health care, employment, and dignity.

Bilateral diplomacy: Negotiations between two countries.

Bilateral (foreign) aid: Foreign aid given by one country directly to another.

Binary (chemical) munitions/weapons: Nerve gas canisters composed of two separate chambers containing chemicals that become lethal when mixed. The mixing is done when the canister is fired. Binary gas is preferred for its relative safety in storage and transportation.

Biosphere: The environment of life and living processes at or near Earth's surface, extending from the ocean floors to about 75 kilometers into the atmosphere. It is being endangered by consequences of human activities such as air and water pollution, acid rain, radioactive fallout, desertification, toxic and nuclear wastes, and the depletion of nonrenewable resources.

Bipolar system: A world political system in which power is primarily held by two international actors.

Buffer Stocks: Reserves of commodities that are either increased or decreased whenever necessary to maintain relative stability of supply and prices.

— C —

Camp David Agreements/Accords: Agreements signed on September 17, 1978, at Camp David—a mountain retreat for the U.S. president in Maryland—by President Anwar al-Sadat of Egypt and Prime Minister Menachem Begin of Israel, and witnessed by President Jimmy Carter.

Capitalism: An economic system based on the private ownership of real property and commercial enterprise, competition for profits, and limited government interference in the marketplace.

Cartel: An international agreement among producers of a commodity that attempts to control the production and pricing of that commodity.

CBN weapons: Chemical, biological, and nuclear weapons.

Chemical Weapons Convention Treaty: Signed in 1993, the treaty requires its 130 signatories to eliminate all chemical weapons by the year 2005 and to submit to rigorous inspection.

Cold war: A condition of hostility that existed between the U.S. and the Soviet Union in their struggle to dominate the world scene following World War II. It ended with the collapse of the Soviet Union in 1991.

Collective security: The original theory behind UN peacekeeping. It holds that aggression against one state is aggression against all and should be defeated by the collective action of all.

Commodity: The unprocessed products of mining and agriculture.

Common Heritage of Mankind: A 1970 UN declaration that states that the "seabed and ocean floor, and the subsoil thereof, beyond the limits of national jurisdiction . . . , as well as the resources of the area, are the common heritage of mankind."

Common Market: A customs union that eliminates trade barriers within a group and establishes a common external tariff on imports from nonmember countries.

Commonwealth of Independent States (CIS): In December 1991 the Soviet Union was dissolved and fifteen independent countries were formed: Armenia, Azerbaijan, Byelorussia (Belarus), Estonia, Georgia, Kazakhstan, Kirghizia (Kyrgyzstan), Latvia, Lithuania, Moldavia (Moldova), Russia, Tadzhikistan (Tajikistan), Turkmenistan, Ukraine, and Uzbekistan. Some of the republics have since changed their names. CIS represents a collective term for the group of republics.

Compensatory Financing Facility: An IMF program established in 1963 to finance temporary export shortfalls, as in coffee, sugar, or other cyclically prone export items.

Concessional loans: Loans given to LLDCs by MBDs that can be repaid in soft (nonconvertible) currencies and with nominal or no interest over a long period of time.

Conditionality: A series of measures that must be taken by a country before it could qualify for loans from the International Monetary Fund.

Conference on International Economic Cooperation (CIEC): A conference of 8 industrial nations, 7 oil-producing nations, and 12 developing countries held in several sessions between December 1975 and June 1977. It is composed of four separate commissions (energy, raw materials, development, and financing). It is the forum of the North-South dialogue between rich and poor countries.

Conference on Security and Cooperation in Europe (CSCE): Series of conferences among 51 NATO, former Soviet bloc, and neutral European countries (52 counting Serbia or rump Yugoslavia). Established by 1976 Helsinki Accords. There are plans to establish a small, permanent CSCE headquarters and staff.

Consensus: In conference diplomacy, a way of reacing agreements by negotiations and without a formal vote.

Counterforce: The use of strategic nuclear weapons for strikes on selected military capabilities of an enemy force.

Countervalue: The use of strategic nuclear weapons for strikes on an enemy's population centers.

Cruise missile: A small, highly maneuverable, low-flying, pilotless aircraft equipped with accurate guidance systems that periodically readjusts its trajectory. It can carry conventional or nuclear warheads, can be short-range or long-range, and can be launched from the air (ALLUM), the ground (GLCM), or the sea (SLCM).

Cultural imperialism: The attempt to impose your own value systems on others, including judging others by how closely they conform to your norms.

Current dollars: The value of the dollar in the year for which it is being reported. Sometimes called inflated dollars. Any currency can be expressed in current value. *See* **Real dollars.**

— D —

Decision making: The process by which humans choose which policy to pursue and which actions to take in support of policy goals. The study of decision making seeks to identify patterns in the way that humans make decisions. This includes gathering information, analyzing information, and making choices. Decision making is a complex process that relates to personality and other human traits, to the sociopolitical setting in which decision makers function, and to the organizational structures involved.

Declaration of Talloires: A statement issued in 1981 by Western journalists who opposed the UNESCO-sponsored New World Information and Communication Order, at a meeting in Talloires, France.

Delivery systems or Vehicles or Launchers: Land-Based Missiles (ICBMs), Submarine-Launched Missiles (SLBMs), and long-range bombers capable of delivering nuclear weapons.

Dependencia model: The belief that the industrialized North has created a neocolonial relationship with the South in which the LDCs are dependent on and disadvantaged by their economic relations with the capitalist industrial countries.

Deployment: The actual positioning of weapons systems in a combat-ready status.

Détente: A relaxation of tensions or a decrease in the level of hostility between opponents on the world scene.

Deterrence: Persuading an opponent not to attack by having enough forces to disable the attack and/or launch a punishing counterattack.

Developed Countries (DCs): Countries with relatively high per capita GNP, education, levels of industrial development and production, health and welfare, and agricultural productivity.

Developing Countries (also called Less Developed Countries): These countries are mainly raw materials producers for export with high growth rates and inadequate infrastructures in transportation, educational systems, and the like. There is, however, a wide variation in living standards, GNPs, and per capita incomes among LCDs.

Development: The process through which a society becomes increasingly able to meet basic human needs and ensure the physical quality of life of its people.

Direct investment: Buying stock, real estate, and other assets in another country with the aim of gaining a controlling interest in foreign economic enterprises. Different from portfolio investment, which involves investment solely to gain capital appreciation through market fluctuations.

Disinformation: The spreading of false propaganda and forged documents to confuse counterintelligence or to create political confusion, unrest, and scandal.

Dumping: A special case of price discrimination, selling to foreign buyers at a lower price than that charged to buyers in the home market.

Duty: Special tax applied to imported goods, based on tariff rates and schedules.

— E —

East (as in the East-West struggle): A shorthand, nongeographic term that included nonmarket, centrally planned (communist) countries.

East-West Axis: The cold war conflict between the former Soviet Union and its allies and the United States and its allies.

Economic Cooperation among Developing Countries (ECDC): Also referred to as intra-South, or South-South cooperation, it is a way for LCDs to help each other with appropriate technology.

Economic statecraft: The practice of states utilizing economic instruments, such as sanctions, to gain their political ends. Economic statecraft is closely related to "mercantilism," or the use of political power to advance a country's economic fortunes.

Economically Developing Countries (EDCs): The relatively wealthy and industrialized countries that lie mainly in the Northern Hemisphere (the North).

Escalation: Increasing the level of fighting.

Essential equivalence: Comparing military capabilities of two would-be belligerents, not in terms of identical mix of forces, but in terms of how well two dissimilarly organized forces could achieve a strategic stalemate.

Eurodollars: U.S. dollar holdings of European banks; a liability for the U.S. Treasury.

Euromissiles: Shorthand for long-range theatre nuclear forces stationed in Europe or aimed at targets in Europe.

Europe 1992: A term that represents the European Community's decision to eliminate by the end of 1992 all internal barriers (between member countries) to the movement of trade, financial resources, workers, and services (banking, insurance, etc.).

European Community (EC): The Western European regional organization established in 1967 that includes the European Coal and Steel Community (ECSC), the European Economic Community (EEC), and the European Atomic Energy Community (EURATOM).

European Currency Unit (ECU): The common unit of valuation among the eight members of the European Monetary System (EMS).

European Economic Community (EEC). *See* **European Union.**

European Free Trade Association (EFTA): Austria, Finland, Iceland, Liechtenstein, Norway, Portugal, Sweden, and Switzerland. Each member keeps its own external tariff schedule, but free trade prevails among the members.

European Monetary System (EMS): Established in 1979 as a preliminary stage toward an economic and monetary union in the European Community. Fluctuations in the exchange rate value of the currencies of the participating countries are kept with a 2¼ percent limit of divergence from the strongest currency among them. The system collapsed in 1993, thus slowing progress toward monetary integration in Europe.

European Union: Known as the European Economic Community, and also the Common Market, until 1994, the European Union has 12 full members: Belgium, Denmark, France, Germany, Greece, Ireland, Italy, Luxembourg, Netherlands, Portugal, Spain, and the United Kingdom. (Austria, Finland, Norway, and Sweden are expected to enter the Union in 1995.) Originally established by the Treaty of Rome in 1958, the Union nations work toward establishing common defense and foreign policies and a common market.

Exchange rate: The values of two currencies relative to each other—for example, how many yen equal a dollar or how many lira equal a pound.

Export subsidies: Special incentives, including direct payments to exporters, to encourage increased foreign sales.

Exports: Products shipped to foreign countries.

— F —

Finlandization: A condition of nominal neutrality, but one of actual subservience to the former Soviet Union in foreign and security policies, as is the case with Finland.

First strike: The first offensive move of a general nuclear war. It implies an intention to knock out the opponent's ability to retaliate.

Fissionable or nuclear materials: Isotopes of certain elements, such as plutonium, thorium, and uranium, that emit neutrons in such large numbers that a sufficient concentration will be self-sustaining until it explodes.

Foreign policy: The sum of a country's goals and actions on the world stage. The study of foreign policy is synonymous with state-level analysis and examines how countries define their interests, establish goals, decide on specific policies, and attempt to implement those policies.

Forward based system (FBS or FoBS): A military installation, maintained on foreign soil or in international waters, and conveniently located near a theatre of war.

Fourth World: An expression arising from the world economic crisis that began in 1973–74 with the quadrupling in price of petroleum. It encompasses the least developed countries (LLDCs) and the most seriously affected countries (MSAs).

Free trade: The international movement of goods unrestricted by tariffs or nontariff barriers.

Functionalism: International cooperation in specific areas such as communications, trade, travel, health, or environmental protection activity. Often symbolized by the specialized agencies, such as the World Health Organization, associated with the United Nations.

— G —

General Agreement on Tariffs and Trade (GATT): Created in 1947, this organizaiton is the major global forum for negotiations of tariff reductions and other measures to expand world trade. Its members account for four-fifths of the world's trade.

General Assembly: The main representative body of the United Nations, composed of all member states.

Generalized System of Preferences (GSP): A system approved by GATT in 1971, which authorizes DCs to give preferential traiff treatment to LCDs.

Global: Pertaining to the world as a whole; worldwide.

Global commons: The Antarctic, the ocean floor under international waters, and celestial bodies within reach of planet Earth. All of these areas and bodies are considered the common heritage of mankind.

Global Negotiations: A new round of international economic negotiations started in 1980 over raw materials, energy, trade, development, money, and finance.

Golan Heights: Syrian territory adjacent to Israel, which has occupied it since the 1967 war and that annexed it unilaterally in 1981.

Gross Domestic Product (GDP): A measure of income within a country that excludes foreign earnings.

Gross National Product (GNP): A measure of the sum of all goods and services produced by a country's nationals, whether they are in the country or abroad.

Group of Seven (G-7): The seven economically largest free market countries: Canada, France, Great Britain, Italy, Japan, the United States, and Germany.

Group of 77: Group of 77 Third World countries that cosponsored the Joint Declaration of Developing Countries in 1963 calling for greater equity in North-South trade. This group has come to include more than 120 members and represents the interests of the less developed countries of the South.

— H —

Hegemonism: Any attempt by a larger power to interfere, threaten, intervene against, and dominate a smaller power or a region of the world.

Hegemony: Domination by a major power over smaller, subordinate ones within its sphere of influence.

Helsinki Agreement. *See* **Conference on Security and Cooperation in Europe.**

Horn of Africa: The northeast corner of Africa that includes Ethiopia, Djibouti, and Somalia. It is separated from the Arabian peninsula by the Gulf of Aden and the Red Sea. It is plagued with tribal conflicts between Ethiopia and Eritrea, and between Ethiopia and Somalia over the Ogaden desert. These conflicts have generated a large number of refugees who have been facing mass starvation.

Human rights: Rights inherent to human beings, including but not limited to the right of dignity; the integrity of the person; the inviolability of the person's body and mind; civil and political rights (freedom of religion, speech, press, assembly, association, the right to privacy, habeas corpus, due process of law, the right to vote or not to vote, the right to run for election, and the right to be protected from reprisals for acts of peaceful dissent); social, economic, and cultural rights. The most glaring violations of human rights are torture, disappearance, and the general phenomenon of state terrorism.

— I —

Imports: Products brought into a country from abroad.

Inkatha Freedom Party (IFP): A Zulu-based political and cultural movement led by Mangosuthu Buthelezi. It is a main rival of the African National Congress in South Africa.

Innocent passage: In a nation's territorial sea, passage by a foreign ship is innocent so long as it is not prejudicial to the peace, good order, or security of the coastal state. Submarines must surface and show their flag.

Intercontinental Ballistic Missile (ICBM): A land-based, rocket-propelled vehicle capable of delivering a warhead to targets at 6,000 or more nautical miles.

Interdependence (economic): The close interrelationship and mutual dependence of two or more domestic economies on each other.

Intergovernmental organizations (IGOs): International/transnational actors comprised of member countries.

Intermediate-range Ballistic Missile (IRBM): A missile with a range from 1,500 to 4,000 nautical miles.

Intermediate-range Nuclear Forces: Nuclear arms that are based in Europe with a deployment range that easily encompasses the former USSR.

Intermediate-range Nuclear Forces Treaty (INF): The treaty between the former USSR and the United States that limits the dispersion of nuclear warheads in Europe.

International: Between or among sovereign states.

International Atomic Energy Agency (IAEA): An agency created in 1946 by the UN to limit the use of nuclear technology to peaceful purposes.

International Court of Justice (ICJ): The World Court, which sits in The Hague with 15 judges and which is associated with the United Nations.

International Development Association (IDA): An affiliate of the World Bank that provides interest-free, long-term loans to developing countries.

International Energy Agency (IEA): An arm of OECD that attempts to coordinate member countries' oil imports and reallocate stocks among members in case of disruptions in the world's oil supply.

International Finance Corporation: Created in 1956 to finance overseas investments by private companies without necessarily requiring government guarantees. The IFC borrows from the World Bank, provides loans, and invests directly in private industry in the development of capital projects.

International Monetary Fund (IMF): The world's primary organization devoted to maintaining monetary stability by helping countries fund balance-of-payments deficits. Established in 1947, it now has 170 members.

International political economy (IPE): A term that encapsulates the totality of international economic interdependence and exchange in the political setting of the international system. Trade, investment, monetary relations, transnational business activities, aid, loans, and other aspects of international economic interchange (and the reciprocal impacts between these activities and politics) are all part of the study of IPE.

Interstate: International, intergovernmental.

Intifada (literally, resurgence): A series of minor clashes between Palestinian youths and Israeli security forces that escalated into a full-scale revolt in December 1987.

Intra-South. *See* **Economic Cooperation among Developing Countries.**

Islamic fundamentalism: Early nineteenth-century movements of fundamentalism sought to revitalize Islam through internal reform, thus enabling Islamic societies to resist foreign control. Some of these movements sought peaceful change, while other were more militant. The common ground of twentieth-century reform movements and groups is their fundamental opposition to the onslaught of materialistic Western culture and their desire to reassert a distinct Islamic identity for the societies they claim to represent.

— K —

Kampuchea: The new name for Cambodia since April 1975.

KGB: Security police and intelligence apparatus in the former Soviet Union, engaged in espionage, counterespionage, antisubversion, and control of political dissidents.

Khmer Rouge: Literally "Red Cambodians," the communist organization ruling Kampuchea between April 1975 and January 1979 under Pol Pot and Leng Saray.

Kiloton: A thousand tons of explosive force. A measure of the yield of a nuclear weapon equivalent to 1,000 tons of TNT (trinitrotoluene). The bomb detonated at Hiroshima in World War II had an approximate yield of 14 kilotons.

— L —

Launcher. *See* **Delivery Systems.**

League of Nations: The first true general international organization. It existed between the end of World War I and the beginning of World War II and was the immediate predecessor of the United Nations.

Least Developed Countries: Those countries in the poorest of economic circumstances. Frequently it includes those countries with a per capita GNP of less than $400 in 1985 dollars.

Less Developed Countries (LDCs): Countries, located mainly in Africa, Asia, and Latin America, with economies that rely heavily on the production of agriculture and raw material and whose per capita GNP and standard of living are substantially below Western standards.

Linkage diplomacy: The practice of considering another country's general international behavior as well as the specifics of the question when deciding whether or not to reach an agreement on an issue.

Lisbon Protocal: Signed in 1992, it is an agreement between ex-Soviet republics Kazakhstan and Belarus to eliminate nuclear weapons from their territories.

Lome Convention: An agreement concluded between the European Community and 58 African, Caribbean, and Pacific countries (ACP), allowing the latter preferential trade relations and greater economic and technical assistance.

Long-Range Theatre Nuclear Forces (LRTNF): Nuclear weapon systems with a range greater than 1,000 kilometers (or 600 miles), such as the U.S. Persing II missile or the Soviet SS-20.

— M —

Maastricht Treaty: Signed by the European Community's 12-member countries in December 1991, the Maastricht Treaty outlines steps toward further political/economic integration. At this time, following several narrow ratification votes and monetary crises, it is too early to foretell the future evolution of EC political integration.

Medium-range Ballistic Missile (MRBM): A missle with a range from 500 to 1,500 nautical miles.

Megaton: The yield of a nuclear weapon equivalent to 1 million tons of TNT (approximately equivalent to 79 Hiroshima bombs).

Microstates: Very small countries, usually with a population of less than one million.

Missile experimental (MX): A mobile, land-based missile that is shuttled among different launching sites, making it more difficult to locate and destroy.

Most Favored Nation (MFN): In international trade agreements, a country granting most-favored-nation status to another country in regard to tariffs and other trade regulations.

Multilateral: Involving many nations.

Multinational: Doing business in many nations.

Multinational corporations (MNCs): Private enterprises doing business in more than one country.

Multiple Independently Targetable Reentry Vehicle (MIRV): Two or more warheads carried by a single missile and capable of being guided to separate targets on reentry.

Munich syndrome: A lesson that was drawn by post–World War II leaders that one should not compromise with aggression.

Mutual and Balanced Force Reductions (MBFR): The 19-nation Conference on Mutual Reduction of Forces and Armaments and Associated Measures in Central Europe that has been held intermittently from 1973 to the end of the 1980s.

Mutural Assured Destruction (MAD): The basic ingredient of the doctrine of strategic deterrence that no country can escape destruction in a nuclear exchange even if it engages in a preemptive strike.

— N —

Namibia: African name for South-West Africa.

National Intelligence Estimate (NIE): The final assessment of global problems and capabilities by the intelligence community for use by the National Security Council and the president in making foreign and military decisions.

Nation-State: A political unit that is sovereign and has a population that supports and identifies with it politically.

Nautical mile: 1,853 meters.

Neocolonialism: A perjorative term describing the economic exploitation of Third World countries by the industrialized countries, in particular through the activities of multinational corporations.

Neutron bomb: Enhanced radiation bomb giving out lower blast and heat but concentrated radiation, thus killing people and living things while reducing damage to physical structures.

New International Economic Order (NIEO): The statement of development policies and objectives adopted at the Sixth Special Session of the UN General Assembly in 1974. NIEO calls for equal participation of LDCs in the international economic policy-making process, better known as the North-South dialogue.

New world order: A term that refers to the structure and operation of the post–cold war world. Following the Persian Gulf War, President George Bush referred to a world order based on nonaggression and on international law and organization.

Nonaligned Movement (NAM): A group of Third World countries interested in promoting economic cooperation and development.

Nongovernmental organizations (NGOs or INGOs): Transnational (international) organizations made up of private organizations and individuals instead of member states.

Nonproliferation of Nuclear Weapons Treaty (NPT): Nuclear weapon states, party to the NPT, pledge not to transfer nuclear explosive devices to any recipient and not to assist any non–nuclear weapon state in the manufacture of nuclear explosive devices.

Nontariff barriers (NTB): Subtle, informal impediments to free trade desinged for the purpose of making importation of foreign goods into a country very difficult on such grounds as health and safety regulations.

Normalization of relations: The reestablishment of full diplomatic relations, including de jure recognition and the exchange of ambassadors between two countries that either did not have diplomatic relations or had broken them.

North: (as in North-South dialogue): (a) A shorthand, non-geographic term for the industrialized countries of high income, both East and West; (b) Often means only the industrialized, high-income countries of the West.

North Atlantic Cooperation Council (NACC): Consists of 37 members, including all members of NATO, the former Warsaw Pact members, and former Soviet republics (Russia, Ukraine, Belarus, Georgia, Moldova, Armenia, Azerbaijan, Kazakhstan, Uzbekistan, Kyrgyzstan, Turkmentistan, and Tajikstan), the Czech Republic, Slovakia, Poland, Hungary, Romania, Bulgaria, Estonia, Latvia, Lithuania, and Albania.

North Atlantic Treaty Organization (NATO): Also known as the Atlantic Alliance, NATO was formed in 1949 to provide collective defense against the perceived Soviet threat to Western Europe. It consists of the United States, Canada, 13 Western European countries, and Turkey.

North-South Axis: A growing tension that is developing between the North (economically developed countries) and the South (economically deprived countries). The South is insisting that the North share part of its wealth and terminate economic and political domination.

Nuclear free zone: A stretch of territory from which all nuclear weapons are banned.

Nuclear Nonproliferation Treaty (NPT): A treaty that prohibits the sale, acquisition, or production of nuclear weapons.

Nuclear proliferation: The process by which one country after another comes into possession of some form of nuclear weaponry, and with it develops the potential of launching a nuclear attack on other countries.

Nuclear reprocessing: The separation of radioactive waste (spent fuel) from a nuclear-powered plant into its fissile constituent materials. One such material is plutonium, which can then be used in the production of atomic bombs.

Nuclear terrorism: The use (or threatened use) of nuclear weapons or radioactive materials as a means of coercion.

NUT (Nuclear Utilization Theory): Advocates of this nuclear strategy position want to destroy enemy weapons before the weapons explode on one's own territory and forces. The best way to do this, according to this theory, is to destroy an enemy's weapons before they are launched.

— O —

Official Development Aid (ODA): Government contributions to projects and programs aimed at developing the productivity of poorer countries. This is to be distinguished from private, voluntary assistance, humanitarian assistance for disasters, and, most importantly, from military assistance.

Ogaden: A piece of Ethiopian desert populated by ethnic Somalis. It was a bone of contention between Ethiopia and Somalia that continued until 1988 when a peace agreement was reached.

Organization of Economic Cooperation and Development (OECD): An organization of 24 members that serves to promote economic coordination among the Western industrialized countries.

Organization of Arab Petroleum Exporting Countries (OAPEC): A component of OPEC, with Saudi Arabia, Kuwait, the United Arab Emirates, Qatar, Iraq, Algeria, and Libya as members.

Organization of Petroleum Exporting Countries (OPEC): A producers' cartel setting price floors and production ceilings of crude petroleum. It consists of Venezuela and others such as Ecuador, Gabon, Nigeria, and Indonesia, as well as the Arab oil-producing countries.

— P —

Palestine: "Palestine" does not exist today as an entity. It refers to the historical and geographical entity administered by the British under the League of Nations mandate from 1918 to 1947. It also refers to a future entity in the aspirations of Palestinians who, as was the case of the Jews before the founding of the State of Israel, are stateless nationalists. Whether Palestinians will have an autonomous or independent homeland is an ongoing issue.

Palestine Liberation Organization (PLO): A coalition of Palestinian groups united by the goal of a Palestinian state through the destruction of Israel as a state.

Partnership for Peace Program: A U.S.–backed policy initiative for NATO formulated by the Clinton administration in 1994. The proposal was designed to rejuvenate the Atlantic Alliance and contribute to the stability of recent independent countries in Eastern Europe and the former Soviet Union. No NATO security guarantees or eventual membership in the alliance are specifically mentioned.

Payload: Warheads attached to delivery vehicles.

Peacekeeping: When an international organization such as the United Nations uses military means to prevent hostilities—usually by serving as a buffer between combatants. This international force will remain neutral between the opposing forces and must be invited by at least one of the combatants. *See* **Collective security**.

People's Republic of China (PRC): Communist or mainland China.

Petrodollars: U.S. dollar holdings of capital-surplus OPEC countries; a liability for the U.S. Treasury.

Physical Quality of Life Index (PQLI): Developed by the Overseas Development Council, the PQLI is presented as a more significant measurement of the well-being of inhabitants of a geographic entity than the solely monetary measurement of per capita income. It consists of the following measurements: life expectancy, infant mortality, and literacy figures that are each rated on an index of 1–100, within which each country is ranked according to its performance. A composite index is obtained by averaging these three measures, giving the PQLI.

Polisario: The liberation front of Western Sahara (formerly Spanish Sahara). After years of bitter fighting over Western Sahara, Polisario guerrillas signed a cease-fire agreement with Morocco in 1990. The UN will conduct a referendum in Western Sahara on whether the territory should become independent or remain part of Morocco.

Postindustrial: Characteristic of a society where a large portion of the workforce is directed to nonagricultural and nonmanufacturing tasks such as servicing and processing.

Precision-Guided Munitions (PGM): Popularly known as "smart bombs." Electronically programmed and controlled weapons that can accurately hit a moving or stationary target.

Proliferation: Quick spread, as in the case of nuclear weapons.

Protectionism: Using tariffs and nontariff barriers to control or restrict the flow of imports into a country.

Protocol: A preliminary memorandum often signed by diplomatic negotiators as a basis for a final convention or treaty.

— Q —

Quota: Quantitative limits, usually imposed on imports or immigrants.

— R —

Rapprochement: The coming together of two countries that had been hostile to each other.

Real Dollars (uninflated dollars): The report of currency in terms of what it would have been worth in a stated year.

Regionalism: A concept of cooperation among geographically adjacent states to foster region-wide political, military, and economic interests.

Reprocessing of nuclear waste: A process of recovery of fissionable materials among which is weapons-grade plutonium.

Resolution: Formal decisions of UN bodies; they may simply register an opinion or may recommend action to be taken by a UN body or agency.

Resolution 242: Passed by the UN Security Council on November 22, 1967, calling for the withdrawal of Israeli troops from territories they captured from Egypt (Sinai), Jordan (West Bank and East Jerusalem), and Syria (Golan Heights) in the 1967 war, and for the right of all nations in the Middle East to live in peace in secure and recognized borders.

Resolution 435: Passed by the UN Security Council in 1978, it called for a cease-fire between belligerents in the Namibian conflict (namely SWAPO, Angola and other front-line states on the one side, and South Africa on the other) and an internationally supervised transition process to independence and free elections.

Resolution 678: Passed by the UN in November 1990 demanding that Iraq withdraw from Kuwait. It authorized the use of all necessary force to restore Kuwait's sovereignty after January 15, 1991.

— S —

SALT I: The Strategic Arms Limitation Treaty that was signed in 1972 between the U.S. and the former Soviet Union on the limitation of strategic armaments.

SALT II: The Strategic Arms Limitation Treaty was signed in 1979. SALT II was to limit the number and types of former Soviet Union and U.S. strategic weapons. It never went into effect, as it was not ratified by the U.S. Senate.

Second strike: A nuclear attack in response to an adversary's first strike. A second-strike capability is the ability to absorb the full force of a first strike and still inflict heavy damage in retaliation.

Secretariat: (a) The administrative organ of the United Nations, headed by the secretary-general; (b) An administrative element of any IGO; this is headed by a secretary-general.

Short-range Ballistic Missiles (SRBM): A missile with a range up to 500 nautical miles.

Solidarity: Independent self-governing trade union movement started in Poland in 1980. It was terminated in December 1981 after radical members of its Presidum passed a resolution calling for a national referendum to determine if the communist government of Poland should continue to govern.

South (as in North-South axis): A shorthand, nongeographic term that includes economically less developed countries, often represented by the Group of 77.

Sovereignty: The ability to carry out laws and policies within national borders without interference from outside.

Special Drawing Rights (SDRs): Also known as paper gold. A new form of international liquid reserves to be used in the settlement of international payments among member governments of the International Monetary Fund.

State: Regarding international relations, it means a country having territory, population, government, and sovereignty, e.g., the United States is a state, while California is not a state in this sense.

State terrorism: The use of state power, including the police, the armed forces, and the secret police to throw fear among the population against any act of dissent or protest against a political regime.

"Stealth": A code name for a proposed "invisible" aircraft, supposedly not detectable by hostile forces, that would be the main U.S. strategic fighter-bomber of the 1990s.

Strategic Arms Limitation Talks. See **SALT I** and **SALT II.**

Strategic Defense Initiative (SDI): A space-based defense system designed to destroy incoming missiles. It is highly criticized because the technological possibility of such a system is questionable, not to mention the enormous cost.

Strategic minerals: Minerals needed in the fabrication of advanced military and industrial equipment. Examples are uranium, platinum, titanium, vanadium, tungsten, nickel, chromium, etc.

Strategic nuclear weapons: Long-range weapons carried on either intercontinental ballistic missiles (ICBMs) or Submarine-Launched Ballistic Missiles (SLBMs) or long-range bombers.

Strategic stockpile: Reserves of certain commodities established to ensure that in time of national emergency such commodities are readily available.

Structural Adjustment Program. See **Conditionality.**

Submarine-Launched Ballistic Missile (SLBM): A ballistic missile carried in and launched from a submarine.

Superpowers: Countries so powerful militarily (the United States and Russia), demographically (Pacific Rim countries), or economically (Japan) as to be in a class by themselves.

Supranational: Above nation-states.

— T —

Tactical nuclear weapons: Kiloton-range weapons for theatre use. The bomb dropped on Hiroshima would be in this category today.

Tariff: A tax levied on imports.

Technetronic: Shorthand for technological-electronic.

Territorial sea: The territorial sea, air space above, seabed, and subsoil are part of sovereign territory of a coastal state except that ships (not aircraft) enjoy right of innocent passage. As proposed, a coastal state's sovereignty would extend 12 nautical miles beyond its land territory.

Terrorism: The systematic use of terror as a means of coercion.

Theatre: In nuclear strategy, it refers to a localized combat area such as Europe, as opposed to global warfare that would have involved the United States and the former Soviet Union in a nuclear exchange.

Theatre Nuclear Forces (TNF): Nuclear weapons systems for operations in a region such as Europe, including artillery, cruise missiles, SRBMs, IRBMs, and MRBMs.

Third World: Often used interchangeably with the terms less developed countries, developing countries, or the South, its two main institutions are the nonaligned movement (which acts primarily as the political caucus of the Third World) and the Group of 77 (which functions as the economic voice of the Third World).

Tokyo Round: The sixth round of GATT trade negotiations, begun in 1973 and ended in 1979. About 100 nations, including nonmembers of the GATT, participated.

Torture: The deliberate inflicting of pain, whether physical or psychological, to degrade, intimidate, and induce submission of its victims to the will of the torturer. It is a heinous practice used frequently in most dictatorial regimes in the world, irrespective of their ideological leanings.

Transnational: An adjective indicating that a nongovernmental movement, organization, or ideology transcends national borders and is operative in dissimilar political, economic, and social systems.

Transnational Enterprise (TNE) or Corporation (TNC). See **Multinational Corporation.**

Triad (nuclear): The three-pronged U.S. strategic weapons arsenal, composed of land-based ICBMs, underwater SLBMs, and long-range manned bombers.

Trilateral: Between three countries or groups of countries, e.g., United States, Western Europe, and Japan; United States, Russia, and China.

— U —

Unilateral: One-sided, as opposed to bilateral or multilateral.

United Nations Conference on Trade and Development (UNCTAD): A coalition of disadvantaged countries that met in 1964 in response to their effort to bridge the standard-of-living gap between themselves and DCs.

— V —

Verification: The process of determining that the other side is complying with an agreement.

Vietnam syndrome: An aversion to foreign armed intervention, especially in Third World conflicts involving guerrillas. This is an attitude that is especially common among those who were opposed to U.S. participation in the Vietnam War.

Visegrad Group: Term used to refer to Poland, Hungary, Slovakia, and the Czech Republic. These countries were subject to the same conditions and status in their recent application to participate in NATO's Partnership for Peace initiative.

— W —

Walesa, Lech: Leader of the independent trade union movement known as Solidarity, which came into existence in August 1980 and was dissolved in December 1981 by martial law decree. He was elected president of Poland in December 1990.

Warhead: That part of a missile, projectile, or torpedo that contains the explosive intended to inflict damage.

Warsaw Pact or Warsaw Treaty Organization: Established in 1955 by the Soviet Union to promote mutual defense. It was dissolved in July 1991. Member countries at time of dissolution were: the Soviet Union, Bulgaria, Czechoslovakia, Hungary, Poland, and Romania.

West (as in the East-West conflict): Basically the market-economy, industrialized, and high-income countries that are committed to a political system of representative democracy. The three main anchors of the West today are North America, Western Europe, and Japan, also known as the Trilateral countries. Australia and New Zealand are also parts of the West.

"Window of vulnerability": An expression often used, but not consistently defined, by President Ronald Reagan and his administration during the 1980s. Military specialists used the word to refer to a period of time in the late 1980s when it was predicted that the United States silo-based ICBMs could be accurately hit by Soviet missiles while the mobile MX system (now scrapped) would not yet be operational, and when the aging B-52 bombers would no longer be serviceable while the Stealth aircraft would not yet be operational. President Reagan planned to close this "window" by MIRVing the silo-based ICBMs, by hardening their concrete covers, by building B-1 bombers, and by the "Star Wars" initiative.

World Bank (International Bank for Reconstruction and Development [IBRD]): Makes loans, either directly to governments or with governments as the guarantors, and through its affiliates, the International Finance Corporation and the International Development Association.

— X — Y — Z —

Xenophobia: A dislike, fear, or suspicion of other nationalities.

Yield: The explosive force, in terms of TNT equivalence, of a warhead.

Zimbabwe: Formerly Rhodesia.

Zionism: An international movement for the establishment of a Jewish nation or religious community in Palestine and later for the support of modern Israel.

SOURCES

International Politics on the World Stage, Fourth Edition, 1993, Dushkin Publishing Group/Brown & Benchmark Publishers.

Global Studies: Africa, Fifth Edition, 1993, Dushkin Publishing Group/Brown & Benchmark Publishers.

Global Studies: Commonwealth of Independent States, Fourth Edition, 1992, Dushkin Publishing Group/Brown & Benchmark Publishers.

Global Studies: The Middle East, Fourth Edition, 1992, Dushkin Publishing Group/Brown & Benchmark Publishers.

Credits/ Acknowledgments

Cover design by Charles Vitelli

1. A Clash of Views

Facing overview—Photo courtesy of NASA.

2. Population

Facing overview—United Nations photo by Shelley Rotner.

3. Natural Resources

Facing overview—United Nations photo by Kate Bader. 117, 119—*Scientific American* graphics by Johnny Johnson. 118—*Scientific American* illustrations by Patricia J. Wynne.

4. Development

Facing overview—United Nations photo.

5. Conflict

Facing overview—U.S. Air Force photo.

6. Cooperation

Facing overview—United Nations photo. 225—United Nations photo by John Isaac. 226—United Nations photo by M. Grant.

7. Values and Visions

Facing overview—United Nations photo by Y. Nagata.

ANNUAL EDITIONS ARTICLE REVIEW FORM

■ NAME: _____ DATE: _____

■ TITLE AND NUMBER OF ARTICLE: _____

■ BRIEFLY STATE THE MAIN IDEA OF THIS ARTICLE: _____

_____

_____

_____

_____

■ LIST THREE IMPORTANT FACTS THAT THE AUTHOR USES TO SUPPORT THE MAIN IDEA:

_____

_____

_____

_____

_____

_____

■ WHAT INFORMATION OR IDEAS DISCUSSED IN THIS ARTICLE ARE ALSO DISCUSSED IN YOUR TEXTBOOK OR OTHER READING YOU HAVE DONE? LIST THE TEXTBOOK CHAPTERS AND PAGE NUMBERS:

_____

_____

_____

_____

_____

_____

_____

■ LIST ANY EXAMPLES OF BIAS OR FAULTY REASONING THAT YOU FOUND IN THE ARTICLE:

_____

_____

_____

_____

■ LIST ANY NEW TERMS/CONCEPTS THAT WERE DISCUSSED IN THE ARTICLE AND WRITE A SHORT DEFINITION:

_____

_____

_____

_____

_____

*Your instructor may require you to use this Annual Editions Article Review Form in any number of ways:
for articles that are assigned, for extra credit, as a tool to assist in developing assigned papers, or simply
for your own reference. Even if it is not required, we encourage you to photocopy and use this page;
you'll find that reflecting on the articles will greatly enhance the information from your text.

We Want Your Advice

ANNUAL EDITIONS: GLOBAL ISSUES 95/96
Article Rating Form

Here is an opportunity for you to have direct input into the next revision of this volume. We would like you to rate each of the 53 articles listed below, using the following scale:

1. **Excellent: should definitely be retained**
2. **Above average: should probably be retained**
3. **Below average: should probably be deleted**
4. **Poor: should definitely be deleted**

Your ratings will play a vital part in the next revision. So please mail this prepaid form to us just as soon as you complete it.
Thanks for your help!

Annual Editions revisions depend on two major opinion sources: one is our Advisory Board, listed in the front of this volume, which works with us in scanning the thousands of articles published in the public press each year; the other is you—the person actually using the book. Please help us and the users of the next edition by completing the prepaid article rating form on this page and returning it to us. Thank you.

Rating	Article	Rating	Article
	1. Preparing for the 21st Century: Winners and Losers		27. NAFTA Is Not Alone
	2. Global Change: Increasing Economic Integration and Eroding Political Sovereignty		28. Chile's Economy Still Bustling
			29. The Continent That Lost Its Way
			30. The Burden of Womanhood
	3. Jihad vs. McWorld		31. Land Mines on the Road to Utopia
	4. Damping the World's Population		32. The Triple Revolution
	5. Megacities		33. We're #1 and It Hurts
	6. Must It Be the Rest against the West?		34. The Future of Europe
	7. Optimism and Overpopulation		35. Japan's Non-Revolution
	8. Vicious Circles: African Demographic History as a Warning		36. Global Village or Global Pillage?
			37. The New Challenges to Global Security
	9. No Refuge		38. Why Yugoslavia Fell Apart
	10. The Killers All Around		39. Central Asia: The Quest for Identity
	11. The Greenhouse Effect: Apocalypse Now or Chicken Little?		40. Islam and the West: The Next War, They Say
	12. Can We Save Our Seas?		41. Rogue States, Criminals, and Terrorists Crash the Nuclear Club
	13. Sacrificed to the Superpower		
	14. Shaping the Next Industrial Revolution		42. Contest over Asia: Search for Security in the Pacific
	15. Green Justice: The Facts		
	16. A Planet in Jeopardy		43. Dismantling the Arsenals: Arms Control and the New World Agenda
	17. Facing a Future of Water Scarcity		
	18. Greenwatch: Red Alert for the Earth's Green Belt		44. The United Nations and the New Global Challenges
			45. Polio Conquered in Western Hemisphere
	19. The Landscape of Hunger		46. Ten Keys to World Peace
	20. Can the Growing Human Population Feed Itself?		47. Hunting for Africa's Wildlife Poachers
			48. Universal Human Values: Finding an Ethical Common Ground
	21. Crowded Out		
	22. Oil: The Strategic Prize		49. Long Walk to Freedom
	23. Energy: The New Prize		50. Preparing Now for a Peaceful 21st Century
	24. Canada Is Ready to Exploit Huge Oil Reserves Locked in Sands		
			51. Women's Role in Post-Industrial Democracy
	25. The Boom: How Asians Started the 'Pacific Century'		
			52. The Post-Communist Nightmare
	26. India Gets Moving		53. The Global Village Finally Arrives

(Continued on next page)

ABOUT YOU

Name_____ Date_____

Are you a teacher? ☐ Or student? ☐

Your School Name _____

Department _____

Address _____

City _____ State _____ Zip _____

School Telephone # _____

YOUR COMMENTS ARE IMPORTANT TO US!

Please fill in the following information:

For which course did you use this book? _____

Did you use a text with this Annual Edition? ☐ yes ☐ no

The title of the text? _____

What are your general reactions to the Annual Editions concept?

Have you read any particular articles recently that you think should be included in the next edition?

Are there any articles you feel should be replaced in the next edition? Why?

Are there other areas that you feel would utilize an Annual Edition?

May we contact you for editorial input?

May we quote you from above?

ANNUAL EDITIONS: GLOBAL ISSUES 95/96

BUSINESS REPLY MAIL

First Class   Permit No. 84   Guilford, CT

Postage will be paid by addressee

**Dushkin Publishing Group/
Brown & Benchmark Publishers**
Sluice Dock
Guilford, Connecticut 06437

DPG

No Postage
Necessary
if Mailed
in the
United States